THE DREAM LIFE

Movies, Media and the
Mythology of the Sixties

J. HOBERMAN

THE NEW PRESS

NEW YORK
LONDON

For Mara and Anna

Published in the United States by The New Press, New York, 2003
Distributed by W. W. Norton & Company, Inc., New York

LIBRARY OF CONGRESS CATALOGING-IN-PUBLICATION DATA

Hoberman, J.
    The dream life : movies, media, and the mythology of the sixties / J. Hoberman.
        p.   cm.
    Includes bibliographical references and index.
    ISBN 1-56584-763-6 (hc.)
    1. Motion pictures—United States—History.   2. Motion pictures—Political aspects—
United States.   3. United States—Politics and government—1963–1969.   I. Title.

PN1993.5.U6H56 2003
791.43'658—dc21

2003045914

The New Press was established in 1990 as a not-for-profit alternative to the large, commercial publishing houses currently dominating the book publishing industry. The New Press operates in the public interest rather than for private gain, and is committed to publishing, in innovative ways, works of educational, cultural, and community value that are often deemed insufficiently profitable.

The New Press
38 Greene Street, 4th floor
New York, NY 10013
www.thenewpress.com

In the United Kingdom:
6 Salem Road
London W2 4BU

Composition by Westchester Book Composition

Printed in the United States of America

2 4 6 8 10 9 7 5 3 1

THE DREAM LIFE

Also by J. Hoberman

The Magic Hour: Film at Fin de Siècle

Entertaining America: Jews, Movies, and Broadcasting
(with Jeffrey Shandler)

On Jack Smith's Flaming Creatures

The Red Atlantis:
Communist Culture in the Absence of Communism

42nd Street

Bridge of Light: Yiddish Film Between Two Worlds

Vulgar Modernism: Writing on Movies and Other Media

Midnight Movies (with Jonathan Rosenbaum)

Contents

Acknowledgments

The Dream Life has its origins in the courses I taught, from the mid-1980s on, in the New York University Department of Cinema Studies. I am grateful to my colleagues, my students, and particularly to the research assistants recruited from those classes. I wish it were possible to thank them all individually.

Each in their way, Karen Durbin, Robert Stam, and the John Simon Guggenheim Foundation encouraged me to write this book; David Schwartz allowed me to program a series of Vietnam Westerns; Joel Wallman gave me an opportunity to develop my thoughts on the "violent" reception of *Bonnie and Clyde*; Andy Hsiao enthusiastically retrieved the project when it appeared to be languishing in limbo; Art Spiegelman was a helpful source of ideas.

Over the years, bits and pieces of *The Dream Life* have appeared, in different form, in the *Village Voice, Sight and Sound*, and the *New York Times*, as well as program notes for the American Museum of the Moving Image. I have also paraphrased material from *Midnight Movies*, which I co-wrote with Jonathan Rosenbaum, from my monograph on Dennis Hopper, and from my piece in the anthology *Why We Watch: The Attractions of Violent Entertainment*.

Although *The Dream Life* is primarily about movies, it pays homage to those writers of the 1960s and 1970s who made cultural journalism into literature: Joan Didion, Michael Herr, Susan Sontag, Pauline Kael, Hunter S. Thompson, Gore Vidal, Garry Wills, Tom Wolfe, and especially Norman Mailer. A number of individual histories also informed my approach. These, more or less in the order that I encountered them, include Julian Smith's pioneering account of Vietnam and the movies, *Looking Away*; Lloyd deMause's provocative *Reagan's America*; Lawrence Suid's prodigiously researched *Guts and Glory*; and Richard Slotkin's magisterial *Gunfighter Nation*. I also learned much from Todd Gitlin's *The Whole World Is Watching*, John Hellman's *American Myth and the Legacy of Vietnam*, Dale Carter's *The Final Frontier*, and Van Gosse's *Where the Boys Are*.

I first read Siegfried Kracauer's *From Caligari to Hitler* in the late 1960s as an undergraduate at the State University of New York in Binghamton. Then, I imagined writing something that would be called *From Strangelove to Wallace or Reagan or Worse*—and I imagine *The Dream Life* is a belated version of that. It was also at SUNY Binghamton that I encountered the great film artist Ken Jacobs, whose ideas regarding the social impact of movies had a decisive influence on my thinking, as well as the brilliantly original Bob Schneider. Between 1971 and 1975, Bob and I not only saw many movies together but produced a number of mixed media pieces, performed under the rubric Theater of Gibberish; in their approach to politics, popular culture, and the period of "the Sixties," those pieces echo throughout these pages.

Finally, I shall be forever grateful to my wife, Shelley, who not only lived through much of this history but, even more intimately, through its writing. This book could not have been written without her love.

—J. Hoberman, May 2003

THE DREAM LIFE

Introduction:

"Suddenly . . . It's 1960!"

"The social world is at all times filled with countless spiritual forces or entities that one can simply call ideas." So the Weimar film critic Siegfried Kracauer wrote in 1932. "They all want to penetrate the extant world; they all want to become reality." Like unmade film scripts, they desire to go into production.

One definition of a movie would be an idea successfully transformed into an industrially produced collective experience. Each movie is the result of a particular process by which an individual fantasy has been realized, first as a scenario and then again as a motion picture. This enterprise is further modified in the social world by the impersonal forces of money, marketing, and bureaucratic inertia—along with the less rational factors of corporate power struggles, personal rivalries, aesthetic arguments, political disputes, and on-set love affairs.

A movie is an idea that accumulates meaning as it is conceived, produced, exhibited, and reviewed. Because it is an idea consumed by millions, a movie can also be a source of group identity. United before the same vision, enthralled by a common illusion, a populace might well believe itself to be a nation. The historian Benedict Anderson has described this vast audience as an imagined community; Marshall McLuhan coined the phrase "Global Village" to describe its imagined intimacy.

The notion of a Global Village is an artifact of the fifteen tumultuous years between the launch of the first satellite, Sputnik, and the media-driven debacle

known as Watergate—a period conveniently designated as "the Sixties." Given
the post-1960 tele-saturation of the American marketplace, the corresponding
development of political image-building and the advent of a self-conscious Pop
Art, as well as the relaxation of the long-standing codes that governed the
protocols of mass-media content, the distinction between passive consumer
and active participant blurred. Movies might be political events, and political
events were experienced as movies.

•   •   •

As the 1950s ended, there was fantastic prosperity—at least for some. A comfortable majority of Americans owned their homes. National income had risen
by 60 percent, while the amount considered discretionary doubled. Racial segregation and inequality remained facts of life (so was the sense of social regi-
mentation understood as "conformity"). Still, the nation felt fully realized—
the now fifty states were wired for trademark saturation and televisual simultaneity.

Three networks irradiated the public with advertisements, political conventions, old movies, and the collective memory manifest in the twenty-odd Western series shown each week on prime time. America was an image of itself—for
itself, a spectacle in which public visions and private hallucinations were simultaneously willed upon millions of screens alongside such other collective
enterprises as wars and political campaigns. Well before the new decade arrived, Americans articulated an impatience to light out and blast off toward
the unknown: The slogan that introduced Chrysler's amazingly long and
forward-thrusting '57 models was "Suddenly . . . It's 1960!"

The Cold War declared during the winter of 1945–46 had mutated into the
more glamorous Space Race. As some new national purpose strove for realization, there were as yet only a few political movements to challenge the dull
consensus of the Fifties. For some, this apparent hegemony itself seemed suspect. In his so-called Black Book the millionaire candy manufacturer Robert
Welch identified President Dwight D. Eisenhower as the dedicated agent of a
vast Communist conspiracy. Welch, self-proclaimed alarmist and merchant of
the jujube, founded the John Birch Society in December 1958—only weeks

before Fidel Castro's beatnik army descended from the Sierra Maestra to take Havana.

Some saw the nation as irredeemably evil. In 1959, CBS newsman Mike Wallace introduced his viewers to the white-devil–denouncing Black Muslims. *Time* had already profiled the Muslims, quoting their leader, Elijah Muhammad: "Every white man knows his time is up. . . . We want unity of all the darker people of the earth." The Muslims, *Time* reported, preached a "doctrine of total hate" while recruiting "trained muscle" from ex-convicts like the New York leader who had renamed himself Malcolm X. The cult had designated 1970 as their D day, assuming that by then "the big white nations will have eliminated each other with atomic warfare and Black Africa will stand unchallenged."

For others, *these* already felt like the latter days. All manner of fallout shelters, artificial satellites, and intercontinental ballistic missile systems promoted a new sense of planetary consciousness and danger. An organization of peace activists, the National Committee for a Sane Nuclear Policy (SANE), campaigned for a halt to Soviet and American nuclear tests as New York's unbelievably wealthy new governor Nelson Rockefeller initiated a massive civil-defense campaign predicated on the building of those backyard bomb shelters that suburban developers, without irony, termed "The Family Room of Tomorrow." On TV, *The Twilight Zone* imagined a post-atomic world three times during its inaugural 1959–60 season. The same eerily deserted cities were found at the movies in *On the Beach* which, arriving just before the new decade, projected Armageddon by 1964.

The nation trembled on the brink of some shining void, primed for some grand, as yet undefined project. A yearning for complete security, consecrated in the video-hearth's blue glow, merged with the fantasy of frontier freedom and absolute mobility—a two-toned, tail-finned, super gasaroony automobile in each suburban garage and an interstate highway system unparalleled in the solar system. After two soothing terms in office, venerable war hero Dwight D. Eisenhower was to pass on the presidency, and in his *Esquire* account of the 1960 Democratic Convention (itself a prime document of new-decade millennialism) Norman Mailer predicted that the "incredible dullness wreaked upon the American landscape in Eisenhower's eight years" would be swept away by a raging torrent—the "subterranean river of untapped, ferocious, lonely, and romantic desires, that concentration of ecstasy and violence which is the dream life of the nation."

• • •

Throughout the Sixties, there was the sense that electoral politics, the mass media, and publicity had combined in a new totality—an additional atmosphere, a second nature, the dream life of the nation. Hollywood first envisioned this as the 1950 movie *The Next Voice You Hear*, an unfunny, apocalyptic situation comedy in which God commandeered the radio to address the American people— and the world—for six consecutive nights: Mass communication as divine creation, programmed for prime time. (The movie evoked television without breaking the Hollywood prohibition against representing its rival medium.)

American movies, abetted by the TV shows, newsweeklies, Top 40 songs, bestsellers, polls, advertising campaigns, and the other scenarios that define the modern polity, produced a social mythology, or realm of shared material fantasy. If U.S. foreign policy could scarcely be conceptualized apart from the nation's quintessential historical genre, the Western, American democracy was appreciated as a form of theater in which political leaders assumed the symbolic weight of movie stars, headline celebrities, and other media phantasms. World War II hero John F. Kennedy was packaged and understood as a potential Hollywood divinity. Kennedy's "New Frontier" scenario appropriated a title that had twice served as a vehicle for real star (but imaginary war hero) John Wayne. Meanwhile, Wayne dreaming his political manifesto *The Alamo* coincided with America's electing him "John Wayne"—the nation's number-one box-office star and more.*

---

*Wayne had spent World War II stateside, but his movies effectively projected him upon the war's representation. He was the Duke, the nation's cowboy warrior, an actor sufficiently iconic to become the superhero of his own comic book. The first of thirty-one John Wayne Adventure Comics was published in early 1949.

The politics of the new totality were the subject of another movie, *A Face in the Crowd*, released in 1957. Directed by Elia Kazan from Budd Schulberg's script, *A Face in the Crowd* concerns Lonesome Rhodes (Andy Griffith), a hillbilly guitar picker discovered in an Arkansas jail who becomes, almost overnight, a major-league demagogue. His personality amplified by the mass media, the raucous hayseed graduates from radio to TV, from making fun of his sponsor's commercials to refurbishing the images of political candidates. Lonesome is on the verge of running for office himself when his jilted mistress (Patricia Neal), the Ivy League radio reporter who first found him, destroys his career by opening a studio microphone so the American people can see the true nature of the monster they've embraced.

In production from the summer of 1955 through the 1956 presidential campaign, *A Face in the Crowd* could be seen to synthesize all manner of current enthusiasms—TV comic Milton Berle and TV confessant Richard Nixon, pioneer televangelist Billy Graham and telemarketing (and telemarketed) pioneer Davy Crockett, the Actors Studio and the anti-advertising exposé *The Hidden Persuaders*. The audience could decide. Although Schulberg told a *New Yorker* reporter, "Don't, for God's sake, identify [Lonesome Rhodes] with Elvis Presley . . . ," that's exactly what *Life* did, calling Rhodes a "guitar-thumping demagogue" who inspired "scenes of frenzied bobby-soxers behaving like Presley fans." How could they not? As played by Griffith with a slavering, avid ferocity that would never again break the practiced affability of his corn pone persona, Lonesome Rhodes is a force of nature—a nightmare vision of pop culture run amok that would continually be reinvented and reinterpreted by audiences and pundits.*

The imagined community entertains itself with shared fantasies and collec-

---

***A Face in the Crowd* is in no way a great movie, but as political rhetoric, its scenario has never ceased to be relevant. The movie was darkly alluded to in 1960 and eight years later reconfigured as *Wild in the Streets*, wherein a candidate for Senate creates a Frankenstein monster in the person of the twenty-two-year-old rock star he has recruited to help him. Rereleased (with a nod to Alabama governor George Wallace) in 1972, *A Face in the Crowd* was invoked to explain Watergate in 1974 and reimagined as *Nashville*

tive memories; it is defined by the articulation of a national narrative and the projection of a leading man. In 1960, these processes coincided with the first fully spectacular national campaign. Narrowly elected that November, John F. Kennedy was not simply the President of the United States or the Leader of the Free World but an idea come to fruition, the protagonist of a collective drama: the Hollywood Freedom Fighter. Kennedy, in collaboration with his audience, established a precedent for the two self-dramatizing presidents who would follow him—even as his assassination rent the national narrative asunder.

The "purest power in America," film historian David Thomson once observed, is that of having one's fantasy realized on screen—and hence played in a hundred million minds. During the Sixties, fantasy was highly contagious. Movie stars made political statements; delusion contaminated and sometimes supplanted reality in Indochina, Watts, Haight-Ashbury, and Washington DC, even as a desire to enter into and make history arose among Third World peoples, African Americans, and Western youth. (As a vehicle for the subjective consciousness instrumental in the development of such countercultures, movies demonstrated that the imagined community might be manufactured.)

By the summer of 1969, Americans were living in a moment of antithetical, competing scenarios—a virtual civil war. The withdrawal from Vietnam and forced resignation of Richard Nixon began the sorting-out of a new national narrative which would find fulfillment with the 1980 election of a second

---

in 1975, and although the movie discharged its prophetic duty with the 1980 election of Ronald Reagan, the idea of a remake floated throughout the Reagan era.

Nor was that the end. As Leonard Quart noted in *Cineaste* after the 1988 election, the sequence where Lonesome shows a prissy Eastern candidate how to smile and comb his hair, instructing him on the need for a nickname and a hound dog, only came into its own in 1988, when Republican handlers Roger Ailes and Lee Atwater remade George Bush by teaching him to talk tough, eat pork rinds, swear by *Hee Haw*, and appear in ads claiming that the President "defines the character of America . . . the heart, the soul, the conscience of the nation." It would take no stretch of the imagination to have seen Lonesome Rhodes as Ross Perot (or *Bob Roberts*) in 1992, and only a mild sense of tabloid melodrama to appreciate Hillary Clinton playing Patricia Neal to her husband's Andy Griffith.

Kennedy, the former movie star and TV personality Ronald Reagan. *The Dream Life* recounts the period of the Missile Crisis and the Space Race, the so-called Black and Sexual Revolutions, the Vietnam War, and Watergate, in terms of this heightened cultural self-consciousness. Against the pageantry of the highly personalized 1960, 1964, 1968, and 1972 presidential elections, as well as the rise of the New Left and the New Right, the book follows the development of those archetypal figures who populated the mythology and haunted the political discourse of the Sixties: The Hollywood Freedom Fighter, the Secret Agent of History, the Righteous Outlaw, the Legal Vigilante, and the Sixties Survivor. Like creatures of classical mythology, these figures were chimerical and hybrid—part imagined, part human. Each would call its antithesis into being.

Although the movies discussed include some by the key Hollywood filmmakers of the period, my emphasis is on cinema as shared fantasy and social myth. In that sense, *Spartacus, The Manchurian Candidate, Dr. Strangelove, Bonnie and Clyde, The Wild Bunch, Sweet Sweetback's Baadasssss Song*, and *Dirty Harry* may be understood as movies that, in effect, directed their directors. (Filmmakers may make movies, but they do not necessarily make them as they please.) Cult films writ large—their meanings determined by the reception and metaphoric use given them by their audience, whether counterculture or silent majority—these are movies that America could be said to have given to itself, films that emanated from, and returned to shape, the nation's dream life.

I

Making Pre-History, A.D. 1960

The most exhilarating thought of the twentieth century:
"We are making History."
—Harold Rosenberg, *Discovering the Present* (1973)

High noon in the century: "In the leap of modern history," *Time* predicts six months into the new decade, "A.D. 1960 will break records in the building of new nations." Only that week, four proud former empires—Britain, France, Italy, and Belgium—"benevolently watched old colonies become independent new countries." Locally, such nation-building is commemorated in the form of Freedomland USA, the world's largest theme park, "a living panorama of the American past," constructed on 205 acres of swampy landfill in the far northeast reaches of the Bronx, New York. Freedomland's $33 million cost is double the tab for Disneyland, which opened five summers ago, and equals who knows what percentage of newly independent Mali's gross national product.

Shaped like a map of the continental United States, its borders ringed by parking lots, Freedomland invites Americans to stroll through the national past—to play at being American. Plastic Indians lurk in the bushes, and costumed pirates patrol the periphery of Little Old New York, a stone's throw from the giant flying saucer that squats at the center of the Satellite City. This monument to freedom is a public movie set, where fantasy is highly regulated. Chicago burns and San Francisco quakes every half hour, even as extras stage a gunfight on the scaled-down streets of a Western town described as a distillation of Tucson, Tombstone, and old Santa Fe.

Freedomland is consecrated to the Hegelian notion that history is rational and that the history of the world has achieved full consciousness—in the existence of the United States. The past is petrified, but so is the future. The present is somewhat less certain. Indeed, Freedomland is under siege. Even as workers hurry to finish the Blast Off Bunker and Space Rover, U.S.-USSR disarmament collapses with the revelation that the Soviets have downed an American high-altitude U-2 spy plane hundreds of miles inside Russian territory. Japanese students stage anti-American riots so severe that President Eisenhower is forced to reroute his farewell trip to the East Asian periphery, where Red China is taking target practice on the tiny Nationalist-held island Quemoy. Meanwhile, only ninety miles from Florida, Cuba's increasingly pro-Soviet leader, Fidel Castro, is preparing to nationalize the island's American oil refineries.

Sunday, June 19, 1960: The day Freedomland opens, the President touches down safely in South Korea. The Strategic Air Command is on alert, U-2 spy planes survey the earth. Senator John F. Kennedy, frontrunner for the Democratic presidential nomination, tells the American Legion State Convention in Sioux Falls, South Dakota, that the United States must increase defense spending, and the *New York Times* learns of an Australian astronomer who believes A SATELLITE FROM ANOTHER WORLD MAY BE IN ORBIT in our solar system. To prepare for the inevitable Soviet invasion, ten Missouri duck hunters have formed an apocalyptic militia known as the Minutemen. Harvard professor Henry Kissinger is arguing that peace can only be maintained by threat of mutually assured destruction—to be known by the acronym MAD—but a faction within the Pentagon secretly advocates preemptive nuclear strike before the global situation changes to favor the Soviet Union. As two Cuban diplomats, expelled from the United States as spies, pack their belongings, the *New York Times Magazine* reveals that their master is himself under mind control! The "Shadowy Power Behind Fidel Castro" is one Major Ernesto "Che" Guevara, a "soft-spoken, Argentinean-born physician with Communist propensities, shoulder-length hair and an indefinably oriental aspect." Guevara is an expert on guerrilla warfare and a "fanatic believer in political indoctrination."

Does Freedomland also believe in political indoctrination? Western motifs are common, and the conquest of space is a given. Curiously, however, the Revolutionary War seems to have no place. Freedomland commemorates America's manifest destiny but, like much Fifties official culture, defends itself against the nation's unruly impulses. As if to ward off some eruption of the dream life, security is unusually high when 60,000 citizens, twice the number expected, storm the Freedomland gate. Does the crowd seek to participate in its own history?

Do they demand Dionysian youth ecstasy, riotous urban insurrection, the pleasures of foreign invasion, the thrill of political assassination? If so, it is still a few years too soon. By then, Freedomland will have folded—too static for the new narrative of the Sixties. Its failure shall be regarded as the greatest debacle in the history of the American amusement park.

•   •   •

In June 1960, great public works and spectacular shows of patriotic might were reaching fruition in Hollywood as well. Such movies not only addressed the American audience but sought to represent that audience to itself—through the materialization of inchoate group fantasies or the articulation of a new national narrative. In the dream life of democracy, movie stars and media personalities nominated themselves for the leading role.

Spartacus, produced by and starring Kirk Douglas, and *The Alamo*, produced by, starring, and directed by John Wayne aka "the Duke," were Cold War scenarios that, years in the making, germinated as American boys did battle in far-off Korea and blossomed during the period of the Missile Gap to ripen in the tropical breeze of the postcolonial freedom struggle. These epic spectacles were the costliest movies yet made in America. Both were budgeted at $12 million, each ran over three hours; inspirational as well as entertaining, they featured rebels who, in losing their great battle, became symbols of ultimate victory in the fight for freedom.

Spartacus chose Freedomland's opening day to run a full-page announcement in New York newspapers:

> In 73 B.C., a Thracian gladiator named Spartacus led 70 followers in an escape from the training school at Capua. For four years, he and his army—soon grown to 90,000—defied the might of the Roman Legions in history's first organized fight for freedom. His struggle made his name a legend, his goals an inspiration.

Scarcely less epochal than the first revolution in recorded history, *The Alamo* dramatized the most famous incident in the Texan War of Independence: Besieged for thirteen days in 1836, the 183 American irregulars defending an old mission in San Antonio were overcome and massacred by 7,000 Mexican soldiers under General Antonio López de Santa Anna. This glorious defeat transformed backwoodsman raconteur Davy Crockett, a Tennessee ex-congressman who had joined the rebels, into a Texas martyr, while inspiring the immortal battle cry: "Remember the Alamo!"

Establishing its action in "the year of Our Lord, 1836," *The Alamo* was John Wayne's attempt to imbue the American national narrative with suitably cosmic significance. *Spartacus*, of course, needed hardly strain to so position its saga—the story unfolds in the Age of the Dictator, at the center of the civilized world, among those, as the press notes had it, "dreaming the death of slavery, 2000 years before it would finally die." The problem was rather to render the story American. These slaves weren't even Christian! Indeed, *Spartacus* was unique among Hollywood's spectacles of antiquity—thanks, in part, to the prestige that its protagonist enjoyed in the Communist world.*

---

*Asked by his daughter to name his favorite heroes, Karl Marx cited the scientist Johannes Kepler and the rebellious slave Spartacus. Where a U.S. missile would eventually come to be called the Davy Crockett, Spartacus lent his name to all manner of grandly

Even in America, the Spartacus scenario—preproletarian uprising against the mightiest ruling class on earth—was imagined largely by onetime Communists. Adapted by blacklisted Dalton Trumbo, a member of the so-called Hollywood Ten, from a book that helped to win the Stalin Peace Prize for its then-Communist author, Howard Fast, *Spartacus* marked a comeback for the Hollywood Left. *The Alamo*, by contrast, was a production of the Hollywood Right. It was conceived by members of the staunchly conservative Motion Picture Alliance for the Preservation of American Ideals (MPA)—including producer-director-star John Wayne, screenwriter James Grant, and composer Dmitri Tiomkin. Founded in early 1944, the MPA had invited the House Committee on Un-American Activities (HUAC) to investigate the would-be Spartacists of Red Hollywood.

Ready-made for Cold War allegory, *Spartacus* and *The Alamo* proposed rival scenarios. One was a story of universal liberation that ultimately reflected on social injustice within America—the legacy of slavery—and, implicitly, on America's potential to right that injustice elsewhere in the world. The other movie recounted a specifically and, some might say, chauvinistic American event as a global object lesson. Such popular uprisings and struggles for national liberation were scarcely irrelevant, within Freedomland or without. "Most of [the non-European] world is already in the throes of social revolution," Harvard professor Arthur Schlesinger wrote in his 1949 Cold War liberal manifesto, *The Vital Center: The Politics of Freedom*. This revolution, Schlesinger explained, was essentially nationalist—a "revolt against the landlords [and] for-

---

marginal Communist parties, not to mention a failed revolution in 1919 Berlin. The anti-imperialist Freedom Fighter appeared in Soviet mass spectacles and was cited in Soviet primary-school textbooks. He haunted the imagination of Red artists. Arthur Koestler's *The Gladiators* was hailed as the "first Marxist historical novel" when it was published in London on the eve of World War II. Koestler's Spartacus is a tragic figure; his greatest desire is to found a utopian state, but he is compelled, by the historical necessity of his battle against Rome, to assume dictatorial powers. Thus the liberator falls victim to what Koestler termed the "law of detours"—allowing the ends to justify the means—though his refusal to accept this law's ultimate logic and purge his political opponents effectively dooms his revolution.

eign economic exploitation"—but also part of a colossal ideological struggle between the United States and Communist Russia.

Kirk Douglas and his associates regarded themselves as America's conscience; with *The Alamo*, John Wayne nominated himself as the nation's martial demiurge. Liberated from their studios in the post–World War II reorganization of the movie industry, confident that images might change the world, newly powerful movie stars might well imagine themselves on history's stage.

Enter the Hollywood Freedom Fighter

The movies had a new mission. As any nation expresses itself through the articulation of a shared narrative and the projection of a heroic leader, so Freedomland demanded a larger-than-life protagonist to personify and glamorize America's global competition with Communist Russia.

Star of the Cold War extravaganza, a Hollywood Freedom Fighter would rally America to its own cause, even while holding aloft a torch to inspire the world's oppressed. This figure was not simply a romantic hero or a man of action, but an embodiment of the zeitgeist—an individual whom Hegel would have termed "world-historic." Each in its way, *Spartacus* and *The Alamo* would advance such a personality. So had the recent Cuban Revolution. And so might the American political drama.

John F. Kennedy was baptized in the dream life, educated in the reality studio, and brought up in the spectacle. His father, Joseph P. Kennedy, was a self-made man with a powerful fantasy and $300 million to realize it. In the late 1920s, the senior Kennedy bankrolled movies for his mistress Gloria Swanson; in the early 1930s, he masterminded the mergers that created the RKO studio; before President Roosevelt appointed him ambassador to the Court of St. James, Kennedy oversaw the reorganization of Paramount Pictures.

There were movies screened every night at Joe Kennedy's house, and young Jack—who shared his father's fascination—spent his college vacations out in the movie colony, fraternizing with stars and chasing starlets. The old man briefly considered hitching his son to Grace Kelly before deciding she was too Hollywood. (One of his daughters did, however, marry the British-born MGM ingénue Peter Lawford.) John Kennedy's successful 1946 campaign for Congress had been predicated on his Pacific-theater heroics as commander of PT-109. Kennedy, who suffered from Addison's disease, actually flunked his first Navy physical and passed a second exam only through his father's influence. Recognizing the publicity value of PT boats, Joseph Kennedy then secured his son's commission—with magnificent results. The story of John Kennedy's wartime valor was first brought to the American people by John Hersey in the post D-Day issue of *The New Yorker* and further disseminated by *Reader's Digest*.

In 1952, the year 300 Washington, DC, correspondents voted him the "handsomest member of the House of Representatives," thirty-five-year-old Jack Kennedy was elected to the Senate from Massachusetts, despite the nationwide Republican landslide. The next summer, *Life* magazine went "courting" with the Senator, featuring him and his beautiful fiancée, Jacqueline Bouvier, on its cover—with more space inside devoted to snapshots of the pair vacationing on Cape Cod than to the Korean War armistice. In September, *Life* returned to document the couple's Newport nuptials. A few weeks later, the newlyweds premiered their telegenic personalities on Edward R. Murrow's interview show, *Person to Person*.*

Some senators still staked their political ambitions on legislative maneuvers. Others, notably Joseph McCarthy and Estes Kefauver—both of whom used publicized committee hearings to promote themselves as national figures—were more sensitive to the nature of the show. But none had the power to transform political reality into something as glamorous as Freedomland. A foretaste of Kennedy's uncanny aura came in October 1956 when, appearing in Louisville on behalf of the Democratic ticket, the thirty-nine-year-old Senator's car was engulfed by a howling mob of college kids proclaiming him

---

*Kennedy's congressional career was undistinguished. Far more important was the bestselling book of popular history published under his name in January 1956. *Profiles in Courage*, a study of a dozen nonconforming senators who voted their conscience at the cost of their careers, solidified Kennedy's image. Written with the uncredited Theodore Sorensen, the book won a Pulitzer prize while providing a useful reminder that the former PT-boat commander had himself exhibited grace under pressure.

"better than Elvis" (who had only just introduced "Love Me Tender" on *The Ed Sullivan Show*).

• • •

With a new Soviet leadership broaching the possibility of "peaceful coexistence" and the Cold War in temporary remission, Americans felt free to dream a new cluster of new images, entities, and icons. There was the gyrating hillbilly cat Elvis Presley, and the dead Rebel Without a Cause James Dean; the serious sex star Marilyn Monroe, and the TV quiz-show genius Charles Van Doren. There were the teenaged freedom fighters who battled their Russian Communist slave masters in faraway Hungary; there was the civil rights preacher Martin Luther King Jr. and the movie-star senator John F. Kennedy.

Davy Crockett was scarcely the least of these mid-decade icons. The three-part Crockett saga, telecast on Walt Disney's new television show, *Disneyland*, during the winter of 1954–55, precipitated TV's first true festival—months before the new nation of television watchers united before the spectacle of *The $64,000 Question*. "With only twenty shows behind it, *Disneyland* has become an American institution," *Newsweek* reported in April 1955. This "first big-budget television show consistently and successfully aimed at the whole family" so mesmerized America's schoolchildren, teachers felt compelled to assign the program for homework—it was instant history.

"An idea bursts out of the darkness and can be formulated," Siegfried Kracauer wrote. Imagined communities yearn to reflect and hence experience themselves—to participate in festivals and to tailor such expressions to the figures of their stars and leaders. The combination of Crockett's amiable heroism, Disney's brilliant packaging, and TV's capacity to construct an audience initiated the children born after World War II into the experience of their own collectivity. It was Davy who first defined the Baby Boomers, an as yet unnamed generation—of consumers not the least.*

---

*The festival known as the Davy Crockett craze generated $300 million worth of toys and other merchandise. Ten percent of all children's wear was associated with Crockett—not to mention the coonskin caps that caused the price of raccoon pelts to

President Dwight Eisenhower was easily reelected amid the late-1956 season of tumult with the Red Army in Budapest programmed against the Anglo-Franco-Israeli invasion of Egypt. It was then that United Artists—the studio that pioneered the post–World War II system of star-driven, big-budget independent production—agreed to risk $2.5 million on John Wayne's vision of *The Alamo*, conditional upon Wayne's company putting up an equal sum and Wayne taking the role of Davy Crockett. Thus drafted, the star set about raising money from a cabal of patriotic oil men—ultimately securing three million dollars from O. J. and I. J. McCullough, one and a half million from Clint W. Murchison, and another million from Murchison's sons—who would help him realize his patriotic destiny.*

The Alamo was not the only epic in production. As the year ended, Fidel Castro, a thirty-year-old erstwhile student radical who had already served prison time for his doomed, romantic attempt to overthrow Cuba's governing regime, embarked upon another adventure—leading a handful of would-be revolutionaries into the mountains of Oriente province. Early in 1957, *New York Times* correspondent Herbert Matthews tracked down Castro and re-

---

jump twenty-four fold. By March, "The Ballad of Davy Crockett" topped three music charts (pop, country-western, and children's). By August, after the Disney studio opened a cobbled-together feature film, *Davy Crockett, King of the Wild Frontier*, in 950 theaters, this new anthem had sold seven million records in twenty different versions.

*As part of a secret campaign undertaken by the Pentagon and National Security Council to encourage the promotion of "freedom" in American movies, the Joint Chiefs of Staff met in late 1955 to discuss the concept of Militant Liberty. According to a classified report, Militant Liberty would "explain the principles upon which the Free World way of life is based" and dramatize "the magnitude of the danger" threatening that way of life. The following summer, representatives of the Joint Chiefs conferred with several Right-thinking Hollywood figures. These meetings were held at John Ford's office on the MGM lot, where he was preparing to shoot the Air Force drama *The Wings of Eagles*, and prominent among the participants was the movie's star, John Wayne. A report made to the Joint Chiefs on July 5, 1956, notes Wayne's assurance that "the [Militant Liberty] program would be inserted carefully" in all pictures, produced by his Batjac company.

ported that the "rebel leader of Cuba's youth, [was] alive and fighting hard and successfully in the rugged, almost impenetrable fastness of the Sierra Maestra." Because the government of corrupt strongman Fulgencio Batista had reported Castro dead, the *Times* ran Matthews's scoop on Page One. Writing like a press agent, the reporter proclaimed Castro to be "invincible." In fact, the revolutionary commanded but eighteen men, some armed only with machetes. What the journalist saw was staged—a form of guerrilla theater. Castro tricked Matthews by recycling his men like extras in a low-budget epic to make it seem as though there were forty and that they were from but one of many camps. Matthews, meanwhile, projected Castro as a charismatic Freedom Fighter.*

The Cuban revolution was front-page news because Cuba had never seemed closer. In late 1954, *Business Week* reported the island awash with "multimillion dollar real estate and transport development schemes," not a few hatched by American gangsters. Havana might become an American pleasure dome greater than Las Vegas, Miami Beach, or Disneyland. Four new luxury hotels were under construction. Some 325,000 tourists, many lured by wide-open prostitution and gambling, were expected for the second winter of Castro's revolt—as well as the handful of young Americans who joined the idealist Cuban revolutionaries.†

Sputnik and the Specter of Communist Earth Control

If the recession that gripped America during late 1957 were a psychological malady, its early signs might be located in the events of the week after Labor Day.

Tuesday, September 5: Nine black students attempt to enter the segregated Central High School in Little Rock, Arkansas, only to be turned away by a

---

*Castro's image was further burnished by the half-hour CBS "special report" *Rebels of the Sierra Maestra: The Story of Cuba's Jungle Fighters*, broadcast on May 19, 1957.

†Senator Kennedy himself would spend a swinging Christmas 1957 in Havana, staying with Ambassador Earl Smith and likely dining with Batista. The subject of *Time*'s December 2, 1957, cover story, "Man Out Front," was already running for the 1960 nomination, helped by $1.5 million worth of newfangled computer sampling and a Soviet technological breakthrough.

jeering, heckling, spitting white mob. That same morning—after years of marketing studies and with much fanfare—Ford Motor Company unveils its new 1958 Edsel.

Throughout September, TV news reports nightly on Little Rock, occasionally showing some hapless correspondent menaced by segregationist zealots. The ongoing spectacle compels reluctant President Eisenhower to order even less willing General Edwin Walker to dispatch U.S. paratroopers into Little Rock. Meanwhile, three million potential customers mob automobile showrooms for a glimpse of Ford's supreme creation—available in Chalk Pink, Ice Green, Jet Stream Blue, and President Red. The Edsel campaign is the largest PR job ever devoted to a single product and thus the most futile. The car appears ridiculous—a shameful, resounding flop.*

Then, on October 4, 1957, with the sight of U.S. soldiers occupying an American city still before the eyes of the world, the Soviets launch humanity's first artificial satellite—Sputnik!

If the Soviets can put a hundred-pound sphere in orbit, are they not equally capable of dropping a hydrogen bomb anywhere on the earth's surface? America, to cite the year's number-one song, is "All Shook Up," and the commotion is loudest at Ground Zero. Hours after news of Sputnik breaks, the most politically ambitious Democratic senators—Estes Kefauver, Stuart Symington, and Hubert Humphrey—are gesticulating at the sky, jabbering that the Republicans lost the exosphere. Call a joint session of Congress! The Free World faces extinction, and the Democrats are blaming Ike—who had capped the Disneyland opening back in July 1955 with the dizzy announcement that the United States would launch a satellite by the end of 1958.

"The Roman Empire controlled the world because it could build roads," explains the former schoolteacher and current Senate majority leader Lyndon

---

*As unemployment climbed to a post–World War II high, American auto sales fell to a decade low. Detroit faced competition from revitalized European industries. Edsel's failure—blamed by some on mechanical failures and others on the vaginal shape of its vertical grill—was exacerbated by the success of the West German Volkswagen, among other small and cheap foreign cars.

Baines Johnson, Democrat of Texas. "The British empire was dominant because it had ships. In the air age we were powerful because we had airplanes. Now the Communists have established a foothold in Outer Space." From that position, Johnson reasons, "total control of the earth may be exercised." The vision alarms even the *New York Times*, which chastises the Texan for propagating such "frightening images" to help fund "American spatial imperialism."*

As 1957 ends, the *Washington Post* exposes a "missile gap," leaking the conclusions of the secret government Gaither Report in suitably hysterical terms: By this scenario, the United States is in "the gravest danger in its history . . . moving in frightening course to the status of a second-class power . . . exposed to an almost immediate threat from the missile-bristling Soviet Union." All America is now the Alamo, with Santa Anna's troops visible just over the ridge.

•   •   •

The Soviets had won a great victory in the image war. If America's allies were rattled, those other nations of Asia, Africa, and Latin America constituted an audience that would be mightily impressed. These viewers were the Third World. The term had been coined by French sociologist Alfred Sauvy in 1952 to describe countries seeking neutrality in the U.S.-Soviet competition. But the phrase attached itself to the undeveloped former colonies that were newly free and already the next battleground. Indeed, the Cold War had scarcely begun when Arthur Schlesinger pondered this arena, wondering in *The Vital Center* how to "prevent the loss of Asia and Africa to the Soviet Union?" The United

---

*Compounding the national humiliation, Russia orbits a second satellite a month later, this time with a canine passenger. There is scant comfort to be derived from Warner Brothers' celebration of the new Air Force nuclear delivery system, *Bombers B-52*, released in late November. Finally, on the eve of Pearl Harbor Day 1957, scientists announce the launch of an American satellite. The nation's hopes are lifted, albeit briefly. After a dramatic countdown, the Vanguard rocket blasts four feet into the air, sinks sickeningly back to earth, and blows up. Through the smoke, the payload is flung clear. America's pride—a three-and-half-pound ball, six inches in diameter—bounces on the launch pad and rolled to a stop, radio signal still chirping. The event is even televised live.

States, Schlesinger implied, would be obliged to back—or even create—popular non-Communist national movements.

How to insure that the Third World—and hence History—developed our way? That was the question of the hour. *The Alamo* was concerned above all with maintaining American vigilance in the worldwide struggle against the international communism. *Spartacus* called for solidarity with the liberation of the oppressed. Wayne's movie culminated a decade-long crusade. (The star may have been an agnostic, but before the cameras rolled, he had his entire cast gather in prayer—"something veteran film men say they have never seen done," noted *Variety*.) *Spartacus* suggested an underground, revolutionary undertaking—it was a conspiracy against the Hollywood blacklist; there were political debates, and even purges.

In early 1958, star-producer Kirk Douglas commissioned Howard Fast to adapt his novel. By April, Fast had turned in sixty pages. But Douglas and his associate Edward Lewis were distraught—the script was a "disaster." Douglas dumped Fast and secretly hired Dalton Trumbo, Hollywood's highest-paid screenwriter prior to the blacklist, to write a new screenplay. Seeking political cover, the star met with Vice President Richard Nixon. Douglas hoped that Nixon, then refurbishing his image in preparation for a 1960 presidential bid, would make a statement against the blacklist. Nixon (the HUAC attack dog of 1947, demanding Jack Warner demonstrate his loyalty by producing anti-Communist movies), informed Douglas that he considered the blacklist an internal Hollywood matter.

Nixon had recently returned from his own post-Sputnik, Third World nightmare, having been heckled, spat upon, and pelted with fruit throughout his Latin American tour. A Caracas mob—acting under orders of the "Communist high command in South America" per Nixon's subsequent account—had surrounded the vice president's car and smashed the windows with apparent intent to drag him out and beat him to death. In response, President Eisenhower sent an armada through the Caribbean while U.S. forces at the Guantánamo base in Cuba were put on alert. Nixon was no Freedom Fighter; his misadventure only underscored the need for *Spartacus*. But, long before Douglas's movie began shooting, another prescription arrived.

A novelistic analogue to Schlesinger's *The Vital Center*, written by retired Navy captain William J. Lederer and Berkeley political-science professor Eugene Burdick, *The Ugly American* was published in July 1958, even as the new Soviet strongman, Nikita Khrushchev, his power consolidated at home, looked toward the undeveloped world abroad. Lederer and Burdick constructed a fiction to change that world. Extending the American frontier to the Indochina jungle, represented by the imaginary country of Sarkhan, their scenario stressed the importance of competing with the Soviets in this primordial wilderness. The authors criticized U.S. foreign service personnel as spoiled ignoramuses, while offering a prescription: American agents must learn the native language, know the indigenous culture, swim like fish among the people, perhaps even practice some form of military counterinsurgency . . . just like Fidel Castro. Otherwise, "the Russians will win without firing a shot, and the only choice open to us will be to become the aggressor with thermonuclear weapons."*

The Ugly American's title character—a big, homely, unaffected construction engineer, a builder of roads and dams—is what a Soviet socialist realist would term the novel's Positive Hero. This Lincolnesque figure is confounded by State Department bureaucrats, as is a second positive model, the character of U.S. Ambassador MacWhite. The capable diplomat is ultimately forced to resign his post—but not before publicly praising the few Americans in Indochina aiding the Cold War struggle. In addition to the engineer, these include a Catholic priest, a manufacturer of powdered milk, and an insouciant Air Force colonel modeled on colorful CIA operative Edward G. Lansdale.

Serialized in the *Saturday Evening Post*, selected by the Book-of-the-Month Club, *The Ugly American* went through twenty printings by November and remained on the bestseller list for seventy-eight weeks, occasioning no small

---

*Even as Kirk Douglas pondered *Spartacus*, *Time* celebrated Castro—the "swashbuckling" leader of the "never-say-die band of anti-Batista rebels," the "romantic near legend" who was the subject of Oriente's "swelling hero worship."

ambivalence. Perhaps no American fiction since *Uncle Tom's Cabin* was more influential. IF THIS WERE NOT A FREE COUNTRY, THIS BOOK WOULD BE BANNED, the paperback edition boasted. Eisenhower read *The Ugly American* and ordered an investigation into America's foreign aid program. The State Department counter-pamphlet published in spring 1960 was too late—Democrats had long since seized upon the book. A few months after publication, Jack Kennedy sent a complimentary copy to every other member of the U.S. Senate.

• • •

New Year's Day 1959: *The Ugly American* rides high on the best-seller list as, having begun his final assault with scarcely more men than died at the Alamo, Fidel enters Havana. On his face, per *Time*, is the "age-old smile of the conqueror."*

The glory of this Freedom Fighter is such that, for one shining moment, Fidelmania is universal. Even the Eisenhower administration hastens to recognize Castro's provisional government. Life puts the "bearded rebel scholar" on its cover and follows up with a pictorial spread: THE LIBERATOR'S TRIUMPHAL MARCH THROUGH AN ECSTATIC ISLAND. TV personalities Jack Paar and Ed Sullivan fly to Havana for interviews. Castro appears on *Face the Nation* and *Person to Person*. Naturally, there is talk of a Hollywood movie. A screenwriter in Havana speaks to Comandante Raúl Castro. Raúl expresses his wish to be played by Frank Sinatra with who else but Marlon Brando as big brother Fidel.

The honeymoon will be brief. Within weeks, *Time* turns. The January 26 cover story characterizes the Cuban as a "spellbinding romantic" with a "natural flair for publicity." One issue later, Castro is "The Scolding Hero," attempting "to run the country from Floor 23 of the Havana Hilton," his ego "big enough to include the hemisphere." Having declared January 21 the Day

---

*Back in Washington, former secretary of state John Foster Dulles, dying architect of the Cold War order, can no longer read the future: "I don't know whether this is good for us or bad for us." In a mad bit of synchronistic hubris, the Soviets choose that very day to hurl their Lunik I at the moon—missing its target, the rocket orbits the sun as the tenth planet.

of Justice, Castro organizes trials in the concrete arena of the Havana Sports Palace. Guerrilla Theater on a grand scale: The newly liberated Third World masses sit in judgment of the deposed neocolonialist regime. "This is the Coliseum in Rome," jeers ex-major Jesús Sosa Blanco, charged with scores of murders in Oriente. Indignant foreign correspondents cite the prejudicial judges, the "popcorn-munching atmosphere," and the mob's bloodlust: "When do the lions come in?" one demands.

That April, Fidel tours the United States. The New York public relations firm hired for the occasion presents him as Spartacus at the Alamo—an "ancient Roman hero" born in Oriente, the Cuban equivalent of Texas. Snubbed by President Eisenhower, this living Profile in Courage is welcomed by enthusiastic crowds in New York and Washington, DC, where he declaims the Gettysburg Address in English at the Lincoln Memorial. Reporters are dazzled, some comparing Castro to the patriots who made the American Revolution. Ordinary citizens, less suspicious than their leaders, greet the Cuban leader as a new Davy Crockett. Fidel addresses the students at a posh New Jersey boys' school—afterward there's a mad scramble to the lectern to grab his discarded cigar butt. The April 13 *Life* reports a toy manufacturer preparing to saturate the kiddy market with 100,000 El Libertador fatigue caps, their chinstraps sporting a luxuriant black beard.*

Back home, Castro acts as if he believes himself the leader of a sovereign nation. Large estates are broken up, foreign investments confiscated—including one billion American dollars. The United States protests, Fidel denounces yanqui imperialism, recognizes Red China, and signs a long-term trade agreement with the Soviet Union. Ike severs economic aid, reduces—and then ends—sugar imports, embargos exports, and increases the American naval presence in the Caribbean. The press panegyrics of 1957–58 give way to a chorus of

---

*The Fidelista cap-and-beard was not the season's only projected craze. Kirk Douglas's press agent told *Newsweek* that the star's Spartacus hairstyle, a crew cut with a short ponytail in the back, designed by Jay Sebring, would start a whole new trend: "We'll give out prizes for the best Spartacut!"

sneering abuse, epitomized by *Life*'s November 1959 description of Castro as a "silly egomaniac" and "tinhorn tyrant."

"How Long Can Castro Last?" implores *Fortune*'s January 1960 issue. This rogue freedom fighter is as big a headache as the Sputnik. In mid-March, less than two weeks after a shipment of Belgian arms blows up in Havana harbor, a new scenario goes into development. Eisenhower approves a CIA plan to train anti-Castro refugees in Guatemala for the inevitable invasion.

When Superman Came to the Supermarket

A week and a half into 1960, the *Hollywood Reporter* provided John Wayne a forum to promote *The Alamo*. The movie, Wayne declared, was a clarion call for "people everywhere who have an interest in a thing called Freedom," and America had never needed it more: "We are all in danger, and have been for a long time, of going soft." The actor was a new recruit to the John Birch Society, but his message was soon reiterated by Senator John Kennedy, who, a few days before, had finally declared his candidacy.

Kennedy's presidential campaign actually began the morning after Dwight Eisenhower's 1956 landslide. No Democratic politician spent Eisenhower II stumping for more local candidates or addressing more Jefferson-Jackson Day dinners—and there was certainly no politician who enjoyed better press. *Time*'s "Man Out Front" cover story described "the Democratic whiz of 1957" as a college girl's dreamboat, mobbed by autograph hounds and even assaulted by amorous admirers: "In his unannounced but unabashed run for the Democratic Party's nomination for President in 1960, Jack Kennedy has left panting politicians and swooning women across a large spread of the U.S."

Even while Time-Life continued to market the Massachusetts senator as a pop star, old Joe Kennedy pitched his son as the "greatest attraction in the country today," rhetorically asking journalists just why it was that when Jack's picture appeared on the cover of *Life* or *Redbook*, the magazines seemed to enjoy record sales. "He can draw more people to a fundraising dinner than Cary Grant or James Stewart," the elder Kennedy bragged. The reporters agreed: John Kennedy had been profiled by more magazines than all his rivals together; he was the star politician of the nation's beauty salons. Avuncular, donnish little Adlai Stevenson was criticized in 1956 for lacking a presidential image. Now, thanks to the ongoing televisualization of America's national narrative, the whole idea of the presidential was to change. Widely predicted throughout the 1950s, the specter of a TV-packaged candidate was knocking at the door.*

Kennedy himself defended the new telepolitics in the November 14, 1959, *TV Guide*:

> Honesty, vigor, compassion, intelligence—the presence or lack of these and other qualities make up what is called the candidate's "image." While some intellectuals and politicians may scoff at these "images"—and while they may in fact be based only on a candidate's TV impression, ignoring his record, views and other appearances—my own conviction is that these images or impressions are likely to be uncannily correct.

Even the obviously less-charismatic Richard Nixon was regarded as a skillful huckster. Nixon, Washington journalist Richard Rovere wrote, was "a politician with an advertising man's approach to his work."

> Policies are like products to be sold to the public. . . . He moves from intervention (in Indochina) to anti-intervention with the same ease and lack of anguish with which a copywriter might transfer his loyalties from Camels to Chesterfields.

Advertising was, however, only part of the program.

Predicated on the image, Kennedy's presential bid naturally inspired instant feedback. Gore Vidal's *The Best Man*, a play set during a presidential convention, opened on Broadway in the midst of the primaries to run through the

---

*The confluence of advertising and politics was the subject not only of Vance Packard's 1957 exposé *The Hidden Persuaders*, but also of John Schneider's 1956 political satire *The Golden Kazoo* (which projected a computer-driven, craze-ridden 1960 election run by rival advertising agencies) and of Elia Kazan's 1956 movie *A Face in the Crowd*.

election and beyond. The upcoming campaign would be experienced as festival and replayed as legend—chronicled by Theodore White's bestselling *The Making of the President, 1960,* recorded by the cinema verité documentary *Primary,* mythologized by Norman Mailer's *Esquire* report "When Superman Came to the Supermarket," and defined by the first television debates.

•   •   •

Everything in the unfolding narrative seemed to break Kennedy's way. During the two months prior to the Democratic Convention, the Eisenhower administration was confounded by a series of foreign-policy PR disasters: the loss of Cuba, the anti-American riots in Japan, the U-2 spy plane shot down over Russia. Ike's denial blew up when it was revealed a week later that, instead of injecting himself with poison, the pilot had more or less bailed into Nikita Khrushchev's arms.

As the Paris Summit collapsed with the Soviet leader dramatizing maximum rage in denouncing the bewildered Eisenhower as a "liar," Wayne's publicist Russell Birdwell quickly suggested inviting world leaders for a make-up summit at the Alamo. Leaving (or was it entering?) the show to mix it up with real politicians, pugnacious Wayne challenged Kennedy directly. Even as the candidate's "jet-propelled bandwagon" prepared to touch down in Los Angeles after "two years of a most expert and relentless pursuit of the Democratic presidential nomination" (per *Time*), Wayne paid $152,000 for a three-page ad folded into the cover of *Life's* July 4th special issue: THERE WERE NO GHOST WRITERS AT THE ALAMO, the headline blared:

> Very soon the two great political parties of the United States will nominate their candidates for President.
>
> Who is the man who, after the political merry-go-round has stopped, will hold in his hand the gold ring of victory?
>
> Do we know him? Have we ever known him? Will we ever know him?
>
> Who has written his speeches? Who—or what board of ghostwriting strategists—has fashioned the phrases, molded the thoughts, designed the delivery, authored the image, staged the presentation, put the political show on the road to win the larger number of votes?
>
> Who is the actor reading the script?

What did this intimation of conspiracy, this confusion of Hollywood movie and presidential campaign, signify? Was the Cowboy Warrior under the influence of the Black Book? It was in that samizdat, circulated for the preceding two years amongst John Birch Society true believers, that founder Robert Welch had identified Dwight Eisenhower as a Communist plant with a carefully constructed patriotic image, positioned by his Kremlin handlers to assume the presidency. Kennedy was likely something far worse. Had Wayne read Richard Condon's 1959 thriller *The Manchurian Candidate*, in which—aided by a rogue plutocrat—Russian and Chinese Communists infiltrate American electoral politics with brainwashed dupes? Or, was the Duke suggesting that Kennedy was an actor like himself? Could he be expressing his own sense of the new totality? Did he suspect that movies, television, newsweeklies, best-sellers, public opinion polls, advertising, and the other scenarios defining America's imagined community had created a fantastic theater of democracy in which Hollywood stars might approach the symbolic valence of political leaders?*

The 1960 Democratic Convention was the first ever held in Los Angeles. Opening night, July 11, the politicians and stars consecrated their union, mingling for dinner at the Beverly Hilton. Milton Berle, Judy Garland, Sammy Davis Jr., and Mort Sahl entertained. Marlon Brando, Harry Belafonte, Henry Fonda, Sidney Poitier, Anthony Quinn, Robert Ryan, Shelley Winters, and Nat King Cole were booked for a later gig. Frank Sinatra—who had sung the national anthem at the convention's opening ceremonies—was seated next to the supreme Star-Pol, almost the candidate's consigliere. An early and prominent Kennedy supporter, Sinatra had partied with and pandered for the senator in Vegas, attended strategy meetings at Peter Lawford's Santa Monica pad, and supplied the campaign anthem, a revised version of "High Hopes," his Oscar-winning song from *A Hole in the Head*.

---

*Wayne himself was using adman rhetoric to proclaim *The Alamo*'s import: "The eyes of the world are upon us. We must sell America to countries threatened with Communist domination."

This was, Norman Mailer thought, conceivably the most important convention in American history. Not only was the writer who aspired to be the
nation's greatest novelist covering the event for *Esquire* magazine, but the man
it nominated was "unlike any politician who had ever run for President." Pondering this apparition with the "deep orange-brown suntan of a ski instructor"
and teeth visible half a football field away, Mailer declared that the Democrats
were poised to advance a candidate who was primarily "a great box-office
actor." Never mind that, for at least eight years, the American public had been
sold the idea that Kennedy was a star and that Mailer's piece was another part
of this process. "The national psyche must shiver in its sleep," the novelist
imagined. "One could vote for glamour or for ugliness, a staggering and most
stunning choice." (What rhetorical heights might Mailer have reached had he
known that—so it has since been written—Kennedy was even then carrying
on with the very Hollywood goddess the writer would later take as his muse:
Marilyn Monroe.)

Polls suggested a dead heat. Appropriating as his brand name the "New
Frontier" (a title Republic had twice used for a John Wayne vehicle), Kennedy
conceptualized this mission in Western terms; evoking "unfulfilled hopes and
unfulfilled threats," the Democratic candidate exploited the moral exhortation
and crisis mongering eschewed by national tranquilizer Ike. "To be an American in the next decade will be a hazardous experience," Kennedy warned. "We
will live on the edge of danger." The candidate demanded sacrifice and hyper-
vigilance, telling a Salt Lake City audience that the Communist system was a
fearsome enemy—"implacable, insatiable, unceasing in its drive for world domination."

September 12 was John Wayne Day in Houston: As the star was named
Texas Salesman of the Year, Kennedy and running-mate Lyndon Johnson made
their first joint Texas trip. The pair visited the Alamo, and that night—in the
campaign's most significant image-event thus far—Kennedy spoke as a Catholic
on live TV before a less-than-friendly audience of three hundred Houston
ministers. In West Virginia, where his Protestant opponent Senator Hubert
Humphrey took "Give Me That Old Time Religion" for a campaign song,

Kennedy had responded to suggestions that his loyalty might be divided between the U.S. and the Vatican by invoking his heroism aboard PT-109. Now
the candidate boldly rewrote the Alamo scenario: "Side by side with Bowie
and Crockett died Fuentes and McCafferty and Bailey and Bedillio and Carey—
but no one knows whether they were Catholics or not. For there was no
religious test there."*

Kennedy's campaign was not the only Hollywood-scale bid to remake history; nor was Wayne's paranoid scenario the lone conspiracy. The CIA had
begun secretly training an invasion force of Cuban exiles; in August, the KGB
warned Castro that an attempt on his life was planned for a rally in Havana's
Plaza Cívica. In September, the CIA dispatched former FBI agent Robert Maheu to offer mobster Johnny Roselli a $150,000 contract on Castro. (An agency
operative had already been assigned to treat a box of the Cuban leader's favorite cigars with botulinum toxin.) Roselli, the mob front at the Stardust
casino in Vegas and once Hollywood's top gangster, put Maheu in touch with
Florida heroin king Santos Trafficante—the syndicate's erstwhile Havana representative—and Chicago's new Boss of Bosses, Sam Giancana. Rome's campaign against Spartacus might seem wholesome by comparison.†

•   •   •

Mid-September, an exotic collection of world leaders descended upon New
York for the fifteenth United Nations General Assembly in what amounted to
a virtual trailer for Kirk Douglas's underdog epic.

---

*This speech was later used in TV spots run mainly in states with significant Catholic
populations. The ads were less to reassure Protestant voters than to mobilize Catholic
ones.

†Giancana already enjoyed common interests with John Kennedy. Both friends of Frank
Sinatra, they had another mutual acquaintance, twenty-five-year-old Judith Campbell.
Sinatra introduced Kennedy to Campbell in Las Vegas that February—their two-year
series of trysts began a month later. In April, Sinatra delivered Campbell to Giancana.
According to Judy, she slept with both men and, at Kennedy's request, even brokered
a meeting at a Miami Beach hotel—waiting in the toilet while the two conferred on,
she surmised, the crucial West Virginia primary. The FBI had already noted Giancana's

"This could be the weirdest, jazziest session of the UN that ever was," an American diplomat tipped *Newsweek*. As a panoply of Third World stars arrived, including Nasser, Nehru, Nkrumah, Sukarno, and Sekou Touré, the journal published a special supplement. "From the ends of the earth they came, each a mighty man in his own far country. There were black men in flowing gowns with tribal scars on their faces, brown men in turbans and fezzes, white men with unkempt beards. . . ." Even Nikita Khrushchev was back. "K," as the tabloids dubbed him, was accompanied by every top dog in the Soviet sphere and preceded by wild rumors of a gigantic new Russian rocket poised to blast the first man into space.

In the 1952 election, Soviet leader Joseph Stalin had been a near-abstract force of evil. Eight televised years later, the Cold War was personalized. Khrushchev's September 1959 American tour—his threats, boasts, and earthy bromides, his trip to Hollywood and tantrum when denied access to Disneyland—gave Communism a human face. K threatened to bury capitalism, and now voters were encouraged to consider which presidential contender might best knock the shovel from his hands. In July 1959, John Kennedy held a twenty-two point lead over Richard Nixon in the polls. But two months later, after Nixon argued capitalism's superiority over socialism with Khrushchev at a Moscow trade fair—the so-called Kitchen Debate—the vice president slipped ahead 51 to 49 percent.

Running to Nixon's right on foreign policy, Kennedy elaborated the post-Sputnik argument implicit in *The Ugly American*. The Soviets were poised to surpass American defense technology, economic growth, and political influence—particularly among the very bloc of nonaligned nations now thronging the UN. *Newsweek* designated three international "Danger Zones": Churning Cuba, Exploding Laos, and the Mad Congo, where a civil war embroiled UN troops in combat for the first time since Korea. It was reported that the nation's belea-

---

involvement; he had dispatched henchman Skinny D'Amato to forgive strategic gambling debts and grease the local Democratic machine. Wiretaps indicated that mob donations were funneled to the campaign with Sinatra himself as bagman.

guered crypto-Communist leader, Patrice Lumumba, was trying to reach New York—another potential Spartacus defying Rome.

Lumumba would be a no-show, but Fidel's *barbudo* horde arrived on a (promptly impounded) Cuban airliner. Showman that he was, Castro pretended to treat the visit as an invasion. He joked of hanging his hammock in the UN garden or establishing a guerrilla camp in Central Park, before booking rooms at Harlem's Hotel Theresa. Two thousand Black Muslims rallied outside as the Cuban hero met with their leader, Malcolm X. Ignored by U.S. Secretary of State Christian Herter, who invited eighteen other Latin American leaders to lunch, Castro dined with the hotel employees while his guerrillas feasted on the chickens they killed, plucked, and cooked in their own rooms. After entertaining Nasser and welcoming Khrushchev to liberated Harlem, Castro headed downtown to deliver the longest speech in UN history—a four-hour, twenty-six-minute diatribe during which he ripped up the U.S.-Cuban military treaty.*

Castro was that weird and jazzy season's first star. But "the Beard" was succeeded by irrepressible K, who, installed in the Soviet consulate on Park Avenue, dominated headlines for three weeks. One afternoon, Khrushchev staged an impromptu press conference, addressing reporters from the consulate balcony. Fielding questions on the World Series and complaining of his "house arrest," he proposed total disarmament. When a group of Hunter College students sang "God Bless America," Khrushchev bellowed the opening bar of the "Internationale."

Khrushchev's UN antics were no less remarkable. He gleefully led his delegation in disrupting a speech by Secretary General Dag Hammarskjöld, heckled the British Prime Minister Harold Macmillan, and, most spectacularly, removed his shoe to bang it on his desk when a representative of the Philippines accused the USSR of having "swallowed" Eastern Europe. Reviewing this

---

*It was after this tirade—which, among other things, insultingly referred to Kennedy as "an ignorant and illiterate millionaire"—that the Democratic candidate decided to make Cuba a campaign issue.

performance in *Esquire*, Saul Bellow would note how K adapted himself to the American media stage, "behaving like a comic artist in a show written and directed by himself." John Wayne was again enraged: "Why don't Kennedy and Nixon take this yelling braggart and boor apart? I'm proud the President of the United States is a gentleman; but I wouldn't care if he walked up and punched Khrushchev in the nose. I'd applaud and holler, 'Attaboy Ike!' "

· · ·

The presidential candidates chose to ignore Khrushchev. Their contest reached its apogee on September 26, with the first-ever televised debate. A Gallup poll put Richard Nixon ahead, but the numbers would shift as an estimated hundred million viewers contrasted John Kennedy's impeccable cool with Nixon's apparent flop-sweat.*

The two campaigns had negotiated an agreed number of reaction shots. There were rules determining when the camera would cut away from the candidate who was speaking to monitor his rival. Kennedy's people initially called for more reaction shots of their guy, just as Nixon's wanted more for theirs. Over the course of the debate, however, they switched sides. As the shifty-eyed, perspiring, seemingly unshaven Nixon experienced what David Halberstam called "cosmetic meltdown," the Kennedy team demanded additional shots of Nixon, while the Nixon men cried for more Kennedy.

Immediately, Theodore White detected a new phenomenon on the ground. Teenage girls were bouncing and squealing as Kennedy's motorcade passed: "From a politician, Kennedy had become, in the mind of the bobby-sox platoons, a thing combining, as one Southern Senator had said, 'the best qualities of Elvis Presley and Franklin D. Roosevelt.' " Reporters soon developed a taxonomy of female responses: There were the Jumpers, who lined the streets and bounded in place. There were the Double-Leapers—women who held

---

*An accomplished debater seasoned by college competition, Nixon was interested in acting and, after law school, performed in a community theater. Nixon had even debated Kennedy. In 1947, the Republican "practical liberal" and Democratic "fighting conservative" held forth on national issues in McKeesport, Pennsylvania.

hands and jumped together. There were the Clutchers, who hugged themselves and screamed, "He looked at me!" There were even Runners that broke through police barricades to pursue the candidate's car.

After the campaign, White wrote a description of Kennedy's effect on the masses in a paragraph that, had it appeared in a paperback whose cover was emblazoned by a wanton beauty, would doubtless have been dog-eared in passing from hand to hand.

> One remembers being in a Kennedy crowd and suddenly sensing far off on the edge of it a ripple of pressure beginning, and the ripple, which always started at the back, would grow like a wave, surging forward as it gathered strength, until it would squeeze the front rank of the crowd against the wooden barricade, and the barricade would begin to splinter; then the police would rush to reinforce the barricade, shove back, start a counter ripple, and thousands of bodies would, helplessly but ecstatically, be locked in the rhythmic back-and-forth rocking. One remembers the groans and moans; and a frowsy woman mutters hoarsely as if to herself, "Oh Jack I love yuh, Jack, I love yuh, Jack—Jack, Jack, I love yuh."

Intimations of an orgy to come: Had thousands of bodies locked into that orgiastic rock 'n' roll of women—however frowsy—jumped, leaped, screamed, clutched, and climaxed in the street for any previous candidate?

October 1960: *Spartacus* vs. *The Alamo*

October 7, the day after John Kennedy raised the campaign's rhetorical stakes by accusing President Eisenhower of permitting "Communism's first Caribbean base," *Spartacus* had its world premiere in New York.

This was a movie awash with free-floating progressive tropes. As the Howard Fast novel gave American Communism a religious credo and a human face, Dalton Trumbo's adaptation provided a retrospective anthology of Popular Front attitudes. The slaves demand a New Deal. Their army is a WPA mural brought to life—all manner and color of kids and dogs, feisty grandmothers and sinewy laborers as virtuous as they are humble.

To add to the Thirties flavor, the villainous Crassus (Laurence Olivier) actually lives in William Randolph Hearst's mansion, San Simeon. As the filmmakers used Hearst's fantasy Greco-Roman palace as the evil plutocrat's home, so the gladiator factory run by droll Batiatus (Peter Ustinov) might have been located in one of Malibu's more secluded canyons. It is tempting to read *Spartacus* as an allegory of Hollywood "swimming pool" Stalinism. The revolution is led by entertainers—the gladiators Spartacus and Crixus (John Ireland), and the poet Antoninus (Tony Curtis). There is even an injunction against informing: the defeated slaves refuse to denounce Spartacus. The House Un-American Activities Committee rules the republic. "Lists of the disloyal have been compiled," Crassus warns, threatening the more moderate and conciliatory senator Gracchus (Charles Laughton) with McCarthyite terror: "The enemies of the state are known. . . . Tomorrow they will learn the costs of their treason."

On the left, the Communist *Worker* criticized apostate Fast as heavy-handed, albeit praising Trumbo for putting the Roman Legions in what the reviewer took to be Nazi regalia. Others found the production itself an instance of working-class heroics. The AFL-CIO touted *Spartacus* as the most expensive movie ever made in Hollywood under union conditions, and hosted a special screening for 1,400 labor leaders. On the right, *Spartacus* was attacked by the American Legion and by syndicated gossip columnist Hedda Hopper: "That story was sold to Universal from a book written by a Commie and the script was written by a Commie, so don't go to see it."

The thaw that Nixon hinted at to Douglas was official when the Daughters of the American Revolution saluted *Spartacus* in their monthly publication as a "Lesson in Freedom," while *Time* went out of its way to praise "longtime Far Leftist" Trumbo.

●　　●　　●

No less than the *Spartacus* collective, John Wayne imagined a role for his movie in the global image war. *The Alamo* would "sell America to countries threatened with Communist domination [and] put new heart and faith into all the world's free people." His immediate purpose, however, was to sell America to the American public. *The Alamo* does not propose to rally the dispossessed but rather remind the privileged of their responsibility to defend themselves.*

Davy, or rather Wayne—who, as the existence of John Wayne Adventure Comics suggests, can never be anyone other than himself—waxes sentimental for the days "when Congress chose the President." Scheduled for release less than two weeks before the people would make their decision, *The Alamo* is an exercise in direct address. "Now," as Wayne liked to tell interviewers, "we've got this democracy. . . . Instead of going in and running his office the way he should, the politician appeals to the popular vote, that being the mob vote. Believe me, this can ruin America."

The star can't resist riding his John Birch hobbyhorse. For years, Robert Welch had insisted on the distinction between a democracy and a republic: "Republic! I like the sound of the word," Wayne's Davy exclaims in *The Alamo*. "It means people can live free, talk free. Go or come, buy or sell, be drunk or sober, however they choose. Some words can give you a feeling that makes your heart warm." Some chose to understand the word as short for Republican—although it is clear that what Wayne has in mind is a form of civic virtue that would be guided by disinterested leadership.

Thus, face frozen in an outsized politician's smile, Wayne's Crockett always knows what's best for his Tennesseans. His first act, when they arrive upon the scene, is leading them to the local cantina—an establishment whose outsized logo might seem immodest on the Las Vegas strip. It soon becomes apparent that, for Wayne, Texas is not simply a nascent republic but a domino; defense of the mission is America's mission. The Alamo is the place to draw

---

Spartacus is a paean to underclass liberation. *The Alamo* is more libertarian in opposing Santa Anna tyranny with the dream of a free, American Texas—although this vision is undercut by a refusal to dramatize the Texans' chafing under Mexican rule, including settler anger at the ban on human servitude. No less than the American Revolution, Wayne's Free World is compromised by tolerance of slavery. The movie's sole black man (Jester Hairston) is an elderly retainer so faithful that, even given liberty, he "freely" chooses to remain in the Alamo to die at his master's side.

the line and take a stand against international aggression. Otherwise, the Mexican dictator Santa Anna might get a notion to march all the way to Tennessee.

Wayne's task—persuading his rowdy crew of naturally self-interested, healthily pleasure-seeking Tennesseans to sacrifice their lives alongside the Alamo defenders—is, in part, a public-relations dilemma. He must articulate the mission for his unwitting followers in such a way that they will freely choose to accept it. Accordingly, Wayne creates a foreign tyrant by forging an insulting letter from General Santa Anna that accuses the Tennesseans of trespassing and threatens them with annihilation if they remain in Mexico.*

The false letter is exactly the sort of deception that Spartacus would never have practiced. But if Wayne's ploy seems morally dubious, the audience has already been inoculated against his high-handed behavior by that of the antidemocratic Colonel Travis (Laurence Harvey), who has been charged with holding off Santa Anna's army. Travis assumes once his "rabble" realizes they are outnumbered seventy to one and required to defend the Alamo to the last man, they will desert. For this reason, he conceals the actual state of affairs.

Wayne's partisanship notwithstanding, *The Alamo* scenario of imminent danger and foreign humiliation was far closer to Kennedy's than Nixon's. As Election Day approached, *Time* noted that no campaign conflict had been sharper than the candidates' "disagreement on national prestige."

• • •

October 19: Fully briefed on the CIA's Cuban plans, John Kennedy confounds Richard Nixon by calling upon "fighters for freedom" to take back the island. As Kennedy grows more strident, Nixon—aware of the Eisenhower administration's plans to eliminate Fidel Castro, but unable to reveal them—is increas-

---

*Once the Tennesseans have sufficiently personalized the fight, Wayne can admit the ruse. That it continues to work only underscores his superior wisdom. The Tennesseans will not go back on their word, and in any case, even if the perfidious Santa Anna didn't write the letter, he might as well have. Hell, he was probably planning to!

ingly agitated. On the eve of the first debate, twenty-seven Batistianos landed in Oriente, but the operation failed when the CIA-sponsored supply drop fell literally into the hands of the local people's militia. Is it possible Castro would still be in place on Election Day?*

Republicans, led by Senator Barry Goldwater, join the Kennedy chorus. Two days later, in the fourth and final televised debate, an outraged Nixon is compelled to argue against his own beliefs, accusing Kennedy of "dangerous irresponsibility" in advocating Castro's removal. Cuba braces for assault. Castro is convinced that President Eisenhower will move to guarantee Nixon's victory by dispatching the U.S.-sponsored invasion force.

October 25: Democratic campaign manager Robert Kennedy receives an anonymous tip that Cuban exiles in Guatemala feel they are being rushed prematurely into invasion. That day, as the Cuban and Soviet UN delegations denounce U.S. interventionism, warning against a manufactured provocation at America's Guantánamo base, the Castro brothers nationalize the remaining U.S. industries and prepare for the island's defense. Their slogan is the same as Travis's at the Alamo: Victory or death.

Perhaps October 27 was D-Day—but, if so, the invasion has been postponed. Meanwhile, in Texas, *The Alamo*'s San Antonio world premiere climaxes a daylong official fiesta, including a ceremony at the new Texas Under Six Flags theme park attended by seven state governors and a U.S. senator. How different it might have been with Cuban freedom fighters storming the beaches and perhaps even Castro throwing his full might against the beleaguered American base at Guantánamo. In New York, the movie opens to mixed reviews. *Newsweek* dismisses *The Alamo* as "the most lavish B-picture ever made," while *Time* is openly contemptuous of "the teary sentiment" that "wallows to a climax of blubbering bathos when a little girl, as the carnage at

---

*Sam Giancana was taped bragging to cronies that he'd met three times with Castro's designated assassin and that the contract would be completed by November. Were these boasts for show? Was the Chicago gangster, who insisted Castro be poisoned rather than shot, stalling? Could he be waiting until his boy Kennedy occupied the White House?

the Alamo concludes, turns to her mother and piteously inquires: 'Mummy, where's Daddy?' "*

Fidel Castro believes that threat of Soviet retaliation that prevented the American attack. Around four in the morning on November 8, 1960, the Cuban leader parties on from a reception at the Soviet embassy to the offices of the newspaper *Hoy* and there reveals himself a Marxist, even since his student days. Well before Fidel concludes his five-hour extemporaneous chat, Americans are going to the polls in record numbers. Nearly 64 percent of the nation's eligible voters cast ballots, the highest percentage since 1908, never again equaled. Moreover, the election is the closest in American history, decided—sometime the next morning—by only 113,000 votes.†

The Year's Best Western: The New Frontier and *The Magnificent Seven*

John F. Kennedy has defeated Richard Nixon. That leaves Fidel Castro. How might one Freedom Fighter dispose of another?

At once idealistic and ruthless, arrogant and insecure, it is the Western *The Magnificent Seven* that offers an epic preview of life on the New Frontier. "Sur-

---

*Many of Wayne's allies saw *The Alamo* as victim of a Kremlin plot. Wayne's MPA comrade, screenwriter Borden Chase, speculated that negative word-of-mouth "was created by the Communists." The John Birch Society's *American Opinion* also rallied to the cause. *Spartacus* was "well-camouflaged" Communist propaganda; *The Alamo*, on the other hand, represented "a return of cinema art, however brief, to the realm of honor and sanity and beauty, from its long sojourn with perversion, subversion, and the myxomycetous companions of those twin depravities." Birch Society members were enjoined to create a demand for the movie—which now joined the pro-HUAC documentary *Operation Abolition* as an educational text.

†As Kennedy's campaign rhetoric was more identified than Nixon's with the warning that was *The Alamo*, he also managed to position himself closer to the underdog sentiments expressed in *Spartacus*. Although many civil rights leaders, including the Reverend Martin Luther King Jr. saw no essential difference between the candidates, Kennedy made a strong symbolic gesture on October 26 with his sympathetic telephone call to Coretta Scott King after her husband's imprisonment in an isolated Georgia jail.

prisingly prophetic," as Richard Slotkin calls it in his exhaustive account of America's twentieth-century cowboy consciousness, *Gunfighter Nation*, *The Magnificent Seven* dramatizes the emancipation of an impoverished Mexican pueblo. The movie opens with the bandit Calvero (Eli Wallach) and his army demanding their regular tribute from the oppressed peons and ends with the nameless village's liberation by six Americans and their impetuous Mexican protégé. Released November 23 on a kiddie show double bill, albeit hailed by *Time* as the year's best Western, *The Magnificent Seven* envisions U.S. foreign policy objectives in the most self-evident and flattering manner imaginable, while introducing a new model for Hollywood Freedom Fighting.

The Alamo visualized America besieged; in *The Magnificent Seven*, it is a distant village instead that is under attack, with America riding to the rescue. *Spartacus* was predicated on civil strife and class warfare within the Empire; *The Magnificent Seven* projects such conflict onto the Third World, an arena wherein visiting centurions or independent gladiators might altruistically resolve the struggle through the introduction of American-style democracy. The film's heroes, the professional gunfighters Chris (Yul Brynner) and Vin (Steve McQueen), arrive respectively from two legendary Western settlements, Dodge City and Tombstone, to meet, bond, and establish their righteous nonconformist credentials in a Texas border town so bigoted the inhabitants won't permit an Indian to be buried on the local Boot Hill. The first mission accomplished by these two super cool freedom riders (who materialized several months before Negro students began desegregating buses in the South) is integrating the local cemetery. Having established that they are capable of fighting injustice in America, Chris and Vin can accept a second mission taking them to Mexico to depose the outlaw strongman Calvera.

The Magnificent Seven does not put forth a heroic, civic-minded loner. Here, almost for the first time, is the notion of a handpicked elite force. (It is a given that the Mexican peons must find their Freedom Fighters in America.) The introduction of this platoon militarizes the Western, although the mission is not for everyone—Chris requires that gunfighters audition for the job. His men will be technicians of Third World liberation.

The Alamo and *The Magnificent Seven* both justified violent intervention in a foreign country, but neither invoked the traditional logic of Manifest Destiny. By incorporating Texas into America's sphere and arguing that the foreign tyrant Santa Anna must be contained, *The Alamo* allegorized the 1947 Truman Doctrine that had effectively declared the Cold War against Communist expansion; by presenting the pueblo as a nascent postcolonial democracy, *The Magnificent Seven* offers a more existential and narcissistic sense of national purpose. Santa Anna was an abstractly cruel military dictator. Calvera, closer in type to the "social bandit" who protects the poor from the authority of the rich, is too cynical for even bogus revolutionary rhetoric. He mixes Khrushchevian peasant vitality with Castroesque posturing bluster. Still, were it not for the prism of Hollywood convention, Calvera would be a distorted reflection of the itinerant gunfighter Chris. Some peons find the two to be morally equivalent—as does Calvera himself, extending the American a remarkable degree of professional courtesy.

With the social bandit Calvera defined as an oppressor, the invaders become a force for liberation—it is through them that the undeveloped world might develop toward Freedomland. Arthur Schlesinger, now a Kennedy adviser, discussed this very possibility in his essay "On Heroic Leadership and the Dilemma of Strong Men and Weak People" (published in the CIA-subsidized journal *Encounter* the month after *The Magnificent Seven* opened). The peoples of the undeveloped world had "a functional need for strong leadership." Indeed, the pragmatic professor pointed out, "it is hardly surprising that heroic leadership should seem the most effective means of charging semi-literate people with a sense of national and social purpose." And, given the circumstances, that heroic leadership could be made by, and imported from, the United States of America.

It was the neoliberal Kennedy who would really put *The Ugly American* to work. From the space program (with its magnificent seven astronauts set to liberate the moon) through the physical-fitness campaign to the Alliance for Progress, New Frontier initiatives were created, as Kennedy said of the Peace Corps, to erase the "Ugly American image." But did *The Magnificent Seven* presage the Peace Corps? Or was it another Kennedy creation, the Army Special

Forces? Personification of counterinsurgency, answer to Lederer-Burdick's call for a small group of well-trained, well-chosen, hardworking, and dedicated foreign-policy professionals, the real Magnificent Seven was the elite military unit who—over Pentagon objections and at Kennedy's insistence—would wear trademark green berets.

Fortifying the pueblo and training the peons, the Seven act as American military advisers: by introducing American-style civic culture, they attempt to foster democracy and win the peons' hearts and minds. Still, in the movie's most prophetic scene, the fearful peons turn on Chris, deciding that Calvera's rule might be preferable to the risk of rebelling against it. At this point, the freelance Freedom Fighter is compelled to overrule the people's nascent autonomy in the name of their town's ultimate independence.

Have the Magnificent Seven descended upon Churning Cuba, Exploding Laos, or the Mad Congo? What are they doing in an undeveloped Third World country? Is it called invasion? Incursion? Intervention? They have been hired to right a particular wrong and rid the pueblo of the oppressive Calvera. Yet only one of the Seven is mercenary—and, in any case, the compensation is so minor as to be meaningless. Why then do these tough-minded professionals take this job? And why, having been asked to leave by the cowardly villagers, do they nevertheless return to the pueblo to finish the job? Calvera dies puzzled by this very riddle: "You came back, for a place like this?" he gasps at Chris. The scenario was so compelling that there would be three follow-ups over the next dozen years—not to mention several real-world sequels.*

•   •   •

In the election's euphoric aftermath, Norman Mailer is inspired to nominate himself as a candidate in the 1961 race for New York's mayor. But Mailer is

---

*Time notwithstanding, most critics were unimpressed. Still, The Magnificent Seven was a popular success and—rereleased in 1961—proved a trove of Western fantasy, generating material for perhaps twenty prime-time cowboy shows. Meanwhile, appropriated by Marlboro cigarettes, the symphonic score enjoyed a long life on the national soundtrack. In 1998, then Speaker of the House Newt Gingrich declared The Magnificent Seven (released early in his adolescence) the best American movie ever made.

more honest than the President elect (for whose narrow victory he believes he might be responsible): He conceives his campaign as a referendum on Fidel Castro.

Spartacus and *The Alamo* are in theaters, *The Magnificent Seven* poised to premiere, when Mailer writes an open letter to Castro, hailing him as conquistador and revolutionary and Kennedy avatar: "You were the first and greatest hero to appear in the world since the Second War. . . . There has been a new spirit in America since you entered Havana. I think you must be given credit for some part of a new and better mood which has been coming to America."

Mailer never gets to read his letter. The huge party that is to launch his campaign turns into an appalling debacle. The writer stabs his wife (fatal only to their marriage) and winds up in the Bellevue psycho ward. Mailer is still there when a series of New Year's bombings in Havana and another invasion scare lead Castro to demand the United States further reduce its consulate staff. In his final days in office, Dwight Eisenhower breaks off diplomatic relations altogether, leaving management of this First Greatest Hero to his young successor.

January 6: Two days after the United States closes its Havana embassy, Nikita Khrushchev declares national-liberation struggles, such as those waged in Algeria and Vietnam, to be "sacred wars." The President elect circulates a copy of this speech among his advisers. The Soviet premier welcomed Cuba to the family of socialist nations and so, with considerable consequences, wed his personal prestige to the survival of the Castro regime. Polls taken at Kennedy campaign rallies had suggested Castro was considered a greater menace than Khrushchev. For his part, Kennedy imagines Castro as his charismatic rival. Both were born to wealth and privilege, but the Cuban Freedom Fighter rebelled against his class—as well as his father, a powerful provincial landowner. Castro is closer than Kennedy to the truth-telling revolutionary Spartacus: As the movie's souvenir book, *Spartacus, the Rebel Against Rome*, described one man "who led an inspired crusade for freedom against the most powerful state on earth," so the Cuban might cast himself as standing alone against the Yankee colossus.

In West Germany, *Spartacus* will be taken for a cultural event and released with the tax-exempt certificate denied such Hollywood apotheoses as *Ben-Hur* and *The Ten Commandments*. But the single most important endorsement *Spartacus* receives is from the new Leader of the Free World. Scarcely two weeks after his inauguration, the President avails himself of an extra ticket proffered only that day by his old war buddy and current undersecretary of the Navy, Paul Burgess Fay, and slips off to a showing.*

It is nearly one hundred years to the day that Karl Marx wrote to Friedrich Engels to express admiration for Spartacus as a "genuine exponent of the ancient proletariat." Leaving the theater, the President pockets the souvenir book and, reminded that his brother Robert had seen the movie a week before, remarks that he'd gone on the Attorney General's recommendation. Asked his opinion, the President pronounces *Spartacus* "fine."

Did Kennedy appreciate the wily old politician Gracchus's frank admission that Rome had "stolen two-thirds of the world from its rightful owners"? Or did he nod with approval at the brutally realist pledge that the wealthy new strongman Crassus gives that Rome will never surrender a single prerogative? Was it possible to watch *Spartacus* and not see Cuba? Shed tears, citizens of New Rome, for noble Spartacus—crucified leader of someone else's rebellion— even as ye shoulder Crassus's tragic burden. The next day, the President shows his adviser McGeorge Bundy the CIA plan for a daylight landing of a thousand exiled Freedom Fighters near the Cuban town of Trinidad.

---

*Legend has it Kennedy crossed an American Legion picket line to see *Spartacus*. In any case, as he arrived at the Warners Theater twenty minutes late, the movie was stopped and restarted from the beginning. Amazing as it is to consider the President attending a public screening on a Friday night, the *New York Times* reported that Kennedy watched the entire film—spending intermission in the theater manager's office, where he learned (1) that *Spartacus* cost $12 million and needed to gross $20 million to break even, and (2) that it was produced 95 percent in the United States with a cast so big there was "an appreciable impact on the unemployment problem around Hollywood."

II

Glamour and Anxiety:
The Kennedy Scenario, 1961–63

America's politics would now be also America's favorite movie,
America's first soap opera, America's bestseller. . . .
—Norman Mailer, "Superman Comes to the Supermarket,"
Esquire (November 1960).

Watcher of movies, lover of actresses, reader (and "writer") of bestsellers, John F. Kennedy was both subject and producer of American mass culture—the first American president to cast himself as a leading man in what often appeared to be his own script. With grudging admiration, Norman Mailer wrote that Kennedy understood that.

The only culture to enlist the imagination and change the character of Americans was the one we had been given by the movies. Therefore a void existed at the center of American life. No movie star had the mind, courage or force to be national leader, and no national leader had the epic adventurous resonance of a movie star. So the President nominated himself. He would fill the void. He would be the movie star come to life as President.

America's first president born in the twentieth century ushered in a new fantasy regime. "The making of the illusions which flood our experience has become the business of America," historian Daniel Boorstin complained in a jeremiad that has remained fresh through the millennium. Kennedy was one such imagined figure in this ongoing spectacle: "the Star-Pol." Even before the new president began his reign, Boorstin pondered the televised face-offs universally believed to have determined the 1960 election. For Boorstin, these so-called "Great Debates" were hot air and sodium vapor—scarcely more than TV quiz shows featuring the candidates.

In *THE IMAGE; or, What Happened to the American Dream*, published as Kennedy began his second year in office, Boorstin made the obvious but influential declaration that a ubiquitous, newfangled "language of images" had displaced the old-fashioned "language of ideals." The citizenry had become an audience. Showmanship was all. Advertising ruled—and entertainment. In politics as in the movies, Boorstin complained, style would inevitably supersede substance. Public interest was piqued more by a candidate's performance—or personality—than by the position articulated.

The famous American Dream was now inseparable from the ordinary aspects of the nation's waking life. In late 1960, a little-known, twenty-seven-year-old painter named James Rosenquist juxtaposed a Kennedy campaign poster image with seductive airbrushed shards from glossy magazine ads for packaged cake mix and a Chevrolet. The canvas might have been the cover for a reissued paperback of *The Hidden Persuaders*, the 1957 bestseller that had meditated on the merger of politics and advertising.

The same month *THE IMAGE* was published, *Art International* complained that artists like Rosenquist were rubbing the "spectator's nose [in] the whole pointless cajolery of our hard-sell, sign dominated culture." Identifying voters with consumers, Rosenquist called his three-panel, billboard-sized painting "President Elect." Kennedy entered the White House already an American icon—confirmed by his new and preferred designation, "JFK."

The spectacular fusion of publicity, stardom, and consumption had a social basis. By 1960, television had fully penetrated the nation's homes, bars, and motel rooms. Less an entertainment medium than a total environment, TV was now the great equalizer, streamlining the imagined community, rationalizing the dream life, offering everybody everything, including something to blame. It was in this context that all events—news as well as movies—occurred. Conceiving America as a nation of starstruck spectators, Boorstin feared that the President would henceforth be the one most adroit in projecting his televised image and performing the role of leader. Indeed, the morning after the first debate, *Newsweek* was already analyzing what was not yet known as body language.

> On the podium, Kennedy uses but two gestures—the common 'chop,' a short downward right jab with finger extended, and the rarer 'swoop,' when he brings his right hand from behind, arcs it over in a flat trajectory, and points his finger at the platform in front of him. . . . Nixon, by contrast, uses his arms and hands constantly.

The Great Debates defined what Boorstin termed the pseudo-event. The pseudo-event was a press release writ large and staged for public consumption, a scenario played out in the mass media, a happening manufactured to become news. The scary thing, for Boorstin, was that pseudo-events naturally proliferated. As corporate culture Coca-colonized ever more space, selling a bottled American identity back to America, so the media tended toward an increasingly self-conscious self-reflexivity. The Great Debates spawned other pseudo-events—all manner of vacuous interpretations, meaningless statements, and idiotic public-opinion polls.

In this new totality, the images themselves were shadows cast by shadows and mirrors of mirrors.

> One interview comments on another; one television show spoofs another; novel, television show, radio program, movie, comic book, and the way we think of ourselves, all become merged into mutual reflections.

So it was written—and so it shall remain.

• • •

In 1945, twenty-seven-year-old future JFK had briefly served as an International News Service correspondent; as a young woman, his bride-to-be, Jacqueline Bouvier, had once been the *Washington Times-Herald*'s Inquiring Photographer. Such dabbling thrilled journalists. The lead article in the post-election issue of *Editor and Publisher* pretended to bemoan the loss of a "first-rate reporter," bragging that, come January 20, the White House would be home to "a President who knows how to write a news story and a first lady who can snap good news pictures."

Indeed, as JFK was a triumphantly self-produced American trademark, so his wife became a media personality in her own right. According to relation-by-marriage Gore Vidal, Jacqueline Bouvier Kennedy had wanted to act in movies but was forbidden to do so by her in-laws. Nevertheless, "she finessed them all by becoming the equivalent of a movie star—and, best of all, a silent star of unmade films." Her face constantly featured on magazine covers, Jackie Kennedy was the first First Lady to have her own press secretary and then her own TV special: The same month *The Image* was published, *A Tour of the White House* was telecast, without commercial interruption, over the CBS and NBC networks simultaneously and rebroadcast by ABC the following Sunday for a total audience estimated at 46 million.

Jacqueline Kennedy was herself a brilliant image maker. It was thanks to the exclusive interview the newly widowed First Lady granted Theodore White in *Life* magazine in the aftermath of her husband's assassination that his thousand-day reign came to be named after a Broadway musical on the court of King Arthur, which had opened two months after the 1960 election and ran into 1963.*

---

*Jacqueline Kennedy not only told White that her husband loved to listen to the original cast recording of *Camelot*—insisting on the lyrics from the musical's final number, "Don't let it be forgot/That once there was a spot/For one brief shining moment that was known as Camelot"—but edited and otherwise supervised his piece. "Seldom," White's biographer, Joyce Hoffman, noted, "would the lines between historical fact and fantasy be quite so blurred or the collaboration between journalist and subject quite so uncondi-

Even before his election, John F. Kennedy had played himself as the star of a new sort of movie. In early 1960, former *Life* picture editor Robert Drew approached the candidate for permission to document his Wisconsin primary campaign. Drew proposed an equivalent to *Life*'s brand of candid photojournalism. His plan was to track the candidates through interviews, TV appearances, and receptions, tag along with motorcades, glimpse their hotel rooms, and take a peek at behind-the-scenes strategy sessions. Promising never to direct the action, Drew asked only for access. Kennedy was canny, confident, and curious enough to agree—and rival candidate Hubert Humphrey was more or less compelled to go along and give permission as well.

"The result," broadcast historian Erik Barnouw later wrote, "was astonishing. No previous film had so caught the euphoria, the sweat, the maneuvering of a political campaign." Camera jammed into the backseat of the candidate's car or tracking in close on a virtual assembly line of handshakes—the filmmakers framing politicians as they courted interest groups and fielded phone calls on live TV—*Primary* invented the essential televisual rhetoric of American democracy in action.

Drew's ostentatiously unscripted and candid celebration of the Image opens by juxtaposing close-ups of Kennedy signing autographs with a poster of his rival, Hubert Humphrey, emblazoned on the back of a receding campaign bus. Although the half-hour film is evenly divided between the two men, it's clear which is the star—and not just in hindsight. As noted by Robert Novak, who covered the primary for the *Wall Street Journal*, Kennedy was a "modern Pied Piper followed through village streets," an apparition at whom "workers [would] continue to stare" after he left their bench during a plant tour.

To watch Kennedy in *Primary* is to marvel at the perfection of his coiffure and radiance of his teeth; to see him work a crowd is to hear explosive gasps

---

tional." According to White's notes, Jacqueline Kennedy described her husband as a "man of magic," who believed that history was the stuff of heroes.

and shrieks. As Norman Mailer recognized at the Democratic Convention, the candidate was even then hyperreal—the perfect image of himself. Backstage, *Primary* had additional significance as an influence on Kennedy's TV aesthetic. Between the election and inauguration, Drew came to Palm Beach to show his subject the film, impressing both the President elect and soon-to-be First Lady with its certification of Kennedy charisma.*

JFK wasted little time burnishing his iconicity. His youthful image, hatless and without a topcoat, beamed across the nation on the freezing morning of January 20, had as much impact as his speech. The only inaugural address since Franklin Roosevelt's first to add a phrase to the anthology of American rhetoric ("Ask not what your country can do for you . . .") was understood as a contribution to the national soundtrack, soon available on nonbreakable LP or 45 extended-play records, "a living, vital historical document in hi-fi." Let those words resound in every American living room.

Thus, Kennedy called for mass political participation even as he consolidated power over the spectator citizenry. Continuing the TV debates by other means, the new President fascinated the viewer nation with the first of sixty-four "live" televised press conferences. According to Press Secretary Pierre Salinger, Kennedy imported a New York "TV consultant" to direct the conference-room mise-en-scène—check the lighting, secure the most flattering backdrop. Kennedy's preparations also included rehearsals. Salinger would anticipate questions and solicit responses to be discussed at a "press conference breakfast" (known in Hollywood as a story conference), allowing the President to practice replies and polish one-liners.

Confirmed as a performer, JFK encouraged photojournalists to hang out on

---

*Drew also screened his *Yanqui, No!*, recently telecast on ABC's *Bell & Howell Close-Up!*. Over footage of a Havana rally, the narrator explained that the revolution was "going to stage a show." And to introduce the Cuban leader: "Fidel Castro, who looks like a raving madman to North Americans, is seen by Latin Americans as a sort of messiah." As the CIA briefed the President elect on the impending Cuban invasion, now to include Castro's elimination, so Drew gave Kennedy a sense of his rival Freedom Fighter.

location and authenticate the new candor. His would be a vérité presidency, world-historic decisions made while children frisked through the Oval Office set! Indeed, Kennedy—who shared his courtship and wedding with millions of *Life* readers—invited Drew to move into the White House with two film crews—one to document public life, the other private. Jackie nixed the latter part of this fantastic scheme, but the President nevertheless starred in several unprecedented TV documentaries.*

Even before *Bell & Howell Close-Up!* telecast Drew's relatively circumscribed look at the presidential workday—enlivened by a contrived get-together with his sisters and clips from *Primary*—one ABC commentator predicted that, having "discovered he's a new TV idol," JFK would use the medium as FDR had radio. In Washington, like Hollywood, stars were observed living the simulation of ordinary life. Kennedy was reported to be placing his own phone calls, dropping in on staff meetings, strolling through Georgetown. A leader who thrived on subterfuge advertised the notion that there would be no secrets on his New Frontier.

Camelot was America's first and most compelling miniseries. Born in manufactured glitz, it ended in televised catastrophe to slowly fissure in an endlessly syndicated half-life of docudramas, factoid novels, fictional reenactments, revisionist biographies, and conspiracy theories. The revelations that emerged a

---

*Broadcast immediately after *The Twilight Zone* one Friday night in February, the half-hour CBS special *Eyewitness to History: Kennedy Close-Up* was, narrator Walter Cronkite explained, the first time TV cameras were allowed in the Oval Office to show "the actual conduct of official business." As JFK awaited a phone call from UN ambassador Adlai Stevenson, visited with the governor of West Virginia, and discussed the budget, the cameras were the most important official business. Later that month, NBC aired its first *JFK Report*, sponsored by what the *New York Times* disapprovingly called a manufacturer of "common household products."

In the fall of 1963, Kennedy took advantage of his wife's absence to invite *Look* photographer Stanley Tretick to shoot a candid photo-essay on his relationship with John Jr. Two weeks after the President's death, these poignant, myth-making pictures ran as a sixteen-page spread, "The President and His Son."

dozen years after the President's murder only confirmed the widespread rumor of Camelot as a shadow land of the vampire industrialists, Hollywood hustlers, militarist maniacs, and CIA-FBI-Mafia scuzzball hit men. Intimations of this dark realm existed even then. As the dream life was at all times percolating with unrealized scenarios that longed to actualize themselves, Kennedy and his court inspired a number of movies—several based on popular novels and most made by men who served their apprenticeships in television. These Kennedy scenarios—*Advise and Consent, The Manchurian Candidate, Seven Days in May, Dr. Strangelove, Fail-Safe*—conceived American democracy as the province of demagogues, extortionists, traitors, megalomaniacs, and assassins.

Shot in sober black and white, such movies were pure delirium, glossy prophetic newsreels that set one American president after another in the midst of some obscurely plotted personal or public Armageddon. For, as John F. Kennedy was Superman Come to the Supermarket, President elect, the Hollywood Freedom Fighter and National Trademark, so he inevitably conjured from the depths of the dream life his mutant, disgruntled double, the mysterious motor force, who (whether programmed by foreign enemies, domestic conspirators, or his own delusions of grandeur) emerged from obscurity to topple the projector and rewrite the show: the other Lone Gunman, the Secret Agent of History.

Camelot Year One: Into the Twilight Zone

"Each day, the crises multiply. Each day, their solution grows more difficult. Each day, we draw nearer the hour of maximum danger. . . ." So John F. Kennedy warned the nation during the course of his first televised State of the Union address, January 30, 1961. This was the most apocalyptic presidential pronouncement since the outbreak of the Korean War. But, as the nation would learn, Kennedy was speaking of himself—albeit in the royal we.

Just before the end, Norman Mailer described Kennedy's adventures, "from the Hairbreadth Harry of his P.T. boat exploits" through "the atomic poker game with Khrushchev last October," as a succession of scenes from the "greatest movie ever made." Careening through the Missile Gap into Cuba,

Berlin, and, finally, Vietnam, while living a high-style melodrama of cynical realpolitik and apocalyptic betrayal, Kennedy presided over a period of glamour and anxiety embodied by another ruthless, suave, and exciting new figure, the espionage agent James Bond. Our young President was an impresario of Crisis—face-to-face confrontation between the two super powers, both on high alert, their nuclear weapons on the table, and the whole world watching.

Kennedy survived two near-cataclysmic crises—one over Berlin and the other over Cuba. But, with the entire globe a field for Cold War competition, there were other potential flash points—the Congo, Laos, the Chinese islands of Quemoy and Matsu, even outer space. As suggested by the volatility with which Soviet premier Nikita Khrushchev responded to the U-2 spy-plane incident of 1960, there was also the possibility that the entire Cold War apparatus might create atomic warfare of its own accord. Michael Beschloss's exhaustive account of Kennedy-era foreign policy is simply called *The Crisis Years*. Kennedy adviser Arthur Schlesinger titled his multivolume biography of Franklin D. Roosevelt's presidency *The Crisis of the Old Order*. Hoping perhaps to coat himself in a bit of JFK glamour, Richard Nixon titled his 1962 memoir of his life in public life, *Six Crises*. (The final crisis was, of course, the 1960 campaign.) Crisis, Nixon suggested, was the essence of politics. Rather, Crisis was the arena in which the Star-Pol lived and breathed and fought—the characteristic public art form of the Kennedy administration.

In the midst of the Kennedy-Nixon debates, Nikita Khrushchev (who had not yet left the great stage that was New York City) created his own pseudo-event by orchestrating a televised one-on-one with talk-show host David Susskind. As a precaution against charges of Commie coddling, the live broadcast was interspersed with plugs for Radio Free Europe while flippant Susskind attempted to tough-talk his guest, using "emotional and colloquial language" that struck *New York Times* reviewer Jack Gould as

Decidedly out of place with a man who, after all, is the head of a world power, not an engaging colleague at Sardi's. At times, one had the sensation of sitting on a keg of dynamite, as if an impulsive miscue might have global reverberations.

Was a crisis an instrumentalized, government-sponsored pseudo-event run amok? Boorstin does not consider this possibility, although he was pleased to credit television with inflating presidential power.*

•   •   •

April 12, 1961: America's new showman in chief loses his first global spectacular when the Soviets upstage NASA's scheduled Mercury flight and orbit cosmonaut Yury Gagarin. Outgunned by Soviet rocketry, JFK finds himself in the same role in which he'd cast Ike. Two days later, the President green-lights "Operation Zapata," the current version of the long-germinating project scripted, produced, and directed by the CIA: Cuba will be invaded, Fidel Castro overthrown. Accepting his world historical mission and acting on the advice of a foreign-policy elite, Kennedy feels obliged to realize his winning campaign scenario.†

The *New York Times* has already gleaned the story, and Castro is preparing for Cuba's defense. Still, the CIA has convinced itself and persuaded the President that Operation Zapata will conjure up what an internal memo characterized as "an organized resistance that did not yet exist." According to the scenario, once the freedom fighters land at the Bay of Pigs in Oriente province, 30,000 Cubans will spontaneously "make their way through the Castro army and wade the swamps to rally to the liberators." The CIA is apparently unaware that their designated landing site is Castro's preferred fishing spot. Nor

---

*Boorstin credited television with encouraging the congressional investigating committees that had conferred celebrity status on senators Nixon, McCarthy, and Kefauver, as well as on Kennedy.

†The initial CIA plan had called for dawn amphibious and airborne assaults on the south Cuban town imagined by the agency to be a hotbed of anti-Castro sentiment. Kennedy deems this operation too cowboy, a would-be World War II invasion. On March 11, he sets new conditions to conceal America's hand—an unspectacular night landing with tactical air support that would appear to originate from a Cuban base. (Meanwhile, the assassination is apparently still on. March 12, the CIA's mobster go-between Robert Maheu tells a friend that the agency has provided him with a vial of poison to pass on to John Roselli.)

does the agency realize that the strike has been scheduled for the very week that the United Nations is to hear Cuba's latest complaint regarding U.S. aggression.

Saturday, April 15, a force of 1,400 Cuban exiles sets sail from a scarcely secret training camp in the Guatemalan jungle. That morning, exiles piloting six unmarked B-26 bombers blast off from Nicaragua to attack Castro's bases—and are unable to destroy even half of his modest air force. Worse, Sam Giancana's hit men have utterly failed to take out the Cuban leader. Sunday afternoon, Kennedy cancels the second air strike. The flotilla, however, cannot be recalled. The exiles land at the Bay of Pigs before dawn Monday. When the New York Stock Exchange opens that morning, there is a bull market in the shares of those American companies whose Cuban property has been expropriated but, with neither air support from above nor popular support on the ground, the invasion quickly collapses.

A pseudo-event with real blood! As journalists Tad Szulc and Karl E. Meyers would report in *The Cuban Invasion: The Chronicle of a Disaster*: "The backdrop was in accord with the rest of the phantasmagoric operation." Lem Jones, a New York press agent formerly with Twentieth Century Fox, "was handing out war communiqués, drafted in the style of a great army's headquarters, that were telephoned to him by an exiled Cuban judge, who in turn was receiving them from the CIA" (in fact, from none other than future Watergate burglar E. Howard Hunt).

> [Jones's] assistants were signing up news correspondents for the trip to the beachhead that was to start any minute, but they never left the lobbies of Miami hotels. In a private house in Georgetown, ten minutes away from the White House, a small dinner celebration was underway—until the news from the elusive front, relayed by walkie-talkies from the bloody and swampy beach to a United States destroyer laying offshore, turned the party into a mournful wake.

The day of the invasion, the CIA explains that the operation had to be launched before Castro could be supplied with Soviet MiG jet fighters. By Tuesday, Jones has beaten the Soviets to it—announcing that nonexistent MiGs have already destroyed "sizable amounts of medical supplies" on the beach. Wednesday, the last invaders surrender. Now it is Fidel's show. At the funerals of those killed in the air attacks, he officially declares Cuba a "Marxist-Leninist state" and then, for five successive nights, parades his prisoners on Cuban TV. "Even Hollywood would not try to film such a story," Castro exults.

The Bay of Pigs is no Alamo—but JFK will never forget it. The greatest political defeat of his life, the failed invasion sets the course of his administration down to its last cataclysmic day. Although the President's approval ratings shoot up, he feels betrayed. Kennedy hints that press reports may have violated national security. There is a touch of paranoia—the shadowy sense of another scenario—as JFK wonders if he'd been set up by Ike, the CIA, the Joint Chiefs, or even his own State Department. The administration, Secretary of Defense Robert McNamara would recall, is now "hysterical about Castro." The President gives his brother Robert F. Kennedy additional powers and reorganizes the National Security Council—approving, before April ends, a recommendation to escalate the anti-Communist counterinsurgency in Vietnam.

JFK also revises the New Frontier script. In late May, after four months in office (and only days before U.S. arms were used, without U.S. fingerprints, to terminate another targeted Caribbean strongman, Dominican dictator Rafael Trujillo), Kennedy delivers a second State of the Union address. Speaking as much to the Soviets as to the American people, he requests more Marines, helicopters, and personnel carriers, asks for a greater emphasis on civil defense, and, in return, promises to land an American on the moon by 1970. The United States is hurtling headlong into the future. Hitching his political star to the Space Race, the President virtually inducts the astronauts into his administration, inviting them to the White House as exemplary New Frontiersmen. In late May, the show goes on the road. President and Mrs. Kennedy visit Paris, London, and Vienna, where JFK holds his first summit with Nikita Khrushchev. The tour makes for sensational TV, but after a tense meeting during which the President and Premier exchanged threats over Berlin, a shaken Kennedy tells his advisers that the United States and Soviet Union are "very close to war."

A well-placed source in the American national-security bureaucracy will inform his Soviet contact that between June 6 and 12, the United States actually scheduled a preemptive nuclear strike on the USSR for September—deterred only by the Soviet announcement of new atomic tests. The heat is on: During this "most fateful summer in America's history," one Isabelle Moore writes a paperback original entitled *The Day the Communists Took Over America*, suggesting that "not even the Roman Empire, in the time of Septimus Severus, when it was well into its final decline, was as willfully blind to its dangers as were the inhabitants of the North American continent." Moore warns that lack of resolution in standing up to the Soviets in Berlin will precipitate a fascist militarist homosexual coup d'etat, followed by America's unconditional surrender and Communist occupation.

Abruptly, JFK materializes on TV in late July to chop, swoop, and (as pictured on the *New York Times* front page) make a gun of his left index finger in the course of the announcement that he'll be fortifying Berlin, calling for an additional 217,000 draftees, and raising military appropriations to levels last seen during the Korean War.

• • •

John Kennedy's anxiety seemed justified when—on August 13, just one week after the day-long seventeen-orbit flight of cosmonaut Gherman Titov left the phrase "space gap" strewn across America's editorial pages—the Soviets and East Germans sealed the border between East and West Berlin and subsequently ringed the city's western zone with a double-tiered wall.

Billy Wilder was in Berlin shooting his Cold War comedy *One, Two, Three* from a script, inspired by the Khrushchev-dominated fall 1960 UN session and originally imagined as a vehicle for the Marx Brothers. The first Kennedy-era film, *One, Two, Three* was at once hysterical and ironic, sophisticated and vulgar, celebrating as it satirized American cultural imperialism—specifically the global expansion of U.S. corporate culture. James Cagney, the great gangster of the early 1930s, had gone legit as the megalomaniacal boss of a Coca-Cola bottling plant in West Berlin, dreaming of a deal with the Kremlin that would open new territories behind the Iron Curtain.

Coca-Cola was, of course, pure elixir of American democracy—Robert Rauschenberg had already incorporated the curvaceous green Coke bottle in several of his combines, and Andy Warhol made it the subject of a 1960 painting. But *One, Two, Three*, in which a belligerent East German beatnik Communist (Horst Buchholz, at one point sarcastically referred to as "Spartacus") must be instantly transformed into an appropriate mate for the dizzy teenage personification of American capital (Pamela Tiffin), is also a fantasy of co-opting Fidel Castro. Indeed, Buchholtz had already been Coca-colonized, playing a U.S.-friendly Mexican peon in *The Magnificent Seven*.

One, Two, Three is essentially good-natured, but by the time it opened at year's end, the *New Yorker* nervously suggested that the filmmakers had pitched their "circus tent on grounds that threaten to become a cemetery." A mushroom cloud shadowed Berlin as the Soviets resumed atomic testing. *Time* had collaged Nikita Khrushchev brazenly standing in front of a nuclear explosion on the cover of its September 8 issue. (Inside, Billy Graham suggested that the "Last Days" were at hand.)

Even as Yankee sluggers Mickey Mantle and Roger Maris chased Babe Ruth's home run record, *Time* reported that Khrushchev's "war of nerves" was rattling the average American: "Across the nation last week, there was endless conversation about the threat of nuclear war." Schoolchildren took cover beneath their desks; black-and-yellow "shelter" signs blossomed like pressed-metal sunflowers in the basements and stairwells of public buildings; *Life*'s cover story, HOW YOU CAN SURVIVE FALLOUT—"97 out of 100 people can be saved," came with A LETTER TO YOU FROM PRESIDENT KENNEDY; *U.S. News and World Report* reassured readers that IF BOMBS DO FALL it would still be possible to write checks on an incinerated bank account.

That fall, *Washington Post* editor and Kennedy confidant Ben Bradlee told colleagues that the President, too, believed "the foul winds of war [were] blowing." The United States resumed underground nuclear testing and, interviewed about Berlin by *New York Times* columnist C. L. Sulzberger in early October, JFK more than once used the phrase "if we push the button." Before month's end, U.S. and Soviet tanks faced off in Berlin at Checkpoint Charlie.

It was a moment when to twist meant to dance, and a panic was an instance of high hilarity. Presidential adviser McGeorge Bundy recalled the season as "a time of sustained and draining anxiety," and Robert Lowell's poem "Fall 1961" included the lines:

> All autumn, the chafe and jar
> of nuclear war;
> We have talked our extinction to death . . .

On TV, *The Twilight Zone* rehearsed "The End" three times in two months. Telecast on November 17, the day that the United States consolidated a drive for "push-button warfare" with the first successful launch of a Minuteman missile from an underground silo, "The Midnight Sun" substituted a kink in the earth's orbit for atomic holocaust. The planet was falling into the sun. "Even at midnight, it's high noon—the hottest day in history!"*

Meanwhile, the Show: As Darryl Zanuck pressed on with *The Longest Day*, his monumental and monumentally publicized re-creation of the American Army's landing on the beaches of Normandy, another Hollywood impresario entered the fray. Otto Preminger (who had campaigned for JFK in 1960) came to Camelot in September to film *Advise and Consent*—the first of the political

---

The Twilight Zone's writer-producer, Rod Serling, was a longtime member of the Committee for a Sane Nuclear Policy (SANE), and from the program's inception, intimations of doomsday were commonplace: The show that opened the third season, September 15, 1961 (two days after the President was briefed on new plans for nuclear war against the "Sino-Soviet bloc") made Adam and Eve the last—as well as the first—couple on earth. Two weeks later, "The Shelter" used the threat of nuclear war to manipulate the denizens of an idyllic small town so that they turn against each other in a murderous frenzy.

In his inaugural address, the President evoked "the burden of a long twilight struggle," and *The Twilight Zone* (which premiered on CBS in fall 1959 and ran through spring 1964) brackets the New Frontier. Although "twilight zone" was Air Force slang, it soon entered American vernacular as a place where logic falters and the sun never shines. Three months into the Kennedy administration, Robert McNamara warned Communist aggressors against starting "twilight zone wars."

thrillers brought to the screen during the Kennedy administration. Allen Drury's 1959 novel, which won the former *New York Times* journalist a Pulitzer Prize and was a bestseller throughout the presidential race, centered on the Senate confirmation of Robert Leffingwell as secretary of state.

When Leffingwell's chances are jeopardized by the revelation that his résumé includes a long-ago flirtation with Communism, his unscrupulous liberal supporters blackmail a younger, conservative senator who had, once upon a time, fallen prey to homosexual temptation. Washington was full of dirty secrets, and politicians were prisoners of past indiscretions. Leffingwell would have been the ideal target for Red-hunter Joseph McCarthy, but Drury's scenario stood McCarthyism on its head. The most egregious demagogue in *Advise and Consent* was a peacenik senator capable of smearing anybody even as he offered to crawl on his belly to Moscow to prevent nuclear war.*

A decade of dramatic televised hearings—culminating in a presidential campaign where four U.S. senators battled for the Democratic nomination—had burnished the Senate with a glamorous patina of power. Hoping to secure government cooperation, Preminger assured the public that he planned to mute the novel's attack on guilty liberals—a bias that had provoked some controversy when the play opened in New York. (Specifically, Preminger promised to make the president less unattractive, drop the corrupt Supreme Court chief justice, and forgo the cautionary futuristic ending, which recapitulated the hysterical onset of the Sputnikchina by having the Soviet cosmonauts land on the moon.)

Preminger enlivened his glorification of imperial realpolitik with a soupçon of backstage sleaze and a well-publicized dash of docudramatic authenticity.

---

*In 1995, the new speaker of the house, Newt Gingrich, included *Advise and Consent* on a reading list for his Republican colleagues. That same year, on *Face the Nation*, Gingrich advocated U.S. recognition of an independent Taiwan—a gambit he later admitted came from Drury's novel. In her Reagan administration memoir *What I Saw at the Revolution*, speechwriter Peggy Noonan cited Drury's importance for herself and her peers: "We had read [his novels] in the 60's when we were young, and they were part of the reason we were here."

The producer offered a $5,000 contribution to the Southern Christian Leadership Conference if Martin Luther King Jr. would play a Georgia senator. Although the ensuing media contretemps compelled King to decline, three actual senators (including Henry Jackson of Washington) appeared in the movie, as did retired eighty-seven-year-old Henry Fountain Ashurst, Arizona's first elected senator, and the wife of FCC Commissioner Newton Minnow. The cast was enormous, with Franchot Tone as the mortally sick but still cagey president and Henry Fonda as the arrogant Leffingwell.

Politics had never been more entertaining. With *The Making of the President, 1960* atop the nonfiction bestseller list, NBC was still running its regular *JFK Report*, and even UN Ambassador Adlai Stevenson had his own biweekly show. Failing to secure permission to film inside the Senate chamber, Preminger used the Senate office building's basement and duped *Time* into reporting that he'd turned down JFK's eager offers of lunch and dinner, before succumbing to a third presidential invitation: "Washington seemed to love being pushed around by Preminger. Even Preminger was surprised." Preminger was even more surprised when Kennedy rescinded a spontaneous offer to let the filmmakers shoot a few scenes in the White House—the scheme was vetoed by Mrs. Kennedy, just as she had scotched her husband's approval of Robert Drew's request to post a camera crew.

Tawdry and grandiose, suffused with the pomp, perks, and piquancy of life at the top, *Advise and Consent* was filled with familiar faces; the vision of old movie stars running the country suggests a modern analogue to Hollywood's megaspectacles of antiquity. (Charles Laughton slipped effortlessly from the toga of a lovably conniving Roman senator in *Spartacus* to the linen suit of an equally flamboyant Southern lawmaker.) Nor was the casting without subtext. While it was hardly common knowledge that the youthful Kennedy had romanced Gene Tierney, here playing a Washington hostess, knowledgeable eyebrows raised at the appearance of presidential brother-in-law Peter Lawford in the role of a bachelor senator with a funny accent and hyperactive sex life. The ultimate inside joke was the voice of presidential buddy Frank Sinatra

wafting out from a jukebox during a key scene in a New York gay bar—
Preminger's most daring touch.

In late September, Sinatra was a weekend guest at the Kennedy compound
in Hyannisport and, among other things, used his Cape Cod visit to secure a
blessing upon the movie that he, writer George Axelrod, and director John
Frankenheimer hoped to make from Richard Condon's wickedly lurid thriller,
The Manchurian Candidate. Laurence Harvey had already signed to play opposite
Sinatra in the role of Raymond Shaw, the war hero programmed by the Red
Chinese to be a political assassin. But then the $2.5 million production, sched-
uled to begin shooting in mid-January 1962, encountered a studio problem.

Published in April 1959, a few months before *Advise and Consent*, *The Manchurian Candidate* was an altogether less responsible political fantasy. *Advise and
Consent* had been received as a serious roman à clef; as with Gore Vidal's play,
The Best Man, reviewers felt obligated to point out that the fictional characters
were modeled on actual politicians like Harry Truman and Joseph McCarthy.
But Condon, a longtime Hollywood PR man, was presciently televisual. He
simply tossed public figures, even President Eisenhower, into the mix—ending
his novel at the 1960 Republican Convention. (Such a strategy would hardly
have seemed unusual to Frankenheimer, who'd been Sidney Lumet's assistant
on *You Are There*, a show in which CBS newscaster Walter Cronkite interviewed actors playing historical personages.)

Most outrageous was the book's paranoid premise. In essence, *The Manchurian Candidate* suggested that the Cold War was a Soviet-American coproduc-
tion. Not only was U.S. electoral politics the province of Communist dupes
and brainwashed killers, the novel's McCarthy figure himself turned out to be
a Soviet creation being cleverly propelled into the presidency. (Condon's scenario thus offered an extreme version of Robert Welch's "Black Book,"
which—envisioning the Secret Agent of History in a particularly outrageous
fashion—held Dwight Eisenhower to be a "dedicated servant of the
international Communist conspiracy.") Sinatra had a deal with United Artists,
but studio head Arthur Krim—who doubled as the Democrats' national finance
chairman—feared *The Manchurian Candidate* might be political dynamite. Ac-

cording to Axelrod, a UA executive called a month before shooting was to begin in January 1962, mysteriously warning that "a year from now, President Kennedy will be on the verge of making a deal with the Russians and to have this film showing will be highly embarrassing to him." The executive backed down when informed by Sinatra that, as a matter of fact, JFK dug the idea.

"That's the only way that film ever got made. It took Frank going directly to Jack Kennedy," Condon told Kitty Kelley years later. According to Sinatra, however, JFK was mainly curious who'd be cast as the movie's arch villain— the zombie assassin's diabolically manipulative mother.

Camelot Year Two: The President's Double Lives

Absurd as Nikita Khrushchev seemed—a potato-faced ogre in an ill-fitting suit, Boris and Natasha's Fearless Leader on the TV cartoon show *Rocky and Bull-winkle*—the American press enjoyed mocking his cult of personality. In October 1961, it was reported that the documentary *Our Nikita Sergeyevich* had opened in Moscow to unanimous rave reviews. In January 1962, the *New York Times* ridiculed a new fiction that featured the Soviet premier as its protagonist: SURE SUCCESS FOR NOVEL—KHRUSHCHEV IS THE HERO. Yet, back in the USA, this sort of hero worship was not altogether foreign, even if the motivation might be partially commercial. President Kennedy's role in the dream life stimulated a proliferation of presidential doppelgängers, stand-ins, and ego-ideals.

Thanks to television, "no official face has ever become so much a part of America's consciousness," *Life* White House reporter Hugh Sidey wrote in a look back at Kennedy's first year in office, even as veteran TV news director Franklin Schaffner supervised a fifty-four-man crew—all wearing ties—in the taping of Mrs. Kennedy's White House tour. Schaffner several times called the First Lady "sweetie," but the President was more concerned with his cameo, insisting on a retake the following day for his "spontaneous" surprise appearance. While no Hollywood producer ever suggested bringing Ike's military exploits to the screen, soon after Kennedy's inauguration, Jack Warner announced that his studio had purchased rights to Robert Donovan's best-selling *PT 109*. The President's wartime craft had figured prominently in the 1960 campaign. It was alluded to in TV ads and one poster showed the twenty-six-year-old skipper, tanned and shirtless, fatigue cap pushed jauntily back, wearing shades and flashing a grin. (That was "the movie before the movie," as political reporter Richard Reeves put it.) For his reelection bid, the President might have the greatest campaign poster ever created—in wide-screen, living color, and stereo sound.

As *PT 109* would be the first motion picture to portray a living American president, Warner gave the White House assurances that he would personally supervise the adaptation, working with veteran producer Bryan Foy. No stranger to presidential mandates (in 1947 Warner told HUAC that his studio made the notorious Stalin apologia *Mission to Moscow* at FDR's behest), the old mogul proceeded with extreme caution. The sixty-five-year-old Foy was the producer of the Oscar-winning docudrama *I Was a Communist for the FBI*; screenwriter Richard Breen had recently written *The FBI Story*. A security check was run on the entire cast. The White House naturally requested and received approval of the script—which JFK was reading even as astronaut John Glenn orbited the globe on February 20. Evidently he liked it. ("Boy, you kill me!" one member of young Kennedy's crew exclaims. "We're beat, burned, and given up for dead living on green coconuts and no water, surrounded by 15,000 Japs, and you think the odds are with us!" "It's a flaw in my character," the future President replies.)

Glenn, personally greeted by the President after his splashdown, and recipient of New York's largest ticker-tape parade since the return of General Mac-Arthur, was one JFK alter ego. The star of *PT 109* would be another, and so the President effectively cast the actor who was to play him. Demonstrating no small amount of prescience and a somewhat reckless acuity, JFK initially requested Warren Beatty, twenty-five-year-old younger brother of Rat Pack gamine Shirley MacLaine, a "brash and rumpled star" whom the *Saturday Evening Post* would that summer anoint "the movies' most sought-after young leading man." (Years later, Beatty slyly maintained—in an interview with John Kennedy Jr.—that it was the First Lady who, having seen him in *Splendor in the Grass*, proposed that he play her husband.)

Beatty expressed oblique interest, having told *Show Business Illustrated* his "earliest childhood ambition was to be President of the United States." But the brash and rumpled star was ambivalent. By one account, when Jack Warner suggested Beatty go to Washington to study the President, Beatty insolently replied that "if the president wants me to play him, tell him to come here and soak up some of my atmosphere." By another, Pierre Salinger met with Beatty and discovered the notoriously particular actor categorically refused to work with a square like Bryan Foy.

For his part, Foy deemed Beatty mixed-up and, consequently, if Beatty played the President, young Kennedy would appear mixed-up as well. Foy told *The Hollywood Reporter* how he put Beatty in his place: "Maybe you'd like it better if we made the President a conscientious objector—or maybe have you fight your way out of the Navy. You're lucky this isn't Soviet Russia." So Beatty was gone and, watching screen tests flown overnight to the White House that March, JFK nixed teen heartthrob Edd "Kookie" Byrnes (the cute parking-lot attendant on the TV detective show *77 Sunset Strip*) and Jeffrey Hunter (John Wayne's "half-breed" sidekick in *The Searchers*, later to play Jesus Christ to Wayne's Roman Centurion in the 1964 *King of Kings*).

The best-known candidate was twenty-two-year-old Peter Fonda, whose father, Henry, had narrated a 1960 Kennedy campaign film concerning *PT 109*—the veteran actor at one point emphatically brandishing a coconut "much like the one" that the future president used to send a message for help. Even before testing, young Fonda disputed Foy's concept of the picture.

> War is insane, I told Mr. Foy, and nothing seemed more insane with the concept of war than the PT boats, yet human bravery rose of this insanity, and one man led his crew to safety through shark-and-enemy infested waters. Commitment to a higher cause despite the insanity of the mission.
>
> Mr. Foy asked me to leave his office, muttering something about New York actors.

Fonda, who refused to use the required Boston accent, was startled to find reporters on the set. His botched screen test made front-page news in the trades. Kennedy tactfully rejected his supporter's son as too young, deciding on the mature-looking Cliff Robertson, who at thirty-six was a decade older than the man he'd be playing.

After Warner Brothers proposed seventy-four-year-old Raoul Walsh to direct, JFK screened Walsh's turgid Korean War comedy-drama *Marines, Let's Go* and was unimpressed. In any case, a memo sent to Salinger by George Stevens Jr., head of the U.S. Information Agency's Motion Picture Division, delicately suggested that Walsh was a Republican and not to be entrusted with so crucial a project: "Bob Donovan's excellent book has sold 40,000 copies. I would estimate that 40,000 people will see *PT 109* in Leopoldville alone." There would be an audience for the movie even in the Congo, and thus projecting the pseudo-event into the chaotic heart of Third World darkness, Stevens proposed either John Huston or Fred Zinnemann to direct, making it clear both were Democrats. In the end, elderly Lewis Milestone—fresh from directing Frank Sinatra's Rat Pack in their Las Vegas caper *Ocean's 11* and Marlon Brando in the lavish, ill-fated remake of *Mutiny on the Bounty*—received the assignment. Midway through the shoot, however, he was replaced by a Warners TV workhorse, Les Martinson.

Kennedy's wartime exploits were to be mythologized at a time when the very idea of combat heroism was coming under fire. Joseph Heller's *Catch-22*, published late in the Berlin Wall hot summer of 1961, shockingly replayed World War II as cynical farce and was selling briskly, despite severely mixed reviews—"an emotional hodgepodge" (*The New York Times Book Review*), "a debris of sour jokes" (*The New Yorker*), "the best American novel that has come out of anywhere in years," (*The Nation*). According to Heller's mad bureaucratic premise, a bomber pilot—such as the book's hipster antihero John Yossarian— might be relieved from active duty for reasons of mental instability, were it not for the fact that the attempt to avoid further missions was itself sufficient proof of the pilot's sanity.

Part theater of the absurd, part service sitcom, its title to eventually enter the dictionary as "a difficult situation or problem whose seemingly alternative solutions are logically invalid," *Catch-22* introduced a crucial concept to the American vernacular and suggested the image war to come. Yossarian was no JFK.

•   •   •

PT 109 was scarcely the only Kennedy scenario in the works during the spring of 1962. Even as Warner Brothers announced plans to portray the President, Twentieth Century Fox purchased the rights to *Enemy Within*, Attorney General Robert Kennedy's account of his investigation into the International Brotherhood of Teamsters and its rogue president, Jimmy Hoffa. But the most ambitious production was Operation Mongoose. On March 14, with *PT 109's* personnel issues finally resolved, the Kennedy brothers approved this new covert anti-Castro project.

Two months before, RFK had informed the CIA's Richard Helms that eliminating Fidel was the administration's top priority. Neither money nor man power would be spared: "We are in a combat situation with Cuba," the Attorney General told a group of CIA ops. Mongoose would be lavishly funded with a budget estimated as high as $100 million. Although RFK was so gung ho on covert action he invited a group of Green Berets to the Hyannisport compound to stage a demonstration, the President was coy, encouraging the use of force against Castro while declining to specify the conditions under which the operation might proceed. Nevertheless, the Kennedys wanted the tropical Spartacus gone by October 1962, in time for the midterm elections. Southeast Asia specialist and model for a heroic *Ugly American* character, General Edward G. Lansdale was tapped to direct Mongoose. The very day John Glenn orbited the earth and JFK perused the *PT 109* script, Lansdale presented RFK with a timetable for infiltration, guerrilla warfare, open revolt, and the installation of a new government.

The old assassination plans were reactivated. PR schemes included composing a catchy anti-Castro anthem and spreading rumors of Christ's imminent Second Coming, to be reinforced by an offshore son et lumière show— although not, evidently, the original idea of rendering Castro delusional with a dose of the powerful hallucinogen LSD-25. Much discussed as a potential chemical weapon by the CIA and other government agencies throughout the 1950s, LSD would have a dramatic impact on American civilians. Even as Lansdale spun his fantasies for Robert Kennedy, Harvard psychology professor Timothy Leary was attacked at a faculty meeting for his "irresponsible" use of students as LSD test subjects—at times taking the drug along with them.

One of Leary's friends, Washington socialite Mary Pinchot—who, unbeknownst to Leary, was married to CIA agent Cord Meyer and, unbeknownst to Meyer, sleeping with his old buddy, JFK—had already introduced the drug to certain members of the government elite. But, just as Operation Mongoose geared up, FBI director J. Edgar Hoover presented the Mafia-phobic Attorney General with an even nastier piece of information. The FBI knew that, for virtually the entire period during which Judith Campbell was a presidential girlfriend, she had been seeing another of Frank Sinatra's powerful pals, namely Sam Giancana.

March 22, three days before a long-awaited state visit to Hollywood where he was to stay at Sinatra's specially refurbished home, JFK lunched privately with Hoover. It will never be known if he was there confronted with Hoover's file, but it was suddenly announced that the President would instead be bunking in Palm Springs with . . . Republican crooner Bing Crosby!

•   •   •

As JFK visited Hollywood, so Hollywood returned to Washington. *Advise and Consent* had a special DC preview with seventy-six senators, two Supreme Court justices, a pair of cabinet officials, and—to Preminger's dismay—only a single Kennedy (Robert's wife, Ethel) in attendance. The movie bugged both liberals and conservatives. Senator Eugene McCarthy deemed it simplistic, while Senator Strom Thurmond objected to the subplot in which a young senator was blackmailed for his homosexual past: "I don't think it will be wholesome for either our people or those abroad."

Even more than most Hollywood movies, the hyperreal *Advise and Consent* was the equivalent of a corporate trademark. The picture purported to reveal the inner workings of American democracy, and when it had its world premiere in May at the Cannes Film Festival, the issue of America's image was much discussed. Where the *London Sunday Express* found *Advise and Consent* "brilliantly and devastatingly frank," the French Communist daily *L'Humanité* saw only the manifestation of a new *"Kennedyste"* style—the celluloid "equivalent to a tactical re-thinking, and only a tactical one, of American policy, no principle of which is put in question."

That spring, Edward R. Murrow, Kennedy's chief of the U.S. Information Agency, asked Hollywood to exercise restraint in making films critical of the United States. The former newsman was likely thinking of the long-ago announced adaptation of *The Ugly American*, already attacked as unpatriotic by Senator J. William Fulbright, chairman of the Foreign Relations Committee. The subject had become only more topical; *Time*'s May 11 issue featured a Vietnam cover story. As *The Ugly American*'s siren song drew the American ship of state closer to disaster on the Indochinese reef, so the movie version plodded inexorably toward the screen. Filming was originally supposed to start in January 1960, but once Marlon Brando became involved, production had to be sandwiched in between the star's stints on *Mutiny on the Bounty*.

As the shoot continued through the spring of 1962, Brando's idealistic, stubborn, well-meaning Ambassador MacWhite was increasingly identified with the New Frontier. Brando adopted a drawling Ivy League delivery; studio press releases stressed that his morning coat and striped paints came from JFK's tailors and his top hat was ordered from the same West German firm that made the President's.

During the 1960 Democratic Convention, Norman Mailer had paid Kennedy the compliment of comparison to Brando. But Brando was only an actor. Once elected, JFK preferred Ian Fleming's Secret Agent 007, James Bond. After a March 1961 *Life* article listed Fleming's *From Russia with Love* ahead of Stendhal's *The Red and the Black* among the President's ten favorite books, the writer's entrée to the White House was regularly cited in the press—particularly once United Artists put its first 007 thriller, *Dr. No*, into production a year later in still-colonial Jamaica.

Holding forth at a Georgetown dinner party in early 1960, Fleming had suggested to JFK that Americans took Castro entirely too seriously. The CIA should deflate his authority through ridicule and innuendo—drop leaflets declaring him impotent, sprinkle depilatory powder in his beard. Fleming's presentation created a buzz so strong that the following morning CIA chief Allen Dulles himself was making phone calls to get his own briefing from the British writer. Fleming had already left town, but a few of his notions eventually found their way into the CIA's plans and then the Cuban scenario being developed by General Lansdale.*

James Bond was another triumph for the image, "as if the social and the theological meanings of grace were really the same," said *Newsweek* of Fleming's hero. Replete with colorful Third World atmosphere, blithely imperialist in its racial assumptions, *Dr. No* bespeaks a time when foreign travel and even airports seemed glamorous. The eponymous half-German, half-Chinese villain (Joseph Wiseman, totalitarian intellectual of *Viva Zapata!*) might run his island "like a concentration camp," but its white-sand beaches are magnificently secluded and his palace is a bachelor pad worthy of a six-page *Playboy* spread. *Dr. No* was not the most extravagant of Bond novels, but it was the timeliest—set in the Caribbean, concerned with a malevolent island despot and his clandestine rocket base. (Meanwhile, Our Nikita Sergeyevich vacationed by the Black Sea, brooding over the Jupiter missiles the United States had placed in Turkey and wondering whether he should plant a few of his own in Cuba's verdant soil.)

Paying lip service to the fantasy that Britain was still a world power, cementing a de facto North Atlantic alliance to make the hemisphere safe for an American moon shot, *Dr. No* proved almost as difficult to cast as *PT 109*. James Bond was to be a New Frontiersman who was neither ugly nor American. UA

---

*As Operation Mongoose percolated and *Dr. No* wrapped, UA chief Arthur Krim organized another presidential bash—the May 19, 1962, Madison Square Garden rally where Peter Lawford served up Marilyn Monroe in a $5,000 skintight, flesh-colored, mesh and rhinestone gown to serenade JFK (who, so secret historians have it, had most recently spent the night with her chez Crosby). Marilyn's suitably steamy version of "Happy Birthday" stole the show, from which Frank Sinatra was conspicuous by his absence.

executives were initially unimpressed by Welsh actor Sean Connery. As staunch Kennedy supporters, they preferred Peter Lawford—who, in turning down the part, lost the sinecure of a lifetime. Lawford's smarminess might have capsized the cycle before it began, but it remains Kennedy's identification with Bond that gives one pause. Suavely cynical, attractively untroubled by doubts, Bond lived in a daydreamer's paradise of beautiful women, high-stakes gambling, and narrowly avoided danger—the excitement amplified by the infectious bit of twangy surf music underscoring his private moments. It is as if Agent 007 were Kennedy's idea of a world historical individual—a two-fisted Sinatra inspiring his presidential follower to feel the irresistible power of his own libido, projected on the screen and running free.

Bond made his own rules—but he was hardly a social rebel. Without being aggressively youthful or overtly anti-authoritarian, 007 seems rather the avatar of a new permissiveness. Women are naturally fascinated by the Secret Agent—he always rates a reaction shot, if not a date. A true professional in his suit and stingy-brimmed fedora, Bond is actually best at beating up people. He endures the vaporization of a native colleague without a thought and coolly dispatches an unarmed adversary (a professor no less), sadistically delivering an extra shot point-blank to make the corpse twitch. James Bond was licensed to kill, and he clearly enjoyed it. That spring, the well-connected Washington pundit Joseph Alsop reported in the *Saturday Evening Post* that JFK had "quietly discarded" U.S. policy against launching a nuclear first strike. Khrushchev evidently took the article literally. Soviet forces were put on alert, and the Premier berated Pierre Salinger: "This warmonger Alsop—is he now your Secretary of State? Not even Eisenhower or Dulles would have made the statement your president made." The temper of the times was such that when *PT 109* began preproduction on Munson Island in the Florida Keys, the construction and beach closings prompted rumors that a sequel to the Bay of Pigs was in the works, while the U.S. Coast Guard mistook the Warners flotilla for a Cuban invasion.*

---

*The attention paid the making of *PT 109* may be deduced by the report Florida lawyer Robert L. Totterdale sent the White House personnel director in late July. Visiting the

• • •

Chickens were flying home to roost. In mid-June, a twenty-two-year-old former Marine mysteriously returned from his inexplicable two-and-a-half-year sojourn in the Soviet Union, having not only defected but also married the niece of a KGB colonel. Where 007 was an imaginary world-historic figure, this Lee Harvey Oswald might actually be one.

Were political events governed by conspiracy? Could there be a conspiracy contained within the mind of a single individual? The Secret Agent of History was pounding on the door, seeking realization, striving to appear—if only for an instant—within the fantasy regime. More weirdness: In late July, Nikita Khrushchev confided in the American ambassador his "genuine fear" that the U.S. military might seize control of Kennedy's government.*

In late July as well, U.S. Navy reconnaissance planes observed a sudden increase in Soviet ships making for the Cuban port of Mariel. The CIA soon discovered that Russian soldiers were guarding the docks as more Russian soldiers unloaded the boats. Some 65,000 American troops participated in Caribbean war games while 7,500 Marines staged a simulated attack on the island of Vieques, just off Puerto Rico. On August 23, the President directed Operation Mongoose to proceed with all due speed toward ousting Castro. Too late. The following week Senator Kenneth Keating, Republican of New York, was loudly warning of Soviet "rocket installations" in Cuba. The Republicans planned to make Castro their number-one issue.

---

set, Totterdale was upset to see "JFK" smoking a cigarette through a long holder. Totterdale's fear that this might create "an IMAGE [of] haughtiness and irresponsibility" was reinforced by concern that the Republicans would politicize the actual wartime incident, suggesting JFK was derelict in duty in allowing his boat to be rammed. There was even an on-set whispering campaign to that effect.

*Little did Khrushchev suspect that the American President and his sometime mistress, the later-murdered Mary Pinchot Meyer, were even then smoking marijuana in a White House bedroom—at least according to their mutual friend, onetime *Washington Post* vice-president James Truitt. Kennedy supposedly declined a third joint, telling Meyer, "No more. Suppose the Russians did something now."

By fall, other scenarios reached completion. The President had clandestine recording systems installed in the Oval Office and the cabinet room. Both could be activated by hidden switches. JFK had a White House secret and a public double: Vaughn Meader, a twenty-five-year-old, Boston-born comedian with a vague resemblance to the President first attracted attention in July performing his JFK impression on CBS's *Talent Scouts* and was booked to appear on both *Steve Allen* and *Ed Sullivan*. Released in November, Meader's comedy album *The First Family*—an amiable send-up of White House domesticity—would sell over four million copies in two months.

Politics was still good show business (ABC premiered a half-hour series updating *Mr. Smith Goes to Washington* to star Fess "Davy Crockett" Parker as a backwoods senator; and Irving Berlin opened his last Broadway musical, *Mr. President*). Even as the October 7 *New York Times* reported a widening breach between the Pentagon and Hollywood, attributed to unfavorable publicity following the use of U.S. troops in *The Longest Day*, *Seven Days in May*—a novel about a military coup d'etat against a pro-disarmament American president—climbed the bestseller list.

Written by Fletcher Knebel and Charles W. Bailey, Washington correspondents for the *Des Moines Register*, *Seven Days in May* was conceived in the Bay of Pigs aftermath, written during the anxious fall of 1961 and set in 1970, JFK's deadline for a U.S. moon landing. Defending their fantastic thesis, shared with the Soviet Premier, and, as it happened, with Senator Fulbright as well, Knebel and Bailey told the readers of *Look* they'd been inspired by Secretary of the Navy John Connally's concern that erosion of individual participation in democratic government might result in dictatorship. The authors further cited the strain between civilian and military leaders that was personified by the case of Major General Edwin A. Walker, the reluctant leader of the troops that occupied Little Rock during the desegregation crisis of 1957 and the subsequent commander of the 24th Infantry in West Germany.*

---

*Walker had been relieved of his commission in spring 1961 and subjected to a widely publicized inquiry after *Overseas Weekly* reported that he was blitzing his men with a

During the summer of 1961, Fulbright confronted Secretary of Defense Robert McNamara, demanding to know what his generals were up to. (Soon after the Arkansas senator spoke out against right-wing "radical extremism," he was targeted by the Dallas-based Minutemen, who advocated periodic assassinations to terrorize those members of Congress not "voting American.") Walker, now a civilian, was arrested for insurrection and seditious conspiracy in the aftermath of the September 30 violence in Oxford, Mississippi, when—in an operation stage-managed by Robert Kennedy—some 400 U.S. marshals escorted James Meredith, the twenty-nine-year-old black Air Force vet who had applied for admission to the University of Mississippi the day after JFK's inauguration.

The Oxford Crisis, which began when a federal court ruled in Meredith's favor and Mississippi Governor Ross Barnett called upon his white constituents to resist, was nearly a domestic Bay of Pigs. Shooting broke out minutes before the President appeared on TV that evening to inform the country that Ole Miss had been successfully integrated. Violence continued until dawn. Two were killed and 375 wounded. TV crews were beaten. From now on, JFK was subject to the same invective militant segregationists had hitherto reserved for his brother.

Intimations of civil war: *Seven Days in May* had been scarcely published before a liberal coalition was assembled to bring it to the screen. The rights were purchased by civic-minded Kirk Douglas, who hired Rod Serling to adapt and *The Manchurian Candidate*'s John Frankenheimer to direct. Producer Edward Lewis assumed a divided government, telling *Variety* the movie would be made despite the Pentagon's "anticipated non-cooperation and stumbling blocks." The government's "executive arm," he thought, "will be in favor." Meanwhile, Eugene Burdick and Harvey Wheeler's *Fail-Safe*, the story of an

---

"propaganda barrage" based on the precepts of the John Birch Society (which he joined in 1959). Senators Fulbright and Goldwater clashed on the military's right to speak out on political issues. Fulbright was concerned about reports linking military commanders—not all retired—to the Birch Society and, noting the coincidence that those most involved in disseminating the Birch line had served under General Douglas MacArthur in World War II or Korea, feared there might be a plot brewing—a coup to install the old soldier as an American de Gaulle.

inadvertent nuclear war that would be the year's other best-selling political thriller, was being serialized in the *Saturday Evening Post*. The President was reportedly reading both, as well he might. It was Boorstin's new totality.

• • •

There is a sense in which the President twice created those bestsellers inspired by the crises that might beset his Camelot—first, by providing a model for these exciting scenarios, and second, by validating them. JFK was the first— but not the last—American president conceptualized as the simultaneous protagonist and ideal consumer of American popular culture. Years later, Gloria Steinem recalled the Kennedy administration as the only time a reporter like herself felt that the story she wrote might actually be read in the White House. Perhaps—by someone. Kennedy himself was actually more interested in the televised news. Feedback time at the White House: Everything ceased, the President was watching his program.

Even as he cultivated his image and burnished his stardom, JFK was evoked on Broadway, mimicked by television comics, glorified in the movies. Brando and Sinatra were his peers. Young actors took him as a model. Not only would Hollywood dramatize the adventures of the young JFK but the Oval Office itself was now a mini reality studio that had been rigged to document the President's escapades (or at least some of them, for Kennedy's personal relationships were rife with subterfuge and cover-up). JFK defined the dream life— and its night terrors. His own top-secret secret-agent fantasies, his ruthless desire to eliminate rivals, might also inspire violent imitation. The presidency, Norman Mailer would observe, was a "primitive office and inspires the tribes of America to pick up the modes and manners of their chief."

Even before Marilyn Monroe was found dead in Hollywood on August 5, James Rosenquist took the President's sometime inamorata for a subject. Scarcely had the goddess given up the ghost than Andy Warhol was opportunistically silk-screening the star's fetishized image—her image as image—for his first New York one-man show. The now-iconic MM assumed her place beside PT-109 and Agent 007 in Kennedy mythology. The cult of personality was such that the imagined community could easily imagine itself as backdrop to the JFK story. When *Dr. No* had its London premiere in October, *Time* called it "almost a certainty" that

> one evening next winter, at perhaps 1930 hours, the President of the United States will enter a small room. For two hours a machine will play with his emotions. He may groan, but he will not be physically hurt. If he is disappointed when he leaves, he will at least emerge into a world where his job seems relatively tame, for he will have seen *Dr. No*, the first attempt to approximate on film the cosmic bravery, stupefying virility, six-acre brain, and deathproof nonchalance of Secret Agent James Bond—the President's favorite fictional hero.

In fact, even as *Time*'s prediction hit the newsstands, the President was straining his own six-acre brain, pondering two-day-old aerial reconnaissance pictures of Soviet missile sites in Cuba.

•   •   •

Tuesday, October 16, 1962, the Cold War narrative approaches its climax. Some, including Secretary of State Dean Rusk and the Joint Chiefs of Staff, are recommending an immediate aerial attack. Kennedy and his advisers spend Wednesday and Thursday debating the morality of such strikes, as Theodore Sorensen writes the speech to be delivered after the bombing. Friday, they discuss the option of blockading Cuba. (Cowboy-talking General Curtis LeMay is increasingly exasperated: "I don't see any other solution except direct military action right now!") Sunday, the President asks his wife if she wished to go to the government bomb shelter. Although JFK personally calls the *New York Times* and the *Washington Post* to keep the story from breaking, Monday morning's *Times* reports "an air of crisis in the capital," the weekend-long, late-night conferences, the agitated comings and goings of far-flung dignitaries, some used as decoys.

The scene is ready-made for a black-and-white nocturne in some futuristic political thriller. To imagine the Missile Crisis is to visualize the windowless War Room with its shiny curvilinear table, blinking telephones, and huge back-lit screen. By noon, American forces are on a worldwide alert, and for the first time, all SAC aircraft armed with nuclear weapons. (Soon, SAC will allow bombers to fly past their customary turnaround points on the Soviet perimeter.) According to intelligence the Soviets later received, military hospitals are being prepared to receive casualties. Kennedy briefs key members of Congress, including Senator Richard Russell of Georgia, chairman of the Armed Services Committee, who tells him that war with the Soviets is inevitable and asks if there'd ever be "more auspicious circumstances."

Franklin Schaffner, director of Mrs. Kennedy's televised White House tour, is flown back to Washington to supervise her husband's presentation. Monday evening, amid rumors of impending war, Kennedy trumps his 1961 State of the Union and Hot Summer of '61 speech with a defining performance, the most frightening television address ever given by an American president. Announcing the presence of offensive missile sites in Cuba, JFK imposes a naval blockade around the island. That the ultimatum is televised—rather than communicated through diplomatic channels—magnifies the crisis. In the midst of Camelot Year Two, *Variety* had declared newsmen David Brinkley, Chet Huntley, and Walter Cronkite the "new heroes of TV today." Now the TV networks are also on alert. NBC, the most mobilized, broadcasts ninety-four bulletins and thirteen news "specials" by the week's end.

Despite wartime security restrictions imposed by the administration, Tuesday's papers buzz with references to Pearl Harbor and D-Day. In New York, the UN Security Council has gone into a televised emergency session. "One looked at the buildings one passed," Norman Mailer later writes, "and wondered if one was to see them again."

The Manchurian Candidate = **The Secret Agent of History**

The Manchurian Candidate had its New York premiere on Wednesday, October 24, even as SAC ratcheted its alert posture up from Monday's Defense Condition 3 to an unprecedented DefCon 2. The administration made public fourteen aerial photographs of the missile installations, Soviet ships steamed toward the U.S. quarantine line, and Undersecretary of State George Ball warned UN ambassador Adlai Stevenson that there could be "a shooting war by tomorrow afternoon." *We'll Bury You!*, a newsreel compilation distributed by Columbia, also opened that day. "It was a grim experience," reported the *New York Times*, "to sit in a darkened theater, watch a chillingly convincing documentary on the spread of Communism and wonder, meanwhile, what was developing on the high seas."

What was it like as the world balanced on edge to sit in a darkened theater at the height of the crisis and watch *The Manchurian Candidate?* Were the streets outside filled with the anxious crowds of *When Worlds Collide?* Were movie houses two-thirds empty? (*Variety* reported that events "hit business badly" on Wednesday and Thursday.)*

Film historian Julian Smith, then a young and "cowardly" English instructor afraid that his reserve unit might be activated, left his apartment and ducked into the most convenient movie theater where, as it happened, *The Manchurian Candidate* had just opened. "From my sullen gloom," Smith remembered, "this picture lifted me as no other had done, before or since."

> When [the programmed assassin] Raymond Shaw swung his rifle from the presidential candidate at the Republican National Convention in Madison Square Garden and shot the Manchurian Candidate through the head, then blasted his mother, I went into a state of glee that held me through a second showing and drew me back the next night, and yet the next. . . .

Why this joy? Was it the inverse of despair, the satisfaction of nihilism fulfilled? The most fantastic elements of American politics were acknowledged at last, just as the nation—even the planet—headed inexorably toward total destruction. The fantasy scenario had arrived in time to make comprehensible so-called reality.

Variety screened *The Manchurian Candidate* in late September and predicted blockbuster results. Director John Frankenheimer remembered the first preview as "hysterical." The movie was denounced by both the American Legion and the Communist Party, then attacked the day before it opened by a syndicated Catholic film critic as "anti-anti-Communism gone crazy, like a fox."

Politics as spectacle, *The Manchurian Candidate* is the quintessential Kennedy-era thriller. In a sense, it is the Kennedy era—a movie that materialized mid–Missile Crisis to conflate right-wing demagogues and the international Communist conspiracy, juxtapose mind-control and assassination; play with PR and televisual reality. The hapless Raymond Shaw is but one secret agent. His mother, married to the dimwitted Senator Johnny Iselin, is an even more powerful clandestine operator. It is she who, duping even the Red Chinese, masterminds a plot designed to mobilize a "nation of television viewers . . . to sweep us into the White House with powers that make martial law look like anarchy."

History does not record if JFK ever saw the movie to which he gave his imprimatur. *The Manchurian Candidate* is a bit Bondlike in its futuristic technology, robotic hit men, sinister Asians, and joking violence. But, given the deadpan non sequiturs—not to mention matter-of-fact integration of dreams, flashbacks, and waking reality—it is far more steeped in the spectacle. Once the spectator realizes that the Cold War is the nightmare from which the hero Frank Sinatra is trying to awake, *The Manchurian Candidate* is genuinely self-reflexive. Just what would the President have made of the movie's ongoing identification of Communists with elderly women? Its mock-vérité political hoopla? The suggestion that marijuana—although not, as would have been more realistic, LSD—was an aid to behavioral modification?

Would Kennedy have appreciated the energy that Johnny Iselin draws from his own televised image? The suave aplomb with which director Frankenheimer mixed TV monitors and "live" action in the same frame to simultaneously orchestrate and deconstruct a pseudo-event? The use of the American national anthem to forestall the hero's prevention of the climactic assassination? How about the idea that Raymond Shaw was a fabricated war hero, not to mention the unwitting dupe of his unscrupulous parent? What would the President have made of the anti-McCarthy satire? The costume party to which the McCarthy-esque Iselin comes dressed as Abraham Lincoln? McCarthy, as Daniel Boorstin noted, built his political career almost entirely on pseudo-events. Indeed, McCarthy was America's preeminent media politician before JFK. Was the President cynical enough to be amused by the movie's notion that McCarthy was a Communist invention—an outright Trojan horse?*

Unlike Richard Condon's mildly futuristic novel, which concerned a Soviet conspiracy to control the nominee of the 1960 Republican Convention, the movie *Manchurian Candidate* was a period piece, set in the years following the Korean War and culminating at an imaginary version of the 1956 Republican Convention. That the movie unfolds in an alternative universe is entirely appropriate to its narrative dependence on implanted memories and overall meditation on the fragility of the human mind. In addition to speculating on how a McCarthy might have been nominated for president, *The Manchurian Candidate* took an extremely literal and highly fanciful view of behavioral modification, or "brainwashing"—a term which, associated with Chinese propaganda and the reeducation of American POWs, was in common usage by the end of the Korean War.†

------

*Once the supreme magic act in the American spectacle, McCarthy had been rendered obsolete. What was all the fuss about? A passé figure of fun, the crypto McCarthy demagogue appeared as liberal peacenik in *Advise and Consent* and drunken stooge in *The Manchurian Candidate*. Two neophyte filmmakers, Daniel Talbot and Emile de Antonio, had already secured rights to the televised Army-McCarthy hearings that captivated America back in the spring of 1954. Of course, the President had numerous associations with the anti-Communist crusader. McCarthy had not only received financial support from old Joe Kennedy, he had visited Hyannisport, employed young Robert on his Senate subcommittee staff, and even dated two Kennedy sisters. JFK was the lone Democratic senator who did not vote to censor McCarthy.

†Eight and a half years before, MGM's low-budget *Prisoner of War* introduced much of *The Manchurian Candidate*'s iconography, including the Pavlovian behavioral modification administered by impassive North Koreans and their sadistic Russian military advisers. Ronald Reagan starred as an American intelligence officer who allows himself to be captured and feigns cooperation in order to expose brainwashing and torture in North Korean POW camps. Released in May 1954, nearly a year after the Korean armistice, the movie was a failure, and defending its documentary accuracy, Reagan blamed liberals for the lack of public interest. In a sense, *The Manchurian Candidate* combined *Prisoner of War* with a far more compelling media event from the spring of 1954: the televised hearings that brought down Joseph McCarthy.

In short, *The Manchurian Candidate* was part of a process. An idea was willing itself into history—or rather several ideas. Condon's title anticipated journalist Edward Hunter's account of the collaboration between Korean brainwashers and Russians in Manchuria to create a "human robot" for secret-agent use. Hunter was a CIA operative and in fact, from 1953 through 1957, the CIA experimented with hypnosis as means for directing potential assassins. Perhaps inspired by *The Manchurian Candidate*, this program for providing history with a hidden motor was revived and expanded in June 1960 and continued into summer 1963 with Fidel Castro as its target.

No less than the Birch Society's "Black Book," a fantasy designed to supplant reality, *The Manchurian Candidate* offered a retrospective survey of Cold War concerns from TV image-building to Communist infiltration of the government. But who was infiltrating whom? The movie's chief brainwasher has a sly habit of paraphrasing American cigarette ads while, thinking like James Rosenquist or Andy Warhol, Senator Iselin gets the number of Communists in the Defense Department from the "57" label on a bottle of Heinz steak sauce. As noted by the philosopher of propaganda Jacques Ellul, brainwashing is not durable "except when the prisoner, once liberated, enters a society with the same *Weltanschauung* as the one imposed on him."

• • •

The Manchurian Candidate drew attention to the nature of a fantasy regime and the notion of a hidden national narrative. A month after the movie opened, the American Legion cited its enigmatic satire as further evidence that the Communists had returned to the movie industry. When asked by *Variety* why the Communist weekly *People's World* had termed *The Manchurian Candidate* the "most vicious attempt yet" to exploit "Soviet-American tensions," a Legion spokesman accused *People's World* of perpetrating a "typical Communist propaganda trick." One brain washed the other. *The Manchurian Candidate* ultimately become an explanation and a historical document—twenty-five years after its release, an ABC-TV documentary on CIA "mind control" used clips to illustrate its thesis. By then, *The Manchurian Candidate* was long out of circulation, withdrawn by Sinatra in the early 1970s. The star's alleged reason—remorse at having produced so prophetic a vision—was naturally incorporated into the movie's meaning.*

Although the mystique of *The Manchurian Candidate* would be burnished by the erroneous assertion that the movie had originally been a failure, it had supplanted *The Longest Day* as national box-office champ by Election Day. Clear-cut victory in World War II was superseded by the Cold War's permanent twilight. Nor was *The Manchurian Candidate* misappreciated. *The New Yorker* seconded *Variety*'s enthusiasm. The *New York Times* was, however, less than amused, charging Sinatra with a "grave sort of irresponsibility"; and when *The Manchurian Candidate* opened in Paris in December, *Le Monde* concurred. This "incoherent" vision of U.S. political insanity was sure to fuel "anti-American propaganda." The critic for *L'Express* was even more blunt in merging the movie with the crisis. *The Manchurian Candidate* so unsettled her, she wrote of leaving the theater praying that something of Europe could survive, given the impending clash between the two super powers.

For the American critic Andrew Sarris, both *Advise and Consent* and *The Manchurian Candidate* reflected a new conception of the United States as "dangerously 'sick.'" Although *The Manchurian Candidate* was well-stocked with Army psychologists and explicitly labeled Raymond Shaw a "sick" character, the movie's cynical, absurdist tone was itself "sick"—in the sense with which the word had been applied for the past dozen years to a distinctive form of American humor.

Back in 1956, *Village Voice* cartoonist Jules Feiffer began calling his weekly strip "Sick, Sick, Sick" in ironic acknowledgment of his neurotic, disaffected characters. Feiffer was the harbinger of nightclub comedians who treated such

---

*At the same time that Frank Sinatra pulled *The Manchurian Candidate* from circulation in the late 1960s, he also withdrew *Suddenly*—an obscure 1954 movie in which he himself played a would-be presidential assassin and which Marina Oswald told the Warren Commission that her husband had watched on Dallas television shortly before Kennedy was shot. When *The Manchurian Candidate* was reissued, after a well-publicized showing at the 1987 New York Film Festival, it was explained that Sinatra had actually withdrawn the movie in a dispute with UA over money.

apparently unfunny subjects as mental (and physical) illness, racial prejudice, religion, and nuclear fallout in their acts. By the summer of 1959, *Time* ran an article on those "Sickniks"—including Mort Sahl, Shelly Berman, Lenny Bruce, Mike Nichols and Elaine May, and Tom Lehrer—who, evincing a "highly disturbing hostility towards the world," trafficked in ghoulish social criticism, cracking jokes "about father and Freud, about mother and masochism, about sister and sadism." A sociologist asked to comment was disinclined to minimize the phenomenon: "It's like the last days of Rome." Others blamed the Sick on the Bomb.*

Even as *The Manchurian Candidate* went into release, *Catch-22*—the great literary expression of the Sick—had inspired quasi-religious devotion. Although Heller's novel never cracked the bestseller list, 32,000 copies were purchased during its first year in print. By the time the novel appeared in its deep-blue paperback edition (weeks before the Missile Crisis), Columbia had paid $150,000 for movie rights and *Newsweek* had run an article on the "zany, unclassifiable" object of the so-called "Heller Cult":

---

*Was the National Committee for a Sane Nuclear Policy (SANE), formed in November 1957, then the contagion's antidote? Throughout the first half of 1960, SANE staged mass rallies in New York, San Francisco, and Los Angeles. Nevertheless, the Sick was so pervasive that the number-one song during the final weeks of the 1960 campaign was Larry Verne's "(Please) Mr. Custer"—a novelty number which travestied the Battle of the Little Big Horn in the person of a presciently timorous cavalryman.

Sick comedy coincided with a new and sympathetic attention toward mental-health professionals in American movies: Krin Gabbard and Glen O. Gabbard's *Psychiatry and the Cinema* finds characters described as "competent, compassionate, and/or lovable psychiatrists" in at least twenty-two Hollywood films released between 1957 and 1963, including the African-American shrink in *The Manchurian Candidate*. (Who better than a black man would understand America's neurosis?)

NBC premiered its psychiatric drama *The Eleventh Hour* in autumn 1962; Sam Fuller's *Shock Corridor*, which began shooting in February (the same month JFK delivered the first-ever presidential message to Congress on the subject of "mental health") and, released the following September, too riven by contradictions to successfully function as anyone's fantasy, literalized the idea of a sick society by dramatizing a number of current American social ills as the delusions of psychiatric patients.

Not since *The Catcher in the Rye* and *Lord of the Flies* has a novel been taken up by such a fervid and heterogeneous claque of admirers. . . . David Merrick wants to do a Broadway version. Anthony Quinn, Jack Lemmon, Ben Gazzara, Paul Newman, Eli Wallach all want to play Yossarian.

Catch-22 was inspired by Heller's own experience as a bombardier in the European theater, but as he often pointed out, the novel was filled with such anachronisms as helicopters, computers, and loyalty oaths, not to mention thinly veiled references to Senator McCarthy and key members of the Eisenhower administration. Rooted in World War II but developed during its aftermath, *Catch-22* was published slightly in advance of a parallel and equally long-germinating scenario: Although the novel gathered prestige during the Missile Crisis, its greatest sequel would be the still-developing war in Vietnam.

Camelot Down: Thinking About the Unthinkable

The Missile Crisis was resolved Sunday, October 28, one day after an American U-2 was shot out of the Cuban sky (while another strayed over Siberia) and twenty-four hours before the planned U.S. air strike. When the Joint Chiefs were informed Khrushchev had agreed to remove his missiles, General Curtis LeMay pounded the table and bellowed, "It's the greatest defeat in our history. . . . We should invade today!" Defense Secretary McNamara remembered looking at Kennedy and noting that the shocked President was "stuttering in reply."*

SAC's former commander, LeMay was virtually acting out the role scripted for him—or, rather, Burt Lancaster—in the adaptation of the military coup thriller *Seven Days in May*. Kirk Douglas, who was to play the "good" soldier, later maintained that although many people advised him to stay away from the project, he received unexpected official support.

---

*This exchange was not included in *Thirteen Days*, the 2000 feature based on actual transcripts from the (secretly bugged) White House offices wherein the crisis was managed.

I went to Washington to talk with the writers. Before I did, I attended a fancy buffet dinner. I was standing with a plate full of hot food, ill at ease. A voice next to me said, "Do you intend to make a movie out of *Seven Days in May?*"

I turned. President Kennedy! "Yes, Mr. President."

"Good." He spent the next twenty minutes, while our dinner got cold, telling me that he thought it would make an excellent movie. If I had had any doubts, this one strong "yea" drowned out all the other "nays."

Frankenheimer similarly recalled Kennedy's interest. White House Press Secretary Pierre Salinger conveyed the message: "The Pentagon didn't want it done. Kennedy said that when we wanted to shoot at the White House he would conveniently go to Hyannisport."

Although the United States maintained its forces at high alert until November 20 and *Seven Days in May* topped the bestseller list into April 1963, the anxiety that gripped the country since the hot summer of 1961 began to dissipate and even turn contemplative—although the Kennedy scenario had yet to reach its critical mass. *PT 109* wrapped. Released on November 13, *The First Family* needed only four weeks to surpass the original-cast recording of *My Fair Lady* as the best-selling LP of all time. A new sensibility, now named Pop Art, was sanctioned—one that reveled in Daniel Boorstin's despairing observation that America's "business" was the making of illusions.*

No less terrified than their subjects by the events of October, the U.S. and Soviet governments negotiated to ban atmospheric testing, establish an emergency hot line, and, in general, rewrite the script for nuclear war. Indeed, two remarkably similar movies were already in production on the subject of acci-

---

*With Pop Art, American artists embraced the image, and the nation celebrated itself as trademark. In the weeks following the Missile Crisis, the Sidney Janis Gallery opened its influential "New Realism" group exhibition, Andy Warhol and Tom Wesselman had their first New York one-man shows, and the Museum of Modern Art devoted a symposium to this suddenly fashionable iconography of comic strips, movie stars, and supermarket products. For those grateful to be alive, even Warhol's paintings of Campbell's soup cans looked beautiful.

dentally produced atomic Armageddon. *Thinking About the Unthinkable*, Herman Kahn's 1962 meditation on subjects thermonuclear, had posited the possibility of an inadvertent war, precipitated by "mechanical or human error, false alarm, self-fulfilling prophecy, or unauthorized behavior" as the most likely of four possible war scenarios.

The first movie on the subject—taken from *Red Alert*, a science-fiction novel published by former RAF pilot Peter George in 1958—was announced in May of that year by Stanley Kubrick. Kahn, among the many experts that Kubrick would consult while making his 1963 *Dr. Strangelove, or How I Stopped Worrying and Learned to Love the Bomb*, playfully suggested that "since the Marxist view of history might incline Soviet planners away from the view that a defective switch could influence history, the Soviets may not be as concerned about this type of problem as the West." Nevertheless, a second evocation of inadvertent nuclear war was being adapted by a group of liberals from the best-selling *Fail-Safe*—a novel in which the United States inadvertently bombs Moscow and is ultimately compelled to apologize by obliterating New York. Max Youngstein, a UA vice president and founding member of Hollywood SANE, read *Fail-Safe* while the novel was in manuscript and acquired the rights, hiring formerly blacklisted Walter Bernstein to write the screenplay.

In their introduction to *Fail-Safe*, Eugene Burdick and his collaborator, Harvey Wheeler, explained that they did not consider their novel an exposé of the Strategic Air Command. Nor was it speculative fiction—the experts agreed that accidental nuclear war was not only possible but increasingly likely: "Hardly a week passes without some new warning of this danger by knowledgeable persons. . . . In addition, all too often past crises have been revealed to us in which the world tottered on the brink of thermonuclear war while SAC commanders pondered the true nature of unidentified flying objects on their radar screens." What could they be thinking of?

> Men, machines, and mathematics being what they are, this is, unfortunately, a "true" story. The accident may not occur in the way we describe but the laws of probability assure us that ultimately it will occur.

Such prophetic gloom struck some as abject defeatism. Professor Sidney Hook, chairman of the philosophy department at New York University, was at work on a pamphlet arguing that the *Fail-Safe* scenario depended on a "conjunction of unrelated improbabilities." Hook considered the novel symptomatic of a mass, irrational failure of nerve—that is, a sickness. How else to explain "the eagerness and excitement of the normally staid publishers?" Or "the raptures of reviewers, movie producers, copywriters, and promotion salesmen?"

> How to explain their willingness to cry havoc!, to celebrate their panic with a fervor whose intensity transcends the synthetic enthusiasms customarily whipped up to attract attention at the box office?

The book was one more pernicious pseudo-event. Although Hook didn't deem it relevant, *Fail-Safe*'s appearance during the season of the Missile Crisis contributed to the million-plus copies sold by the time his hardcover pamphlet *The Fall-Safe Fallacy* was published in October 1963.

Complaining that Burdick and Wheeler scripted the Soviet leader to "sound like a noble Roman Senator and have him accept, with appropriate Stoic sentiments, the sacrifice of New York in exchange for the sacrifice of Moscow," Hook suggested that were *Fail-Safe* translated into Russian, the authors might be eligible for a Lenin Peace Prize. Indeed, "the odds that this would happen seem to me to be greater than the likelihood of the kind of accident occurring about which *Fail-Safe* has frightened the nation."

Who then had the right to frighten the nation? The sense of Hollywood divided—a pop psychoanalyst might term it schizoid—was palpable throughout the Kennedy administration. Total mobilization was a given. Even so liberal a movie as *The Manchurian Candidate* understood military culture as all-encompassing. It was the good soldier played by Frank Sinatra who foiled the conspiracy. The movie industry was operating as though prepared to go to war but seemed unsure which branch of the government—the Pentagon or the President—it was to obey. Armed with the knowledge that two films on accidental nuclear warfare were in preparation, General LeMay encouraged

Universal producer Sy Bartlett (a World War II bomber pilot with twenty-one years in the Air Force) to make *A Gathering of Eagles*—dedicated to the Strategic Air Command and starring future Barry Goldwater–supporter Rock Hudson as a fanatically hard-nosed, wife-neglecting wing commander.

As Hollywood's first post-Sputnik report, *A Gathering of Eagles* was pleased to introduce audiences to the iconography of B-52s phalanxes, minimum interval takeoffs, flashing alerts, ominous red phones, and cryptic transmissions from Omaha: THIS IS JUMBO WITH A SILVERFLASH MESSAGE FOR MOONBEAM. For all its Pop Art space-age pageantry and dogged hyperrealism, reportedly including a scene shot in the War Room itself, *A Gathering of Eagles* was basically a cavalry Western with hypothetical Indians. Instead of a Soviet sneak attack, dramatic tension was provided by the wing commander's anticipation of a "no-notice" Operation Readiness Inspection (ORI). If this didactic celebration of twenty-four-hours-a-day, seven-days-a-week nuclear defense did not achieve its intended result, it was in part because the Hunter character's anxiety compelled him to ignore regulations in responding to the ORI and in part because *Catch-22* rendered such regulations absurd. "Is SAC really all that sick?" *Time* quipped when *A Gathering of Eagles* opened in July 1963.*

---

*A Gathering of Eagles was not the first Pentagon update SAC shepherded through Hollywood. MGM's *Above and Beyond* (1953) told the story of Colonel Paul Tibbets, the pilot who dropped the bomb on Hiroshima, with emphasis on his domestic difficulties. As *The New Yorker* observed, well before the colonel reached his target, "his wife has kicked up such a row about his taciturnity that a security check on her is ordered and she is drummed out of Wendover, along with her two small sons." LeMay himself was a supporting player, played by Jim Backus (cartoon voice of the nearsighted Mr. Magoo).

Paramount's spectacular *Strategic Air Command* (1955) introduced the key to Freedomland security as SAC's B-36 and new B-47 bombers—greeting the first shot of the latter with a peal of sacred organ music. Shot in Vista Vision—bigger and sharper than Cinemascope or Cinerama—*Strategic Air Command* interspersed awe-inspiring sequences of midair refueling with more earthbound drama. Major league baseball player Jimmy Stewart was recalled to service with SAC—a cause for some domestic friction with his wife, June Allyson (who played Mrs. Stewart in two previous movies). Frank Lovejoy was cast as the tough SAC General—not named LeMay, although *Time*, which called

A *Gathering of Eagles* was perhaps Universal's attempt to balance their production of *The Ugly American*, which opened in April—two days after a Dallas sniper (later identified by a government commission as Lee Harvey Oswald) took a pot shot at former General Edwin Walker as he sat at home filling out his income tax return. By the time the movie reached the screen, Americans had lived through the Bay of Pigs, the Berlin Wall, and the Missile Crisis, while JFK had rather less spectacularly dispatched 15,000 American "military advisers" to Indochina. (Signs protesting this involvement first appeared April 14, 1963, at New York's annual Easter peace march.)

The very title, *The Ugly American*, was an accusation. Just as its original meaning had been lost, the movie's script collapsed the novel's multiple protagonists into one, Ambassador MacWhite (Brando), while splitting the imaginary Indochinese land of Sarkhan into a communist North and tenuously democratic South. Thanks to MacWhite's self-righteous bungling, revolution breaks out in South Sarkhan and the Ambassador is compelled to call in the Seventh Fleet. But, thanks to television, exotic Sarkhan is no further away than the dusty pueblo of *The Magnificent Seven*. *The Ugly American* closes with MacWhite's image beamed into an ordinary American living room.

> If the Cold War ended right now, the American people would still be in this fight against ignorance, hunger, disease, because it's right. It's right to be in it, and if I had one appeal to make to every American it would be that. . . .

His impassioned pitch is terminated with a resounding *click!* as a drumstick-gnawing Joe Six-pack turns off the TV, signaling a new manifestation of the

---

the movie "one soaring, super colossal recruiting poster," knowingly observed that the actor "does an excellent imitation of that famous cigargoyle."

LeMay not only endorsed *Strategic Air Command* but, according to *Variety*, participated in its promotion. The more modest *Bombers B-52*, released by Warner Brothers two years later and somewhat overshadowed by the first Soviet satellites, showcased the latest SAC weaponry while shifting the domestic drama to the conflict between a tough career sergeant (Karl Malden) and his winsome daughter (Natalie Wood).

Ugly American. (To drive the message home, the end credits are accompanied by "America the Beautiful.")

The Ugly American received mixed reviews, and its neophyte director, George Englund, the personal friend to whom Brando had entrusted the production, announced a more positive follow-up pegged to the activities of the Peace Corps in Africa. Eugene Burdick was working on the script. Within a month of The Ugly American's release, the situation in South Vietnam had deteriorated. President Ngo Dinh Diem and his brother Ngo Dinh Nhu resented the infringement of their sovereignty exercised by the U.S. Special Forces. Beginning in May, the Diem regime engaged in repressive actions against the nation's Buddhist majority. JFK was concerned lest Vietnam become a campaign issue in 1964. By summer, he and his advisers were discussing Diem's ouster.

●   ●   ●

More American ugliness, this time closer to home: TV news images of Birmingham, Alabama, police in riot gear turning dogs and high-pressure fire hoses on peaceful marchers, many of them children. That spring, the "most thoroughly segregated city in the U.S.," per Martin Luther King (who had been assaulted there by an American Nazi in late 1962), was shown as the most violent as well. George Wallace, inaugurated governor of Alabama in January 1963 with the mantra "Segregation now . . . segregation tomorrow . . . segregation forever," would become a national figure. Wallace flew the Confederate flag over his statehouse and was, for King, the "most dangerous racist in America."

The spring of 1963 initiated America's nine-year season of domestic violence—which would end, more or less, with an attempt on Wallace's own life. The New Yorker published James Baldwin's report on the Black Muslims and coolly apocalyptic meditation on the state of race relations in America, ending with the warning God gave Noah: No more water, the fire next time! The ongoing Birmingham demonstrations made Time's cover in May and again in June. While symbolically pitting himself against King all that spring, Wallace raised the stakes in an April 25 meeting with Robert Kennedy, during which he attempted to maneuver the Attorney General into threatening that federal troops would enforce the University of Alabama's court-ordered integration. In June, Wallace used an appearance on *Meet the Press* to further enflame the issue by repeating his campaign promise to "stand in the door" to block the two black students.

Even before Wallace so informed the public, filmmaker Robert Drew had sniffed out the "crisis" and secured permission to film a TV documentary recording both sides of the unfolding drama. Wallace was understandably suspicious but media-savvy enough to agree, staging an interview beneath a portrait of die-hard secessionist William Lowndes Yancey and explaining to the Yankee TV crew that he'd rather "live a short life of standing for principle than live a long life of compromise. Of course that may not mean much to you folks." Alabama was the last holdout—the Alamo of state-university segregation—and Wallace meant to make the most of it.

Posturing for the camera while the Kennedy brothers were filmed mapping out a legal strategy, Wallace set the stage for the June 11 confrontation—or rather performance. The Governor blocks the doorway, the Assistant Attorney General, Nicholas Katzenbach, serves him with a federal "cease and desist" order. Wallace stands his ground until told to step aside by the now-federalized Alabama National Guard. "It could not have been better scripted," according to Wallace's biographer Dan T. Carter. "Alabama's governor was given the opportunity to act like a particularly disgraceful alley cat prancing back and forth in front of a firmly chained pit bull." (In fact, albeit enjoying himself, Wallace appears in Drew's film as self-controlled—and even statesmanlike—in his call for peace and order.)*

---

*Although the stand in the schoolhouse door would eventually exist in the public mind as an episode in the 1994 movie *Forrest Gump*, Wallace reaped considerable national publicity while, after two and a half years in office, JFK was compelled to take a personal stand against segregation. The same night the President made his televised address, NAACP leader Medgar Evers was shot dead in Mississippi. Discord rose at home even as Kennedy launched a pre-election international peace offensive. In late April, the last Jupiter missiles were quietly removed from Turkey. June 9, JFK made a speech invoking, as no U.S. president had since 1945, the Soviet World War II effort. (In July, his rep-

A day before the White House–Kremlin hot line was established in June 1963, *PT 109* had its world premiere. *Time* joked that the movie was filmed with a "reverence usually reserved for a New Testament spectacle," while *Variety* dutifully reported that the Loew's Orpheum, where it opened in New York, saw the "greatest local mob scene since V-J Day." Scarcely anyone else was convinced. It was tedious to see that which was already in existence—JFK as youthful star politician—trying so arduously to actualize itself. Although *PT 109* seemed an obvious pseudo-event, too dull and inflated to stir much enthusiasm, the *New York World-Telegram and Sun* predicted it would "make a formidable campaign document in next year's election." Meanwhile, NBC drew attention to another Kennedy campaign text by announcing plans for a TV series based on *Profiles in Courage*.

Still, JFK's approval ratings had declined from a post–Bay of Pigs high of 82 percent to 59 percent, the lowest of his presidency. The test-ban treaty was being debated in the Senate, but a Gallup poll suggested that Kennedy's proposed civil rights legislation was responsible for denting his popularity: Some 46 percent of the American public felt the President was "pushing integration too fast." As King and the Southern Christian Leadership Council prepared to march on Washington, August 28, in support of the Civil Rights bill, Senator Barry Goldwater expressed concern that anti-integration unrest would spread to the north and the west.

Wallace warned that if the Civil Rights bill passed, Congress should prepare to withdraw American troops from Berlin and Vietnam. The boys would be needed to keep order at home. Indeed, the Birmingham-based neo-Nazi National States' Rights Party had been calling since March for the execution of Supreme Court justices. Suddenly, the *New Orleans Picayune* ran a four-column story on a recent interview with Fidel Castro. The Cuban leader was furious that the Americans were still trying to roll back the revolution and do away with him. Castro even issued a warning, surely read by Lee Harvey Oswald,

---

resentatives sounded out the Kremlin on a possible joint strike against China's not-yet-operational nuclear facilities.)

secretary and single member of the Fair Play for Cuba Committee, New Orleans chapter: "United States leaders should think that if they are aiding terrorist plans to eliminate Cuban leaders, they themselves will not be safe."

The contagion was spreading. Now was the moment for Sam Fuller's *Shock
Corridor*, in which an ambitious reporter feigns madness and has himself committed to a mental hospital in order to solve the murder of an inmate. At once
floridly written and boldly cartooned, outrageously lurid and rigorously mini-
mal, *Shock Corridor* was shot entirely in interior—the outside world only present as hallucination. But however hermetic the harshly lit hospital ward, there
was the sense that violence could erupt at any moment.

The events of late 1962 had percolated in writer-director-producer Fuller's
imagination. His mental hospital is haunted by doomsday visions, war games,
and race riots. A guilt-ridden nuclear physicist has regressed to age five. A
brainwashed Korean War traitor imagines he is a heroic Confederate general.
Trent, the first black to integrate a Southern university, believes himself
founder of the Ku Klux Klan. Social pathology merges with individual delusion.
Pillowcase over his head, the black Klansman chases a black janitor through
the ward, screaming "Catch that nigger before he marries my daughter!" and
fashions signs directed at himself: BLACK BOMBS FOR BLACK FOREIGNERS! AMER-
ICA FOR AMERICANS!

Shock Corridor was an LSD bummer before the term was coined. America
was so sick that, following Catch-22 logic, the hero must go crazy to solve the
mystery—or even want to. The reporter wins the Pulitzer Prize but, now an
"insane mute," is rewarded with a lifetime assignment in the mental hospital.
Critics were not kind. "*Shock Corridor* Should Never Have Been Made," one
review began. The movie was not simply "outright trash" but "one of the
most vicious and irresponsible pieces of film-making that the screen has given
us in many years." September 15, the first Sunday after *Shock Corridor* opened,
a bomb exploded in a Birmingham church, killing four black children.

How satisfying to rerun June's civil rights triumph in Alabama. If *Primary*
certified the birth of a Star-Pol, Drew's 1963 *Crisis: Behind a Presidential Commitment* dramatized the unfolding events in Alabama as a new politics of photo

opportunity. The movie sparked controversy even before *Show* magazine's six-page spread ("Television Goes Backstage with History") or its premiere at the first New York Film Festival. In late July, two days after breaking the story on page one, the *New York Times* editorialized on the "astounding" fact that this "highly inappropriate"—still unseen—documentary had been made. "The process of decision-making is not the occasion for the creation of an 'image.' . . . The White House isn't Macy's window." Broadcast by ABC with appropriate hoopla the evening of October 21, *Crisis* was presented as an imagistic civil war—opening with rival anthems and crosscutting between the antagonists, the Kennedy brothers and Governor Wallace, at home. However tedious and anticlimactic, the documentary triggered a firestorm.

"The President has no business in show business," the *New York Herald-Tribune* tartly complained, while *New York Times* critic Jack Gould called the show "a prime example of governmental surrender to the ceaseless and often thoughtless demands of the entertainment world." As General Curtis LeMay used *A Gathering of Eagles* to promote SAC, so JFK deployed *Crisis* to push his civil rights agenda. Gould, like Daniel Boorstin, was concerned that spectacle had supplanted substance: "A viewer could not forget that Federal officials and Governor Wallace knew that the cameras were there, and under such circumstances, the hour seemed an incredible bit of play-acting." Crisis indeed. It seemed as though history was being made—or perhaps manufactured—under the klieg lights.

At one point, Wallace warned the camera—and hence the President—that the next national election would be decided by the South and there were some people, no names named, who weren't very popular there. The day *Crisis* was televised, the *New York Times* reported that the President had begun targeting Senator Barry Goldwater—principal critic of the current U.S. Soviet "thaw" as well as the Civil Rights bill—as his likely opponent in 1964. Wallace was barely part of the equation. Yet, slick-haired and scowling, the dapper little governor was receiving invitations to speak at colleges across the country. If, as Pierre Salinger later wrote, Kennedy was abashed by *Crisis*, Wallace was confirmed in bona fide celebrity. Embarking upon his northern tour, the Alabama governor hinted what his allies in the White Citizens Council already knew: Wallace was planning to enter the Democratic primaries and who knows what after. . . .

In October, United Artists's second, more elaborate 007 adventure, *From Russia With Love,* had its London premiere. ("Half the world is trying to kill him!" the trailer proclaimed.) The following month, two nights after *Crisis* was telecast, JFK previewed the new Bond at a private Washington, DC, screening. Ben Bradlee, who was there, noted with apprehension that the President seemed "to enjoy the cool and the sex and the brutality"—not to mention Bond's insouciant realpolitik. JFK had anticipated a coup in South Vietnam since August, especially once Ngo Dinh Diem and Ngo Dinh Nhu began to explore a negotiated settlement with North Vietnam. Yet, cool as he was, the President was shocked on November 2 when, less than twenty-four hours after dissident generals converged on Saigon, the captured South Vietnamese leader and his brother were simply taken out and shot.

Coups d'Etat: Four Days in November, *Seven Days in May*

And suddenly, Everything is Now. On the afternoon of Friday, November 22, 1963, and in the three days that follow, the imagined community known as America experiences itself viscerally as a collective entity. The JFK death event is watched in 96 percent of America's TV homes for an average of thirty-one hours and thirty-eight minutes. Not since the great comets brushed planet Earth to destroy the dinosaurs has there been such simultaneity. The drama played out in the Ford Theater April 17, 1865, was but a dress rehearsal for the events in Dealy Plaza, Dallas. History is made, and as promised by Walter Cronkite, we are there—together.

Initially it seems as though the violence in Birmingham and elsewhere in the South might have lit the fuse that blew the President away. But only hours after Kennedy expires, Dallas authorities capture a lone gunman—one Lee Harvey Oswald—whom they believe to have assassinated JFK for his own obscure political motivations, possibly related to Cuba. Along with comforting biographical material on the new President, Lyndon Baines Johnson, the grimacing, weasel-like suspect is shown to the national audience until—as part of a return to the scene of the crime—NBC broadcasts a live telecast of the alleged assassin's own assassination at the hands of mob-connected, cop-friendly strip-club-owner Jack Ruby. Amid continuous television coverage, a second Secret Agent enters history.

The long weekend special—from Dallas shooting to Washington funeral—offers, as Frederic Jameson will write, the "Utopian glimpse into some collective communicational 'festival.' " The video technology of the instant replay originates in the endlessly televised stop-motion repetition of squat Ruby stepping out of the crowd, gun in fist, and Oswald crumpling in death agony. Television provides much short-term therapy—the medium promotes the illusion of participation while the sheer there-ness of its soothing continuity relieves anxiety, dispelling, for the moment, any fear of conspiracy. There is some comfort to be taken in this ultimate Crisis. Still, as the national narrative has ruptured, the upcoming film version of *The Best Man* will require retakes, and *PT 109* must be withdrawn from release. The spectacle is hastily rewritten. A *Joey Bishop Show*, taped the previous week with Vaughn Meader as guest star, is erased. Even as Fidel Castro places his military on high alert, fearing the United States will blame him for the President's death, NBC postpones a new documentary on the Bay of Pigs fiasco, substituting a telecast of the Grammy awards originally scheduled for Sunday, November 24. Meader's segment is, of course, deleted.

WAS "MANCHURIAN" FILM A PROPHET?, the *Hollywood Citizen-News* wonders. Certainly, for anyone monitoring the dream life's secret history, Dallas had been filled with signs and portents on the morning of November 22. Many of these possible behavioral "triggers" were provided by America's richest man, oil billionaire and John Birch Society–supporter H. L. Hunt, who, only days before, was heard to complain that there was "no way left to get those traitors out of our government except by shooting them out." Hunt's daily radio show, *Life Line*—which that week accused the Moscow-directed tyrant Kennedy of forcing American taxpayers to subsidize World Communism—warned that, were the President successful in creating a Soviet America, he would certainly ban firearms.

Friday's *Dallas Morning News* had presciently run a full-page, black-bordered attack on the President, paid for by H. L.'s son, Nelson Bunker Hunt. The elder Hunt's sometime protégé, former General Edwin Walker, flew the American flag on his lawn upside-down to protest the presidential visit—it was, of course, raised full-staff during the official period of mourning—even as an associate distributed handbills that captioned JFK's photograph WANTED FOR TREASON.

• • •

Announced the very morning of the assassination by a full-page ad in the *New York Times*, *Seven Days in May*'s release was delayed until early 1964—opening in New York on February 19. "Kennedyste" without Kennedy, filled with liberal rhetoric and ominous drum rolls, the movie was paranoid yet idealistic. More sober than *The Manchurian Candidate*, *Seven Days in May* presented its scenario of attempted military coup d'etat with a clipped immediacy.

As the title *Seven Days in May* anticipated the concept of the TV miniseries, so the movie looked and sounded like teledrama—Rod Serling's script returned John Frankenheimer to his origins. The opening scene of right-wing pickets scuffling with Ban-the-Bombers outside the White House was shot a few days after the 1963 Nuclear Test Ban Treaty was initialed in Moscow, and according to *Variety*, actual anti–Test Ban demonstrators had to be dispersed to facilitate the staged disturbance.

Realer than real, *Seven Days'* wise, liberal heroes—the President (Frederic March), his press secretary (Martin Balsam), and the Star (producer Kirk Douglas, here a more modest and self-effacing Hollywood Freedom Fighter)—save American democracy through televised appeals to the American people. Despite this demonstration of faith in the media, however, *New York Times* critic Bosley Crowther complained that "the movies [were] out to scare us all to death with dire and daring speculations on what might happen any day in Washington." Like the similarly postponed, just-released *Dr. Strangelove*, *Seven Days in May* offered the "fearsome prospect of the crisis that might occur if another Air Force general planned to seize control of the Government."

Although producer, Edward Lewis, would get to rework this particular conspiracy, with Burt Lancaster once again cast as the heavy in the 1973 thriller *Executive Action* (a fictional recreation of the Kennedy assassination itself), *Seven Days in May* seemed designed as a rhetorical preview of the '64 campaign. Like JFK, the incumbent Democrat risks signing a test-ban treaty with the Soviets—thus offending Lancaster's chairman of the Joint Chiefs, a combination of Curtis LeMay and Edwin Walker, who appears at Senate hearings to deliver the line then most publicly identified with aspiring Republican candidate Barry Goldwater.

Such carping was momentarily forgotten. This was the fleeting moment of the LBJ consensus—the period of the new President's first hundred days. (Like his predecessor, Johnson consecrated his elevation to supreme leadership by reconfiguring his name as a logo.) Martin Luther King Jr. was proclaimed *Time*'s Man of the Year. The Hat Corporation of America prepared to saturate the market with scaled-down, unisex versions of LBJ's five-gallon Stetson. Thus, *Seven Days in May* served to put a stamp of approval on America's new leader— and not just because the movie's president was named "Jordan Lyman." (As if acknowledging that America might still be stuck in the Twilight Zone, Rod Serling was drafted to write the U.S. Information Agency's hurriedly produced Johnson bio-pic, *Let Us Continue*.) *Dr. Strangelove*, on the other hand, dramatized the catastrophe the nation had been dreading since the hot summer of 1961 and fully expected in October 1962.

Stanley Kubrick's movie opened in New York on January 30, one day after the new South Vietnamese junta was overthrown by a group of young military officers led by the American-trained thirty-seven-year-old General Nguyen Khanh. Having evolved from straightforward thriller to daring black comedy, *Dr. Strangelove* was at once austerely didactic in its demonstration of (largely invented) military codes, security procedures, and chains of command, and broadly farcical—when not extravagantly puerile—in tone. To the image of the futuristic War Room, the movie added that of implacable B-52 bombers flying over the Siberian tundra, the idea of a top-secret government fallout shelter, and the premise of the radioactive Doomsday machine.

In the original novel, the fatal nuclear device was finally too damaged to detonate. But *Dr. Strangelove*—which, unfolding between 3:30 AM and dawn as a comic nightmare that (like *High Noon*) takes place in more or less real time—projected its premise all the way to Armageddon. In the *New York Times*, Bosley Crowther predictably called the movie the "most shattering sick joke" he'd ever experienced, expressing unhappiness with its anti-authoritarian "contempt for our whole defense establishment, up to and even including the hypothetical Commander in Chief."

Dr. Strangelove's Prescription

During the Cuban Missile Crisis, an Air Force psychiatric officer had characterized the mood on his base as one of exhilaration. It was the same sensation experienced by Julian Smith. The mounting tension, the constant simulation of combat preparedness finally gave way to an actual alert. Similarly, with the assassination of JFK, the worst had occurred—or at least a version of it. *Dr. Strangelove* was another exorcism.*

The country had a few remaining jitters. When LBJ visited Florida, he flew in an unmarked helicopter, thanks to rumors that a Cuban missile or kamikaze pilot had targeted the presidential plane. (Johnson was astonished to learn, after he became president, that the CIA was "running a damn Murder Incorporated in the Caribbean" but, just as Fidel feared, suspected Cuba was behind his predecessor's assassination.) Still, Lewis Mumford wrote to the *New York Times*, *Strangelove* was a "break in the catatonic cold war trance that has so long held our country in its rigid grip." In the *New York Review of Books*, Robert Brustein called *Strangelove* "extraordinarily liberating." Antonin Artaud would have admired this movie, which released "through comic poetry, those feelings of impotence and frustration that are consuming us all."

---

*So, too, Andy Warhol's giddily transgressive Pop Art silkscreen "Sixteen Jackies," which repeated images culled from the same post-assassination issue of *Life* that premiered selected frames from the color 8mm home movie that Abraham Zapruder happened to shoot of the President's assassination. In August 1999, the U.S. government paid Zapruder's heirs $16 million for this sacred relic—reportedly the highest price ever commanded by an historical artifact—despite the fact that the film was too fragile to be projected and the Zapruder family already owned all licensing rights.

Strangelove had been extensively previewed in New York during the autumn of 1963. Then, according to Susan Sontag, who wrote on the movie in *Partisan Review*, imaginative liberals wondered whether such political daring might not set off riots with "American legion types storming the theaters, etc." However, "as it turned out, everybody, from *The New Yorker* to *The Daily News*, has had kind words for *Dr. Strangelove*; there are no pickets and the film is breaking records at the box office." The movie was appreciated for its optimism. "Intellectuals and adolescents" alike loved *Dr. Strangelove*, Sontag reported. "But the 16-year-olds who are lining up to see it understand the film, and its real virtues, better than the intellectuals, who vastly over praise it." Compared to *Point of Order*, a condensed version of the 1954 televised Army-McCarthy hearings (and for Sontag, "the real comédie noire of the season"), Kubrick's movie was scarcely even political in treating the "OK targets of left-liberals (the defense establishment, Texas, chewing gum, mechanization, American vulgarity)" from a "*Mad* magazine point of view."*

Characterizing *Strangelove* as a particularly American movie, Brustein found that it overwhelmed the "weary meanderings of Resnais, Fellini, and Antonioni"—the first and last, Sontag heroes. Burying a tired Euro-modernism (while sending up Texas), *Strangelove* was Pop Art. "Fun—this is its one debt to Hollywood," *Strangelove* turned the World War II movie upside down. Approvingly, Brustein noted that Kubrick had "managed to explode the right-wing position without making a single left-wing affirmation: the odor of the Thirties [had] finally been disinfected." Brustein found *Strangelove*'s cheerful lack of moralizing something new—at least in movies. But what was truly fresh in 1964 was the post-Kennedy euphoria. The apocalypse had happened and we remained. The fever broke. The crisis passed—anything seemed possible.

Where *The Manchurian Candidate* anticipated the fearful Kennedy scenario,

---

*Sontag, who had not yet written her essay on lowbrow sci-fi movies and the "imagination of disaster," termed *Dr. Strangelove* "nihilism for the masses. . . . The film's 'matter-of-fact' apocalypse and flip soundtrack reassures in a curious way, for nihilism is our contemporary form of moral uplift."

Dr. Strangelove simply dismissed it. The entire movie-mediated Cold War, from the dramatic Manhattan Project thriller *The Beginning or the End* and the paranoid *I Married a Communist*, through the soft apocalypse of *The Next Voice You Hear* and the sci-fi extravaganza *When Worlds Collide*—with its wheelchair-bound, Strangelove-like industrialist—to *On the Beach* and the Cuban Missile Crisis, was replayed at high-speed . . . for laughs. The invocation of "doomsday" and "mine-shaft" gaps even parodied JFK's election scare tactics. But Kennedy was dead and we lived on!

Dr. Strangelove's "wry" attitude, as Brustein called it, was most apparent in the smutty, desecratory humor of the movie's title and the names of its principal characters: Premier Dmitri Kissoff, President Merkin Muffley, Generals Buck Turgidson and Jack D. Ripper. Had the Cold War been nothing more than one long pissing contest? (JFK so personalized the long twilight struggle that his audience might well think so.) This insolent perspective, Brustein wrote, was familiar, too, from certain comic novels and cabaret acts. It had "rumbled a little bit under the conventional noises of *The Manchurian Candidate*" but had yet to enter the mass media. The thirty-five-year-old critic hailed *Strangelove* as the first Hollywood movie to speak for his cohort—although, actually, his beatnik generation was itself about to be displaced.

"Everything went young in '64," was how Andy Warhol began his account of the year. The old were fixated on the kids and the kids had fixated, most obviously, on a cute quartet of longhaired, perhaps self-parodic, British rockers; not since the Davy Crockett craze nine years earlier had the Baby Boom expressed itself so uniformly. Jack Ruby went on trial for shooting Lee Harvey Oswald. *The Manchurian Candidate* was rereleased throughout the country. The "ugly guerrilla war" in Vietnam worsened. *The Spy Who Came In from the Cold* was the number-one bestseller, but the post-JFK winter and spring of 1964 were ruled by the Beatles—at least so far as the national soundtrack went.

In some sense, the festival remained ongoing. The Beatles' comforting "I Want to Hold Your Hand," released in America on the day after Christmas, reached number one by February and lodged itself there for seven weeks— during which time the group appeared twice on *The Ed Sullivan Show* and, in another victory for youth, Cassius Clay took the heavyweight boxing crown from befuddled "old" Sonny Liston. "I Want to Hold Your Hand" was succeeded by the also reassuring "She Loves You," which held the top spot for two weeks before being displaced by the idealistic anthem "Can't Buy Me Love," the nation's number-one song well into May. *Time* reported on the fashionable New York discotheques, where dances like the Frug and Hully Gully had superseded the Twist. Out in LA, the Whisky A Go Go introduced the Watusi. Birth-control pills proliferated; the stock market was healthy.

A manifesto for that giddy season, Robert Benton and David Newman's "The New Sentimentality" appeared in *Esquire*'s July issue. "The New Sentimentality" began, of course, with JFK: "Suddenly it was 1960 and John Kennedy was there. . . ." Ike had been replaced by a tough guy who knew what he wanted and went for it—a "pro," an "operator," "the man who made his score," the man who knew the score.

Dr. Strangelove partook of the New Sentimentality, but French *nouvelle vague* movies—*Breathless, Shoot the Piano Player, Jules and Jim*—were the key Benson and Newman texts. Directors like Antonioni and Hitchcock were their old masters. Rock 'n' roll merged with Pop Art. The only example of a New Sentimental writer was Robert Lowell: "Beauty of destruction. The sanitarium as a setting for a poem." Significant New Sentimentality purveyors included the Beatles (heralded as masters of The Put-On), Malcolm X (who "gets publicity and fights"), Lenny Bruce ("the hipster, trouble with the cops"), dead Marilyn ("We mourn her neuroticism"), and model Jean Shrimpton ("makeup all day long"). The idea was not to decry the Image but to dig it!

Forget the Hollywood Freedom Fighter. New Sentimentality eschewed patriotism even as it romanticized the clandestine realpolitik of the CIA and thus, without having to say so, the Secret Agent of History! Moreover, presaging the New Wave gangster script based on the exploits of Depression desperados Bonnie Parker and Clyde Barrow that Benton and Newman were brainstorming, the New Sentimentality redefined friendship: Now "we have accomplices. Friends are not for escape, they are for conspiracy."

III

South by Southwest:
Lyndon Johnson's Trip, 1964–66

In September 1964, the Warren Commission determined that Lee Harvey Oswald, acting without apparent motive, was the lone assassin of President Kennedy. Not everyone was convinced. Gangsters bragged to each other over wiretapped phones that they had ordered the hit; witnesses interviewed by the Dallas police, the FBI, and the Warren Commission were dropping like flies.

Some people suspected rogue CIA elements while, according to KGB files released decades later, Attorney General Robert F. Kennedy's friend William Walton had been dispatched to Moscow in December 1963 with word that the Kennedy family believed JFK the victim of a right-wing conspiracy; the message was corroborated by information an American businessman furnished Polish intelligence that Texas oilmen Sid Richardson, Clint Murchison, and H. L. Hunt organized the assassination.

No less than in 1864, the nation would require a new foundation myth to explain the rupture in the American narrative. Perhaps this is why the last New Frontier political spectacle, *The Best Man*, which opened four months after the Kennedy assassination, in early April 1964, proved to be a commercial disappointment. Franklin Schaffner's adaptation of Gore Vidal's highly successful 1960 play—in which a Stevensonian egghead battled a Nixonian opportunist

for their party's nomination—seemed hopelessly anachronistic in its representation of an imagined 1964 presidential convention. America, as predicted by
The Manchurian Candidate, had graduated to the coup. *The Best Man* offered the
nostalgic fantasy of an open political convention—something that would never
happen again. Even before 1960, major party conventions had become televised
spectacles designed to anoint candidates who had already been chosen. Yet, if
only in its subject matter, Vidal's scenario acknowledged that the spectacle was
itself significant (or at least entertaining).

The more sympathetic of Vidal's candidates, mandarin Secretary of State
William Russell (Henry Fonda), is similarly antiquated. Russell is an intellectual
who doesn't believe in God, feels superior to public opinion polls, and is
dismayed by the new image politics of the 1960s. He's vulnerable, not because
he once attended a Communist cell meeting or is a compulsive womanizer,
but because he's suffered a nervous breakdown. (Unlike the New Sentimen-
talists Robert Benton and David Newman, *The Best Man* doesn't regard this as
cool.) Russell's demagogic rival, the so-called Boy Crusader, Joe Cantwell, is a
more contemporary figure—a young Southern senator whose best-selling exposé *Enemy Around Us* links the Mafia with the Communists.*

The villainous Cantwell character is as suggestive of the Kennedy brothers
as he is of Richard Nixon, especially since he is portrayed by the post–*PT 109*

---

*UA purchased the rights to *The Best Man* in June 1960 with the proviso that the picture
would not be released until 1962. In the interim, designated director Frank Capra and
his co-writer, Myles Connolly, decided to improve Gore Vidal's original. Their script
introduced a new character—the innocent young Eurasian governor of America's new-
est state, Hawaii—as a positive alternative to the flawed candidates of Vidal's scenario.
UA executive Max Youngstein bluntly informed Capra this new Best Man was a cliché-
spouting "schnook Boy Scout"; still, Capra remained involved with the stalled project.
Vidal met with the director during the summer of 1961 and was appalled: "He wanted
the [Hawaiian] candidate to dress up as Abraham Lincoln reciting the Gettysburg Address." By the end of 1961 Capra was gone. William Wyler turned down the assignment,
which ultimately went to Franklin Schaffner. Aptly, Schaffner had supervised the live
television feeds for both the 1948 and 1952 Democratic and Republican conventions,
and had directed the Broadway version of *Advise and Consent* and Jacqueline Kennedy's
1962 *Tour of the White House*—not to mention the President's Missile Crisis address.

Cliff Robertson. Not nearly as outrageous as Alabama governor George Wallace, the Boy Crusader is, from a political perspective, closest to Senator Barry Goldwater. Like the Arizona Republican, Cantwell is a charismatic conservative who wants to increase military spending, get tough with Castro, and cut the income tax. (Civil rights is not an issue.) Unfortunately for Russell, the God-fearing, happily married Crusader appears to have no vices. Then an unctuous old Army buddy, played by sick comedian Shelly Berman, shows up to hint that the Crusader was a onetime "degenerate." Will Russell use this information to force Cantwell to withdraw his candidacy?

In the revised universe of 1964, Russell's type is old-fashioned—and not simply because he is too morally fastidious to exploit a weaknesses in an opponent's character. Whether or not a conspiracy was in place, the 1960 campaign demonstrated that image ruled. National politicians were characters in an ongoing television series. The issue was not backstage blackmail but straightforward marketing. Might not Lyndon Johnson prevail by identifying a characterological defect in the product known as "Barry Goldwater"?*

Jet-Age Bronco Busters and Twilight Westerns

Autumn 1963 had been the season of Southern police riots and vigilante church bombings. Positioning himself for the next year's presidential election, JFK had gone to Dallas on a political mission. Texas Democrats were squabbling amongst themselves while the *New York Times* reported the state "abuzz with Goldwater enthusiasm." The morning of November 22, a *Houston Chronicle* poll showed the Arizona senator leading the Kennedy-Johnson ticket in Texas 52 to 48 percent.

Barry abuzz! The New Frontier's most persistent critic was a decade older than the President, born in 1907—three years before Arizona became a state—

---

*The sexual blackmail that figured in *Advise and Consent*, *Seven Days in May*, and *The Best Man* was the specific manifestation of the more flamboyant, globalized sickness in *The Manchurian Candidate* and *Dr. Strangelove*. But *The Best Man* was prophetic in suggesting the formula Vidal would articulate years later: "As real politics [are] entirely excluded from public life, private lives are all that we are allowed to talk about."

to one of the territory's wealthiest clans. Episcopalian grandson of Polish-Jewish immigrant "Big Mike" Goldwasser, who founded his fortune on a La Paz dry goods emporium, the future senator dropped out of college after two semesters, but he had a gift for promotion. Joining the family enterprise, young Barry introduced Gold Water cologne and developed the cattle-brand design emblazoned on Goldwater's towels, kitchenware, and wrapping paper. This "creative merchandising dynamo," as *Women's Wear Daily* described him, understood the West as a style. Goldwater pioneered denim women's wear and even launched a national craze for "antsy pants," boxer shorts printed with a fiery insect design.

The ruggedly good-looking, affably easygoing Goldwater also marketed himself. An amateur photographer, he developed a slide lecture on local history. By 1940 (as Columbia Pictures prepared to release an epic Western shot in, devoted to, and named for his home state), he averaged two shows a week—with added presentations of a 16mm movie made rafting on the Colorado. Some 20,000 Arizonans saw the show in 1941, and Goldwater, who piloted his own plane to screenings, became a regional celebrity—meeting "so damn many Arizonans" as he later put it, that politics seemed "a natural step."

The Goldwaters had been Democrats, but in 1952, Barry successfully ran for the Senate as a Joe McCarthy Republican. Like fellow freshman John Kennedy, Goldwater took no significant role in the Senate's business. He remained more interested in promotion and, like Kennedy, pressed flesh for candidates across the country. No important piece of legislation bore the Goldwater brand. He understood his role as essentially negative, "not to pass laws but to repeal them."

At home as an image, Goldwater served on the same high-profile Senate rackets committee that provided a platform for the Kennedy brothers. In 1956, his campaign manager, Stephen C. Shadegg, cast him in the anti-Communist infomercial *For Freedom's Sake*; the Senator got to browbeat an actor impersonating the three-years-dead Soviet dictator Joseph Stalin. By spring 1957, after Goldwater attacked President Eisenhower's budget as socialistic, *Time* reported that the new spokesman for the Republican old guard was the "handsome"

Senator from Arizona—conservative yet Space Age, the "only qualified jet pilot in Congress." In the dream life, Goldwater resembled the similarly square-jawed, pipe-smoking comic strip Air Force ace Steve Canyon—the Cold War poster boy created by the Senator's contemporary, Milton Caniff.*

Unfortunately for Goldwater, however, the senator whose fictional doppelgänger appeared in *Steve Canyon* (under the name Pipper the Piper) was John F. Kennedy. Nevertheless, the Arizonan was encouraged by Birchites and Dixiecrats alike to seek higher office. Youthful supporters promoted his candidacy at the 1960 Republican Convention; GOLDWATER IN '64 bumper stickers appeared within weeks of Richard Nixon's defeat. The manifesto *The Conscience of a Conservative*, ghosted by Goldwater's speechwriter, *National Review* editor L. Brent Bozell, was a bestseller throughout Camelot—3.5 million copies in print.

"I'm not a philosopher," Goldwater liked to say. "I'm a salesman trying to sell the conservative view of government." Because the Arizona senator spoke both the language of images and the language of ideals, some thought him a peculiar hybrid that, as Richard Hofstadter wrote, dwelt "half in the world of our routine politics and half in the curious intellectual underworld of the

---

*Heralded by *Time*'s cover story, the strip began in January 1947, the same year Goldwater was appointed to the Phoenix Charter Revision Committee. A 1950 *Newsweek* cover juxtaposed Steve Canyon with the headline "Why We Are Losing Asia." A few months later, the handsome pilot was recalled to active duty in Korea. Reenlisting throughout the Fifties, at one point in the CIA, Canyon battled Communists off Formosa and in Indochina—while serving a "seven-day-a-week recruiting poster" carried by 600 American newspapers and another 150 abroad.

Lt. Colonel Canyon came to life (or rather TV) during the same fall 1958 season that Goldwater was reelected in a campaign partially underwritten by Robert Welch and H. L. Hunt. Sponsored by Chesterfield cigarettes, *Steve Canyon* had the misfortune of being programmed Saturday nights opposite Walt Disney's *Zorro*. The "semidocumentary" show was advised by U.S. Air Force personnel, was shot on actual bases, and featured the latest Air Force planes performing their regular functions using authentic dialogue for all pilot-crew communications. The show's writers were promised access to Air Force files immediately upon declassification. Whether it focused on UFOs or bombing strategy, each episode was identified with the name of a specific operation.

pseudo-conservatives." Or was it half in the routine world of cattle-brand bath towels and half in the dream world of the prime-time cowboy shows, to which Goldwater was addicted? In a *Saturday Evening Post* profile notorious for the subject's engaging confession that he hadn't "a first-class brain," Goldwater recalled trying out a political speech on his wife, Peggy. She was unmoved, explaining he'd be addressing "a sophisticated audience, they're not a lot of lame-brains like you, they don't spend their time looking at TV westerns. You can't give them that corn."

Ah, but he could. Goldwater was "handsome as a movie star" per the March 25, 1961, *Business Week*. And, that June, after he helped elect John Tower, the first Republican since Reconstruction to the Senate seat vacated by Lyndon Johnson, Goldwater graced *Time*'s cover as the "hottest political figure this side of Jack Kennedy." Having risen out of the West, from "leader of a die-hard sect" to his party's upper echelons, the Arizonan was nearly iconic, Steve Canyon gone to Washington: Barry Goldwater, Action Hero. Gore Vidal, who interviewed Goldwater for *Life* that spring, saw another contradiction: the Senator was "perhaps the first American politician who, though spokesman for an unpopular minority" (as Vidal considered conservatives) was personally popular nonetheless. Goldwater came across as "sincere, a vague quality far more admired by the lonely crowd than competence or intelligence."

The campus-based Young Americans for Freedom (YAF)—founded by activist veterans of Students for Goldwater on the Connecticut estate of *National Review* publisher William F. Buckley—had, over a single academic year, swollen from 100 zealots to a national membership of 23,000. By the next term, the *New York Times* acknowledged Buckley and Goldwater as the two most popular campus speakers. "You walk around with your Goldwater button and you feel the thrill of treason," the president of the University of Wisconsin Conservative Club told *Time*, explaining that he was in rebellion against his liberal parents. So, as the title of the senator's second ghostwritten book asked, *Why Not Victory?* In a further turn of the dialectic, Goldwater planned to run against Kennedy as Kennedy had run against Eisenhower. The Arizonan proposed to treat the President as a dude. A tan and twangy jet-age broncobuster, Goldwater would zoom out of the comic-strip past to insist the United States was still badly defended and hemorrhaging international prestige. It was only lack of fortitude that kept America from, once and for all, winning the Cold War.

Barry Goldwater had, *Time* thought, "more than his share of political sex appeal." Yet John Kennedy saw someone else in his magic mirror: New York governor Nelson Rockefeller, scion of a family a hundred times richer and more powerful than his own. JFK even believed Rocky could have beaten him in 1960. Hoping to have Goldwater as his foil in 1964, JFK was afraid the impetuous senator would self-destruct en route to the election. But it was Rockefeller who wore the antsy pants and whose billion-dollar bandwagon ran off the road once he dumped his first wife and embarked on a remarriage to a newly minted divorcée. Thus, *Life's* November 1, 1963, cover story anointed Goldwater as Republican front-runner, quoting Richard Nixon's oracular belief that the nomination was Goldwater's to lose: "The Arizonan," *Life* proclaimed, was "All Saddled Up for His First Primary. Hi-Ho New Hampshire! Barry Goes Galloping In."

Life's cover portrayed Goldwater in a favorite publicity pose—wearing a Stetson, a denim work shirt, and dungarees, and holding a golden palomino. "Hopalong Cassidy all baby fat removed," Norman Mailer wrote. "Kennedy was now to be combated by Sheriff B. Morris Goldwater, the Silver Gun of the West. It was one of those pictures worth ten thousand speeches—it gave promise of delivering a million votes."

●　　　●　　　●

Two weeks after *Life* put the Jet-Age Bronco Buster on its cover, John Wayne projected his Goldwater scenario onto the nation's movie screens. *McLintock!*, a brawling Western comedy which went into production in the senator's home state at the white-knuckle height of the Missile Crisis, opened November 13, 1963. (Fellow conservative Republicans and collectors of Hopi kachina dolls, Barry and the Duke had rubbed shoulders in the dream life. Wayne ranked Goldwater with General MacArthur in his political pantheon; when the Duke passed away in 1979, Goldwater eulogized him as a friend of fifty years.)

Wayne's first self-produced vehicle since *The Alamo* was another family affair—written by the star's buddy James Edward Grant, produced by his son
Michael Wayne, and directed by old pal Victor McLaglen's forty-two-year-old
boy, Andrew. The cast boasted two more Wayne children, with the Duke
himself playing the testosterone-fueled Cowboy Father of His Country—forth-
right, overbearing and insufferable, the self-made mine-owner timber-baron
cattle-king George Washington McLintock. This living spirit of America carved
an empire out of the wilderness and defended it against a locust swarm of
would-be homesteaders encouraged by a tinhorn bureaucrat to imagine a claim
to a few hundred acres of his boundless property. McLintock's town, the same
Old Tucson built for *Arizona*, is named for him, and he rules it as John Wayne
ruled the hyperreal *Alamo* set. The interests of the pioneer tycoon are identical
with the general good; the local sheriff (played by a favorite stuntman) is his
earthly vicar.

Just before the 1964 campaign, British critic Philip French proposed a Western schemata based on the personae of several American politicians, including
Kennedy and Goldwater. An admirer of JFK, French characterized Kennedy
Western rhetoric as "elegant, ironic, laced with wit." The pace was "taut and
fast-driving" and, like a Kennedy campaign speech, the "carefully composed"
images emphasized "the harsh challenge of the landscape." As enlightened as
a Western might be, the Kennedy model was "penetrating" in its moral tone,
"cool with an underlying note of the absurd." The Kennedy hero was complex—outwardly "diffident" but "prone to a sense of anguished failure," a solitary figure obsessed by personal tragedy, yet capable of emotional growth.
High Noon and *The Magnificent Seven*, both predicated on a sense of civic responsibility, were exemplary Kennedy Westerns.

French's paradigmatic Goldwater Western was, of course, the "slack and
expansive" *McLintock!* As opposed to Kennedy sophistication, Goldwater rhetoric was "broadly humorous." Goldwater mise-en-scène involved a "casual acceptance of the landscape"; Goldwater morality was seemingly "generous but
ultimately unforgiving." Where the Kennedy past was rendered "without regret," the Goldwater mood was nostalgic. As for the Goldwater hero—"rock-

like" in his sense of virtue and self-image—John Wayne was axiomatic. The key Goldwater Westerns were *The Searchers*, *Rio Bravo*, and *The Alamo*—movies in which rugged individualism was prized above all, with inequality and aggression understood as the natural order.

Newsweek called the outspoken Goldwater "The Fastest Gun," and McLintock, too, thinks with his fists, impugning the manhood of all who cross him, even as he embodies a movement already present in society. A paradigm of truculent patriotism, free enterprise, and moral certainty, G.W. is a politician whose constituents include hardworking white settlers (most in his employ), a volatile Chinese cook, and, in a tip of the Stetson to "Big Mike" Goldwasser, a Jewish storekeeper named Birnbaum—smart, but not enough to keep McLintock from trouncing him at chess. The only other authority figure is the territory's ineffectual "side-saddle governor"—called Cuthbert H. Humphrey after a liberal senator and soon-to-be vice-presidential nominee whose autographed picture Wayne affixed to his guest-room toilet tank.

Sleazy as he is, Humphrey dares put the make on McLintock's estranged wife, the shrewish Kate (Maureen O'Hara, named for her Shakespearean counterpart). According to *McLintock!*'s relentlessly patriarchal premise, in which Wayne's actual son Patrick keeps pestering him for a job (sufficiently frustrated at one point to take a wild swing so Dad might knock him on his keister), G.W.'s real adversaries are Kate—an uppity Eastern-identified snob—and a couple of dumb college kids, including his daughter.*

There is even a hint of countercultural politics in the person of a Comanche who rebels against the Bureau of Indian Affairs. But while McLintock and the Comanche share contempt for Washington, the Great White Father is not about to go native. G.W.'s task is to cultivate Patrick's character ("I don't give jobs, I hire men") while keeping his own "!" up—by insuring that wife and

---

*Six months before *McLintock!* went into production, *Time* identified the folk singer and the Goldwater supporter as two poles of campus idealism, and in its way, the movie recognizes a conflict to come. G.W. is labeled "reactionary" by one such Ivy League banjo-picking idiot.

daughter get their comeuppance. The climactic confrontation between Mc-
Lintock and the increasingly humiliated Kate is staged as a shoot-out on Main
Street. Awarded the *Box Office* magazine Blue Ribbon as December 1963's out-
standing family release, *McLintock!* deemed it healthier to spank a girl than kiss
her—preferably on the Fourth of July.

• • •

Variety dismissed *McLintock!*, which borrows shamelessly from John Ford's
Wayne vehicles, as a "cinematic fricassee." But as premised, per *Time*, in "seeing to it the old frontier does not become too New," John Wayne's second
contribution to a presidential campaign had an agenda. For the New Frontier
had had the effect of rendering the Old archaic. The youthful President was
Gary Cooper's junior by some fifteen years, a decade younger than even
Wayne. Moreover, unlike his predecessor, John Kennedy was no fan of Westerns—already past their peak as prime-time TV fare. Astronauts, secret agents,
and counterinsurgents were JFK's preferred action heroes. The 1964–66 espionage shows—*The Man From U.N.C.L.E.*, *Get Smart*, *I Spy*, *Mission: Impossible*—
were conceived under his spell.

The New Frontier's characteristic expressions included a cluster of self-
conscious post-Westerns, contemporary in setting and shot like art films in
black and white, as well as the first melancholy "twilight" Westerns (suffused
with unfulfilled hopes and unfulfilled threats). The post-Westerns were ambivalent unto neurosis and conceived by liberals, some just returned to Hollywood: *The Misfits* (1961), was directed by self-exiled John Huston from
HUAC-harassed Arthur Miller's screenplay; *Lonely Are the Brave* (1962) was produced by star Kirk Douglas and written by Dalton Trumbo; *Hud* (1963) was
directed by the gray-listed Martin Ritt. All featured estranged—even alienated—
protagonists hung up on the idea of cowboy integrity that men like Wayne
and Barry Goldwater projected as birthright.

Characterized by confused individualism and clucking dismay over an America lost to commercialization, the post- and twilight Westerns articulated what
G. W. McLintock would deplore as disgraceful self-pity. The wranglers in the
prolonged drunken binge that is *The Misfits* are reduced to killing mustangs for

Navajo drag, painted their faces, and performed sacred dances with
akes clenched in their teeth, the Democrat was the descendant of
s and Indian-fighters who battled the Comanche on the banks of
les. Johnson's grandfather, a former Confederate private, was for
reigning cattle baron west of San Antonio. His uncle was a Texas
father a Texas state representative. LBJ himself was a horse-trading,
ting, bushwah-spouting riverboat pol.
eekend 1964, the new President entertained members of the press
Ranch. At one point, he packed his cream-colored Lincoln Conti-
ertible with four reporters—including the blond Hearst scribe Mar-
s, whom he invited to ride shotgun beside him—and, leading a
ive other automobiles, took off on a tour of his domain. Johnson
d Pearl beer and ran oncoming traffic off the road, holding forth
e on the sex life of his prize steer. Like the beef stock baron
LBJ took the bull for his totem.
! signaled a certain Pop Art joie de vivre by making its title an
and its star a national monument. But McLintock was no longer
ding rant into metaphor, the Free World Leader demonstrated his
car horn: a bawling bovine mating call attracting a thunderous
cattle. "Mr. President, you're fun," Means cooed, providing *Time*
You bet: Johnson tricked photographers into tangling with an irate
lasting off at ninety miles per hour to get more beer.

oy Election of 1964

ontier having gone down in a hail of bullets on a Texas street just
oon, the stage cleared for the first Cowboy Election in the History
lic, and in the Saturday afternoon universe of movie matinees and
e was no question which candidate wore the white hat.
rry Goldwater who was the campus idol and fired the idealism of
uth. A high school senior in the affluent Republican town of Park
ls, seventeen-year-old Hillary Rodham was one such Goldwater
d *pasionaria* in straw boater and button-bedecked sash. John Ford

dog food, while the dim-witted cowboy hero of *Lonely Are the Brave* has himself
jailed in order to break out a buddy imprisoned for aiding Mexican illegals.
The cowboy escapes alone to be run over on a rain-slicked highway by a truck
carrying a load of toilet seats. "Natural man going down in defeat under the
continual brutal assault of the industrial-capitalistic-governmental juggernaut,"
jeered Brendan Gill in the *New Yorker*. No less masochistic, *Hud* allowed liberalism to preview its own exhaustion. The venerable cattleman Homer (Melvyn Douglas) lacks the strength to pass on his scarcely defined principles to
his son (Paul Newman), the unscrupulous, if attractive, antihero for whom the
movie was named.

McLintock! saw a generation of Ivy League pinkos to be spanked; *Hud* worried that youth might sell its soul to the *National Review*. Hud was not just a
selfish rake but, worse, a laissez-faire opponent of government regulation—a
young and sexy McLintock. "Somewhere in the back of my mind," Berkeley
film critic Pauline Kael wrote in *Film Quarterly*, "*Hud* began to stand for the
people who would vote for Goldwater, while Homer was clearly an upstanding
Stevensonian. And it seemed rather typical of the weakness of the whole message picture idea that the good liberals who made the film made their own
spokesman a fuddy-duddy." Perhaps *Hud* was intended as a preemptive strike
against Goldwater, but although the President was absent from Kael's rumination, the movie's antihero might equally have been a hostile vision of JFK.

More ambiguous in their politics were the twilight Westerns. John Ford's
The Man Who Shot Liberty Valance made the astounding statement that American history was founded on a necessary lie. "When the truth becomes legend,
print the legend," the newspaper editor concludes upon being told who really
shot the criminal maniac called Liberty. Although the line echoed the conclusion of *Fort Apache*, it had an entirely new meaning in the image-saturated
environment of 1962. The purity of the Westerner's image was predicated on
falsehood.

Ford's going-out-of-business sale liquidated all manner of illusions—its loquacious action largely confined to a soundstage. If *The Misfits* derived additional piquance for being both Clark Gable and Marilyn Monroe's last

completed feature, so *Liberty Valance* gave new meaning to the term "ghost town." The narrative—bracketed by shots of the coffin holding the Unknown Cowboy Warrior that is John Wayne's character—was almost entirely flashback. Trapped in his lone Kennedy Western, Wayne is something of a romantic figure from the distant past. Indeed, all of the principals (played by actors far older than their characters) appear aged phantoms animated by the spirit of historical inevitability to reenact a ritual in a deserted theater. Sam Peckinpah's MGM quickie *Ride the High Country* similarly dramatized the closing of the frontier with the presence of two veteran Western stars—Randolph Scott and Joel McCrea (a charter member of Americans for Goldwater). Peckinpah's elderly lawmen, like the forgotten hero of *The Man Who Shot Liberty Valance* and the marginal cowboys of *The Misfits* and *Lonely Are the Brave*, were an endangered species. So, too, the movies *Ride the High Country*, *Liberty Valance*, and *Lonely Are the Brave* were all dumped by their distributors during spring 1962.

Further intimations that the Western was over: Opening in March 1963, MGM's inadvertently twilight *How the West Was Won* was an extravaganza that involved three directors, spanned three generations of heroic pioneers, and required three hours to chronicle the conquest of the wilderness. But? "Everything in this latest feature on the king-size Cinerama screen is a dutiful duplication of something you've already seen," Bosley Crowther wrote in the *New York Times*.

> The fur trapper that James Stewart plays is not an authentic character; he's a rubber stamp of Mr. Stewart. The same is true of Gregory Peck's gambler, Debbie Reynold's dance-hall girl, Richard Widmark's railroad builder, Thelma Ritter's cheery pioneer, John Wayne's General Sherman, [and] Henry Fonda's buffalo hunter.

The flashback parade of simulacra wound up in a bizarre echo of the downbeat *Lonely Are the Brave* closer, by climaxing with the thrilling vista of bulldozed construction sites and traffic-clogged LA freeways.

"A black humorist could scarcely have come up with a bleaker, more satirical ending," Philip French noted. And yet, by casting its eye upon the Pacific

rim, *How the West Was Won* left off p
had its U.S. premiere weeks later, w
built by American advisers through th

•

Barry Goldwater versus John Kenned
fest; it had geographic elegance: The
Southwest, smoke-filled backroom or
carried South and West, he'd both de
in the Republican base.*

But the Secret Agent of History in
election became a contest between
swilling, steak-scarfing professional
equally comfortable campaigning in b
barren hills where Confederate and C
Johnson was even more profane, co
masculine—in a word, more McLint
the "fun" went out of the election on

Johnson's great-grandparents had
year after the Lone Star Republic join
lican dry-goods heir belonged to a fra

---

*Kennedy vs. Goldwater would have dra
rized in his 1976 book *The Yankee and Co*
occurred fifteen years into the Cold W
oriented "Yankees" and militarist, entrepr

> In Europe and the industrial world
> live with communism. In Asia and
> that we could not, that we had to
> face terrible consequences at home

So long as the brain's warring hemispher
could wear a look of reasonable integrati
States could not win its way militarily in
challenge in the North Atlantic, the makin

dressed in
live bull s
slaveholde
the Peder
a time the
Ranger, hi
crony-coll

Easter
at his LBJ
nental cor
ianne Me
caravan o
chug-a-lug
all the w
McLintoc

*McLint
exclamati
alone. Ex
customize
herd of L
its headli
sow befo

The Co

The New
past High
of the Re
rodeos, t

It was
American
Ridge, I
Girl, a co

dog food, while the dim-witted cowboy hero of *Lonely Are the Brave* has himself jailed in order to break out a buddy imprisoned for aiding Mexican illegals. The cowboy escapes alone to be run over on a rain-slicked highway by a truck carrying a load of toilet seats. "Natural man going down in defeat under the continual brutal assault of the industrial-capitalistic-governmental juggernaut," jeered Brendan Gill in the *New Yorker*. No less masochistic, *Hud* allowed liberalism to preview its own exhaustion. The venerable cattleman Homer (Melvyn Douglas) lacks the strength to pass on his scarcely defined principles to his son (Paul Newman), the unscrupulous, if attractive, antihero for whom the movie was named.

McLintock! saw a generation of Ivy League pinkos to be spanked; *Hud* worried that youth might sell its soul to the *National Review*. Hud was not just a selfish rake but, worse, a laissez-faire opponent of government regulation—a young and sexy McLintock. "Somewhere in the back of my mind," Berkeley film critic Pauline Kael wrote in *Film Quarterly*, "*Hud* began to stand for the people who would vote for Goldwater, while Homer was clearly an upstanding Stevensonian. And it seemed rather typical of the weakness of the whole message picture idea that the good liberals who made the film made their own spokesman a fuddy-duddy." Perhaps *Hud* was intended as a preemptive strike against Goldwater, but although the President was absent from Kael's rumination, the movie's antihero might equally have been a hostile vision of JFK.

More ambiguous in their politics were the twilight Westerns. John Ford's *The Man Who Shot Liberty Valance* made the astounding statement that American history was founded on a necessary lie. "When the truth becomes legend, print the legend," the newspaper editor concludes upon being told who really shot the criminal maniac called Liberty. Although the line echoed the conclusion of *Fort Apache*, it had an entirely new meaning in the image-saturated environment of 1962. The purity of the Westerner's image was predicated on falsehood.

Ford's going-out-of-business sale liquidated all manner of illusions—its loquacious action largely confined to a soundstage. If *The Misfits* derived additional piquance for being both Clark Gable and Marilyn Monroe's last completed feature, so *Liberty Valance* gave new meaning to the term "ghost town." The narrative—bracketed by shots of the coffin holding the Unknown Cowboy Warrior that is John Wayne's character—was almost entirely flashback. Trapped in his lone Kennedy Western, Wayne is something of a romantic figure from the distant past. Indeed, all of the principals (played by actors far older than their characters) appear aged phantoms animated by the spirit of historical inevitability to reenact a ritual in a deserted theater. Sam Peckinpah's MGM quickie *Ride the High Country* similarly dramatized the closing of the frontier with the presence of two veteran Western stars—Randolph Scott and Joel McCrea (a charter member of Americans for Goldwater). Peckinpah's elderly lawmen, like the forgotten hero of *The Man Who Shot Liberty Valance* and the marginal cowboys of *The Misfits* and *Lonely Are the Brave*, were an endangered species. So, too, the movies *Ride the High Country*, *Liberty Valance*, and *Lonely Are the Brave* were all dumped by their distributors during spring 1962.

Further intimations that the Western was over: Opening in March 1963, MGM's inadvertently twilight *How the West Was Won* was an extravaganza that involved three directors, spanned three generations of heroic pioneers, and required three hours to chronicle the conquest of the wilderness. But? "Everything in this latest feature on the king-size Cinerama screen is a dutiful duplication of something you've already seen," Bosley Crowther wrote in the *New York Times*.

> The fur trapper that James Stewart plays is not an authentic character; he's a rubber stamp of Mr. Stewart. The same is true of Gregory Peck's gambler, Debbie Reynold's dance-hall girl, Richard Widmark's railroad builder, Thelma Ritter's cheery pioneer, John Wayne's General Sherman, [and] Henry Fonda's buffalo hunter.

The flashback parade of simulacra wound up in a bizarre echo of the downbeat *Lonely Are the Brave* closer, by climaxing with the thrilling vista of bulldozed construction sites and traffic-clogged LA freeways.

"A black humorist could scarcely have come up with a bleaker, more satirical ending," Philip French noted. And yet, by casting its eye upon the Pacific rim, *How the West Was Won* left off precisely where *The Ugly American*, which had its U.S. premiere weeks later, would open: A new superhighway being built by American advisers through the primeval jungle of far-off Indochina.

·   ·   ·

Barry Goldwater versus John Kennedy was not only a prospective charisma fest; it had geographic elegance: The moribund Northeast against the rising Southwest, smoke-filled backroom or buttermilk skies. Moreover, if Goldwater carried South and West, he'd both defeat Kennedy and effect historic change in the Republican base.*

But the Secret Agent of History intervened, and thus the Yankee-Cowboy election became a contest between a pair of lean and leathery, bourbon-swilling, steak-scarfing professional Westerners—two Sons of the Pioneers, equally comfortable campaigning in bolo ties and ten-gallon hats. Born in the barren hills where Confederate and Cowboy Texas meet, six-foot-plus Lyndon Johnson was even more profane, colorful, folksy, hard-drinking and hyper-masculine—in a word, more McLintock—than Goldwater (who complained the "fun" went out of the election once Kennedy was shot).

Johnson's great-grandparents had migrated west from Georgia in 1846, a year after the Lone Star Republic joined the United States. Where the Republican dry-goods heir belonged to a fraternal order of Arizona white men who

---

*Kennedy vs. Goldwater would have dramatized the scenario Carl Oglesby later theorized in his 1976 book *The Yankee and Cowboy War*—namely, the power-elite split that occurred fifteen years into the Cold War between détente-ist, monopolist Atlantic-oriented "Yankees" and militarist, entrepreneurial Pacific-focused "Cowboys."

> In Europe and the industrial world, the evident truth was that we could live with communism. In Asia and the Third World, the evident truth was that we could not, that we had to fight and win wars against it or else face terrible consequences at home.

So long as the brain's warring hemispheres were kept apart, "American foreign policy could wear a look of reasonable integration. But when it became clear that the United States could not win its way militarily in the Third World without risking a nuclear challenge in the North Atlantic, the makings of a dissolving consensus were at hand."

dressed in Navajo drag, painted their faces, and performed sacred dances with
live bull snakes clenched in their teeth, the Democrat was the descendant of
slaveholders and Indian-fighters who battled the Comanche on the banks of
the Pedernales. Johnson's grandfather, a former Confederate private, was for
a time the reigning cattle baron west of San Antonio. His uncle was a Texas
Ranger, his father a Texas state representative. LBJ himself was a horse-trading,
crony-collecting, bushwah-spouting riverboat pol.

Easter weekend 1964, the new President entertained members of the press
at his LBJ Ranch. At one point, he packed his cream-colored Lincoln Continental convertible with four reporters—including the blond Hearst scribe Marianne Means, whom he invited to ride shotgun beside him—and, leading a
caravan of five other automobiles, took off on a tour of his domain. Johnson
chug-a-lugged Pearl beer and ran oncoming traffic off the road, holding forth
all the while on the sex life of his prize steer. Like the beef stock baron
McLintock, LBJ took the bull for his totem.

McLintock! signaled a certain Pop Art joie de vivre by making its title an
exclamation and its star a national monument. But McLintock was no longer
alone. Extending rant into metaphor, the Free World Leader demonstrated his
customized car horn: a bawling bovine mating call attracting a thunderous
herd of LBJ cattle. "Mr. President, you're fun," Means cooed, providing *Time*
its headline. You bet: Johnson tricked photographers into tangling with an irate
sow before blasting off at ninety miles per hour to get more beer.

The Cowboy Election of 1964

The New Frontier having gone down in a hail of bullets on a Texas street just
past High Noon, the stage cleared for the first Cowboy Election in the History
of the Republic, and in the Saturday afternoon universe of movie matinees and
rodeos, there was no question which candidate wore the white hat.

It was Barry Goldwater who was the campus idol and fired the idealism of
American youth. A high school senior in the affluent Republican town of Park
Ridge, Illinois, seventeen-year-old Hillary Rodham was one such Goldwater
Girl, a corn-fed *pasionaria* in straw boater and button-bedecked sash. John Ford

cast his first-ever Republican vote for Goldwater while, according to a report on the new Native American militancy, "some of the fieriest Red Muslims" supported Barry Sundust, as he translated his name into Hopi. Goldwater presented himself with cartoon bluntness: "The trouble with the so-called liberal today is that he doesn't understand straightforward simplicity. The answers to America's problems are simple." LBJ was an altogether more complex and duplicitous animal—ordering, for example, the presidential seal emblazoned on his cowboy boots, then issuing a panicky denial that he had ever made so crass a request. Where Goldwater wanted less government and more defense, Johnson was the master of legislative coercion, orchestrating greater government *and* armed intervention.

"LBJ is Old Sentimentality," Benton and Newman explained in *Esquire*. "FDR; the big ranch king; cowboys; *The Last Hurrah*; humble beginnings." When the President floated his vision of the Great Society, proposing greater government spending than at any time in the last thirty years, Goldwater called it the Fast Deal. The same season popularized the term White Backlash. The Civil Rights bill occasioned the longest filibuster in American history before the Senate approved it on June 19. LBJ identified himself with integration. Goldwater—who voted against the bill—benefited from the Backlash. So did Alabama governor George Wallace. Campaigning in Wisconsin, a state whose primary allowed crossover voting, the Alabaman solicited support from "Democrats, Republicans, and members of the John Birch Society." The Civil Rights bill, he maintained, would "bring about the ultimate in tyranny." As the South grew Republican, so the North was becoming . . . Southern. Hidden turning point of American political history: George Wallace greeted at South Milwaukee Serbian Memorial Hall, site of a triumphant JFK manifestation during the 1960 primary, by 700 partisans singing "Dixie"—in Polish! April 7, the governor received over one-third of the Democratic vote.

The 1964 presidential campaign, which coincided with the Mississippi Summer organized by the Student Non-Violent Coordinating Committee (SNCC), was a struggle over the quintessential American word. Freedom Now versus Young Americans for Freedom. "The tide has been running against freedom,"

Goldwater warned the Republican Convention in the course of an acceptance speech which employed the words "free," "freedom," and "liberty" forty times without mentioning the Civil Rights struggle. Goldwater's delegates were nearly all white, predominantly from the South and West. They dominated the Republican Convention, yet their candidate was not magnanimous. Rather than make a conciliatory gesture toward the party's defeated moderates, Goldwater baited them: "Anyone who joins us in all sincerity we welcome. Those who do not care for our cause, we don't expect to enter our ranks. . . . Extremism in the defense of liberty is no vice."

Pondering the ecstatic shower of inch-square gold foil pieces that greeted the placing of Goldwater's name in nomination, Norman Mailer—once again covering a convention for *Esquire*—recognized a savage beauty, "as if a rainbow had come to a field of war, or Goths around a fire saw visions in a cave." It was the vision of race war.

> Civilization was worn thin in the center and to the Left a black man raised his primitive cry; now to the far Right were the maniacal blue eyes of the other primitive. The jungles and forests were readying for war. . . . It was certain beyond certainty now that America was off on a ride which would end—was it God or the Devil knew where.*

---

*There were intimations of that crazy trip in the expedition organized that summer by California novelist Ken Kesey, author of *One Flew Over the Cuckoo's Nest* and, for the past few years, a user of LSD-25, the powerful hallucinogen he nicknamed "acid." Kesey, who had been introduced to LSD as a subject in a government laboratory experiment, promoted the unsanctioned use of acid as a "revolt of the guinea pigs." He purchased a 1939 International Harvester school bus that he and his beatnik friends outfitted with a sound system and painted with Day-Glo psychedelic swirls. The fantasy, as these self-proclaimed Merry Pranksters called it, was to drive across America—dropping acid and making movies—to arrive in New York for the mid-July publication of Kesey's new novel, *Sometimes a Great Notion*. The bus destination-sign read FURTHER; the rear panel was emblazoned CAUTION: WEIRD LOAD. The Pranksters drove through Phoenix just before the Republican Convention. Festooning their bus with American flags, they backed it slowly down the city's main drag, unfurling a banner that declared A VOTE FOR BARRY IS A VOTE FOR FUN. After all, the official Goldwater campaign slogan was a blatant appeal to the irrational: *In your heart you know he's right.*

Other portents of disorder: Two days after the Republicans nominated Gold-water, declaring their extreme intentions on network television, the national nervous system was jerked by a racial disturbance that began in New York City's Harlem, jumped upstate to Rochester and across the Hudson to Jersey City, then all the way out to Dixmoor, Illinois, before flashing back east to Philadelphia. It was another guinea pigs revolt, and like the RepCon, the riots were amplified by TV.

Thanks to television, Theodore White explained, "one sees the event in the now . . . the cop beating the rioter over the head. . . . There is a jazz to the immediate news which is unsettling, and this jazz dominated the last weeks of July and early August 1964." Instant information: The jazz that White experienced had been theorized by Professor Marshall McLuhan in his *Understanding Media*. McLuhan, as one bemused colleague explained in *The National Review*, had "carved out a topic [he says "The Topic"] virtually by naming it." Just as Isaac Newton identified gravity, McLuhan pointed out the so-self-evident-as-to-be-invisible organizing principle of the cultural universe: Media.

Daniel Boorstin contended that the journalist had usurped God's role in creating an interesting universe; it was McLuhan's more cheerful thesis that the electronic mass media was altering human consciousness. Print man was dead; TV babies were being born. Dwight Macdonald's notice in *Book Week* predicted that, albeit "nonsense adulterated by sense," *Understanding Media* was "almost certain to be a succes d'estime" and perhaps a bestseller. *Time*'s review foretold a fad—McLuhan's categories (radio as a "hot" medium, television as a "cool" one) could be used to classify everything.

Neither write-up predicted the degree to which McLuhan's name would become shorthand to account for everything. *Understanding Media*, which the author reworked from the final section of his more scholarly *Gutenberg Galaxy*, was topical enough to cite the JFK funeral as proof of TV's capacity to involve entire populations in a particular ritual. Timothy Leary, surely familiar with McLuhan, was explicating the consciousness-expanding miracle drug LSD in televisual terms. On one hand, Leary maintained, LSD exposed the theatricality of our social existence. The drug induced the "science fiction paranoia" realization that one was a robotic role player living life as if "on camera in an ancient television show." On the other hand, Leary proposed the material notion that we were ourselves wired like so many TV sets with electronic brain impulses flashing on our nervous-system video screens. (To transcend television, one had to *be* television.)

For those who thought television simply a narcotic, McLuhan explained that TV was actually stimulating the senses as it provided "Western man" with "a daily session of synesthesia." The despised boob tube cast a unifying spell over highly literate populations and, just as Mailer feared, re-tribalized them. According to McLuhan's formulation, the new age represented a post-rational return to some collective wholeness of preliterate paradise—a regression to a higher level, the Global Village. Perhaps that was why the 1964 campaign played so well as a prime-time Western. There was disorder in the village. There were outlaws. And who looked most like the sheriff who might straighten it out?

• • •

A major general in the U.S. Air Force Reserve, Barry Goldwater was unusually close to the military brass. "The phrases of the Air Force High Command pepper his thinking," Theodore White noted in his campaign account.

> Distances, tonnages, mileages, maps, settings, communications, ranges, payloads, missiles. . . . [Goldwater's] sound in conversation echoes the sound of alert-shacks where pilots chatter about their trade, or, as he ages, the select dining rooms of the Pentagon where generals generalize about combat.

But while Goldwater talked the talk, Lyndon Johnson walked the walk. Goldwater urged U.S. victory in Vietnam; LBJ (who insisted that "we're not about to send American boys nine or ten thousand miles from home to do what Asian boys ought to be doing for themselves") effectively stage-managed the August 2 Gulf of Tonkin "incident," in which North Vietnam fired on an American destroyer conducting electronic espionage in their territorial waters, to pass a Senate resolution supporting all necessary retaliation.

In between the Incident and the Vote, the President appeared on TV—a dramatic postscript to the eleven o'clock news—to announce the bombing of four North Vietnamese ports. LBJ magically reduced a Crisis to an Incident even while unleashing U.S. jets. Then, three weeks after Goldwater was nominated, Johnson demonstrated total control over the Democratic Convention held in Atlantic City—a tawdry town of ancient fan-dancers and geriatric flagpole-sitters where, in addition to kewpie dolls and saltwater taffy, the boardwalk's souvenir stands hawked plastic wall hangings inscribed with JFK's imagined beyond-the-grave message to his wife.

Officially consecrated to the memory of the party's fallen leader, the DemCon was described by one anonymous wag as *"I've Got a Secret* organized by Caligula."* LBJ was notorious for habitually watching the network news simultaneously on three TV sets, phoning a newsman or even the network president to vent his displeasure. During the convention, Johnson attempted to further micromanage the television coverage even as he orchestrated a guessing game over his selection of a running mate. Privately, LBJ was filled with self-pity, complaining to Texas governor John Connally that the South thought him a traitor and the North despised him because he was Southern. Johnson even pretended he might withdraw. But, for all his bizarre, autocratic conduct, the President successfully reduced the election to the question of which Cowboy was more responsible—whose McLintock finger should be on the nuclear trigger. Such was Marshall McLuhan's post-TV wisdom: Instead of the voting bloc, we have the icon. Instead of a political platform, there was the political stance.

As described by his in-house intellectual adviser, Eric F. Goldman, Johnson's stump speech would reach its climax with a tall-tale version of the great Cuban Missile Crisis:

> "As President Kennedy and the leader of the Soviet Union came eyeball to eyeball and the thumbs started inching up"—and LBJ's big thumb would start inching up—"as the thumbs started getting closer to that nuclear button, the knife was in each other's ribs, and neither of them was flinching. . . ." Then he would ask, "Which man's thumb do you want to be close to that button now?"

At least once, the President bellowed that "the world you save may be your own."

When *Fail-Safe* went into production in 1963, some suggested the Kennedy administration might not smile upon a movie showing an American president—even one played by Henry Fonda—nuking New York City to compensate for the unintentional obliteration of Moscow. Producer Max Youngstein was refused Pentagon assistance and, with film libraries cautioned against co-operation, unable to obtain the necessary stock footage. But, appearing as it did in mid-campaign at a moment of heated-up Indochinese involvement, *Fail-Safe* served the Democrats well. For, the Gulf of Tonkin notwithstanding, Johnson was running as the peace candidate.

The public impression was that Goldwater—who advocated using atomic weapons as a means to "defoliate" the Vietnamese jungle—had not imagined the implications of nuclear war. For a man so distressed by the breakdown of law and order, he seemed strangely casual about the prospect of mass annihilation. Steve Canyon had become a mouthpiece for Dr. Strangelove. *Fact* magazine devoted its entire September–October issue to the Goldwater mindset: "The Unconscious of a Conservative." Editor Ralph Ginzburg solicited diagnoses from thousands of psychiatrists, psychoanalysts, and psychologists. (Professionalism was evidently a vestige of the Old Sentimentality.) Ginzburg inverted the premise of *The Best Man*: Emotional maladjustment was introduced as a legitimate issue in a presidential campaign except that in this case, liberals were questioning the stability of a right-wing candidate.*

The President agreed, suggesting that his opponent was a madman capable

---

*Ginzburg asserted that Goldwater had suffered two nervous breakdowns. Meanwhile, the polled shrinks had no problem diagnosing the candidate as a "dangerous lunatic" or a "paranoid schizophrenic" given to "unconscious sadism" and "suicidal tendencies." Goldwater was characterized as "mentally deranged," "grossly psychotic," a "severe obsessive-compulsive," "authoritarian, megalomaniac, grandiose, [and] basically narcissistic." He was compared to Hitler. His opposition to disarmament was based on fear of castration. The doorknocker on his Washington home was a brass pistol, pointing upward.

of precipitating planetary war. In a Labor Day speech in Detroit, LBJ provided a vivid image. Forget fallout shelters: "In the first nuclear exchange, 100 million American and more than 100 million Russians would be dead. And when it was over, our great cities would be in ashes, and our fields would be barren, and our industry would be destroyed, and our American dreams would have vanished." A week later, LBJ raised the casualty figure to 300 million, plus those "unborn generations forever maimed."

The Democrats purchased time that evening during NBC's *Monday Night at the Movies* presentation of the suitably Old Testament *David and Bathsheba* to air the soon-to-be notorious campaign spot known as "The Daisy." Although shown only once, "The Daisy" remains the most famous of all American political commercials. Counting down from ten, a little girl pulled the petals off a flower. When she reached zero, a mushroom cloud filled the screen and the President was heard solemnly warning Americans to vote as though their world depended on it. Thus, the unmentioned Republican candidate was linked to the nuclear obliteration of a five-year-old child.*

Eight days later, *Fail-Safe* had its world premiere at the New York Film Festival. Even before the movie's October 7 release, *Time*'s cover featured the nuclear "issue"—a crude collage including images of both candidates, as well as the Daisy girl, divided Berlin, *Dr. Strangelove*, and the new Davy Crockett atomic rifle capable of launching a .01 kiloton bomb at battlefield range. *Fail-Safe* was the final bit of Missile Crisis fallout, although after the outrageous *Strangelove*, it could not but appear anticlimactic. The sober absence of music, overarticulated fear that technology was developing its own logic, relatively staid resident mad-scientist, and humanist SAC General were hopelessly square. The movie infused the baggage of B-52s and War Room computer screens with a European existential ennui; the sophisticates at a Georgetown party argue over the Bomb until dawn.

---

*"The Daisy" was remade, with similar imagery, by the Republicans during the 2000 presidential election, accusing Democratic candidate Al Gore of having sold out U.S. security for campaign contributions from China.

In late September, shortly before *Fail-Safe*'s general release, vice presidential candidate Hubert Humphrey recommended the movie to presidential press secretary Bill Moyers ("the more millions of people who might see it in these next few weeks, the better will be their understanding of the crucial role of the Chief Executive in preserving the peace"). Moyers sent a memo to LBJ reiterating *Fail-Safe*'s favorable impact "since it deals with irresponsibility in the handling of nuclear weapons." At the same time, *Fail Safe* dramatized one of Norman Mailer's more radical suggestions, proposed in the *Village Voice* in the Missile Crisis aftermath. Mailer wrote an open letter to JFK, requesting Jackie as hostage: "The moment an invasion is let loose, and you as the Commander in Chief go to your deep bomb shelter, why not send us your wife and children to share our fate in this city?" Kennedy, of course, had prepared to protect his family, but as *Fail-Safe*'s Kennedy-surrogate, Fonda was more resolute. Despite the First Lady's presence in New York, he allowed the Soviets to destroy the city as payback for America's inadvertent incineration of Moscow.

Albeit tepid at the box office, the movie was Fonda's apotheosis—a quarter century after embodying Young Mr. Lincoln, the actor was President at last. When *Advise and Consent* had opened, Andrew Sarris had deemed it "perverse" to cast Fonda as the ambitious liberal with a guilty past. Fonda's forte, Sarris explained, had "always been truthfulness and virile sincerity, and yet he has served also as one of the heroic paladins of the New Deal–Popular Front Left."

> He fought the Fascists in Spain in *Blockade*, fought organized society in Fritz Lang's *You Only Live Once* and embodied the aspirations of the rural proletariat as the heroic Tom Joad in the Ford-Steinbeck *Grapes of Wrath*. There is something a bit wicked, perhaps too wicked, in casting our most truthful actor as a liar.

Indeed, our most truthful actor had grown into the perfect image of a corporate liberal. In the courtroom drama *12 Angry Men* (1957), Fonda played the quintessential consensus builder. Initially the only jury member to question the guilt of the underprivileged juvenile delinquent accused of murder, Fonda's character patiently forges a centrist coalition for acquittal.

Embodiment of Arthur Schlesinger's vital center, Fonda tracked the trajectory of tormented liberalism—forged in the crucible of the 1930s, tested under fire during World War II, purged of its Communistic tendencies in the late 1940s—as he failed upward in what might be called his JFK trilogy. Defeated in his bid to become Secretary of State in *Advise and Consent*, Fonda appeared in that position in *The Best Man*; rejected in that movie as a presidential nominee, he returned, in time for the 1964 election, as *Fail-Safe*'s agonized Doomsday leader. *Fail-Safe* represented the culminating Kennedy scenario. Afterward, Fonda became a post-apocalyptic liberal. Thanks to his crazy, mixed-up kids, Jane and Peter, he wound up as personification of the as yet unnamed Generation Gap.

●   ●   ●

Soon after *Fail-Safe*'s release, Kennedy's great adversary also vanished. The Soviets lost their human face even as NBC's *The Man From U.N.C.L.E.* gave its secret agent hero a cute Russian sidekick.

LBJ was only helped by the mid-October purge of Nikita Khrushchev and subsequent detonation of a Red Chinese nuclear device. In vain, Goldwater counterpunched on social issues. The defender of states' rights now presented himself as candidate for sheriff, promising to enforce law and order on "the federal level." Republican strategist Clif White had advised his candidate that the Missile Gap of 1964 was Moral Decay. What's more, the crisis was amplified—in a continuous, rising drone—by the media. "The nation's newspapers are filled with stories of crime and violence, ranging from rape to riots, from juvenile delinquency to embezzlement," White noted. "We have, in fact, the built-in, national reservoir of hundreds of millions of dollars's worth of publicity working for us."

Late in the campaign, the Republicans organized a front group of frontier schoolmarms—Mothers for a Moral America, whose members included Hollywood activists Nancy Reagan and Hedda Hopper. Some $45,000 funneled through the Mothers was used to cobble together a sensational twenty-seven-minute montage of TV news clips baldly called *Choice*. As written by Otis Carney and produced in a week, *Choice* was pure feedback—the sound of quotidian media babble reverberating with the stridence of a police-car siren.

To narrate, Nancy Reagan recruited Raymond Massey, who had played the Great Emancipator in *Abe Lincoln in Illinois* and, more recently, *How the West Was Won*. Massey spoke over a phantasmagoric montage juxtaposing footage of muggers and gamblers with covers of dirty books and material on the new topless bathing suit. "Now there are two Americas," Massey intoned, just short of hysteria. "One is words like *allegiance* and *republic*. This America is an ideal, a dream. The other America, the other America, is no longer a dream but a nightmare."

Choice's nightmare included a staged shot of the producer's own black 1963 Lincoln Continental careening down a backcountry road, the unseen driver chucking beer cans out the window. Ruled by a brazen, usurping Texan, the Great Society is the province of bacchanalian beatniks, gyrating strippers, Negro vandals, and society degenerates dancing the Twist. "In eight short months there are more riots in the United States than in the last eight years. In the streets, the mobs, mobocracy. . . ."

Whatever their disagreements, candidates Nixon and Kennedy had been contained in the same frame. But now there were two Americas—the Armageddon of "The Daisy" and the apocalypse of *Choice*. To combat the fantasy-inflamed readers of sleazy paperbacks like *Jazz Me Baby*, sonorously frothing Massey conjures an alliance of clean-cut astronauts and manly laborers, the Statue of Liberty and an all-white class of smiling school kids pledging allegiance. Patriotic anthems drown out raunchy bump-and-grind. In one America, blacks are shown as wanton looters; in the other, they constructively pick cotton.

Just as George Washington was resurrected for the finale of Goldwater's 1956 Stalin-bash *For Freedom's Sake*, so *Choice* recruited George Washington McLintock—who had just had a cancerous lung removed. John Wayne was barely returned from the hospital when Carney propped him up in his living room, a rifle visible on the wall behind. Wayne wrote his own lines. "You've got the strongest hand in the world," he reminds the nation. "The hand that pulls the voting lever. Use it, will you! The choice is yours, America."

Operation Choice, Otis Carney recalled, was as "secret as a CIA plot" (or John Wayne's medical condition), a veritable 007 movie of "code names," "furtive" hotel meetings, and "clandestine" editing rooms. The filmmakers ran into a conspiracy to embargo footage of the grafting Johnson cronies, Bobby Baker and Billy Sol Estes. *Choice* was hardly back from the lab before the Democrats burglarized a print and mobilized against its being shown: "Overnight, they pushed their buttons in the press," Carney would maintain. Although 200 prints were sold to local groups and *Choice* was shown by stations in California and Wisconsin, the planned national telecast—Thursday afternoon, October 22—was derailed. First, NBC demanded *Choice* be edited for obscenity; then, on the eve of the broadcast, it was canceled by the candidate. Goldwater refused to press the button. Years later, Otis Carney maintained that the bad press terrified Wayne as well. "He commanded me to get him off the thing. I said: 'But, Duke, I read you every word of the script. You loved it.' " But to read the script was not to see the images. Prime-time prophecy of the Orgy to come, *Choice* was too hot for TV. Its visual clarion call for a Cowboy jihad ran counter to the current mood of national hedonism—not to mention the public's longing for peace.*

The only solace hip Republicans could take was the late-campaign TV speech given to rally the troops and billed as "A Thoughtful Address by Ronald Reagan." Stressing that he was speaking without a script, the host of TV's *Death Valley Days* insisted that there was no longer Left and Right, only up or down.

---

*It took another sort of Western to simultaneously celebrate frontier individualism and treat violence seriously. Kennedy content served à la Goldwater yielded the Johnson Western. Philip French imagined these as John Ford movies without John Wayne— especially *Sergeant Rutledge* and *Cheyenne Autumn*, which, in preproduction during the 1963 March on Washington, suggested an appreciation of Martin Luther King Jr.'s nonviolent crusade. But as the world was to discover, the real LBJ Western was far more monstrous.

We're at war with the most dangerous enemy that has ever faced mankind on his long climb from the swamp to the stars. . . . Freedom has never been so close to slipping from our grasp . . . this is the last stand on earth.

Thus paraphrasing the Missile Gap scare tactics of Kennedy's 1960 campaign rhetoric, Reagan attacked the Democrats as "socialists" and accused them of reducing the presidential election to the contest of personalities. The day after Goldwater's overwhelming defeat—Johnson receiving 61 percent of the popular vote—a group of conservatives in Owosso, Michigan, formed Republicans for Reagan. One Star-Pol had died, another slouched toward Bethlehem to be born.

Major Dundee—Great Society Abroad

The Cowboy Election over, some mega Cowboy Scenario yearned for realization. Lyndon Johnson's fantastic promise of a Great Society was manifest in two wildly overwrought, would-be world-historical Westerns: Sam Peckinpah's 1965 *Major Dundee* and Arthur Penn's 1966 *The Chase*, both eagerly anticipated debacles.

For a brief period, but not quite yet, Penn and Peckinpah would be the hippest directors in Hollywood—bold genre-wreckers and purveyors of bloody mayhem. Peckinpah, born in 1925 to a prosperous family of California pioneers, was a professional Westerner; Penn, two years older and the son of a first-generation Jewish watchmaker, was an Eastern intellectual. Peckinpah enlisted in the marines and studied at Fresno State. Penn was drafted into the infantry, then attended experimental Black Mountain College, the University of Perugia, and the Actors Studio. Both men broke into show business via television; each initiated his Hollywood career with a self-consciously nouveau Western. Penn's 1958 *The Left Handed Gun*, adapted from Gore Vidal's teleplay, featured the young Method actor Paul Newman as a neurotic Billy the Kid. Peckinpah's first feature, *The Deadly Companions* (1961) was an undistinguished piece of hack work—used by the neophyte director to get into pictures, then butchered by its crude producer—but his 1962 *Ride the High Country* attracted attention for its poignantly autumnal deployment of veteran Western stars.

Major Dundee took place during the Civil War, albeit opening on a different battlefield—the scene of a Texas massacre. *The Chase*, at once Southern gothic and grandiose post-Western, superimposed Mississippi racial politics on Texas affluence—Hollywood's LBJ Ranch set. Both movies were sprawling embodiments of New Deal hubris and artistic bravado, each a foredoomed, violent, misshapen expression of rampant megalomania—suffused in racial anxiety, shot through with intimations of personal and public disaster, the disruption of law and order. Both suffered for the director's loss of control and yet were compelling for that very reason.

•   •   •

February 7, 1965: Two days after *Major Dundee* has its preview at the Egyptian Theater in Los Angeles, Lyndon Johnson again orders the retaliatory bombing of North Vietnam, and never mind that the new Soviet premier, Aleksey Kosygin, is visiting Hanoi!

Now a duly elected president, LBJ is under pressure from his National Security Adviser, McGeorge Bundy, and Defense Secretary Robert McNamara to escalate American involvement. "Both of us are now pretty well convinced that our current policy can lead only to disastrous defeat," Bundy had warned in a January 27 memo. The night of February 6, the Viet Cong attacked a U.S. base in the spooky central highlands. Eight Americans were killed and one hundred wounded, with ten aircraft destroyed. Bundy's next memo reiterates that the prospect of "inevitable" defeat demands "sustained reprisal."

Projecting the imminent collapse of South Vietnam and, by extension, what remains of the national narrative, LBJ opts for full-scale intervention. The scenario is now writing him. The first series of sorties is too modestly titled Flaming Dart. McNamara, however, wants it understood there will be "unlimited appropriation available for the financing of aid to Vietnam. March 2, these air-attacks expand into Operation Rolling Thunder—massive B-52 raids on military targets, complete with carpet bombing and napalm. Intended to last only eight weeks, Rolling Thunder has what the movie industry called "legs"—it will run for three-and-a-half years, right through the 1968 election.

Thanks to the voter registration drive organized by Nobel laureate and *Time* Man of the Year Martin Luther King Jr., March 1965 marks the apex of the President's moral authority. Sunday night, March 7, ABC interrupts their telecast of *Judgment at Nuremberg*—Stanley Kramer's all-star condemnation of Nazi war crimes—with a fifteen-minute report on the clash that day between Alabama police and civil-rights marchers en route from Selma to Montgomery. Just over a week later, LBJ delivers his "We Shall Overcome" speech to Congress, and for a moment, homely, homespun Lyndon Johnson is the Hollywood Freedom Fighter.

The idea, however, is already obsolete. The day after the United States bombs North Vietnam, an obscure leftist organization, Students for a Democratic Society (SDS), calls for an April 17 March on Washington. The counterforce begins to build. A March 24 teach-in at the University of Michigan attracts 3,000 participants—five times more than organizers expected. There are 30,000 American troops in Vietnam, and the guarded optimism of 1963 has evolved into something less rational. "Escalation" is a newly minted coinage (Herman Kahn's *On Escalation: Metaphors and Scenarios* has just been published) but despite, or rather because of, McNamara and Bundy's intimations of disaster, the money keeps pouring—lighter fluid on the barbecue.

By now, McNamara and the Joint Chiefs are committed to escalating on the ground as well. April 6, Johnson signs National Security Action Memorandum No. 328, approving twelve covert CIA operations, twenty-one Army actions, and a 20,000-man increase in support troops. The bombing is extended to Laos. The next night, LBJ is televised live from Johns Hopkins University. In very nearly the biggest communicational festival since the Kennedy funeral, an estimated 60 million Americans tune in to watch their President explicate a "war of unparalleled brutality."

> Simple farmers are the targets of assassination and kidnapping; women and children are strangled in the night because their men are loyal to their government.

And helpless villages are ravaged by sneak attacks. Large scale raids are conducted on towns. . . . It is the new face of an old enemy.

That enemy is older than Communism. Out on the frontier, groups of peaceable settlers—members of "the Free World family"—are besieged by bloodthirsty savages. We need Indian-fighters, gunslingers, tough sheriffs, the magnificent Seventh Cavalry!

• • •

The day of the President's speech, *Major Dundee* opened at New York's Capitol Theater. The most sympathetic review called the movie "ugly," "brutal," "gory," and "pessimistic," as well as "costly."

Indeed, Johnson's description of Vietnam might have been transposed to the screen as the Apache carnage with which *Major Dundee* begins—a torched, corpse-strewn settlement complete with American cavalry corpse hung by his heels. Slack-jawed and slavering in his moment of triumph, the demented-looking Apache chief, Sierra Charriba, contemplates his dead American adversary and brazenly taunts the viewer, "Who will you send against me now?" An answering title—MAJOR DUNDEE in crimson letters—is branded on the image of flaming Cinemascope destruction, accompanied by a jaunty choral command, delivered by TV personality Mitch Miller's Sing Along Gang, to "Fall in behind the Major" and pursue the Apache phantasm.

Commonweal hazarded that *Major Dundee* "must have started with a good idea and then [gone] haywire in the execution." Peckinpah was fascinated by the spectacle of smashed ambitions—he'd wanted to make a movie on General Custer as a great man motivated by selfish ambition, a perverse hero whose greatest triumph was a legendary defeat. *Major Dundee*'s action unfolds almost exactly a century before the season during which the movie was released. This historical framework enabled Peckinpah to comment on the Civil Rights crusade while reflecting, consciously or not, the current leadership crisis.*

Major Dundee intuited Lyndon Johnson's dilemma—although it originated, mid-Camelot, in Columbia producer Jerry Bresler's search for a new Charlton Heston ve-

Peckinpah caught the wave and capsized; his Great Society scenario was a movie about confusion and failure that, grossing a pitiful $1.6 million, was itself a confusing failure. But how could it have been otherwise when the production conflicts so mirrored those of the narrative?

An ambitious Southerner in the service of the Union, the overbearing Dundee commands a Texas prison camp to which he was transferred for creative insubordination—trying to "fight his own war" at Gettysburg. He repeats the pattern by illegally commandeering weapons to cross into Mexico in pursuit of two white children taken captive by the Apaches. The resident Indian scout (James Coburn) gives the major "one chance in a thousand to recover the boys," thus raising the stakes. Dundee's mission is to recover the white captives, wreak vengeance on the Apache, and restore American honor. But in this cavalry, American civil discord is a given.

Unlike John Ford's *Fort Apache*—where soldiers spend as much time dancing as fighting and are identified with tender domesticity—*Major Dundee* offers no positive evidence of American civilization. Peckinpah was imagining a new sort of Western, savage, spectacular, charged with magical desire. As in Antonin Artaud's imagined Theater of Cruelty, the first production of Peckinpah's cinema of cruelty could be called "The Conquest of Mexico" and, as Artaud promised, it would "stage events, not men." *Major Dundee* can be considered a surrealist irrational enlargement of a Ford cavalry film. Once the Major crosses the Rio Grande, pursuing Sierra Charriba into Mexico, he goes through the looking glass. Peckinpah contaminated the self-contained classicism of Ford's *Fort Apache* with the geopolitical aspirations of *The Magnificent Seven*. Like the latter, *Major Dundee* enhanced its importance with an international

---

hicle. Bresler turned up Harry Julian Fink's thirty-seven-page treatment, which—once Heston expressed interest—was imagined as a road show, like the spectacular *How the West Was Won*. John Ford, inevitable first choice to direct any cavalry movie, was already working on his final Western, *Cheyenne Autumn*. Thus, the script found Peckinpah, who spent the Civil Rights Summer of 1963 elaborating a scenario that would place America's preeminent epic star (*Moses/Ben-Hur/El Cid*) in the role of a maladroit, embittered, overreaching loner.

cast. But Peckinpah had an even madder vehicle in mind—hiring twenty-five stuntmen, the most ever assembled for a single movie (per *Life*'s five-page spread).

Production was originally set to begin December 1, 1963; additional rewrites and miscellaneous tumult, including the Kennedy assassination, pushed the date to February 6, 1964. Charlton Heston, having read the revised script after attending the JFK funeral, confided in his diary that he didn't know what the heck *Major Dundee* was about. Two days before the shoot opened in Durango, the studio underwent a shake-up. Yet, even as *Major Dundee*'s budget suffered a last-minute cut from $4.5 to $3 million, Peckinpah fought to keep the movie in Mexico. There, he could recapitulate the reign of terror at Columbia. Production assistant Gordon Dawson recalled being "scared to death." Peckinpah "was firing people right and left," fifteen crew members in all.

On his own initiative, Dundee pulls together a motley regiment of Confederate prisoners of war, Union deserters, Texas horse thieves, and free black soldiers. The American army is violently integrated yet grossly divided. Northerners and Southerners sing rival anthems while, in another dig at Ford, the degenerate civilians bellow "My Darling Clementine." All that binds these Americans is their fear and loathing of a racial foe. Dundee's men will be united only "until the Apache is taken or destroyed." Indeed, Dundee's worst enemy isn't Sierra Charriba but his former fellow officer, the Confederate prisoner Tyreen (Richard Harris).*

---

*Peckinpah likened Dundee's pursuit of Sierra Charriba to Ahab's mad quest for Moby Dick. But there were other such figures in American history. Did anyone remember Captain L. H. McNelly, the Texas Ranger and Indian fighter who, in 1875, was charged with driving cattle rustlers from southeast Texas? The enthusiastic McNelly led thirty Rangers in hot pursuit across the Rio Grande and, once in Mexico, used torture to exact information, performed summary executions and, perhaps to provoke war, ignored orders to return. LBJ himself was a McNelly fan; the old captain was even on his mind that spring. Johnson praised him in the foreword he signed for the re-publication of Walter Prescott Webb's 1935 *The Texas Rangers*, a book that whitewashed McNelly, explaining that "affairs on the border cannot be judged by standards that hold elsewhere."

Fall in behind the Major! Like an action painter or a jazz musician, Peckinpah planned to find Major Dundee's main theme even as his movie was
being made. But the new regime at Columbia feared that they had inherited
a runaway production with a lunatic at the helm. No less than Dundee, Peckinpah led his men into Mexico—the underdeveloped world where anything
was possible. Studio left behind, the film became a conquest of this wild landscape. The deeper into Mexico, the fewer the civilized constraints—despite the
parade of sweating Columbia suits who ventured south of the border to see
what was happening. After five weeks, the Apaches deprive Dundee of his
rationale by setting free the captives. But still, fueled by the Major's desire for
glory and revenge, his overweening vanity, and a certain giddy inertia, the
quest goes on. So did the movie, although midway through production the
star was compelled to intervene to save his director's job. Threatening to walk
off the picture if Peckinpah were discharged, Heston wound up offering to
forfeit his salary—a gesture without parallel in Hollywood history. The idealistic actor had come to believe that this movie meant something: *Major Dundee*
and Major Dundee would demonstrate the "strength and flexibility of the
Union" that had enabled the United States to "survive the bloody trauma" of
Civil War.

The making of *Major Dundee* coincided with the Republican primary season,
the prolonged Senate debate on the second Civil Rights bill, the emergence of
George Wallace as the national personification of White Backlash, and LBJ's
introduction of the Great Society—a period when the United States was looking inward and only two maverick Democrats, Senator Wayne Morse of
Oregon and Senator Ernest Gruening of Alaska, questioned the nation's involvement in Vietnam. There was as yet no crisis—no international incident
in the waters off Vietnam. In the *Major Dundee* scenario, the return of the
captives has effectively nullified the rationale for the Major's self-declared war.
To secure arms to continue their now-pointless pursuit of the Apaches, Dundee's men incidentally liberate a village held by another interventionist
power—the French.

What are all these foreigners doing in Mexico? Are they searching for some obscure self-actualization? Dundee hasn't "the temperament of a liberator," claims his rival, Tyreen, taunting the Major as the two compete for the attentions of the German beauty (Senta Berger) that the plot has marooned in this desert pueblo. On-set accounts that Heston and Harris actively disliked each other only improve these scenes, but the woman is not really the issue. *Major Dundee* is, after all, a Western—a genre that exists to rationalize the use of deadly force. Each and every Western necessarily divides the world into good guys and bad, defining the bad guy in such a way that, by the movie's end, the good guy is morally justified and absolved by history in wreaking vengeance as judge, jury, and executioner. But who are the heroes and villains in *Major Dundee*?

The French subsequently punish the pueblo for welcoming Dundee's soldiers by massacring its inhabitants. Thanks to the triangulation now afforded by the Europeans and the Apache, Dundee stands between civilization and the wilderness. A true American, he first uses Indian strategy to confound the French and then, in the film's penultimate battle, demonstrates his cavalry's superiority to the Apache. Only a greater savage can defeat the savage Sierra Charriba.*

The climactic irony has Dundee and Tyreen poised to fight their long-delayed personal duel when, suddenly, instead of the Seventh Cavalry it's France redux. In a bizarre bit of geopolitical allegory, Dundee and his men must break through the French lines to reenter the United States. This absurdist finale is an exercise in tropistic patriotism. For the first time since entering Mexico, Dundee's forces unfurl their colors and Tyreen—introduced in the movie cursing the Stars and Stripes—dies having recaptured the American flag from the French.

Major Dundee wrapped on April 30, 1964, fifteen days late, $1.5 million over

---

*Dundee operates like those Indochinese guerrillas who, for four years, armed themselves with captured American weapons. But now, as in their own revolution, the Americans are the "Indians." This triumph of counterinsurgency, Richard Slotkin points out, has a true mirror logic: "The guerrilla is induced to think like an American planner and tricked into abandoning guerrilla fight/flight tactics for frontal assault."

budget, and a week after Lyndon Johnson conjured up his fantasy of the Great Society. That summer, as LBJ was coronated in Atlantic City, Peckinpah found himself eighty-sixed from the Columbia lot while his original cut—including fantastic slow-motion battle sequences inspired by Akira Kurosawa's *Seven Samurai*—was shortened by nearly half an hour. Entire scenes were deleted, mainly dealing with Dundee's extravagantly neurotic motivations. There was no more talk of a road show. The Cowboy Election not withstanding, epic Westerns were passé. Over at Warners, *Cheyenne Autumn* was similarly downgraded to a conventional release.

●   ●   ●

As brutally as liberal intellectuals were now reversing themselves on the candidate they had supported in 1964 and even applauded for his stand on civil rights as recently as March, so *Newsweek*, which had named Sam Peckinpah's *Ride the High Country* the best movie of 1962, turned on its director: "Think of Yosemite Falls or suicides from the top of the Empire State Building, or streaking meteorites downward toward the earth and you'll get some idea of the decline in the career of Sam Peckinpah. *Major Dundee*, his third film, is a disaster." The movie was pure death wish—"as if Peckinpah were enjoying his ruin."*

Peckinpah's blighted blockbuster was enjoying its final days in release, playing New York neighborhoods on a bill with the Three Stooges in *The Outlaws Is Coming*, when the CIA-directed government of the Dominican Republic was overthrown in a late April coup led by the nation's last elected president, Juan Bosch (himself deposed by a U.S.-supported coup in the fall of 1963). The CIA set up an alternative junta on a Dominican air base, which followed the nec-

---

*For the *Saturday Review*, *Major Dundee* was not simply inept but camp. The title character's ridiculous toughness was "too much"—an increasingly common view of LBJ. Investigating the mood on campus for the *New York Post*, Pete Hamill would report that, while the public overwhelmingly approved of their President, "not a single student" he interviewed, whether "left, right, [or] indifferent" respected Johnson. "They think of him as vain, cornball, intellectually muddled, power-mad, paranoiac at times, an agent of the Lawrence Welk gang."

essary protocol in asking the American ambassador for American troops to protect American lives. Just like *Major Dundee*: Recover the captives, restore honor, wreak vengeance. Thus informed, the Great Cowboy ordered in the marines—employing his favorite phantasmagoria on the National Security Council, "it's just like the Alamo"—and interrupting the TV Western *Bonanza* to so inform the American people.

Not even six months after Johnson's stunning electoral victory, he was being openly reviled. On May 2, as part of the spring's climactic campus teach-in, Berkeley's Vietnam Day, organized by Jerry Rubin, Norman Mailer made a fabulously insulting speech. Mailer received a standing ovation in part because he attacked not only Johnson's policy but his personality—and even his public image. Mailer proposed that, as a gesture of contempt, opponents of the war invert the President's photographs. The Vietnam Day organizers had buttons prepared; when the speech was published in *The Realist*, the magazine's cover featured an upside-down LBJ. (Mailer "qualitatively changed the event," Rubin recalled in an interview two decades later by "giving us permission to insult a father figure, indicating that it's okay to ridicule the President.")

Mailer recognized Johnson's "monstrous vanity" and media-driven mega-lomania. The President was known to keep three TVs in his office and another three in his bedroom. Frequently interrupting regular programming or com-mandeering the prime-time schedule, LBJ went on television more often during his first year in office than his predecessor had in the course of his entire foreshortened term. (By the end of 1965, Johnson would log more TV ap-pearances than Dwight Eisenhower made in eight years.) Moreover, he de-manded the camera catch his right profile.

In the face of this personality cult, Mailer had proposed, in effect, a modest form of guerrilla theater—a concept recently developed by the San Francisco Mime Troupe. The guerrilla theater action would erase distinctions between public and private behavior to create social change, not by representing it but by living it. The Mime Troupe called this "breaking the glass." According to their theorist, Peter Berg, performers had to become life actors, consciously creating the roles they enacted in everyday existence—not unlike the Merry

Pranksters' acid-inspired desire to confound conditioned responses or Timothy Leary's LSD revelation that all social behavior was a form of game playing.

A counterculture was coming into existence, and consciousness was the battlefield. In his "Guerrilla Theater: 1965," written soon after Vietnam Day, Mime Troupe founder R. G. Davis warned that "social theater is a risky business. . . . Operative paranoia is our appropriate state of being." So it was with Mailer, who explained the War in Vietnam in terms that were not so much simple as primal. On the one hand, Johnson—a vainglorious, image-obsessed President who believed the headline more real than the event—had decided to upstage the Civil Rights movement. On the other, the Kennedy assassination had driven America nuts: "Our country was fearful, half-mad, inauthentic—it needed a war or it needed a purge." As he had at the 1964 Republican Convention, Mailer prophesied upheaval to come.

> Something in the buried animal of modern life grew bestial at the thought of this Great Society—the most advanced technological nation of the civilized world was the one now closest to blood, to shedding the blood and burning the flesh of Asian peasants it had never seen.

June 14 brought the Great Society's suitably grandiose White House Festival of the Arts, organized by historian-in-residence Eric F. Goldman. LBJ had intended to orchestrate another TV extravaganza, but even before this thirteen-hour marathon got under way, it was a source of embarrassment. Robert Lowell searched his conscience and made public a letter explaining to the President why, after originally accepting an invitation, his opposition to Johnson's Vietnam policy precluded any participation. Caught between God and Caesar, Lowell's fellow intellectuals scrambled to stake out their own moral positions. Lillian Hellman, among others, signed a telegram in support of the poet.

The wildly ambitious White House event included painting, sculpture, music, dance, photography, and even cinema. Major Dundee was on hand to narrate a forty-minute compilation of clips from Hollywood classics *North by*

Northwest, On the Waterfront, Shane, Friendly Persuasion, and *High Noon.* The movies were the last presentation before the outdoor buffet dinner. The critic Dwight Macdonald was circulating a two-sentence petition suggesting that one's presence at the festival need not be construed as support for LBJ and opposition to Lowell. Catching up to Heston in the Rose Garden, Macdonald invited the actor to add his name to the meager list. The actor's refusal resulted in a toe-to-toe, eyeball-to-eyeball shouting match, with Macdonald insulting Heston's intelligence. ("I had an exhilarating chance to fence with Dwight Macdonald, who was fussing around like a petulant bumblebee," Heston confided in his diary.)

That same evening, CBS broadcast the hour-long documentary *The Berkeley Rebels,* which gave a platform to several student radicals. Michael Rossman baffled his interviewer by suggesting—at age twenty-five—that he was something other than an adult and claiming that his generation had "no ideology" beyond the realization that "society stinks." But it was the glimpse of the grafitto MAKE LOVE, NOT WAR that startled one reviewer: "What will these kids think of next?" Reality seemed increasingly elastic.

The current White House buzz word was "scenario"—thanks not only to Herman Kahn but to the former PR man Jack Valenti, who was among Johnson's closest aides. All that summer, the White House resonated with talk of an image crisis. The overt emphasis on credible scenarios and public relations constructs promoted a powerful sense of disassociation. The South Vietnamese government was overthrown once more, this time by Catholic militants who installed General Nguyen Van Thieu as chief of state and Air Vice Marshal Nguyen Cao Ky as prime minister. Soon, General William Westmoreland and Secretary of Defense McNamara were again informing the President that his only option was to expand America's involvement.

On July 27, Johnson approved McNamara's recommendations and the following day scheduled a high-noon press conference to inform the American people that their nation was at war—kind of. The monthly draft call doubled. There had been 23,000 American soldiers in Vietnam at the end of 1964. By the end of 1965, there would be 184,000. More than just an anti-Communist extravaganza, the U.S. presence began to suggest something hyperreal—a second Texas, a simulated wild frontier.

The Chase—Great Society at Home

May 1965, with the first of an eventual 20,000 U.S. troops in the Dominican Republic, Hollywood's second great Great Society fiasco went into production. "Few films of recent vintage have attracted as much interest and gossip," the *New York Times* reported in June. No less than the Vietnam War, *The Chase* involved the Best and the Brightest. The producer was Sam Spiegel, returning to Hollywood after the Oscar-winning triumphs of *The Bridge on the River Kwai* and *Lawrence of Arabia*. The star was Marlon Brando, still considered the greatest actor of his generation.

For Brando, the big draw was working with the outspokenly anti-Hollywood, Method-oriented Arthur Penn. For Penn, the attraction was directing from a screenplay by his friend, the venerable dramatist Lillian Hellman. Although the script was Hellman's first since she was blacklisted, her unhappiness with the project was already known—she received a single credit, yet her work had been revised by another blacklisted writer, Michael Wilson, and then the original author, Horton Foote. As *Major Dundee* elaborated, only to explode, the cavalry and Indian movies of the early Cold War, so *The Chase* took off from the town Westerns of the same period. The movie was based on a play that had run thirty-one performances on Broadway in the spring of 1952. Foote's spare parable opened several months before the release of *High Noon*, to which it bore marked resemblance: Over a twenty-four-hour time period, a small-town Texas sheriff awaits the return of Bubber Reeves, an escaped convict who has sworn to kill him. The sheriff is committed to Bubber's nonviolent apprehension. Yet, in the course of trying to save the criminal from a lynch mob, the lawman panics and winds up shooting Bubber himself.

This story percolated throughout the Eisenhower era. First, Foote reworked the material as a novel. Then, producer Sam Spiegel acquired the property in

1959 and commissioned a script on which he would not focus for another five years. By then it was a time of heightened Texas consciousness. Spiegel's interest in *The Chase* was reawakened by an incident occurring in Dallas a month before the Kennedy assassination, when UN ambassador Adlai Stevenson was jeered, shoved, and spat upon by right-wing demonstrators. Even before November 22, 1963, Texas had suffered an image crisis—ridiculed as the domain of chauvinist braggarts and ignorant oil millionaires, Hud-quarters for a cabal of gun-toting crazies. Soon, per the *Nation*'s Washington correspondent, Robert Sherrill, the state was understood to be a "proud, fertile desert of social reaction," with Lyndon Johnson its Pharaoh in Chief.

A volatile frontier community inflated by sudden oil wealth seemed to Spiegel to be a metaphor for the nation—even as Texas came to represent the all-American death and violence trip. *The Chase*'s town, Tarl, is a Western set—two-block Main Street, adobe jail, ornate bank, and rowdy saloon complete with golden-hearted scarlet woman living upstairs. The characters are recognizable Western types—the taciturn sheriff, Calder (Marlon Brando), the boyish misunderstood outlaw, Bubber Reeves (Robert Redford), the domineering local plutocrat, Val Rogers (E. G. Marshall), and the requisite gaggle of fearful citizens. The situation, predicated on Bubber's presumably vengeful return to Tarl, is similarly generic. But the moment is Now.

The Chase was *High Noon* as modified by a number of current events—the struggle for civil rights, the Kennedy assassination, and the war being waged by his Texan successor. But where *High Noon* was a Sunday morning sermon, *The Chase* was one long Saturday night in the world's steamiest small town. Val Rogers celebrates his birthday with a grotesque soiree—his palatial mansion filled with rich old gargoyles doing the Frug. Down the hill, there's a wild party at the home of Rogers's emasculated bank employee, Edwin Stewart (Robert Duvall), full of drunken wife swappers. Allegory is brazen—the errant Mrs. Stewart (Janice Rule) torments her husband with a mock flamenco dance, snipping a pair of scissors as her castanets—and nearly everybody packs a gun. Yet another shindig—this one for provocatively unchaperoned teenagers—is going on across the street. Meanwhile, an addled hymn singer wanders around the set, whose obvious back-lot quality was, for Penn, a continual source of dismay.

As in *High Noon*, the failure of nerve is displaced onto the town—here even more flamboyantly venal and corrupt. As the beleaguered sheriff mumbles to his loyal wife, Ruby (Angie Dickinson): "Some of those people out there are just nuts." The citizens accuse Calder of being owned, as they are, by Val Rogers—who not only defines Tarl with his corporate logo, but dreams of creating a mega university so no child will ever have to leave his Great Society. Bubber—scarcely a dangerous criminal, hardly even a crazy, mixed-up kid— embodies Tarl's guilty conscience. Bubber has taken the rap for more than a few of his schoolmates, even as the plutocrat's son, his erstwhile best friend, Jake (James Fox), has taken up with Bubber's wife, Anna (Jane Fonda).

Bubber's unwilling return has the quality of chickens coming home to roost, to use the phrase Malcolm X made famous in relation to the JFK murder. The locals are haunted by the memory of the convicted man's stare: It's "like everything's gone all wrong and he just can't figure out why." Who can? Like the Apaches in *Major Dundee*, Bubber is a much-discussed yet largely invisible threat. Still, the buried animal is stirring. Although Jake ventures from the family oil field into its cotton fields to wish his Mexican workers a perfunctory *vaya con Dios*, *The Chase*'s lone instance of social integration comes when half the cast settles down to watch a stilted TV news report on Bubber's escape— their imagined community defined by collective fear and a common familiarity with the media.

As *Major Dundee*'s mad plunge into Mexico seems prophetic of Lyndon Johnson's foreign policy, so the anxious, ineffectual paternalism of *The Chase* suggests the domestic chaos of the Great Society. Brando, identified with liberal causes in general and Civil Rights in particular, may look and act like a hero, but he cannot enforce the law; Bubber may be headed for the border, but Mexico's freedom is never more than an illusion. What we have instead—once Bubber's mother makes a scene amid the drunken, adulterous couples and her hysteria galvanizes the town—is the breakdown that the Goldwater campaign visualized in *Choice*, the state *Newsweek* would describe, in reviewing *The Chase*, as an "orgiastic night of lawlessness."

Looking for Bubber, a fear-crazed mob invades the jail and Val Rogers bludgeons an innocent black man. Meanwhile a gang of drunks opportunistically assaults the sheriff: Civil order collapses with this prolonged and extremely convincing attack on the movie's star. Penn told one interviewer that the fight was only partially "staged." There were takes in which Brando, who suggested shooting in slow motion, was really being slugged—that the star had taken up with the girlfriend of Richard Bradford, who plays the mob leader, helped fuel the scene—but this material was too "unbearable" to use. Still, the sudden explosion of rage and anti-authoritarian hatred gives this sequence an unexpected jolt.

It is as if anything can happen—starting with Brando's bravura slow roll over and off the desktop whereon he'd just been beaten. The sheriff's face has been battered to a bloody pulp and the townspeople are shown subjectively through his eyes—promise of LSD bummers to come. A ranting, out-of-control Val Rogers leads the populace, turning out "Roman games–style" (as Columbia publicity put it) to capture Bubber in the automobile graveyard where he has holed up, along with his generational and sexual cohort, Jake and Anna. Penn shot the town sequences on the Warners back lot, while the junkyard was assembled on an outlying "movie ranch," used mainly for Westerns. On the hot summer evening of Wednesday, August 11, as *The Chase* lurched toward closure, the colored equivalent of the movie's "Saturday night" arrived: A terrifying riot broke out in another part of Los Angeles—namely the black ghetto of Watts—and, building in intensity each night, continued through Monday, August 16.

• • •

A minor traffic arrest had ignited the conflagration. On the first night there were nineteen cops and sixteen civilians injured, and thirty-four arrests, before an audience of . . . millions? Incredibly, in a permutation that transformed events into a communicational festival, the riots were telecast live.

"One of the Los Angeles stations, Channel 5, performed a technical near miracle from its flying helicopter," Theodore White wrote. Anyone in LA could turn on the tube to "see looters carrying off sofas, furniture, television sets, appliances, groceries as if in a barbarian carnival." By Thursday night, the citizens of Watts were alternately performing for the camera and showering the news crews with rocks. The festival was now TV interactional. Crowds were drawn to stores where looting had been reported and to buildings shown burning. Even white spectators appeared. Meanwhile, the Fire Department had ceased responding to alarms, relying instead on live relays from the Channel 5 helicopter.

The radio—Marshall McLuhan's tribal drum—fanned the flames with crazy rumors: Snipers were reported on the Harbor Freeway, looters said to be heading for white neighborhoods. "Burn baby burn," the catch phrase used by the soul-music DJ who called himself the Magnificent Montague, was the password and the rallying cry. Once the looting got going, even children of eight or nine were seen drinking cheap wine and malt liquor.

There were more fires on Friday night—perhaps 10,000 rioters torching their own neighborhood. LA police chief William Parker compared the situation to "fighting the Viet Cong" and admitted "we haven't the slightest idea when this can be brought under control." The John Birch Society was no small presence in the LAPD, and Parker's men were prone to fantasy. A ten-car convoy of Negroes with red armbands was hallucinated on the Ventura Freeway; another group in a yellow school bus was reported on the Golden State Freeway. Some cops thought they had discovered a Muslim sect; others believed the red armbands were VC agents. Nor were these the only imaginary presences. For two days, the *Los Angeles Herald-Examiner* carried accounts of nonexistent gun battles.*

---

*This was truly guerrilla theater. A year later, Thomas Pynchon wrote, Watts residents recalled their riot in aesthetic terms: "Some talk now of a balletic quality to it, a coordinated and graceful drawing of cops away from the center of the action. Others remember it in terms of music; through much of the rioting seemed to run, they say, a remarkable empathy; or whatever it is that jazz musicians feel on certain nights;

Friday evening, Lieutenant Governor Glenn Anderson called up the National Guard. As the riot spread throughout the weekend, north toward the Civic Center and even Pasadena, the white inhabitants of Los Angeles and Orange County frantically stocked up on rifles, knives, bows and arrows—"even slingshots," according to the owner of one store, who reported selling seventy-five shotguns in a day. By the time the smoke cleared, there were 34 dead, over 1,000 reported injuries, nearly 4,000 under arrest, and $40 million in property damage.

Had society begun to mirror *The Chase*? Or did Penn imagine that he was making a documentary? It was perhaps with Watts in mind that, after weeks of indecision, the director figured out how to shoot *The Chase*'s climax. The Alamo implodes. Texas napalms itself. Burn baby burn! Following their elders down to the junkyard, Tarl's teenagers stage a spontaneous hootenanny, chuck Molotov cocktails, roll flaming tires into the assemblage as a gasoline leak sets the junkyard ablaze. It's almost a flashback to November 23, 1963, as the escalating series of metaphors culminates with the apprehended Bubber's vigilante assassination on the Tarl jailhouse steps, with Penn's composition and Redford's body language evoking Jack Ruby's murder of Lee Harvey Oswald. Bubber may be innocent of the killing he's accused of committing, but it was, after all, the JFK assassination which brought the real Val Rogers to power and our national Tarl to its sorry state.

Years later, the critic Robin Wood recognized *The Chase* as a key vision of "American apocalypse"—the first Hollywood movie wherein "the disintegration of American society and the ideology that supports it" is shown as "total and final, beyond hope of reconstruction." And poor Bubber—the wronged innocent, open and attractive, doomed from the start and identified with the black man in his existential victimhood—was the harbinger of all-American

---

everybody knowing what to do and when to do it without needing a word or a signal."

Whether, as Senator George Murphy believed, the looting was so "expert" as to suggest rehearsal, a script for such activities had already been prepared—albeit by the FBI, which, back in February, two days after the assassination of Malcolm X, published a manual, *The Prevention and Control of Mobs and Riots.*

outlaws to come. Back in June, even as *The Chase* was in production and Benton and Newman rewrote their script for *Bonnie and Clyde*, which would be Penn's next project, Students for a Democratic Society (SDS) held its annual national convention in Kewadin, Michigan. Rather than organize against the draft or even focus on opposing the war, the organization opted for its own grandiose project—the attempt to transform American society in its entirety. The conclave was swelled by hundreds of new members and a hitherto unseen breed of activist. According to movement historian Kirkpatrick Sale, this was the first SDS meeting where people openly smoked marijuana. Many militants had a new uniform: Men and women wore blue denim work shirts, dungaree jackets, and heavy boots, and it was then that "those droopy Western-movie [mustaches] that eventually became a New Left cliché, made their first appearance in quantity."

> These were people generally raised outside of the East, many from the Midwest and Southwest, and their ruralistic dress reflected a different tradition, one more aligned to the frontier, more violent, more individualistic, more bareknuckled. . . .

This New Frontier tendency was dubbed "Prairie Power." Many of its adherents, Sale noted, were the children of Goldwater supporters.

The Cowboy President made the notion of the Western outlaw increasingly viable. More radical role-playing: All summer, a bunch of crazed bohos in the half-deserted old mining town of Virginia City, Nevada, lived another sort of Western. The Red Dog Saloon, conceived during the course of a snowed-in two-day LSD trip, was a folk-rock club modeled on the saloon set for TV's *Gunsmoke*. The joint opened June 29 and—less a bar than a way of life—attracted all manner of San Francisco hipsters before being shut down at summer's end amid rumors of teen sex and drug orgies.*

---

*The Red Dog Saloon was an avant-garde Freedomland—elaborating on the psychedelic light shows, free-form dancing, and continual dress-up developed by the Merry Prank-

Social breakdown was impending. Sam Spiegel took out an ad in the September 1 *Variety*: THE WAITING IS OVER . . . *THE CHASE* IS ON THE WAY! That same week, the folk-rock protest-song "Eve of Destruction" entered the Top 40, where, reaching number one in late September, it remained into November, a baleful warning that "the Eastern world—it is explodin', violence flamin', bullets loadin'." Just as the antiwar kids began to imagine themselves as Western bad guys, *Choice* was globalized, put to music, appropriated by the Left, and delivered over and over and over again on the national soundtrack.

Written by nineteen-year-old former surfer P. F. Sloan and hoarsely declaimed by former folksinger Barry McGuire, "The Eve of Destruction" was the counterculture anthem of 1965—a deliriously apocalyptic conflation of nuclear anxiety, civil rights agitation, and Vietnam protest, equating Red China with Alabama, invoking slaughter in the Middle East, and promising that "there'll be no one to save with the world in a grave." Intended as a B-side, the song was on the airwaves only hours after a tape was passed to a sympathetic Los Angeles disc jockey. Selling 10,000 copies a day as the nation's students returned to school, "Eve of Destruction" was consequently attacked by the Young Republicans and Citizens for Conservative Action, and banned by ABC network affiliates and at individual radio stations in Chicago and L.A.*

"Eve of Destruction" was exhibit A in *Newsweek*'s mid-September report on

---

sters as it anticipated the Trips Festivals staged in San Francisco that fall. Don Works, a member of the peyote-eating Native American Church, reconfigured himself as Comstock McLoaded, growing a handlebar moustache and tending bar in a striped shirt with sleeve garters. LSD was plentiful, the fantasy pure cinema. As Red Dog co-founder Chan Laughlin told employees, "when your feet hit the floor in the morning, you're in a Grade B movie."

*There was even a patriotic answer-song, "The Dawn of Correction," which maintained that,

> The Western world has a common dedication
> To keep free people from Red domination.
> Maybe you can't vote, boy, but man your battle stations
> Or there'll be no need for votin' in future generations.

the new craze for message-oriented folk rock and also received particular attention in Reverend David A. Noebel's tract, *Rhythm, Riots and Revolution*. Reverend Noebel, a preacher with the Christian Anti-Communist Crusade, had revealed "a systematic plan geared to making a generation of American youth mentally ill and emotionally unstable" in his 1965 pamphlet, *Communism, Hypnotism and the Beatles*. According to Noebel's argument, the Beatles were a new form of Manchurian Candidate:

> The Communists, through their scientists, educators and entertainers, have contrived an elaborate, calculated and scientific technique directed at rendering a generation of American youth neurotic through nerve-jamming, mental deterioration and retardation. . . .
> The Beatles' ability to make teenagers weep and wail, become uncontrollable and unruly, and take off their clothes and riot is laboratory tested and approved.

Music, Noebel warned, might one day destroy America. Change the soundtrack and change the scenario. Folk rock was a further refinement in the Communist conspiracy.

Of course, folk music had been a Communist staple since the days of the Popular Front, and the March 9, 1965, issue of *The Worker* daringly bestowed a measure of political correctness on rock 'n' roll.

> What "new" music will be created as the growing youth movement for jobs and equality rocks our cities. Will it echo the croons of Irving Berlin or the twang of Kentucky bluegrass? Or will it seek expression in the "soul" music of our sidewalks.

Scarcely five months later, Reverend Noebel noted, the seed had borne fruit. *Billboard* headlined ROCK + FOLK + PROTEST = AN ERUPTING NEW SOUND, while Bob Dylan, identified by Noebel as "a faithful disciple of identified Communist Woody Guthrie," transformed his image from that of "a sloppy, disheveled Castro-looking cultist" to a "more respectable rock 'n' folk composer."

It had all come together that August, according to the Christian Crusade theorist, as Fidel Castro orchestrated an unholy alliance of Communists and Black Muslims directed by radio transmissions: "Trained revolutionists, with their disgruntled lackeys and always present dupes, destroyed acres of Watts territory with gasoline bombs and a bloodcurdling riot cry borrowed from a Los Angeles disc jockey, 'Burn, baby, burn.' "

Meanwhile, there was the Dodge Rebellion that the advertising agency BBD&O declared on behalf of Chrysler Motors. Dodge had been a car for middle-aged squares—its spokesman was TV bandleader Lawrence Welk. Suddenly gramps vanished and the car was promoted by Pam Austin, a twenty-four-year-old California blonde whose résumé included two movies with Elvis Presley. In her form-fitting dark gray jumpsuit and kicky boots, the Dodge Girl was a go-go terrorist, slipping from rooftops, dropping through drawbridges, colliding with trains to recruit revolutionary followers: THE DODGE REBELLION WANTS YOU! Watts blew up while the first spots were in production.

"There's a revolutionary leader whose face is getting to be better known than Fidel Castro's, and is certainly less bearded," the *New York Times* noted with giddy approval. Created the same year that Herbert Marcuse published his notorious formulation of repressive tolerance ("the publicity of self-actualization . . . encourages non-conformity and letting-go in ways which leave the real engines of repression in the society entirely intact"), the Dodge Rebellion was the original baby boom–directed instance of what would later be called "liberation marketing": Consumers unite, you have nothing to lose but the inability to change your image.

Herbert Philbrick—the FBI informant who inspired the TV show *I Led Three Lives*—warned a Christian Crusade rally that the Communists were planning riots in twenty American cities for October 15 and 16. Philbrick was referring to the International Days of Protest, the first national event organized by a consortium of antiwar groups. The New York demonstration was notable not only for its size and newly felonious draft-card burnings, but for the virulence of the counter-pickets who, sometimes pelting the 25,000 marchers with eggs, brandished signs advising them to GET A HAIRCUT and GO BACK TO CUBA.

•   •   •

The Chase's New York preview that winter was scarcely less acrimonious. The movie was received as an abomination. The hooting, wisecracking audience jeered so loudly the final reel was nearly inaudible—the mob placing itself in the same relationship to the movie as Tarl did its beleaguered sheriff.

Five days before *The Chase* opened, February 18, 1966, Arthur Penn was quoted in the *New York Times* maintaining that he had directed *The Chase* only as a favor to Lillian Hellman and had never "made a film under such unspeakable conditions." Penn told interviewer Rex Reed he had to fight to get "decent actors" and was compelled to use a Hollywood back lot: "They wouldn't let us go to Texas to shoot it properly; there was no privacy, the film became a public event. Each day 20 people saw the day's rushes before I did. . . ." Producer Spiegel had even taken the footage to Europe and edited it there. Penn issued a disclaimer.

> I've only seen a rough cut of *The Chase* in London and I don't know what the hell it means. The final decisions in editing were not mine. Lillian is not speaking to me at all. It's the end of big studio moviemaking for me. I'll never do another one, unless I really need the dough.

The Chase seemed incoherent. Writing in *Life*, Richard Schickel called it "a disaster of awesome proportions," using terms that might have described *Shock Corridor*: Had *The Chase* only "consciously set out to evoke the malfunctioning of the fevered mind," it might have been "an interesting experiment." But this surreal atmosphere was rather a "by-product of desperation and ineptitude." Reed, attacked by Penn for reporting the director's distaste for the project, termed *The Chase* a "disaster so total I pray for the professional futures of everyone involved in making it."

With a bit more perspective, Penn concluded in a 1969 interview that what he, Hellman, Spiegel, et al. were really acting out was the "death rattle of

Hollywood." The sheriff and his bride leave town at the end of *High Noon* to let their fellow citizens stew in the juice of their flop-sweat moral failure. The sheriff and his wife depart Tarl as *The Chase* ends, the way Lot and his wife might have split Sodom—an analogy suggested by the movie's lone religious fanatic, the elderly woman who wanders through town preaching from her Bible. According to Robin Wood, Sam Spiegel reversed *The Chase*'s last two scenes. The released movie ends not, as written, on the image of Ruby and Calder but with stricken Val Rogers emerging from his mansion to inform Anna that not only is her husband, Bubber, dead but so is her lover, Rogers's son, Jake. As *The Chase* was made during the year America's involvement in Vietnam stormed past the point of no return, we might consider Spiegel's switch an improvement.

Vietnam: "An Oriental Western"

February 5, 1966, with the bombing of Vietnam resumed after a Christmas break, the President—along with members of his cabinet, the Joint Chiefs, assorted diplomats, and various national security cowhands—flew to Honolulu to hobnob with the Vietnamese junta.

Timed, on two days' notice, to divert attention from the relatively low-budget and critical Foreign Relations Committee Vietnam Hearings chaired by Senator William Fulbright, this spectacular conference reiterated the President's Great Society war aims: "We have helped and we will help [the Vietnamese] to stabilize the economy, to increase the production of goods, to spread the light of education and stamp out disease." The pledge was the same LBJ had made ten months earlier on the eve of the *Major Dundee* premiere. America's intervention was inspired by a desire to eradicate not Communism but poverty, ignorance, and disease. As soon as the war ended, the President would ask Congress for a billion dollars for new schools, "modern medicine," a Mekong River equivalent of the Tennessee Valley Authority, a New Deal for both Vietnams! This apparent contradiction was explained by historian Eric F. Goldman; the idea of rural, impoverished Indochina stirred LBJ's childhood memories: "When President Johnson looked at Asia he saw central Texas."

And, when Lyndon Johnson thought about Texas, he remembered the Alamo. It was his birthright. In 1904, three years before the President was born, his father, State Representative Sam Johnson Jr., introduced a bill in the Texas legislature authorizing the state to purchase and restore the deteriorating adobe shrine. The boy Lyndon visited the holy tomb many times with his father. He was present in Austin when Sam was honored as the Alamo savior, along with the philanthropist Clara Driscoll.*

During World War II, the future President had invoked William Travis by asking his fellow Texans to once again "step over the line" in defense of liberty. Some twenty years later, LBJ inevitably saw his commitments in the same terms, telling his National Security Council that Vietnam—like the Dominican Republic—was "just like the Alamo."

> Hell, it's just like if you were down at the gate and you were surrounded and you damn well needed somebody. Well by God, I'm going to go—and I thank the Lord that I've got the men who want to go with me, from McNamara right on down to the littlest private who's carrying a gun.

Was LBJ an improved version of Texas commander-in-chief Sam Houston, sending reinforcements to the besieged mission? Or, in comparing U.S. troops to the Alamo's doomed defenders, had he cast himself as the commander who, by drawing that line in the sand, resolved to fight to the last man? At the conclusion of the year that brought America's full-scale commitment to the Indochinese war, John Wayne had addressed himself to the President in precisely those terms.

•   •   •

December 28, 1965, America's greatest American took pen and boldly reminded the nation's number-one Texan of a previous John Wayne production:

---

*Lyndon Johnson's first congressional campaign cited the Alamo bill as his father's sole legislative achievement. When he first ran for Senate (a campaign partially underwritten by Driscoll), Johnson and his mother campaigned at the Alamo.

Perhaps you remember the scene from the film *The Alamo*, when one of Davy Crockett's Tennesseans said: "What are we doing here in Texas fighting—it ain't our ox that's getting gored." Crockett replied: "Talkin' about whose ox gets gored, figure this: a fella gets in the habit of gorin' oxes, it whets his appetite. May gore yours next." Unquote. And we don't want people like Kosygin, Mao Tse-Tung, or the like "gorin' our oxes."

One can but imagine LBJ's response to this insolent instruction in his own family history by a gussied-up Republican actor.

Wayne was now Johnson's rival. He was determined that, as *The Alamo* came to stand for American history, his next film would make American history. Despite his political differences with the President, the Duke was prepared to produce a movie in support of Johnson's war, and despite those differences, LBJ was willing to accept the offer. Such was the necessity for a viable Vietnam scenario. The basis for the movie was Robin Moore's best-selling novel *The Green Berets*—1.2 million paperback copies in print.*

The Green Berets was published in May 1965, just as the phrase "credibility gap" began to gain currency. No less than the President, Moore had fashioned a Vietnam scenario. Full of daring exploits, both military and sexual, his jungle-initiation soldier-of-fortune saga was marketed as an updated version of James Michener's World War II *Tales of the South Pacific*—as well as a post–James Bond sequel to *The Ugly American*. The author's introduction insisted that *The Green Berets* was firsthand reportage. It had been "planned and researched" as a "factual book based on personal experiences." But Moore decided he "could present the truth better and more accurately in the form of fiction," protecting

---

*Scion of the Sheraton hotel family, a onetime ad executive who claimed to have roomed with Robert Kennedy at Harvard, Moore alternately maintained that he undertook a celebration of the Special Forces at the request of the Kennedys or LBJ, whom he'd met in Jamaica in summer 1962. Moore trained at Fort Benning, then traveled to South Vietnam in 1963 as an accredited—if unconventional—correspondent. Over his four-month tour, he was permitted to carry a rifle and was ultimately awarded his Green Beret.

the identities of his Green Beret protagonists while providing the reader with additional narrative context. Then, there was the official response. Claiming that the book contained sixteen breaches of national security, the Pentagon had paradoxically insisted it be labeled fiction.*

Wayne was only the latest player to express interest in Moore's novel. But earlier plans had come to naught. Loathe to celebrate the Special Forces and unhappy with Moore's accounts of Green Beret forays into North Vietnam, the Pentagon made its cooperation contingent on screenplay approval—and this approval would not be lightly granted. Hence, Wayne's man-to-man missive to the President. In mid-January, Jack Valenti sent a memo to LBJ advising support for Wayne's project. It was during this exchange of messages that RCA released Staff Sergeant Barry Sadler's recording "The Ballad of the Green Berets." Finally the undeclared war had an anthem.

A high school dropout who spent four years in the Air Force before joining the Special Forces, Sadler composed "The Ballad" before he was sent to Vietnam—adding exhortatory lyrics to a melody cribbed from a German marching song. Sadler was trained as a combat medic but professed to prefer killing, telling *Time* the satisfaction he derived from "a good shot, leading a man across a field and bringing him down." He himself was put out of commission by a dung-tipped pungi stake and, assigned to Fort Bragg as a public information officer in June 1965, sent his ballad to a music publisher sufficiently impressed to contact RCA.†

Released on January 11, "The Ballad of the Green Berets" was the fastest-

---

*Moore's "sly commingling of fact and fiction" (*Time*) celebrated the methodology as well as the tough pragmatism implicit in the New Frontier, but two years after the assassination of JFK, such Bond-like derring-do struck some as excessive. *The Green Berets* was an admission of torture, border violations, indeed "every conceivable crudity and stupidity that might possibly be charged against American soldiers by their worst enemies," wrote *Commonweal*'s reviewer.

†Some have seen signs of conspiracy. Robin Moore—whose tour of Vietnam coincided with Sadler's—arranged for the RCA session, where Sadler required but three takes to

moving RCA single since the Elvis era. The 45 sold half a million copies even before Sadler—relieved from duty (or perhaps reassigned) to promote the record—appeared on the January 30 *Ed Sullivan Show* to sing what struck some as a concluding stanza, less rollicking than robotic, to "The Ballad of Davy Crockett." Had the war turned a corner? "The folk-rock of anti-Vietnam-war ballads has been drowned out by a best-selling patriotic blood-churner," *Life* crowed in its approving four-page spread a month after Sandler's TV debut, noting that two million copies of the single and album had been sold.

By March, when Robert McNamara announced that he was sending another 30,000 recruits to reinforce America's Vietnam garrison, LBJ had come to believe that public opinion was growing ever more hawkish. *The Chase* was still enjoying its first run on March 5, when "The Ballad of the Green Berets" displaced Nancy Sinatra's "These Boots Are Made for Walkin' " for a month-long stay atop the pop music charts. The number-one single for 1966, ultimately the most popular topical song of the decade, the Green Beret anthem would be recorded in seventy-five different versions by year's end, including a German-language rendition that sold 600,000 copies.

There seemed a desire, appreciated by some as absurd, for living trademarks and costumed icons: Comic book heroes had a sudden panache, even as their two-dimensional heroism was ridiculed. The campy *Batman*, telecast in prime-time two nights a week, was a stunning unexpected success. The musical *It's a Bird . . . It's a Plane . . . It's Superman*, written by David Newman and Robert Benton, was poised to open on Broadway. ("The Whole Country Goes Super-mad," *Life* proclaimed in its March 11 issue: "Pop art and the cult of camp have turned Superman and Batman into members of the intellectual community.") Sadler, who relocated to Hollywood after his 1967 discharge, was their flesh-and-blood equivalent, licensing his name for T-shirts and toy guns.

---

record his song. Certainly book and ballad already enjoyed a symbiotic relationship: As Sadler's stern visage graced the cover of *The Green Beret*'s November 1965 paperback edition, so Moore was co-credited with the lyrics to Sadler's "Ballad."

"I'm the only hero of the Vietnam war," Sadler told the *Washington Post* in 1978. "Name me two Medal of Honor winners. You can't. But everybody remembers me." Together, the "Ballad" and the novel—not to mention the new Green Berets comic strip—spoke to the need for a martial myth that only Cowboy Warrior Davy Crockett George Washington McLintock Wayne could bring to fulfillment.

●   ●   ●

As intuited by the Red Dog Saloon and the rise of Prairie Power within SDS, the Cowboy fantasy was overdetermined. Even as John Wayne and the White House exchanged memos, the January 23, 1966, *New York Times Magazine* published a colorful article by British journalist Anthony Carthew, titled "Vietnam Is Like an Oriental Western."

There were now over 200,000 American troops in South Vietnam, and the first year of full-scale U.S. commitment dwarfed all previous Indochinese wars. ("It seemed to dwarf Vietnam itself," Frances FitzGerald wrote.) A colossus bestrode the earth. Indeed, as Carthew observed, "the tiny Vietnamese, whose hips are no wider than a Texan's thigh, gazes up, always up, at the phenomenon, and somewhere behind his eyes there is wonder."

> He sees his little towns spread and shake with violent life. . . . In places like Pleiku and Ankhe, half-a-dozen saloons open up every week. Bar girls wiggle into town, dressed at midday as for midnight. It is all rather like the set for one of the old-style, clear-cut Westerns. You catch yourself expecting to see John Wayne ride in at any moment.

The Duke would not, however, arrive for another six months.

It was June 1966, a few weeks after the President mocked his critics as "Nervous Nellies," that Wayne first visited Vietnam—part of a seventeen-day tour organized by the Department of Defense. He spent his first few days in the country commuting from the Rex Hotel in Saigon to the village that served as the location for a government documentary that he was to narrate. *Variety* reported that "every time [Wayne] steps outside, the traffic stops and there are yells from the kids, 'Hey, Number One Cowboy!' " Duke modestly attributed this recognition to the popularity of *The Alamo*. On June 17, he left Saigon to visit the aircraft carrier *John Hancock*. Then he returned inland, touring the Special Forces camp at Da Nang and the Marine base near Chu Lai, where, on June 20, snipers fired several rounds—some bullets even hitting the ground near where Wayne was signing autographs. The Duke's coolness was widely reported, although not his remark that "the yella bastards do all their shootin' from hidin', don't they?"

The star was living his image—unlike the habitués of the Red Dog Saloon, he needed no LSD to believe himself "John Wayne." Pleased that some men hailed him as Stryker, after the tough Marine sergeant he played sixteen years before in *Sands of Iwo Jima*, the Duke traveled on to Pleiku, where he hosted a screening of *Fort Apache* for an audience of Green Berets and Montagnard tribesmen. The Green Berets presented the Duke with a lighter engraved FUCK COMMUNISM; the tribesmen gave him the Montagnard bracelet he wore in subsequent Westerns. Wayne subscribed to Moore's romantic view of the loincloth-clad, teeth-filing aboriginals as noble savages, indulgently noting that as most did not speak English, they instinctively cheered when the Indians attacked the U.S. Cavalry.

• • •

John Wayne was now part of the war—the unwieldy .45-caliber service pistol was called a John Wayne rifle, the tasteless biscuits included in C rations were known as John Wayne cookies.*

Home from the War, Robert Jay Lifton's psychological study of Vietnam veterans published in 1973, details the effect of the "John Wayne thing," particularly among Marines and recruits from the South and Southwest. The Wayne thing involved "a whole constellation of masculine attitudes" founded upon being "tough" and "tight-lipped" as well as

> physically powerful, hard, ruthlessly competitive, anti-artistic; a no-
> nonsense sexual conqueror for whom women were either inferior, inscru-

Elsewhere on the national movie lot, another Western star was planning an ambitious project. Still host of the long-running TV series *Death Valley Days*, Ronald Reagan formally announced his candidacy for California governor on January 4, 1966. A second-tier movie star since the early 1940s and a Hollywood spokesman throughout the Cold War anti-Communist crusade, Reagan emerged as a national political force during the waning days of the Goldwater campaign. In his *Life* magazine election postmortem, Loudon Wainwright described the actor's last appearance on behalf of the Republican ticket.

> It had been a long and dismal electoral season, and Mr. Reagan, flushed with catastrophe and glowing in boyish middle age, brought it to a petulant and somehow threatening close. "Isn't it a shame," he asked a crowd made up mostly of teen-agers in yellow Goldwater sweatshirts, "isn't it a shame that there isn't someplace in a campaign for quality to pay off? But we're just starting out." Mr. Reagan waited for the whistles to subside before he delivered his benediction. "God bless all of you," he said, "and I'm sure that in the days ahead we won't lack for ammunition."

Wainwright was haunted by this martial image. Reagan himself was more impressed by the California race in which, bucking the Democratic landslide, movie actor George Murphy trounced the epicene New Frontier press secretary Pierre Salinger, who had been appointed to fill a briefly empty Senate seat.

Reagan initiated discussions with political public relations consultants Stu Spencer and Bill Roberts in April 1965. By the time "Eve of Destruction" hit number one, the actor was committed to run. Leo Litwak's November 1965

----

table, or at best weaker creatures; and, above all, unquestioningly loyal to one's immediate (often all-male) group. . . .

The John Wayne thing was predicated upon perpetuating old victories, avenging old defeats, and repaying "the 'debt of honor' [the young man] owes his father and his nation." As Ron Kovic—a twenty-year-old Marine whose favorite movie was *Sands of Iwo Jima* and who was wounded and paralyzed from the chest down around the time the Duke toured Nam—wrote in his 1976 memoir, *Born on the Fourth of July*: "I gave my dead dick for John Wayne."

New York Times Magazine article predicted Reagan's success as a campaigner: "He glows with good health. His appearance is statuesque. He will overwhelm the ladies and charm the men." Litwak was particularly impressed by Reagan's rendition of the pledge of allegiance and his command of one-liners. Spencer-Roberts appreciated this talent, investing most of the campaign budget in TV, with a series of intentionally unpolished spots. Projecting an aura of friendly concern, glowing like the tube itself, fulfilling Daniel Boorstin's warning that "the making of the illusions which flood our experience has become the business of America," hyperreal in every emotion, Reagan proved a televisual Medusa whose amiable gaze had the power to transform rival politicians into crumbling fossils.

Spencer-Roberts engaged two psychology professors, Dr. Stanley Plog of UCLA and Dr. Kenneth Holden of San Fernando Valley State College, to direct their candidate and tune his message. Plog and Holden honed the set speech that Reagan first began delivering as a General Electric corporate spokesman in 1954—"one of the longest-running acts in show business," the *New York Times Magazine* noted. The professors weaned the candidate from pet bellicosities like "the totalitarian ant heap" and reinforced such positive concepts as the "Creative Society," focusing Reagan's assault on big government, welfare, high taxes, and crime while emphasizing his visionary faith in an unregulated marketplace. "We were with him every waking moment," Plog recalled of the campaign.

There were many on the Right, Reagan among them, who held the image-makers and hidden persuaders responsible for the mass deception that the Democrats used to defeat Barry Goldwater. But social programming worked. Now, in a neat turn of the dialectic, Goldwater's political heir assimilated and elaborated that same political technology.

•   •   •

Ronald Reagan, who handily won the Republican primary in June 1966, was the first American politician to accept the regime of behavioral psychology. Lyndon Johnson, meanwhile, practiced a cruder form of persuasion. RAISING THE PRICE OF AGGRESSION per *Time*'s July 8 cover, the tough-talking President sent forty-five F-4 Phantom jets to bomb the Hanoi-Haiphong oil refineries. "Your daddy may go down in history as having started World War III," he told daughter Luci.

The war was a flaming backdrop to a season of senseless violence. "The whole slumscape erupted in open warfare," *Newsweek* wrote of Chicago, where month-long racial disturbances included a white riot, replete with Confederate flags and swastika regalia, in which Martin Luther King Jr. was struck by a thrown stone. The old Student Nonviolent Coordinating Committee (SNCC) slogan "Freedom Now" was superseded by new leader Stokely Carmichael's call for "Black Power"—a "catch phrase with the immediate effect of titillating Negroes and frightening whites" per *Newsweek*'s "Crisis of Color" cover story.

Even as Chicago police exchanged gunfire with black residents of the West Side, the city hosted the cold-blooded murder of eight student nurses by twenty-five-year-old Dallas drifter Richard Speck. It was, as *Time* put it, "an incredible, nearly soundless orgy of mutilation and murder." Then, only weeks later at the University of Texas in Austin, came the "Madman in the Tower." Another twenty-five-year-old, this one an erstwhile altar boy, former Eagle Scout, ex-Marine, and current student of architectural engineering, named Charles Joseph Whitman, purchased ammunition to, as he told the clerk, "shoot some pigs." After killing his mother and his pregnant wife, Whitman installed himself atop the library tower in the middle of the campus and began picking off victims—killing twelve and wounding another thirty-one in a ninety-seven-minute "mad orgy of violence" (*Newsweek*).

The news cycle accelerated. The Whitman sniper attack superseded the Speck killings as "the crime of the century" according to *Time* (which pointed out that the year's most controversial bestseller was Truman Capote's "nonfiction novel" of senseless slaughter, *In Cold Blood*). In late July, a song written and performed by a former mental patient who called himself Napoleon XIV began careening up the charts. Selling half a million copies during its first week of release, the lunatic rant "They're Coming to Take Me Away, Ha-Haaa," inspired an equally hysterical response, banned from the radio after hitting number three on August 13.

The August *Esquire* ran David Newman and Robert Benton's proposed moratorium on the zeitgeist: "Has it really been just six years, or are we all going crazy. It seems like it's been the Sixties forever. . . ."

Luminaries come and go faster than a speeding bullet. Fads and fashions flame up and burn out in a week. The last six years have been so filled with places, people, and things you have forgotten about that this seems a good time to call for a halt. We have had enough! Enough!

And so we benevolently announce that the Sixties are over. Let six years be a decade. Let the next four be a vacation.

Speeding bullets and flaming fashions: Lenny Bruce was dead of a drug overdose; Bob Dylan broke his neck in a motorcycle accident. The economy, too, was showing signs of exhaustion. Inflation surged while stock prices sagged.

With a hint of the New Sentimentality, Newman and Benton acknowledged the Kennedy assassination as "the definitive event of the Sixties, one that, as they used to say, 'altered and illuminated our time . . . and you were there.' In fact, you always will be there until the day you die." The festival was forever. The narrative refused to come together. *Inquest*, Edward Jay Epstein's critique of the Warren Commission report, had been followed by *Rush to Judgment*, an even more elaborate debunking by civil rights lawyer, peace activist, and one-term New York assemblyman Mark Lane.*

Lane noted the fantastic mortality rate of Warren Commission witnesses—

---

*After publishing a 10,000-word brief in Lee Harvey Oswald's defense, Lane was retained by Oswald's mother to represent her son's interests before the Warren Commission. Refused permission to observe the commission's workings, he consequently began his own investigation—working simultaneously on a book and documentary film—which concluded that the Commission had covered up a conspiracy to murder the President. Published in early summer, *Rush to Judgment* went through six printings and sold 225,000 hardcover copies by year's end—introducing such key elements as the Grassy Knoll from which fifty-eight of ninety eyewitnesses believed the fatal shots were fired and the pristine bullet which supposedly wounded both Kennedy and Governor John Connally (twice).

but at least Kennedy consciousness lived. Public opinion polls showed registered Democrats preferred Senator Robert Kennedy to the President as their 1968 candidate. Setting the stage for his own comeback, Richard Nixon was speaking openly of an RFK-LBJ split even as he goaded Johnson to further escalate the war in Vietnam. On that front, South Vietnam's premier, Nguyen Cao Ky, told *U.S. News & World Report* he believed war with Red China to be inevitable.

The President, meanwhile, was hemorrhaging popularity. Scarcely two years after Lyndon Johnson's electoral triumph, *Time* would note that LBJ's "pettiness and peevishness, his displays of deceit and conceit have been so frequently documented that what was once a nebulous attitude of indifference on the public's part has crystallized into active dislike." Johnson's presence made JFK's absence all the more painful. Back during the summer of 1965, Barbara Garson—a veteran of the Berkeley Free Speech movement who in addressing an antiwar rally inadvertently referred to "Lady MacBird Johnson" and immediately realized the power of this slip—began writing an elaborate agitprop that went Norman Mailer one better by suggesting that LBJ was responsible not only for the war in Vietnam but for murdering his predecessor as well.

That same month, *The Nation* quoted an unidentified Eastern senator's bracketing the President with Shakespeare's usurper: "It's not so much that Mrs. Johnson reminds me of Lady Macbeth. But the parallel is there. Macbeth was power-mad. Johnson is power-mad."

•   •   •

October 17: Air Force One is loaded with racks of Texas steaks and cases of sugar-free Dr Pepper as the President leaves on his own seventeen-day tour of Southeast Asia. LBJ flies first to Hawaii, then on to Pago Pago, New Zealand, and Australia (where demonstrators hurl paint at his limo). Finally, two-score renditions of "The Yellow Rose of Texas" later, he lands in the Philippines to confer with the leaders of South Vietnam. The show is on the road.

Pravda terms the presidential trip a "Hollywood panorama." *Time* deems it "more like a Bob Hope extravaganza (The Road to Manila?) than a diplomatic errand of potential historical significance." While in Manila, however, the President spontaneously decides to visit his boys. On the morning of October 26, forty-five reporters are summoned to a briefing, then impounded and boarded on a charter plane. Minutes later, Air Force One takes off with four Phantom jets flying cover and every U.S. ship in the China Sea on full alert. The President lands at Cam Ranh Bay, fifty miles from the nearest combat zone. He reviews the troops, hands out medals, refers to the "vicious and illegal aggression across this little nation's frontier," visits a hospital, eats lunch in the enlisted men's mess hall, goes to the Officers' Club in the company of General Westmoreland, and there directs his commanders to "go out there and nail that coonskin to the wall."

LBJ's entire Vietnam visit lasts two hours and twenty-four minutes—only three minutes longer than the eventual running time of *The Green Berets*. The tour proceeds on to Thailand, Malaysia, and South Korea, where, in the course of an exhortatory speech to the troops, Johnson gets so fired up he fabricates the notion that, like John Wayne, his "great-great-grandfather died at the Alamo." If John Wayne was playing Johnson, Johnson is playing Wayne to a live audience of epic proportion.*

Here, if not in America, LBJ is a movie star. There are scores of handmade posters of the American President (and none of them upside down) labeled WELCOME THE KING OF KINGS, hailing THE TEXAS BULL or THE WORLD MARSHAL (this over a picture of Johnson as a cowboy, with two guns drawn) and proclaiming WE LIKE BIG SHOT OF WORLD.

Life correspondent Hugh Sidey speculated that the President's megalomania was fed by his spectacular reception, particularly in South Korea. I've never seen so many people. . . . They were like ants coming across the rice paddies on the dikes. Streams of humanity, crowded, just massed on the mountain. You could see them for miles either way.

> Johnson, whenever he saw a crowd that size, was in heaven. Sure as hell, what he saw for them was a Texas scene. You know, we'll build a dam down here, grow a little corn, put highways in—all that.

Gathering the Tribes: Diggers, Panthers, Outlaws

As China was convulsed by Mao's Great Proletariat Cultural Revolution, *Time* had wondered if the world's largest nation had "finally been driven mad by mounting U.S. pressure in Vietnam." Perhaps the CIA had dropped LSD in the water supply. The newsweeklies reported mobs of the chanting, banner-waving teenaged militants known as Red Guards running wild in Beijing and Shanghai—closing down schools, defacing shrines, breaking into private homes, insulting Party officials, beating bourgeois opponents and parading them through the street in the name of revolutionary purity: Youth Power had struck even China. Could this happen here? Late-summer HUAC hearings into alleged Communist involvement in the opposition to the war in Vietnam were reduced to travesty when—acting on the advice of guerrilla-theater theorist R. G. Davis—Jerry Rubin presented himself as a walking pseudo-event by showing up in a tricorn hat and Revolutionary War costume. ("They might not report what he had to say," Davis explained to Todd Gitlin, "but they would take a picture of him.")

But nowhere was Youth Power more evident than in California. Through-out the spring and summer of 1966, newcomers swelled the psychedelic bo-hemia of San Francisco's Haight-Ashbury, a district where life had begun to fulfill Antonin Artaud's desire for the convulsive "poetry of festivals and crowds." It was as if the Red Dog Saloon had taken over an entire urban neighborhood. Newcomer Emmett Grogan, who joined the San Francisco Mime Troupe that spring, wrote that "the longhairs were all changing their names to more romantic-sounding, rough 'n' ready, American tags—like Wil-liam Bonney, Mitzi Gaynor and John Wesley Harding." By fall, Grogan, the Mime Troupe's Peter Berg, and Peter Coyote—who changed his name from Cohon—were calling themselves Diggers (after the millennial seventeenth-century English sect) and staging all manner of street events as part of their mind-blowing guerrilla-theater cultural-revolutionary outlaw agenda.

In Los Angeles, dubbed by *Time* the "holy temple of the American cult of youth," police regularly dispersed the longhaired kids who thronged Sunset Strip while, in the course of their research on behalf of Ronald Reagan, professors Plog and Holden discovered that campus unrest was what they termed a sleeper issue: "Wherever we went, people wanted Reagan to say how he would handle the student uprising." California's state university system entered the campaign when the candidate delivered an address, published as "The Morality Gap at Berkeley," in which he asserted that "a small minority of beatniks, radicals and filthy speech advocates" were attempting to seize the university as "a rallying point for Communists and a center of sexual misconduct."

Was it odd that a candidate guided in every particular by two university psychology professors would attack the Berkeley faculty for not upholding "those ethical and moral standards demanded by the great majority of our society"? Paraphrasing *Choice* and running against the chaos of *The Chase*, Reagan warned of campus "drug usage" and "sexual orgies"—alluding to doings at a student antiwar rally that were "so contrary to the accepted code of morality" that he could not discuss them.

Misjudging the source of Reagan's appeal, the Democrats attacked him as an actor. One ad cribbed an image from the 1941 *They Died with Their Boots On* to show the young Reagan—absurdly clad as a Civil War officer—as General George Custer. Another TV spot had incumbent governor Pat Brown shamelessly compare his opponent to actor-assassin John Wilkes Booth.

Even more out of touch was the Democratic attempt to link Reagan to right-wing extremism. It wasn't the John Birch Society that started that riot in Watts. Moreover, while Negroes were readily identifiable, Birchers mainly looked like . . . us. The point was reinforced by a Reagan radio spot that began, "every day the jungle draws a little closer." Reagan's election was clinched during the last three days of September by the riot that broke out in San Francisco's Hunt's Point ghetto after white cops shot and killed a black sixteen-year-old fleeing in a stolen car.

•   •   •

The old Hollywood of Ronald Reagan; the new Hollywood of *Bonnie and Clyde*: For over three years, the *Esquire* writers Robert Benton and David Newman had developed and shopped a screenplay about the Depression-era desperados

Clyde Barrow and Bonnie Parker. This was a story Benton was born to write—
he'd been an infant in the very East Texas territory where (and when) Bonnie
and Clyde began their criminal career.

Benton and Newman were inspired by John Toland's *The Dillinger Days*, a
history of the 1933 crime wave published in spring 1963, to write a self-
consciously nouvelle vague screenplay. Struck by Bonnie and Clyde's reckless
violence, fascination with publicity, and unconventional sexual arrangement,
Benton and Newman found these Depression outlaws weirdly contemporary—
noting in their treatment that, "if Bonnie and Clyde were here today, they
would be hip." (Hip enough to hang at the Red Dog Saloon? Join the San
Francisco Mime Troupe? Represent the ascension of Prairie Power?) Star-
producer Warren Beatty—who bought the script and enlisted Arthur Penn to
direct—also had his eyes on the not-yet-defined youth market.*

Two days before the California election, a *Los Angeles Times* production story
confirmed the movie's contemporary spin by explaining that, "the gun was
[the outlaw couple's] needle, splattering bullets their LSD, the excitement of
the chase and the escape their 'kicks.'

> To them citizens were the 1934 equivalent of squares. They imagined themselves
> in revolt against all authority. . . . Clyde Barrow was contemptuous of other con-
> temporary outlaws in Chicago and New York because they were "old men over
> thirty."

Youth culture gangsters were not the only new phantasm percolating in the
dream life. The Black Power Maoists that LA cops had only hallucinated in
Watts came into existence on October 15 as two Oakland college students—

---

*Evidently, the role of C. W. Moss, the third gang member who "can't make up his
mind whether he prefers Bonnie or Clyde" was first offered to pop singer Jordan Christopher, a hot property since his marriage to Richard Burton's abandoned wife, Sybil.
Years later, Beatty maintained that he originally envisioned Bob Dylan in the role of
Clyde.

Huey P. Newton and Bobby Seale—drafted a Ten Point Program for their newly founded Black Panther Party for Self Defense.*

A few weeks after Ronald Reagan was elected California governor with 57 percent of the votes, the man who would appoint himself Reagan's nemesis—convicted rapist and jailhouse writer Eldridge Cleaver—was paroled from Folsom Prison to join first the staff of *Ramparts* magazine and then the Black Panther Party as their Minister of Information. Two masters of illusion, Cleaver and Reagan both projected themselves as possible presidents in 1968. (Within ten days of his victory, the governor-elect convened his inner circle to discuss the next step.)

How did Reagan happen? "California was awash with Reagan money, with the former Goldwater people eager to prove they could make it here," Herbert Gold explained. Gold argued that, "Reagan's name and face began to seem plausible simply by repetition on billboards, radio, television, stickers, posters. One estimate is that he spent ten times the money spent on the Brown campaign." But money was not everything. As a prisoner, Cleaver welcomed the Berkeley uprising.

> The characteristics of the white rebels which most alarm their elders—the long hair, the new dances, their love for Negro music, their use of marijuana, their mystical attitude towards sex—are all tools of their rebellion. They have turned these tools against the totalitarian fabric of American society—and they mean to change it.

Reagan's rise combined with Fear of the Young in "The Day It All Happened, Baby," a story about a demagogic pop star who uses generational warfare to

---

*This was another idea longing to realize itself. During the summer of 1965, the Lowndes County Freedom Organization—an independent political party based in rural Mississippi—adopted the symbol of the black panther. Some ten months later, Marvel Comics had introduced the first African-American superhero—the Black Panther—in *The Fantastic Four* #52 (July 1966).

make himself president, written by Robert Thom (a thirty-six-year-old Yale-educated playwright), published in the December 1966 *Esquire*. Later that month, *Time* declared America's "under twenty-five generation" its collective Man of the Year.

Early in 1967, Lyndon Johnson audited his books and realized Robert Mc-Namara had underestimated the war's cost by some $11 billion! Rolling Thunder alone consumed over a billion dollars in 1966—nearly ten dollars paid for each dollar of damage inflicted. (Saddled with a king-sized economic migraine, the President asked Congress for $12 billion more and then, because he was unable to raise taxes, had to slash Great Society programs by $2.5 billion.)

There were nearly 400,000 American troops in Vietnam—the Oriental Western swollen to epic proportions. Such scale should have insured victory. Yet, despite a concerted military offensive—a half-dozen major search-and-destroy operations, successful engagements in which the Americans inflicted eight times the casualties they absorbed—something was wrong. Existing only so the United States might defend it, South Vietnam was the ultimate Freedomland, a pure projection of America's will.

January 19, 1967, five days after the massive Golden Gate Park "Human Be-In," a homemade Prankster Digger hippie festival dubbed the Gathering of the Tribes, *MacBird!*—which had already sold 100,000 copies and was a text used at seven colleges—began previews in New York City, with Stacy Keach in the title role. The production was housed in a "filthy, stinking Greenwich Village flophouse," reported the *Sunday News*, calling *MacBird!* "one of the most revolting displays of political slander to ever come out of the American theater."*

---

*The producers had difficulty finding a printer for their program. The *New Yorker* refused to list *MacBird!* in its weekly calendar or accept advertisements. Local intellectuals were in disagreement: Dwight Macdonald praised the play in the *New York Review of Books* and Lionel Abel attacked him for it in *Partisan Review*. The best notice was J. Edgar Hoover's in the FBI's April *Law Enforcement Bulletin*: "We should be alarmed when widespread recognition and monetary awards go to a person who writes a 'satirical' piece of trash which maliciously defames the President of our country and insinuates he murdered his predecessor."

MacBird! coincided with heightened attacks on Johnson's policies. "Napalm" was now a household word. The January issues of magazines as disparate as *Ramparts* and *Ladies' Home Journal* included features on Vietnam's suffering children. While *MacBird!* was in previews, the real Robert Ken O'Dunc returned from a trip spent hobnobbing with European leaders on the subject of Vietnam and had a tense meeting with the actual MacBird. February 10, the day before *MacBird!* opened, 100 students staged a sit-in at the University of Wisconsin office used by recruiters from napalm-manufacturer Dow Chemical. After nineteen were arrested, twice as many as those involved in the original sit-in barricaded the university chancellor in his office. February 25, Martin Luther King Jr. delivered his first speech attacking the war—appearing along with the dove senators Ernest Gruening, Mark Hatfield, Eugene McCarthy, and George McGovern. Before the week was out, Senator Kennedy joined the chorus.

General William Westmoreland requested 210,000 more troops to bring his forces to 665,000. (After months of internal debate, Johnson agreed to reinforce the Alamo only to 525,000.) The Pentagon finally approved the script for *The Green Berets*, but Hollywood felt nervous. The project moved from Columbia to Universal. Even though the Harris Poll, for the first time, reported greater support for victory in Vietnam than for supervised withdrawal of American forces, Universal backed out two weeks before shooting was to start. In mid-June, Warner Brothers took on the burden.

That spring, SDS National Secretary Greg Calvert staked out an aggressive Cowboy (or was it Indian?) position when, invoking the example of Che Guevara, he told the *New York Times Magazine* that SDS was "working to build a guerrilla force in an urban environment [and] actively organizing sedition." Following the lead of Black Power theorist Stokely Carmichael, SDS searched for the "source of its own oppression," organizing around draft resistance. (On June 23, when LBJ addressed a Democratic fundraiser in LA, SDS sponsored the first antiwar protest to provoke police violence.) Picking up on the guerrilla theatricality of the San Francisco be-in, these manifestations took the form of grassroots festivals. Indeed, the counterculture seemed to have achieved historical inevitability when, on June 2, the Beatles turned unmistakably hippie with the release of their druggie concept album *Sergeant Pepper's Lonely Hearts Club Band*.

The same month, the SDS "Back to the Drawing Boards" conference— organized by the old guard to mark the organization's fifth anniversary and held at a camp in the Michigan woods—was rudely disrupted by a contingent of Diggers, who commandeered the meeting. While Peter Berg explained that media was "more dominant than reality and the way to retake the media was to create alternative realities," Tom Hayden only saw that the Diggers' guerrilla stagecraft was their message. The Digger viewpoint was that "no meetings, no plans, no talk was necessary, that chaos was splendid. And they came in dressed like Indians." Former SNCC activist Abbie Hoffman was transfixed; onetime SDS president Todd Gitlin titled his account of the event, "The Theater of Outlaws." The moment of *Bonnie and Clyde* had arrived.

IV

Born to Be Wild:
Outlaws of America, 1967–69

Variously characterized by early reviewers as "reprehensible," "stomach-turning," "grisly," "gross and demeaning," "gruesome," and "dementia praecox of the most pointless sort," Arthur Penn's *Bonnie and Clyde* appeared midway through the hippie Summer of Love—only weeks after the worst riots yet consumed the black ghettos of Newark and Detroit.

Penn's disavowal of *The Chase*—published in the *New York Times* six days prior to the movie's opening—was for *Variety* "an industry 'crime' so unprofessional" that no apology could erase the stigma. But the director effaced the memory of *The Chase* by committing a far worse offense with his next picture, which spent six months polarizing critics, packing theaters, and producing new fantasies. But first, *Bonnie and Clyde* invited viewers to reconsider screen violence.

Bloody mayhem now seemed integral to national self-understanding. Tom Wolfe's contribution to *Esquire*'s July 1967 special issue "Why Are We Suddenly Obsessed with Violence?" argued that the continuing fascination with the Kennedy assassination exemplified a new "pornoviolence." *Life* had published excerpts from the Zapruder film three times, and Wolfe complained of the "incessant replay, with every recoverable clinical detail, of those less than five seconds in which a man got his head blown off." Such pornoviolence was not just vicarious but megalomaniacal: "You do not live the action through the hero's eyes. You live with the aggressor."

But those few moments in Dallas, preserved for all time on 8mm film, were a sacred mystery—the founding moment of a new America. As profoundly abrupt and disorderly as the Kennedy assassination was, it rewrote the national narrative forever.

On one hand, the JFK murder supported the notion—advanced in the early twentieth century by French revolutionary theorist Georges Sorel—that historic change was necessarily marked by bloodshed. On the other, it seemed a plausible segue to the cowboy reign of Lyndon Johnson. Mayhem was Johnson's heritage: Like his contemporaries Bonnie and Clyde, the President was born in central Texas at the end of a half-century of sustained violence encompassing Civil War, Indian attacks, vigilantism, banditry, feuds, and lynching.

●   ●   ●

Bonnie and Clyde had its world premiere August 4, opening the Montreal International Film Festival. *New York Times* critic Bosley Crowther was there, declaring himself amazed that "so callous and callow a film should represent [the] country in these critical times." *Bonnie and Clyde* was "an embarrassing addition to an excess of violence on the screen." But was it only the screen?

Crowther was already in the midst of a campaign against movie mayhem, until then exemplified by Robert Aldrich's World War II commando caper *The Dirty Dozen*, which had opened in New York on June 16, set house records at the Loew's Capitol, and, released nationally over the July 4 holiday, enjoyed the highest grossing week of any picture in MGM history: Indeed, *The Dirty Dozen* sold an unprecedented $15 million worth of tickets during its first two months of release—a period coinciding with a dramatic increase in American civil violence, much of it racial and directed against police.

The summer of 1967 was previewed on the afternoon of May 2, when eighteen representatives of the Black Panther Party staged a stunning photo opportunity by appearing in full regalia, armed with M-1 rifles and 12-gauge shotguns, at the California state capitol building in Sacramento. This was a further permutation of guerrilla theater. Governor Ronald Reagan, caught on the lawn delivering a speech to a group of young people, was whisked inside as the TV news crews crowded around to record the Panther leader Bobby Seale's warning that the "American people in general" and "black people in particular"

> take careful note of the racist California Legislature which is now considering legislation aimed at keeping the black people disarmed and powerless at the very same time that racist police agencies throughout the country are intensifying the terror, brutality, murder, and repression of black people. . . .
>
> The Black Panther Party for Self-Defense believes that the time has come for black people to arm themselves against this terror before it is too late.

Two weeks later, a Houston policeman was killed by sniper fire during disturbances at the predominantly black Texas Southern University. That same night in Washington, DC, SNCC chairman Stokeley Carmichael declared that, "we're going to shoot the cops who are shooting our black brothers in the back." Over the next month, Boston, Tampa, Dayton, Atlanta, Buffalo, and Cincinnati all experienced racial disturbances.

June's incidents were but prologue to the Newark disorders which were sparked by the arrest of a black cab driver, at around 8 PM on Wednesday night, July 12. Just past midnight, a fire bomb hit the police station, and an hour later, the looting began—"the largest demonstration of black people ever held in Newark," according to Tom Hayden, who'd spent the past four years there as a community organizer. A refugee from the Haight's Summer of Love, Digger performance artist Emmett Grogan claimed to have been present: Newark was what was happening, a Fillmore rock show in the streets, an "explosion of flashing lights, flickering flames and fast-moving silhouettes. The sound of running, laughing, screaming, glass-breaking, bottle- and brick-throwing young black bloods was a constant uproar."

But Hayden thought the rioting—which recurred Thursday—was extremely focused. "The 'rampaging' was aimed almost exclusively at white-owned stores." This was a very particular form of be-in. "People on the street felt free to take shelter from the police in homes of people they did not know." Touring the scene at 5 AM, New Jersey governor Richard Hughes was dismayed by the "carnival atmosphere." As looting continued into the next day, Hughes called up 3,000 National Guardsmen and, assigning 500 state troopers to Newark, put the black wards under martial law. (Once the fires died down, the ongoing occupation was justified by the presence of mysterious snipers—none of whom were ever caught.)

For Hayden, this was not just an ad hoc orgy of destruction—a riot "without ideas"—but a positive intervention. "To the conservative mind the riot is essentially revolution against civilization," he theorized.

> To the liberal mind it is an expression of helpless frustration. While the conservative is hostile and the liberal generous toward those who riot, both assume that the riot is a form of lawless, mob behavior. . . . Against these two fundamentally similar concepts, a third one must be asserted, the concept that a riot represents people making history.

The fantasy was contagious.

Leaving twenty-three dead and $10 million in property damage, Newark gave new meaning to the Doors' hit single "Light My Fire"—a musical burn-baby-burn which, released in early June, surged to the top of the national soundtrack by the weekend following Newark's pacification, when Detroit erupted in the worst domestic disturbance since the labor and race riots of 1919. Detroit doubled Newark's casualties, quadrupled the estimated cost of destruction, and ultimately required a pacification force of nearly 13,000. July 30, the same day order was officially restored, the *New York Times* published the latest missive in Crowther's crusade under the oxymoronic headline AN-OTHER SMASH AT VIOLENCE. Here, the critic took issue with those readers who wrote the *Times* to attack his attack on *The Dirty Dozen*. To those who argued that the new violent movies reflected American social reality, and particularly the war in Vietnam, Crowther replied that

> by habituating the public to violence and brutality—by making these hideous exercises into morbid and sadistic jokes, as is done in *The Dirty Dozen*—these films of excessive violence only deaden their sensitivities and make slaughter seem a meaningless cliché.

Was the violence in Detroit and Vietnam, then, a meaningful cliché?

The Dirty Dozen evoked World War II in a drastically revisionist fashion. Not since *Catch-22* was the myth so desecrated. *The Dirty Dozen's* eponymous antiheroes were murderers, rapists, and other violent misfits, released from the brig and commanded by a tough colonel (Lee Marvin) ordered by the cynical American brass to lead a suicide mission behind German lines. It was a tough Major Dundee leading a lumpen gang of crypto Green Beret counterinsurgents. Moreover, the movie had an attitude.

On one hand, *The Dirty Dozen* mocked society's ambivalence regarding the killer instinct. An Army psychologist, pronouncing the Dozen "the most twisted bunch of anti-social psychopaths" imaginable, adds that he "can't think of a better way to fight a war." Thus the movie endorsed a tough-minded realpolitik. "Dirty" violence was not only necessary but also free to be enjoyed. Moreover, it was authentic. At the same time, *The Dirty Dozen* attacked authority—of any kind. American commanding officers, no less than German, are shown as essentially corrupt and callous.

Although *The Dirty Dozen* opens with a graphic representation of a hanging, extraordinary mayhem is withheld until the slapstick final mission when the Dozen trap the German generals in an underground bunker—together with a number of innocent civilians, most of them women. The Americans pour gasoline through ventilator shafts and toss in grenades. Unfolding in an atmosphere of frenzied cruelty, this sequence manages to invoke mass death by a combination of gas chamber asphyxiation, saturation bombing, and napalm. When *The Dirty Dozen* opened in New York, many critics were shocked.

Crowther was but the most outspoken in labeling the film a "raw and pre-posterous glorification of a group of criminal soldiers who are trained to kill and who then go about this brutal business with hot sadistic zeal." For Crowther, *The Dirty Dozen* was a vulgar, irresponsible celebration of war.

> To bathe these rascals in a specious heroic light—to make their hoodlum bravado and defiance of discipline, and their nasty kind of gutter solidarity, seem exhila-rating and admirable—is encouraging a spirit of hooliganism that is brazenly antisocial, to say the least.

Newsweek similarly complained that the "orgy of unrestrained violence" with which the film climaxed was designed "to stir only the atavistic passions of this audience." The *New York Post* termed *The Dirty Dozen* "roughage [sic] for an audience needing entertainment increasingly hyped for the hardened." The *Daily News* reported that the movie opened to "the loudest blast of applause ever heard on old Broadway," while *The New Yorker* observed that "the moronic muggings [sic] of the title characters were hailed by colleague thugs in the audience with gales of comradely laughter." No American critics saw fit to observe that their own country was even then engaged in a military operation. *The Dirty Dozen* was understood less as picture of war than incitement to criminality. So it was with the even more "political" *Bonnie and Clyde*.

•   •   •

Considering *Bonnie and Clyde*'s carnage, *Variety* recommended a "hard-sell ex-ploitation campaign." Warner Brothers complied, taunting critics with one of the most outrageous slogans of the period: THEY'RE YOUNG . . . THEY'RE IN LOVE . . . AND THEY KILL PEOPLE.

Crazier than even the most extreme SDS rhetoric, this daringly disjunctive sell line appeared almost simultaneously with new SNCC chairman H. Rap Brown's formulation that "violence is necessary and it's as American as cherry pie." Such flippancy was provocative, and when *Bonnie and Clyde* opened the-atrically on August 13, the response was no less strong. The "blending of farce with brutal killings is as pointless as it is lacking in taste," Crowther wrote.

Then something unusual happened. "We got advertising we never could have afforded," Arthur Penn recalled. The *Times* was flooded with letters attacking Crowther, who felt compelled to write a third denunciation that accused *Bonnie and Clyde* of distorting history and pandering to a fashionable anti-establishment anger. Warner Brothers ran ads in which the Barrow Gang thanked New York for its support, while *Variety* gleefully reported the fracas as "Crowther's 'Bonnie'-Brook." The *Times* published another half-dozen letters praising *Bonnie and Clyde*, plus an interview with Penn in which he trumped Crowther: "The trouble with the violence in most films is that it is not violent enough." Let *Films in Review* call *Bonnie and Clyde* "evil," *The New Yorker* had two positive reviews: critic Penelope Gilliatt's notice was followed two months later by Berkeley-based freelancer Pauline Kael's 9,000-word manifesto.

> The innocuousness of most of our movies is accepted with such complacence that when an American movie reaches people, when it makes them react, some of them think there must be something the matter with it—perhaps a law should be passed against it.

The dream life overflowed. *Bonnie and Clyde* had not only fans but partisans.

By linking Penn's movie to the issue of free speech, while implicitly endorsing the overthrow of the Motion Picture Production Code, Kael raised the rhetorical stakes. She maintained that *Bonnie and Clyde* was perceived as dangerous because it popularized a hitherto rarefied coterie attitude toward criminal behavior: "*Bonnie and Clyde* brings into the almost frighteningly public world of movies things that people have been feeling and saying and writing about"—the justification for political violence articulated by H. Rap Brown or, more philosophically, in Frantz Fanon's Third Worldist manifesto *The Wretched of the Earth*.

As the anxious response to *The Dirty Dozen* suggested, a movie might speak for, as well as to, its audience. Like political demagogues or world-historic individuals, such movies might articulate ideas that an imagined community had only felt. These movies might even reconstitute the imagined community.

If You Are a Bonnie-and-Clyder . . . : The Birth of Radical Chic

"Once something is said or done on the screens of the world, once it has entered mass art, it can never again belong to a minority, never again be the private possession of an educated, or 'knowing' group," Pauline Kael warned her *New Yorker* readers. As *Dr. Strangelove* legitimized pop nihilism, so the even stranger love story that was *Bonnie and Clyde* celebrated illicit thrills and glamorized forbidden roles.

The bored waitress Bonnie Parker (Faye Dunaway) and brash ex-con Clyde Barrow (Warren Beatty) meet on a dusty, depressed West Dallas afternoon when she foils his casual attempt to steal her mother's Model T. The scene—which opens with a Warholian close-up of Bonnie's lips—is fraught with erotic suggestion and narcissistic display. Bonnie, who observes Clyde from her bedroom window, is first seen nude. When the barely abashed Clyde proudly flashes his revolver, Bonnie suggestively fondles the barrel and, excited by his admission that he served time for armed robbery, taunts him into knocking over a grocery store. Clyde does so and Bonnie is so aroused she literally hurls herself upon the gunman as they career off together in their newly stolen getaway car.

Bonnie and Clyde wastes scant time establishing a social basis for its protagonists' criminal behavior, the better to dwell on that behavior itself. As guns bestow power, so the automobile conveys freedom. The capacity for criminal violence is, from the onset, a factor of desire—shown alternately as a substitute for, or stimulant to, sexual relations. For, to Bonnie's bewildered disappointment, this handsome hunk proves unresponsive. "Your advertising's just dandy," she complains, "Nobody would guess you don't have anything to sell." In an exchange charged with psychosexual anxiety, Clyde reasserts control of the courtship by appealing to Bonnie's secret yearning to be a star—successfully seducing her as his accomplice in criminal glamour. *Bonnie and Clyde* proposed a daringly blatant connection between violence and sexual repression, but its real originality lay in the realization that the lust for celebrity in the Global Village might be a drive as potent as sex.

The movie's initial tone is saucy and lighthearted, with frequent use of bluegrass artists Flatt and Scruggs's rollicking banjo piece "Foggy Mountain Breakdown" to accompany the outlaw pair's comic mishaps. Holding up a second grocery, Clyde narrowly avoids having his head split by a clerk who attacks him from behind with a meat cleaver. After attempting to rob a bank that has already failed, the couple pick up a loveably stupid accomplice, C. W. Moss (Michael J. Pollard), as a driver, only to be confounded in their next job when he parallel-parks the getaway car on Main Street. Here, the fun becomes too real. A bank teller pursues the outlaws to their automobile's running board and panicky Clyde is compelled to shoot him point-blank in the face. Hitherto, *Bonnie and Clyde* took pleasure in broken glass and overturned automobiles and promoted the enjoyment of reckless cowboy behavior. Now a cloud passes over the sun.

Pursued by the Texas Rangers, the increasingly celebrated couple joins forces with Clyde's older brother, Buck (Gene Hackman), and his wife, Blanche (Estelle Parsons). After an initial flurry of enthusiasm, the mood again darkens. The Barrows are twice trapped in rustic motor courts by small armies of lawmen and compelled to shoot their way to freedom, killing several police officers. Here, Penn raises the firepower to wartime dimensions, thus allowing for some painful verisimilitude—as when Buck is shot in the head and Blanche, herself wounded, launches into what would be an Oscar-winning rant of denial.

Simultaneously victims and aggressors, *Bonnie and Clyde* personified Tom Wolfe's pornoviolence. As the movie's attractive star performances preclude other viewpoints, *Bonnie and Clyde* struck some as less overly gruesome than excessively glamorous. "Pretty people who kill, and the killing they do is pretty too," Jimmy Breslin snarled in *New York* magazine, suggestively—if irrationally— adding that if "you want to see a real killer, then you should have been around to see Lee Harvey Oswald." None other than the once-banned author Henry Miller joined the fray, publishing an attack, "Make Love Not Gore," in *Penthouse*: "Worse than cold-blooded murder, in my opinion, is the presentation of murder as a form of entertainment. . . . I feel compelled to look upon the viewers as even more sick than the killers they are watching." Rather, let us have "obscene films, the more censorable the better. . . . What a relief it would be to see some real warm-hearted fucking on the screen," Miller exclaimed, calling for precisely the form of liberation initially denied the movie's protagonists.

Just as Bonnie and Clyde's sexual frustration is shown to fuel their outlaw violence, so their hard-won happiness must be punished by the authorities— as presaged by the police gun battles that disrupt their attempt at motor-court domesticity. Indeed, once Bonnie and Clyde triumph over internalized repression to achieve normal sexual relations, the capacity for outrageous—and outrageously punitive—violence resides entirely with the state. The outlaw couple's climactic, bloody ambush-execution has tremendous finality. Their bullet-perforated automobile is evidence of official vengeance upon taboo desire. The shooting stops, the lawmen emerge and advance toward the car. The movie ends; consciousness extinguished, the screen goes black.

•   •   •

Bonnie and Clyde divided American critics, but the civil war was brief. Bosley Crowther retired at the end of 1967; Pauline Kael went on staff at *The New Yorker* to become the most influential American movie critic of the next two decades. Certified Pop Art, *Bonnie and Clyde* was featured on the cover of the December 8, 1967, *Time*, as interpreted by Robert Rauschenberg, for an essay on "The New Cinema: Violence . . . Sex . . . Art." *Time*, which had panned *Bonnie and Clyde* as a "purposeless mingling of fact and claptrap," blandly reversed itself to proclaim Arthur Penn's movie "sleeper of the decade." *Time*'s original review parroted Crowther's outrage at *Bonnie and Clyde* representing the United States in Montreal; the newsweekly now echoed Kael's assertion that audiences left the movie in a state of stunned reverie.*

That same week, the *New York Review of Books* cover featured David Levine's

---

*By some accounts, the anonymous *Time* staffer who reviewed *Bonnie and Clyde* was subsequently relieved of such responsibilities. Ironically, the actual Bonnie and Clyde were among the first "stars" featured by *Time*'s crime page. Distancing itself from other media, *Time* reported that, "an awe-struck Press magnified [Clyde Barrow] into one of the 'worst Killers of the Southwest.'" In 1934, the Barrows' fatal ambush precipitated a primitive festival as 20,000 cops, reporters, and celebrity-worshippers descended upon the Arcadia, Louisiana, crime scene.

caricature of President Johnson as a suitably degenerate Clyde, with Secretary of State Rusk his demure Bonnie. Stanley Kauffmann made a similar connection at a lower level, noting in *The New Republic* that Gene Hackman's Buck Barrow looked and sounded like "a young LBJ"—LBJ was but a year older than fellow East Texan Clyde Barrow. Indeed, the month *Bonnie and Clyde* opened, H. Rap Brown called the President "an outlaw from Texas." But that got things backward.

Television, in *Time*'s McLuhanesque formulation, had assumed Hollywood's traditional function, and "cinema" was now the "favorite art form of the young." This generational relationship was clinched when the newsweekly's December 26 issue ran a letter by an eighteen-year-old college freshman from Peoria maintaining that *Bonnie and Clyde* was "not a film for adults"—which was why it incurred such Establishment wrath. Nor was it *Bonnie and Clyde*'s violence that shocked her peers: "The reason it was so silent, so horribly silent in the theater at the end of the film was because we liked Bonnie Parker and Clyde Barrow, we identified with them and wanted to be like them." What did that mean? Can one imagine such a letter written in defense of *The Dirty Dozen*—and imagine it being published?

Like *The Dirty Dozen*, *Bonnie and Clyde* was a movie with a new attitude. The former featured war criminals as war heroes. Now, here were outlaws looking photogenic as pop stars: In one sequence, the Barrow Gang playfully cluster around the car of a hapless undertaker (Gene Wilder) and his date, pushing their faces against the windows as though imitating the Beatles in *A Hard Day's Night*. Good looks, swell clothes, actorly assurance, and charismatic cool set *Bonnie and Clyde* apart from their dowdy environment. Scarcely a pair of Dustbowl losers in faded gingham and overalls, *Bonnie and Clyde* recalled the rich young couple in *The Great Gatsby*, motoring heedlessly through the hinterlands, smashing the lives of lesser little folk, then retreating into their money. But who remembered the 1920s or the 1930s?*

---

*In generational terms, Bonnie and Clyde were the children of Davy Crockett: In March 1968, the *New York Times* noted that five teenage boys in dress "apparently inspired by

Self-conscious myth, *Bonnie and Clyde* crystallized a shift not only toward movie violence but toward the movies themselves. *Bonnie and Clyde* was steeped in movie-ness. The past was the "movie" past. The shock image of the perforated bank teller recalled that of the elderly woman shot in the face during the Odessa Steps sequence of Sergei Eisenstein's *Battleship Potemkin*, and this killing was followed by an even more obvious quotation—Bonnie, Clyde, and C.W., taking refuge in the movies, watching the campy opening number, "We're in the Money," from the musical, *Gold Diggers of 1933*.

Bonnie and Clyde's hyperreality is allegorized by the very credits, punctuated by a camera shutter's click, as sepia snapshots of the original *Bonnie and Clyde* are gradually replaced by their iconic stand-ins Beatty and Dunaway. From the onset, Penn's Bonnie and Clyde act as though they are living a movie. Star-making is a process. For virtually the entire period they are on the run, the couple construct public images—posing for photos, introducing themselves as celebrities, enjoying their press clips, and, in the case of Bonnie, recounting their exploits as doggerel verse.

Narcissism is its own justification. *Bonnie and Clyde* signaled a new complicity, a willingness to go with the flow, a sense of crime as a game ruined by grown-up society's tedious insistence that acts had consequences. Reporting from London in the December 21, 1967, *Village Voice*, theater critic Charles Marowitz summed up a new *mentalité* manifest in the local counterculture.

> If you are a bonnie-and-clyder, you are pro-camp and anti-Ugly; pro-permissiveness and anti-authoritarian; an advocate of the easy, improvised approach to life rather than a Five Year Planner. You pledge allegiance to Pink

---

the movie *Bonnie and Clyde*" were arrested in a wealthy Connecticut suburb having created a "disturbance" by brandishing a toy gun as an armored car pulled up to a bank. That spring, male-female hold-ups were reported in Atlantic City and the Bronx as part of a 50 percent rise in bank robberies. Just as the authors of the discarded MPAA code feared, the attractive protagonists of *Bonnie and Clyde* succeeded in seducing viewers into complicity in criminal violence.

Floyd and the Rolling Stones and all they stand for, and walk imperturbably toward the exit-doors while the National Anthem is playing.

Bonnie and Clyde were too beautiful to grow up, become domestic, join the middle class. Their vehicle was all about going over the edge, hence the cartoon that ran in the January 13 *New Yorker*. A couple of pear-shaped middle-aged bourgies laughingly announce themselves on an apartment intercom: "Open up. It's Bonnie and Clyde!" To dig *Bonnie and Clyde* was, at the very least, to declare yourself a kid-symp.

For Robert Benton and David Newman, Bonnie was a "strange and touching vision: a pretty girl who was both tough and vulnerable, who was both Texas and universal, who wrote poetry and shot policemen, who loved life and courted death." Bonnie broke the prison of gender to commit crimes like a man; posing for snapshots with a captured Texas Ranger, she mocked cowboy authority. Was Bonnie an icon of female liberation? Even before *Harper's Bazaar* showcased "The Gangster Game," the January 12, 1968, *Life* put Dunaway on its cover as "Bonnie: Fashion's New Darling." *Newsweek*'s March 4 Dunaway cover hailed the "with-it girl of the '60s" and first American woman since Marilyn Monroe to "electrify the world's moviegoers." But was it the actress or the role?

As *Women's Wear Daily* proclaimed spring's hot shade the "gun-barrel gray of Bonnie's pistol," so the March *Mademoiselle* celebrated Dunaway, explaining in suitably Kracauerian terms that "every so often a new look comes into being."

> It may float on the air unlabeled, unclaimed in origin, before it crystallizes and people say, 'That's it. That's what we're talking about.' Which is what happened with *Bonnie and Clyde*'s Faye Dunaway. Suddenly she brought a look to life, focused it by the way she walked and talked and wore her clothes. . . .

Bonnie and Clyde ignited clothing fads on both sides of the Atlantic—calf-length "maxi" skirts, revivals of fedoras, wide ties, and (seized back from Barry

Sadler) berets. Nor did viewers fail to notice that Faye Dunaway wore no brassiere.*

As Bonnie and Clyde discotheques proliferated, California supermarkets held Bonnie and Clyde sales—"everything a steal"—and Cartier's displayed gems in the context of fake bullets and a Bonnie beret. On TV, TWA showed the Barrows driving to the airport and escaping in a jet, Flying A gasoline had the Barrows delayed by an overfriendly service-station attendant, GM cast a Pontiac dealer in the Gene Wilder role, abducted by the gang (to whom he sells a new car). "Not in a generation has a single Hollywood movie had such a sudden decisive and worldwide impact," the *Hollywood Reporter* opined.

This instant feedback was not so much a pseudo-event as a Global Village festival. In a manner only hinted at by *Dr. Strangelove*, *Bonnie and Clyde* was a Happening. It was new. It was Now. It was Us—or Them. Marowitz compared "the heady ecstasy" with which the Barrows broke the law to "the arcane pleasure that attends pot parties in north and southwest London." In the United States, of course, youthful outlaw activity might encompass not only taking drugs but demonstrating against the state, evading the draft, and, in the case of the Black Panthers, shooting it out with the police. Although the Barrows did not take up arms against the state with any particular purpose, their revolt was an inspiration. These outlaws humiliated authority and expressed solidarity with the dispossessed. "You ought to be home protecting the rights of the

---

*In London, Carnaby Street's November 17 Christmas preview provided a unified field—the leading shops, boutiques, and even bistros, filling their display windows with mannequins sporting Bonnie hairdos and mid-calf skirts, along with Clyde slouch fedoras and sharp-cut, chalk-striped double-breasted suits. A band called the St. Valentine's Day Massacre played Depression tunes like "Brother Can You Spare a Dime," although Dunaway—present for the occasion—spooked some of her fashion-followers by wearing a mini.

Across the Channel, Brigitte Bardot set off the fashion revolution even before *Bonnie and Clyde*'s gala Paris opening. The star devoted a chunk of her annual New Year's Day TV show to the movie, wearing Bonnie fashions and, of course, singing the new "Ballad of Bonnie and Clyde," written by Serge Gainsbourg.

poor folks, not chasing after us," they taunted their robotic Texas Ranger nemesis, reminding him of a time (unseen in the movie) when "poor farmers kept you laws away from us with shotguns."

Eric Hobsbawm—whose study of peasant resistance, *Primitive Rebels,* was already a Berkeley cult book—had described social banditry as an assault on state authority enacted for a politicallly powerless audience. Embodied by (and promoting themselves as) stars, the young and beautiful Bonnie and Clyde acted as if they had politics and were perceived as world-historic figures: Righteous Outlaws.

● ● ●

Violence, in the libidinal economy of *Bonnie and Clyde,* is a consequence of thwarted desire—sexual and otherwise. For the sexually dysfunctional Clyde, gunplay is compensatory. But what of the politically repressed? Andrew Kopkind might have been experiencing himself as Clyde when he wrote in the September 28, 1967, *New York Review of Books* (notorious for its cover diagramming the recipe for a Molotov cocktail) that "to be white and a radical in America this summer [was] to see horror and feel impotent." Interviewed by *Newsweek,* Faye Dunaway claimed a protofeminist identification with Bonnie: "She was up against a stone wall—a girl with potential who is blocked."*

In its contempt for the state, *Bonnie and Clyde* was embraced as a film of the left. Penn himself made the link to Black Power, proudly telling *Cahiers du Cinéma* that "five Negroes present" during a preview screening "completely identified with *Bonnie and Clyde.* They were delighted. They said: 'This is the way; that's the way to go, baby. Those cats were all right.' " There can be no greater validation for a white American than black American approval, and Penn's pleasure was capped by his observation that African Americans were themselves at "the point of revolution." As *The Dirty Dozen* had anticipated the

---

The New Left Notes published for the June SDS 1967 convention anticipated Fashion's Darling by including in its crude cover collage the image of a laughing, carbine-toting "New American Woman." Appropriating a term from the Black Panthers, the September 25 *New Left Notes* characterized the authorities as pigs.

summer riots, so *Bonnie and Clyde* presaged autumn's escalated antiwar rhetoric. (In Kansas, an SDS leader was arrested for threatening to assassinate the President; in Baltimore, Father Philip Berrigan led the first raid on a Selective Service office, dousing draft records with animal blood.) And as the Barrow Gang contested the government monopoly on violence, so *Bonnie and Clyde* popularized the attitude Tom Wolfe would derisively label "radical chic."*

Bonnie and Clyde was in release but a few weeks when an alert SDS militant, Gerald Long, published a piece in the September 9 issue of the Old Left weekly *Guardian*, explaining that the movie's subject was the "violation of bourgeois property relations." This was not a liberal or sociological tract like the old Henry Fonda vehicle *You Only Live Once*, which had suggested that times were hard and criminality the unfortunate result. This was something far more exciting.

> [Bonnie and Clyde] are just out there doing their thing, the thing they should be doing, and the camera and the audience are digging it and zooming along with them on the flight of the banjos plunking in the background. The banjos are freedom, integrity, spirit, all the things that bourgeois bankers, sheriffs and undertakers are not.

When these two "consciousness-expanding outlaws" drive into the service station where C. W. Moss pumps gas, it's as if "a Mustang convertible pulls up with Luis Turcios, Frantz Fanon, and Nguyen Van Troi inside and they hold the door open and say, 'Hop in man, we're driving on down to the Pentagon.'" Clyde Barrow, People's Hero.

The New Left experienced *Bonnie and Clyde* as a miraculous vision. "Here I was," wrote Berkeley activist Michael Rossman of Stop the Draft Week, "trying to sing what it's like to see the vectors of the war, the breaking black

---

*The February 19, 1968, *New Left Notes* included a sympathetic review of Georges Sorel's *Reflections on Violence*: "Proletarian violence makes the future revolution certain." But that was scholasticism. For the radical intelligentsia of the 1960s, Sorel had been supplanted by Frantz Fanon—one of the seven New Left heroes designated by the May 5 *New York Times Magazine*—who, in *The Wretched of the Earth*, asserted that "national liberation is always a violent phenomenon."

thing, the incipient hippy pogrom focus on our heads, and us on the streets of Oakland and at *Bonnie and Clyde* for the third time, trying to learn what to do next while the culture decides to eat its young." The movie had an oracular quality. The first line of Abbie Hoffman's proposed advertisement for the scheduled "exorcism" of the Pentagon was "Don't miss *Bonnie and Clyde*."

The 1967 March on Washington would climax the yearlong countercultural festival. In late August, the National Mobilization Committee Against the War in Vietnam, familiarly known as the Mobe, announced its intention to shut down the Pentagon on Saturday, October 21. Jerry Rubin, brought east as a Mobe coordinator, recruited his new pal, Abbie Hoffman. (Only four days earlier, the pair made international news by showering the New York Stock Exchange with dollar bills and thus sowing hilarious greedfest consternation.) Elaborating on a scenario by poet Gary Snyder, Hoffman declared that a band of Lower East Side hippies would form a magic ring around the Pentagon, levitate the building ten feet, and cast out its evil spirits.

October 21, with the Army in the streets of Washington for the first time since disgruntled World War I veterans marched on the White House in 1932, some 50,000 protestors massed at the Lincoln Memorial. "The hippies were there in great number," Norman Mailer wrote in *Armies of the Night*, his LSD-obsessed, first-person account of the event. Mailer appreciated their theatricality. "Many dressed like the legions of Sgt. Pepper's Band, some were gotten up like Arab sheiks, or in Park Avenue's doormen's greatcoats, others like Rogers and Clark of the West, Wyatt Earp, Kit Carson, Daniel Boone in buckskin." The Red Dog Saloon mobilized. Halloween was ten days away. Mailer saw "soldiers in Foreign Legion uniforms" and "hippies dressed like Turkish shepherds," "gurus and samurai"—"assembled from all the intersections between history and the comic books, between legend and television, the Biblical archetypes and the movies." Many were, of course, tripping.

After the rally, thousands marched from the Mall half a mile over the Arlington Memorial Bridge into Virginia. (Not all followed. John Lewis of SNCC declined to join in, saying, "We don't want to play Indian outside the white man's fort.") The Pentagon, already ringed by national guardsmen, was surrounded by the protestors. The poet Ed Sanders and his band, the Fugs, arrived on a flatbed truck chanting: "Out, demons, out!" The crowd shouted with them. "End the fire and war. End the plague of death." Others contributed to the sustained, growling *ommmmmmmm*. After Sanders declared the exorcism a success and called for a "grope-in," the protestors staged the war's largest mass draft-card burning—as well as the antiwar movement's most iconic photograph, the image of a longhaired hippie placing the flower of peace in the barrel of a youthful guardsman's gun. As night fell, the guardsmen (reinforced by a number of Southern marshals) used tear gas and beat the largely nonviolent demonstrators. The 683 arrests were the greatest number so far; the high was such that a follow-up march organized in New York declared the war over.

Mailer got his best reviews in twenty years and won a National Book Award for *Armies of the Night*. Hoffman and Rubin were launched as counterculture Star-Pols. The CIA initiated Operation CHAOS, aggressively infiltrating and spying on New Left groups to determine how closely they were controlled by the Soviet Union. In fact, the fiftieth anniversary of the October Revolution could scarcely have seemed less relevant. Forget Lenin. The world's greatest revolutionary was Fidel's former comrade, Che Guevara, missing from the media stage for over a year and bound for death-trip glory. An international revolutionary martyr was born October 7 when Bolivian soldiers captured and executed Che. A Christ-like picture of him flashed around the world—"the corpse of the last armed prophet laid out on a sink in a shed, displayed by flashlight," wrote Robert Lowell.

Che posters were prominent in the march on the Pentagon, *Time* observed. The same issue's report on "campus celebrities" noted that the "most desirable speaker, if only he were available, insisted one Berkeley student leader, would be Ho Chi Minh. Almost as good, a Harvard student sighed sadly, would have been another Communist, the newly deceased 'Che' Guevara."*

---

*According to Graham Greene, Che's death saddened even those without Marxist sympathies. He "represented the idea of gallantry, chivalry and adventure in a world more and more given up to business arrangements between the great world powers."

Was martyred Che the real Hollywood Freedom Fighter? "For the first time in its

While still in Cuba, Che told some American visitors his greatest desire was to become an urban guerrilla in the United States, fighting imperialism in the "belly of the beast." That was where his image came to rest. Darryl Zanuck, touring Europe in the aftermath of Che's death, became aware of the dead revolutionary's "tremendous appeal" for young people and instructed his son Richard to develop a Guevara bio-pic.

• • •

Collective fantasies yearned for realization. Che was a revolutionary icon, a counterculture poster personality to rival the reclusive Bob Dylan, who, having dropped from sight since his motorcycle accident during the summer of 1966, was recording *John Wesley Harding*—his first album in almost two years, a paean to the Righteous Outlaw, filled with apocalyptic Wild West imagery.*

Bonnie and Clyde was only the season's most popular example of desperado revisionism. Rock critic Paul Williams, founder and editor of *Crawdaddy!* magazine, published a lengthy state-of-the-art appreciation of the Doors, Rolling Stones, Jefferson Airplane, et al., entitled simply—and without explanation— *Outlaw Blues*. American icons were recast as countercultural heroes. Michael McClure's *The Beard*, a play in which archetypal Western bad-boy Billy the Kid

---

history," Herbert Read declared, "the communist movement has found a romantic hero, a man in the tradition of Count Roland or the Black Prince." Or was Che the greatest of Righteous Outlaws? Jean-Paul Sartre declared him "the most complete human being of our age." Not to be outdone, Susan Sontag proclaimed the dead hero "the clearest, most unequivocal image of the humanity of the world-wide revolutionary struggle unfolding today."

*In its idiocy, ABC launched their 1967–68 season with a new dramatic Western series, *Custer*. The youthful Indian-fighting general was presented as a rebel—described in the network's promotional material as "long-haired, headstrong, flamboyant, and a maverick." Well before its debut, *Custer* was attacked by Indian organizations and even criticized in *TV Guide*. The National Congress of the American Indian demanded equal time. "Glamorizing Custer is like glamorizing Billy the Kid," the head of the Tribal Indian Land Rights Association told *Newsweek*. Not so. The social bandit, however murderous, did not act in the name of the state.

and Hollywood goddess Jean Harlow faced off in a "blue velvet eternity," opened in New York three days after the Pentagon exorcism—and a year after battling censorship in San Francisco.

McClure's glamorous outlaws were Bonnie and Clyde in the guise of Haight-Ashbury hippies. The Kid had shoulder-length locks, a black suit with a frilly Western shirt, and cowboy boots. The Depression sex star Harlow resembled psychedelic blues singer Janis Joplin—her wild corona of spun-sugar hair and thrift-shop gown offset by an oversized, ratty-looking boa. *The Beard's* content was explicitly sexual, with dialogue "as 'dirty' as anything the American stage has ever known" per one review. After an hour of verbal sparring, the Kid performs oral sex on Harlow; the play climaxing with her climax, ecstatic moans of "STAR! STAR! STAR! STAR! STAR!" as the curtain falls.

For literati, the fall's main event was William Styron's controversial *The Confessions of Nat Turner*—a first-person novel based on historical accounts of the African slave who led an 1831 uprising in Virginia. An authentic Third World revolutionary was exhumed from the American past. Specifically thinking of Mao and Castro, as well as Stokeley Carmichael, Styron made Turner a tragically flawed figure whose capacity for violence, like Clyde Barrow's, was fueled by his own sexual repression. Although reviews were generally favorable, Styron's conception of a neurotic Nat was attacked by black intellectuals. Black actors even threatened to boycott the never-made film version.

Meanwhile, *Newsweek* detected another, more menacing manifestation of black revolutionary energy in a newly released Italian movie, Gillo Pontecorvo's quasi-documentary re-creation of mid-1950s Third World struggle, *The Battle of Algiers*: "At the recent New York Film Festival at Lincoln Center and later at a first-run theater on Manhattan's East Side, many young Negroes cheered or laughed knowingly at each terrorist attack on the French, as if *The Battle of Algiers* were a textbook and a prophecy of urban guerrilla warfare to come."*

---

*Other critics, including Bosley Crowther, made a connection to the U.S. "involvement" in Vietnam, as well as the situation in American cities.

Certainly, *The Battle of Algiers* offered invaluable instruction in the language of communiqués, organization of cells, placement of terror bombs, and use-value of cop killing. Indeed, Che was scarcely in his unmarked grave when Black Panther leader Huey P. Newton was wounded in, and imprisoned after, a gunfight with the Oakland police. Although "Free Huey" soon became a ritual New Left demand and, thanks to the personality poster designed by Eldridge Cleaver, Huey an icon, his movie—Mario Van Peebles's *Panther*—would not arrive for another twenty-eight years.

Gerald Long, a future signer of the Weatherman manifesto, had expressed hope, in his *Guardian* piece, that *Bonnie and Clyde* would break attendance records. The movie was superb agit-prop: "The audience really gets angry when the anonymous Minions of Bourgeois Order blast down the Blythe Spirit of the Revolution." But Long's comrades were not monolithic in supporting his position—particularly those of the older generation. One letter published in the *Guardian*'s September 16 issue was pure generational rage: "I have never read a more obscurantist ill-digested bit of nonsense in all my years." Didn't Long understand that "lumpenproletariat" scum like the Barrow Gang (or, perhaps, the Panthers) were the "excrescence of a heartless exploitative society?" No less than the movie, Long had sullied the memory of the Thirties—those who had stood up for Okies and the Forgotten Men were the real revolutionaries, or rather, progressives.

Penn had stocked *Bonnie and Clyde* with knowing references to Thirties icons, quoting Dorothea Lange and Walker Evans's photographs for the Farm Service Administration and re-creating scenes from the 1940 movie *The Grapes of Wrath*, directed by John Ford. But *Bonnie and Clyde*'s slapstick violence and dismissive put-downs of square authority desecrated this socially conscious Old Sentimentality. John Howard Lawson, doyen of the Hollywood Ten, published an essay contrasting "our film," *The Grapes of Wrath*, with "theirs." *Bonnie and Clyde*, Lawson wrote, was the first American film to express "total alienation." The movie made no distinction between "socially motivated" and "criminal" violence. From the "startling" close-up of Bonnie's lips to the final machine-gun fusillade, the protagonists were motivated by "blind impulse."*

How ploddingly literal-minded! For Marx and Engels, crime was an ineffectual individualistic response to poverty and oppression—while crime stories served only to titillate the jaded bourgeois palate. It was Marx's rival, Bakunin, who realized that the bandit was "always the hero, the defender, the avenger of the people, the irreconcilable enemy of every State, social or civil regime, the fighter in life and death against the civilization of State, aristocracy, bureaucracy and clergy." Certain criminal acts might be clear expressions of class warfare—demonstrations that it was possible to turn oppression upside down.

Long's celebration of *Bonnie and Clyde* was topped four months later when *New Left Notes*, which had never before reviewed a commercial movie, devoted a quarter of its January 8, 1968, issue to Neil Buckley's analysis. Long, Buckley

---

*Lawson found it significant that, following the "absurd" debacle of an early hold-up, the Barrow Gang took refuge in a movie theater. Exactly! *Bonnie and Clyde* has almost nothing to do with *The Grapes of Wrath* and practically everything to do with 1950s delinquency films like *The Wild One* and *Rebel Without a Cause*. (That Clyde would have been a perfect part for James Dean was made clear in the 1973 *Bonnie and Clyde* remake, *Badlands*, which portrayed its doomed outlaw couple as misunderstood yet sensitive Midwestern teens.) The major difference was that, at once pre- and post-1950s, these new rebels had neither chastened parents nor a therapeutic society to welcome them back.

For his part, Penn, who envisioned *Bonnie and Clyde* as a mythic re-creation of the Great Depression he'd experienced as a child, told one interviewer he wished he'd listened to the Library of Congress recording of Woody Guthrie talking about Dust Bowl bandit Pretty Boy Floyd before making *Bonnie and Clyde*. Guthrie "solved the whole picture for us. . . . He gave the sociological background in terms of people's attitude towards the banks in a way that it had taken me months of working with Benton and Newman to finally come around to."

Pointing out that the historical Barrow Gang had inadvertently helped create the conditions whereby the FBI might wage a federal war on crime, Penn suggested that someone make a movie about Pretty Boy Floyd—as it was, his own next film would be about, and star, Guthrie's folk-singing son, Arlo.

declared, gave Hollywood "more ideological credit than it deserves." Unlike
the Old Left hero Spartacus, for example, *Bonnie and Clyde* neither realized
their human potential nor understood their enslaved condition. Moreover,
Penn's film made no mention of a ruling class.

And yet, Long was not entirely wrong. Such was the cunning of reason
that *Bonnie and Clyde* turned out to be revolutionary beyond the filmmakers'
intentions. Historical context overdetermined the movie's reception. Prerevo-
lutionary violence in America precluded viewing *Bonnie and Clyde* as just a
"tragedy of youth gone bad." If anything, *Bonnie and Clyde* was the "political
equivalent of a horror movie," demonstrating that those who challenged the
state-sanctioned capitalist order were punishable by death: "The viewer leaves
the film with a tingling sensation where the bullet holes might have been in
his body had he too gone wrong—had he too violated property rights."

Reading *Bonnie and Clyde* as political prophecy, Buckley was hung up on
the prospect of violence to come: "That we have not suffered many deaths in
our ranks is both surprising and encouraging. To suspect that this state of
grace of liberal society will continue much longer is to be overly optimistic."
Long merely blurred the distinction between Clyde Barrow and Frantz Fanon;
Buckley's analysis demolished the separation between the scenario and the
show.

> In its essential element, *Bonnie and Clyde* is revolutionary because it defines pos-
> sible futures for us based on the reality of conditions under which we struggle.
> The film does not depict a revolutionary ideology. It does much more than that;
> it defines a revolutionary's lot.

Arthur Penn's movie was not just an unprogrammed youth festival. As the
admen would hype Coca-Cola several years hence, this collective fantasy was
the Real Thing. "We are not potential Bonnies and Clydes," Buckley declared
with the lunatic, lysergic certainty that sought to levitate the Pentagon, "we
are Bonnies and Clydes."

Spring 1968: Shooting *Easy Rider*, Going *Wild in the Streets*

As antiwar protest escalated throughout the fall, U.S. ambassador to Vietnam Ellsworth Bunker and commander of American forces General William Westmoreland had waxed optimistic: The end was in sight; there was light at the end of the tunnel. The success of this government propaganda offensive was evident in the polls. Demonstrators were blamed for encouraging the Communists and prolonging the war. For the first time in over a year, LBJ's popularity began to rebound. But, a few weeks into 1968, when Warren Beatty prevailed upon Warner to rerelease *Bonnie and Clyde* with a new, more dignified ad campaign stressing his movie's artistic merit, cowboy authority would be on the ropes.

Washington, DC, January 23: Clark Clifford, the designated new secretary of defense, attends President Johnson's regular Tuesday national security lunch. *MacBird!* has finally closed after 386 performances at various Greenwich Village venues; Johnson's approval rating is approaching 50 percent. Yet, Clifford thinks, the President seems exhausted and morose. The day before, a B-52 armed with four hydrogen bombs missed the runway at Thule Air Force base in Greenland and plunged into the Atlantic; neutral Cambodia lodged an international protest after U.S. forces crossed its border; and Senator Mike Mansfield, Johnson's successor as Majority Leader, delivered a speech blaming the war for the "national disaster" facing America's cities. LBJ is about to present Congress with a record $186 billion budget, including a tax increase to offset his second consecutive $20 billion deficit.

That very morning the President had been shaken awake at 2 AM to learn of the Navy intelligence ship *Pueblo*'s capture by North Koreans within their territorial waters. LBJ had just called up 14,000 reserves even as newspapers are reporting on the 5,000 Marines—most eighteen and nineteen years old— besieged behind sandbags at the isolated base at Khe Sanh. This token outpost had been reinforced in November for the officially leaked purpose of drawing an enemy force.*

---

*Was the war a co-production? Both sides had the same idea. The North Vietnamese imposed the siege on Khe Sanh as a ploy to divert U.S. attention to the remote strong-

Clifford deems Johnson, who has a terrain model of the Marine stronghold installed in the White House situation room, unduly suspicious—if not downright paranoid. LBJ is convinced the North Korean provocation and the Khe Sanh siege are part of a grand scheme to surround and Alamo-ize the United States. Containment has come home. The next target, the President believes, will be Berlin. In fact, it is Saigon: At 3 AM, Wednesday, January 31, nineteen VC commandos storm the U.S. embassy, kill five Americans, and hold the building for six hours—long enough for TV news crews to document the action.

The panicky reporting, the raw footage of corpses in the rubble, the images of dazed soldiers exchanging automatic gunfire are something new: Watts on TV in the Nam. A chasm opens between the administration narrative and telereality. These chaotic transmissions contributed to the "huge collective nervous breakdown," that Michael Herr will describe in *Dispatches*: "Every American in Vietnam got a taste." Or, as *Life*'s cover haiku reads:

> New frenzy in the war
> Vietcong terrorize the cities
> SUICIDE RAID ON THE EMBASSY

During their Tet offensive, the North Vietnamese attacked thirty-six South Vietnamese cities, marching around the garrison at Khe Sanh to occupy—and virtually destroy—the ancient university center at Hue. Now, Michael Herr wrote, Vietnam was

a dark room full of deadly objects, the VC were everywhere all at once like spider cancer, and instead of losing the war in little pieces over years we lost it

---

hold even while Westmoreland, eager for a classic military engagement, hoped to lure 20,000 North Vietnamese regulars to that same location. And so the war's greatest battle began on a red clay plateau six miles from the Laotian border, just south of the DMZ. Khe Sanh was bombarded around the clock from the surrounding hills; by night, North Vietnamese patrols crept forward from jungle cover toward the perimeter.

fast in under a week. After that, we were like the characters in pop grunt mythology, dead but too dumb to lie down. . . .

Although the American forces struck reflexively to regain the illusion of control, it was a costly proposition: "We took space back quickly, expensively,
with total panic and close to maximum brutality. Our machine was devastating.
And versatile. It could do everything but stop."

The so-called "Tet Photo"—an image of a South Vietnamese police chief
summarily executing a nameless Viet Cong suspect, taken February 1 in the
middle of Saigon by AP photographer Eddie Adams—was splayed across four
columns above the fold on Page One of the next morning's *New York Times*
under the headline, STREET CLASHES GO ON IN VIETNAM, FOE STILL HOLDS PARTS
OF CITIES: JOHNSON PLEDGES NEVER TO 'YIELD'. (Later that week Adams's photo
was published in *Time* as a "picture that will go into the history books.") The
same shooting was recorded by an NBC crew and telecast for twenty million
viewers on that evening's *Huntley-Brinkley Report*. The split-second impact of a
bullet entering a man's brain—with its unavoidable echo of the JFK assassination—became synonymous with the instant when, as Harold Evans would
put it in his memoirs years later, "Western opinion about the Vietnam war
shifts fundamentally."*

Tet prompted an investigation by the most trusted man in America, CBS
news anchor Walter Cronkite—still remembered for breaking into the afternoon soap opera *As the World Turns* with the bulletin that President Kennedy
had been shot. Cronkite's mission was more important than any congressional

---

*Commenting on fighting around a city in the Mekong delta later that week, a U.S.
major gave the image its caption when he told an AP correspondent that it had been
necessary to destroy Ben Tre in order to save it. The next day, Senator Robert Kennedy
cited the Tet Photo—which eventually won Adams a Pulitzer—in addressing the Chicago Book and Author luncheon: "The photograph of the execution was on the front
pages all around the world—leading our best and oldest friends to ask, more in sorrow
than in anger, what has happened to America." It was after Tet, as well, that U.S. forces
in the field would fully experience the effect of widespread drug use and heightened
racial tensions.

fact-finding junket. His four nights of Vietnam broadcasts culminated with a February 27 prime-time report, concluding that "it seems more certain than ever that the bloody experience of Vietnam is to end in stalemate." Watching this performance on one of his three TVs, LBJ was said to have told his press secretary that if he'd lost Cronkite, he'd lost the country.

Indeed, the President's improved approval ratings immediately plummeted to 36 percent, as newspapers reported Westmoreland's secret request for another 200,000 troops. At home, the swelling army was that of Senator Eugene McCarthy's supporters. America, McCarthy felt, had become like the Roman Empire, policing its periphery while the inner cities decayed at home. As Senator Kennedy declined to challenge LBJ, McCarthy proposed to enter the Democratic primaries himself, running against the President's war. Before Tet, the McCarthy campaign had seemed a quixotic enterprise—a few Ivy League professors and students gone "clean for Gene" spending winter break organizing New Hampshire. (Adding to their urgency, LBJ abolished graduate deferments on "Black Friday," February 16.) McCarthy was expected to pull 12 percent of the vote; on March 12, the Minnesota senator came within a few hundred ballots of out-polling the President. Psychologically, it was the electoral equivalent of Tet; although Johnson was the technical winner, he was fatally weakened by his adversary's unexpected show of strength. Suddenly, Kennedy reassessed his position. On March 16, RFK decided he, too, would challenge Johnson.

Nor were the McCarthy and Kennedy juggernauts the only crusades. Martin Luther King, who spoke approvingly of McCarthy's candidacy in January, was organizing the Poor People's Campaign, a massive march on Washington scheduled for late April. And Richard Nixon's comeback would not be denied. He won in New Hampshire with 79 percent of the Republican vote and topped that showing in Wisconsin, where his only competition was a half-hour documentary promoting California Governor Ronald Reagan. The Beatles' trippy Christmas TV special and follow-up LP provided an all-purpose metaphor: *The Magical Mystery Tour*. As Bob Dylan's *John Wesley Harding* peaked at number two on the album charts, the Barrows were back on the road, en route to selling the $23 million worth of tickets that made *Bonnie and Clyde* the thirteenth highest-grossing American movie in history.

As the winter ended, other filmmakers were experiencing a certain restless energy. Sam Peckinpah was in the saddle, headed for deepest Mexico. Peckinpah had sold the new Warners honcho, Kenneth Hyman, on making a Western *Dirty Dozen—The Wild Bunch!*—but the director had something more fantastic in mind. His ambition, so he confided, was to out–*Bonnie and Clyde* *Bonnie and Clyde*. The *Bonnie and Clyde* scenario also impressed Michelangelo Antonioni; the Italian maestro's magical mystery tour twice crossed the United States in late 1967 and early 1968, scouting locations and meeting counterculture celebrities in preparation for his first American film, *Zabriskie Point*. And now Henry Fonda's boy, Peter, and Peter's crazy pal, Dennis Hopper, were making their drugged-out motorcycle Western, *Easy Rider*.

•   •   •

Peter Fonda would have been the biggest star on the American-International Pictures lot if the home of degenerate youth cinema had had one. This low-rent studio, created in the year of *The Wild One* 1954, was the first to appreciate the post World War II teenage audience and—by specializing in juvenile delinquency melodramas, sci-fi monster movies, and primitive rock musicals, mostly directed by the incredibly efficient Roger Corman—had more or less invented the drive-in picture.

As the youth culture mutated, AIP abandoned the beach party mode of the early Sixties in favor of topical exploitation flicks populated by bikers and acidheads. Dennis Hopper, a thirty-one-year-old beatnik Method actor whose up-and-down Hollywood career extended back to *Rebel Without a Cause*, had played both types, but it was Fonda who top-lined AIP's two blockbusters, *The Wild Angels* and *The Trip*. Resplendently posed in leather and chrome, young Fonda made a personality poster that became a dorm-room icon. *The Wild Angels*, which cost $350,000, grossed over $5 million during the crazy summer of 1966; *The Trip*, somewhat artier, was released a year later to coincide with the Summer of Love, realizing ticket sales ten times its $400,000 budget.

Mid-September 1967, while Fonda was in Toronto to promote *The Trip*, the star had another vision. By his own account, he was smoking pot in his hotel room at 3 AM when he realized that the real cowboys of today were . . . bikers. Fonda imagined a movie about a cool pair of motorcycle dudes who make a big dope score and go on the road, riding across the country, digging on America, planning to retire to a Florida orange farm—only to be shot and killed by two hippie-hating redneck duck poachers.*

No less than Bonnie and Clyde, Fonda's bikers were doomed Righteous

---

*In his memoir, *Don't Tell Dad*, Peter Fonda writes that he envisioned *Easy Rider* as a contemporary version of *The Searchers*. Ex-Digger Peter Coyote proposes another origin in his memoir *Sleeping Where I Fall*, explaining that, while visiting Hollywood with a delegation of Diggers that included the Hell's Angel known as Sweet William, Fonda and Hopper came to check them out.

> These guys were our age, sons of the film community, caught somewhere between their home base and their imaginings of free life, seeking to connect with a pure strain of the underground. We discussed "what was happening" for some time and how it might be translated into film. . . . Chat was easy and things felt good. Then Sweet William took the floor, magnificent in his Angel colors, his hard-chiseled face and poetic eyes mesmerizing even those of us who knew him well.
>   "You know what I'd do?" he said. "I'd make a movie about me and a buddy just riding around, just going around the country doing what we do, seeing what we see, you know. Showing the people what things are like."

Coyote considers this the "germinating idea" for *Easy Rider*, although his account is clouded by vague chronology. Coyote also writes that Hopper and Fonda asked him to write and direct a scene for the movie with the Mime Troupe. "Several months later, they called with an offer: twenty dollars a week and a place on Fonda's couch for me, but nothing for my friends—'because this is a real low-budget thing.'" Coyote angrily refused, noting that "the finished film added insult to injury" in its portrait of a commune which

> entertains itself by watching a clutch of dodos clump through a mindless commedia-type stage play announced by a crudely lettered sign as 'Gorilla Theater'—an obvious travesty of the Mime Troupe's guerrilla theater and a backhanded slap at the communards, who are less hip than the individualistic, wandering biker heroes.

Outlaws. Fonda was so excited by his idea that he called his buddy in the middle of night to share the revelation. Hopper, a talented photographer who had long nursed the desire to direct and had been unsuccessfully peddling a script about movie-making he'd cooked up on the set of the 1965 John Wayne Western *The Sons of Katie Elder*, refined Fonda's concept. That fall, the pair took the project—working title *The Loners*—to their employers at AIP.

Easy Rider was the logical extension of the AIP motor-psychedelic youth flick but proved to be the greatest film AIP never made. Studio chief Sam Arkoff was not pleased that the basis of the bikers' big score was cocaine (rather than pot) and also demanded a contract allowing him to replace Hopper as director if the movie went over budget. Known for frugality, AIP was about to release its most lavish movie ever, *Wild in the Streets*. The title, lifted from an abandoned project for which promotional material already existed, conflated those of the two most celebrated motorcycle flicks—*The Wild One* and *The Wild Angels*—with a pet Goldwater phrase ("crime in the streets"); the script had been adapted by Robert Thom from his 1966 *Esquire* story, "The Day It All Happened, Baby."

Thom and director Barry Shear, a forty-seven-year-old TV veteran, were neither part of the Hollywood establishment nor its antithesis. Deploying a scenario recently used in the British film *Privilege*—wherein a pop singer fronted a fascist takeover—Thom and Shear updated the demagogic threat film *A Face in the Crowd* for the 1960s. *Wild in the Streets*, already in production when *Bonnie and Clyde* had its premiere and the hippies exorcized the Pentagon, was a new sort of AIP horror film: *I Was a Teenage Spartacus*. Rock stars and hippies take control of the state.

The Loners was stalled at AIP when Fonda and Hopper sought to raise money for another project. *The Queen*, written by Hopper's pal Michael McClure, went *MacBird!* one better. LBJ and his cowhands—McGeorge Bundy, Dean Rusk, and Robert McNamara—would sit around in off-the-shoulder evening gowns plotting to assassinate JFK. Mid-January, Fonda and Hopper had pitched *The Queen* to independent producers Bob Rafelson, thirty-three, and Bert Schneider, thirty-four, the masterminds behind *The Monkees*—a high-concept sitcom about a band of ersatz Beatles. Schneider had no interest in *The Queen*, but after he read Hopper's twelve-page outline for *The Loners*, he blew Fonda's mind by writing a check for $40,000 in advance of a promised $360,000.

The script—which now involved black humorist and *Dr. Strangelove* screenwriter Terry Southern, who came up with the title *Easy Rider*—was not yet complete when filming began, on Fonda's twenty-eighth birthday. The signs were not auspicious. Because the neophyte producer miscalculated the date of Mardi Gras, the New Orleans sequence had to be shot first and in 16mm. Walter Cronkite was rattling Lyndon Johnson on TV. Hopper, too, was on edge, opening the hastily organized production by haranguing the cast and crew: "This is MY fucking movie!"

Easy Rider's five days in New Orleans have become a mythologized orgy of violent, drug-addled, hotel room–trashing paranoia. Seventeen crew members quit. In his account of the debacle, Peter Biskind describes Hopper demanding that one of the project's three cameramen, Barry Feinstein, turn over the first day's exposed stock: "I don't trust you—gimme all your film, I want it in my room!"

> Feinstein started throwing the film cans at him, whereupon Dennis jumped him, kicked and pummeled him. They went flying through a door into the room shared by [actresses Toni] Basil and [Karen] Black. According to Dennis, Peter was in bed with both women. The two men paused for a second to contemplate this spectacle, and then Feinstein heaved a television set at Dennis.

("I was never in bed with Peter Fonda," Black told Biskind. "Believe me.")*

On the shoot's last morning, Hopper and several survivors of his shell-

---

*Fonda's recollection is only slightly less dramatic. Depressed by Hopper's antics, he'd gone to visit Basil and Black to smoke pot and play guitar when he heard a disturbance outside the door.

> Dennis was trying to take Barry's personal Arriflex-and-lens combo to shoot some shots of neon lights in the water reflections, as it was raining. . . . The fight spilled into Karen and Toni's room, and Dennis

shocked company sneaked into the city's St. Louis Cemetery to film an improvised acid trip. According to Fonda, "Dennis was directing while acting in character, pulling from a bottle of wine and popping speed." He browbeat actress Toni Basil into taking off her clothes to cower in a sunken grave while Fonda curled up in the stone lap of the statue atop the Italian Society tomb, persuaded by Hopper to articulate, for the first time, his feelings about his mother's suicide. Then the director himself flipped out. What manner of heroes were these? The sixteen hours of incoherent rushes were screened in Los Angeles—a disaster compounded by Hopper's pot bust on Sunset Boulevard. Fonda, who had secretly taped his partner's psychotic tirades, was looking for another director, but Schneider—having already sold the picture to Columbia—refused to panic. Hopper would remain.

In late March, as Fonda, Hopper, and Southern wrestled with the shooting script, Peter's sister Jane graced *Life*'s cover in form-fitting latex astronaut drag: FONDA'S LITTLE GIRL JANE AS A FUTURISTIC SPACE TRAVELLER IN THE MOVIE BARBARELLA. Inside, her uninhibited posing was parsed for maximum generation-gap titillation.

> It wasn't so much [Jane's] right-out-there-in-the-open nudity that smarted but the fact that this was, after all, Henry's daughter. As everybody knows, he is American bedrock—Young Abe and Jesse James and Mr. Roberts and the Male Animal and the farmer who took a wife on the trail of the lonesome pine.

From dad's appearances in *Advise and Consent* to *The Best Man* to *Fail-Safe* to ... topless bondage gear in intergalactic space? Jane's trip would take far further out, but in the meanwhile, she patronized her brother: "It's a hell of a lot harder to be Henry Fonda's son than Henry Fonda's daughter," although, she

---

> broke Karen's guitar over Barry before he picked up the TV set and threw it at him.

Breaking up the scuffle, Fonda medicated Hopper with "a doob—he'd been doing whites and wine all day"—followed by a 1,000-milligram dose of Placidyl.

reported, Peter had been liberated by LSD. He "writes, he sings, he plays the guitar very well, he's got a photographic studio. He will be a good actor, too." But acting was not the point—at least not the way Jane meant it.

Easy Rider's script was completed during the three-week period in March when, as Theodore White put it in his account of the 1968 presidential campaign, "U.S. politics became unhinged." In the days after McCarthy's near-win in New Hampshire and RFK's announced candidacy, America's Vietnam casualties surpassed those suffered in Korea while B-52s pounded the hills around Khe Sanh with more explosives than had ever been dropped in the history of mankind. Saturation bombing plus napalm and chemical defoliants— the skies above Khe Sanh were filled with airborne sci-fi command stations as well as transports and armed choppers. Then, 9 PM Sunday, March 31, the Death Pharaoh LBJ materialized on TV and, after announcing the cancellation of his long-running Rolling Thunder, appeared to abdicate power.

The next morning's *New York Times* reported that the nation's normally loquacious television commentators were "stunned into virtual incoherence" by the President's surprise announcement that he would not run for reelection. The polls put McCarthy over LBJ 60 percent to 40 percent in the April 2 Wisconsin primary, yet some wondered if Johnson's renunciation wasn't some sort of trick. The stock market soared—the nearly eighteen million shares sold surpassed the volume on Black Tuesday 1929. The new record lasted two days, broken on word that LBJ was now prepared to start peace talks with North Vietnam. Universal euphoria! The *Times* ran a picture of Robert Kennedy and wife, Ethel, mobbed by ecstatic supporters. BOBBY IS GROOVY, the signs read. Scarcely anyone noticed that George Wallace had declared his independent candidacy.*

---

*The week was golden: *Time's* cover featured reform Communist leader Alexander Dubcek: Self-determination for Red Czechoslovakia. The planets were in alignment! Self-proclaimed tribal rock musical *Hair* was moving its Age of Aquarius vaudeville uptown to Broadway where Stanley Kubrick's *2001: A Space Odyssey*, not yet advertised as THE ULTIMATE TRIP but still the most visionary American movie of the decade, opened at Loew's Capitol.

Although it felt almost as though the war was over, fighting in Vietnam intensified with LBJ's announcement. General Westmoreland ordered commanders to apply "maximum pressure" in the field. No matter, the public mood lasted only until the evening of Thursday, April 4, when the bulletin went out that Martin Luther King Jr. had been shot dead by a sniper in Memphis. There were riots that night in 125 cities—although not, significantly, in Indianapolis, where RFK was campaigning in the city's black wards and, speaking extemporaneously to the stunned crowd, made his first public reference to his brother's murder.

From then on, race rivaled the war as a campaign theme—in Vietnam as well. "The death of Martin Luther King intruded on the war in a way that no other outside event had ever done," Michael Herr reported.

> In the days that followed, there were a number of small, scattered riots, one or two stabbings, all of it denied officially. . . . We stood around the radio and listened to the sound of automatic-weapons fire being broadcast from a number of American cities.*

Bonnie and Clyde won only two Oscars at the Academy Awards ceremony, delayed two days by the King funeral. It was with some relief to Hollywood savants that the designated best picture turned out to be *In the Heat of the Night*, a liberal racial melodrama with Sidney Poitier as a Philadelphia cop who has to solve a murder case in racist Mississippi. Hollywood's only black leading man had starred in two other 1967 hits (*To Sir with Love* and *Guess Who's Coming to Dinner*). He received no nominations but was much in evidence along

---

*The worst disturbance was in Washington, DC—over 700 fires and widespread looting. Ten were killed, including a white man pulled from his car and stabbed to death. Sunday, twenty-two-year-old Georgetown senior and RFK supporter Bill Clinton volunteered for a student relief program, driving a white Buick convertible marked with a homemade red cross, past burnt-out storefronts to Fourteenth and U Streets to distribute food. Whether or not, as has been suggested, the future president had enlisted to impress a visiting girlfriend, he was, one friend would recall, "numb and shocked" by what he saw.

with Dustin Hoffman—youth star of the amazingly successful comedy *The Graduate*—who brought as his date Eugene McCarthy's daughter Ellen.

RFK was campaigning in Michigan. The morning after the Oscars, a sniper was spotted on the rooftop outside his Lansing hotel. Later that day, the candidate's motorcade was mobbed in downtown Kalamazoo. A twenty-seven-year-old mother of five hoisted herself into Kennedy's convertible and pulled off his shoe.

•   •   •

Mid-April: Peter Fonda and Dennis Hopper resume production, around the time Operation Pegasus breaks the siege of Khe Sanh. Ten thousand Vietnamese and 199 Marines have died during the seventy-seven-day assault on the base that the United States will abandon in June. Fonda and Hopper shoot the New Orleans bordello interiors, some billboards on Hollywood Boulevard, and the hippie commune scenes. The partners had planned to use New Buffalo commune, near Taos, as their location, but after the Buffalo is torched by irate locals, they fabricate a commune—bringing a gaggle of Hollywood hippies to Topanga Canyon. Then they go on the road, searching for America with a new cameraman, a professional crew, and, in Fonda's case, a personal bodyguard.

Easy Rider is, even in 1968, a costume movie. Fonda's modern cowboys—Wyatt and Billy—are self-conscious archetypes, successors to Marlon Brando's Wild One and James Dean's Rebel Without a Cause as conceived by the Wild One and Rebel themselves. Hopper, dressed like Wild Bill Hickock in Stetson and buckskin, plays gibbering sidekick to the leather-clad, flag-bedecked Fonda.*

As *Easy Rider* works its way from California through Arizona to New Mexico, AIP rolls out its Demagogue a Go Go. Appropriately, *Wild in the Streets* has its April 17 world premiere in Chicago—designated site of the 1968 Dem-

---

*Taking the idea of a flag sewn on his jacket from John Wayne in *Flying Tigers*, Fonda complained of being hassled for this sacrilege by various cops, all of whom, he pointed out, would themselves be wearing the flag within a year of *Easy Rider*'s release.

ocratic Convention and already a youth cult target. On the last day of 1967, Abbie Hoffman, Jerry Rubin, and Paul Krassner had founded the Youth International Party, or Yippie!, to plan for that summer's "revolutionary action-theater." As a sequel to the March on the Pentagon, the Yippies proposed to counter the Democratic Convention with the greatest guerrilla extravaganza ever devised—a "free rock orgy" featuring the Rolling Stones, the Beatles, and Bob Dylan to end in "a huge orgasm of destruction atop a giant media altar."

Rubin had an acid vision of the Convention held behind barbed wire and defended by paratroopers rushed back from Nam. The day after Bobby Kennedy declares his candidacy, the Yippies call a press conference: "We will create our own reality. And we will not accept the false theater of the Death Convention." Meanwhile, Chicago mayor Richard J. Daley is already waging his media war. Having made the national press by ordering police to "shoot-to-kill" during the disturbances that followed Martin Luther King's assassination, he will gain more publicity on April 27 when his cops club and Mace peaceful antiwar demonstrators and then arrest twenty-six at the benefit a week later.

April 24, *Wild in the Streets* opens in LA. That same day militant students—led, in part, by the campus SDS—occupy their second building at Columbia University. Generational solidarity with a vengeance, *Wild in the Streets* recasts juvenile delinquency as a political movement—like the Lower East Side SDS chapter formed around the time of the October 1967 Barrow Gang March to Levitate the Pentagon, as a "street gang with an analysis." The cell, which included Herbert Marcuse's son-in-law, Tom Neumann, adopted the slogan "Armed Love," borrowed their logo from Zig-Zag rolling papers, and, in reference to a poem by black nationalist LeRoi Jones, took the name Up Against the Wall Motherfucker.

Were *Wild in the Streets* not so lurid, the movie might also—as *New Left Notes* said of *Bonnie and Clyde*—define a possible future based on the Reality of the Conditions Under Which We Struggle. For one thing, its revolution is media-determined. For another, the demagogic rock-star protagonist, twenty-two-year-old multimillionaire Max Frost (Christopher Jones, star of Don Siegel's short-lived TV series *The Legend of Jesse James*) personifies the youth market. *Wild in the Streets* is both an allegory of a movie industry that calculated 52 percent of its audience to be under twenty-five years of age and a compensatory fantasy: "They won't draft us," Max sneers, "we'll draft them." The kids apply force against their parents, fomenting mass confusion by putting LSD in the nation's drinking water and ultimately confining everyone over thirty to psychedelic concentration camps.

Released during the primary season, *Wild in the Streets* will remain in theaters through the election and, over the course of this extended run, serve to prophesy and allegorize many things: Yippie fantasies, Wallace nightmares, student uprisings at Columbia and in Paris, Chinese Red Guards, the McCarthy and Kennedy campaigns, and Chicago. If *The Chase*, per *Newsweek*, fobbed off "sensationalism for significance," *Wild in the Streets* treats social problems as entertainment. Pauline Kael notes that *Wild in the Streets* parodies the hysteria of anti-hippie newspaper editorialists "by blaming everything on the parents," specifically Max's overbearing yet permissive mother (Shelley Winters). "My son has a good reason for shutting down the country," Mrs. Frost proudly explains, anticipating the moment when Columbia SDSnik Mark Rudd's mother would be quoted in the press referring, with fond irony, to her son, the revolutionary.

Wild in the Streets offers an intoxicating fantasy of youthful autonomy. There is a vague sense in the culture at large that this might actually be happening somewhere—perhaps in China?—as at Columbia, where the SDS militants who have liberated university president Grayson Kirk's office put their feet on his desk, drink his sherry, smoke his cigars, and investigate his shelves. There, hidden behind another text, they discover a book on masochism. "I get up and shave with Grayson Kirk's razor, use his toothpaste, splash on his after-shave, grooving on it all," James Simon Kunen writes in his diary of the occupation, whimsically titled *The Strawberry Statement.*

Max's politically correct retinue—whose integrated members include a character played by the young Richard Pryor—suggests that generation transcends race, class, and sexual orientation. Everybody wants to be young. As if to demonstrate this universality, *Hair* opens on Broadway on April 29. The cast has barely finished partying when, at 4 AM, New York police storm the occupied buildings at Columbia. It is a bloody process. "The kids thought the cops were gonna throw tear gas in and the police thought that the kids had Molotov cocktails ready to throw out," Mayor John Lindsay's aide, Sid Davidoff, recalled. There were seven busloads of tactical police—"storm troopers in those days. . . . If we had held them in that bus much longer, they would've hit us."

Columbia falls, but the virus is contagious. May 3, student demonstrations in Paris shut down the Sorbonne. Three days later, French students battle police in the Latin Quarter. International cataclysm of school-is-out springtime liberation! The Columbia radicals can't believe what they believe they've triggered: May 1968. (It is the same magic month that Beatle John Lennon and conceptual artist Yoko Ono spend their first night together and are thereafter inseparable.) The French kids, suddenly in the generational vanguard, shake the de Gaulle government—challenging the planetary balance of power—even as the U.S. presidential race pretends to be normal. In the midst of the Columbia occupation, Hubert Humphrey had announced his candidacy, ludicrously attempting to co-opt the Yippies with his "politics of joy." Nelson Rockefeller has thrown his hat into the ring five weeks after promising not to run. But now, the Gallup poll shows him more popular than Richard Nixon—and the one Republican candidate who can beat any Democrat. (His campus supporters include the young Newt Gingrich.)

RFK meanwhile is battling to win the Indiana primary, where, according to *Variety*, his hastily organized campaign has budgeted $3 million to spend, with another $15 million in reserve. Erstwhile director of *The Manchurian Candidate* and *Seven Days in May* John Frankenheimer is RFK's media adviser. But Frankenheimer's 16mm campaign film, documenting Kennedy's whistle-stop tour through the Indiana heartland, looks as though it were directed by Arthur Penn. RFK supposedly visited the barber before coming to Indiana, but with his hair blowing in the wind and his wife, Ethel, in her miniskirt, he could be the fifth Beatle. Sound of manic banjo picking; ecstatic crowds lining the train tracks. Inevitably, the *Indianapolis Star* ran an editorial cartoon picturing Ethel and Bobby as Bonnie and Clyde, roaring through the state tossing money from an open roadster.*

As the most powerful newspaper in the state, the ultra-conservative *Star*, owned by Eugene Pulliam (Goldwater partisan and grandfather of future vice president Dan Quayle), is RFK's implacable foe. Journalists joke that "the only way Kennedy could get on the *Star's* front page would be by getting shot." But to run against LBJ, RFK assimilated some of the Goldwater message. Kennedy calls for jobs instead of "welfare handouts" and, reminding audiences that for four years he served as the nation's top cop, campaigns against "lawlessness and violence." Despite this vaguely anti-Washington rhetoric, RFK demonstrates fantastic appeal for the impoverished and dispossessed—urban blacks, Chicano farm workers, and youth. It is Kennedy, not McCarthy, who campaigns for a draft lottery and promises "to tell it like it is." The RFK campaign song, "This Man Is Your Man," takes its melody from Woody Guthrie. The RFK campaign book, *To Seek a Newer World*, is salted with citations from Dylan, Lennon, and the Berkeley Free Speech Movement.

Kennedy presents himself as a bridge over troubled waters, mediating between the generations and the races. "As the car swept along, he was, obviously, The Kennedy, of The Family and Blood Royal, the Prince Coming to Town," Theodore White would write. "In a working-class district he was Robin Hood. At night, in such places as Gary and South Bend on the final weekend, he was the Prince, Robin Hood and Pied Piper all combined. One remembers the children in the streets who followed him." This alliance, too, has been anticipated by *Wild in the Streets*. Craftily, Max Frost organizes "the

---

*Kennedy's chief rival in the charisma sweepstakes was neither McCarthy nor LBJ's surrogate, Governor Roger Branigin, but McCarthy's advance man, Paul Newman, campaigning since New Hampshire and even featured on *Life's* cover the week of the primary. "The Star-Spangled Look of the '68 Campaign" revealed McCarthy's Hollywood contingent to include Tony Randall, Eli Wallach, Elaine May, Robert Ryan, and Dustin Hoffman, while RFK had lined up Rod Steiger, Shirley MacLaine, Sammy Davis, Bobby Darin, Peter Lawford, and hippie songbirds Sonny and Cher. Both campaigns, *Life* noted, "hope to get Marlon Brando who is mounting his own antipoverty crusade."

biggest block party in history" to benefit the thirty-seven-year-old candidate for California senator, Johnny Fergus (McCarthy supporter Hal Holbrook).*

Kennedy beats McCarthy in Indiana and will win again the following Tuesday in Nebraska. In the weekend between, May 10 and 11, French students take the world stage. Thirty thousand march through Paris, then—fearing police attack—rip up paving stones, overturn cars, and barricade themselves in the Latin Quarter. After midnight, the police respond with tear gas and grenades, bursting into Red Cross posts and even private homes. A twenty-four-hour general strike begins Monday as the United States and North Vietnam open long-delayed talks in Paris. Back in Nam, it has been a rough fortnight. The 1,800 American casualties double those of Tet.†

May 28: RFK loses Oregon to McCarthy, in part because the war has reemerged as an issue. McCarthy has traced the mess back to JFK, pointing out

---

*Wild in the Streets presents this as a case of mutual exploitation. Rich and ruthless, a sleazy Bobby Kennedy run amok, Fergus wants to lower the voting age to eighteen. Jones uses his teenage army to bully him into supporting a drop to fourteen. But what was RFK's relation to the counterculture?

During a congressional hearing, Kennedy openly questioned the government's decision to curtail LSD research (and it was rumored that Ethel had herself undergone LSD therapy). Concerned about other anti-narcotic legislation, Allen Ginsberg visited Kennedy's office in early 1968 to discover that the Senator had his own agenda: "He wanted to know the relationship between the flower-power people or the hip-generation people and the black-power leaders. He wanted to know if there was any kind of political relationship or any political muscle behind such a coalition." In fact, RFK had already approached the "beards," as he called them, consulting Tom Hayden and Staughton Lynd before his March 1967 attack on Johnson's prosecution of the Vietnam War. If Hayden found Kennedy "incredibly appealing," Kennedy likely deemed Hayden reasonably useful. A July 20, 1968, FBI memo reported that the RFK campaign had funneled money to Hayden and Rennie Davis to create demonstrations in Chicago.

†Worldwide synchronicity: May 18, militant cineastes shut down the Cannes Film Festival. By May 22, nine million French workers are on strike and over 100 factories occupied. May 24, Charles de Gaulle addresses the nation on TV. That night, the Bourse is set afire. Street fighting in the Latin Quarter spreads to Lyons. May 26, the Nantes strike committee declares a people's republic.

that RFK ads even used a Robert McNamara testimonial. As Kennedy and McCarthy head on to California, Humphrey travels from state to state, lining up delegates chosen by the local political machine. Don't trust anyone over thirty. Learning that Johnny Fergus plans to betray them, Max and his cohorts successfully run their commune's senior member, twenty-five-year-old Sally LeRoy—played by beatnik anti-star Diane Varsi—for Congress.

In her maiden speech, Sally addresses the House of Representatives as though performing at the Fillmore. Wearing a Napoleon hat and shaking her tambourine, she can't help giggling at the sight of these fogies: "America's greatest contribution has been to teach the world that . . . getting old is . . . such a drag." It is the movie's supreme moment. One alternative weekly concludes a negative review by saluting this "rhetorical grandness that for a minute or two almost makes [*Wild in the Streets*] seem real." Congress is dosed with LSD; Sally's bill passes. The voting age lowered, Max runs for president as a Republican. His troops mass on Washington. There is a massacre. The kids are galvanized. Max wins.*

Wild in the Streets opens in New York on May 29, the day that De Gaulle disappears from Paris, and for the next thirty-six hours, the revolution seems on the verge of triumph. The *New York Times'* new film critic, Renata Adler, considers *Wild in the Streets* "by far the best American film of the year so far,"

---

*Dangerous as this demagogue might be, his libido is largely sublimated. Max is not a sex star. Closer to Dylan than Elvis Presley, he sings protest songs and is transparently modeled on James Dean—Jones's demonic scratch-and-mumble imitation peaks with a mock-Hitler speech. Or was Robert Thom frequenting the Whiskey a Go Go during the spring of 1966? Jim Morrison anticipated *Wild in the Streets* with the cri de coeur ending of "When the Music's Over": We want the world and we want it . . . Nah-ow-OW!!! Indeed, the night of May 10 (the very Night of the Barricades in Paris), Morrison and the Doors performed in Chicago for 15,000 crazed fans. Had Morrison seen *Wild in the Streets*? According to one biographer, he gave his material maximum force— "falling and leaping, writhing in mock agony, throwing himself against the stage floor with such force that he hurt his side"—before concluding his inflammatory set with "When the Music's Over." The crowd joined in on the final demand; the concert ended with the audience twice storming the stage, beaten back each time by Mayor Daley's cops.

almost a comic version of *The Battle of Algiers*. But where the rejuvenated *Times* saw sympathy with the young, *The Nation*—which had been spooked by *Bonnie and Clyde*—was apprehensive. "The effect is unambiguous," Robert Hatch writes. "It is to make anyone over 30 hate and fear the rising generation." Anticipating *Easy Rider*, Hatch worries the movie might result in an epidemic of hippie lynching.

A similar fatalism surrounds Robert Kennedy's magical mystery tour. "There are guns between me and the White House," the candidate was heard to remark at the Martin Luther King Jr. funeral. In fiercely overheated prose, Theodore White describes Kennedy as the Liberator of the Ghettos in America's heart of darkness. "Touring a deep ghetto with Robert Kennedy was like being in the eye of a hurricane, and as dangerous. . . ."

> Hands would reach for him, grabbing for a thread, a shoelace, a shoe; in the near-hysteria, anyone in the car with Bobby would become a bodyguard, protecting him. If he stooped to shake a single black hand, six more would clutch at him, at his fingers, up his wrist, to the elbow, tugging. They loved him, but the frenzy of their love was a danger in itself, for an accident was always instantly possible, anywhere, as the black youngsters climbed over the car, got into the seat with him, and crusted themselves on the hood and fenders. When the car tried to pick up speed and they tumbled to the ground, rolling over like bouncing balls as they fell or jumped from the vehicle, there was always, constantly, the danger that a child would be run over—and the frenzy might turn instantly to hate at the sight of blood.

The dream life is a white-water torrent. According to Pierre Salinger, Jacqueline Kennedy is convinced Bobby is targeted for assassination. The *San Francisco Express Times* runs a mock interview—written by Barbara Garson's husband, Marvin—with the ghost of President William McKinley. "Don't waste your vote on Kennedy," McKinley says. "They're going to kill him." June 5, less than a week after *Wild in the Streets* opened in New York, one day after Andy Warhol is shot point-blank in the reception area of his new Union

Square "factory" and only minutes after defeating Eugene McCarthy in the California primary, RFK meets death in the crowded pantry of the Ambassador Hotel.

•   •   •

Robert Kennedy spent the last day of his life in Malibu, relaxing around John Frankenheimer's pool. Standing before his jubilant supporters, RFK was that Hollywood Freedom Fighter returned to life—the shining star who would dissolve the distinction between races, generations, and classes (not to mention show business, political authority, and sexual desire). Bobby's final speech ended with the New Left exhortation "On to Chicago!" His charisma promised to restore the lost national narrative. What powers could prevent it?

Pete Hamill, standing next to Kennedy in the Ambassador pantry, thought the assassin, Sirhan Sirhan, looked like a trained gunman. Five others were wounded in the struggle for the weapon, but all survived. Somehow in the confusion, the words THE ONCE AND FUTURE KING appeared scrawled in crayon on the wall near where the heir to Camelot lay dying. By the time the East Coast woke to the news, the army had 10,000 troops stationed around Washington in anticipation of the riots. There were none. "One of [Robert Kennedy's] possibilities was that he was always doomed," Robert Lowell would remark. "It's very strange when you sort of anticipate something; then, when it happens, you're almost more astonished than if you hadn't."

Some saw the conspiracy: June 13, Truman Capote went on *The Tonight Show* and explained to host Johnny Carson that all three assassinations—Kennedy, King, and Kennedy—were connected. Citing *The Manchurian Candidate*, Capote suggested that Sirhan Sirhan was a brainwashed hit man. The *New York Times* television critic Jack Gould was outraged. "Idle speculation over the guilt or innocence of murder suspects who are in custody but have not yet been brought to trial surely is not within the acceptable province of entertainment television shows," he wrote. TV was adding to the confusion that it itself created. Some took an even more radically McLuhanist position. Robert Scheer noted that Sirhan Sirhan had "spent his whole life watching television in Los Angeles [and] the only reason Kennedy entered his life was because Kennedy was always on TV." Others blamed the pseudo-event. *Life*'s June 21 cover story, "The Psycho-biology of Violence" by psychologist Albert Rosenfeld, linked the RFK murder to a climate "where real life and fictional—as in the popular movie *Bonnie and Clyde*—are filled with images of brutality."

Indeed, the first page of Rosenfeld's piece was illustrated with a frame enlargement of Bonnie's death spasm: The "casual acceptance of violence" epitomized by *Bonnie and Clyde*, might "arouse susceptible people to violent acts." Similarly, Arthur Schlesinger's broadside *Violence: America in the Sixties*, an elaboration on a commencement address given the morning after RFK's assassination, deplored *Bonnie and Clyde* for its "blithe acceptance of the world of violence—an acceptance which almost became a celebration."

The imaginary relationship between *Bonnie and Clyde* and the RFK murder was clinched by Jimmy Breslin, who recalled that "in all the months that [*Bonnie and Clyde*] was around big, I only heard of one person who was against the picture so much that he wouldn't even go and see it."

> He was riding in a car in December in Chicago, going to the Book and Author luncheon at the *Chicago Sun-Times* and the car went past a theatre playing the movie and Bobby Kennedy said, "What about that movie?"
>
> "I hear it's terrific," somebody in the car said.
>
> "Best picture of the year," somebody said.
>
> Kennedy stared at Chuck Daly, one of the people in the car.
>
> "I hear it's the most immoral movie ever made," Bobby Kennedy said quietly.

Within a week of Kennedy's death, Executive Order Number 11412 established a National Commission on the Causes and Prevention of Violence. At the hearings, *Bonnie and Clyde* was cited repeatedly—if frequently sight-unseen.*

Creating Our Own Reality: *The Green Berets* and the Battle of Chicago

The vibes of the spring tumult surely reached Mexico, where Sam Peckinpah was shooting *The Wild Bunch*, the movie meant to displace *Bonnie and Clyde* as the epitome of Hollywood violence. Drinking heavily, nursing hemorrhoids, and flying concubines in and out of his movie-set pueblo, mad Sam was having the time of his life making the movie of his career. *The Wild Bunch*'s unbelievably violent and complicated final scene, which the crew called the Battle of Bloody Porch, involved six cameras and required eleven days of shooting—or was it, as some would recall, an entire month?

The shoot concluded in June. Cast and crew returned to a changed America, although as production assistant Gordon Dawson confessed, "We didn't know any of that shit was happening. We were totally wrapped up in the film." Peckinpah edited his martial Western as John Wayne rolled out with his. SO YOU DON'T BELIEVE IN GLORY, the posters blared. AND HEROES ARE OUT OF STYLE. AND THEY DON'T BLOW BUGLES ANYMORE. SO TAKE ANOTHER LOOK AT THE SPECIAL FORCES IN ANOTHER SPECIAL KIND OF HELL.

June 19, nearly two and a half years after the Duke first wrote to the President, *The Green Berets* opened at the Warner Theater on Broadway. Some 150 protestors turned out, most from Veterans and Reservists to End the War in Vietnam, Youth Against War and Fascism, and the antiwar serviceman's paper, *The Bond*. Brandishing a Viet Cong flag and placards reading UP AGAINST THE WALL JOHN WAYNE, the demonstrators were excited by the rumor that the Duke had promised to personally deck anyone carrying antiwar posters to his premiere. The demo was generally peaceful, with only thirteen arrests and a single organizer who claimed to have been beaten by police. Not so the re-

---

*Meanwhile, Jerry Rubin automatically included stills of the outlaw couple in his 1970 manifesto *Do It!*, while, on the college circuit, Abbie Hoffman regularly identified himself with Clyde.

views. *The Green Berets*, Renata Adler wrote in the *New York Times*, was "so unspeakable, so stupid, so rotten and false in every detail that it passes through being fun, through being funny, through being camp, through everything and becomes an invitation to grieve. . . ." Adler was clearly talking about the war itself. "It is vile and insane."

The Green Berets became the focus of a divided America—a highly charged event both in the United States and abroad. The response in Paris was predictably vitriolic, with the Communist *L'Humanité* denouncing the movie as a "provocation" that spit upon the North Vietnamese flag. There were anti-American demonstrations in Sweden and West Germany, where the movie's run was cut short. A Stuttgart daily compared *The Green Berets* to Nazi propaganda, and one antiwar group demanded that, given its "massive falsification" and unmistakable incitement to "racial hatred and murder," the Ministry of Interior Affairs ban all Wayne movies. But back in New York, *Variety* reported, *The Green Berets* was doing "excellent business," with two cops stationed at the Warner Theater.

LBJ's abdication left Wayne the lone authority figure standing. *Time*'s August 8 cover story—"The Last Hero"—offered the endorsement of SDS organizer Terry Robbins, an advocate of the militant Prairie Power faction who, twenty months later, would blow himself up while manufacturing a homemade bomb: "He's tough, down to earth, and he says and acts what he believes. He's completely straight and really groovy. I mean, if they really want to make a movie about Che Guevara, they ought to have Wayne play him." While gracing *Time*'s cover, Wayne came to Miami Beach to deliver an oration—"Why I Am Proud to Be an American"—to the dull Republican Convention at which, edging out the combined forces of governors Rockefeller and Reagan with ten votes to spare, Richard Nixon was nominated on the first ballot.

There was a generally unnoticed riot in Miami's black ghetto that night, and the former vice president delivered an acceptance speech that lamely plagiarized Martin Luther King Jr., eight times repeating the phrase "I see a day." But mainly Nixon presented himself as a tribune for white America, a vehicle for the "voice of the great majority of Americans, the forgotten Americans, the non-shouters, the non-demonstrators." This, too, was borrowed rhetoric. The concept of the "forgotten American" had been one of Barry Goldwater's themes in 1964.

•   •   •

Searching for a way to describe America's jungle war in his Vietnamese reportage, Michael Herr came up with John Ford's 1948 cavalry film *Fort Apache*. In particular, Herr liked the scene where Henry Fonda's newly arrived colonel, a stand-in for General George Custer, tells John Wayne's veteran Indian-fighter that he spotted some Apache as he neared the Fort, and Wayne politely replies, "If you saw them, sir, they weren't Apache."

> But the colonel is obsessed, brave like a maniac, not very bright, a West Point aristo, wounded in his career and his pride, posted out to some Arizona shithole with only marginal consolation: he's a professional and this is a war, the only war we've got. So he gives the John Wayne information a pass and he and half his regiment get wiped out.

"More a war movie than a Western," *Fort Apache* was Herr's "Nam paradigm," complete with the wisdom of John Wayne.

The Green Berets begins where *Fort Apache* ends, with a military press briefing. *Fort Apache*'s final scene makes clear that newspapers could usefully spread patriotic disinformation by portraying the Fonda character as heroic martyr rather than arrogant fool; thus, in *The Green Beret*'s opening scene, journalists have been invited to the John F. Kennedy Center for Special Warfare so they may learn to print the legend. In *Fort Apache*, the newspapermen were fools; in *The Green Berets*, they are dangerous knaves. The worst—grim, twitchy David Janssen—taunts one Green Beret as a "military robot."

The Green Berets nonsensically suggests that journalists don't know what's going on in Vietnam because they haven't seen Vietnam, and they haven't seen Vietnam because, presumably, their newspapers don't want to know what is really happening there. But the disjunction between official pacification reports and the war as reported was a factor of the media's free access—particularly the TV crews allowed to accompany American troops in the field who returned with vivid images of battlefield confusion and search-and-destroy missions where cheerful GIs set villages aflame with their Zippo lighters.

Perhaps to monitor the press, an ordinary housewife shows up at the JFK Center: "It's strange we never read of this in the newspapers," she muses after a Green Beret invokes the threat of Communist world domination. Hence the necessity for this movie: *The Green Berets* is as much about winning the hearts and minds of the American people as about winning the war. A continual emphasis on terminology and semantics mirrors Wayne's own concern. "If they would call this a war, the American people would get behind it," the star told the *New York Times*. But there is a problem in motivating kids to fight: The United States hasn't been invaded. Our ox hasn't been gored. America's women haven't been raped and murdered—yet. No less than Davy Crockett's Tennesseans, we need Santa Anna's letter.

Just as *Fort Apache* was a crypto combat film, so *The Green Berets* is a crypto Western. All the clichés are welcome. *The Green Berets* even ends with Wayne heading into the sunset—a problem in that he's supposedly gazing at the South China Sea, which is east of Vietnam. Like the Great Cowboy, Wayne envisioned Khe Sanh as the Alamo, although here, the besieged American base is nicknamed Dodge City, and, as Wayne explains to Janssen, tossing a bit of frontier boilerplate at this ridiculous dude in his safari jacket, "due process is a bullet." The South Vietnamese commander (George Takei) speaks pidgin English. He's a good Indian. The Viet Cong, who hoist their ladders against the walls of Dodge City like Mexican soldiers storming the Alamo, are howling savages.*

Hardly unaware of these parallels, producer Michael Wayne explained to *Esquire* that, contrary to expectation, he was not "making a picture about Vietnam" but "a picture about good against bad. . . . It's the same thing as the

---

*John Ford's last film—the documentary *Vietnam! Vietnam!* (1971)—made for (and shelved by) the U.S. Information Agency, also drew explicitly on this mythology. According to Ford biographer Joseph McBride:

Indians. Maybe we shouldn't have destroyed all those Indians, I don't know, but when you're making a picture, the Indians are the bad guys." *Esquire* obligingly registered *The Green Berets*'s release by running young Wayne's statement along with Edward Sorel's caricature of the old man perched atop a stagecoach fleeing a diminutive, pinto-riding Ho Chi Minh poised to shoot an arrow into his hide.

Filmed at Fort Bragg, South Carolina, and Fort Benning, Georgia, *The Green Berets* enjoyed much Pentagon assistance, which it repaid by sanitizing Robin Moore's novel to stress South Vietnamese devotion and Viet Cong corruption. Much of it is laughably staid. The camera rarely moves. Almost everything is in middle shot. James Simon Kunen, self-identified revolutionary chronicler of the Columbia occupation, saw the movie soon after it opened, noted the audience's perfunctory applause, and, assuming that *The Green Berets* was "essentially made by the government," felt a twinge that the U.S. Ministry of Truth was "a failure at even being evil."*

Yet, turgid as it is, *The Green Berets* has a measure of delirium. "This trip is gonna make LSD feel like aspirin," someone promises, invoking Wayne's sar-

---

> The Vietcong are the bad guys, the peasants are the terrorized farmers, the Americans are the Earp Brothers come to clean up the territory so that decent folks can go to church and set up schools. Such an innocent vision of society is charming in the archaic context of the Western genre, but debilitating and ridiculous in a documentary of modern war.

*Edited as Khe Sanh was besieged and the North Vietnamese made final preparations for the Tet offensive, Wayne's movie telescoped the war: The 1965 escalation merged with the 1968 crisis of representation. Indeed, as suggested by Richard Slotkin, *The Green Berets* documents the Credibility Gap. However the movie fictionalized the actual war, it faithfully reproduced official phantasmagoria. The opening scene was taken from transcripts of the February 27, 1965, State Department White Paper, "Aggression from the North." Understanding the need to establish a North Vietnam infiltration scenario, the CIA fabricated evidence: A phony firefight was staged off the coast of South Vietnam, where 100 tons of boxed Chinese and Czechoslovak arms had been sunk in a fake North Vietnamese ship. Foreign correspondents were invited to inspect; the story was presented in the White Paper. Shown the document in advance, Max Frankel

castic nickname for LBJ. The opening scene has a nutty internationalism. As if to reinforce the Teutonic marching song Barry Sadler cribbed for his melody, the movie has one Green Beret report in German. Elaborating on LBJ's 1965 Johns Hopkins speech, the movie reiterates that the VC rape children and torture prisoners, use poison, burn villages, and debauch native girls. The mass carnage of the American air strike is thus divine retribution. In the closing heart-wrencher, the war orphan Hamchuck is vainly looking for the grunt who adopted him and who has just been killed in the last triumph of American counterinsurgency. Wayne gets to plant the dead man's green beret on his head: "You're what this is all about." For Renata Adler, *The Green Berets* was insane precisely because it assumed these images only need be produced to manipulate the audience into a patriotic frenzy.*

For Americans, the war is ennobling: A counterinsurgency mission out of *The Dirty Dozen*, a Green Beret team parachutes into Indian country to capture a North Vietnamese general who has been trapped by his libido. Although the war in Vietnam displaced half the South Vietnamese peasantry, there is no sense of this disorienting urbanization in Wayne's hilariously chaste version of a Saigon nightclub. There is, rather, the patriotic sexuality of the South Vietnamese woman—the desire for her displaced onto the degenerate North Vietnamese commander who moves through the jungle in a chauffeur-driven limousine en route to a secret villa stocked with Champagne, caviar, and female companions dressed for an evening at the opera.

As in *The Alamo*, the Wayne character is the film's highest authority. His

---

cited this "conclusive proof" of North Vietnamese aggression in the same day's *New York Times.*

*Adler was incredulous to see Wayne deploying "machine killing of men who have won fairly hand-to-hand," as though this were the stuff of heroic fantasy. However violent the traditional Western hero, he was never the aggressor; the Westerner was moved to action by injustice or personal threat. Now, as Adler noted, "the left-wing extremist's nightmare of what we already are has become the right-wing extremist's ideal of what we ought to be."

approval is crucial. He cues George Takei to forgive his sister-in-law for patriotically going to bed with the North Vietnamese general and endorses the South Vietnamese commander's gung-ho formulation: "We build many camps, clobber many VC. Affirmative?" "Affirmative! I like the way you talk." Everything is affirmative. This is the best of all possible Vietnams—the most moving death during the air strike is that of a pet dog. In the spirit of revolutionary conversion, Janssen ultimately picks up a gun and joins the fight. ("If I say what I feel I may be out of a job," he tells Wayne. "We can always give you one," the Duke replies.) *The Green Berets* made more money for Warners that year than any movie save *Bonnie and Clyde*. This success proved Wayne's point: Give the public Vietnam the way it should be—the way it could be, the way it would be if only the media let it—and the war was a hit.

• • •

August's new North Vietnamese offensive was overshadowed by the Warsaw Pact invasion of Czechoslovakia. After a national security meeting on August 20, LBJ lectured Hubert Humphrey on his dovish tendencies. Humphrey feared—not without reason—that the President might reconsider his abdication. Days after the Soviets occupied Prague, Yippies began arriving in Chicago. "The police killed this teenager, half American Indian down from the upper Midwest, and called him a Yippie," eco-activist Keith Lampe recalled. "It was like throwing a dead body on your doorstep as a warning."

Friday, August 23, the Yippies gathered near City Hall to nominate their candidate, the hog Pigasus (promptly seized by the police). Confrontation was overdetermined. Paul Krassner remembers Mayor Daley's assistant, David Stahl, asking him and Abbie Hoffman about the Yippies' real plans. "Didn't you see *Wild in the Streets?*" Krassner inquired, to which Stahl grimly answered, "We've seen *Battle of Algiers*." Where the Yippies threatened to dose reservoirs with LSD, Chicago officials anticipated a scenario in which urban guerrillas blew up ice cream parlors. All spring, Jerry Rubin had been concerned with the RFK threat: " 'What if Bobby shows up at our Festival of Life and wants to dance?' some Yippies wondered. . . . Interest in Czechago went DOWN. Down. Down," he recalled in his manifesto-memoir *Do It!* "Bobby was bringing life back into the Democratic-Death Convention." But the planned festival gained new momentum after the assassination. Rubin excitedly telephoned Ed Sanders with the "good news." Not for nothing would they riff that Sirhan Sirhan was a Yippie.*

Still, only 5,000 demonstrators came to Chicago to join forces with about as many locals. Daley had nearly doubled their numbers with 12,000 police on the streets and 6,000 National Guardsmen on alert. Delegates were obliged to clear six security checkpoints to enter the Convention Hall—surrounded, as in Rubin's acid vision, by barbed wire, a wall of helmeted police, and a horde of suspicious plainclothesmen. The show also involved a small media army. CBS alone brought a total of 800 engineers, camera operators, directors, producers, and correspondents. Transportation was complicated by simultaneous taxi and transit strikes. Communication was also problematic. Daley had another walk-out against the telephone company temporarily lifted—but only inside the hall. Thus, the networks were prevented from installing feeds from their hotels. Moreover, the city refused to issue parking permits for the networks' mobile units. (Daley had arranged for a live TV relay from O'Hare Airport, but only if and when Lyndon Johnson arrived.)

Democrats had scheduled their convention in late August to coincide with the President's sixtieth birthday. His presence was powerfully invisible—the eerie absence of Johnson's portrait gave some the sense that he was stage-managing the entire event from his Texas ranch. Even as the DemCon opened on Saturday night with Senator Daniel Inouye's surprisingly downbeat keynote address, Humphrey feared that LBJ might be orchestrating a draft. The next afternoon, the Yippies staged their Festival of Life in Lincoln Park—sans stage

---

*Nor were the Yippies the only beneficiaries. Within days of Kennedy's elimination, George Wallace's ratings began to rise—"the surge nobody foresaw" per *Life*'s August 2 piece. Pollsters put Wallace's numbers at 16 percent, and when a group of British journalists asked Washington pundits if the former Alabama governor had enough support to deadlock the electoral college and, for the first time since 1828, throw the election into the House of Representatives, they were amazed to discover that many believed the scenario not only credible—but likely.

and sound system—and, that night at curfew, had their first confrontation with the police. "We didn't like these filthy hippies from San Francisco and New York," a local, then-"greaser," Bob Zmuda, would recall.

> Then, stapled on every telephone pole in the neighborhood, was a one-shot thing that said, "Come to Lincoln Park for the Love-In. Grass. Free love." I was maybe eighteen years old, so I probably was the fastest-radicalized person you could ever see.

That was the first stage of conversion. The cops, who roughed up TV crews, photographers, and reporters, took care of the next. The Yippie scenario worked. "From every direction the Yippies' own brand of rock music started: the rhythm of rocks rending copcar metal and shattering windshields," Rubin exulted.

> The Battle of Czechago was on. Creatures from the Smoky Lagoon, grotesque, massive machines like tanks lit with powerful lights, entered the park and shot tear gas that made you vomit. Pigs with masks—looking like sinister spacemen— led the way, ghouls in hell, turning the park into a swimming pool of gas.

On Monday, after *Bonnie and Clyde* opened in Saigon to set a one-day box-office record, and Tom Hayden (who had warned Rubin that "people are gonna die in Chicago, we're gonna have to go underground, we'll have to form armed units") was arrested in Lincoln Park, organizer Rennie Davis led a Viet Cong flag–carrying march through the Loop. That night, police again used clubs and tear gas on the Yippies who refused to leave the park. A few SDS honchos were present. For the organization's bewildered ex-president, Todd Gitlin, the barricades seemed "part Eisenstein, part Paris—so what was real?" Meanwhile, as Warren Beatty and Norman Mailer partied at the Playboy mansion and a credential fight between rival state delegations wore on, LBJ was informed that he, too, was running six points behind Nixon.

The RFK delegates were led by George McGovern—"the friendliest man in

Chicago," per Mailer. The South Dakota senator had "an honest Midwestern face, a sobriety of manner, a sincerity of presentation, a youthfulness of intent, no matter his age, which was reminiscent of Henry Fonda." He was "a Boy Scout leader who could play Romantic lead in a ten-million-dollar movie." But the time for a Fonda presidency was long gone. Mailer had been covering the conventions for *Harper's* only a month after he'd finished shooting his own political movie. The writer's third and most ambitious feature was conceived in the aftermath of the RFK assassination. Reflecting his belief that American presidential candidates would now come from those used to projecting their images through on-screen scenarios, *Maidstone* was Mailer's contribution to the fantasy of 1968. The novelist cast himself as famous director Norman T. Kingsley, "an American Buñuel with an unsubstantiated proclivity towards Greek love."

Maidstone had no script—it was pure existential psychodrama, shot over five days at several Long Island estates. Mailer explained to the cast that his character was both making a film about a male brothel and contemplating a run for the White House. *Maidstone* was an exercise in egotism, paranoia, and magical thinking. Kingsley, Mailer made clear, was being shadowed by PAXC, an acronym for the Prevention of Assassination Experimentation Control, and attended by a group of hangers-on called the Cash Box. Participants drew straws to discover whether they were PAXC agents (or double-agents), part of the problem or part of the solution. Mailer's own entourage included two of three ex-wives, current spouse Beverly Bentley, plus future wife number five—along with critic Dwight Macdonald, playwright Michael McClure, boxer José Torres, and Warhol superstar Ultra Violet. ("It's all so organized, Andy's films are never like this," she explained to whomever would listen.)

There were a few professional actors—Rip Torn, cast as Kingsley's perhaps treacherous half-brother, Harris Yulin, and a guy from Provincetown whose jaw Mailer wound up breaking. At once the director, star, and candidate, Mailer strutted around bare-chested—having himself filmed as he chatted up a middle-aged woman wearing a McCarthy button or compared himself favorably with economist John Kenneth Galbraith, informing a bunch of black kids that he was "the best white man around." Mailer imagined his set as a hothouse of orgies and intrigue and, indeed, his camera operator D. A. Pennebaker remembered a uniquely hostile environment: The cast members were

> like fish driven around and around and ready to jump out of the pond. I could feel the tension. The evenings at the Hilltop Acres Motel in Sag Harbor where everyone was staying were tortuous: Who was in? Who was a success? Who was a failure?

Who was a PAXC agent? Who was not?*

As late as Tuesday, some still wondered if the Great Cowboy would arrive in Chicago. With Mailer representing *Harper's*, *Esquire* commissioned reports from Terry Southern, William Burroughs, and Jean Genet. For them, the action was all in the street. "We are bathed in a Mallarméan blue. This second day imposes the azure helmets of the Chicago police," Genet rhapsodized. Even veteran Theodore White seemed disoriented. "By Tuesday night," he would write, "convention, media, police, authorities, innocents were all adrift."

> And as the convention came out of control on the floor and television spread an authentic feel of its dislocation, the police in the evening moved on the campers

---

*Later, Mailer maintained that *Maidstone* was a "military operation." As the filming ended, he explained that what he'd been orchestrating was a five-day "attack on reality." The finished movie, he promised, would be a Pirandellian roller coaster. But, as noted by biographer Carl Rollyson, *Maidstone* replicated a familiar Mailer pattern. Violence was courted but avoided. Having flirted with assassination, the director retreated into an abstruse lecture on filmmaking—until, outraged by this bad faith, Rip Torn refused to accept the movie's spurious ending. July 23, the morning after Mailer declared *Maidstone* over—while he was having Pennebaker take home-movies of him with his wife and four children—Torn charged across the lawn and attacked Mailer with a hammer, shouting, "I must kill Kingsley." Torn pulled his blows but still drew blood. Mailer leapt upon the actor, knocked him down, and nearly chewed off his ear. The adversaries glared at each other. "You're just a fraud, aren't you?" Torn said at length as Pennebaker racked focus on his wound.

at Lincoln Park [only just addressed by Black Panther leader Bobby Seale], driving once again the forlorn, the crazy and the calculating from Lincoln Park to sanctuary at Grant Park.

Joined by demonstrators from the LBJ unbirthday party at the Coliseum, the crowd remained in Grant Park, chanting slogans below the Hilton until three in the morning.

In addition to the media, there were two camera crews in the street: Michelangelo Antonioni's and Haskell Wexler's. Not altogether unfamiliar with the territory, cinematographer Wexler was born in Chicago in 1922 and had shot *The Best Man* for Franklin Schaffner. But *Medium Cool* was an even riskier project than *Maidstone*—one that Wexler had remortgaged his home to finance. Although, according to the filmmaker, the entire script—which concerns the radicalization of a callow TV news cameraman—was written in advance, he shot a number of quasidocumentary scenes at Resurrection City in Washington, DC, as well as at the RFK funeral. Once the production returned to Chicago, George Stevens Jr. secured Wexler a limited convention pass. "So many of the guys in my crew had long hair, the cops thought it was all a hippie plot," the filmmaker recalled. In addition, Wexler filmed National Guardsmen in the midst of riot training, an apartment full of black militants, the Roller Derby, and the Mothers of Invention performing at a local rock club. The filmmaker maintained that, for the entire seven-week Chicago shoot, he was under surveillance by some combination of the police, Army, and secret service—and, adding another level of reality, they frequently shot him shooting.

●   ●   ●

For Haskell Wexler, television trafficked in sensation and promoted passivity. *Medium Cool* opens with a scene in which a TV crew first tapes a car wreck and only then decides to call an ambulance. To the degree that *Medium Cool* has a narrative, it concerns the adventures of the cameraman, John (Robert Forster), seen at one point frolicking with a girlfriend beneath a Tet Photo poster. Still, John believes in an independent press, and after discovering that the television station for which he works is making his tapes available to the cops, he blows up and gets fired. This enforced leisure allows him time to further raise his class awareness, hanging out with Eileen (Verna Bloom), a recent migrant from West Virginia who has a small son and a fondness for RFK. Then, John gets a freelance gig to cover the DemCon.

Wednesday, August 28: the convention approaches critical mass. Ted Kennedy makes it clear that he will neither allow himself to be drafted as an anti-Humphrey candidate nor join Humphrey's ticket as vice president. Thomas Whiteside, a print journalist covering the TV journalists, reports a peculiar symbiosis, noting that after a few hours of network correspondents talking up Kennedy's candidacy, hand-lettered DRAFT TED KENNEDY signs dutifully materialized on the convention floor. "When the signs appeared, the television cameras that were endlessly panning around the hall searched them out as visual confirmation of the so-called boom."

As the peace plank introduced by Democratic opponents of the war is defeated, war breaks out between CBS and Daley's security. In a repetition of the previous night's broadcast, when correspondent Dan Rather was punched and thrown to the floor by a plainclothes security man, reporter Mike Wallace is shoved while reporting the on-air arrest of a New York delegate. "I think we've got a bunch of thugs here!" exclaims anchor Walter Cronkite on air from his sky booth. Meanwhile, after someone raises a red flag at the Mobe rally in Grant Park, the police attack. Battling back, the crowd is bottled up, trapped, and tear-gassed. This is the climax of *Medium Cool*, with Eileen wandering through the melee wondering what it's all about. "The whole world is watching," demonstrators shout, begging the NBC camera crew to "stay with us." Dodging army tanks, Eileen acts like Alice in Wonderland. "Look out, Haskell, it's real!" someone yells off-camera. (Hit full on with tear gas, the filmmaker will be blinded for twenty-four hours.) Some manage to escape onto Michigan Avenue, where, with surreal timing, the Reverend Ralph Abernathy is leading a mule train to dramatize the Poor People's Campaign. Then the protestors are cornered in front of the Hilton. It is five minutes to eight. TV floodlights are turned on—the street, per one CBS man, transformed into a "movie set"—as all hell breaks loose.

The attack, per Mailer, is "sudden, unprovoked, and total." From his Olympian vantage point on the nineteenth floor, White scribbles impressions: "Like a piston exploding from its chamber, comes a hurtling column of police." The cops are clubbing demonstrators, reporters, even passers-by, to the ground. Some get pushed through a ground-floor window—breaking the glass, the Diggers might say. Gazing down from his Hilton window, Mailer watches "children, and youths, and middle-aged men and women being pounded and clubbed and gassed and beaten."

> It was as if the war had finally begun, and this was therefore a great and solemn moment, as if indeed even the gods of history had come together from each side to choose the very front of the Hilton Hotel before the television cameras of the world and the eyes of the campaign workers and the delegates' wives, yes, there before half the principals at the convention was this drama played. . . .

Guerrilla theater will never again achieve this scale. As in *Medium Cool* (or Vietnam), the media is radicalized by its very presence. But although demonstrators chant, "The whole world is watching," the riot is not televised live. As McCarthy's name is placed in nomination, word arrives at master control that downtown Chicago is "blowing up." Some seven commercials later, the first videotape of the violence outside the Hilton is broadcast with Cronkite's avuncular commentary: "There seems to be a minister in trouble with the police, they're manhandling him pretty severely. . . . There seems to be a wounded man there."

An hour after the attack, another seventeen-minute clip is shown, preempting Cleveland mayor Carl Stokes's speech seconding Humphrey's nomination. Forty minutes later, CBS telecasts a videotape shot by a mobile unit in Grant Park. "There has been a display of naked violence in the streets of

Chicago," Cronkite announced, adding that a CBS eyewitness termed the melee unprovoked, "police just charged the demonstrators, swinging at the crowd indiscriminately." (Thereafter, the networks punctuate the convention oratory with reaction shots of Daley.) At 11:47, Humphrey is nominated, the National Guard positioned outside the hall with machine guns.*

The following day, McCarthy addresses the demonstrators in Grant Park. Dick Gregory leads a march that, turned back on Michigan Avenue, has a violent confrontation with the National Guard. As protestors hang Daley in effigy, the delegates are shown a short movie on RFK: "Even dead and on film, he was better and more moving than anything which had happened in their convention, and people were crying," Mailer would report. Humphrey delivers his acceptance speech, but the Chicago police have the last word and cap the week by bursting into McCarthy headquarters for a predawn raid on the mainly sleeping campaign workers.

●   ●   ●

Chicago's mayor justified the police riot by invoking history's secret force. He was, he claimed, acting on a discovered plot to assassinate Hubert Humphrey, Eugene McCarthy, and himself. But this scenario paled by comparison to the one Abbie Hoffman and his cohorts had broadcast to the world—described years later by Yippie organizer Jim Fouratt as a "bloodbath" staged for TV.

> It was very few people and it looked like a billion people on television and it played in history as an epic moment. . . . Chicago was exactly what [Abbie] always wanted it to be, a media event.

---

*Theodore White would complain that "delayed intercutting created the most striking and false political picture of 1968—the nomination of a man for the American Presidency by the brutality and violence of merciless police." But if the violence in downtown Chicago is accentuated for being reported in the context of more decorous happenings on the convention floor, TV coverage of the mayhem demonstrably alters the mood. When Senator Abraham Ribicoff denounces Daley in his speech nominating McCarthy, cameras show Daley mouthing obscenities in response.

A few days later, Hoffman wrote *Revolution for the Hell of It*, which described the Festival of Life as a spectacle produced by Marshall McLuhan and directed by Mayor Daley and Antonin Artaud.

The Election: Calling *Coogan's Bluff*

A mere four years after the Goldwater debacle, Democrats had replaced Republicans as the party of extremism and seemed destined for a comparable defeat. The Labor Day Gallup poll put Richard Nixon at 43 percent. Hubert Humphrey was at 31 percent and George Wallace at 19 percent. As the Democrats left Chicago, some proposed that Eugene McCarthy's star delegate, Paul Newman, pick up the gauntlet. In early September, a few McCarthy advisers met to explore the senator's return for an independent run.

And then there was a party not on the ballot: the party of *Bonnie and Clyde*. SDS had received tremendous publicity—not all of it negative. In late September, *Newsweek* published a special report on "campus rebels." The next month, *Life* profiled "The Defiant Voices of S.D.S." SDS membership was conservatively estimated at between 80,000 and 100,000. The new academic year brought a dozen new college and high school chapters; the National Office was swamped with applications. At the University of Michigan, 200 showed up for the term's first SDS meeting. Their mood was militant and memory of the DemCon fresh.

The students demanded action. Impatient with the current SDS leadership, the most militant announced a new caucus, named for the most celebrated of American social bandits. The Jesse James Gang (which included future Weathermen Bill Ayers and Terry Robbins) was committed to "aggressive confrontation politics." A month of disruptive meetings resulted in two rival SDS chapters. This schism—at the very university that hosted the key SDS teach-in of 1965—was prophetic, coinciding with the hard-line Progressive Labor Party's infiltration of SDS in New York, Boston, and California.

Investigating the connection between the Chicago demonstrations and international Communism, HUAC subpoenaed a number of Mobe and Yippie leaders. The hearings convened October 1 with Jerry Rubin as first witness. "I was dressed as a world revolutionary," he recalled. "Beret, buttons, rifle, bare-chested. I got Vietcong pants from [SDS militant] Bernadine Dohrn, straight from the Vietcong." Rubin also wore a bandolier of live cartridges. Although these were confiscated, he was permitted to keep his toy M-16. On the second day, Abbie Hoffman went his Yippie associate one better, showing up in a custom-made American flag shirt an irate Washington cop ripped from his back as he entered the congressional office building. In addition to his other credits, Hoffman was now the first to be arrested under a new federal flag-desecration statute.

A *Fortune* survey taken in October showed a million kids identifying with the New Left. Some *Fortune* readers might have blanched but not Twentieth Century Fox chairman Darryl Zanuck. For, according to the survey, Che Gue-vara was more popular on campus than LBJ, Nixon, Humphrey, and Wallace. The dead revolutionary was a campus demigod and Zanuck had him! Back in May, with the Cannes Film Festival shut down by militant students, matinee idol Omar Sharif was playing in a bridge tournament on the Cote d'Azur. Looking up from his cards, the Egyptian profile spotted "two dusty, haggard-looking creatures" climbing out of a "big car with German license plates." Sharif recognized his supplicants as Zanuck and director Richard Fleischer. "Three times before they'd offered me the part of Che Guevera. I'd turned it down three times." Finally, Sharif submitted to the demands of history, which evidently included a sense of solidarity with his fellow Third World superstar. Sharif stipulated that his contract contain a special "conscience clause"—Che's integrity or lack of same would be guaranteed by the actor himself.

Now *Che* was in production. FILM ABOUT GUEVARA A BOON TO PUERTO RICO, the *New York Times* reported in November. John Leonard's dispatch, published a month later in the *New York Times Magazine*, noted that Fox's production budget was bigger than Castro's. "It costs more to make a movie about a revolution than it does to make a revolution . . . about $10,000 an hour." Like *Maidstone's, Che's* set was filled with reporters: "It's exactly as if something important was going on," Leonard joked. This "symphony of green fatigues" might be the radical students and dropouts who massed daily on Berkeley's Telegraph Avenue.

Che was the first movie fifty-nine-year-old Sy Bartlett produced since his 1963 SAC tribute *A Gathering of Eagles.* The fifty-four-year-old screenwriter Michael Wilson—once upon a time the leader of Hollywood's beleaguered Communist Party—had survived the blacklist to rebuild his career on uncredited work for Sam Spiegel. Richard Fleischer, the fifty-two-year-old director of twenty-six movies in all genres, had no such political past. "No one had ever heard of Che Guevara until he died," he told Leonard, imbuing his subject with the posthumous superstardom of adolescent idol James Dean. Accordingly, *Che* opens with the image of the hero's corpse, swathed in mysterious mutterings and intercut with images of Third World children. Various witnesses are heard. One compares Che to a "Hindu holy man."

Demonstrating the revisionist power of a dead hero, *Che* suggests that Fidel (a clownish, overbearing Jack Palance) ripped off Che's ideas and persona. A tough guy who can shoot a traitor point-blank and talk strategy even as he yanks out Fidel's aching tooth, Che is so disgusted by the Missile Crisis that he insults the Soviet ambassador and turns off the sound when Fidel goes on TV. Ultimately, Che equates yanqui and Soviet imperialism. "I've had enough," he tells Castro. The Beard begs him to stay, but Che is unmoved. "You want to build socialism on one flea-speck in the Caribbean?" he sneers before leaving for Bolivia, where he will die, betrayed by those he wished to liberate. The last word is given to the old peon who, hating both Che and the government, had informed the authorities. "Why do people in your country flock to see a dead gangster?" Why indeed?

When this cautiously pandering bore premiered in the spring of 1969, *Variety* deemed it less anti-Communist than anti-Che, suggesting that "were the Nixon Administration to consider a rapprochement with Castro, they could hardly hope for a better film to 'prepare' the American people." The Left, however, was outraged. *Rat,* the New York underground weekly edited by former SDS honcho Jeff Shero, devoted its May 16, 1969, issue to the movie—

CHE! STOLEN FROM THE GRAVE—printing an annotated "liberated script" that a "disgusted" Fox employee had furnished the paper. In any case, *Che* was a box-office disaster. One morning at 4 AM, during its opening week, someone lobbed a hand grenade into Loews Orpheum. The gesture was superfluous.

•   •   •

Che's protagonist was the Sixties' lamest Hollywood Freedom Fighter, embalmed in a tediously self-important and old-fashioned bio-pic. The stiffly portrayed revolutionary bore scant relation to glamorous outlaws like Bonnie and Clyde, let alone the pop-star demagogue Max Frost. Moreover, *Che* seemed impervious to the disorder and delirium that made it seem a viable property.

More attuned to the moment were Don Siegel's *Coogan's Bluff* and Andy Warhol's *Lonesome Cowboys*—self-consciously contemporary Westerns, produced during the winter 1968 crisis of Cowboy Authority and premiered during the campaign's dispirited final weeks, that made a travesty of the genre, presenting it as a form of Pop Art.

Siegel described his film as a "fish out of water" story; the same was true of *Lonesome Cowboys*, the first Warhol movie shot west of the Hudson. Both movies were predicated on recognizing the West as a fantasy realm, each inverting the other: In *Coogan's Bluff*, an Arizona deputy sheriff (Clint Eastwood) is dispatched to New York City to extradite an LSD-crazed hippie fugitive; in *Lonesome Cowboys*, a gaggle of New York "degenerates" visit Arizona to enact their own particular sort of Western.

A familiar figure in the long-running, cattle-drive TV series *Rawhide* (CBS, 1959–66), Eastwood made three Westerns for Italian director Sergio Leone during the mid 1960s, achieving international icon status as the grungy, nameless bounty hunter in *A Fistful of Dollars*, *For a Few Dollars More*, and *The Good, the Bad, and the Ugly*. Like the Beatles and the Sony Trinitron, these "spaghetti" Westerns partook of an international American pop culture—although they were both more abstract and violently naturalistic than current Hollywood equivalents. Bosley Crowther had bracketed *For a Few Dollars More* with *The Dirty Dozen* as evidence of the new cine-sadism in his summer 1967 run-up to *Bonnie and Clyde*. By then, Eastwood was back to make his first Hollywood vehicle, *Hang 'Em High*. Released—and attacked for its mayhem—a year later, the movie was still playing when *Coogan's Bluff* opened October 2 by threatening the residents of America's most liberal city: CLINT EASTWOOD GIVES NEW YORK 24 HOURS . . . TO GET OUT OF TOWN. (That same day, Mexico City police fired on a student demonstration, killing some 200. The Year of the Barricades was not yet over.)

Coogan's Bluff quickly establishes the Eastwood character's mastery of the wilderness, personified by the renegade Navajo, Running Bear [sic]. The deputy tracks, tricks, and traps the Indian—then gratuitously knocks him down. This vengeful pattern is elaborated once Coogan is dispatched to the city to bring back Running Bear's equivalent, the longhaired killer, Ringerman. That Eastwood's Arizona deputy is in some sense a parody Westerner is reinforced by his reception in the land of filthy streets and even dirtier-mouthed kooks. Coogan is cheated by cabbies, insulted by hookers, camped on by homos, and attacked by Ringerman's aggressive, vaguely Jewish mother. He is dismissed by a hostile black detective as "Buffalo Bill in a fancy hat" and chastised by Susan Clark's bleeding-heart probation officer, a misguided feminist unable to recognize a real man when she sees one. Coogan is even arrested for impersonating a cop. Nevertheless, the Westerner remains an ideal—at least compared to these denizens of the urban jungle.

Lonesome Cowboys opens with another sort of tussle in the Arizona wilderness. Viva, the film's lone female, and Tom Hompertz, cast as its universal object of desire, embrace naked in the sagebrush. As this is a Warhol film, their lovemaking is explicit but desultory. Later, Viva and her "nurse" (Taylor Mead) stroll through an empty frontier town. Five mounted cowboys approach, and Viva appraises their leader (Louis Waldon) as New York's hardboiled whores did Eastwood in his Western drag: "I think he's wearing makeup." Much of *Lonesome Cowboys* is a literal camping trip, but the movie has a documentary quality. Some of this is self-reflexive: "Stop it! You're gonna hit the tape recorder!" one crewmember yells as Viva is thrown to the ground by Waldon's boys. Other scenes are spontaneously authentic: The gang-rape, beer breakfasts, pot smoking, and wrestling matches the cowboys engage in suggest ordinary behavior ordinarily repressed by Hollywood Westerns.

Lonesome Cowboys' location was often described as a ghost town—a location *Newsday*'s Joseph Gelmis found "unintentionally significant." In fact, it was shot in Old Tucson, the same set that served as McLintock, Arizona. For Gelmis, Warhol's "amoral fun and games" signified the end of the Western: "The past is dead. The myths are being perverted. The inheritors are like a race of mutants who have lost their humanity and regressed to primitive conscious-ness." In other words, the Indians had captured the fort. "It was misty the day we started shooting," per Warhol.

> The dialogue the boys were coming out with was going along the lines of "You dirty cocksucking motherfucker, what the hell is wrong with you?" and in the middle of this type of thing, we saw that they were bringing a bunch of tourists in, announcing "You're about to see a movie in production . . ." Then the group of sightseers marched in to "You fags! You queers! I'll show you who's the real cowboy around here, goddam it!" They started going nuts, rushing their kids away and everything.
>
> Eventually, the grips, the electricians, and the people who built the sets formed a vigilante committee to run us out of town, just like in a real cowboy movie. . . . They monitored every move we made. The sheriff came in a heli-copter and stood on top of the water tower with binoculars, watching to see if anybody took their clothes off. Pretty soon we just left, it got to be too much of a hassle to work there.

Unbeknownst to Warhol, the sheriff had notified the Federal Bureau of Investigation, and as a result of these wild shenanigans, the FBI began a file on Warhol and *Lonesome Cowboys*, including a detailed account of its world premiere at the San Francisco Film Festival on November 1, four days before the election.*

---

*Even before their release, the disco Westerns *Lonesome Cowboys* and *Coogan's Bluff* were synthesized in John Schlesinger's *Midnight Cowboy*, adapted from James Leo Herlihy's

•   •   •

In *Coogan's Bluff*, the acme of social disintegration is the hero's visit to a psychedelic disco called The Pigeon-Toed Orange Peel. In this Hollywood vision
of Andy Warhol's multimedia Exploding Plastic Inevitable—shot on Universal's
largest soundstage with 125 extras and 400 hippies—movies are projected upon
the walls, the floor lights up, and bare-chested boys cavort with girls nude
beneath their Day-Glo body paint. This chaos is contagious. *Coogan's Bluff* has
little moral gravity—and was, indeed, condemned as "socially irresponsible"
by the National Catholic Office for Motion Pictures. Coogan triumphs through
a combination of illegal and unethical means. He lies to the NYPD, rifles a
therapist's personal files, and exacts information by seducing a zonked-out hippie chick—sitar-accompanied sex on the crash pad floor! But whatever the
cowboy does, the system is even worse.

The day *Coogan's Bluff* opened in New York, George Wallace was at his
absolute height—battling City Hall for the right to hold a rally at Shea Stadium.
John Wayne was so enthusiastic that he sent the Wallace campaign three
checks for $10,000—the last inscribed, in the phrase of the day, "sock it to 'em,

---

1965 novel. The naive would-be gigolo, Joe Buck (Jon Voight, in a role Warren Beatty
supposedly campaigned for) leaves Texas to wind up hustling New York's 42nd Street
and bonding with Ratso Rizzo (Dustin Hoffman), a filthy, tubercular petty thief. Like
the suburban squares who once rented beatniks to enliven their cocktail parties, Schlesinger hired a gaggle of Warhol regulars to grace the film's requisite pot orgy of depravity. (Adding to the craziness, the movie was on location in New York when Andy
was shot in June 1968.)

Midnight Cowboy pushed the Camelot post-Western further into dress-up and travesty. If *The Misfits* and *Lonely Are the Brave* intimated the Western's demise, *Midnight
Cowboy* presented its props as pure masquerade. "That's faggot stuff," Ratso sneers of
Buck's rodeo ensemble. The aspiring hustler is amazed: "John Wayne—you gonna tell
me he's a fag?" This exchange, not found in the novel, may be the revenge of once-
blacklisted screenwriter Waldo Salt on the personification of Hollywood anti-
Communism. *Midnight Cowboy* would be highly decorated—winning Best Picture and
two other Oscars, despite being the first major studio production released with an X.
Perhaps the extent of the Academy's anxiety over the movie's unwholesome implications was assuaged by the simultaneous honoring of Wayne as Best Actor for *True Grit*.

George." The late-September polls reduced Hubert Humphrey's support by three points—and gave two of them to the Alabama governor. At this rate, Wallace would have 30 percent by Election Day. Moreover, with a seemingly impregnable hold on eleven Southern states and perhaps 170 electoral votes, his base appeared secure. Now, like Lee marching toward Gettysburg, Wallace invaded the North.

This was the rock 'n' roll campaign. As noted by a team of British journalists in their 1968 campaign history *American Melodrama*, Wallace rallies infused "revivalist excitement" with the "perfume of erotic adventure." Jan-Neen Welch left her advertising agency job in Hammond, Indiana, to join the Wallace caravan when it passed through town in mid-August. A voluptuous blonde dressed as a gold-lamé cowgirl, Jan-Neen offered a kiss for each $20 campaign contribution, inaugurating the fund-raising by caressing the microphone and inviting all red-blooded men to STAND UP FOR AMERICA and enlist in the crusade: "I want you for the Wallace rebellion!" Having enlisted the Duke and the Dodge Rebellion, Wallace's campaign appropriated "The Battle Hymn of the Republic":

> He stands up for law and order, the policeman on the beat.
> He will make it safe to once again walk safely on the street.
> He'll uproot the seeds of treason, he'll restore the courts of law
> So justice can prevail.
> Won't you stand up with George Wallace!
> Won't you stand up with George Wallace!
> Won't you stand up with George Wallace!
> So all men can be free!

Unlike his rivals, Wallace appreciated the value of antiwar protestors. He thrived on melees between his supporters and the hecklers who pelted him with everything from rocks and eggs to peace medallions and miniature whiskey bottles. (TV crews knew to employ two cameras—one for Wallace, the other to cover his brawling audience.) Hippie-baiting was part of the act: "Come on down. I'll autograph your sandals," Wallace taunted longhairs. "Hey

sweetie pie! Oh sorry, I thought it was a she." Why do the established parties
"kowtow to these anarchists?" he wondered. "One laid down in front of President Johnson's limousine last year. The first time they lie down in front of
my limousine it'll be the last time. . . ."

Thursday, October 24, Wallace came to Madison Square Garden. The arena
was ringed by 3,000 police—some thought security even tighter than at Chicago. The scene was a magnet for crazies. A klavern of Klansmen up from
Louisiana took their place beside a platoon of Minutemen and a cell of American Nazis. Two thousand, mainly youthful, protestors, some carrying signs
reading FREE HUEY! SMASH WALLACE!, taunted the cops with cries of "Sieg Heil."
At least twenty-five were arrested in scuffles with police; at one point, a group
of kids stormed a Wallace bus from Long Island. Wallace hats and Confederate
flags were wrested from the Alabaman's partisans and set aflame with cries of
"Burn baby burn." Inside the Garden, the 17,000 supporters waved their dime-
store Stars and Bars and screamed for "White Power." Their numbers included
gun-packing off-duty cops. The *New York Times* reporter who questioned one
was told that "Wallace is the only guy who stands for law and order; he's
telling it like it is. I'm a cop, and 80 per cent of the force is for him." As was
their custom, Wallace's people had handed tickets to a hundred white longhairs
and black demonstrators. In one ugly outbreak, a dozen Wallace supporters
attacked a small group led by the pastor of a Harlem church, shouting, "Hey
niggers, get out of here!"

Suddenly, the Pigeon-Toed Orange Peel: Madison Square Garden rocked
on its foundation as Wallace appeared—a tumultuous welcome bringing him
eight times to the flag-bedecked stage's edge. "I've been waiting to fight the
main event in the Garden for a long time," he quipped. Speaking without a
text from behind a bulletproof lectern, the exultant candidate assured the
crowd he would not spend their taxes "to educate students to raise money for
the Communists." Then he removed his jacket, bobbing and weaving across
the stage like the bantam-weight fighter he'd been in his youth.

Right fist clenched, left fist jabbing, Wallace delivered a flurry of punchlines: "We don't have a sick society, we have a sick Supreme Court. We ought to register Communists, not guns. We ought to turn this country over to the police for two or three years and everything would be all right." The crowd was ecstatic. "We don't have riots in Alabama," Wallace shouted above the din, effacing the memory of Birmingham and Selma. "They start a riot down there, first one to pick up a brick gets a bullet in the brain!"

•   •   •

George Wallace received over a dozen standing ovations, but his New York rally was a last hurrah. As a political phenomenon, he was already over. For much of the campaign, the Alabaman ran without a vice presidential candidate. (His first choices were J. Edgar Hoover, who ignored him, and Texas governor John Connally, who mulled the possibility, waiting until late October to endorse Humphrey.) Then, October 3, Wallace presented his old commander, General Curtis LeMay, and plunged from his pinnacle of menace.

Wallace's campaign could not recover from LeMay's threat to bomb North Vietnam back to the Stone Age. Within a week, Humphrey supporters salted a *Dr. Strangelove* telecast with an ad citing Richard Nixon's opposition to the nuclear nonproliferation treaty. Then the Democrats revived the nuclear bomb ads of 1964, captioning a mushroom cloud in psychedelic color with the slogan "Humphrey, there is no alternative." By mid-October, Wallace's polls dropped from 20 percent to 15 percent, most of the shift coming from Northern and border states, as Humphrey rose by nearly the same percentage. Nixon began to woo Wallace supporters with attacks on busing to achieve school integration.

One of the most heavily advertised products on television, Nixon had been working on his TV skills as well as honing his relevance. Gore Vidal was amused when the Republican candidate used his acceptance speech to enjoin the great majority of nondemonstrators "to see it like it is and tell it like it is." Reporting on the RepCon for the *New York Review of Books*, Vidal noted the phrase was "just slightly wrong for now," but imagined that, for Nixon, it "must sound positively raunchy," as though he were hanging out in Vegas with Frank Sinatra. After reappropriating the two-finger V-for-Victory sign from the antiwar movement, the so-called New Nixon stunned America by intoning "Sock it to ME?" on the season premiere of the top-rated *Rowan & Martin's Laugh-In*—his cameo followed by a paid endorsement from faded pop singer Connie Francis.*

A month later, after *Laugh-In* was featured on *Time*'s cover, the Republicans revisited the show with a political spot that offered an abbreviated version of the Goldwater campaign's infamous *Choice*. Abbie Hoffman had called Chicago "an advertisement for revolution." The Republican commercial took him at his word: A ridiculously ebullient Humphrey was juxtaposed with footage of Chicago streetfighting, as well as Vietnam, accompanied by "There'll Be a Hot Time in the Old Town Tonight" and, as a punch-line, the old LBJ exhortation to "vote like your whole world depended on it."

In the end, the election—like the DemCon—was defined by absence. Dion's pop dirge "Abraham, Martin, and John," replete with reference to "my old friend Bobby," peaked in November at number four. The streets, however, were quiet and turnout lighter than anticipated. For a brief moment, Humphrey led in the vote totals—but it was soon apparent that a constitutional crisis was averted. Whatever the popular vote, Nixon would win the Electoral College. The final results gave him 43.4 percent to Humphrey's 42.7 percent. Wallace received only 13.5 percent; his thirty-nine electoral votes far from forcing a deadlock. Close as the election was, some Democrats suspected that— encouraged by the opportunism of then-LBJ policy adviser Henry Kissinger— the South Vietnamese had insured a Republican victory by deliberately sabotaging the Paris peace talks.

No Future: The Children of *Bonnie and Clyde*

The Hollywood Western seemed as though it might be played out during the Kennedy administration, but five years of Lyndon Johnson brought the genre back from the grave: *Major Dundee* abroad, *The Chase* at home. The Great Cowboy left the White House in January 1969 at the peak of U.S. involvement

---

*Nixon's single line reportedly required five takes.

in Vietnam. Back in the World—short for Real World, as the 542,000 service-men pursuing the Viet Cong Sierra Charriba called the United States—almost everyone was living some form of the LBJ-LSD Western.

Dodge City was universal, along with the Dodge Rebellion. Frontier may-hem was popularly understood as national narrative's central trope. The Na-tional Commission on the Causes and Prevention of Violence report, published in June 1969, argued that American history was predicated upon "a series of violent upheavals." That same month, the cover of *New Left Notes* featured two young men, black and white, crouched together on a rooftop above a burning city, both armed with automatic rifles.*

The fourth and fifth largest hits of 1967, *Bonnie and Clyde* and *The Dirty Dozen* mixed ultraviolence with blatant anti-authoritarianism. And as *The Dirty Dozen* spawned a cycle of crypto Vietnam War movies concerning pariah groups sent on morally ambiguous missions, *Bonnie and Clyde* engendered a number of vehicles for the Righteous Outlaw, including the movie—opening June 28, 1969—that *Variety* opined the "most violent U.S. film ever made." *The Wild Bunch*, in which a collection of aging gunfighters jump from the frying pan of the closed American frontier into the fire of the Mexican revolution, synthesized *Bonnie and Clyde* and *The Dirty Dozen*. Sam Peckinpah imbued a twilight Western with war-movie carnage, manifesting a new license regarding the representation of sex, use of language, and extent of permissive movie-star behavior in Third World countries. Dirtier (and far less attractive) than the Barrow Gang, devoid of even token Magnificent Seven altruism, his movie's antiheroes were mercenaries, counterinsurgents, invaders, and rebels. And the only freedom for which they fought was their own.

Village Voice critic Andrew Sarris praised *The Wild Bunch* as one of the few recent movies that didn't seem "concocted by a market-research computer." The opening sequence was a case in point—children playfully torturing insects,

---

*Meanwhile, the Museum of Modern Art concluded a retrospective on the postwar Hollywood action movie—having dropped the rubric "Violent America" after one dis-tributor refused to furnish prints for presentation in a program so called.

bank robbers disguised as American soldiers, hostages forced to sing John Ford's favorite hymn, "Now Let Us Gather By the River," the Temperance Union marching smack into the middle of an elaborate stakeout that makes clear the entire town is being sacrificed to the interests of a railroad company.

More passionate and convulsive than *Major Dundee*, *The Wild Bunch* evokes a Mexico of dusky whores and tequila sunsets. This is the real Oriental Western, the last New Frontier. "I came to Mexico to look for a new idea of man," Antonin Artaud wrote, and as a wise old peon tells the Bunch leader, Pike (William Holden), "We all dream of being a child again, even the worst of us. The worst of us most of all." All is permitted under the regime of the bandit-general Mapache (Emilio Fernández), ranging from the innocent orgy of two Bunch members and three fat, compliant señoritas splashing around in a wine vat, to the more complicated and brutal joke wherein Angel, the Bunch's token Mexican member, sees his "woman" with Mapache and shoots her dead as she licks the lobe of the old monster's ear.

The savage Mapache makes *The Magnificent Seven*'s Calvera seem like an ascetic philosopher king. Whereas his protection-racket parodies state power, the anarchic Bunch claim no such official status. On the contrary. As Pike's lieutenant, Dutch (Ernest Borgnine), explains, "We don't hang nobody!" Bunch code is founded upon the pragmatic camaraderie that obliges them to return for Angel after he is captured by Mapache, insuring that the climax of this greatest LBJ (which is to say, Vietnam) Western would be one more version of the Alamo— gallant Americans fighting to the last man against Mexican hordes. But where in this scenario was a role for the John Wayne thing? The Cowboy Warrior played the obsessive Indian-hating racist Ethan Edwards in *The Searchers*; he could have portrayed Major Dundee. Those were men of vengeance and justifiable homicide. The Duke, however, never killed an innocent bystander.

Had there ever been an American Western in which humanity was so consistently venal, cowardly, and cruel as in *The Wild Bunch*? The law is represented by the railroad company; its agents are moronic bounty hunters riding behind the unwilling ex-convict Deke Thornton (Robert Ryan). The Bunch are less like Wayne's Green Berets than the Comanches that Wayne battled in *The*

Searchers; they kill their own wounded and leave them unburied. Western morality is obliterated. In this scenario, there are no good guys. A postscript shows Thornton recruited to the Mexican revolution, but this faint echo of *Magnificent Seven* idealism glosses *The Wild Bunch*'s real pleasures—the thrill of invasion and massacre of foreigners.*

•   •   •

Summer 1969 replayed "1968" most programmatically with the oracular *Easy Rider*, which—both within Hollywood and without—presented itself as generational statement and outlaw vision of the Great Society. Reveling in countercultural values, *Easy Rider* featured drugs, sex, and rock 'n' roll, as well as guerrilla theater, communes, and the *I Ching*—not to mention the sort of brown-rice millennialism predicting civilization's imminent collapse and the fatalistic sense that longhaired freaks would have to fight for their lives against George Wallace's killer redneck straights. This apocalyptic scenario was, of course, a fervent desire. Yet, made by two children of the dream life, *Easy Rider* felt like a caper. In interviews, director Dennis Hopper stressed that his Billy and Peter Fonda's Wyatt (aka Captain America) represented a fundamentally criminal society and embodied a spurious freedom. Was Hopper speaking of the movie industry?

---

*The Wild Bunch consolidated the inversion of values initiated by *Bonnie and Clyde*—as did the enormously popular *Butch Cassidy and the Sundance Kid*, which, opening in September, would be the year's top box-office attraction. Butch (Paul Newman) and Sundance (Robert Redford), the glamorous heroes of George Roy Hill's insipid twilight Western, are whimsical hipsters—the *nouvelle vague* ménage à trois they establish with schoolteacher Katherine Ross suggests a gutless *Jules and Jim*. Sepia-tinted and interspersed with old movie footage, *Butch Cassidy* is less brutal than *The Wild Bunch* in presenting the unregenerate criminal as sympathetic and expressing regret at his elimination. The state and its agents are far more abhorrent than the killers and lawbreakers they pursue.

Like *The Wild Bunch*, *Butch Cassidy* winds up south of the border, in Bolivia. The boys haven't killed anyone—they've been robbing banks in pidgin Spanish—but these expatriated Americans are naturally tougher, as well as technologically more advanced, than the locals. A regiment of Bolivian soldiers is required to dispatch the two gringos— image freezing on their mad dash for freedom—just as the Wild Bunch take an entire Mexican army with them when they go.

Wyatt and Billy were freaks and heads and true Americans on the road with rock 'n' roll. Arthur Penn's *Alice's Restaurant*, released five weeks later, was milder in its emphasis on motorcycles and marijuana, less fearful than contemptuous of small-town America. Perhaps in reaction to *Bonnie and Clyde*, Penn sought to demystify the Outlaw glamour that *The Wild Bunch* and *Easy Rider* took for granted. A movie of fretted instruments rather than acid rock, *Alice's Restaurant* evoked the passé pre-folk-rock scene of 1965. Longhaired troubadour Arlo Guthrie (playing himself) becomes vulnerable to the draft after he's kicked out of college somewhere out West and, in another flight from the frontier, returns east to join a commune in Stockbridge, Massachusetts. In part, the movie dramatizes Guthrie's original ballad—an anti-authoritarian satire in which Arlo's arrest for illegally dumping the garbage left over from a Thanksgiving feast has the unintended but fortunate effect of criminalizing him and thus rendering him unfit for the army (and, not incidentally, making him a star).

A second narrative concerns the failed community created by manic Ray (James Broderick) and earth mother Alice (Pat Quinn) around the deconsecrated church they've purchased in Stockbridge. Alice and Ray are, according to the formulation Yale professor Charles Reich had begun to develop, attempting to establish a new group "consciousness"—or collective fantasy. Hipster parents to a hippie brood, they are a domesticated Bonnie and Clyde whose Renaissance Fair remarriage is the most benign of orgies—a zonked jam. Penn directed this saga from the perspective of an empathetic outsider, and in *The New Republic*, Stanley Kauffmann complained that, just as *Easy Rider* presented Peter Fonda as a "young sage-martyr," Penn's movie uncritically bought "all the hippie tenets of innate superiority and purity." *Easy Rider* was a lifestyle advertisement—an invitation for a generation to dress up and play Davy Crockett once more. More detached, *Alice's Restaurant* was the recording of that desire.*

---

*Penn's movie is too distanced to approach *Easy Rider*'s classic howlers, most delivered by sanctimonious Fonda. "You do your own thing in your own time," he solemnly

Shot during the exhausted final months of the Johnson presidency rather than the crazy post-Tet spring, *Alice's Restaurant* is more dispirited than *Easy Rider*. Still, equally devoid of political analysis and deep in political denial, both movies articulate a general sense of failure. "You know this used to be a hell of a good country," reflects the *Easy Rider* straight man played by Jack Nicholson. "I don't know what went wrong with it." Kauffmann mocked the snowy graveyard scene in *Alice's Restaurant* in which folk chanteuse Joni Mitchell sang "Songs to Aging Children" while the commune's resident junkie was laid to rest "as if some special holy innocence were being committed to the earth." Why, the critic wondered, was he any more a martyr than a dead "Puerto Rican slum-dweller or a Bowery derelict?" The reason was that this self-destructive youth represented the righteous promise of an entire generation—already understood as doomed.

Penn cited the hippies' burden, having grown up on the Eve of Destruction under the shadow of the atomic bomb: "Nobody makes any mention of it. But it's the bottom line for a certain instability, the sense that the world really may not be there on a given day, if Curtis LeMay has his way." In *Easy Rider*, the sense of narcissistic paranoia is clinched by Roger McGuinn's rendition of Bob Dylan's "It's Alright Ma (I'm Only Bleeding)" moments before outlaws Wyatt and Billy are dispatched to oblivion by their vigilante doppelgängers—a fate linking them to Martin Luther King Jr. and Robert Kennedy.

As self-adoring as this show biz martyrdom might be, the *Easy Rider* scenario was characterized by a concern, however selective, with authenticity. As a director, Hopper encouraged improvisation and used non-actors, most extensively in the scene where the protagonists are insulted by the habitués of a

---

informs the rancher who feeds him and his buddy lunch. Fonda has a clear sense of himself as a Hegelian force, granting consciousness and direction to a movement already present in society. Thus he bestows his approval on the hippie commune as well, telling Hopper, "Dig. They're gonna make it." *Alice's Restaurant* is more skeptical. Ray's cry, "We're beautiful and we're doing it," is less self-congratulation than self-delusion. The movie's painful ending has him still dreaming of reinventing his commune, this time in Vermont.

Louisiana diner. With a sure instinct for publicity, Hopper assured the *New York Times* that he, Fonda, and Nicholson were smoking real pot on-camera. Indeed, *Easy Rider*'s dealing scenes struck reviewers as incredibly naturalistic: "When [Fonda] is sniffing the white powder during his first drug transaction, and later, by the edge of the airport where he's selling the stuff [to Phil Spector], it's happening. It's not a movie at all," Archer Winsten marveled in the *New York Post*.

Alice's Restaurant, too, was received as a semidocumentary. The *Saturday Review* claimed to be disoriented at "never being quite sure when fact ends and fiction begins." Penn used amateur performers, including Arlo's nemesis, Officer Obie (William Obanhein), and extras drawn from a group of local hippies known as the Cadre. Meanwhile, the real Alice and Ray were getting divorced and their on-set presence heightened the hyperreality. "As filming went on, people began to accept the movie Alice as the real Alice," screenwriter Venable Herndon noted. "This was sometimes hard on Alice." Co-producer Joe Manduke explained that "the movie became more real to them than a reality which had faded into fantasy. We re-created events which happened to them two or three years ago. Sometimes they broke into tears." It was a Warhol moment. The whole world was watching.

The new naturalism meant telling it like it was. It meant creating one's own reality. But it also meant—as in *Easy Rider, Maidstone,* and the upcoming *Zabriskie Point*—learning to act as though one were living in a movie. Hollywood life-acting: Audience and phantoms dwelt in the same allegorical landscape.

•   •   •

The twilight Westerns of the New Frontier had been recast as youth films. Pondering *Alice's Restaurant, Life* detected a curious nostalgia: "The costumes bring on memories of a young and just-settling America." And, when Arthur Penn asked Arlo Guthrie where he learned the hymn "Amazing Grace," Guthrie informed him that "we sing all the old, old songs of the church and the early settlers."

As at the Red Dog Saloon, hippies returned to the West, outfitted in appropriate get-ups. America was starting over in its mind—this time without slaves or Indian fighters. Penn imagined Arlo and his cohort as pioneers who had no frontier. In retreating from the stockade that was Vietnam, the counterculture preferred to remythologize their heroic forebears as Native Americans. "They love ritual," Penn explained. "They have a lot in common with Indians." (Switching back and forth between Cowboy and Indian, the director was diagramming his next movie, the long-delayed *Little Big Man*.)

The original Americans had been drafted by Black Power activists as archetypal victims of white-supremacist imperialism and praised by New Left theorists as an indigenous alternative, in their tribal social structure, to U.S. capitalism and Soviet totalitarianism. For the counterculture, Indians represented a superior civilization—more organic, spiritual, and communal than white settler society. No less than the Sons of Liberty who perpetrated the Boston Tea Party, the Haight-Ashbury hippies impersonated Native Americans—adopting long hair, headbands, and beads, taking up so-called tribal lifestyles, promoting ecological concerns, and rationalizing the use of marijuana, mescaline, and peyote as Indian sacraments. The Righteous Outlaw was a red man in Abraham Polonsky's *Tell Them Willie Boy Is Here*. Opening soon after the publication of Sioux activist Vine Deloria Jr.'s "Indian manifesto" *Custer Died for Your Sins*, *Willie Boy* was no less polemical in its view of American history.

Directing his first film since 1948, Polonsky told one interviewer that his Western was a cautionary story "intended for young people not yet committed to the disasters of history." A former Communist and longtime blacklistee, the writer-director had been involved in the abortive Yul Brynner adaptation of *The Gladiators* and, briefly, its rival *Spartacus*. *Willie Boy* was, however, a more complicated tract. "Civilization," Polonsky explained, was "the process of despoiling, of spoilation of people, which in the past we considered a victory, but we now suspect is a moral defeat for all." Racism, violence, imperial conquest all figured in Polonsky's modest post-Western. Set in southern California

1909, *Willie Boy* was the allegorical reworking of a fossilized news item—the several-week pursuit of a twenty-six-year-old Chimeheuvis Indian accused of kidnapping his bride after murdering her father. The manhunt becomes additionally sensational with the discovery of the girl's body and the assumption that an alcohol-inflamed Willie Boy has killed her. The incidental drama of a presidential visit (with its inevitable assassination anxiety) feeds the hysteria, amplified by the media into fear of a full-scale Indian revolt.

A literate Old Leftist, Polonsky drew on the precedent of Richard Wright's 1940 novel *Native Son*, with its psycho-socially constructed African-American murderer Bigger Thomas. The movie opens when, having served a month in jail for drunkenness, Willie Boy (Robert Blake) returns home, in time for fiesta, to the Morongo reservation—a sterile parody of white civilization designed to control the Indians that requires no imaginative stretch to conceptualize as the hippie reeducation camp that the protagonists of *Easy Rider* had died to avoid. Blake's Willie Boy is cool, unreconciled, and angry. "Out of step in a white man's world" per the trailer, he is set apart—like Bonnie and Clyde—from the depressing environment by his contemporary attitude. This "man who wouldn't crawl [or] hide his arrogance" experiences racial hostility and responds in kind. Hassled in a pool hall, Willie Boy clobbers whitey with a billiard cue. Nor does he respect tribal elders—shooting his woman Lola's father when the old man arrives, rifle in hand, to catch the couple en flagrante. Make love and war, while you can.

Willie and Lola (played in red-face by Hollywood's leading counter-culture ingénue Katharine Ross) flee to the hills. Meanwhile, egged on by Lola's mentor, Dr. Arnold (Susan Clark, *Coogan's Bluff* probation officer, here promoted to reservation superintendent), the local sheriff, Coop (Robert Redford), organizes a pursuit. One nostalgic member of Coop's posse reminisces about the old-time *Major Dundee* fun of going down to Mexico and bringing back scalps. Son of a celebrated Indian-fighter, Coop is too civilized to fit into this scenario but too civilizing to ignore it. He is the Western lawman who cannot, as Polonsky explained, "develop a new consciousness." In any case, his character's name—an unsubtle reference to Gary, if not

James Fenimore, Cooper—suggests the impossibity of separating national narrative from its mythic representation.

When *Tell Them Willie Boy Is Here* opened in December 1969, *Variety* declared it the "most complex and original American film since *Bonnie and Clyde*," as well as the "closest any American filmmaker has come to the Godard-Pasolini-Duras idea that our present civilization must be destroyed and built anew." *Bonnie and Clyde* prophesied the gun-toting hippie commune on wheels: Armed Love. But, lacking the slightest hint of rock 'n' roll patriotism or folkie nostalgia, Polonsky's film offered no place for fantasy. Hippies notwithstanding, Willie Boy is the last Indian, a one-man guerrilla insurrection. Hence Coop's bitter final line, when criticized for allowing the Chimeheuvis to cremate Willie Boy's corpse: "Tell them we're all out of souvenirs."*

• • •

No less than the protagonists of *Easy Rider* and the patrons of *Alice's Restaurant*, Michelangelo Antonioni had gone in search of America. MGM was anxious to bankroll the maestro's follow-up to his astonishing hit, *Blowup*, and flew Antonioni to Los Angeles in May 1967 to discuss plans. Knocked out by the infinite freeways, plenitude of used-car lots, and "steel buildings shining through clouds of pollution," Antonioni plucked the idea for his movie from an item in a Phoenix newspaper about a hippie who was killed by police while trying to return a stolen airplane.

---

*Writing in the *New Yorker*, Pauline Kael found Polonsky's movie at once old-fashioned and ultra-fashionable—an apocalyptic mix of "schematic Marxism and Freudianism and New Left guerrilla Existentialism and just plain new-style American self-hatred." The movie struck Kael as supremely detached.

> The numbing hopelessness of *Easy Rider* has emotional appeal; the irrationality and the cool, romantic defeatism are infused with an elegiac sense of American failure. It's easier to dismiss the programmed ideological negativism of *Willie Boy*, which stays on a conscious (almost abstract) level while attempting to demonstrate that we are a nation with bad instincts. There's no regret—not even the facile tone of regret that made Peter Fonda's Captain America such a sham hero.

Antonioni returned to the United States in the heroic days of late 1967 to meet with off-off-Broadway playwright Sam Shepard in New York. Shepard gave the hippie-outlaw-martyr story an environmental exploitation angle by introducing the character of a wealthy real estate developer, a George Washington McLintock foil to the hero's Billy the Kid. Antonioni then continued his investigation, flying back to California to hang out with militants in Berkeley and hippies in Golden Gate Park. While there, he found his leading lady in anthropology student Daria Halprin, eighteen-year-old daughter of avant-garde choreographer Ann Halprin.

Zabriskie Point, which Antonioni named for the lowest spot in Death Valley and hoped to open with footage of a real urban race riot, had been scheduled to start shooting in June 1968, but production was postponed while the director searched for Daria's co-star, imagined as an American Che, the Hollywood embodiment of the New Left. Some 1,300 hopefuls mobbed the Electric Circus in New York's East Village one Friday afternoon. "To join in the mass hallucination of grandeur all you had to be was a male, between the ages of 19 and 23, and five feet 10 inches tall," Steven Lerner wrote in the *Village Voice*. Waiting on line, Lerner deduced that Antonioni's desired type was a "tall, gaunt, hollow-eyed youth (preferably with dark hair) who looked shifty enough to be an Algerian bomb-thrower and mean enough to slit your throat if you couldn't light his cigarette."

Lerner further noted that, during their auditions, prospects were often given the line "fuck you," and he advanced far enough in the audition process to learn that rage was crucial. He was asked what made him angry and if violence tended to "happen" around him. Meanwhile, as Antonioni's scouts scoured the nation for the personification of enraged white youth, the director himself flew to Chicago for the DemCon and got tear-gassed in Lincoln Park. Finally, Mark Frechette was discovered one night in the midst of a heated argument at a Cambridge, Massachusetts, bus stop. ("I've got one who really knows how to hate," the scout reported.) A twenty-year-old carpenter who had only recently joined musician Mel Lyman's Fort Hill commune—publishers of Boston's un-

derground weekly, *Avatar*, as well as the group later immortalized in *Rolling Stone* as an exemplar of "acid fascism"—Frechette had never heard of Antonioni, but he had the chiseled looks of a young Peter Fonda and a history of violence that included two stints in a mental hospital. Shooting finally began in late summer and continued from the post-Chicago apotheosis of the New Left for nine months into the early regime of Richard Nixon.*

Characterized by continual conflict between the Italian filmmaker and his American crew, *Zabriskie Point* was treated as an alien invasion. Antonioni had barely begun when copies of his script disappeared from a locked MGM office and word spread that he planned to desecrate the American flag atop the Mobil Oil building in downtown LA. No sooner were Mobil's lawyers placated than Antonioni had to deny a report that he'd been filming on the RFK death site in the Ambassador Hotel kitchen. When production moved north to Marin County, Antonioni was accused of fomenting a riot on the campus of Costa Costra College. To the sound of a tribal drum, Kathleen Cleaver and other Black Panthers taunted a group of white students, telling these would-be radicals that if they want to be "real," they should chuck a Molotov cocktail into the ROTC office. Mark (Frechette) stuns the meeting by announcing his readiness to die and splits to buy a gun. The students occupy the library building, but after a policeman cold-bloodedly guns down a black kid, Mark (or someone) shoots the pig. Then Mark flees just as, by some accounts, Antonioni's crew split before the local police could serve warrants for their arrest.

Mid-November, Antonioni retreated to Death Valley—importing Joseph Chaikin and twenty members of New York's Open Theater, as well as a number of teenagers from Salt Lake City and Las Vegas, for a nude "love-in." By now the production's phones were being tapped and its mail opened. As *Za-*

---

*By now, even Jean-Luc Godard had launched a magical mystery tour; he was in New York, filming interviews with Tom Hayden, Eldridge Cleaver, LeRoi Jones, and a woman employed on Wall Street, documenting an actress walking through Harlem and Jefferson Airplane performing on a hotel roof, for his never-completed *One American Movie*.

briskie Point inspired its own Operation Chaos, so Frechette waged a personal guerrilla war—trying to persuade Antonioni to hire Mel Lyman to score the movie and littering the set with copies of the *Avatar*, open to his guru's picture. To add to the paranoia, the star—classified 4-F—was being harassed by his draft board and, summoned to Phoenix for a physical, had to stage an Arlo Guthrie freakout. Back in LA, Antonioni felt police everywhere: "The cop is looking at you. In the streets. In your houses. Everywhere. It's incredible. They arrest you if you say 'fuck.' Everyone is afraid of the police."

Sumptuous and alienated, *Zabriskie Point* is scarcely more than a violent anecdote unfolding over the course of one long afternoon. The TV references to Mark's crime, the ease with which he steals a plane, only add to the science-fiction ambience. Daria (Halprin), who works for Sunnydunes Enterprises in the police-state skyscraper of total surveillance, is driving through Death Valley to Phoenix in her 1954 Buick for a rendezvous with her boss and lover Lee Allen (Rod Taylor). In a scene that might have come from a Doors song, she stops in a desert town populated by disturbed children. They attack her but she manages to escape.

Mark, who proves an extremely competent pilot, flirtatiously strafes Daria's car, then lands so they can meet. She lights a joint and offers him a toke, but Mark demurs. His is a "reality trip." Neither particularly expressive, they engage in arid repartee and then make love in close-up, occasioning a lyrical interlude of other naked couples—the Orgy as a vision of the new order. Daria tells Mark that he's "beautiful," and together, they paint the plane. Mark is planning to return it, but just as with Bonnie and Clyde, Wyatt and Billy, and Willie Boy, the Great Society will not let him live. As he lands in LA, Mark is shot down by the cops. Daria hears the news on her car radio.

Zabriskie Point ends in the desert's plastic pleasure spa. Arriving in Phoenix, Daria proceeds to a mountaintop ranch, and there has another vision—the Eve of Destruction. She imagines the ranch house exploding and, as though watching her own personal movie, has only to look at it to make it happen. Three times, the place blows up in slow motion: A television, a refrigerator, patio furniture, a box of cereal, a loaf of Wonder Bread, even a copy of *Look* (which

later would place Daria and Mark on its cover), float in space. Then, having brought down the world, Daria disappears into the sunset.*

Some attempted to storm the reality studio with riots; others hallucinated themselves inside the control room. Quintessential movie protagonists were now the very people whom Major Dundee might have pursued into Mexico—a doomed assortment of criminals, crazies, draft dodgers, dope dealers, and Indians. Bringing home the Green Berets might not be sufficient. As prophesied by George Wallace and *Coogan's Bluff*, these new types would soon be opposed by vigilantes and equally extreme representatives of law and order.

By some sorcery of example or consent, the Great Cowboy in Washington had created an incredible new national narrative. America—which is to say the World—was a Texas frontier, both violent and absurd. Shadowed by a sense of inevitable catastrophe, *The Wild Bunch* most vividly articulated this collective fantasy. Sam Peckinpah framed his narrative with the spectacle of hapless civilians caught in a murderous crossfire and repeatedly invited viewers to savor the spectacle of unfolding disaster—the botched stakeout that provides the

---

*Frechette did too. Angry that Antonioni was portraying America's youth revolution as political rather than spiritual, he went AWOL and returned to Fort Hill, refusing to take calls from MGM for six days until Antonioni himself phoned. "I told him he wasn't making a film about any America I knew," Frechette remembered lecturing his director. "I told him things just had to change before I would come back." Finally, after Antonioni agreed to spend ten days reshooting dialogue deemed overly political as well as promising to visit Fort Hill at the earliest opportunity, Frechette returned to California.

Throughout the filming, Halprin and Frechette had been, naturally, conducting a love affair. As soon as *Zabriskie Point* wrapped in April 1969, the couple decamped for Fort Hill, where Frechette had left his wife and baby. That month, in Berkeley, an amalgam of hippies, students, politicos, and vagrants began tilling the empty lot they declared "People's Park." In May—foretaste of Nixon hardball—*Zabriskie Point*'s producers were served with subpoenas, charged with violating the Mann Act by transporting persons for immoral purposes across state lines. May 15, People's Park was bulldozed and Berkeley occupied by the National Guard. Antonioni, meanwhile, had taken his footage to Rome, where he spent the next seven months editing. He did not stop in Fort Hill. Nor did he use the dialogue that Frechette went on strike to force him to reshoot.

opening bloodbath, the collision on the railroad tracks allowing the outlaws to capture a shipment of U.S. Army weapons, the exploded bridge flinging men and horses into the river, the climactic slow-motion massacre—an ecstatic, orgasmic finale wherein more people are killed than could possibly live in the pueblo of Agua Verde and the same extras die over and over. The image of a Gatling gun gone out of control provided a metaphor for the movie's overall love of mayhem.

Although aestheticized to an unprecedented degree, Peckinpah's stylized violence was perceived as a form of naturalism. Just as Bonnie and Clyde were the real thing, *Wild in the Streets* foretold the future, and *Easy Rider* seemed to be truly happening, a movie had finally revealed the truth. Hence producer Phil Feldman's grandiloquent pronouncement after *The Wild Bunch*'s stormy preview at a press junket in late June 1969: "The era of escapism is over; the era of reality is here. . . . The entertainment industry has a right and duty to depict reality as it is."

V

Nixon Time:
The War at Home, 1969–71

Richard Nixon was finally president. But now there were two Americas—each defined against the other. From Maine to California, the land resounded with strident calls for armed struggle. The antiwar movement had grown so alienated that many openly identified with the Viet Cong.

Two distinct nations, yet scarcely any division between reality and fantasy: On March 22, the new President contemplated the counterculture and declared that "this is the way civilizations begin to die." Nixon quoted Arthur Schlesinger quoting William Butler Yeats: *Things fall apart; the center cannot hold.* As the 1968–69 school year ended, the President told an audience at General Beadle State College in Madison, South Dakota, that America's "fundamental values [were] under bitter and even violent attack." He conjured an apocalyptic vision of "a deeply troubled and profoundly unsettled time. Drugs, crime, campus revolts, racial discord, draft resistance . . . old standards violated, old values discarded." Indeed, the struggle for the university-owned vacant lot renamed People's Park that preoccupied Berkeley during the spring of 1969 brought the first state-sanctioned use of guns against white demonstrators and the first student fatality. Emboldened by the new regime in Washington, Governor Reagan declared that "if it takes a bloodbath, let's get it over with."

Bloodbath or orgy? In the midst of the 1968 presidential campaign, the Living Theater returned from Europe to spend the next half year touring the United States—confronting their audiences by stripping naked and calling for Paradise Now. The Doors' lead singer, Jim Morrison, saw one such performance at the University of Southern California on February 28, 1969. The next night, when the Doors played in an old airplane hangar in Miami, Morrison followed the Living's lead—drunkenly taunting his audience as a "bunch of slaves" and pulling down his leather pants before inviting everyone up on stage. The Doors left the arena littered with what would be described by Morrison's biographers as "a thousand empty wine and beer bottles and panties and brassieres in sufficient quantity to open a well-stocked lingerie store." The singer was now Public Enemy Number One.

Pop stars imagined themselves revolutionaries and vice versa. In late '67, there had been only the Black Panthers and the Diggers. Then came Yippie! and the great media spectacle of Chicago, and now new political cells took names like rock bands: the Crazies, the White Panthers, the Red Guards, the Jesse James Gang, the May Day Tribe, Alice's Restaurant Marxist-Leninist, the International Werewolf Conspiracy. The annual SDS convention that would be the organization's last opened June 18 in Chicago and ended, amid multiple schisms, with the creation of the Weathermen.

History was being made; the war came home. The Righteous Outlaw would spawn the Legal Vigilante.

The End of the Sixties

"There was a melancholy to the end of a century," Norman Mailer sighed in his paean to the space race, *Of a Fire on the Moon*.

> The French, who were the first to specify a state for every emotion, would speak of the fin de siècle. It was the only name to give his own mood, for Aquarius [as Mailer was calling himself] was in a depression which would not lift for the rest of the summer, a curious depression full of fevers, forebodings, and a general sense that the century was done—it had ended in the summer of 1969.

Yes—and with a portrait of Aquarius on the cover of *Life* magazine.

For those going through the changes that made the Sixties so heady, the decade might well feel as momentous as a century. (*Esquire* had begged for a moratorium as early as August 1966.) At any rate, the first summer of Richard Nixon's belated presidency brought the acme of a particular cosmic consciousness. It was inevitable, perhaps, that a million pilgrims gathered, along with Aquarius, on July 16 in Cocoa Beach, Florida, to witness the launch of Apollo XI, the manned moon-rocket that JFK had promised the American people in May 1961—a lifetime before. Less predictable was the other public event that defined the summer of '69—the 350,000 freaked-out kids who, exactly one month after the moon launch, trekked to a muddy field in upstate New York for what was advertised as THREE DAYS OF PEACE AND MUSIC—AN AQUARIAN EXPOSITION, Woodstock.

This was the summer of myth made material. The *New York Times* editorialists were sufficiently delirious to imagine the last half of July 1969 "the most revolutionary and significant fortnight of the entire twentieth century." Covering the Apollo launch for *Life*, Mailer scarcely hesitated in calling the moon mission "the climax of the greatest week since Christ was born."

For others, Woodstock was even more amazing. (The moon launch had, after all, been preempted fifteen months before by Stanley Kubrick's "space odyssey," *2001*.) Indeed, Mailer's moon report in the August 29 *Life* was somewhat upstaged by a ten-page color spread on "The Big Woodstock Rock Trip," while Abbie Hoffman defined his hastily written manifesto, *Woodstock Nation*, as a counter-report to *Of a Fire on the Moon*: "Mailer is off writing his book on the space program for $1,000,000 for *Life* magazine, while I try to sort out the most remarkable event in our history. . . ." Hoffman furrowed his brow. Woodstock obviously followed from Chicago, but where was the dialectic? "Functional anarchy, primitive tribalism, gathering of the tribes. Right on! What did it all mean? Sheet, what can I say brother, it blew my mind out."

Hoffman's reading of Woodstock's revolutionary potential was wildly exaggerated. In *The Birth of Tragedy*, Nietzsche notes "that whenever a group has been deeply touched by Dionysian emotions, the release from the bonds

of individuation results in indifference, or even hostility, towards political instinct." Hoffman himself had been kicked off the stage at Woodstock when he interrupted a set by the Who to tell the people about his jailed disciple, White Panther martyr John Sinclair. Even then, Woodstock was understood as less Dionysian than its propagandists proclaimed. With the god's followers running amok, actual Dionysian mysteries might climax in madness, murder, and mutilation. Still, for arch-rationalist Ayn Rand, the summer of 1969 provided the perfect counterpoint of Apollo and Dionysus as explicated in *The Birth of Tragedy*. The moon landing was the triumph of intellect; Woodstock, the nadir of primitive instinct. "It is man's irrational emotions that bring him down to the mud," Rand wrote in her *Objectivist Newsletter*. "It is man's reason that lifts him to the stars."

Richard Nixon assumed the presidency believing he'd be able to end the war in Vietnam within a year. Excited by the moon flight, Nixon began stressing a fresh White House public-relations offensive predicated on the astronaut term "all systems go" and sent a secret message to Ho Chi Minh, offering some sort of settlement, but only up until November 1. Three weeks later, national security adviser Henry Kissinger threatened his North Vietnamese contacts with "measures of the greatest consequence" if there was no solution by November.

The Moon Shot and Woodstock scenarios were equally redolent of innocence and megalomania, making history and the conquest of new worlds. Both were realized as uniquely participatory media events. You had to be there. Each was a science-fiction festival. ("I took a trip to our future," Hoffman wrote.) If the moon landing was an epic, billion-dollar TV special, complete with "live" presidential phone call, broadcast into every Freedomland motel room and bar, the Aquarian Exposition was, in essence, created to be repackaged as a movie (and soundtrack). The counterculture regarded the moon show as the ultimate in imperial smoke and mirrors. Pop iconographer Peter Max attempted to cash in with a series of Day-Glo commemorative posters, but Peter Collier's *Ramparts* column offered a more typical expression of dissident cynicism: "The whole expedition could just as easily have been acted

out on the back lot of Universal Studios. . . . One could not forget that he was watching television."*

•   •   •

ALL THE WORLD IN THE MOON'S GRIP, the *New York Times* caroled on July 21, 1969, the day after astronaut Neil Armstrong took his world-historic step for mankind. But that was scarcely the lone manifestation of lunacy.

It was the summer of the Righteous Outlaw: Not just Abbie Hoffman's "almost perfect propaganda film" *Easy Rider*, but *The Wild Bunch*! For onetime SDS activist Stew Albert, *The Wild Bunch* was a fantasy sequel to *Bonnie and Clyde*, as the "vanguard" embodiment of "revolutionary soul." Where did these illusions come from? "The best American flicks are a couple years ahead of the American revolution's reality," Albert explained in *The Berkeley Tribe*.

> The film rebels don't argue about the need for self-defense. They have already taken up the gun while a lot of us still give flowers to pigs, sign petitions, and pray for rain to save the polluted planet.
>
> Armed defense began with Bonnie and Clyde's tour of Oklahoma banks. They left a lot of dead pigs but never really understood why they took up the gun except depression unemployment was a drag. . . .

Albert had assimilated the earlier SDS critique. Where "Bonnie and Clyde could only fight the enemy in single fragmented encounters along a lonely nihilist

---

*This conception reached its epitome with *Capricorn One*, a 1978 thriller that embellished the idea of the moon launch as made-for-TV spectacle with post-Watergate notions of conspiracy and cover-up. The presence of Elliott Gould and Karen Black as kooky anti-establishment reporters only underscored the exhaustion. Such druggy paranoia was totally played out—superseded the year before by the arrival of a new pop culture dialectic. In 1977, the counterculture was successfully neutered and massified by a couple of ex-hippies. As George Lucas's *Star Wars* rationalized Dionysian mysticism with Apollonian technology, so Steven Spielberg's *Close Encounters of the Third Kind* used love-zaps from the sky to transform members of the Middle American Silent Majority into hippie dropouts. It was Woodstock all over again, only this time on the Moon.

road," the rebels of *The Wild Bunch* "join forces with humanity, see the enemy as a systematic monster, and take him on all at once."

"You can say the movies are daydreams, a substitute for real politics," Albert wrote, but *The Wild Bunch* was "truer to the way we must live and what is to be done than the Memorial Day March of Fools (including myself) which left the fence standing and the People's Park at the mercy of bulldozers." Did *The Wild Bunch* offer a model? Do you believe in magick? As with the last fin de siècle, there was a revival of occultism. The Kali Yuga was at hand. Soviet and Chinese troops had clashed on March 2 along the Ussuri River; relations between the two Communist powers so deteriorated by summer that Americans believed the Soviets were considering a preemptive strike on Chinese nuclear installations.

The gods demanded human sacrifice. Over the weekend that preceded Woodstock's Three Days of Peace and Music, the Hollywood starlet Sharon Tate—best known for her role in the 1967 *Valley of the Dolls*—and five of her friends were ritually butchered in a secluded Benedict Canyon home at 10050 Cielo Drive. Their killers left the letters P-I-G scrawled in blood on the back door. (The next night, in another part of LA, Leno and Rosemary LaBianca were stabbed to death, found beneath similar bloody slogans—DEATH TO PIGS, RISE, and, misspelled on the refrigerator, HEALTER SKELTER. The letters W-A-R were carved in Leno's corpse, a fork stuck in his abdomen.) *Life*'s August 29 Woodstock issue ran a feature on the return of Tate's husband, director Roman Polanski, to the scene of the crime. "This must be the world famous orgy house," was Polanski's reflexively sardonic remark. For *Life*, the living room where the slaughter occurred was the "dark side of the moon."

Some years later, Joan Didion would recall that, for many Angelenos of her acquaintance, the Sixties ended the morning of August 9, "when word of the murders on Cielo Drive traveled like brushfire through the community." For Hollywood, the Tate massacre was comparable only to the first Kennedy assassination. "The tension broke that day. The paranoia was fulfilled."

America's Night of the Living Dead (My Lai, Manson, *Myra Breckinridge*)

The Moon Shot was a spectacular within another, even more fearfully expensive one. (In 1969, the Pentagon calculated that each enemy casualty cost American taxpayers $60,000. The U.S. share of world trade, once nearly half, had fallen to 10 percent. Inflation rose to a post-1951 peak. Richard Nixon's budget had a $3 billion deficit—modest compared to the $23 billion projected for 1971—and although the stock market slide was yet to come, *Business Week* observed that "few hawks [were] left in the business world." The movie industry suffered its own crisis. Average weekly attendance was 18 million—barely a third of what it had been in 1950. Five studios were in the red. The remaining audience was a cipher, nearly two-thirds between the ages of fifteen and twenty-nine. Testing limits, scrambling after current attitudes, groping in the dark for the youth market, Hollywood contributed to the prevailing delirium. As *Bonnie and Clyde*'s offspring would not appear until summer 1969, the first six months of the Nixon era brought numerous failed experiments. While Jules Dassin's *Up Tight* transposed the Irish revolutionary situation of *The Informer* to a Midwestern black ghetto, Otto Preminger's drug comedy *Skidoo* and the crazy sex farce *Candy* (based on Terry Southern and Mason Hoffenberg's underground 1958 novel) attempted to represent the counterculture. All opened the month before Nixon's inauguration, even as their prospective audience puzzled over the transmission that was the Beatles' "White Album."

Candy had been optioned by French actor Christian Marquand, who recruited his friend Marlon Brando to play a fake Hindu guru. Brando attracted such $50,000 per week luminaries as Richard Burton, James Coburn, and Walter Matthau, not to mention John Huston, Charles Aznavour, Ringo Starr, and Anita Pallenberg (the once and future consort to several members of the Rolling Stones). The folk-rock superstar Byrds and proto heavy-metal band Steppenwolf contributed to the soundtrack. Even the Living Theater, then in Italy developing *Paradise Now*, participated in a few scenes, including an orgy in drag. Southern, however, withdrew after Marquand cast seventeen-year-old

Ewa Aulin in the title role—the former Miss Teen International with the cow-eyed, kewpie-doll stare was Swedish, and for Southern, Candy's untarnishable innocence could only be American.*

Skidoo—on which Southern worked uncredited—began production in early 1968, as Hollywood civilization headed toward the rocks. The elderly cast— Burgess Meredith, George Raft, Cesar Romero, Mickey Rooney—was aug-mented by the televisual presence of authority figures John Wayne and Ronald Reagan, while, in the ultimate head joke, Groucho Marx appeared as a criminal mastermind named God. *Skidoo* employed a gangster family to represent Amer-ica's doomed establishment. Retired mobster Jackie Gleason and his moll Carol Channing played the parents of a wayward teenybopper. The plot dictated that Gleason share a jail cell with an acidhead draft dodger while Channing moth-ered a gaggle of flower children and, in the film's most shocking scene, vamped junior gangster Frankie Avalon.

Introducing the possibility of intergenerational sex and drugs as part of its new Freedomland, *Skidoo* remains the most LSD-tolerant movie ever produced in Hollywood, while, given its requisite anti-militarism, multiple orgy se-quences, incidental psychedelia, rock montages, and climactic be-in, *Candy* an-ticipated images from almost every self-consciously Sixties film—including Hollywood's most remarkable assault on popular taste, *Myra Breckinridge.*

•   •   •

---

*Shooting began in Rome in late 1967 and continued through spring, with a hiatus while Aulin went to an Adriatic sanitarium for a week of sleep therapy to recover from her scenes with Brando. According to James Coburn, the star had been relentlessly coming on to the teenager: "He tried everything, being the father, the psychiatrist, the stern disciplinarian. She was so besieged and befuddled that all she did was laugh and laugh, so uncontrollably that she couldn't get through her lines. She would look at [Brando] in this fright wig and just get hysterical. He was so funny and ingratiating to begin with—only now he wanted to fuck her. . . . She just went over the edge." Aulin's exploitation was the ruling metaphor. *Candy* elevated smarminess to a universal prin-ciple. Titillation was predicated on panty flashing and peek-a-boo nudity while the surplus of father figures, together with the prolonged incest and sex-abuse fantasies, suggested a particularly sleazy gloss on the generation gap.

Based on Gore Vidal's saga of a transsexual heroine who arrives in Hollywood with a program to "realign the sexes," *Myra Breckinridge* was an even more "impossible" adaptation than *Candy*. Nevertheless, Fox outbid Warners and National General Pictures for the rights—thus, *Myra* joined the film biographies of revolutionaries Che Guevara and Malcolm X as part of the Twentieth Century Fox youth slate orchestrated by studio boss Darryl Zanuck and his son Richard.

Having secured *Myra*, Fox spent eighteen months wondering whom to cast in the lead. Finally, in July 1969, a year after Vidal delivered a first draft, the part went to Raquel Welch, who, thanks to well-orchestrated publicity and her cavegirl turn in the 1966 remake of *One Million B.C.*, was Hollywood's reigning sex goddess. Welch was under Fox contract—and so was Mae West. In fact, the sensation of 1933 still owed the studio a movie! To make *Myra Breckinridge*, West stipulated top billing, secured the movie's highest paycheck, and wrote her own dialogue. Fox completed the stunt casting with celebrity film-journalist Rex Reed as Myra's pre-sex-change alter ego, Myron.

The director, Michael Sarne—born to Austrian refugee parents in the blitzed London of 1940—was a former teen actor and faux Cockney pop singer. Sarne had made two previous films, most recently *Joanna*, an ode to swinging London which *Time*'s late-1968 review deemed the "most dazzling directorial debut of the year." Unhappy with Vidal's script, Sarne wrote his own, promising "a dirty, sexy and funny picture," while keeping Vidal's idea of using old film clips from the Fox vault.

Embodiment of Hollywood's crisis, still without a final draft, *Myra* began shooting September 22. Two days later—on the opening of the season's other madcap spectacle of transgression, the Chicago Conspiracy Trial—the *Los Angeles Free Press* ran an interview with Sarne in which he slagged his cast. For months thereafter, *Myra Breckinridge* provided fantastic gossip fodder. A week into production, *Variety* reported producer Robert Fryer's attempt to replace Sarne. Another youth, twenty-six-year-old David Giler, was hired to synthesize the Vidal and Sarne screenplays. Giler wanted to recuperate the movie as a musical, but Sarne refused to shoot the changes. Continually reintroducing his

own excised material, he told a British journalist that he didn't want "subtlety" but "vulgarity."

On the ninth day of production, Hollywood reporter Joyce Haber was invited to lunch with Richard Zanuck. Fox had just opened its tremendously successful *Butch Cassidy and the Sundance Kid*, but Haber detected a "feeling of hysteria." Lunch was delayed while Zanuck held an "emergency meeting" with Welch and Fryer. En route to the studio's private dining room, she and Zanuck bumped into Fryer with Reed, who, as if on cue, begged Zanuck to go on set and "see what Sarne is doing to morale. Everyone hates him."*

Still, Sarne—whom Giler called the "best exploiter of the generation gap [he'd] ever seen"—retained the Zanucks' backing. Even as the project went through ten scripts, Sarne told *Variety* he got the screenplay he wanted: "I didn't compromise. . . . The studio decided to do something revolutionary and I'm simply helping them to do it."

Elsewhere on the revolutionary front, the Weathermen introduced themselves to America that October: The self-appointed vanguard of the fissured and dying SDS capped the demonstrations around the Conspiracy Trial with four Days of Rage during which several hundred representatives of militant white youth chanting HO! HO! HO CHI MINH! DARE TO STRUGGLE, DARE TO WIN! smashed car and store windows in downtown Chicago.

The decade ending, monstrous combatants lumbered to the fore. Myra was but one of the pop-cultural freaks and mutants to storm the stage. As Sarne mocked the "intellectual pygmies" who ran Hollywood, so Vice President Spiro Agnew denounced the antiwar movement as an "effete corps of impudent snobs." Meanwhile: PIG AMERICA BEWARE: THERE'S AN ARMY GROWING RIGHT IN YOUR GUTS, AND IT'S GOING TO HELP BRING YOU DOWN, the Weathermen warned in the October 21 *New Left Notes*. With the LA Police Department

---

*"I'm not worrying about the dividing line between reality and fantasy," Sarne explained. "Bobby [Fryer] is. He's terrified I'll go too far." Nevertheless, Sarne agreed to drop Myra's appearance as a "Biblical Charlton Heston figure" and the scene where she dashed down Wall Street and got raped by a cop—or was it Myron who ran naked and, castrated by Myra outside the Stock Exchange, bled a horde of precious stones?

closing in on the killers of Sharon Tate, Calvin Trillin investigated *Myra Breck-inridge* on behalf of *Life*:

> Knowing that people walk around film studios in all sorts of bizarre costumes, I was not surprised that the first person I noticed on the set of *Myra Breckinridge* was wearing an orange beard, stringy blond hair down to his shoulders, boots, suede bell-bottoms in two shades of brown and a sleeveless, brownish garment that looked like a pre-dirtied undershirt. He turned out to be the director, Michael Sarne. Sarne is playing an angry young British film maker [and] like everyone else in Hollywood, he dresses carefully for the part.

The morning after Halloween, Sarne staged his orgy. "The set was closed but it was the hottest thing in Hollywood if you could get in," Reed wrote.

> There was one girl walking around, a suit drawn on her body, with four sequins pasted on for buttons. A man in an Indian hat had pinned an enormous fur contraption over his genitals. A singer named Choo Choo Collins wore nothing but a polka-dot bikini painted on her body. There was a man in a jockstrap with a fingerlike thing hanging down from his crotch. A group of nudes stood around a grand piano singing 'The Star-Spangled Banner' and there was one man in a bra and panties and another in a half-slip. . . . *

West was in her dressing room, but when she heard what was going on, she wrote herself an entrance in which, descending the stairs to universal applause, she looked down, patted her hair, shifted her hips, and drawled, "This must be what's called 'letting it all hang out.' " The appearance was extraordinary in that the star otherwise refused to appear with Welch. Their scenes

---

*Nor did Reed fail to note the naked man riding a pogo stick or the self-proclaimed witch who prophesied Mae West would suffer a heart attack so that she could replace her. According to Reed, Sarne encouraged extras to say whatever came into their minds. "One girl was asking: 'Do you masturbate in the shower?' Another said, 'Let's burn all the pubic hair off her body with lighter fluid.' And one extra, who used to come to the studio regularly in a catatonic state, and never spoke, finally broke her silence. She stood up in the middle of the group and asked, 'Do you fuck or suck?' "

were shot on different days with the dialogue-coach feeding each actress her lines. For Welch, dubbed the "Old Raccoon" by Sarne, making *Myra* was a nightmare: "I cried until my stomach would feel as if it were dropping out." John Huston, cast over Sarne's objections as Myra's uncle, Buck Loner, would not take direction or, indeed, talk to anyone on the production—finishing a take, he locked himself in his dressing room. Script doctor Giler had Pauline Kael's pan of *Joanna* prominently displayed in his office. "This whole town is like a vast piranha pool," Sarne told one reporter. To another, he complained he had no friends on the set—while asserting "people are dying for me all over town as a director."

"People are dying for me all over town": Was Sarne enacting some sort of nervous collapse? Was it survivor guilt? The director had been a guest at the wedding of Roman Polanski and Sharon Tate. He and his wife, Tanya, were friendly with the Polanskis. They had even planned to stay in the Polanski residence that summer—Tanya, too, was pregnant—but changed their minds to rent a Malibu beach house, thus leaving 10050 Cielo Drive to heiress Abigail Folger and her Polish boyfriend, Frykowski. The Sarnes entertained Sharon, Voityck, and Abigail for dinner two days before the murders—Sarne even considered dropping by Cielo Drive that fatal Friday night!

The terror swept through LA's piranha poolside at the very moment when Sarne bested Vidal in the battle over *Myra*'s script. No wonder the director felt confident and acted insane: "They can't get rid of me," he told *Women's Wear Daily* in January, as if he had some occult power. "I deliberately shot the film in such a way so that no one else could cut it."

•   •   •

November 3: In a much-ballyhooed nationally televised address, the President conjures the bloodbath consequences of the "first defeat in our nation's history." Richard Nixon was originally to announce a new offensive, but the October 15 moratorium, an antiwar manifestation observed by millions across the nation, has forced him to postpone his plan. Instead of attacking North Vietnam, the President lashes out at the peace movement. The war is now his war. In the most effective speech of his presidency, Nixon designates two forces contending for

the nation's soul—a "vocal minority" of antiwar demonstrators and the "Great Silent Majority" of patriotic Americans. "North Vietnam cannot defeat or humiliate the United States," he warns. "Only Americans can do that."

Gallup puts the President's approval rating at 68 percent as the White House accelerates its PR offensive by declaring a mid-November National Unity Week to rally the Silent Majority around the country, the flag, the war, and Richard Nixon. Then, on November 13—the very day Agnew contemptuously denounces the TV networks' "instant analysis" of Nixon's November 3 address, and two days before a half million antiwar protestors march on Washington in the largest demonstration to that point in American history—thirty newspapers carry Seymour Hersh's report on the My Lai massacre.

The incident had occurred in South Vietnam on the morning of March 16, 1968 (just as Sam Peckinpah's convoy converged on Parras, Mexico, to begin rehearsing *The Wild Bunch*). Members of Charlie Company of Task Force Barker, 11th Brigade of the Americal Division, under the command of Captain Ernest Medina and Lieutenant William Calley, went berserk during a routine search-and-destroy mission in a "free-fire zone," shooting 347 unarmed men, women, and children in the hamlet My Lai 4—returning that afternoon to burn the village and slaughter the livestock. (Meanwhile, Bravo Company was murdering civilians at My Khe 4, a few miles away.) The massacre had been reported in France as early as May 1968. Still, Army brass maintained a cover-up for nearly twenty months—despite photographs taken by public-information officer Ronald Haeberle.

Once the story breaks, My Lai makes the covers of *Time* and *Newsweek*, and Haeberle's color photos are published as a multi-page spread in the December 5 *Life*. Among the atrocities Peckinpah could not have imagined was the attempted gang rape of a thirteen-year-old girl prevented by the presence of Haeberle's camera but escalating into her murder as soon as the photographer turned away.

More evil omens: December 4, a few days before the Conspiracy defense team calls its first witness, Fred Hampton—the charismatic twenty-one-year-old leader of the Chicago Black Panthers—and his associate Mark Clark are shot dead in their beds by Chicago police. Two days later, the Rolling Stones end the

most financially remunerative rock tour in history with a free concert at the derelict Altamont Speedway, forty miles east of San Francisco. Four people die—one drowned in a puddle, two run over by cars, and one bludgeoned to death by members of the Hell's Angels motorcycle gang, whom the Stones engaged to guard the stage. Then, the Los Angeles Police Department announces the apprehension of the parties responsible for the Tate-LaBianca murders.

This is the way the century that is the 1960s ends. December 1969 reeks of blood and the memory of blood. The December 19 *Life* trumps My Lai by introducing America to the pure personification of evil—Charles "Jesus" Manson, the wild-eyed, bearded, ex-con LSD Svengali of a "Love and Terror" hippie cult, or maybe harem, that called itself "The Family."

•   •   •

How could any of this be visualized? The last week of December, as the Weathermen convened their National War Council in a ballroom located in the black ghetto of Flint, Michigan, the *Village Voice* favorably reviewed an obscure horror film with the unappetizing title *Night of the Living Dead*.

First released over a year before, *Night of the Living Dead* was still playing on double and triple bills in the sticky-floored theaters of New York's Forty-second Street, grossing out audiences with its unrelentingly gruesome Judgment Day vision of the dead returning from their graves: Cannibal Zombies Run Amok in Rural Pennsylvania. "The gluey, bottomless horror of the film oozes from an amalgam of studiedly derivative elements," *Voice* reviewer Richard McGuinness noted. "The plot—people with clashing personalities trapped together in a shabby country house by the ambulatory, flesh-eating corpses lurching outside—is secured in the gruesome psychology of those EC comics banned in the '50s." The "unrestrained" narrative "kills all the characters in what, near the end, becomes an avalanche of atrocities." Adding to the effect, the movie seemed "made in a state of frenzy"—if not inside the brain of a maddened Mansonaed.*

---

*Produced outside the movie industry, *Night of the Living Dead* was not bound by Hollywood decorum. The rough-hewn style was closer to the raw immediacy of un-

Shopped to distributors during the *Wild in the Streets* spring of 1968, *Night of the Living Dead* embodied the Eve of Destruction: battlefields, riots, and mass demonstrations. The movie brought the war home with a vengeance. Was social breakdown ever more luridly visualized? Not for nothing does one dazed character, traumatized by a ghoul attack in an American flag-bedecked cemetery, continually mumble, "What's happening?" It was the question of the hour. No less than the Mansons, *Night of the Living Dead* offered a cannibal nightmare—the most literal possible image of America devouring itself. Black against white, child against parent, hawk against dove—and that was just in the besieged farmhouse that served as the movie's main location. Meanwhile, the marauding zombies provided a grimly hilarious cross-section of ordinary Americans—if not a metaphor. (As Gore Vidal pointed out, the phrase Silent Majority was a Homeric term for the dead.)

Night of the Living Dead was a piecemeal production that, financed by pooled savings, shot in black and white on weekends and between projects, had taken almost a year to complete. With only two professional actors in the cast, everyone else doubled and tripled up on jobs. This was a collective effort that, the then twenty-eight-year-old director George Romero would later recall, was "so fucking democratic, it got sort of crazy."

Just like SDS. Convening their War Council in Flint, the Weathermen decorated the Giant Ballroom with iconic Day-Glo personality posters of the Third World revolutionary saints Che, Ho, Mao, and Malcolm X. In a mania of applied Pop Art, an entire wall was consecrated to a red-and-black checkerboard of Fred Hampton images. Another display offered an array of bullets, each marked with an enemy name: Nixon, Johnson, Humphrey, Reagan, Sharon Tate. A six-and-a-half-foot cardboard machine gun dangled from the

---

derground movies and cinema verité than to any studio production. Similarly, the narrative offered no happy ending, nor any reassurance whatsoever. What's more, the movie asserted its marginal status by casting a black actor as the smartest, most capable, and most sympathetic character. Nothing prior to *Night of the Living Dead* encouraged the audience to cheer when a black character shot and killed an unarmed white man.

ceiling. Every night for a week, the Weathermen held frenzied mass meetings called "wargasms," featuring group calisthenics and sing-alongs. The seasonal "White Christmas" received new lyrics:

> I'm dreaming of a white riot
> Just like the one October 8
> When the pigs take a beating
> And things started leading
> To armed war against the state . . .

The travesty ended with the heartfelt, paranoid, and eerily survivalist sentiment "May you learn to struggle and fight/Or the world will off you 'cause you're white."

In the midst of one wargasm, Weather leader Bernadine Dohrn expressed hallucinated solidarity with the Manson Family: "Dig it: first they killed those pigs, then they ate dinner in the same room with them, then they even shoved a fork into the victim's stomach. Wild!" Oh bottomless, gluey, bloodbath horror! Eternal darkness and mutilated corpses!

•   •   •

Night of the Living Dead was not the only exploitation film to seize the time. New year dawned on Sunset Boulevard to community outcry against a billboard that sprouted among the other movie posters and commercial messages. (These included the benign seasonal greeting WAR IS OVER! IF YOU WANT IT. HAPPY CHRISTMAS FROM JOHN AND YOKO.) The offending sign: THE FAMILY THAT SLAYS TOGETHER STAYS TOGETHER—BLOODY MAMA. It was removed after four days.

Bloody Mama was American-International Picture's last topical outrage—a degenerate child of *Bonnie and Clyde*, directed by Roger Corman from Robert Thom's screenplay. Rather than celebrate a glamorously doomed outlaw couple, *Bloody Mama* provided the opportunity for Shelley Winters to top her *Wild in the Streets* persona as the monstrous Ma Barker, mother hen to a Depression-era criminal brood of sexually anarchic, drug-addled hillbilly trash. As much

cult leader as matriarch, Winter's Ma sings to her offspring while masterminding their violent escapades, she sports an ostentatious crucifix and piously declares each Barker atrocity—from casual murder to fishing for gators with live piglet bait—to be God's will. She's also something of a philosopher: "This is supposed to be a free country—but unless you rich, you ain't free." Still, as suggested by the prologue showing the child-Ma raped by her own father, class resentment is subsumed by a sense of generational sin and overall sexual pathology. Ma bathes her grown sons, demands their bisexual friend (Bruce Dern) for the night, and displays open carnal interest in the small-town banker (Pat Hingle), whom the gang abducts.

The *Bloody Mama* sign was a disturbing addition to the allegorical landscape because, as AIP doubtless realized, their movie's postproduction coincided with an insatiable public curiosity regarding what *Life*'s December 19 cover story called THE LOVE AND TERROR CULT, THE WRECK OF A MONSTROUS 'FAMILY.' For those unfamiliar with the effects of LSD, the everyday life of the Manson Family—their bizarre attachment to the Beatles' "White Album," for example—was almost inexplicable. The counterculture was, of course, most susceptible to Manson fascination. The *Los Angeles Free Press* accorded the acid guru a regular column; the rival *Tuesday's Child* declared him Man of the Year. Chicago Seven defendant Jerry Rubin used a recess during his trial to visit Manson in jail because, as he put it, "I fell in love with Charlie Manson the first time I saw his cherub face and sparkling eyes on TV." While Los Angeles district attorney Vincent Bugliosi complained that Manson had become a "cause," the *Berkeley Barb* noted that prison authorities fostered Manson's countercultural image, permitting the monster to keep his long hair, bellbottoms, and fringe leather shirts, repeatedly presenting him to be photographed in full hippie regalia.

Released from prison in March 1967, the then-thirty-two-year-old thief, hustler, and would-be superstar gravitated to the Haight in time for the Summer of Love, there to drop acid and gather the flock of runaway children with whom he ultimately settled at the derelict Spahn Movie Ranch outside LA. But was Manson really a hippie? Liberation News Service's "Fourteen Ways

to Make Out Manson" attempted to explain the source of Manson's daemonic appeal: "Whatever is disgusting and revolting to the average man in decaying Amerikan society, whatever is evil in the eyes of Richard Nixon and Pat Nixon, that's what we dig, that's what we are."*

•   •   •

Further evidence of image war and positive polarization: On the evening of January 14 in New York, Leonard and Felicia Bernstein held a cocktail party at their Park Avenue home to support the twenty-one Black Panthers charged with a conspiracy to implement the *Battle of Algiers* scenario by bombing five midtown Manhattan department stores. The Bernstein bash, whose guests included wealthy socialites and show-business personalities—Otto Preminger, Sidney Lumet, and Mrs. Arthur Penn among them—inspired Tom Wolfe's essay on "radical chic" and was cited as symptomatic of liberal lunacy in a secret memo Daniel Moynihan was then writing the President on race relations. Had not the year's first issue of *Time* designated the Panthers the "most authentic villains" in white America?†

"American self-hatred has reached such a point that the movies are selling it, and projecting it onto the American past," Pauline Kael complained in her review of *Tell Them Willie Boy Is Here*. Whereas the critic had praised *Bonnie and Clyde* for popularizing contemporary attitudes toward violence and authority, she attacked *Willie Boy* as if frightened of the revolution *Bonnie and Clyde* wrought. The audience believed that America was collapsing.

---

*The notion of Manson as ultimate Righteous Outlaw reminded LNS "of some people's brief—or not so brief—romance with John Dillinger and Bonnie and Clyde." Less widely known was Manson's jailhouse connection with the last living member of the Barker Gang, Alvin "Creepy" Karpis. It was Karpis who—six years earlier, when both were incarcerated at the Terminal Island Penitentiary in San Pedro, California—taught young Charles to play steel guitar.

†Over the course of the lengthy Panther 21 trial, the prosecution introduced *The Battle of Algiers* as evidence and screened it for the jury. According to juror Edwin Kennebeck, "the film did more to help me see things from the defense point of view than the DA suspected."

They're on the side of apocalypse: since they feel it's all going down anyway, it seems to make them feel better to see these movies saying that it should go down, that that's right. And now here's a movie that goes all the way—turning white Americans into a race carrying blood guilt, a race whose civilization must be destroyed.

May you learn to struggle and fight. Or the world will off you 'cause you're white.

Willie Boy was only the first. The most overtly ideological of revisionist Westerns addressed the subject of the Indian wars. In their open identification with Native Americans, such movies were the equivalent of marching for peace beneath a Viet Cong flag. Hollywood contra Hollywood: Cavalry Westerns *Little Big Man* and *Soldier Blue* were in production when My Lai was exposed, and the revelation of American atrocities only reinforced their argument that the slaughter of Native Americans was the essence of the white man's war. Arthur Penn had purchased the rights to Thomas Berger's novel *Little Big Man* in 1965, but—now shooting outside Billings, Montana—he could not have picked a more propitious time to bring it to fruition.

Little Big Man, a picaresque vaudeville starring generational symbol Dustin Hoffman, was designed as a series of escalating massacres to climax, like Buffalo Bill's Wild West Show, with a representation of Custer's Last Stand. A settler child brought up by the Cheyenne, Hoffman's character might have been one of the white kids captured by Sierra Charriba: "For a boy it was a kind of paradise—I wasn't just playin' injin, I was livin' injin!" Over the movie's course, Hoffman shuttles between white and Indian culture. In the former (shown as hypocritical, brutal, sexually repressed, ridiculous, and ultimately insane), he is variously a snake-oil salesman, a gunfighter, a wino, and a muleskinner; in the latter, he is, as the Cheyenne call themselves, a "Human Being." More than any previous Western, *Little Big Man* dramatized what Paul Zimmerman described in *Newsweek* as the "split between the defenders of the faith and the apostles of a new life-style." Satirizing religion, the army, and John Ford, demonstrating the moral superiority of the Cheyenne (and, by extension, the

audience), the movie arrived complete with *Look*'s cover story—"A Strange Role for Dustin Hoffman"—that announced, "Red power has begun to assert itself. . . . [Viewers] will get a new experience, the losing of the West." Hoffman, who had to learn to ride a horse for the movie and was compared to the Kennedys and the Beatles in *Esquire*'s production piece, was as far from John Wayne as any star one could imagine.*

Kael had called *Willie Boy* an incitement to "genosuicide" made for "black kamikazes and masochistic white Americans." What, then, was *Soldier Blue*, a conflation of the Sand Creek Massacre and Battle of Wounded Knee, which Ralph Nelson was then filming in the Mexican high sierras? Sole survivors of a Cheyenne ambush, a released captive (Candice Bergen) and cavalry private (Peter Strauss) make their way through Indian country to the fort, only to arrive as the cavalry ignores a white flag to slaughter a Cheyenne village. Paraplegics and amputees were bused in from Mexico City for this climax. In her memoirs, Bergen recalled the "prosthetics truck" stocked with wooden legs, severed heads, and blood bags. She herself was required to wear "lifelike plastic breasts."

Predicting the "most gut-clutching film in history," *Time*'s February 2 production story described one of *Soldier Blue*'s more sensational bits in which a cavalryman rapes and mutilates an Indian maiden, noting that, "even the Sharon Tate murderers might have blanched at such a scene."

Spring 1970: *Patton* over Cambodia

Could *Soldier Blue* and *Myra Breckinridge* be Hollywood's future? Were the old entertainment verities gone? Hollywood seemed fixated on the events of "1968": "Gutter language, nudity, casual permissiveness point up the fatal mugging of puritanism on stage, on screen, and in rock music," *Variety* complained in their January 7, 1970, front-page story, B.O. DICTATORSHIP BY YOUTH. "There

---

*March 6, 1970, the same day the *Berkeley Tribe* editorialized that, "To defend ourselves against mounting pig terror, we must take up the gun," the Weather Underground inadvertently blew up a Greenwich Village townhouse. The building next door belonged to Hoffman—scarcely a fortnight returned from Montana when the clandestine bomb factory blasted a hole through his living room wall.

are no subtleties in today's young. Theirs is the vocabulary of anger, violence, destructiveness."

The counterculture mega-hits *Easy Rider*, *Midnight Cowboy*, and *Butch Cassidy* were still in release, and straggler *Zabriskie Point* had just unfurled its colors to a fusillade of derision. As the horrifying Manson was promoted for the role of America's number-one hippie, so My Lai commanding officer Lieutenant William Calley came to personify the Vietnam War. America needed a military hero, and like a miracle, one suddenly materialized. Now there was *Patton*—the last Twentieth Century Fox road show but the first true Nixon movie—which premiered at New York's Criterion Theater, two days after the opening of the Panther 21 trial, on February 4, 1970.*

In his celluloid portrait, subtitled *Portrait of a Rebel*, the colorful and controversial four-star general George Patton was positioned not only as an authority figure but even as a Righteous Outlaw. Although *New York Times* critic Vincent Canby called *Patton* "the story of a man about whom only the Establishment would become genuinely sentimental," reviews were mainly favorable. Unlike *The Green Berets*, *Patton* created a consensus: *Variety* marveled that the movie appealed to hawks and doves, "ultra-liberals" as well as the American Legion. Director Franklin Schaffner, writer Edmund North, and even producer Frank McCarthy thought *Patton* was antiwar—at least, considering its hero's dubious behavior, by implication. But that questionable subtlety was soon lost.

---

*Patton was a long-germinating project. As far back as Korea, Fox mulled a Patton biopic. Warner Brothers then pursued the project until it became clear the Pentagon disapproved. A dozen years later, Fox reactivated the scenario (offering it first to the iconoclastic Sam Fuller). Then in 1965, as Johnson's war escalated, producer Frank McCarthy hired fresh-from-film-school Francis Coppola to write a screenplay for venerable William Wyler to direct. Budgeted at $10 million, this multigenerational production suffered delays throughout 1967, including Wyler's departure due to conflicts with star George C. Scott. (As Wyler was replaced by Franklin Schaffner, Edmund North revised Coppola's script.) For a while, Scott quit as well. The lead was offered to Burt Lancaster, Lee Marvin, Rod Steiger, and John Wayne. All turned it down, although Wayne later confessed this a blunder. Would history—or just the movie—have changed if the Duke had played Patton?

Time's January 5 issue had named the Middle Americans as their Man and Woman of the Year—choosing, over the Silent Majority, a term coined by pundit Joseph Kraft in late 1967.

> Everywhere they flew the colors of assertive patriotism. Their car windows were plastered with American-flag decals, their ideological totems. In the bumper-sticker dialogue of the freeways, they answered MAKE LOVE NOT WAR with HONOR AMERICA or SPIRO IS MY HERO. They sent Richard Nixon to the White House and two teams of astronauts to the moon. . . .
>
> While the rest of the nation's youth has been watching Dustin Hoffman in *Midnight Cowboy*, Middle America's teen-agers have been taking in John Wayne for the second or third time in *The Green Berets*.

By mid-March—when *Patton* went wide and General Lon Nol deposed Prince Sihanouk in Cambodia—Schaffner's movie was widely understood to articulate Silent Majority yearnings. Observers were struck by the long lines of middle-aged or elderly whites queued to see the movie, zombie ghouls tottering back to the box office.

Why? Like *Major Dundee*, *Patton* began on the grisly battlefield of national defeat—a massacre in the Sahara with Bedouins and buzzards stripping American corpses. But, far more satisfying than *Dundee*, *Patton* ended three hours later in total American victory. How did the General prevail? Like the Major, he had to first create a fighting force. "They don't look like soldiers, they don't act like soldiers," was Patton's first response to the lackadaisical American troops. *Patton*'s key scene, played just before intermission, has the General browbeat, slap, and nearly pull his gun on a sniveling "yellow-belly" private hospitalized for battle fatigue. (Patton actually struck two such soldiers, one suffering from malaria.) The scandal becomes a national issue. The U.S. Senate delays Patton's promotion, and he is further humiliated by the Allied Supreme Commander, General Dwight D. Eisenhower—compelled to make a public apology to the private, the medical staff, and the entire unit. His career seems over, but in the movie's second half, the irascible general bounces back to win the Battle of the Bulge. In the end, Patton's former adjunct promoted to be his superior officer, General Omar

Bradley (Karl Malden) tells him that the slapped soldier "did more to win the war than any other private in the army."

As impressive as *Patton*'s triumphant narrative was the movie's Pop Art prologue. The first image is the screen-filling red, white, and blue of a monstrous American flag—greeted, Stanley Kauffmann noted in *The New Republic*, by a smattering of "defiant applause." Presently, to the cry of "ten-SHUN!," the tiny figure of Patton emerges. Close-ups feast on the fetishistic details of his outfit—the shiny helmet embossed with four stars and the letter A, the blue sash, the riding crop, the jodhpurs and boots, the pinky rings, the ascot, the pearl-handled revolvers, the chest layered with medals. Canby joked that this bizarre presence might be mistaken for "a member of the chorus of *The Student Prince*." Yet the critic "felt the audience lunge toward [Patton] with relief. Everything was all right again, the old values were safe."

By now the so-called old values had come to encompass telling-it-like-it-is. Framed by the flag, the General bids his audience be seated, then launches into an outrageously tough-talking speech: "I want you to remember that no bastard ever won a war by dying for his country. He won it by making the other poor dumb bastard die for his country." Although wearing the orders and decorations given to him after the war, Patton speaks as if the war were just getting under way. "Men, all this stuff you've heard about America not wanting to fight—wanting to stay out of the war—is a lot of horse dung," he rasps. The recruits to whom Patton speaks are never shown; it is the viewer who is addressed.

> Americans traditionally love to fight. All real Americans love the sting of battle. When you were kids, you all admired the champion marble-shooter, the fastest runner, the big-league ballplayer, the toughest boxer. Americans love a winner and will not tolerate a loser. Americans play to win all the time. I wouldn't give a hoot in hell for a man who lost and laughed.

At this point, Canby noted, the audience giggled in embarrassment. But titters stopped as Patton continued: "That's why Americans have never lost and will

never lose a war—because the very thought of losing is hateful to Americans."
How long had the nation been waiting to hear that?*

Even "before [*Patton*] had really begun," Kauffmann wrote, "it was a solid,
unassailable hit." When the Oscar-bedecked picture was re-released fourteen
months later on a double bill with Fox's other military success *M*A*S*H*, a
significant portion of the audience was reported remaining in their seats to
savor *Patton*'s opening exhortation a second time.

• • •

Movies continued to offer imaginary solutions to real problems. *Variety* suggested that audiences were flocking to *Patton* to see "a hero who is egocentric
and personally unpleasant, but has the know-how in achieving military victory." In England, the *Times of London* stated the obvious: "I daresay the Americans now fighting in Asia could do with him if he could manage another of
his reincarnations."†

Patton's most public fan was, however, the President of the United States.

---

*Now framed in close-up, Patton plunges on.

> I actually pity the poor bastards we're going against. By God, I do. We're
> not going to shoot the bastards. We're going to cut out their living guts
> and use them to grease the treads of our tanks. We're going to murder
> those lousy Hun bastards by the bushel. . . . Wade into them and spill their
> blood. Shoot them in the belly. When you stick your hand into a bunch
> of goo that a moment ago was your best friend's face, you'll know what
> to do. . . . We're going to hold the enemy by the nose and kick him in
> the ass. We're going to kick the hell out of him, go through him like crap
> through a goose.

There is a pause. "All right," Patton concludes, "Now you sons of bitches know how I
feel. I will be proud to lead you wonderful guys into battle anytime, anywhere. That's
all." Although this routine could almost have been written for Scott's Buck Turgidson
(who resurfaced when *Dr. Strangelove* was theatrically rereleased that summer), the
speech was a compilation of actual Patton statements.

†Indeed, the hero's own son, Colonel George S. Patton III, commanded the 11th Armored Cavalry Regiment in Vietnam. Prone to encouraging his men with Pattonesque
exhortations like "I do like to see the arms and legs fly," George III surpassed his father

Richard Nixon would repeatedly screen the three-hour movie throughout the spring of 1970. The most conservative estimate has Nixon watching *Patton* twice—on April 1 and then again on April 25. (In between, as the nation thrilled to the spectacle of the disabled Apollo 13 moon flight, he grandly promised to withdraw 150,000 more troops from Vietnam before year's end.) Other commentators, noting that the President obtained a personal print, believe he projected *Patton* at least a half-dozen times, both at the White House and at his San Clemente, California, retreat.

Nixon's biographer Stephen Ambrose tactfully writes that the President "started watching" the film in late March. Months later, Secretary of State William Rogers told Darryl Zanuck that the President found a way to bring almost every conversation around to *Patton*—he was a "walking ad for that movie." Soon, syndicated columnists Evans and Novak revealed that presidential assistant H. R. Haldeman had advised young White House staffers to see *Patton* if they wanted a handle to grasp the Commander in Chief's mindset; the movie persuaded the President that "the true American spirit was Patton, not the New Left."*

The same day the Evans and Novak column ran, a jury convicted five of

---

with a 1968 Christmas card on which a color photo of stacked Viet Cong corpses was captioned "Peace on Earth."

Life's White House correspondent Hugh Sidey saw a more personal component: Ike was the unseen presence who rejected Patton's Sicily plan, the demiurge that cast down Patton and raised him up. Nixon, too, was publicly humiliated by Eisenhower, who similarly compelled his young running mate to go on TV to defend his spot on the 1952 Republican ticket. Sidey thought Nixon's insecurities promoted an admiration for tough guys like John Connally and John Wayne. The President suffered "an inferiority complex" and "cast around for stronger people. . . . Then the Patton film comes along. Here's a man in battle. Here is an argument for boldness, innovation, ready-made."

On the other hand, as Garry Wills noted, *Patton* may be less "about male aggression satisfied" than "the baffling of a good man's energies." The President braced himself with "shared rejection. He was stiffening his spine with the surest medicines for it— resentment of his critics, and self-pity." In any case, according to Kissinger, Chinese leader Zhou Enlai screened *Patton* in preparation for Nixon's 1972 visit.

the Chicago Seven of crossing state lines with intent to foment a riot. Patton, too, had also had to contend with undisciplined, cowardly young people—and when he lost his temper and attacked the hospitalized "yellow belly," it was for the bastard's own good, as well as the country's. After the "slap heard round the world," liberal journalists had called for Patton's court martial, but as the movie points out, Patton was supported by a great Silent Majority; the mail that followed the slap was 89 percent in his favor! Nixon likewise endured an acrimonious adversarial relationship with the treacherous press—like Patton, he was forever drawing unwelcome, unsympathetic media attention. Only two days after the President ordered B-52s to secretly bomb the Plain of Jars in mid-February, the *New York Times* blew his cover.

Patton survived an image crisis, endured disappointment, withstood personal attack, and came back to win World War II. He was absolved by History as well as by Hollywood. Patton had even designed a uniform, just as Nixon proposed one for the White House guards. More: Patton's eccentric belief in reincarnation, his mystical connections to ancient battlefields, were part of a larger pattern. "The men can't tell you're acting, sir," an aide-de-camp informs him after one cursing, screaming display. "It's not important for them to know," is Patton's reply. "It's only important for me to know." Thus, Patton anticipated what Nixon privately called his Madman Theory. "I want the North Vietnamese to believe I've reached the point where I might do anything to stop the war," he explained to Haldeman in 1969.

As spring arrived, power barometers registered mounting pressure. The same day that Majority Leader Hale Boggs denounced FBI surveillance of Congress and rock star Grace Slick attempted to sneak Abbie Hoffman into the White House tea to which, as Tricia Nixon's former classmate at Finch College, she'd been invited, Nixon was spooked by his own vice president. Spiro Agnew was asserting that anything less than total invasion of Cambodia was mere "pussyfooting." With stocks falling on Wall Street, the April 25 screening proved crucial. JFK had *Dr. No*, LBJ had *The Alamo*, SDS had *Bonnie and Clyde*, the Panthers had *The Battle of Algiers*, Abbie Hoffman and Tom Hayden had *Wild in the Streets*, Norman Mailer had *Maidstone*, and the President had . . . *Patton*.

The movie, so Evans and Novak later revealed, served to reinforce Nixon's "resolve to risk the Cambodian intervention." National Security adviser Henry Kissinger understood that he had gained admittance to the President's inner sanctum when he was asked to join Nixon, Attorney General John Mitchell, and Florida businessman Bebe Rebozo, on the presidential yacht for an official wargasm—a martini-fueled, pre-invasion Potomac River cruise of which Kissinger wrote that "the tensions of grim military planning were transformed into exaltation by the liquid refreshments." The outing was capped by a White House presentation of *Patton*, which Kissinger's memoirs hint may actually have been Nixon's second screening of the day.*

Thursday evening, April 30, five years and twenty-three days after LBJ offered his Indochina rationale; the President went on television to announce he had ordered American ground troops into Cambodia. The *New York Times* reported Nixon seemed as "grim" as Johnson in using the "toughest" rhetoric of his presidency. Other viewers were less restrained. Nixon appeared at once drunk and hungover, perhaps even suffering the DTs. The President was "strident." He slurred his words. His upper lip was beaded with sweat, and "his vision" was apocalyptic.

> We live in an age of anarchy. We see mindless attacks on all the great institutions which have been created by free civilization in the last five hundred years. Even here in the United States, great universities are being systematically destroyed. Small nations all over the world find themselves under attack from within and from without . . .

---

*Haldeman's notes reinforce Kissinger's account of the President's overwrought state. Nixon was on a manic jag—drinking heavily and going without sleep, throwing tantrums, worrying where to put his new pool table, cursing his aides, and invoking *Patton*, who, he told Haldeman, was, for him, an inspiration. In an unusual psychological analysis of the presidential mood swing away from the optimism of mid-April, Max Frankel noted in the *New York Times* that despite the ongoing war which he had inherited, Nixon "had gone longer into his term of office than either President Kennedy or President Johnson without some militant demonstration of his resolve to act strongly abroad."

So do larger ones.

> We will not be humiliated. We will not be defeated. It is not our power but our
> will and character that is [sic] being tested tonight.
>   If, when the chips are down, the world's most powerful nation, the United
> States of America, acts like a pitiful, helpless giant, the forces of totalitarianism
> and anarchy will threaten free nations and free institutions throughout the world.

Thus presenting the invasion of Cambodia as the ultimate measure of the national purpose, Nixon articulated the doctrine of credibility more directly than any previous American president (even as he widened his own credibility gap by strenuously denying the past six months' secret bombings of Cambodia).

Rather than speak from his Oval Office desk, Nixon chose the White House War Room, standing with a pointer before a map, as though it were a military briefing. The President cast himself as Patton: Total victory or political death!

> I would rather be a one-term President and do what I believe was . . . right than
> to be a two-term President at the cost of seeing America become a second-rate
> power and to see this nation accept the first defeat in its proud hundred-and-
> ninety-year history.

The White House switchboard reported that incoming phone calls supported the President six to one; antiwar demonstrations began on many college campuses within the hour.

May Day: The following morning, the President met at the Pentagon with the Joint Chiefs of Staff, Secretary of Defense Melvin Laird, and Kissinger. The assembled officials were disquieted by their commander's behavior. Nixon didn't appear to pay much attention to their briefing. Distracted, he broke into the discussion with a disjointed, impassioned, profane monologue worthy of you-know-who. Nixon reiterated his determination to "clean up those sanctuaries," and shouted at his mortified advisers that "you have to electrify people with bold decisions. . . . Let's go blow the hell out of them!" Was he still acting? As the President left the Pentagon, he suddenly turned to reporters, shifting his focus from the Viet Cong to their student supporters: "You see these bums, you know, blowing up the campuses . . ." he mumbled. Had the President recalled General Bradley's last line about the slapped soldier winning the war?

• • •

The invasion of Cambodia compounds tension at Yale, where, with Black Panther Bobby Seale set to go on trial in New Haven, students are already on strike. All manner of revolutionary celebrities—including the reunited Conspiracy—have come to town, and the apprehensive administration cancels the alumni weekend. The first issue of *The Yale Review*, whose associate editors include first-year law student Hillary Rodham, was timed for May Day publication and largely devoted to the upcoming trial. Sunday, a mass rally calls upon the nation's students to shut down the universities. By then, however, some sixty colleges are already on strike. Antiwar demonstrations produce the worst disturbances in the history of Stanford. The National Guard is called out to restore order at Ohio State.

At nearby Kent State, students (who, only weeks ago, responded tepidly to Jerry Rubin's call for revolution) celebrate Saturday night by torching the two-story wooden barracks that serve as the campus ROTC building. The town firemen are prevented from putting out the blaze. The structure burns to the ground in a carnival atmosphere, accentuated by the live ammunition exploding inside. The next morning, Governor James Rhodes—a senatorial candidate in the upcoming Republican primary—declares student demonstrators "worse than Brown Shirts and the Communist element. . . . They're the worst type of people we have in America." Rhodes dispatches National Guardsmen to Kent State, where, on Monday, May 4, four students are shot dead and nine more wounded.

Each day for the rest of the week sees a hundred new campus demonstrations. Some thirty ROTC buildings are burned or bombed. Over 500 colleges are closed. According to the May Gallup poll, campus unrest is now regarded

as the nation's leading problem. Before dawn Friday morning, the sleepless
Richard Nixon materializes amid the youthful demonstrators camped out at
the Lincoln Memorial. They are stunned as the President rambles on about
football and reminisces over his own student days. Some seven hours later on
the steps of the New York Stock Exchange—where, after news of Kent State,
the Dow Jones Industrial Average suffered its worst one-day loss since November 22, 1963—an antiwar rally is attacked by 200 laborers from a nearby construction site, who assault demonstrators and bystanders, tear down the
Episcopal banner at Trinity Church, invade City Hall to demand the American
flag be raised to full staff, and smash windows at nearby Pace College. The
Deputy Borough President of Manhattan observes police joining ranks with
rampaging workers and laughing as students are beaten. The following week
brings prowar demonstrations every lunch hour in New York's financial district, culminating in a Friday march where several thousand construction workers parade in support of the President. Among the signs observed: WE LOVE
NIXON, AGNEW, MITCHELL, HIS WIFE, AND REAGAN.*

The people have spoken, and the construction worker's hard-hat is an instant icon. The following week, Conservative Party leaders appear at a midtown rally wearing star-spangled helmets. Magical and democratic, the hard-hat
confers a masculinity that is almost Pattonesque. Beer manufacturers will soon
feature helmeted actors in their advertisements. In a May 26 ritual induction,
the President meets with leaders of the New York Building and Construction
Trades Council and is crowned with a hard-hat labeled Commander in Chief.
The Dow hits bottom that day at 621 (then, after Nixon confers with business
leaders, rebounds an impressive 34 points). Henry Kissinger fears that not only
the nation but also the erratically behaving President teeters on the brink of

_____

*Other placards characterized the city's liberal, antiwar mayor, John Lindsay, as a
"Commy rat," a "faggot," and an "idiot." May 20, 100,000 workers staged a prowar
march through Lower Manhattan. It was billed as a spontaneous demonstration, although virtually every Manhattan construction site was shut down and some wondered
where the men got their U.S. flags and professionally printed signs (which included the
slogan NATIONAL GUARD, 4; KENT, 0).

collapse. For H. R. Haldeman, "Kent State marked a turning point for Nixon, a beginning of his downhill slide towards Watergate."

•   •   •

On June 5, the President summons the directors of the FBI, the CIA, the National Security Administration, and the Defense Intelligence Agency, and informs them that "hundreds, perhaps thousands of Americans—mostly under thirty—are determined to destroy our society." In essence, he is anticipating the critical response to the long-awaited *Myra Breckinridge*. Using the novel's original sell line—"Everything you've heard about Myra Breckinridge is true," the movie (which, over the course of its nine-month gestation, had doubled its budget from $3 to $6 million) is unveiled June 23 in the most tumultuous New York premiere since *The Green Berets'*.

It is four days short of the first anniversary of the epochal Stonewall Riot, and the crowd outside the Criterion (so recently *Patton's* bastion) is filled with brazen drag queens. Indeed, *Myra's* opening previews the Christopher Street Liberation Day March held later that week. The *East Village Other* finds a "festive, often violent atmosphere" reminiscent of the Columbia building seizures—"cops, pickets, police barricades, press, television cameras, pushing, showing-off, camaraderie, hurt feelings, and heroes." The *New York Times* reports that between two and ten thousand "screaming" citizens blocked Times Square, "crashing through barricades and breaking store windows." Two policemen are sent to the hospital.

Myra Breckinridge compounds this orgy of confusion the morning after when it nearly doubles the Criterion's previous record for an opening-day box office while garnering the most hostile notices ever accorded a Hollywood release. The story of a homosexual film critic who undergoes a sex change and moves to Hollywood in order to, first, seize control of his uncle's acting school and then orchestrate a realignment of the sexes is received with fear and loathing by all reviewers.*

---

*In LA, where *Myra Breckinridge* smashed *The Dirty Dozen's* opening-week record at the Loew's Hollywood, the *Los Angeles Times* deemed it sui generis, "beyond or beneath

•   •   •

Myra Breckinridge besmirched, as it fetishized, all Hollywood history. Considering that its first dramatic sequence is a public castration, that a later scene—revealing the heroine's absent penis—makes a cowboy and his lawyer faint, and that the movie's director was driven from Hollywood never to return, it seems amazing that *Myra* has never been recuperated by film theorists.

Beginning with the image of Raquel Welch and Rex Reed dancing along the Walk of Stars, the movie is demystifying on a grand scale. Welch's bad acting is given a deeply pathetic dimension by the pathos of her dialogue, characterizing movie stars as "gods and goddesses." Reed, whose ineptitude somewhat burnishes his female alter-ego's talent, revealed that Welch craved the part of Myra so desperately that she tested for it—appropriate in that *Myra* is a movie founded on a dialectic of yearning and exploitation, the class relations between idols and their fans, the pitting of glamour haves against glamour have-nots. Mainly taking place on a blatant movie set, where, amid all manner of ridiculous acting routines, would-be stars study to appear in porn films or Westerns, *Myra* expresses an unprecedented contempt for make-believe—the insult capped by the unprecedented spectacle of seventy-seven-year-old Mae West lasciviously babbling on about "stud banks" and "lay-a-day plans."*

---

the usual forms of criticism" and the *Los Angeles Herald-Examiner* called Myra "repulsively neurotic." *Time* found the X-rated *Myra* "about as funny as a child molester . . . an insult to intelligence, an affront to sensibility and an abomination to the eye." The newsweeklies attempted to outdo each other in characterizing *Myra*'s perversions. *Newsweek* termed it "the perfect picture of an industry that's down for the count, flat on its back and playing with its sorry self." *New York* called *Myra* the "creation of an infant smearing about in its own excrement." Finally, the movie was singled out for attack in *Life*'s July 4 editorial as "unforgivable" in its vulgarity. "As I walked out of the theater," managing editor Ralph Graves wrote, "I heard a woman behind me say, 'We might as well slit our throats if we've come to this.' "

*An icon who never appeared out of character, West is here the return of the repressed. As the greatest star of 1933, she projected a pioneering image of confident, free, outspoken sexuality. Her vehicles, *She Done Him Wrong* and *I'm No Angel*, not only saved Paramount but also were largely responsible for the 1934 enforcement of the Production

The acting academy wherein hippie students learn to communicate "real honesty," or "experience" a tree, might be the Manson Family's Spahn Movie Ranch. Even without LSD, Hollywood is a cult writ large, allowing such cynical predators as the super-agent Leticia Van Allen (West), the cowboy acting teacher Buck Loner, and his nephew-turned-niece, Myra, to feed upon corn-fed idiots like would-be movie stars Rusty Godowsky (Roger Herren) and his girlfriend Mary Ann (Farrah Fawcett). The whole notion of "normal love" is ridiculed throughout—not the least at Buck Loner's academy, which, among other things, teaches "cinema love-making." Even the obligatory orgy scene— intercut with the first "medical" examination Myra gives Rusty—is provocatively desultory.

Myra's anti-Americanism is indistinguishable from post–Pop Art attitudes regarding American mass culture. How to explain Myra's worship of the old movies that formed the American mentality she loathes? After referring to the "entire range of human—which is to say, American behavior," Myra goes even further: "Could the real Christ have possessed a fraction of the radiance of H. B. Warner or Jeffrey Hunter?" Still, her professed goal is the "destruction of the traditional man."

Is Myra a drag queen, a transsexual, a lesbian, a feminist? Stripping down to American-flag bikini briefs in the movie's most outrageous scene, the monster straps on an unseen, if clearly monstrous, dildo and appears to penetrate Rusty (who believes his eccentric acting teacher is giving him a posture exam). Cowboy authority is utterly debauched. Myra smacks Rusty's flanks with her Stetson as their unnatural act is subsumed by a montage including images of a battering ram, a crumbling dam, a roller coaster, an atomic blast, the pit of hell, and Alice Faye singing "America, I Love You."

America might be irresistible, but *Myra* was not. "There is a little something here to set everyone's gorge agurgling," *Time* gasped—even if it's just the vial

---

Code. Thus West's presence conflates two turbulent periods—the Great Depression and the Great Society. In this, *Myra* followed *Bonnie and Clyde*. (Indeed, many extras feature the Clyde "look.")

of Rusty's urine specimen placed in the center of the frame. (This was part of the sequence that the newsweekly proposed as the "nadir" of Hollywood cinema.) *Myra Breckinridge* was not just the worst moment in American movie history but the expression of the whole dread sexual revolution. Who was it that ravished poor Rusty? The feminist Myra or the homosexual Myron? This new public enemy conflated and hyperbolized the most outrageous aspects of women's liberation, gay rights, and the porn pandemic—the bra-burning attack on Miss America, the appearance of counterculture sex tabloid *Screw*, the revolt of the Stonewall drag queens.*

Time, which had hailed Michael Sarne for the "most dazzling directorial debut" of 1968, now assigned him "special discredit for the repulsive dildo rape scene and the obscene device of interspersing the film with clips from movies of favorite old stars." (One, Loretta Young, successfully filed suit to have her image removed from the film.) In the context of *Myra*, "Laurel and Hardy are made to look like fags," *Time* complained, failing to note that, in the clips used, Laurel and Hardy were costumed as soldiers. Released during wartime, *Myra Breckinridge* was filled with anti-patriotic sentiment. Another old movie shard interpolated in the rape montage has a uniformed man declare "that's what I call disgusting," to which a woman coyly responds "why don't you show them how, sergeant?"

---

*On January 7, 1970, *Variety* reported that there were already "some 800 skinemas all over the U.S. specializing in homo and 8–16mm amateur stag flix which grind around the clock and get up to a straight $5 admission," and *Myra Breckinridge* was but one step away. (After the Motion Picture Association of America branded Myra with the first X rating in Twentieth Century Fox history, MPAA chief Jack Valenti took the unprecedented precaution of issuing a personal endorsement: "I personally found the film a very funny spoof but a picture children should not view.") Three minutes into the movie, the soundtrack coyly bleeps "mother" and keeps "fucker." Throughout, *Myra* identifies itself with pornography. An outrageously phallic Carmen Miranda sequence is followed by a cut to a porn theater marquee—SOMETHING NEW IN SIN, BEAVERS GALORE—as though the Miranda number were playing inside.

Generational War in the Dream Life: Hey *Joe* (Where You Goin' with That Gun in Your Hand?)

In its January 1970 paean to the "Men and Women of the Year," *Time* allowed that white Middle Americans were particularly angered by black militants.

> During 1969, job militants at construction sites in Pittsburgh came up against phalanxes of hard-hatted white workers determined to prove that they were capable of counterviolence. "The threats strike me as blackmail," says Al Braselton, an Atlanta advertising man. "Negroes have got to confront the white community strongly, but it had better not be with shotguns, because we've got a lot more of them than they have."

Having made a seamless, free-associational segue from Northern white-ethnic working-class resentment to the ruminations of a Southern white professional image-maker, *Time* veered into another imaginative scenario.

> Without exactly meaning to [sic], white Middle America rests upon the unspoken threat of sheer presence and the six-gun deterrent, Gary Cooper's fingers twitching two inches from his holster. No wonder the Middle Americans recoil when the twitching fingers are black. . . .

Proletarian rage, upper-middle-class paranoia, twitchy trigger fingers: *Time* had anticipated *Joe*. Then in production, this murky-looking, low-budget independent feature opened in New York seven months later on July 15, 1970, the day after J. Edgar Hoover, also reliving the 1930s, declared the Black Panther Party the "greatest threat to the national security in the history of this nation."

Named for another character unafraid to tell it like it was, *Joe* was conceived during the fin-de-siècle summer of 1969 by forty-two-year-old Harvard-educated advertising executive and unproduced playwright Norman Wexler. Prodded by John Avildsen, an agency colleague whose recent experience included directing a skin flick, Wexler began shopping his three-page treatment, then called *The Gap*, which pitted a middle-aged adman against his wanton hippie daughter—taking *Candy* down to the real nitty-gritty. By September, the idea caught the attention of the exploitation-film company Cannon, which, sensing a quick killing, stipulated that Wexler deliver a finished script in eight days. Avildsen was recruited to shoot the movie for a modest $106,000 in six weeks during the dreary winter of 1970.

The so-called Gap was already the name of a dungarees-only emporium opened that summer by a San Francisco real-estate developer. Wexler and Avildsen promised to be equally of the moment: *Joe* opens by introducing a suitably degenerate Bonnie and Clyde, hippies Frank (Patrick McDermott) and Melissa (Susan Sarandon), sharing a bath in the kitchen area of their squalid East Village apartment. But, instead of lovemaking, explicit close-ups show Frank cooking and shooting smack. The Orgy is pharmaceutical. Neglected Melissa ingests too much speed and, after freaking out in a neighborhood sundries store, winds up in the hospital. Her father, haute WASP account executive Bill Compton (Dennis Patrick), ventures downtown to collect her effects from the pad of depravity. At that moment, Frank returns to taunt him with Melissa's unresolved family drama ("When I met her she was balling her way up the aisle at the Fillmore and every once in a while she used to like to try an old cod"), driving the White Father berserk. In a splendidly cheesy effect, complete with crude psychedelic superimpositions, the enraged adman bludgeons the hippie scuzzball to death.

This was new! Anything now seems possible. Compton picks up Frank's dope-filled shopping bag and flees. Cut to the dank, nearly empty neighborhood tavern where, inexplicably absent from work, steamfitter Joe Curran (Peter Boyle) holds forth, his mind crammed with phantom antagonists. "The niggers are getting all the money!" he announces, instantly capturing the viewer's attention. Ignored by a weary bartender, Joe's harangue continues. "Fuck work when you can screw, have babies, and get paid for it."

> Welfare! They get all that welfare money. They even get free rubbers. You think they use them? Hell no. The only way they make money is making babies. They sell the rubbers and then they use the money to buy booze.

Joe is grinning like a Halloween pumpkin when haggard Compton—desperate himself for an alcohol fix—enters the establishment (whose single object of decoration is a framed photograph of the Iwo Jima flag-raising). Could this be a lost liberal? Joe turns to the impeccably dressed newcomer. "Find me a liberal who isn't a nigger lover and I'll massage your asshole—and I ain't queer!"*

Was there a way to bottle this essence of Middle American outrage? As Columbia had already registered *The Gap*, Wexler's original title was changed. According to Susan Sarandon, *Joe* was not only retitled but reconfigured in the wake of May's Wall Street rumble: "They saw that they had a godsend in Peter Boyle and they re-edited it to emphasize him." In addition to the requisite soundtrack album, Mercury Records rushed out a release devoted to Joe's diatribe—which escalates to a call for vigilante vengeance.

Joe's repeated assertion that he is ready to kill "just one hippie" allows him to bond with Compton. When, in a paroxysm of alcohol-induced bravado, the adman confesses his crime, Joe is ecstatic: "I just talk about it, but you did it!" He assures Compton that Compton is a hero—after all, Frank was a dope dealer and how many had he already murdered with that shit? Anyway, as Joe later reassures Mrs. Compton: "The police in this town ain't gonna bust their ass over one junkie murder. See, a guy who kills one junkie, might kill another junkie . . . heh, heh."

Joe has the red, white, and blue titles of a poor man's *Patton*, and like Patton, Joe expresses sentiments no American politician—not even George Wallace—

---

*What can restore the initial excitement provided by this heavyset, bald, working stiff installed on a barstool in the middle of a New York City afternoon shooting off his mouth? "The dollar ain't worth shit!" Summing up the Great Society (and its economic aftershocks), *Joe* gave presence to those blue-collar workers whose income was eaten away by wartime inflation even as the counterculture eroded their moral code. The spring demonstrations in New York and St. Louis, during which, for the first time, American civilians fought in the streets over Vietnam, truly brought the war home. As the conflict entered its sixth year, the white working class came to seem the last bastion of traditional manliness—their Alamo besieged by an unholy alliance of threatening women, militant blacks, and liberal "faggots." There is a strong sexual content to Joe's denunciation of both the bleeding hearts ("42 percent of all liberals are queer, the Wallace people took a poll") and the rich college kids who spend their vacations at fancy resorts and have orgies—a word Joe pronounces with a hard *g*.

had the nerve to articulate in public. (Four days after *Joe* opened, Richard Nixon jotted on a legal pad, "Need to Handle Wallace.") Patton was Middle America's commander in chief. Joe, as suggested by the movie's minimalist country-western title tune ("Hey Joe, don't it make you want to go to war . . . once more?") was the infantryman of that Emerging Republican Majority that political analyst Kevin Phillips detailed during the 1968 campaign.*

Despite his gun collection, Joe lacks the political consciousness to become a Minuteman. Rather, his anger seems the expression of an unacknowledged—albeit only newly discovered—psychological ailment, the midlife crisis. In the movie's key moment of class-transcendent bonding, Joe asks Compton if he, too, ever has the "feeling that everything you do, your whole life, is a crock of shit?" Amazingly, Compton agrees.

•   •   •

Generational struggle in the dream life, *Joe* is filled with intimations of media warfare. Frank is a painter-manqué while Compton is a professional image-maker. For Joe, the TV news confirms the reality of Compton's crime, but television is not the only thing that brings the men together. As Joe's wife, Mary Lou, blurts out when the Comptons are invited for Chinese takeout chez Joe: "Everything is kids." That's the problem in this Global Village. Opening

---

*The "liberal coalition of Negroes and silk-stocking voters" provoked a "conservative (and increasingly Republican) counter trend among working-class and lower-middle-class Catholics," Phillips wrote. Noting that this segment of the electorate was just as "anti-establishment today (albeit less obviously) as it was upon disembarkation a century ago," he declared that the decade's "great political upheaval" was not

> Senator Eugene McCarthy's relatively small group of upper-middle-class and intellectual supporters, but a populist revolt of the American masses that have been elevated by prosperity to middle-class status and conservatism. Their revolt is against the caste, policies and taxation of the mandarins of Establishment liberalism.

Pointing out that even in liberal New York City, Nixon and Wallace won a combined 40 percent of the vote, Phillips cited working-class "resentment of the blyth [sic] nihilism of the children of the affluent society" and "Negro-Democratic mutual identification."

on the same day as Paul Williams's sober view of campus radicalism, *The Revolutionary, Joe* waded into theaters in a season of rampant youth exploitation. *Love Story*, thirty-two-year-old Yale professor Erich Segal's treacly campus romance—resulting in the doomed marriage of an uptight Harvard preppie and a smart-mouthed, working-class Cliffie—had been a bestseller since March and, first written as a script, was already in production for its Christmas release.

Segal's own vision of campus protest, directed by Stanley Kramer as *R.P.M.*, would not appear until the fall semester. It was *Getting Straight*—directed by UCLA-educated former AIP-hand Richard Rush, with Elliott Gould as a hip Viet-vet grad student and Candice Bergen as his co-ed girlfriend—that had the good fortune to open ten days after Kent State. Two weeks later, *The Magic Garden of Stanley Sweetheart*—a first film by zoom-happy TV director Leonard Horn—managed to recount the picaresque adventures of a longhaired college junior (Don Johnson) without mentioning either the draft or Vietnam. The movie was shot on the Columbia campus, unlike *The Strawberry Statement*—another first feature, also from MGM—which transposed James Simon Kunen's account of Columbia 1968 to San Francisco, after the university refused to serve as a location.*

Small wonder Joe was pissed. These draft-dodging, self-indulgent rich kids were being presented as the crown of creation—not only heroes but victims,

---

*Directed by the former commercial maker Stuart Hagmann with a hyperactivity enabling him to incorporate everything from tap-dancing radicals singing "God Bless America" to newsreel footage of the mortally wounded Robert Kennedy, *The Strawberry Statement* had its world premiere at the Cannes Film Festival and opened at a New York art theater in mid-June. The movie's climax, en route to an inevitable freeze frame, has the student protesters occupying the school gymnasium, thus prompting Vincent Canby to compare this MGM production to the college musicals the studio produced in the late 1930s, except that here the "big show [was] a police bust." The students await the cops, sitting cross-legged and, as led by their black militant leader, chanting John Lennon's "Give Peace a Chance." Suddenly, Hagmann cuts to an overhead angle. "The camera peers down from the ceiling, showing us—not people with ideas and attitudes— just a Busby Berkeley flower arrangement."

whose opposition to the war threatened to obliterate the event that defined their fathers. Joe and Compton drink and bond across the class divide, the movie reaching its comic highpoint when (playing *The Searchers* for a night) they tour the East Village in search of runaway Melissa. "Look at that shit—Cowboys and Indians," Joe sneers, peering into the window of a St. Marks Place boutique, perhaps even the recently opened emporium called Outlaw. "Well, they grew up on television—Hopalong Cassidy at age three," Compton recalls thoughtfully. (The adman is a McLuhanite.)

After dinner at a macrobiotic restaurant, the pair are picked up by a gaggle of hippies and wind up partying with Frank's stash. Joe wants to get high—he offers the hookah to Compton and, displaying his own familiarity with demographic hard sell, advises the adman to "get with the Pepsi generation." (Thanks again to TV, both men know how to smoke pot.) When the girls start dancing naked, Joe is transfixed: "This is an or-gee isn't it?" Neither bothering to phone home, Joe and Compton each gets himself a chick, only to discover, by the dawn's early light, that the girls' male confederates have made off with their wallets. The two guys are now living in the moment. After violently extracting a commune address, they drive to the hippies' rural farmhouse. There, in a scene that struck some as a domestic My Lai, Joe invades the premises and, a porcine avenging angel, begins murdering all inhabitants. Kids are cowering in the corner begging for mercy as Joe persuades Compton to pick up the gun. A final freeze frame has Compton shoot a just-arrived hippie chick—it is, of course, Melissa.

Hailing *Joe* as "a film of Freudian anguish, biblical savagery and immense social and cinematic importance," *Time* thought the final sequence rivaled the *Bonnie and Clyde* climax. Getting away with murder, as at Kent State, might not be impossible. "A lot of Joes sit in jury boxes these days," the reviewer darkly warned. And in movies: Unlike *Patton*, *Joe* polarized, as well as fascinated, audiences. Stanley Kauffmann noted in *The New Republic* that at the downtown Murray Hill Cinema, "Joe's mouthings drew laughs, and the East Village swingers drew applause." But that same night "a friend saw the picture at its Broadway theater [the Embassy] where, she reports, Joe was a hero to at least some and where one woman said, after the final shoot-up, 'We should kill 'em all.' "

The initial response to *Joe* was so strong that the Embassy screened the movie around the clock. Peter Boyle recalls attending a 2 AM show to find people "screaming at the screen." The previously unknown actor was an instant celebrity. He was hailed—"Hey, Joe!"—as a long-lost buddy by New York hard-hats and profiled as a rising star in *Life*, where he confessed to being "horrified" to overhear one middle-aged man explain Joe as "a movie about a guy like me who's sick and tired of all this crap." Rather than revel in his new identity, Boyle spent the summer afraid for his life.

> Kids are standing up at the end of the movie and yelling, 'I'm going to shoot back, Joe.' In fact, the other night I was walking down 46th Street and I had a flash of myself being shot down in the street, just because someone thought I really was Joe.

A week after *Joe* opened, presidential aide Tom Charles Huston presented Richard Nixon with a plan to coordinate all domestic intelligence-gathering— including wiretaps and break-ins—under White House direction. Nixon didn't approve the plan for ten months, but the issue of extralegal justice was on his mind. The first weekend in August, the President screened the latest John Wayne vehicle, *Chisum*. A day or two later, speaking to reporters in Denver, where he was participating in a four-day Law Enforcement Assistance Administration conference on crime control, Nixon cited *Chisum* while discoursing on the news media's infatuation with the Righteous Outlaw.

> What I say now is not to be interpreted as any criticism of the news media. What I say now is simply an observation of the kind of times we live in and how attitudes develop among our young people.
>   Over the last weekend I saw a movie—I don't see too many movies but I try to see them on weekends when I am at the Western White House or in

Florida—and the movie I selected, or, as a matter of fact, my daughter Tricia selected it, was *Chisum* with John Wayne. It was a Western.

Had any previous American president ever made a public pronouncement based on a movie? Nixon was a student of the culture!

Allowing that *Chisum* was "basically another Western" (albeit "far better than average movies [or] average Westerns"), Nixon permitted himself to wonder why it was that the genre had continued to survive year after year: "This may be a square observation, [but] the good guys come out ahead in the Westerns, the bad guys lose." Nixon clarified an essence, but as the hard-hats already worried, would this always be the case? The ballad sung by country singer Merle Haggard (known throughout the land for his conservative anthems "Okie from Muskogee" and "The Fightin' Side of Me") beneath *Chisum*'s opening credits, posed that very question. "Chisum, Chisum, can you still keep goin' on?" The movie answered by arranging to have Wayne's eponymous frontier patriarch hoist himself on his horse and descend from his hilltop domain into the weak, divided town below to reassert that just order he'd established a quarter-century before.

Although much concerned with issues of law and order, *Chisum* was not precisely an establishment Western. Billy the Kid was among the good guys and, "curious" thing, as the then-liberal *New York Post* put it, the villains included many authority figures—"corrupt sheriffs, racially bigoted military men, gutless politicians and an octopus-like capitalist who had enough money to buy the law" until the Duke literally takes the law into his own hands and punches him out a window to his death. How fitting that the movie was set in the New Mexico territory which, from the Civil War's end to the twentieth century's dawn, had been the only place in America—until now!—wherein political assassination was a key element of the system.

Chisum was Hollywood's first serious Billy the Kid movie since Arthur Penn adapted Gore Vidal's *Left Handed Gun* in 1957. Penn's Billy was an anguished illiterate; Wayne's is a nice young fella trying to go straight and even telling a former crony that "it ain't like old times." For a while, the Kid is Wayne's protégé. Wayne respects Billy's loyalty—however extreme. After the Kid shoots the bad guys who bushwhacked his saintly boss, he rides into town and finishes the job by killing the contemptible old sheriff who abetted the crime.

Although Wayne might have been more inclined to go out and, in the course of making a citizen's arrest, beat the crooked lawman to a pulp, he recognizes the connection between his notions of law and order and Billy's more impulsive brand of summary justice. But John Wayne was not quite a vigilante. He sent money to George Wallace but he stuck with Richard Nixon. After the Kid shoots the bounty hunter (a cold and grizzled Clint Eastwood type) come looking for him, Wayne has no choice but to kick the killer off his land.

Not without reason, Nixon was concerned that today, when John Wayne no longer dwelt among us, young people were encouraged to glorify criminals (even if this was not done "intentionally" by the press, radio, and television).

> I noted, for example, the coverage of the Charles Manson case when I was in Los Angeles, front page every day in the papers. It usually got a couple of minutes in the evening news. Here is a man who was guilty, directly or indirectly, of eight murders without reason. Here is a man, yet who as far as the coverage was concerned, appeared to be rather a glamorous figure, a glamorous figure to the young people. . . .

"As Mr. Nixon recounted all this, his face darkened, his eyes flashed, his voice grew more intense," the *New York Times* noted. The speed with which reporters ran for the phones as the President concluded his remarks—all but knocking him down in the stampede—alerted the White House press office to trouble. The next morning, a smirking Charles Manson displayed the *Los Angeles Times* headline, MANSON GUILTY, NIXON DECLARES. Where was the Wayne to shoot him?!

Nor was Manson the lone glamorous outlaw. August 5, Huey Newton was finally released on bail. Ten thousand supporters massed outside Alameda County Jail as, luxuriating in freedom, Newton climbed atop a car and stripped off his shirt. The crowd went wild. "It was like one massive orgasm," one participant recalled. Soon the Panther idol met *Easy Rider* producer Bert Schneider, already a major supporter of the LA Panthers. Schneider recognized Newton as a true Star-Pol: "He's my hero. If he's not Mao, I'll eat it."*

Manson did not precipitate the week's only courthouse commotion. Two days after Brother Huey tasted freedom, the trial of two black nationalist Soledad prison inmates was disrupted by a shoot-out in the Marin County courthouse. Attempting to secure the release of his brother, prison activist George Jackson, seventeen-year-old Jonathan Jackson took the judge, several jurors, and an assistant district attorney hostage—before being shot down by police, along with the judge and two defendants.

The Weather Underground's first "communiqué," published in the July 31 *Berkeley Tribe*, had declared A STATE OF WAR: "Revolutionary violence is the only way." Among other things, the communiqué proclaimed "guns and grass are united in the youth underground. Freaks are revolutionaries and revolutionaries are freaks." September 12, the Weather Underground engineered Timothy Leary's escape from the California minimum-security prison in San Luis Obispo, where he was serving a six-month to ten-year sentence for marijuana possession. Days later, Leary's statement appeared in *San Francisco Good Times*: "I declare that World War III is now being waged by short-haired robots whose deliberate aim is to destroy the complex web of free wild life by all and every means possible against the genocidal machine. . . . To shoot a genocidal robot policeman in defense of life is a sacred act." Soon, the fugitive guru would surface in Algiers, where Eldridge Cleaver had already established his own political exile.

Theirs was not the only new front. September 4, even as radical Palestinians made a second failed attempt to assassinate King Hussein of Jordan, Marxist

---

*Hollywood had first rallied behind the Panthers at a series of fundraising parties organized that spring by Shirley Sutherland, wife of *M*A*S*H* star Donald. Guests included Schneider, Candice Bergen, Warren Beatty, Peter Fonda, Jane Fonda, Jack Nicholson, and Jon Voight, as well as Elizabeth Taylor.

candidate Salvador Allende won a plurality in Chile's three-way election. September 15 (the same day Nixon gave the CIA carte blanche to prevent Allende's coming to power), Hussein turned on the Palestinians and for the next ten days, it seemed that full-scale war might break out in the Middle East.

• • •

The spring semester had ended in riot and confusion. The fall term had scarcely begun when a stoned-on-something Jimi Hendrix choked to death on his own vomit. History was slipping away. Autumn 1970 was the season of dead icons as well as radical desperados.

Brandeis senior Katherine Ann Powers spent her summer as part of a gang that crisscrossed the country, stealing cars, holding up motels, and pulling bank jobs as far afield as LA, Philadelphia, and Evanston, Illinois. They planned to use the money to arm Black Panthers and sabotage military transports. Had their path crossed the Medicine Ball Caravan, rock 'n' roll magical mystery tour heading east from San Francisco under Warner Brothers auspices? Perhaps they took a break from daredevil criminality to catch *Soldier Blue*, hailed by white radical Dotson Rader in the *New York Times* as "among the most significant, the most brutal and liberating, the most honest American films ever made."*

Although *Soldier Blue* opened with Indian folksinger Buffy Sainte-Marie proclaiming "This is My Country," it was a song for Katherine Ann, the story of a revolutionary white woman. Captured by the Cheyenne, Candice Bergen's Cresta Lee is profane, sexually experienced, street smart, unsentimental, and vociferously antiwhite (anticipating, in her acerbic attitudinizing, Bergen's later TV persona, Murphy Brown). Three days after the Rader piece appeared, Pow-

---

*According to Rader, *Soldier Blue* confronted "the indecent complicity of the American film industry in a racist falsification of history," destroying "the phony myth of Cowboys and Indians, Good Guys and Bad Guys." Rader wrote as though reporting on the Revolutionary People's Constitutional Convention held in Philadelphia over the Labor Day Weekend. As *The Black Panther* explained in announcing the conclave, "The United States of America is a barbaric organization controlled and operated by avaricious, sadistic, bloodthirsty thieves."

ers and her cohorts robbed a bank outside Boston. A policeman was killed; Powers escaped to spend the next twenty-three years underground.

The 1970 election was dominated by events of the previous May—as the *New York Times* suggested with a piece on the semiotics of construction-work apparel, A NEW HAT IN POLITICAL RING. In mid-September, Spiro Agnew went on tour, accompanied by White House speechwriters William Safire and Pat Buchanan, the former Goldwater activist who was the principal author of Nixon's Silent Majority speech and Cambodia announcement, as well as Agnew's attack on the networks. Out on the hustings, the Vice President was playing a rhetorical Compson to the electorate's blue-collar Joes. Would the nation "be led by a President elected by a majority of the American people?" Agnew asked a San Diego audience. Or would America be "blackmailed into following the path dictated by a disruptive, radical, and militant minority—the pampered prodigies of the radical liberals in the United States Senate?"*

Agnew might have been addressing *The Greening of America*, a treatise by a Yale professor, more youth-loving than youthful, which attributed an entirely new consciousness to his students. *The Greening of America* elaborated on a vision Charles Reich had while in Berkeley during the Summer of Love. The nation was in the midst of an unstoppable, pot-smoking, love-making, bellbottom-wearing, essentially nonviolent revolution against the Corporate State and its zombie supporters. We all live in a yellow submarine!

Reich's analysis had little interest in racism or the War in Vietnam but much to say about the stunted consciousness of the Joe generation. Peering out from the quad, the professor advised his readers to "look again at a 'fascist'—tight-lipped, tense, crew cut, correctly dressed, church-going, an American flag on his car window, a hostile eye for communists, youth, and blacks."

---

*Yale student Bill Clinton furthered his political education working for the antiwar Democratic candidate for senator from Connecticut, the Reverend Joseph Duffey. Attacked by Agnew as a "revisionist Marxist," Duffey was dogged throughout his campaign by hard-hat demonstrators.

Unlike the evolved hippies he hated, the average Joe "has very little of love, or poetry, or music, or nature, or joy."

> He has been dominated by fear. He has been condemned to narrow-minded prejudice, to a self-defeating materialism, to a lonely suspicion of his fellow man. He is angry, envious, bitter, self-hating. He ravages his own environment. He has fled all his life from consciousness and responsibility. He is turned against his own nature; in his agony he has recoiled upon himself. He is what the machine left after it had its way.

After excerpting *The Greening of America*, the *New Yorker* was inundated with the greatest flood of mail since it published Rachel Carson's *Silent Spring*. All autumn, the *New York Times*'s new Op-Ed page ran articles debating Reich's thesis, and for one week, Reich and Segal, two fellows of Yale's Ezra Stiles College, simultaneously topped the *Times*'s fiction and nonfiction bestseller lists.

October 5 (twenty-four hours after Janis Joplin died of an apparent drug overdose, the day defendant Charles Manson leapt ten feet over the counsel table and, screaming for "Christian justice," made to attack the judge with a pencil), Richard Nixon returned from a trip to Europe. The law-and-order President was, of course, devoted to the blue-ing of America.

Plunging into the campaign, Nixon visited twenty-two states over the next twenty-one days, promising to bring home 40,000 more American troops by Christmas as he attacked the "fawning approval" of violence, hijacking, and cop-killing that in certain "fashionable circles has become the mark of being 'with it.'" Everywhere, the President was trailed by the student demonstrators, who unwittingly served as campaign props. Nixon had taken a leaf from the 1968 Wallace playbook. Reporters noted that shortly before the President was to speak, small groups of protesters were suddenly admitted into the auditorium and escorted to the remaining seats in the rear. Once inside and within earshot of the President, the students performed as expected—shouting epithets and, in thus defining the Silent Majority, enabling Nixon to answer them.

Five days before the election, Nixon taunted demonstrators in San Jose by flashing the V sign: "I could not resist showing them how little respect I had for their juvenile and mindless ranting." His entourage was pelted with debris, one rock hitting the fifth car from the President's. The local police chief claimed that it required "an act of God" to secure Nixon's escape, although journalists had been warned there might be trouble and some thought the President's staff pleased—especially as three windows on the press bus were broken by stones.

Nixon was running for sheriff against the hippie outlaws. Two days later in Phoenix, he invoked the San Jose melee in his final campaign speech: "Let's recognize these people for what they are. They are not romantic revolutionaries. They are the same thugs and hoodlums that have always plagued the good people." The rhetoric was black and white, but the election proved inconclusive. The Republicans lost nine House seats while gaining two in the Senate, where eight "peace" candidates won and six were defeated.

Still, *Joe* was scarcely played out. In New York, the movie concluded a twenty-one-week run at the Murray Hill and New Embassy and then moved to Flagship Showcases over Thanksgiving—a few days before shorthaired robot J. Edgar Hoover placed Bernadine Dohrn on the FBI Most Wanted list.

●   ●   ●

After the election, the President authorizes a daring rescue mission. Colonel "Bo" Gritz and fifty-six Green Beret volunteers launch a helicopter attack on the Son Tay prison complex, twenty-three miles from Hanoi, hoping to liberate a hundred POWs, mainly B-52 pilots. This is the movie John Wayne hadn't thought to make. But the camp is empty; the Vietnamese had relocated their prisoners back in July.

Richard Nixon is less concerned with the mission's success than its repercussions. Is Son Tay another Cambodia? Will there be demonstrations? "This time they will probably knock down the [White House] gates," the President fretted in a meeting with advisers before authorizing the raid. "I'll have a thousand incoherent hippies urinating on the Oval Office rug." It is, however, a different youth-culture representative who comes calling that winter. Four days before Christmas, the President has a visitation. Elvis Presley, who'd written Nixon a six-page letter requesting a meeting and suggesting he be made a "Federal Agent-at-Large" in the Bureau of Narcotics and Dangerous Drugs, is ushered in for the greatest photo opportunity in Oval Office history.

According to Egil Krogh's memo on the meeting, the Hillbilly Cat (now known as "the King") presents himself as an ardent patriot who denounces the Beatles as "a real force for anti-American spirit."

> He said that the Beatles came to this country, made their money, and then returned to England where they promoted an anti-American theme. The President nodded in agreement and expressed some surprise. The President then indicated that those who use drugs are also those in the vanguard of anti-American protest.

Perhaps taken aback, Elvis assures the President that he is on his side. He, too, admires *Patton*, and has seen the movie many times. Impressing Krogh with his "emotional manner," Elvis tells Nixon that he has been studying Communist brainwashing and the drug culture for the last ten years. He asks the President for a Bureau of Narcotics badge (for his collection) and, at the conclusion of the meeting, spontaneously hugs him.

On New Year's Day, Elvis and seven associates drop by FBI headquarters. The King is wearing a fur-trimmed bellbottomed suit and carrying his Bureau of Narcotics badge, but J. Edgar Hoover is not there to receive him. Disappointed, Elvis declares the FBI Director to be "the greatest living American" and offers his services as an FBI informant. According to notes in the Bureau's file, Elvis blames the troubled state of American youth on the Beatles' "filthy unkempt appearance and suggestive music," adding that the Smothers Brothers and Jane Fonda will "have a lot to answer for in the hereafter for the way they have poisoned young minds by disparaging the United States." Elvis has merged with Joe. The King has a premonition, but he is not yet our Legal Vigilante.

A stone cast into the limpid pool of American consciousness, *Joe* has a continuing ripple effect. January 20, 1971, the movie goes into wider release. (The next night, a new situation comedy has its network premiere—it features a domesticated Joe and is called *All in the Family*.) The night after that, the President—still thinking of Elvis?—delivers a State of the Union message calling for a "New American Revolution" to restore "power to the people." St. Patrick's Day 1971, *Joe* is rereleased to an even larger circle of theaters. By then, however, a trio of Righteous Outlaws has materialized to mount their last stands. To shoot a genocidal robot policeman in defense of life . . .

The Last Round-Up: Counterculture Psychodrama and Hippie Westerns, 1971

Like Michael Herr's imaginary grunt, the countercultural revolution was history but didn't yet know it. The corpses still walked—as in *Night of the Living Dead*, recently resurrected as a midnight cult film in Washington, DC. The "suppressed" special issue of the new New Left monthly, *Scanlon's*, devoted to Guerrilla War in the U.S.A. was finally printed by a press in Quebec and available in liberated bookstores, while, in further opposition to Joe, early 1971 saw the candidacy of militant dove Senator George McGovern and a cluster of kamikaze heroes, each the star of his own particular psychodrama.

The sleep of reason brought forth the Third World shaman-gunslinger El Topo, the messianic half-Indian Billy Jack, and the revolutionary black hustler Sweet Sweetback. Each scenario was a work of total involvement, a guerrilla production conceived and micromanaged by its hitherto obscure, self-directed star in militant defiance of the American movie industry—anti-Hollywood Freedom Fighters, as well as Righteous Outlaws, looking for the Alamo and waging image war in the Belly of the Beast. Each movie would spawn not simply a cult but a revolution . . . in marketing.

El Topo was first to arrive. In December 1970, New York's Elgin Theater took advantage of the hippie crowds flocking to a three-night presentation of avant-garde films by John Lennon and Yoko Ono to announce an added feature. Mexican director Alejandro Jodorowsky's *El Topo* (The Mole) would be shown at midnight because, as the first small *Village Voice* ad announced, it was "too heavy to be shown any other way." The counterculture felt the weight. *Little Big Man* opened only four days before *El Topo*'s premiere. But this Greening of the Western—in which the Cheyenne embodied Charles Reich's Consciousness III—offered scant respite from the winter's weary science-fiction scenario. A third manned mission landed on the moon in February even as it was revealed that the United State had unleashed a South Vietnamese invasion of Laos. Richard Nixon threatened North Vietnam with unlimited bombing (and ordered his Secret Service to install a secret recording system in the Oval Office). Nixon's approval ratings fell below 50 percent as winter ended; Democratic front-runner Senator Edmund Muskie pulled even in the Gallup poll. "The first months of 1971 were the lowest point of my term," the President recalled. "The problems we confronted were so overwhelming and so apparently impervious to anything we could do to change them that it seemed possible that I might not even be nominated for reelection in 1972."

Nixon's problems, as any hippie might have told him, were in his head. Go to the desert, fast, speak to the scorpions and the snakes. Such was Jodorowsky's way. He not only wrote, directed, and scored *El Topo*, but also appeared on screen in virtually every scene as a character none too subtly identified with Moses, Buddha, Jesus, and the Magnificent Seven. Later, the filmmaker revealed that *El Topo* had been shot in sequence and that he'd worn throughout special under shorts with holes for his testicles and a green circle stitched around his anus "to make sure I wouldn't act like John Wayne."

A mystical Western (an Eastern Western), *El Topo* picks up where *The Wild Bunch* ended. The eponymous hero, bearded and dressed entirely in black leather, rides into a movie-set pueblo strewn with human corpses and butchered animals. El Topo seeks out and guns down the three bandits responsible for the massacre, castrates the colonel who is their leader, and takes the colonel's woman, Mara. A witchy dominatrix in her own right, Mara demands the hero prove his worth by killing the four Master Sharpshooters of the Desert, and betrays him once he does. El Topo is crucified by a sinister lesbian who has replaced him in Mara's affections. He is left for dead but rescued by a bedraggled band of dwarfs and cripples.

For some, *El Topo* had intimations of those South American urban guerrillas—the Tupamaros in Uruguay and the Montoneros in Argentina—then engaged in political abductions, assassinations, and bank robberies. For others, it was more powerful sorcery. Hidden in the mountains, El Topo sleeps for twenty years. When he wakes, he resolves to liberate his newfound community by digging a tunnel out of their subterranean prison, raising money for this project through street performances in the degenerate Western settlement at the foot of the mountain. Worse than *The Chase*'s Texas Sodom, this town is the province of sex-starved harpies and epicene cowboys. Blacks are sold into slavery, Indians slaughtered, executions treated as theater, and El Topo forced to perform public sex with a dwarf—all beneath the same eye within a pyramid found on a greenback dollar bill. At the movie's climax, the freaks escape into this little America and are butchered. El Topo arrives too late and finds the street littered with their corpses. Enraged, he grabs a rifle and single-handedly decimates the citizenry. Then he sets himself ablaze, Buddhist monk style, on Main Street.

Living in Paris in the mid-1960s, Jodorowsky had staged more than one happening under the sign of Antonin Artaud, and *El Topo* presented itself as an orgiastic initiation which spoke both to the counterculture's love of the arcane and its collective paranoia, while investing hippie violence with a religious aura. If *El Topo*'s audiences identified with the holy killer in the movie's first and second parts, by the third he presented himself as their savior. *El Topo* was the Che the tripped-out denizens of the Red Dog Saloon might have imagined—champion, literally, of the freaks.

Even before the cult went public in late March 1971, when an ecstatic report appeared in the *Village Voice*, Dennis Hopper and Peter Fonda were palling around with this new genius, while John Lennon was spotted among the Elgin regulars. Soon the former Beatle had encouraged his manager, Allen Klein, to purchase *El Topo* for distribution.*

---

*That very month, Lennon used an interview in the British underground paper *Red Mole* [sic] to announce his solidarity with the New Left: "I'd like to incite people to break the framework, to be disobedient in school, to insult authority."

• • •

Word-of-mouth kept *El Topo* running seven midnights a week until Allen Klein yanked it from the Elgin to prepare for an official opening the next fall. By then, *El Topo* had been joined by an even more outrageous call to bloody revolution. *Sweet Sweetback's Baadasssss Song*—written, directed, edited, and scored by Melvin Van Peebles, who also starred under the name Brer Soul—was another self-induced desert revelation.

Driving through the Mojave during February 1970, Van Peebles paused to masturbate: "I unbuttoned my fly, leaned back against the front fender of the car getting myself comfortable, and pulled out my pecker and began to beat my meat." It was then that his muse "rolled the stone away from the cave. I peered into me and saw I was tired of the Man." Inspired, Van Peebles composed a Guerrilla Cinema manifesto:

> 1) NO COP OUT. I wanted a victorious film. A film where niggers could walk out standing tall instead of avoiding each other's eyes. . . . 2) MUST LOOK AS GOOD AS ANYTHING CHUCK EVER DID. 3. ENTERTAINMENT-WISE, A MOTHER FUCKER. 4. A LIVING WORKSHOP. I wanted 50% of my shooting crew to be third world people.

John Wayne making *The Alamo* could scarcely have had more attitude. The movie was shot over the course of nineteen days in May and June 1970, a period that included the Kent State aftermath and the May 14 killing of two black students by the Mississippi Highway Patrol on the National Guard–occupied campus of Jackson State College. Editing, which took five and a half months, began as Fox released *Myra Breckinridge*.*

Like *Myra* and *Joe*, *Sweetback* had a particular relationship with pornography

---

*While raising money for his movie, Van Peebles was offered a shot at a project originating in the days of Darryl Zanuck's youth slate. In late 1968, James Baldwin was brought to Twentieth Century Fox to adapt *The Autobiography of Malcolm X*. The screenplay had since migrated from Fox to Columbia, where it remained until resurrected two decades later for still another studio by Spike Lee.

and hence the Orgy. Van Peebles hired a known porn-film camera operator and began by filming his most sexually explicit scenes. The motion picture unions assumed the project was pornographic—which was also how the Motion Picture Association responded. *Sweetback* was screened for the MPAA on January 4, 1971, and branded with an X rating. As no distributor would take it, Van Peebles went with the exploitation company Cinemation. Even then, only two theaters booked the movie. Nine days before *Sweetback*'s planned release, Van Peebles held a press conference in Los Angeles, challenging the MPAA rating system on racial grounds. The filmmaker accused the MPAA of participating in "cultural genocide" by imposing a white judgment on black subject matter, demanded that the X rating apply to white patrons only, and threatened to sue.

Van Peebles dedicated his movie to "all the brothers and sisters who have had enough of the Man." The Man, meanwhile, was sowing discord among the brothers. March 8, the Black Champ and outspoken Third World icon Muhammad Ali returned to the ring after three and a half years in exile for refusing induction into the army. But Ali's comeback was thwarted when Joe Frazier knocked him down in the fifteenth round. The Black Panthers, too, were on the ropes. Even as Van Peebles battled the MPAA, members of the New York Panther 21 (or was it the FBI?) wrote a letter criticizing Huey Newton and praising the Weathermen—who, a year before, had fire-bombed the home of presiding judge John Murtaugh. Newton purged the 21 as well as the Panther's flamboyant, Stetson-wearing, Viet-vet, LA leader Elmer "Geronimo" Pratt. A month later, the split between Brother Huey and Eldridge Cleaver erupted on live TV. Newton and his lieutenant, David Hillard, were on *AM San Francisco* when Cleaver phoned in from Algiers, demanding the Panther 21 be reinstated and calling for Hilliard's expulsion. Newton expelled Cleaver instead.

March 1971, which began with the Weather Underground detonating a bomb in a Capitol building toilet, ended with another explosion. Lieutenant William Calley had been found guilty of murdering twenty-two Vietnamese civilians and sentenced to life in prison while, in California, the longest murder trial in American history wound to a tortuous conclusion with Charles Manson convicted and condemned to death. Two days later, on March 31, *Sweet Sweetback* had its world premiere in a city synonymous with flaming insurrection, Detroit. Advertised over black radio, *Sweetback* set a house record, and April 2, a day after the President ordered Calley released from the Fort Benning stockade, *Sweetback* opened big in Atlanta. April 23, Van Peebles's movie had its New York release at three theaters—in Greenwich Village, Times Square, and Harlem. Thus, *Sweetback* targeted three potential constituencies: counter-cultural, lumpen, and black.

Crediting the Black Community as its star, *Sweetback* was shot on the streets of Watts and LA's skid row. Raw and grainy, switching stocks between 16 and 35 millimeter, the movie was filled with handheld zooms, split screens, and psychedelic freeze-frames. *Sweetback* was even murkier and more lurid than *Joe*, and reviewers couldn't decide whether Van Peebles was any good as a filmmaker. Unlike *Right On*, a 1970 performance documentary of the incendiary Last Poets, which (described by producer Woodie King Jr. as "the first 'totally black film' " making "no concession in language or symbolism to white audiences") opened quietly in New York on April 8, *Sweetback* received violently mixed notices from both white and black critics.*

Van Peebles offered numerous instances of degradation—including a live sex show performed for a white audience and a scene played with a character sitting on the toilet. A woman questioned by police about one of her children

---

*Reviews often took cues from the audience. Many white critics denied they were even addressed by *Sweetback*. *Variety* insisted it was "clearly intended first and foremost for members of the black community, some of whom are bound to find it presumptuous for a white reviewer to deal with the sociological and political problems in the script." *Ebony* maintained that "if a white man had made the film, they'd burn the theater down." In a *New York Times* think piece, Clayton Riley called *Sweetback* a "terrifying vision [that] Black people alone will really understand." This black *El Topo* was "designed to blow minds." Van Peebles had contrived a "blasphemous parade of brilliantly precise stereotypical Blacks and Whites." It was a provocation: "Shock. Disgust. Towering rages everywhere."

can only mumble, "I might have had a Leroy, I don't rightly remember." A grinning Sambo uses the seat of his pants to shine his white customer's shoes. The movie crystallized all manner of class, ideological, aesthetic, and gender conflicts in the African-American audience—as well as on the cultural Left. Where *The Militant* praised the movie's anti-colonial message, *Women's Liberation* ran a graffiti'd ad marked with slogans like FUCK THIS RACIST BULLSHIT, while *Muhammad Speaks* called *Sweetback* a "mangled, crippled, white supremacist, non-thinking, savage, inhuman vision of Black people." The film's black militant Moo Moo is an ambiguous figure—and yet, if Sidney Poitier (biggest star of 1967) was an analogue to Martin Luther King, Sweetback embodied Black Power, the Black Muslims, the Black Panthers.

The police are an official lynch mob. The black hero is trapped in a world of cloddish whites where, as in Marxist eschatology, "the tradition of all the dead generations" (the Silent Majority) "weighs like a nightmare on the brain of the living." But here, unlike *Night of the Living Dead*, the protagonist shoots a cop and escapes, body oozing, into the desert and across the border. This was the black Righteous Outlaw at last—even if the libidinal economy was less than romantic. In *Bonnie and Clyde*, violence substituted for sex. In *Sweetback*, sex is a sublimated form of violence. It is also survival. The priapic Sweetback has to service a woman before she'll file off his handcuffs, and he subsequently saves his life by bringing a biker mama to climax. The opening scene, as Van Peebles described it, has "women lined up like a sort of a feminine wild bunch [sic], standing in a semicircle around a kitchen table." The child Sweetback (played by Van Peebles's son, Mario) is sexually initiated—and named—by a maternal whore. Were it not for the accompaniment of the gospel song "Wade in the Water," the scene could have been lifted from a contemporary porn film. Is it an act of love, an Oedipal fantasy, a rite of passage, an example of child rape?

Officially, the emphasis was on liberated black manhood, an interpretation favored by Huey Newton, who argued that the women recognize the boy as their future and so baptize him into manhood. In an analysis that filled the entire June 19, 1971, issue of the *Black Panther*, Newton allegorized *Sweetback's* sex scenes as Sweetback's absorption of the community's love and his silence as a space to be occupied by the audience. It might be "mischievous and reactionary," as *Ebony* thought, "to suggest to black people in 1971 that they are going to be able to screw their way across the Red Sea." If that were the case, "black people would have celebrated the millennium 400 years ago."

But Brother Huey saw *Sweetback* as another *Battle of Algiers*—a new scenario—and, just as the earlier film was required Panther viewing (entered as evidence in the trial of the Panther 21), so *Sweetback* became a Panther text. Newton, twice tried on charges of killing an Oakland cop, urged his followers to see the "first truly revolutionary Black film made," with his critique as a guide. A lumpen figure becomes a revolutionary hero by offing a pig and gets away with it. Sweetback is the quintessential Black Panther. Like the social bandit, he demonstrates the possibility of turning oppression upside down. And if Sweetback was a nickname signifying sexual bravado—well, wasn't Malcolm X a pimp hustler turned revolutionary?

In May, Van Peebles successfully sued *Sweetback*'s Boston distributor for trimming nine minutes from the film. For the next two weeks, *Sweetback* was America's number-one movie—although *Time*, *Life*, *Look*, or even New York's *Daily News* had not yet reviewed it. The director was profiled in *Newsweek* (which proudly noted that all three nighttime network talk shows had refused to book him). By summer, however, *Sweetback* could no longer be ignored— the movie was the equivalent of a celluloid riot and, having already made more than $10 million, the top-grossing independent picture of all time. *JET* extolled Van Peeble's mixture of profanity and revolution as a black business venture that beat the system at its own game: "In its first nine weeks of showing . . . [*Sweetback*] grossed $2.6 million, wiping sneers of derision from the lips of skeptical white theater owners and replacing them with beaming smiles of servility." Van Peebles noted, "For the white man, my picture is a new kind of foreign film. . . ."

The main thing is to build a black movie industry. Black people need a mirror they can watch themselves in, a mirror the white man can't distort. I've proved that a black man can make it in this business with no help from Whitey. In the next couple of years a lot of black directors gonna do the same thing.

In fact, *Sweetback* was almost instantly recuperated. MGM's black detective thriller *Shaft* opened a few months later and—thanks in part to its conventional narrative structure—crossed over commercially to attract whites as well as blacks, grossing $12 million, helping to save the financially troubled studio and forging a template for the blaxploitation films of the early 1970s. Meanwhile, as predicted by the end-title—Watch Out! A Badass Nigger is Coming Back to Collect Some Dues—*Sweetback* joined *Myra* as a durable figure of terror, to be conjured up in one form or another during five of the next six presidential elections.

•   •   •

Mid-summer 1971, *Billy Jack* arrived unheralded in New York. Warners had begun releasing the movie, mainly at drive-ins, in April, the same month that the Vietnam Veterans Against the War (VVAW) broke into media consciousness. For five days, a thousand vets camped out on the Washington Mall. The VVAW operation involved marches, a ceremony on the Capitol steps for the return of Vietnam service medals, and testimony before the Senate Foreign Relations Committee. The police were startled by the sight of longhaired veterans, and the vets were subsequently mocked by Vice President Agnew, who told an audience that "I heard one of them say to the other: 'If you're captured by the enemy, give only your name, age, and the telephone number of your hairdresser.' "

The hero of *Billy Jack* was himself a Viet-vet as well as a multiple oxymoron—a cowboy Indian on a motorcycle, a practitioner of Korean martial arts inducted into the Shoshone "priesthood of the snake," a one-man tribe, an antiwar Green Beret, the Great Spirit given human form. A sequel to the American International Pictures biker flick *Born Losers*, which had introduced Billy Jack during the same month that Bonnie and Clyde made their convulsive reappearance on the American scene, Tom Laughlin's movie—written and produced in collaboration with his wife, Delores Taylor—began, like *Easy*

Rider, as an AIP production. *Billy Jack* started shooting during the tumultuous fall of 1969, in Prescott, Arizona, but a dispute with the studio caused Laughlin to shut down production.*

Laughlin next made a short-lived deal with Avco Embassy, but before shooting restarted, the production moved on to Twentieth Century Fox as a late addition to the Zanuck youth slate. In April 1970, Laughlin hired a new cinematographer and moved his location to Santa Fe, Land of Billy the Kid, where Peter Fonda was then making *The Hired Hand*. *Billy Jack* wrapped after six weeks, at a cost of $650,000. But, even more than Jodorowsky or Van Peebles, Laughlin was forced to play the Righteous Outlaw. After Fox decided to recut his film and impounded the negative, he held the soundtrack for ransom, informing the studio "we would send them one erased reel of tape a week until the soundtrack was totally destroyed." Fox relented, giving Laughlin and Taylor a deadline to raise nearly one million dollars to buy back their picture. The filmmakers made a deal with Warner Brothers, but this, for Laughlin, was "the worst phase of our troubles." Warners released *Billy Jack* without advertising—in New York it disappeared after two weeks. (In 1972, *Billy Jack*'s makers filed a $51 million antitrust lawsuit against the studio.) And yet, in small cities across the South and Midwest, *Billy Jack* proved to be a hit. It opened in a suburb of Dayton, Ohio, in June and ran at the same theater for over a year.

---

*Like the Indian it celebrated, *Billy Jack* would be subject to continual hassling and white-man treachery. Laughlin explained that his fate was ordained when an owl alit on an illuminated Shell sign at the tiny Prescott Airport. "This is highly unusual for an owl. The Navajo regard the owl as a messenger of death. Though my crew pretended to scoff at all such superstitions, none of them was about to get on the airplane that was due in at any moment."

The scene could have been scripted by Alejandro Jodorowsky or Melvin Van Peebles. Laughlin's Iroquois spiritual adviser retired to "a dark part of the parking lot, spread out his medicine, and smoked." Laughlin asked if it was safe to board the plane and was informed it was. "The owl had come to give me a message." *Billy Jack* would "do more good for the youth of America than any picture in recent times." But there were demons who did not wish the kids to receive his message. "I would be put through unbelievable hell for the next three years as they tried to keep the picture from being made."

Disarmingly artless, even affecting in its abrupt transitions and documentary improvisations, *Billy Jack* dramatizes the struggle between two types of vigilante justice. The local sheriff is a flawed embodiment of Cowboy Authority. His daughter, Barbara, returns home from Haight-Ashbury sick and pregnant. (As in *Joe*, generational warfare is a father-daughter thing.) The town is actually run (as well as owned) by a McLintock named Posner, who delegates authority to his wimpish son, Bernard. Civilization is embodied by Jean Roberts (Delores Taylor) and the children's crusade she leads. She is associated with Martin Luther King Jr., and her utopian creative Freedom School, located on a nearby Indian reservation, is an integrated counterculture of longhaired folksingers— a more purposeful, less neurotic Alice's Restaurant.

Laughlin and Taylor create the sort of extended family that Charles Reich imagined for the essential Consciousness III social structure (and which, he believed, found its most successful expression in rock groups that not only worked but lived together). Brutalized by her lawman father, runaway Barbara seeks refuge at the Freedom School. Tensions are exacerbated each time the school's bus drives the singing and clapping students into the bigoted and bully-infested town, where, in a further intimation of the civil rights movement, the locals refuse to serve them. The heart of the film is a tumultuous confrontation between hippies and town elders, resulting in an invitation out to the school for a round of theater games and role-playing.

The *New York Post* cited the spell *Billy Jack* cast on audiences—not only did they cheer and hiss, but they listened intently to philosophical monologues and left the theater debating the film's message. "We may have learned to resist the adorableness of Disney-style kids, but this infant counter-culture is harder to resist, because the kids are like our own—they scatter tough phrases and four-letter words, and their fresh faces take all the obscenity out," Pauline Kael wrote, having experienced a shock of recognition. "This infant idealism is widespread in the country; the Laughlins have put it on the screen, and the kids must be overjoyed to see themselves there."

Billy Jack and Jean Taylor resemble the marshal and his Quaker wife in *High Noon* (although their love is chaste), but, as Kael pointed out, *Billy Jack* was "unlike the Westerns in which the hero shoots the villains and thus demonstrates to the schoolteacher that her pacifism won't work." In *Billy Jack* it was the Gandhian schoolmarm whose principles prevailed—although, as in a John Wayne movie, these feminine values were preserved by traditional macho. Billy Jack karate chops Bernard—who, among other villainies, has raped Jean—and guns down the sheriff. When (as at Kent State), the governor calls out the state militia, Billy Jack barricades himself, with Barbara, in the church: "Today's as good as any to die," he tells her, Indian-style. The siege is complete with live TV coverage. In the end, Billy Jack surrenders. As he's walked to the patrol car, the kids raise their clenched fists. Are they engaging in the symbol of armed resistance, or appropriating it for peace?

"Here at last is an anti-drug, anti-war movie that shows both sides of the generation gap in uncompromising terms," wrote Rex Reed, who would be paid to endorse *Billy Jack* in its TV advertisements. The movie's message was simply, "the hypocrisy of America, the stupidity and lies creeping out of Washington, and the need for compassion and understanding between people if life is to survive on this planet." Kael appreciated the movie's positive hero, so unlike Willie Boy and those other cynical, fatalistic, or introspective protagonists who rejected the possibility of meaningful action.

> To be hip has meant to feel that nothing external could be changed, and the movies have been ending in violence or failure or death. The character of Billy Jack combines the good man of action with the soul-searching mystic. He appears to be armed, rather than disarmed, by his studies with an Indian holy man. . . . The movie restores the—by now welcome—tradition of the (relatively) happy ending.
>
> In a primitive and original way, *Billy Jack* is hip. It's probably the first hip movie for teen-agers (and sub-teen-agers) since the Beatles' films, which were also hopeful.

By the end of 1971, *Billy Jack* had grossed $9 million, making it the year's number-six box-office attraction. At once a beleaguered independent production and a monster of mass saturation, the movie was no less schizoid than its hero. *Billy Jack* "can be seen as both Marxist and Fascist," Stuart Byron pointed out in Boston's *Real Paper*. "It's left-wing, it's right-wing, and yet it never unites these impulses into a convenient philosophy such as 'populism.' " Even Elvis was a fan.

●   ●   ●

As anticipated by Sam Peckinpah, the dying Western was now the vehicle for new Hollywood ambitions. Freedomland was redesigned to include My Lai and Route 66, heroic Mexicans and holy outlaws. Throughout 1970, Arthur Penn, Robert Altman, Warren Beatty, Peter Fonda, and Dennis Hopper were all playing Cowboys and Indians. As the gang of old cowboy stars complained in the deeply anti-authoritarian *Myra Breckinridge*, "We were Saturday afternoon for the whole world—and what has taken our place? Communist perversion." Long live the Red Dog Saloon . . . but only through summer 1971. When Hopper's *The Last Movie* was released in late September, the *Easy Rider* revolution was over.

As *El Topo* and *Billy Jack* built their cults through spring 1971 in tandem with *Sweet Sweetback's Baadasssss Song*, a trio of explicitly hippified studio Westerns—Altman's *McCabe & Mrs. Miller*, Fonda's *The Hired Hand*, and Frank Perry's *Doc*—were saddled to ride into theaters. Provocatively "naturalistic," even as they featured the new Hollywood stars of *Bonnie and Clyde* and *Easy Rider*, all three shamelessly revised the past according to present dogma. The settling of the West pit a libertarian, cautiously feminist, mildly multicultural realm of sex and dope against the forces of the uptight, patriarchal, all-encompassing, implicitly white-supremacist regime of corrupt capital that Charles Reich called the Corporate State. Naturally, the good guys were doomed.

Altman's *McCabe & Mrs. Miller*, the most nuanced of the three, opened in late June with Beatty in his first (and only) cowboy role. A true American entrepreneur, John McCabe introduces gambling and prostitution to a raw Northwestern mining town—aided in this civilizing venture by an acerbic English madam, Constance Miller (Julie Christie). Mrs. Miller, whose hard-headed practicality is belied by a secret opium habit, proves even more visionary than McCabe. Her project .is to make the West safe for a "proper sportin' house—class girls, clean linen, and proper hygiene!" The partners' casino-bordello is a virtual hippie commune of music and dancing, birthday parties and hot-tub frolics. But paradise is short-lived. As the execution of one contented young customer (Keith Carradine) dramatizes the slogan MAKE LOVE NOT WAR, so McCabe is destroyed by hypocritical religion and soulless corporations.

"There are no 'tough guys' among the youth of Consciousness III," Reich marveled. "Hitchhikers smile at approaching cars, people smile at each other on the street, the human race rediscovers its need for each other." How was it possible to make a Western about such creatures? In the aftermath of *Easy Rider*, Universal studio head Lew Wasserman created a "youth" unit headed by Ned Tanen, whose first three projects—Hopper's *The Last Movie*, Fonda's *The Hired Hand*, and Monte Hellman's *Two-Lane Blacktop*—were all some sort of Westerns, perhaps of the Martian variety.*

Arriving in early August, *The Hired Hand* was overtly druggy ("a literal trip for turned-on audiences," per *Variety*). Opening with a sunburst, Fonda's directorial debut reveled in ultra slow-mo lap-dissolves, multiple superimpositions, and male sensitivity: Bruce Langhorne's score suggesting a suite for banjo, fiddle, and sitar as a trio of saddle tramps skinny-dip and talk wistfully

---

*"We blew it," Peter Fonda's Captain America had declared. *Two-Lane Blacktop* was proof. Months before completion, Hellman's account of an existential drag race was hailed by a *Rolling Stone* production story as "an instant classic." *Esquire* made Rudy Wurlitzer's screenplay its April 1971 cover, declaring *Two-Lane Blacktop* the "movie of the year." The movie was targeted directly at the counterculture but, when it finally opened on July 7, audiences proved indifferent. Most critics were underwhelmed, although the *Village Voice* praised Hellman's "feeling for the vast inhuman distances which form the face of America and the character of her people." Warren Oates received the best notices for his portrayal of a speed freak con man racing his 1970 Pontiac GTO cross-country against the souped-up 1955 Chevy driven by one rock star, James Taylor, and serviced by another, Dennis Wilson. (Far more fascinating than Wilson's role here was his cameo in the Charles Manson story; the Beach Boy drummer hosted the Family at his palatial Sunset Boulevard pad for several months during the spring and summer of 1968 while he tried, unsuccessfully, to promote Charlie's recording career.)

of California. Bugs skitter across the sand dunes. The oasis shimmers. The atmosphere is soulfully lugubrious. This lazy desert mirage is a far-out cowboy paradise of surpassing tenderness—as though Captain America and Billy have died and gone to heaven.

Like all hippie Westerns, *The Hired Hand* sought to tell it like it was. Fonda's desire to break through to a greater naturalism may be deduced from his explanation of the movie's prelude: "We used the four classical elements and signs of the zodiac—earth, air, fire, and water, going from one to the other in slow motion, until finally, from the water—the water from which life first came—comes a man," namely the star-director. Enigmatic and withholding, *The Hired Hand*'s Harry is (according to the movie's press notes) "facing what contemporary society would call an 'identity crisis.' " The dropout drifter expresses his desire to leave cowboy paradise and return to the wife, child, and farm he abandoned seven years before. But Amerika won't leave him in peace. On the way home, Fonda and his two buddies stop in the wretched hellhole of Del Norte, a ghost town controlled by an evil merchant (Severn Darden), who shoots one guy for his horse and is shot by Fonda—but not fatally. Fonda and his surviving buddy (Warren Oates) push on to the farm run by Fonda's wife, unglamorous Verna Bloom, playing a woman a decade older than he. To make amends for his desertion, Fonda masochistically offers to work as Bloom's hired hand but freaks when he learns that, in his absence, she slept with the help.

The Hired Hand insists on Bloom's sexual needs and knowledge—she teaches Fonda that his relationship with Oates was essentially romantic. But the star's longhaired, bearded, narrow-hipped Harry is the resident sex object: The bath Fonda takes before his second wedding night provides the occasion for a second nude scene. (When Bloom expressed anxiety about what she might have to do in *The Hired Hand*, Fonda had reassured her: "Only one person took their clothes off in a Peter Fonda film, me.") Still, when Fonda learns that Oates, who has again left for California, is being held captive by Darden, he is obliged—over Bloom's protests—to return to Del Norte. There, after a spastic shoot-out, *The Hired Hand* ends with a homoerotic pieta, Oates cradling dead Fonda.

Consciousness III once again was too pure to live. A week later, on August 18, *Doc* stumbled in from its desert odyssey. FOR THE PAST 90 YEARS THESE THREE PEOPLE HAVE BEEN HEROES, the newspaper ads proclaimed, a promise to debunk Wyatt Earp (New York actor Harris Yulin), Doc Holliday (Stacy Keach), and Katie Elder (played by Faye Dunaway as a whore earthy enough to complain that "beans make you fart"). *Doc* opens with its antihero emerging from the windy wastes, making toward a miserable cantina. A professional gambler, Doc wins Katie in a poker game and rides off with his prize to arrive on Tombstone's dirty, teeming main street. As the new girl in town, Katie draws an enthusiastic crowd—complete with mariachi band—while Doc is reunited with his buddy Wyatt, a cold and calculating wheeler-dealer with unpleasant political ambitions.

Doc was arguably the last Great Society movie. Pete Hamill's script was inspired by his coverage of LBJ's 1966 Far Eastern tour. Two years later, Hamill met director Frank Perry at a literary soiree and they further brainstormed the project, with Hamill finishing his script the night of the moon landing. Announced that November, *Doc* was scheduled to roll June 1970, in Mexico, then put off until autumn. Germinating for the equivalent of an entire presidential term, *Doc* had swollen on years of bile—finally shot in Spain, where Perry constructed the "largest western town ever built for a movie," which proved to be an alcohol-fueled Con II Red Dog Saloon for a particular New York scene. (Rex Reed visited in October 1970 to find the cast recovering from sundry "affairs, bed-hopping, drugs, and brawls." Among other scandals, Hamill "cold-cocked one actor in a local tavern for knocking another actor's wife off a barstool.")

The movie is dutifully stoned—as the tubercular anti-hero medicates himself with opium, the fumes reduce the movie to slow motion—and also has a homosexual undercurrent. Once roused, Doc grabs Katie from beneath a sweaty john and drags her to his room—feeding Wyatt's jealousy. (Katie, however, is an old-fashioned girl. No ménage-à-trois free-love communes for her, she wants to go with Doc and have his baby, storming the opium den and setting it aflame to prove her point.) Ultimately, vacillating Doc is recruited by Earp in his feud with the criminal Clanton clan and, unable to move to a higher consciousness, enters into the spirit of the event by drilling the youngest Clanton—even though the kid has put down his gun. "I guess he reminded me of too many things," Doc muses as he rides off toward death and dissolves into his portrait.

Variety hailed *Doc* as potentially therapeutic, even a litmus test for mental health: This blatantly revisionist Western "may shock the naive, outrage the super-patriotic, offend those who prefer the clichés of the 19th Century American West, but satisfy the well-adjusted." Other reviews were less positive. But if no one missed the political allegory, specifics were open to interpretation. *Life* called Earp "the 1969 model Nixon," while Andrew Sarris noted Earp's "LBJish lust for self-justification." The *New Yorker* was most annoyed with what Penelope Gilliatt took to be *Doc*'s nihilistic attitude toward the recent American past: "The dialogue is so tinged with double meanings and historical anticipation that its thoughts about the frontier spirit almost become remarks about Kennedy's New Frontier."

> After the final shoot-up at OK Corral, Wyatt looks at his brother Morgan's corpse and says, in an accent that is joltingly an imitation of the Kennedy voice, "I tell you that my brother did not die in vain. We are going to build a better town. We are going to build a better Tombstone." . . . [Faye Dunaway] doesn't seem within a mile of the blowsy woman of the lines and of historical fact; she belongs to Camelot and to a system of stylish hope which the film holds out by hindsight.

The Western was dying, and yet, outside the genre, there was hardly another way to conceptualize American politics.

•   •   •

Newsweek called *Doc* "so callowly conceived, poorly written and flaccidly directed" as to provoke laughter, but the biggest bomb would be Dennis Hopper's long-awaited *Easy Rider* follow-up. Like Clint Eastwood, Hopper was among the last Hollywood stars to serve an apprenticeship in the Western. But where Eastwood fused Outlaw and Lawman, Hopper was less ambiguous. As an actor and a director, he combined the Cowboy with the Juvenile Delinquent, living out a revolt against Hollywood that seemed virtually reflexive.

Rooted in the megalomania of the Great Society, *The Last Movie* was actually to be Hopper's first. Inspiration came to him in Durango while appearing in the 1965 John Wayne vehicle *The Sons of Katie Elder*: "I thought, my God, what's going to happen when the movie leaves and the natives are left living in these Western sets?" Hopper had hoped to make *The Last Movie* in 1966 with Wayne and *Katie Elder* director Henry Hathaway in cameo parts, but the project fell through when music producer Phil Spector withdrew financial support. In the wake of *Easy Rider*, Universal gave Hopper $850,000 and total autonomy so long as he remained within budget. Hopper wanted to film in Mexico but feared government censorship—thus, most of the movie was shot during the breakdown spring of 1970 in the remote Andes village of Chincheros, Peru.

Was any location ever further out? Chincheros was a second plane ride from Lima and had no electricity. As Peru was the world capital of cocaine, Hopper had little difficulty attracting Hollywood's druggie elite, although, according to Peter Fonda, the cast was mainly stoned on the local, 190-proof white lightning—particularly after paranoid Hopper confiscated everyone's stash. Despite logistical difficulties including the impossibility of viewing dailies, Hopper finished on schedule—taking forty hours of rushes to Taos, New Mex-, ico, where he drove Universal crazy by mulling over his footage for the next sixteen months. *The Last Movie* was the Tanen unit's key project. With the studio still hoping for an Easter 1971 release, Ned Tanen showed up at Hopper's place to see how things were going: "I walked in, and this enormous orgy was going on."*

---

*The orgy had been arranged at Hopper's request by Lawrence Schiller and L. M. Kit Carson as part of their documentary, *The American Dreamer*. In this portrait of the artist

Ignoring his producers, Hopper sought advice elsewhere. In early 1971, he
had screened *The Last Movie* for Alejandro Jodorowsky, and after the maker of *El
Topo* dismissed it as conventionally Hollywood, began reediting. Thus, incorporating Universal's planet-earth logo into the action (while withholding a title
credit for nearly half an hour), *The Last Movie* became three interlocking films.
The first is a studio Western directed by Sam Fuller on location which shuts
down after the actor playing Billy the Kid is accidentally killed. The stuntman
Kansas (Hopper) stays behind, imagining he might develop Chincheros as a production site, but the only subsequent movie is one conceived by the local Indians. Having watched Fuller's production, they restage it as a ritual on the
abandoned set, using make-believe equipment to "film" actual violence. Kansas
is designated "El Muerte" and chosen to die at the climax of this second movie.*

Hopper is not content to stay within this allegorical framework. A third
movie begins with Kansas's death. Narrative evaporates as *The Last Movie* turns
into a comic documentary of its own making. The death scene is played over
and over, actors go out of character, the set photographer wanders on camera.
This collapse of the fictional is superseded by the disintegration of cinematic
representation. The movie loses sync, the camera is heard, editing dissolves,
the emulsion is scratched. The shadows refuse to be anything more than shadows, leaving the audience to its own devices.

---

at "put-up-or-shut-up" time, Hopper plays prophetic outlaw artist—an acid cowboy
dressed in Stetson, denim, and flowered shirt, taking target practice, quoting Charles
Manson, and driving his pickup truck through the New Mexico desert. The tension is
palpable.

*Like *The Wild Bunch*, to which it alludes with a bit of slow-motion pseudo-carnage,
The Last Movie is set south of the border and suggests that Americans must extend the
frontier beyond their boundaries if they are to continue to be Americans in the traditional sense. Hopper is, however, less sentimental than Peckinpah. Whereas *The Wild
Bunch* tends to treat whoring around as boyish fun, *The Last Movie* dwells unpleasantly
on the relationship between sex, power, voyeurism, and money in a foreign land—
including a tepid orgy staged for the benefit of some visiting Americans in the local
brothel.

Universal smelled catastrophe. A test screening at the University of Iowa was inauspicious. When Hopper took the stage after the movie, the audience hurled garbage and abuse. As Tanen hustled the director out, a teenage girl working the popcorn concession asked him if he'd made this movie. When Hopper answered in the affirmative, she busted him in the nose. *The Last Movie* won an award at the Venice Film Festival and opened in New York on September 30, where it broke the single-day box-office record at the RKO Fifty-ninth Street theater, site of *Easy Rider's* triumphant engagement. Within two weeks it had vanished, having been attacked and ridiculed by virtually every reviewer in America as an incoherent string of apparent non sequiturs.

The Legal Vigilante: *Dirty Harry* and Tricky Dick

There remained 140,000 U.S. troops in Vietnam when *Dirty Harry*—Don Siegel's new Clint Eastwood vehicle—opened on December 21, 1971. But they were not the only uniformed Americans under fire.*

SUPPORT YOUR LOCAL POLICE, a John Birch Society bumper-sticker mantra since the mid-Sixties, had thus far inspired only Burt Kennedy's parody Westerns, *Support Your Local Sheriff* (1969) and *Support Your Local Gunfighter* (1971), and the cops had taken to staging their own demonstrations. In October 1970, as the Hard-hat Election approached its climax, some 3,000 police officers from forty-four states massed on the Capitol steps, protesting the American Civil Liberties Union, attacking liberal Supreme Court decisions, declaring the country in the midst of violent revolution, exposing a national conspiracy by radical groups to murder policemen, and demanding legislation to make attacks on law officers a federal crime.

After testifying at a House Internal Security Committee hearing on the Black Panthers, John H. Harrington—thirty-year veteran of the Philadelphia police

---

*Five days later, Operation Proud Deep brought the heaviest bombing of North Vietnam since 1968. Protests included a forty-two-hour occupation of the Statue of Liberty by fifteen Vietnam Veterans Against the War who, among other things, hung the American flag upside down.

force—told the rally that the ACLU and Supreme Court were dividing the nation by promoting legislation that "condones flag burning, outlaws prayer in public schools and advocates the open display of pornography" while ignoring the conspiracy to "assassinate us pigs." *Dirty Harry*—which had its world premiere to benefit the San Francisco Police Activities League—acknowledged such resentment even as it fulfilled the Silent Majority's eight-year longing for a heroic cop. *Sweet Sweetback's Baadasssss Song* was dedicated to "all the brothers and sisters who have had enough of the man"; *Dirty Harry* opens by scrolling the names of those San Francisco policemen killed in the line of duty— even though no cops are slain in the movie itself.

Cobbled together from four scripts, *Dirty Harry* was in production throughout the late spring and summer of 1971. A few weeks into the shoot, Washington police launched a preemptive sweep of the antiwar protestors who'd come to the capital at the behest of the May Day Tribe, by revoking a permit for their use of West Potomac Park. As protestors rallied on Sunday, May 2, 5,000 police were reinforced by 1,500 National Guardsmen and 10,000 soldiers, including paratroopers. The next morning, the Tribe invaded downtown Washington, planning to disrupt traffic and march on the Pentagon. By nightfall, in the largest such operation in American history, some 7,000 demonstrators and bystanders were arrested, most held in the Washington Coliseum and RFK Stadium.

Dirty Harry's production also coincided with the extra-legal activities precipitated by the *New York Times'* June 13 publication of the so-called Pentagon Papers. Culled from a forty-three-volume classified study commissioned by Robert McNamara in 1967, the papers explicated the policy-making rationales of the JFK and LBJ administrations. Motivated by the secret bombing of Cambodia, former Defense Department employee Daniel Ellsberg gave these documents first to Senator William Fulbright and then to *Times* reporter Neil Sheehan. Although the White House understood Ellsberg's revelations as far more damaging to previous Democratic administrations than the current Republican one, Richard Nixon believed Ellsberg and the *New York Times* were engaging in "criminally traitorous" behavior and had his special counsel Charles

Colson draw up lists of other "enemies" in the press, antiwar movement, and liberal intelligentsia.*

Meanwhile, per the President's instructions, domestic adviser John Ehrlichman formed an anti-leak unit jokingly known as the Plumbers. Former CIA operative E. Howard Hunt, the information officer on the agency's ill-fated Bay of Pigs operation, was directed to break into the Brookings Institute to secure other Vietnam papers. The strategy was to discredit Camelot. Nixon proposed to release unknown material behind the Cuban invasion, the Missile Crisis, and the coup that toppled Ngo Dinh Diem. Railing against cautious "goddam lawyers," Nixon pointed out that his advisers had been worried the previous summer when he had intervened in the Manson trial. But "I knew exactly what we were doing on Manson. You've got to win some things in the press." Some thought Nixon was goaded by Henry Kissinger, who felt implicated by the behavior of his onetime student Ellsberg, but the President needed no prompting: "We're up against an enemy, a conspiracy," he told aides. "They're using any means. We are going to use any means. Is that clear?" The night of September 3, the Plumbers burglarized the Beverly Hills office of Ellsberg's psychiatrist.

The President had been making dramatic public gestures all summer. His trip to China was announced on July 15; a month later, he imposed wage and price controls and, by severing the dollar from the gold standard, unilaterally terminated the Bretton Woods Agreement. Timed to preempt the nation's former number-one TV show, *Bonanza*, the announcement was framed as a Sunday night TV special. Nixon's performance, economist Herbert Stein recalled, "had to be dramatic and smooth as possible. . . . But it was not regarded as a step in the continuing process of government. After the special, regular programming would be resumed."

---

*Casting Ellsberg as another Alger Hiss, the President sought to indict him and asked the Supreme Court to enjoin further publication of the papers—even, at one point, proposing to argue the case personally. The White House planned to link Ellsberg to "radical revolutionary" groups and, Nixon promised his staff, "destroy him in the press."

The next day, European stock markets crashed and currency exchanges shut down. As a national mood-changer, however, the President's speech had considerable short-term gains. Having trailed Senator Edmund Muskie in a three-man race with George Wallace, Nixon pulled ahead by six points. The administration even produced two new political stars. Secretary of the Treasury John Connally, former LBJ protégé and Texas governor, emerged as Nixon's designated economic "quarterback." Meanwhile, the heady atmosphere of secret diplomacy coalesced into a media cult around Kissinger, increasingly appreciated as a combination of James Bond and Dr. Strangelove.

Summer 1971 was also marked by grim acts of terror and desperation in the arena of the nation's penal system. August 21, George Jackson—Black Panther hero and best-selling author of *Soledad Brother*—was killed attempting to escape San Quentin. The Weather Underground responded nine days later by bombing the San Francisco Department of Corrections. In early September, 1,200 inmates of the Attica Correctional Facility in upstate New York seized fifty hostages, mainly guards, and took over the prison's D Yard. Negotiations stalemated, and on September 13, National Guards charged in, killing thirty-two prisoners and ten hostages. (Four days later, the Weather Underground bombed the Department of Corrections in Albany.)

It was a moment when the nation's laws and protocols—abroad as well as at home—were broken at the highest levels. Even John Wayne felt required to make the ultimate sacrifice. Wayne's late Westerns had been as absorbed with personal mortality as contemporary social upheaval. *The Cowboys*—directed by non–Wayne employee Mark Rydell and originally to star George C. Scott—conflated both concerns. Once more, the Duke cast himself as a two-fisted entrepreneur, the successful venture capitalist as self-made cattleman. But here, his enterprise is in crisis. Wayne's mega-rancher, Wil Andersen, has been let down by his feckless hired hands and is forced to save his cattle drive by drafting a bunch of teenagers—teaching them to drink, shoot, kill, and otherwise conduct themselves as men.

It's an unsentimental business arrangement and yet a film to tear the Presidential eye. Petersen finds his recruits at the local primary school—no student deferments in this territory! A varied group, the inductees include a skinny kid, a fat one, a stutterer, a Jew, a Mexican, a runt, a four-eyes, and a lad who plays Vivaldi on the guitar. The platoon is complete when a jolly black cook (Roscoe Lee Browne) shows up to administer the chuck wagon. Like the troops in Vietnam, these cowboys will grow to manhood under John Wayne's tutelage. Their education is completed in a delirious scene of *lèse majesté*, where the film's villain, a scurvy jailbird known as Long Hair (played by AIP biker-hippie Barker gang-member Bruce Dern), shoots Duke four times in the back. Wayne's death—his first onscreen since *The Alamo*—provides *The Cowboys'* most naturalistic, brutal, and exploited aspect. Legend has it that the Duke warned Dern that he'd be the most-hated man in America. "Yeah," Dern supposedly replied, "but they'll love me in Berkeley."

Wayne was now the last of the old-time Hollywood Freedom Fighters, and his sacrifice offered a drastic solution to an imaginary problem. The crisis in American troop morale was increasingly publicized as ground forces were withdrawn. Nixon's Army was largely composed of teenaged draftees, chosen by lot and concerned mainly with surviving their twelve-month tour of duty. No one, *New York Times* correspondent Donald Kirk reported after going on patrol with the grunts, wanted to be the last man killed in Nam. The prevailing slogan was "CYA (cover your ass) and get home." Alienation was particularly pronounced among black recruits—who, despite the nursemaid role assigned Browne in *The Cowboys*, were both overrepresented in combat units and underrepresented as officers corps. What now would be the myth of the American experience? An article published by retired Marine Corps Colonel Robert D. Heinl Jr. in the June 7, 1971, *Armed Forces Journal* maintained that "morale, discipline and battleworthiness" were "lower and worse than at any time in this century and possibly in the history of the United States."

> By every conceivable indicator, our army that now remains in Vietnam is in a state approaching collapse. . . .
>
> Intolerably clobbered and buffeted from without and within by social turbulence, pandemic drug addiction, race war, sedition, civilian scapegoatese, draftee

recalcitrance, malevolence, barracks theft and common crime, unsupported in
their travail by the general government, in Congress as well as the executive
branch, distrusted, disliked, and often reviled by the public, the uniformed services today are places of agony . . .

Before the Tet offensive, recruits were relatively distanced from the home-
front Orgy. By 1969, however, the troops were Orgy veterans—no cordon
sanitaire existed between the nation's armed forces and its riotous youth culture. Cheap pot, opium, and even smack abounded in Nam. (The Pentagon
eventually revealed that a third of all enlistees had tried heroin, with nearly
two-thirds of those developing a habit.) Reported incidents of insubordination
had doubled since 1968: The American presence entered its final year amid
increased atrocities against civilians, refusal to follow combat orders, and the
fragging of overly enthusiastic officers. As Heinl noted, "word of the deaths of
officers will bring cheers at troop movies or in bivouacs of certain units." Still,
the Duke did not die in vain. Forced to maturity, his kids not only complete
their mission, driving his cattle to market, but wreak vengeance on the Long
Hair gang by taking the law into their own hands.

•   •   •

The week *Dirty Harry* opened, *Box Office* declared Clint Eastwood "star of the
year." Originally, Frank Sinatra was to have played the part of the embittered
lawman. By 1971, the social fabric was so tattered that even an inveterate cop-
hater like Sinatra could be considered police-detective material. (Indeed, bonding with Spiro Agnew, Sinatra had turned Republican.) After Sinatra dropped
out with an injured hand, John Wayne was offered the role. But the Duke
declined. He had something else in mind—namely *The Cowboys*.*

Thus, *Dirty Harry* presented Eastwood in a role alternately imagined for two
venerable attractions on the allegorical landscape—the fading Vegas neon glitz

---

*In addition to Wayne, Siegel wanted Audie Murphy ("the killer of all time, a war hero
who killed over 250 people") to play the serial killer Scorpio. Although this was nixed
by the studio, the idea of opposing two World War II icons is a clue to the movie's
use of doubling and complementary psychologies.

of Sinatra's antiauthoritarian id and the weathered Mount Rushmore of Wayne's ponderous superego. Compared to these two, laconic Eastwood was still appealingly blank territory. Cooler than Sinatra, more morally ambiguous than Wayne, the forty-one-year-old star embodied a new attitude. He was not only grimmer than America's previous number-one Cowboy but also more beaten down.

The original dirty Westerner, Eastwood first mined box-office gold playing a grizzled bounty hunter, the Man with No Name. The baroquely violent and cynical Sergio Leone Westerns which made Eastwood an international icon were almost Maoist in their assertion of power relations: "There are two types of people in this world," Eastwood hisses in *The Good, the Bad, and the Ugly*, "Those with a loaded gun and those who dig." In the course of a rambling analysis of *Easy Rider* and the new Western published in Seattle's underground paper *Helix*, Asian-American militant Frank Chin spoke of his immediate identification with Leone's Eastwood.

> He could care less about progress, the course of civilization, work, money, most women, home, settling down, down payments on a late-model horse, clothes. . . . His role says, "I am Nobody and you better not fuck with me." Society takes this as a challenge and sets out to absorb or kill him.

Articulate only in negation, the Man with No Name is an anti-bourgeois loner with a gun, a Righteous Outlaw without a cause.

According to Chin, indigenous Third World revolutionaries like the Black Panthers and the (American) Red Guards were "often at the drive-in, whooping it up with Sergio Leone." These abstract, gritty Westerns provided would-be urban guerrillas with spiritual armament "against the monstrous brutality of the civilization that hates men, hates the land, hates America the Country, and America the Dream." In *Dirty Harry*, however, that civilization is the monstrous excrescence of the Great Society, and Eastwood's "Dirty Harry" Callahan is stuck cleaning up its mess—including Panthers, hippies, and the liberal decisions of the Warren Court.

No less than the Man with No Name, Dirty Harry is a stylized creature—
an uptight cop who chews gum and wears shades. His off-the-rack sports jacket
is unnaturally close-fitting, as if to accentuate the permanent chip on his shoulder. Harry had been anticipated by Popeye Doyle, rogue cop of the enormously
popular *French Connection*. (Doyle was introduced beating up a black suspect
and consequently, in the course of busting an international heroin ring, shooting one unarmed man in the back and a federal agent by mistake.) But, as
embodied by Eastwood, Dirty Harry had a glamour the low-rent Doyle could
never approach. Reviewing *Coogan's Bluff* in the *New York Times*, Vincent Canby
compared Eastwood to a taller, older, "tranquilized" James Dean, suggesting
that his "fathomless cool" was unconscious parody. In fact, Eastwood trumped
Elvis in proposing a new synthesis between hipster and enforcer.

Richard Nixon had campaigned on the issue of law and order in 1968 and
1970. But, in that, he was only following Barry Goldwater, George Wallace,
and Robert Kennedy (who ran in the 1968 Democratic primaries as the nation's
onetime chief law officer). Opening, according to the protocols of the new
national narrative, with an assassin's high-powered rifle pointed at the camera,
Dirty Harry was no less demagogic. The senseless—but not unsensuous—
execution of a nubile young woman in a bikini brings Dirty Harry into the
picture. An individualist thwarted by bureaucrats, Eastwood's lone lawman
suggests an updated, downgraded Gary Cooper in *High Noon*. Indeed, the *Dirty
Harry* scenario is reminiscent of *High Noon*'s, but unlike *Dirty Harry*, *High Noon*
did not make the viewer a party to an extortionist serial-killer's reign of terror.
The sniper, known as Scorpio, is beyond pathological. He's totally demonic
and no one in the pueblo is safe; in his most egregious crime, Scorpio kidnaps
a presumably virginal fourteen-year-old girl, whom he rapes, tortures, and possibly buries alive.

Dirty Harry burst out of the darkness at a time when cops were being
celebrated as heroes and vilified as pigs and somehow managed to be both—
the Dirty Dozen reduced to a single combatant, Patton and the soldier whom
Patton slaps, the synthesis of the *Patton/M*A*S*H* double bill. There's a Nietz-

schean quality to Siegel's tawdry vision. The struggle is played out against such epic locations as the deserted Kezar Stadium, Golden Gate Bridge, the gigantic cross in Mount Davis Park, the Fort Mason Tunnel, and the roof of the fifty-two-story Bank of America building that was San Francisco's tallest skyscraper. Pauline Kael, who published an influential attack on *Dirty Harry* in mid-January, called the movie a hard-hat version of Ayn Rand's *The Fountainhead*. Although Kael and others characterized *Dirty Harry* as a fascist movie, it may be more useful to understand Harry as a fascist hero. This cop thinks with his blood. When he's assigned a new partner, he worries that the man's college degree will get him killed. Harry's hatred of nuance is intrinsic to his appeal. *Dirty Harry* offers an extreme definition of masculine behavior and a pathological loathing for everything else. Harry twice spies on couples making love, and it's emphasized that he has no wife. As isolated in his way as Scorpio, he's pure—a celibate gunman.

Patton, Joe, and *Dirty Harry* were all war movies, and in each case, the war was waged against the young—although *Dirty Harry,* as opposed to Dirty Harry, operates by surrogate. (From the movie's first victim on, violence is directed against two uppity groups, blacks and women.) An establishment outsider with the capacity to single-handedly overrule institutional law and order, Dirty Harry was a new breed of cop—just as Patton was a new sort of military commander. The forced jog around San Francisco in order to deliver Scorpio's undeserved payoff is as cruel as basic training. More grunt than Green Beret, this police officer with a biker's nickname endures considerable abuse: "When are you going to get a haircut?" his supervisor demands. For much of the movie, Harry accepts his lumps—attacked by irate citizens who mistake him for a Peeping Tom, used as a bagman, humiliated by Scorpio.

Worshipping authority in the abstract while flaunting it in the specific, invoking the Law but spitting on the brass, *Dirty Harry* reproduced the brutal class distinctions created by Vietnam. Barely half of all American troops were classified as infantrymen, and most of these were menaced mainly by long-distance mortar fire. Only a minority of those who served in this lavish, hallucinatory war experienced actual combat: Grunts sent in-country to search-and-destroy slogged, sometimes for weeks, through rain forest and rice paddy to endure the cannon-fodder terror of serving as live bait—drawing VC fire so that American air power could target the enemy. This recapitulated a larger situation.

America was involved in the nation's most elaborate military operation since World War II, except that only a small percentage of society seemed directly affected. There was no food rationing, no gas coupons, no Liberty Bonds, no real home front. *Dirty Harry*'s belligerent invocation of martyred police—a prophecy, in its list of names, of the eventual Washington, DC, Vietnam Memorial—proposed cops as our foot soldiers. (*Dirty Harry*'s concern for the war at home is reinforced by those images, then unique, of choppers hovering over San Francisco, as if the city itself were a free fire zone—which is what it turns out to be.)

Harry articulates neither ideals nor ideology. His job is thankless and badly paid. The risks he runs are ridiculous. He's even less able to express his reasons for remaining a cop than Cooper's marshal in *High Noon*. Cooper was disgusted because the townspeople won't live up to the law; in the updated *High Noon* of *The Chase*, Marlon Brando was disgusted because the townspeople flout the law. But Dirty Harry is disgusted because he can't live within the law. Whatever the Eastwood character did in *Coogan's Bluff*, the system was worse; in *Dirty Harry*, the system is actually an obstruction. In the Panther idiom, it's part of the problem, instead of the solution.

As in Vietnam, the situation in which Harry finds himself is not inherently unwinnable. The war has not been lost on the battlefield but somewhere else by a failure of nerve. They're not letting him win. This is the official reason why Dirty Harry loathes the brass as well as the politicians, personified by San Francisco's whining liberal mayor and myopic district attorney—a pair of nattering nabobs, prating elitists, and bleeding-heart Ellsbergs. A paradox: Harry's hatred of the power structure is far more pronounced than Cooper's in *High Noon* or Brando's in *The Chase*, and yet the scenario, Andrew Sarris suggested, could have been written by lawmen John Mitchell or J. Edgar Hoover.

Dirty Harry was deemed important enough for a report in the American Civil Liberties Union newsletter, which observed that the movie really begins at the point where the fourteen-year-old girl is discovered dead and the idiot DA attacks Harry: "Does Escobedo ring a bell? Miranda? Ever hear of the Fourth Amendment? That man had rights." Harry (and we) have nothing but exasperation for the pointy-headed Berkeley law professor who tries to educate him in the niceties of constitutional protection—which, in Scorpio's case, has been violated under the Fourth, the Fifth, the Sixth, and possibly, the Fourteenth Amendments. As the ACLU pointed out, this sequence is the movie's turning point. The "torrent of legalistic rhetoric" serves to overwhelm Harry and enrage the audience.

Like *Patton* and *Joe*, *Dirty Harry* proposed an agenda: The complications of urban life were solvable by direct action, if only the radical chic fools who run the show would stand aside. The mayor is so mealy-mouthed he can't even say the word "nigger" when he reads Scorpio's extortion letter aloud. The police chief is a wimp who warns Harry to remember that Scorpio is "no animal of any kind." The media is ridiculously credulous, constantly taking the infinitely duplicitous Scorpio at his word.

A dirty man for a dirty time, Dirty Harry is the only available hero in a corrupt, degenerate, cowardly civilization; Eastwood is the Last Cowboy, his persona emerging from the Great Society's rubble at the twilight of liberalism. The Frankenstein monster lurched on through the Indochinese jungle, but the rational ambitions that set it in motion are long exhausted. A man with a badge and a vision, Harry was the hero of whom Joe dared only to dream: the Legal Vigilante.

●　●　●

The Legal Vigilante can break the rules, suspend constitutional guarantees, engage in illegal searches, torture, stalk, and even execute a suspect—all in the name of the greater good. "You're lucky I'm not indicting you for attempted murder," the DA tells Harry, citing some absurd statute. To which Harry replies, "The law is crazy," and finally, "I don't know what the law says, but I do know what's right and wrong." Defending the imagined community against the corrupt, effete power structure that has betrayed it, Harry is our protector, if only the authorities would let him be. He alone

understands the necessity for violence: "Nothing wrong with shooting so
long as the right people get shot." The determination of just who the right
people are would be problematic were Harry not infallible. Indeed, when it
comes to crime, Harry can be psychic—as when he senses that a bank job is
in progress and has an uncomprehending lunch-stand counterman telephone
for reinforcements. The Eastwood character visits a disco in *Coogan's Bluff*,
towering over the writhing, degenerate crowd. Dirty Harry enlarges the image. San Francisco—Siegel's specific choice as the film's location—is the
wacky, ultra-permissive city of hippies, liberals, homosexuals, and Black Panthers, not to mention the topless dancers advertised in Dirty Harry as "college coeds."*

Unlike the Arizona out-of-towner, Harry has to live with this scum. "One
day, I'd like to throw a net over the whole lot of them," he snarls to his
partner as they drive through the sleaze zone. Orgy Time and no shortage of
enemies—Bonnie and Clyde, Myra and Manson, Billy Jack, Sweetback, and El
Topo, Easy Rider, Bloody Mama, and the whole Weather Underground of
Crazy, Mixed-up Kids. Nevertheless, as someone points out, "Harry hates
everybody." In this equal-opportunity misanthropy, the detective resembles
another media hero of 1971: Archie Bunker, the disgruntled paterfamilias of
the number-one TV show, *All in the Family*. Bunker, like his neighbor Joe,
personified—albeit in diminished form—the white ethnic Catholic blue-collar
worker described by Kevin Phillips in *The Emerging Republican Majority*. As
Archie was a domesticated Joe, so Archie's daughter, Gloria, was a less-
threatening version of Melissa Compson. Not shacked up with a junkie in an
East Village slum, Gloria had married (and brought home) grad student Mike
Stivic, a McGovernik avant la lettre, whom Archie dubbed "Meathead," and
this reflexive defender of the Enlightenment (upholding, in David Marc's

*The trope would enter national political discourse in 1984 when President Ronald
Reagan, recapitulating his gubernatorial campaigns, ran for reelection against the "San
Francisco Democrats." Ironically, the city was also the site of the most extensive vigilante movement in American history—the San Francisco "vigilance committee" of 1856,
organized by leading merchants to eradicate crime and political corruption.

phrase, "every modernist position from the theory of evolution to abortion on demand") served to highlight Archie's uncomprehending opposition to secular humanism.

All in the Family was thus a liberal counterweight to the restorationist *Patton*: The World War II veteran Archie was a dinosaur headed for extinction, while Mike and Gloria represented the wave of the future. Archie got the laughs, but in the didactic tradition of the American sitcom, it was the younger generation's "liberal" views that were positioned as correct and reasonable. Harry, who is unchallenged by a Meathead in the house (or on the force, once his younger and more moderate Chicano partner resigns), articulates hard-hat values with an even juicier contempt for liberal solutions.

Albeit tougher than Bunker, Dirty Harry nevertheless projects the same mixture of outraged innocence and nostalgic resentment. Harry may be less voluble, but the perhaps politically motivated bank robbery that he foils on his lunch break occasions a masterpiece of tough-guy rhetoric. The spectacle of controlled violence on a crowded downtown street, screams and crashing glass counter pointed by the orgasmic eruption of the fireplug, is merely a prelude to Harry's confrontation with one of the perpetrators, a black man with a Panther-style beret and a distinct resemblance to Sweet Sweetback. "I know what you're thinking," Harry hisses at the sullen perp who sits on the pavement wondering whether to lunge for his carbine. "Did he fire six times or five?"

It's a playfully sadistic invitation to Russian roulette. After a brief testimonial for his .44 Magnum, Harry issues his challenge: "You have to ask yourself 'Do I feel lucky?' Well do ya, punk?" This is Harry's equivalent of reading a suspect his rights—and far more satisfying. Harry sets up the confrontation for his pleasure and that of the audience (which savors the humiliation of a once-frightening figure). The perpetrator declines Harry's dare and feebly calls after him, in an anachronistic Negro dialect, "Hey, Ah gots to know." Mouth still stuffed with hot dog, smirking Harry strides back to discharge his empty gun at the punk's head.

So much for the Panthers. Harry's nemesis Scorpio is an amalgam of Sixties demons: the San Francisco serial murderer known as the Zodiac Killer (and still at large), the Madman in the Tower, the kidnappers who buried alive Florida heiress Barbara Jane Mackle in 1968, Lee Harvey Oswald, even Charles Manson. Iconographically, Zodiac is a hippie—he has long hair and wears a crooked peace sign. As George Bush's scriptwriters intuited during the 1988 campaign, *Dirty Harry* is *Easy Rider* in reverse—Dennis Hopper as killer rather than victim.*

•   •   •

Great Society monster to the end, Scorpio caps all of his previous crimes by hijacking a transport of schoolchildren—the ultimate in forced busing. Dirty Harry has appeared in the nick of time, just as the 1972 campaign is gearing up.

December 23, 1971: Two days after *Dirty Harry*'s opening, Richard Nixon releases RFK's old nemesis, disgraced Teamster Union boss Jimmy Hoffa, from prison—and will later be endorsed by the 2.5 million-member union. Front-runner Edmund Muskie announces his candidacy on January 4, and a week later the eternally hopeful Hubert Humphrey follows suit. Headed by Attorney General John Mitchell, the Committee to Re-Elect the President (soon to be known by its acronym CREEP) opened its office in late 1971. Discrediting Muskie is an early priority, as well as neutralizing George Wallace.

Two weeks before the most militant of Plumbers, G. Gordon Liddy, will present Mitchell with a million-dollar secret campaign intelligence plan involving the use of electronic bugs, call girls, and the strategic kidnapping of radical activists, the Justice Department drops its lengthy investigation of Wallace's brother Gerald, dismissing a grand jury that had already spent close to eighteen months hearing evidence of corrupt financial practices in Alabama. The next

---

*Bush would give President Reagan credit for transforming America from a society that tolerated movies like *Easy Rider* to one that appreciated *Dirty Harry* movies. On the one hand, this is an absurd statement—as *Easy Rider* and the original *Dirty Harry* appear, both during Nixon's first term, less than two and a half years apart. On the other hand, it's true in the sense that *Sudden Impact*—Dirty Harry's greatest hit, the "make my day" film—was released in 1983. The Dirty Harry-ization of America was an ongoing process.

day, the Alabama governor announces that he had rejoined the Democratic Party to seek its presidential nomination.

It is while the President visits China and Dirty Harry pursues Scorpio that Muskie's masculine image dissolves. The front-runner is set up by a letter— describing him laughing to hear French Canadians compared to blacks—published in the state's main daily, the right-wing *Manchester Union Leader*, as well as by the newspaper's repeated attacks on his wife. Flying back into New Hampshire, Muskie stands on a flatbed truck outside the *Union Leader* office and denounces the newspaper's publisher as a "liar" and a "gutless coward." Snowflakes are falling, and the candidate's voice breaks with emotion. Is it a sob? Could those be tears??

In preparation for the 1972 election, Nixon's men cast themselves as patriotic insurgents, if not Legal Vigilantes. Although they control the government of the United States, the President and his advisers still regard the nation's capital as a hostile place. "This hasn't been our town," Washington native Pat Buchanan complains. It belonged to Them.

> They live in Georgetown, with their parties; they never invited us, they ignored us. We were the vanguard of Middle America and they were the liberal elite. It's a schism that's cultural, political, social, emotional. When we came in 1968, they dominated American society—the media, the Supreme Court, the bureaucracy, the foundations. They left us with our cities burning, and inflation going, our students rioting on the campus. And Nixon challenged all this.

And yet power, according to Buchanan, seemed to reside elsewhere.

> We came in talking togetherness and now they attack us for divisiveness. But we can talk togetherness until we're blue in the face. It does no good if every night they see on the tube blacks attacking whites, or whites attacking blacks, students in demonstrations, picket lines, war riots. The tube is doing it, the tube is dividing us. . . .

Indeed, a new hippie antagonist appears on television that month.

During the summer of 1971 ex-Beatle John Lennon and his wife, Yoko Ono, had relocated to New York City and were soon acquainted with the full range of countercultural celebrities—rapping and getting high with all manner of Yippies, Panthers, feminists, underground artists, and political activists. Jerry Rubin recruited Lennon and Ono to appear, along with most of the Chicago Seven, jazz saxophonist Archie Shepp, protest singer Phil Ochs, and Motown star Stevie Wonder at the December 10 "John Sinclair Freedom Rally" in the liberated zone of Ann Arbor, Michigan. Albeit disorganized, the event was a success. Sinclair—serving a ten-year sentence for selling two joints to an undercover narcotics agent—was freed, pending appeal, two days later. Follow-up plans were made for a national Lennon-Ono rock 'n' roll caravan anti-Nixon tour to culminate at the 1972 Republican Convention in San Diego. Perhaps Allen Ginsberg and Bob Dylan would join. The idea was to mobilize the newly enfranchised eighteen-year-olds against Nixon! A week later, John and Yoko sought another alliance, playing Harlem's Apollo Theater at a benefit for the families of the prisoners shot during the Attica uprising. By February 4, Senator Strom Thurmond sent a secret memo to John Mitchell suggesting that the Justice Department look into deporting Lennon. Then, in a Global Village event as unlikely in its way as the following week's Nixon in China miniseries, John and Yoko co-host the popular *Mike Douglas Show*.

Each afternoon throughout the week of February 14, the Lennons turn on America to a mix of pop avant-gardism and countercultural rhetoric. The couple's "frequent displays of short-term memory loss" lead one observer to deem them "obviously stoned"; their guests include revolutionaries Bobby Seale and Jerry Rubin. In a segment recorded and transcribed by the FBI, Rubin explains that "Nixon has automated the war in Vietnam so that it's machines killing people; created a situation where 43 people can be murdered; created a situation where four kids can be killed at Kent State." On March 6, the Immigration and Naturalization Service refuses to renew Lennon's visa.

•   •   •

The Plumbers had already devised a plan to kidnap Jerry Rubin and take him to Mexico to keep him away from the San Diego convention. Let Dirty Harry handle that would-be Scorpio punk. Was it ironic, then, that one of *Dirty Harry*'s few favorable notices appeared in the March 2 *Rolling Stone*? Only four years before, the *New Left Notes* had saluted Bonnie and Clyde as revolutionary heroes. Now, the official voice of the counterculture recognized Don Siegel as an auteur and expressed appreciation for Harry's anti-bourgeois anti-authoritarianism.

A similar point was made by the rival rock journal *Crawdaddy*, where, referencing *The French Connection*, critic Foster Hirsch compared Gene Hackman's demotion to Fonda and Hopper's murder at the end of *Easy Rider*. Hackman's Popeye was also the "victim of a mummified status quo except this victim isn't a visionary hippie or a romanticized rebel, he's a grubby, beer-guzzling, pizza-eating reactionary." But where *Crawdaddy* characterized Harry as a "real pig," *Rolling Stone*'s reviewer Paul Nelson bracketed him with the outlaws of *The Wild Bunch* as a "dignified" and "honorable" anachronism.*

Overshadowed commercially and critically by *The French Connection*, *Dirty Harry* had also been surpassed as so-called fascist cinema by Stanley Kubrick's *A Clockwork Orange* and Sam Peckinpah's *Straw Dogs*, as well as *John Wayne and the Cowboys*, which materialized at Radio City Music Hall the same morning George Wallace declared his candidacy. But just as *Sweetback*, *El Topo*, and *Billy Jack* mobilized followings over time, so *Dirty Harry* developed into a mainstream cult film: Eastwood and Siegel were invited to address police gatherings, and the movie inspired a craze for the foot-long, three-pound Smith &

---

*For Nelson, Harry was a "proud son of John Wayne, James Stewart, Gary Cooper, and Henry Fonda—but the difference is that in today's cities, more violence is required." The critic compared Siegel's "philosophical position" to that of Daniel Ellsberg: "The law itself is not sacred; in certain instances, it would be immoral for an honorable man not to break it." Small wonder Siegel, who considered himself an anti-establishment liberal, wrote appreciatively to the editor that "Of all the reviews I have read, [Nelson's] seemed to understand more fully what I was trying to say in the picture than any of the others."

Wesson .44 Magnum—a weapon whose use-value was less practical than magical.*

As with *The Dirty Dozen* and *Sweet Sweetback's Baadasssss Song*, many reviewers felt compelled to note *Dirty Harry's* audience response, pointing out
that the movie's ostensible targets were loudly appreciative. *Dirty Harry's* fantasy of omnipotence was popular on Forty-second Street. It was "cheered and
applauded by Puerto Ricans in the audience, and they jeered—as they were
meant to—when the maniac whined and pleaded for his legal rights," Pauline
Kael noted.

> Puerto Ricans could applaud Harry because in the movie laws protecting the
> rights of the accused are seen not as remedies for the mistreatment of the poor
> by the police and the courts but as protection for evil abstracted from all social
> conditions—metaphysical evil, classless criminality. The movie shrewdly makes
> the maniac smart, well-spoken, and white. . . .

For all his crypto-racist rhetoric, Dirty Harry justified minority paranoia regarding police and the power structure. Profiling Eastwood a few years hence
in the *Village Voice*, Larry Cole remembered watching *Dirty Harry* with a "gang
of Lower East Side street kids." Amazed that they identified with Harry, Cole
realized that "it wasn't the violence that propelled [them] into Eastwood's role
but the justice that came from it."

> The prisoners at Attica who instinctively threw themselves on top of their hos-
> tages when Rockefeller's troops began to shoot did it because they shared the
> same romantic sense of justice I had seen in the kids and that the kids had seen

---

*Dirty Harry was a hit, grossing $18 million, but it mainly created a character and a
series of increasingly successful sequels—*Magnum Force* (1973), *The Enforcer* (1976), *Sudden Impact* (1983)—while contributing to the movie and TV cop craze of Nixon's second
term, when even John Wayne "jumped on the paddy-wagon," per Carlos Clarens, with
McQ (1974) and *Brannigan* (1975). Throughout the Seventies, *Dirty Harry* was cited as a
stimulus to both criminal violence and police brutality. The ultimate endorsement came
in 1981 from the Goskino projectionist who reported *Dirty Harry* the movie most
screened by Leonid Brezhnev and the Soviet politburo.

in Dirty Harry. Fuck intellectualized ethics, rationalized right and wrong, proxied retribution. Right is right and wrong is wrong.

Fascism works!

Having broken the law to save civilization, the Legal Vigilante looks at his police badge and then, just as the *High Noon* marshal dropped his star in the dust, chucks it into the same fetid lake where the grotesque, no-longer Righteous Outlaw has fallen. There isn't anyone on the screen to witness this act— the American public is the only audience for Dirty Harry's final gesture.

VI

After the Orgy,
from *Blowup* to *Blow Out*

The fifties were the real high spot for the U.S. ('when things were going on'), and you can still feel the nostalgia for those years, for the ecstasy of power, when power held power. In the seventies power was still there, but the spell was broken. That was orgy time (war, sex, Manson, Woodstock). Today the orgy is over.

—Jean Baudrillard, *America* (1986)

As directed by the Next Voice You Hear and enforced by the Seventh Cavalry, the Pax Americana took hold, bringing forth the Imperial Presidency. First there was General Ike, beloved Christian Soldier who kept the peace and built the great network of interstate highways. Then, as the sputnik rose in the sky and intercontinental ballistic missiles were stockpiled in the earth, the youthful Star-Pol JFK emerged from the dream life to warn all rival empires that we were prepared to defend the most remote frontiers of Freedomland.

Come to Marlboro Country! Remember the Alamo! The Western scenario inspired the most grandiose crusade in human history. So what if imperial Rome became overextended in guarding an increasingly far-flung perimeter?

America could patrol the entire globe. Americans, as Garry Wills would point out, "had things the Romans lacked—jet planes, helicopters, napalm, defoliants, one-man water-walking rockets, computers, and theoreticians of the strategic hamlet." Brushfire wars flared along the watchtowers, silver spaceships hurtled toward the moon. The nation was bombarded by cathode rays as first the Great Cowboy and then President Madman bombed one rebellious outlaw state (as well as several neighboring provinces) into not-quite-submission.

As prophesied in *The Manchurian Candidate* and *Shock Corridor*—movies that projected Freedomland as a conspiratorial labyrinth or an unknowable mental hospital—the Republic had mutated. Not long before the 1964 and 1968 elections, a leading candidate for president was somehow eliminated by assassination. It would happen again in 1972 unless, of course, the election was canceled first, as some savants feared. Davy Crockett was dead, replaced by The Godfather. Our leaders were Lords of Misrule and Masters of War, dazzling in duplicity yet befuddled by their roles in the murky national narrative. President Madman even visited Red China—living out a Black Panther Weather Underground New Hollywood revolutionary fantasy. While Nixon was toasted in the Forbidden City, his leading challenger shed tears defending his wife's honor. Some speculated that he, like much of the populace, had been dosed with LSD.

Realness was demanded but hallucinations were endemic. Wonder Bread and Circus Circus no longer sufficed. Cities had burned, the populace smoldered, the Cavalry was pinned down, the Voice no longer heard in the land. Now came the moment of pornographic display, Dionysian cults, a zonked-out children's crusade, unisex, dope, motorcycle Indians, black men born to be wild in the streets, armed love, orgy time. . . . A face in the crowd, running for California's governor in 1966, Ronald Reagan had identified the Berkeley campus as the site of orgies "so vile" that he dared not describe them. Campaigning against student "advocates of sexual orgies, drug usage, and filthy speech," the movie-star candidate promised, if elected, to "investigate the charges of Communism and blatant sexual misbehavior"—two classic Hollywood sins conjoined on the state university campus. Some crimes were even cinematic. Reagan told a woman's club in April 1966 that he had proof that the Alameda County district attorney investigated a student dance cum "orgy," with projected images of "men and women, nude, in sensuous poses, provocative, fondling." As the Berkeley activist Jerry Rubin explained in his manifesto *Do It!*, "Riots, campus struggles, demonstrations—the longer, the better—are social, community orgies." Orgy: the ultimate, uncontrollable collective desire. The movement proposed sex as a weapon. To get naked in public was a moral act.*

But while a 1970 presidential task force on obscenity reported that the new pornography "strongly [paralleled] the rise of certain extremist groups of nihilists"—Myra, Sweetback, Manson—middle America was enjoying its own porn pandemic. Universal Choice! By 1972, there was a startling proliferation of skin flicks, massage parlors, swingers clubs, live sex shows. One might read signs of the Orgy in the sweaty entrails of *The Chase*. The riotous Great Society farrago of vengeful patriarchal petro-plutocrats, saintly escaped convicts, guntoting wife-swappers, victimized Negroes, and helpless lawmen culminated in a contrived conflagration on the Columbia back lot (filmed even as Watts burned) and, then, a tasteless reprise of the Kennedy assassination. Evoking the waste and piety of Pax Americana Cold War spectacles, Pauline Kael mocked this authorless disaster—released even as hallucinations were endemic and the Oriental Western swelled to monster proportions—as a newfangled epic of imperial antiquity, exploiting the licentious behavior it piously decried.

Flash-forward to 1968: *Shampoo*

The first periodization of "1968"—year of the Righteous Outlaw and Cowboy Authority on the ropes—starred three still-viable Sixties icons, Julie Christie (ever since her turn as a model in *Darling*, the signifier of Swinging London), Goldie Hawn (whose body-painted midriff was a staple of TV's potted Orgy, *Rowan & Martin's Laugh-In*), and producer–star–co-writer Warren Beatty (Weatherman avant la lettre in *Bonnie and Clyde*).

---

*"Our program of rock and roll, dope, and fucking in the streets is a program of total freedom for everyone," White Panther martyr John Sinclair proclaimed before being jailed.

That the Christie character was named "Jackie" provided another powerful Sixties connection—particularly as she played the lost love of the actor who'd been JFK's chosen stand-in a dozen years before. But that was scarcely *Shampoo*'s lone political referent; its action was restricted to a frantic twenty-four-hour period in the life of Beverly Hills hairdresser George Roundy (Beatty), Election Day 1968.

Juggling a complex round of professional and personal assignations, George lives with Jill (Hawn), a sweetly dim aspiring actress—another bit player in the show—and, over the movie's course, betrays her with her best friend and his former lover, Jackie, now mistress of Lester Karp (Jack Warden), a middle-aged financier of powerful political-cum-mob connections; with Lester's sex-starved wife, Felicia (Lee Grant), who is one of George's preferred customers; and, almost inadvertently, with the Karps' teenage daughter, Lorna (Carrie Fisher).

No simple pagan servant of the Orgy, George seeks to institutionalize it. He ineptly strives to go into business and is encouraged by Felicia to seek Lester's help in setting up his own beauty salon. (Was Lester, then, a parody of Jack Warner, the studio boss before whom Beatty was forced to grovel to get his *Bonnie and Clyde* rereleased?) Lester leads George to believe he might consider investing in this project, but at the moment George approaches him, Lester is more interested in having the hairdresser, whom he naturally believes a homosexual, act as a beard and escort Jackie to a swank banquet—a Republican victory celebration to be held at a Beverly Hills restaurant that night. Even Republicans are in on the Orgy!

Back in the real November 1968, a major Hollywood studio run by a fellow not unlike Lester was actually shooting a fake biography of revolutionary martyr Che Guevara. Contriving to get Jackie to the banquet, Lester is as great a risk-taker as Darryl Zanuck. It's madness—Felicia will, of course, be present—but somehow Lester wants to flaunt his exquisite harlot, her backless gown cut nearly to the cleft of her perfect buttocks. To compound the comedy, Jill also turns up, escorted by a young producer who is proposing to cast her in a cigarette commercial that, like *The Ten Commandments*, will be filmed on location in Egypt.

Dinner is a fabulous disaster. The women rebel! Felicia attempts to drag

George into the toilet for a quick fuck. Jackie drinks too much and makes an outrageous scene, after which Felicia promises Lester a very expensive divorce. In the ensuing confusion most of the principals move on to a psychedelic extravaganza at a vast Beverly Hills estate. Here, events come to a head. Lester discovers that George has been sleeping with both his wife and his mistress; Jill understands that George has been continually unfaithful to her; George realizes that he truly loves Jackie. Unfortunately for him, Jackie has decided to marry Lester. As day breaks, George is abandoned by all three women: Nixon time.

Pauline Kael, who very much cared for *Shampoo*, praising its "yummy" premise as "something a smart porno filmmaker would come up with," feared the movie might be dismissed as frivolous precisely because it was so serious. "In its way, *Shampoo* is a very uncompromising film and it's going to cause dissention. People who are living the newer forms of the *Blowup* style, or want to, won't like this view of it." But what did Kael mean by the *"Blowup* style," based as it was on a film she had disliked?*

Seven years before, Kael synopsized the *Blowup* style as a frenetic yet sterile round of sex, drugs, rock 'n' roll, and celebrity. What were its newer forms? Had it become even more fashionable, promiscuous, narcissistic, and distracted? Was it now more democratic? Was it institutionalized—not simply a style but a lifestyle? Or was it simply over?†

● ● ●

The original zeitgeist film, Michelangelo Antonioni's *Blowup* was shot in London in the spring of 1966 and was so current that it was all but dated from

---

*"Was there ever a good movie that everybody was talking about?" Kael wrote in early 1967, as though *Bonnie and Clyde* would never happen. "People identify with [*Blowup*] so strongly, they get upset if you don't like it—as if you were rejecting not just the movie but them."

†Kael was not alone in making this connection. *Time* titled its review of *Shampoo* "Blow Dry," and, writing in *Film Quarterly*, David Ehrenstein compared George's "inability to distinguish casual promiscuity from deep emotional commitment" to *Blowup*'s Thomas.

the moment of its world premiere a week before Christmas at the Coronet Theater in New York. *The Chase*, released ten months earlier, had hinted at some new public derangement, but *Blowup* was the first commercial release to celebrate the Orgy. The counterculture was in place, Nam totally Texafied. Here was the full dream-life flowering of zombie hedonism, amoral affluence, guerrilla theater, body paint, micro-minis, raga rock, and group-grope. Pure Spectacle of the Sixties, *Blowup* celebrated the put-on; it valorized impulse behavior, promoting the druggy sense that reality was individual and subjective rather than social and objective. Everyone was his or her own star.

Blowup opened the same month *Time* declared the under-twenty-five generation Man of the Year and *Esquire* published "The Day It All Happened, Baby." Out in the next youth capital, the acidheads of San Francisco were organizing a vast pageant, a Gathering of the Tribes, tens of thousands tripped-out and milling around Golden Gate Park—the first Human Be-In. Musing on his subject, Antonioni told a London reporter he found youth culture "most interesting" but wondered what it all meant. "Often I think of the Roman Empire." London, famous not only for its rock 'n' roll aristocrats but a supporting galaxy of models, photographers, designers, and boutiques, had only recently been the fashion capital of the Western world. *Time*'s April 1966 cover story on its designated City of the Decade reported Antonioni scouting locations for "a film on—of all things—the swinging London scene." Postdating even *Time* by nine months, *Blowup* arrived late in the day and, among other things, set out to be a critique of the Image, an explication of pseudo-events. Understandably, London critics attacked it as "shallow," "fabricated," and "laughably absurd," "the adman's tawdry, swinging city." But for everyone else, Antonioni invented a juvenilopolis as stylized and vacant as the set for a Samuel Beckett play (and yet how wondrously verdant, how freshly scrubbed).*

---

*Although based on a story by Julio Cortazar, *Blowup* originated in a profile of fashion photographer David Bailey that ran two years earlier in the *Times of London* and concerned the ways in which photographers simultaneously document and create events.

The movie's first scene has a flamboyant band of mimes engaging in obnoxious street theater, even as the protagonist, a young fashion photographer identified in the credits—if nowhere else—as Thomas (David Hemmings) leaves the flophouse where, disguised as a beggar, he had spent the night gathering material for a picture book. Thomas is a spy, but like the hero of a latter-day *Arabian Nights Entertainment*, escapes in the chariot of his magnificent Rolls Royce, returning to the mod palace of his duplex studio where a gaggle of mannequin houris are already waiting for a fashion shoot. In *Blowup*'s signature sequence, adapted for the early print ads, Thomas dismisses the models, preferring to concentrate his attention on the statuesque and celebrated Verushka (playing herself), whom he photographs with an intensity that is a parody of the sexual act, straddling her writhing torso to climax in a frenzy that leaves them both spent. Then it's back out into the crazy, empty outside world. After dropping in on an antique shop to buy, on a whim, a wooden airplane propeller, Thomas strolls into a lushly deserted park where he idly photographs an apparent pair of lovers. The woman, identified in the credits as Jane (Vanessa Redgrave), disengages herself from her companion—an older man whom we barely see—and agitatedly demands that the photographer turn over the film.

But secret agent Thomas believes that his camera licenses him to do anything: "Some people are bullfighters, some people are politicians—I'm a photographer." This hero is a soft James Bond, wielding a Nikon instead of a Beretta, although his Rolls, complete with then-futuristic car phone, is worthy of 007: He shakes insistent Jane, but she is waiting at his studio when he returns, offering herself in exchange for the film. The photographer cleverly fobs her off with another roll, but before they can do more than remove their shirts—let alone begin to make love—Jane remembers a prior appointment and flees. Free now to develop and print the object of her desire, curious Thomas discovers what could be a shadowy gunman hidden in the grassy knoll behind Jane's lover. His narcissistic conclusion is that his presence in the park prevented a murder.

There is then an interlude where Thomas stumbles across two teenage girls nervously hanging around his studio in hopes of becoming fashion models and tumbles into a spontaneous dalliance—both birds at once!—before returning to the darkroom. Further enlargements reveal a body on the ground and suggest that a murder did take place. By now it is night. Thomas returns to the park and finds a corpse. Frightened and exhilarated, he goes back to his studio to discover the place ransacked—although at least one of the incriminating photographs remains. Thomas leaves again, wishing to inform his publisher of his adventures (for he has decided to conclude his book with the murder photo), but en route to a party at the publisher's home, he is distracted by the sight of a woman he imagines to be Jane, and so briefly strays into a subterranean rock club. As he watches, the band—who are, in fact, the Yardbirds—sacrifice their instruments upon the altar of a faulty amplifier and, without meaning to, the photographer finds himself in possession of a precious guitar shard. Hysterical fans chase him to the street, where, eluding them, he chucks the relic into the gutter.

Arriving finally at the party, Thomas discovers host and guests in a marijuana-stupefied haze. No one seems to know or care what he's babbling about. ("I thought you were supposed to be in Paris," the photographer snaps at Verushka. "I am in Paris," is her hilariously dreamy reply.) At dawn, Thomas makes his third visit to the park. The body has vanished. Was it ever there? The mime troupe arrives and—like a band of fey Diggers—begins playing an imaginary game of tennis. Thomas, again a bystander, is coaxed to join. He hesitates, does so, and as the camera tracks back, vanishes from the screen, leaving an aerial view of an empty green field.

Early audiences found *Blowup* delightfully unfathomable, and to add to the confusion, it came courtesy of MGM. "Bizarre" was a recurring media characterization, used as a sell word in the movie's print ads. Critical focus tended to be literal—much clucking over the new permissiveness or wondering whether the murder was truth or illusion. *Blowup* had significance. People argued over it and it was widely overinterpreted because, in part, it blatantly proposed that movies and reality were in the head. Those who saw *Blowup* a second time ventured all manner of paranoid connections. For, as its tumble of events made retrospective sense, *Blowup* also might allegorize America's disrupted national narrative.

At least three early reviews connected Antonioni's murder mystery to the Zapruderized confusion around the Kennedy assassination—the alternative scenarios of Mark Lane's *Rush to Judgment* and Edward Epstein's *Inquest* were both bestsellers during the autumn of 1966. It was as if (as *The Manchurian Candidate* promised, Beatlemania suggested, and *The Chase* spelled out), the unsolvable murder of the President had been the occult signal to let the games begin. Even Antonioni found a way to allude to JFK's loss, telling *Life* of his fascination with the American space program: "For many years I've wanted to do a film on the first man to land on the moon. I received an answer in which the President invited me to spend five days discussing the project. Then he was killed."

•   •   •

With its lugubrious pot party and kicky fashion craziness, sublimated camera sex and dissolute rock club, *Blowup* introduced grown-up Hollywood's "contemporary" set pieces for the next five years—and beyond. (*Candy*, *Skidoo*, *Midnight Cowboy*, *Myra Breckinridge*, and *The Strawberry Statement* were each an aspiring *Blowup*.) Appropriately, the industry that would pillage Antonioni's hit initially received it as a slap in the face. Reporting on the movie's Hollywood preview, *Playboy*'s critic Arthur Knight observed that the audience seemed to hate what they saw—"almost as if Antonioni had insulted them personally."

> Famous directors, writers and producers buzzed from group to group, drink in hand, asking each other what the picture was all about, and shrugging humorously when an immediate answer was not forthcoming. Obviously, the feeling was that both they and Metro had been had by an Italian upstart who had made his film deliberately obscure as a kind of spiteful, anti-Hollywood joke.

Variety's reviewer considered *Blowup* "a bust."

In the late 1950s (when power held power), urban Americans patronized European and Japanese art cinema in part because these films were more sexually frank than those made in Hollywood. Still, the distribution of these imports—including a relative blockbuster like Fellini's *La Dolce Vita*—was restricted to large cities and college towns. *Variety* predicted less for *Blowup*: Because distributor MGM refused to cut explicit material, the best *Blowup* could hope for was "the most select of selected situations . . . it goes far beyond the limits of good taste." Instead, *Blowup*, produced by Italians but made in English, became the first Euro-art film mass success, grossing $7 million. *Blowup* was also the first studio release to open without the imprimatur of the Motion Picture Association of America's newly revised, soon obsolete, production code.

That *Blowup* was condemned by the National Catholic Office only enhanced its notoriety. Several scenes were particularly objectionable—one in which Thomas observes his neighbors making love, the other in which the photographer cavorts with the two teenyboppers. The latter scene opens with a dream of consumption as the would-be models try on a closet full of dresses, proceeding through momentary abandon and ecstatic destruction to climax in confused boredom: the Orgy in miniature.

Within a month, everyone in America was in on the scene. *Blowup* opened as strongly in LA, Washington, and Boston as New York, while a *Life* spread covered the "naked rompings" that cost the movie its MPAA seal. With smug wonderment, the French journal *Positif* reported the festival—it was "not unusual to see Americans freezing in line for over an hour" to see *Blowup*.

•   •   •

Shampoo was conceived in *Blowup*'s wake, even as Antonioni's 1970 *Zabriskie Point* would be made under the spell of *Bonnie and Clyde*. Beatty was spending much time in London—having rented a flat there in late 1967—where he became taken (and had taken up with) the realm's hottest international star, Julie Christie. One can only imagine Beatty's mindset. Opening in London on

September 7, *Bonnie and Clyde* took what for three years had been the capital of youth style by storm.

Within weeks, the title was appearing in news stories, editorials, and headlines. The *Daily Express* reported *Bonnie and Clyde* "the number one topic of conversation in the pubs and discotheques . . . the Bonnie Look is the first to really capture the kids since the bikini and the skin-tight blue jean." Not just kids. "Even at the royal premiere of *Doctor Dolittle*, attended by Queen Elizabeth II in diamonds and glittering ball gown, there was one couple attired in the bizarre '30s costumes." The same week in December that *Bonnie and Clyde* graced *Time*'s cover, the *Los Angeles Times* reported BRITAIN BALMY OVER *BONNIE AND CLYDE*. It was then that Beatty and Robert Towne, *Bonnie and Clyde*'s script doctor deluxe, began a screenplay called *Hair*.

Retitled and delayed a half dozen years, *Shampoo* finally emerged as costume drama, transplanted to LA, where, thanks to its freeways, the whole city enjoyed the same continual distraction as Antonioni's hero. (Jill to George: "You never stop moving, you never go anywhere.") If the imaginary tennis courts were found on Lester's Beverly Hills mansion, the *Blowup* lifestyle was otherwise domesticated and democratized. In *Blowup*, Thomas's work was indistinguishable from his leisure; his dream-life pad was fashion boutique, photo lab, harem, and house beautiful. In *Shampoo*, George's downfall was precisely his hapless, utopian attempt to—in millennial Digger parlance—*live as though the day were here.*

George mistakes the beauty salon that employs him for an artist's atelier. "I never know when you're working and when you're not," Jill whines. Nor does George. He has an appointment at Felicia and Lester's Louis XIV–furnished mansion to prepare Felicia's coiffure but is sidetracked, first by their daughter, the dour dumpling Lorna, who poses the hostile question "Do you wanna fuck?" and next, by Felicia herself, intuiting her daughter's Oedipal power play and trumping it by mounting George, still in her mink, with the bedroom door left strategically ajar. The impulsive transformation of work into love is repeated when George subsequently visits Jackie on a mission to redo her 'do.

George is an image-maker to be sure—if more than a few rungs down the hipness-and-status ladder from Thomas's fashion photographer. In fact, George is largely peripheral to the real Orgy of wealth and power, although he has the power to make women anxious merely by mentioning their hair. *Shampoo* is profoundly deflationary. The sight of George suggestively blow-drying a client's wet coiffure, manipulating her compliant head at the level of his crotch, is an appropriately diminished version of Verushka's camera-ravishment in *Blowup*. Similarly, George's frantic sprint around the grounds of an expansively psychedelic lawn party parodies Thomas's cooler pursuit of truth in *Blowup's* finale. But the pot party, already satirized in *Myra Breckinridge*, was staged in *Shampoo* for period pathos.

Where the recycling of the Beatles' "Yesterday" as background cha-cha for the Republican banquet may be a complicated joke about memory and cooption in the U.S.A., the party scene—like the Beach Boys songs which frame the movie—is deeply sentimental. *Shampoo* represents the moment of Che's apotheosis and the illusion of Cowboy Authority's overthrow. Still, unconsciously transposing the action to the world of 1975, *Time* would identify George as "the last shabby survivor of the age of grooviness"—the Sixties Survivor.

The 1972 Campaign: Warren, George, Jane, and *The Candidate*

Scarcely unfolding in some vague and universal Now, *Shampoo* signaled its allegorical ambitions for being set November 4, 1968 A.D. to end as the sun rose on the Nixon Era. Much was made of this, particularly in unfavorable commentaries, yet it is more fruitful to consider *Shampoo* as Warren Beatty's response to Richard Nixon's reelection. The 1972 campaign not only featured a loveable loser named George and marked the end of the Sixties, but established Beatty as a significant and innovative political operative. Indeed, Beatty enjoyed greater influence, both as strategist and organizer, on the 1972 campaign than any Hollywood figure would have on a major party's presidential candidacy until the inevitable election of Ronald Reagan in 1980.

Beatty first met George McGovern in 1968 at the most disastrous of Democratic conventions and, like his older sister, Shirley MacLaine, became one of the South Dakota senator's earliest supporters. Accompanying McGovern from primary to primary—the surprise second-place finish in New Hampshire on March 7, the Florida debacle a week later, the April 4 upset victory in Wisconsin—Beatty was more than a magnet for media attention. He was part of the candidate's inner circle, treated with respect by even the gonzo likes of Dr. Hunter S. Thompson, who, covering the campaign for *Rolling Stone*, reported with approval that Beatty was "blossoming fast in his new role as one of McGovern's most valuable and enthusiastic organizers." McGovern's campaign was managed by Frank Mankiewicz—son of screenwriter Herman Mankiewicz and nephew of director Joseph Mankiewicz. But Beatty established a particularly close relationship with McGovern's thirty-one-year-old junior campaign-manager, Gary Hart—or maybe it only appeared so. The two were natural alter egos; if Beatty enjoyed the satisfaction of being taken seriously as a politician, Hart occasionally had the thrill of being mistaken for a movie star. A *Rolling Stone* photograph shows them hanging out, deep in conversation— two unsmiling narrow-hipped studs with perfectly tousled, collar-length shags (Hart in a neatly pressed work shirt, Beatty wearing a denim suit), just a pair of Sixties cowboys living the *Blowup* lifestyle.

It was during the McGovern campaign that Beatty rewrote the *Wild in the Streets* scenario. Where angry young pop star Max Frost organized "the biggest block party in history" to promote the candidacy of the Kennedyesque sleaze Senator Johnny Fergus, serious youngish movie star Warren Beatty perfected the rock benefit (which the Yippies had fantasized as their path to power) to support Kennedy heir George McGovern. The soundtrack was perfect because, as if on schedule, the war was heating up! Just after the Wisconsin primary, President Madman resumed bombing.

•   •   •

April 15, 1972: Richard Nixon sends B-52s to destroy the oil depots at Hanoi and Haiphong. That night, at the Inglewood Forum in LA, Warren Beatty stages the first of five McGovern benefits, which, over the next few months, will raise a million dollars—not to mention his candidate's profile among the nation's newly enfranchised teens. For it can hardly escape notice that while such youthful favorites as Carole King, Joni Mitchell, and James Taylor are performing for McGovern, the pop star who will open Richard Nixon's Los Angeles campaign headquarters is Rudy Vallee, singing sensation of 1927.

George McGovern places second to Hubert Humphrey on April 25 in Pennsylvania, and once-designated front-runner Senator Edmund Muskie suspends his campaign (which has been dogged by White House operative Donald Segretti's dirty tricks). The next day, Nixon announces a 20,000-troop withdrawal to bring U.S. forces below 50,000 for the first time since 1965. The McGovern candidacy is turning out to be what Hollywood calls a sleeper, and Beatty's rock concerts, the *New York Times* notes, are "one of the [campaign's] most celebrated surprises," with Beatty the surprise within the surprise. As the *Times* reports, the star has "astonished Senator McGovern with the success of his bold approach to major contributors."

> After a concert in Cleveland last Friday night, Mr. Beatty went to a party at the home of Mr. and Mrs. George Gund Jr. Early Saturday morning, Mr. Beatty, who played Clyde Barrow in the movie *Bonnie and Clyde*, asked Mr. Gund directly for $100,000.
>
> "Are people really giving that kind of money?" asked Mr. Gund, whose late father was one of the richest bankers in Cleveland.
>
> "People like you aren't giving any less," Mr. Beatty replied.
>
> Mr. Gund then handed Mr. Beatty a personal check for $30,000, apologizing that he would have to take a closer look at his cash balance before coming up with the rest.

Beatty soon informs the *Times* that "a great deal of the leadership of this generation comes from music and film people, whether people like that fact or not." The *Times* doesn't seem to like it—the wonderful reviews the newspaper gave *Wild in the Streets* during the last presidential campaign notwithstanding. The *Times* imagines Beatty a brash desperado. Nearly five years after *Bonnie and Clyde*'s release, he remains Clyde Barrow, insouciantly holding up a sleepy Cleveland bank. And yet, for anyone who knows *Shampoo*, the scene described equally suggests George-the-hairdresser's fantasy of borrowing money from Lester. (Or is this painful sequence Beatty's illustration of that other George's inability to hustle the Gunds of the world?)

Less than two weeks later, at a campaign rally in a Maryland parking lot, would-be assassin Arthur Bremer—a twenty-one-year-old unemployed assistant janitor—guns down and seriously wounds one more George, Governor Wallace of Alabama. As a primary candidate, Wallace has more total votes than either McGovern or Hubert Humphrey. "Every dog has its day and ours is next," the real Democratic front-runner had boasted after placing second in Wisconsin and Pennsylvania, while winning Tennessee, Alabama, and North Carolina. Even as he lays in intensive care, Wallace takes Maryland and Michigan. Still, with those five shots, Nixon's reelection is assured.*

McGovern, meanwhile, rolls on. Beatty's greatest triumph follows the crucial, if uncomfortably close, win in California. June 14, eight days after McGovern edges Humphrey and two nights before the fateful Watergate burglary, Beatty stages a concert at Madison Square Garden that brings out half the radical activists in New York and brings in $400,000. The evening is called "Together with McGovern" and to dramatize his insolent appropriation of Nixon's 1968 pledge to "bring us together," Beatty temporarily reunites three famously sundered acts—Simon and Garfunkel, Mike Nichols and Elaine May, and Peter, Paul, and Mary. No less impressively, he has seduced a posse of Hollywood stars to act as celebrity ushers: Candice Bergen, Gene Hackman,

---

*Wallace's elimination occurs in the midst of heightened Plumber activity. Two nights before, Frank Sturgis burglarized the Chilean Embassy; the first attempt to break into the Democratic headquarters at the Watergate complex will be two weeks later. The night of the failed assassination, the President calls aide Charles Colson to inquire after Bremer's politics. "He's going to be a left-winger by the time we get through," Colson assures Nixon, apologizing for not having thought sooner about "planting a little literature" on the suspect.

James Earl Jones, Stacy Keach, Shirley MacLaine, Paul Newman, Jack Nicholson, Ryan O'Neal, Diana Sands, Marlo Thomas, Jon Voight, and Raquel
Welch.*

Raquel never shows. But more striking and less predictable is that the ushers
include George the Hairdresser's three future concubines: Julie Christie, Lee
Grant, and Goldie Hawn. Even Carrie Fisher deserves a footnote. Her father,
singer Eddie Fisher, was a public Nixon supporter. Do you wanna fuck, indeed.

• • •

It was after "Together with McGovern" that, writing in the July 8 issue of *The
Saturday Review*, Richard Reeves anointed Beatty "the most prodigious fund
raiser in American politics" and delivered the backhanded compliment that
"there has always been an instinctive bond between politicians and actors—
both callings attract people with the same kind of suffocating egos." So it is
in *Shampoo*'s banquet scene. TV monitors are scattered among the diners. The
obvious irony of a televised Spiro Agnew—compelled to resign after allegations
emerged in the summer of 1973 that he'd accepted bribes while governor of
Maryland—lambasting "permissive attitudes" and crediting the President with
setting "the moral tone of the country" is less significant than the tension his
spectral presence creates between figure and ground. Which image is imaginary
and whose is the most inspired performance? Who is lending whom a basis in
reality?

The stars pretend to join us in the audience even as they cast themselves
in the show. New-minted journalist Abbie Hoffman called the 1972 DemCon
"an orgy for celebrities." Participants included Beatty and MacLaine, Jack Nicholson, Art Garfunkle, Allen Ginsberg, Jerry Rubin, and himself: "At any time
in any room you almost felt like dividing the people into celebrities and non-

---

*Compare these to the troglodyte army of toupees and face-lifts supporting Nixon: John
Wayne, Frank Sinatra, Susan Hayward, Zsa Zsa Gabor, Jack Warner, Jimmy Stewart,
Charlton Heston, Bob Hope, Dorothy Lamour, Bing Crosby, Jack Benny, Lawrence
Welk, June Allyson, Edgar Bergen, Cary Grant, Art Linkletter, Fred MacMurray, Ethel
Merman, Debbie Reynolds, Cesar Romero, Danny Thomas, Jane Russell, Red Skelton.
The youngest was likely Clint Eastwood.

celebrities. It got so bad that sometimes you'd ask someone for their name and they'd answer, 'I'm nobody.' "

Pols and stars jostled each other in the charisma bazaar. Robert and Jane Squier, media consultants for Hubert Humphrey in 1968 and Edmund Muskie in 1972, told Reeves the relationship between the two types was deeper than the makeup many politicians had taken to wearing: "Actors think politicians have the only high better than theirs [while] the only person who really impresses a politician is someone like Paul Newman." Robert Squier was there when Humphrey met Newman in 1968: "I never saw Hubert so in awe. Both of them were. I thought they were going to ask each other for autographs." But Robert Redford informed Reeves that he, for one, eschewed the power celebrity conferred: "Actors are suckers for politics. You've just begun to see what's going to happen. Ronald Reagan is only the beginning."

Redford may have been the only star in America more Kennedyesque than Beatty. (He wasn't asked to audition for *PT 109*, but he did serve Arthur Penn as a sacrificial victim—part JFK, part Lee Harvey Oswald—in the mad confusion of *The Chase*.) Some three years later, when Beatty went on the road to flack *Shampoo*, he would justify the relatively few pictures he made in telling the *New York Post* that, over the years, he'd been offered *Butch Cassidy and the Sundance Kid*, *The Sting*, *The Way We Were*, and *The Great Gatsby*: "Robert Redford's hits are all the pictures I turned down." Beatty's biographer David Thomson calls these the "body of Redford's screen career." But Thomson overlooks one movie that Beatty, were he still brooding over 1972, might not have forgotten. Redford supported Eugene McCarthy in 1968 and in 1972 told reporters he thought McGovern the best available choice. And yet, irresistible Beatty was unable to enlist Redford in the McGovern crusade. Redford had his own election-year project going: *The Candidate*.

Like the McGovern campaign itself, *The Candidate* was rooted in the madness of 1968. Redford recalled watching the candidates' last-minute TV appeals, switching channels between Nixon, "so absolutely staged," and Humphrey "scrambling around with that bizarre end-of-the-line fatigue." And, earnest joker that he was, the actor thought: This would make a good movie. To script his scenario, Redford commissioned Jeremy Larner, a former McCarthy speechwriter who had relocated to Hollywood after Bert Schneider bought his novel *Drive, He Said* for Jack Nicholson. The director Michael Ritchie had worked with Redford on *Downhill Racer* but, even better, served as media adviser for John Tunney in his successful 1970 race against California senator George Murphy. Tunney's campaign manager, Nelson Rising, came along as associate producer.

Redford cast himself as Bill McKay, a left-wing advocate lawyer and son of a former California governor, tempted by the Mephistophelean political operative Marvin Lucas (Peter Boyle) to run against the arch-conservative senator, Crocker Jarmon. First seen, McKay is a shaggier Gary Hart, wearing a blue denim work shirt as he attends to the legal needs of the underprivileged. "Politics is bullshit," his belligerent Chicano pal tells Lucas, who, looking for a new face to promote, cleverly appeals to McKay's underdog vanity. Everyone knows young McKay is unelectable; still, he is charismatic as a movie star. (The movie's opening credits are "Robert Redford as *The Candidate*.") At the very least, a campaign—even symbolic—would, like this movie, permit McKay to directly address the people of California and publicize the issues in which he believes.

A pro-busing, pro-welfare, pro-abortion, anti-Vietnam eco-freak, McKay wins the Democratic nomination. He may be an awkward campaigner—ineffectual at pressing flesh, tedious in his position papers—but he is, of course, radiantly telegenic. Thus begins a campaign by photo opportunity—intercut with cameos by real-life candidates McGovern and Humphrey in support of that "fresh new talent" Bill McKay, as well as ersatz reports by actual TV newsmen (Howard K. Smith commenting on the phenomenon of political "packaging"), and a scene, based on an incident during the Tunney-Murphy race, where the challenger races to a raging forest fire to be upstaged by the incumbent's helicopter arrival to announce that he has arranged for federal relief.

Newsweek found the movie's performances naturalistic enough "to erase the essential and perhaps illusory distinction between the actors and politicians in our society." Redford's star quality was "all-too-readily transferable," while Don Porter played Crocker Jarmon "with a fervor that would win him a Senate seat in half the states of the Union." In fact, Porter's rhetoric was a demonstrated winner—his lines were largely patched together from those delivered by California's recently reelected governor, Ronald Reagan. McKay's media handlers construct an image of unthreatening activism, all-purpose concern, and beautiful, virile youth. "They're gonna take a look at the Crock and think maybe he can't get it up any more," Lucas chuckles. *The Candidate*, like *Shampoo*, is an Oedipal movie. No less than the New Left, nonconformist Hollywood stars like Redford and Beatty experienced themselves in combat against a paternal establishment. The scenario generated by McKay's handlers is generational warfare, with Crocker Jarmon initially supported by McKay's father (Melvyn Douglas).

Intimations of assassination abound. McKay is stalked by elderly white men, harassed by one in a men's room and punched by another after a campaign rally. The script dictates the Candidate be forced to trim his sails as well as his hair. Still, as helped by a televised debate in which the incumbent projects as an old windbag, McKay winds up the surprise winner. Racing through a hotel kitchen in such a manner as to recall the circumstances under which Robert Kennedy was shot, the Candidate seems almost traumatized. A premature Sixties Survivor, he turns to Lucas and wonders, "What do we do now?"

•   •   •

Robert Redford, Jeremy Larner, and Michael Ritchie saw *The Candidate* as a form of guerrilla theater, an intervention in the 1972 campaign, a warning to voters—presumably against glamour, glitz, packaging, TV, and Hollywood itself. *The Candidate* was an anti-pseudo-event that its makers wanted in release as Democrats and Republicans staged their conventions, back to back, in Miami Beach. For Warner Brothers, the election was a means to promote the movie. There were plans for Redford to take part in ticker-tape parades. The studio hoped to lure New York City mayor and ex-presidential candidate John Lindsay back into the ring to launch Redford on Broadway. Warners spent $270,000 to set up a chain of McKay campaign storefronts in twenty American cities and hired associate producer Nelson Rising's R.P. Media, a firm specializing in political candidates, to handle public relations.

Redford and his entourage chartered a train in July and made a whistle-stop tour from Jacksonville to Miami Beach, dispensing balloons, buttons, and posters emblazoned with the slogan "McKay—The Better Way." Over 100 reporters, both political and entertainment, were along for the ride on this million-dollar Digger production; Redford's speeches, it was said, drew larger crowds than collected by any Democratic candidates during the Florida primary, even though the star regularly wound up with the grinning declaration that he had nothing to say.*

The McKay bandwagon arrived in Miami Beach the weekend before the DemCon opened. As she rushed from the station to the Fontainebleau, whose majestic marble-and-gold, crystal-chandeliered lobby was crammed with the youngest, least male, and most racially mixed group of delegates to ever attend a Democratic convention (as well as a media horde in sci-fi regalia, a supply of Secret Service agents, and a gaggle of half-clad Yippies in full-lotus postures), the reporter for *The Christian Science Monitor* found herself thinking *The Candidate* understated: "This is the real Hollywood production." Still, the lobby was plastered with enough McKay posters for delegates to begin asking about this apparent dark horse.

Well in advance of the DemCon, the Republicans had characterized McGovern's candidacy as that of "Amnesty, Acid, and Abortion," and indeed, such a convention could not contain its Orgiastic potential. There were times that Jerry Rubin—inside with press credentials—thought he'd died and gone to heaven. Walking through the Convention floor was "a multi-media psychedelic experience as high as any acid trip." Czechago '68 had been bottled. Gary Hart

---

*Jeremy Larner recalled that the audience of extras assembled at the Paramount Theater in Oakland for the scene in which McKay gives his final campaign speech seemed genuinely overwhelmed. Larner warmed up the crowd, reading them Redford's script paragraph by paragraph and indicating the appropriate reaction. As delivered by the star, however, the speech "evoked not only spontaneous applause but tears."

would remember Bill Clinton, the twenty-six-year-old Yale Law School senior coordinating the Arkansas delegation for McGovern, as "the one person in that period who had as much or more hair than I did." Not likely. Rubin saw "the hairiest Convention since the Founding Fathers thought the whole idea up . . . a sea of jeans [and] dashikis." These delegates, Norman Mailer decided, were "a bona fide new species." Four out of five had never attended a convention. Nearly 15 percent were African-American, with Latinos and Native Americans another 6 percent. Women made up 38 percent, and a third of all delegates were younger than thirty-five. The enemies list was out in force. On the first night, as national chairman Larry O'Brien welcomed them, Allen Ginsberg sat beneath the podium, chanting a Buddhist mantra. "The wonderful thing about going into a McGovern headquarters is to find that there is no ego-tripping," young Clinton told a reporter. No ego, perhaps; no tripping, perhaps not.

Underground journalist Jay Levin recalled the DemCon as a nonstop party. "You could score any kind of drug you wanted, there was a transvestite section"—Myra herself!—and "lots of kids who'd been on the streets in 1968 were now delegates. Abbie and Jerry were greeted as heroes." Hoffman was particularly enthusiastic. Unaware that the President had already sent a memo to his campaign manager, John Mitchell, with specific instructions to use Hoffman and Rubin's McGovern endorsement to embarrass the Senator, he believed that the Yippies could "take over the Democratic Party."

In order to avoid a Chicago replay, the Miami police had gone through year-long sensitivity training. "There were plainclothes police everywhere," Rennie Davis noted, but they allowed the demonstrator encampment in Flamingo Park to become a mini Woodstock. In this controlled theme park, amid the skinny-dippers and lovemaking couples, cops dispensed Quaaludes—a powerful tranquilizer that was suddenly the counterculture's drug du jour. Nor was this the only collusion. According to police officer Walter Philbin, most arrests were made "by scenario." Hoffman and Rubin promised the cops a specific number of demonstrators at an agreed location in time for the nightly news broadcast: "This is what they wanted, news time, the publicity of arrests."

On the convention's final night, a spontaneous outburst of bottled-up tensions sent the proceedings out of control with a parade of increasingly ridiculous vice presidential nominations in opposition to McGovern's designated choice, Senator Thomas Eagleton, that effectively delayed McGovern's acceptance speech until 3:30 AM. Among other things, Rubin noted that

> When they were calling the roll call on the Vice-Presidential nomination, folks wearing bright purple tee-shirts that said 'Gay Power' were hugging and kissing in the aisles. . . .
> During the California credentials battle, a long-haired freak from Arizona grabbed Abbie and lifted him into the air. 'I'm the first, man!' he shouted.
> 'The first what?'
> 'The first fucker to ever cast a vote on acid.'

But, for Hunter Thompson, the scene which "the press mistook for relaxed levity was actually a mood of ugly restlessness [that bordered] on rebellion."

> All over the floor I saw people caving in to the lure of booze, and in the crowded aisle between the California and Wisconsin delegations a smiling freak with a bottle of liquid THC was giving free hits to anybody who still had the strength to stick their tongue out.

According to Thompson, half the delegates had begun to lose control. "Leaning against the now-empty VIP box once occupied by Muriel Humphrey, a small blonde girl who [had] worked for the Lindsay campaign was sharing a nasal inhaler full of crushed amyls with a handful of new-found friends."

Such blatant Dionysian behavior was not shown on TV, although the images broadcast were scarcely better. "I thought the convention was great," McGovern recalled.

> But what came across on television, apparently, to many of these guys was they saw a lot of aggressive women, they saw a lot of militant blacks, they saw long-

haired kids, and I think that combination, which helped win the nomination for me, I think it offended a lot of them.

Not to mention creating the image of the Democratic Party that would persist for decades.

•   •   •

The Candidate received a mixed response. Writing in the July 23 *New York Times*, Congresswoman Bella Abzug worried that young people might "find their worst fears confirmed by this simplistic film, and see politics as a determinist process that forces its participants from compromises into doubletalk and sell-outs."*

Newsweek wondered why Vietnam was mentioned only once and, tartly suggesting the film should be called "The Softening of the Candidate," linked it to the McGovern campaign's ultimately pyrrhic attempt to abandon the moral high ground and storm the political center. *The Commonweal* found *The Candidate* a primer on running for senator from California that looked as though it were made by media hucksters rather than about them—which indeed it was. *Life*, more star-struck, agreed that the film was a "handbook for today's image-conscious politics" but gladly played along, asking readers "Would You Vote for This Man?" The magazine hired a PR firm to evaluate candidate McKay, while suggesting that Redford himself was a potential Reagan warming up to run for governor of Utah.

The 1972 Democratic candidate caught Redford's vehicle at a movie house

---

*Abzug's concerns were misplaced. Four presidential elections later, *Vanity Fair* revealed that two Indiana law students, Frank Pope and J. Danforth Quayle saw *The Candidate* at a bargain matinee and, "all fired up" by Redford's scenario, directly "repaired to one of Indianapolis's better restaurants." The source of their fascination was scarcely candidate McKay's last-gasp liberal agenda.

> While Danny drank scotch and Frank alternated between bourbon and Coke, they spent eleven hours analyzing how to use what they'd learned. "Danny thinks he has more perfect features than Robert Redford," says Pope. "We were aware the day-of-media was coming, and if you could handle that, you'd have an edge."

in Custer, South Dakota, where he had gone to relax and plan the fall campaign. As it turned out, McGovern would scarcely have time to catch his breath. Hardly a week after Senator Thomas Eagleton was announced as his running mate, the story was all over Washington that the Missouri senator had been treated for depression with electroshock therapy—most recently at the Mayo Clinic in the early autumn of 1966. Eagleton hadn't thought to inform McGovern, and now that he had been revealed to be a mental Manchurian Candidate, the not-so-Best Man, a worst-scenario Goldwater, McGovern was under siege. After a weekend of staff meetings, the vice presidential nominee flew into Custer for a joint press conference with his running mate. On Wednesday, July 26, McGovern made the mistake of declaring himself "1,000 percent" for Eagleton. Now the media fury began.

According to Hunter Thompson, McGovern and his family had laughed hardest during *The Candidate* when one McKay handler instructs another to "Get all the reporters on the press bus . . . and drive them over the nearest cliff." Still, McGovern didn't really care for *The Candidate*, telling a newsman that it showed "the sicker side of politics." Indeed. That Sunday morning, Eagleton appeared on CBS's *Face the Nation*, learning after the show that the Democratic National Committee had just dumped him on NBC's *Meet the Press*. Eagleton was officially off the bus on Monday, but McGovern was unable to secure a replacement until Saturday. Finally, former Peace Corps head Sargent Shriver accepted the job—after Ted Kennedy, Governor Abraham Ribicoff, Hubert Humphrey, and Edmund Muskie all declined. *Time's* McGovern/Shriver cover bombed; *Newsweek* ruled with a story on the Chinese science of acupuncture. Meanwhile, the Gallup poll put Nixon ahead, 57 to 31 percent.

•   •   •

Although the Republican Convention was originally planned for San Diego, it had been switched to Miami in late 1971—as a result, some claimed, of the planned national John Lennon–Yoko Ono tour to free John Sinclair. Others, however, believed San Diego had been designated as the site of a right-wing coup to assassinate Red China–placating traitor Richard Nixon. In any case, the Miami RepCon was the most rigorously planned pseudo-event thus far. As Abbie Hoffman and Jerry Rubin explained it, "Control the Imagery was the word from the top."

No detail of the media scenario was too inconsequential. A special elevator behind the speaker's rostrum—designed by the producers of TV's *Dating Game*—insured that no one would appear taller to the broadcast audience than the President. Above the podium were three twelve- by twenty-five-foot screens that replayed the RepCon's defining moments: Nixon's arrival in Miami, a pro-Republican rock concert, the President embraced by Sammy Davis Jr. Whenever important images were shown—like the campaign film *Portrait of a President*—the hall lights were shut off, compelling the networks to transmit the Republican programming rather their own "live" reporting.

In *Shampoo*, TV is the icon of pure power, the instrument of context, history's maker and repository. For the White House, 1972 was the year of TV. The President had been amazingly successful at determining his media coverage. As aide Charles Colson explained: "Nixon had a fetish about wanting to try to dominate the news. . . . He would call me a lot and say, 'What story is going to be our story next Thursday?' " The President intended to script the nightly news scenario. David Gergen (then a young speechwriter working with Colson, later Director of Communications in the Gerald Ford and Ronald Reagan administrations, as well as an adviser to President Bill Clinton) explained that before any public event was put on the President's schedule, "you had to know what the headline out of that event was going to be, and what the lead paragraph would be."

In February, Nixon took the TV audience on a guided tour of hitherto forbidden China and, three months later, brought the nation with him to Moscow on his Mission of Peace. Nixon learned his lesson in the 1970 campaign—he would run for reelection as a remote and powerful leader, the personification of national purpose. While TV showed the Democrats attacking each other throughout the primary season, Nixon barricaded himself behind a wall of privacy, appearing only as The President. This was known as the Rose Garden strategy. The convention film *Portrait of a President* was exactly that. Washington, Lincoln, Theodore Roosevelt and . . . Nixon!, with the Red Chinese and Soviet politburos in supporting roles.

While the noncandidate President minimalized contact with the press, his campaign spots elevated him to a realm above partisan politics. Not unlike the supreme leader in a series of Socialist Realist canvases, Nixon was shown listening to his subjects, engaging in solitary contemplation, and, together with associates, orchestrating farsighted projects. He was a statesman who took decisive action in matters that concerned the nation's welfare (and indeed the entire planet), but he was also seen in the Oval Office chatting on the phone or at the piano playing "Happy Birthday" for Duke Ellington.

The convention news analysis was preempted. Nothing was left to chance. "We actually prepared, down to the minute, a script for the whole convention," Gergen recalled. A team of BBC reporters was mistakenly handed a copy, complete with applause cues, scheduled "spontaneous" floor demonstrations, and specified prime-time features. There was even an "alternative script." If the podium action seemed dull, Nixon's team provided its own counter-programming by offering the networks interviews with prominent individuals considered "good copy."

Despite Jerry Rubin's threat to flood Collins Avenue with naked longhairs, the scene outside hardly matched the intensity of the 1968 Democratic convention. The 3,500 hippies, Yippies, Zippies, druggies, Progressive Labor types, feminists, and gay liberationists camped in Flamingo Park could not find a way to write themselves into the Republican scenario. Although the demonstrators taunted delegates as "war criminals," attacked a bus carrying Strom Thurmond and the South Carolina delegation, staged a puke-in, and repeatedly stormed the convention center, they attracted far less media coverage than the smaller demonstrations of four years before.*

Hunter Thompson was singularly unimpressed, writing that

> With the lone exception of the Vietnam Veterans Against the War, the demonstrators in Miami were a useless mob of ignorant chicken-shit ego-junkies

---

*But Norman Mailer felt that the promise of TV coverage had already destroyed the demonstrators' authenticity: "Television pollutes identity, and television cameras are

whose only accomplishment was to embarrass the whole tradition of public protest. They were hopelessly disorganized, they had no real purpose in being there,
and about half of them were so wasted on grass, wine, and downers that they
couldn't say for sure whether they were raising hell in Miami or San Diego.

Tuesday afternoon, 1,300 uniformed Vietnam veterans, some on crutches and
others in wheelchairs, marched on the Fontainebleau. Ron Kovic and two other
partially paralyzed VVAW members managed to get inside the hall Wednesday
night for Nixon's acceptance speech, but their demonstration was ignored by
the TV cameras. That night, the denizens of Flamingo Park—self-described
"liberated zone of revolutionary living, organizing and non-violent direct action"—took to the streets. The tear gas was uncorked, there were 1,129 arrests,
and the next morning's polls put Nixon's lead at 64–30 percent.

Newsweek reviewed the show the following Monday: "With production lo-
gistics that rivaled *The Greatest Story Ever Told*, Republican media planners surrounded the President with more young faces than he'd ever been seen with
before," movie critic Joseph Morgenstern wrote. Even the idea of youth had
been co-opted, rewritten, and cast to suit the Nixon campaign.

> The Republican kids looked older, more knowing and less spontaneous than
> their Democratic counterparts. Among those few youthful extras with speaking
> parts, not one used the interjection 'like,' except as it applied to liking the
> President. . . .

> If the Democratic convention was improvisational theater, the Republican pri-
> metime production was a Hallmark Hall of Fame: tightly scripted, expensively
> mounted, often hollow but star-studded.

---

about them all the time. So the most serious cannot even finally know if they protest
the war or contribute to the entertainment of Nixon's Epic." Hunter Thompson's report
supported the latter possibility. "Every time the Fontainebleau lobby started buzzing
with rumors about another crowd of demonstrators bearing down on the hotel," he
wrote, "the boats across Collins Avenue would fill up with laughing Republican delegates." Approaching the hotel, the demonstrators "found themselves walking a gauntlet
of riot-equipped police on one side, and martini-sipping GOP delegates on the other."

Morgenstern's favorite moment came when Stewart introduced the film *Pat—Tribute to a First Lady* and then the First Lady.

> As she walked to the rostrum, Ray Bloch's orchestra played "Lovely To Look At" in an odd kind of stripper's tempo, medium slow with heavy drums and cymbals.
>
> It was a deliciously discordant note, one of the few in an extraordinary attempt to create a controlled media environment.

This hint of orgy not withstanding, the Republicans had learned well the lessons of 1968. Norman Mailer left the Republican Convention's "three-day spectacular of celebration" ritually convinced that Nixon was

> the first social engineer to harness and then employ the near to illimitable totalitarian resources of television. . . . Never before in history had a prepared tide of sentiments so similar in direction been washed for so long across the American brain.

The Hollywood metaphor so startling twelve years before was impossible to avoid. "Being next to McGovern was like being in a movie film next to Gary Cooper," Norman Mailer wrote, while Senator Bob Dole, chairman of the Republican National Committee ("perhaps the best-looking of the Republicans") struck him as "a ringer to play Humphrey Bogart's younger brother."*

The September 23 *Newsweek* put McGovern-supporter Shirley MacLaine on its "Show Biz in Politics" cover, but she was scarcely movie land's most cel-

---

*As the ultimate Star-Pol election, 1972 was John Wayne's 1960 nightmare—and yet, Mailer noted, the Duke attended the RepCon "in a blue yachting jacket and grey pants, cheeks red, dark hairpiece on, and eyes as wide open, expressionless and sleepy as a lion digesting a meal." There were plenty to keep Wayne company: Charlton Heston, James Stewart, Frank Sinatra, and Sammy Davis, Jr. (who had grabbed the President so suddenly that Nixon flinched in inadvertent terror). And there was also Ronald Reagan. His "easy voice," Mailer thought, was "full of the chuckles of good corporate living," while his mastery of one-liners "gave every evidence of being managed by Bob Hope."

ebrated firebrand. It was during the summer of 1972 that Henry Fonda's only daughter, the actress who played Robert Redford's wife in *The Chase*, achieved her apotheosis as Hollywood Freedom Fighter. Just after the DemCon, the *New York Times* and the *Washington Post* broke the story that Jane Fonda had been in Hanoi, making radio broadcasts for the North Vietnamese government. Ten days later, on the same morning George McGovern pledged undying support for Thomas Eagleton, the actress returned home to face the music. Arriving in Miami on the second day of the Republican Convention to speak at a rally honoring George Jackson, Fonda was already the personification of political protest.

Since late 1970, the actress had crisscrossed the country, appearing at campuses and donating her speaking fee to the VVAW. "You cannot help but be impressed by how audiences, particularly college students, regard her with something approaching reverence," *Life* observed. Fonda made her first attempt to travel to Hanoi in February 1971. The following month, she and Donald Sutherland organized a new antiwar group, the Entertainment Industry for Peace and Justice, which, although its first meeting drew 1,200 Hollywood dignitaries to the Beverly Hilton, collapsed a few months later. By then, Fonda had opened another front with *The FTA* (for "Fuck the Army") *Show*, a "political vaudeville" that had its premiere just outside Fort Bragg in North Carolina. Designed as a response to Bob Hope's Christmas Show, its theme song was "Insubordination." Fonda won an Oscar for *Klute* weeks later, but it was her politics that rated an article in *Life*: "Nag, Nag, Nag! Jane Fonda has become a nonstop activist." There was "scarcely an evil—be it racism, sexism, capitalism, or the war in Vietnam—she has not taken on."

Relentless as she was humorless, Fonda proclaimed herself "a revolutionary woman" ready to support all radical struggles. John Wayne had finally met his match. The Duke was not only the top box-office attraction of 1971 but the most outspoken. "I believe in white supremacy until the blacks are educated to a point of responsibility," he told *Playboy* in a notorious interview published that April. It was the spring of *Sweet Sweetback* and *Billy Jack*, of Lieutenant

Calley's trial and the antiwar Viet-vets, and Wayne used *Playboy* as a platform to propose his own rhetorical orgy—attacking *Midnight Cowboy* and the Righteous Outlaws of *Easy Rider* and *The Wild Bunch*, blaming the press for the My Lai massacre and comparing the plight of the South Vietnamese to that of Jews in Nazi Germany. The Duke was approaching his sixty-fifth year on planet Earth. "I thought you wuz dead," is how more than one cowardly lowlife greets him in *Big Jake*, opening in May as Fonda began rehearsing with Sutherland and Boyle in her latest latest vehicle, *Steelyard Blues*—"a film which says stealing is not theft, property is theft," she told *Life*.*

That fall, Fonda embarked on the month-long FTA Pacific tour, with stops at bases in Hawaii, the Philippines, Okinawa, and Japan. The twenty-one performances (which were filmed for a subsequent movie) were seen by some 64,000 servicemen. Vivian Gornick, who covered the tour in the *Village Voice*, reported that

> As the month progressed it became clear, even to me, that indeed the FTA was surrounded, wherever it went, by agents of the CID, the OSI, the CIA, the local police, the various national investigating agencies of the countries it visited. In fact, one of the most incredible elements in the entire Asian tour of the FTA was the miracle of frightened attention that it received from the U.S. military.... Men were confined to base, "riot conditions" were declared, GIs were photographed.

Mocking the military brass and attacking male chauvinism, these obscenity-rich shows were not subtle. (According to Gornick, Fonda was enamored of a

---

*Steelyard Blues went into production in the summer of 1971, directed by Alan Myerson in Oakland and Berkeley. It was there Jane encountered radical feminism, spending time at the Red Family collective on 3016 Bateman Street. (The most celebrated of Berkeley's political communes, ostentatiously stocked with shotguns and the writings of North Korean Communist leader Kim Il Sung, the Red Family had recently expelled one of its founders, Tom Hayden, either for "male chauvinism" or the "bourgeois privatism" of his relationship with the ex-wife of fellow-communard Robert Scheer.

particular phrase, forever speculating on the "political correctness" of everything she observed.) Sutherland reported on the war as if it were a football game and read excerpts from Dalton Trumbo's pacifist novel *Johnny Got His Gun*. Fonda played Pat Nixon, singing "Nothin' could be finer than to be in Indochina makin' mon-ey." Denied permission to enter South Korea or South Vietnam, the tour returned home just before Christmas.

Fonda, however, was just beginning. July 8, she deplaned an Aeroflot jet at Hanoi airport. There, she offered to make ten radio broadcasts to be aired beginning July 14—the same day that AIP premiered the *FTA* movie in New York. The next morning, the story broke. Fonda held a press conference on her return, screening a twenty-minute silent film showing the ruined North Vietnamese dikes—as well as Jane herself, the image of radical chic in guerrilla-style black pajamas, laughingly pretending to aim an anti-aircraft gun at an American bomber. Despite this publicity, *FTA* ran only a week in New York, and AIP pushed back the national opening to the fall, when Fonda and Tom Hayden were in the midst of their Indochina Peace Campaign, a nine-week, ninety-city tour to get out the antiwar vote.

Fonda had informed the world that she would "passively" support McGovern as someone preferable to Nixon if no more prepared to make fundamental social change. Despite this lack of enthusiasm, she was hung around McGovern's neck like a poison-ivy lei. William Buckley proposed that a President McGovern might name her Secretary of State. Two Republican congressmen demanded she be convicted for treason. Not to be outdone, Richard Ichord, the Missouri Democrat who chaired the House Committee on Internal Security, declared her a criminal and introduced legislation to prevent American citizens from traveling to the war zone. It was, after all, an election year, and Fonda remained a congressional issue throughout September. Nightmare of *Advise and Consent* guilt-by-association: The FBI even put her mortified and disapproving father under surveillance.

There was one other outlaw Hollywood production that fall, namely the Black Panther Party. In the aftermath of the Panther civil war, Huey Newton grew closer to the movie industry, traveling down from Oakland with his bodyguards to hobnob poolside with his main patron, producer Bert Schneider, as well as stars Warren Beatty and Jack Nicholson. Moreover, Newton's thinking had evolved in ways that might be considered cinematic. Not just *Sweet Sweetback's Baadasssss's Song* but *The Godfather* was now a text, providing Newton with a paradigm for reorganizing the Panthers into "political" and military wings.

In early August, Warner Brothers opened Gordon Parks Jr.'s *Superfly*—an independent feature made in Harlem during the winter of 1972 with money raised among black business people. Whether or not these investors included local pimps and drug merchants, the movie projected a fabulous vision of successful criminality. With his Zapata mustache and flowing hair, coke dealer Youngblood Priest (Ron O'Neal) looked like a Righteous Outlaw and dwelt in *Blowup* heaven. Priest drove a giant car, occupied an incredible pad (color TV in every room), took bubble baths with beautiful women of all races, and snorted coke off a golden crucifix. He was tough, too, beating up junkie muggers, facing down political activists, and making a mockery of the honky police.

Produced for under $500,000, *Superfly* grossed twice that playing to black audiences at two New York theaters. Hailed by *Variety* as "the phenomenon in the phenomenal new black feature market," *Superfly* coincided with a new Panther scenario. Revolution gave way to a fantasy of orgy enforcement. Schneider rented the increasingly coked Newton a penthouse above Oakland's Lake Merritt, while, looking to survive the Sixties, Panther rank and file traded leather jackets for wide-lapelled three-piece suits: Bobby Seale was campaigning for Oakland mayor in a chauffeured pimp-mobile and broad-brimmed fur hat.*

The Nixon Western

American ground troops departed Vietnam by August's end. Bomber death planes might yet ride shotgun in the sky, but 43,500 Air Force personnel aside,

---

*If the Panthers were studying *Superfly*, the movie's feeble sequel *Super Fly T.N.T.*, written by Alex Haley and released in June 1973, gave the coke dealer a modicum of political consciousness, recruited to aid African revolutionaries in their struggle against French imperialists.

Fort Apache was left to the Indians. The ruling myth of the past quarter-century dissolved. Now, after the My Lai, disco, and hippie Westerns, came the Last Western, the Nixon Western. Less grandiose but more cynical than the Johnson Western, this terminal mode was characterized by unmistakable weariness even in its enhanced carnage and desire for vengeance. Nixon himself suggested its origins in praising John Wayne's *Chisum* two years before, when liberal tolerance for rampant Righteous Outlawism infected the populace with the virus of juvenile delinquency—or worse.

The Nixon Western was founded upon an aggravated sense of racial and generational division. The typical setting was a shabby, morally bankrupt town, and even the natural world might seem as blasted as an inner-city ghetto. The landscape was muddy realist and dangerous to the point of absurdity. Every farmer was a potential killer. Freedomland was the province of mixed-up kids, religious crazies, profit-hungry entrepreneurs, duplicitous con artists, and twisted loners—not unlike the President himself.

The Culpepper Cattle Company and *The Great Northfield Minnesota Raid*, both titled like historical panoramas and released in spring 1972, pronounced a pox on Cowboy Authority and Righteous Outlaw alike. As made apparent by their credit sequences, these movies filtered the past through the sepia prism of *Bonnie and Clyde* and set history banjo-dancing. The soggy, autumnal *Northfield*, a revisionist account of the bank-robbing James brothers, written and directed by erstwhile independent Philip Kaufman, even opened with a black-and-white mock-documentary of families driven from their farms like 1930s Dustbowl refugees.*

The social bandit who inspired John Dillinger and Clyde Barrow (and gave

---

*Outlandishly representing the last stand taken by legendary Missouri outlaws Frank and Jesse James and their cousins, the Younger brothers, *Northfield* was named for their scheme to rob the biggest bank in Minnesota. Although, for *New York Times* critic Roger Greenspun, *Culpepper* did not so much evoke the Old West as its current representation—the time (perhaps only a year earlier) "when American rock stars wanted to look like Wyatt Earp"—*Northfield* was even more topical in representing the James brothers as tattered, mystical quasi-hippies.

his name to the SDS militants of Ann Arbor, Michigan) is here depicted as a violent, amoral, delusional, religious fanatic, still waging a guerrilla war behind enemy lines eleven years after the Civil War's end. The eponymous raid, of course, is a sodden, murderous disaster. The good people of Northfield turn vigilante, raiding their local whorehouse and lynching some innocent cattle buyers, even as Jesse escapes in drag.

Culpepper, the first feature by TV-commercial director Dick Richards, was a bildungsroman in which a sixteen-year-old would-be cowboy enlists in the capitalist Culpepper cattle drive as a cook's helper—partaking in what one reviewer called an "unglamorous, lonely, miserable existence." It was a Nixonian world-view, and the scenario previewed the presidential election. After various violent adventures, the hero drops out of Culpepper's heartless enterprise to defend a bedraggled pacifist sect, *Strawberry Statement* on the prairie. These crypto McGovernite, proto flower-children, abjectly fearful and pitifully dependent on hypocritical charismatic leadership, are to be slaughtered by a barbaric McLintock figure whose rapacity confounds even Culpepper. Once the shooting starts, the cowering cultists let down the boy as well. The movie ends with an ironic chorus of "Amazing Grace," underscoring the inability of these Christians even to bury their dead.

Moral confusion was rampant. Realpolitik reigned supreme—along with vigilante justice. The President had launched a diplomatic offensive with his February 1972 Chinese trip. But that spring, the North Vietnamese mounted their strongest attack since Tet 1968. Some analysts, Henry Kissinger among them, felt South Vietnam would have fallen then—six months before the election!—had the United States not deployed massive air strikes. Back on a high, Patton at the switch, madman Nixon wanted the Chinese, Soviets, and North Vietnamese to believe him capable of anything. Intimidation abroad, intimidation at home. The White House Plumbers were directed to "incapacitate" Daniel Ellsberg to prevent his participation in the May 3 Capitol Hill antiwar rally at which he correctly predicted Nixon's next step. Five days later, the President denounced the North Vietnamese as "international outlaws," expanded the bombing, and mined Haiphong harbor against Russian and Chinese ships—the most provocative challenge one super power had issued another since the Cuban Missile Crisis.

• • •

The final stage of America's withdrawal from Vietnam played out against the acrimonious tumult of a presidential election. George McGovern cast his campaign as a struggle between the forces of darkness and light. He was an Old Testament prophet denouncing a corrupt, hypocritical Caesar.

McGovern's was a hippie operation. His Washington headquarters, Theodore White sniffed, "could only be described as filthy. Wastebaskets spilled over; cigarette butts littered the floor; paper cluttered offices; the corridors smelled." Less-fastidious Hunter Thompson recalled that all activity ceased each evening for the "daily bummer" as the staff gathered around a lone color TV to watch the network news. Appropriately, the set itself was "fucked," so McGovern's face appeared "as if he were speaking up from the bottom of a swimming pool full of cheap purple dye." Thompson did not find this reassuring. That the candidate had no control over his image was also suggested by the Republican TV spot in which a weathervane affixed with McGovern's photo spun wildly—just as the senator's unpopular positions on busing, amnesty, and marijuana seemed buffeted by public opinion and media coverage.

By mid-September, John Connally's Democrats for Nixon were running an ad in which an incredulous hard-hat was informed of McGovern's plan to extend welfare benefits to 47 percent of the population. Meanwhile, as revealed years later in White House tapes, Charles Colson planted irate blue-collar Joes to confront the hapless candidate as he toured the factories of the industrial Midwest. In a related form of political theater, the President revived the old George Wallace ploy of setting up longhaired protestors as props—sometimes to be roughed up by spectators. *Wild in the Streets* remained an issue, in a negative sense. Democrats and Republicans spent $24 million in 1960; the tab for the 1972 campaign was $100 million and climbing. But where 1960 saw a record 64 percent voter turnout, 1972 brought the lowest percentage in a quarter century—only 55 percent, despite, or perhaps because of, the newly enfranchised youth vote. What of the kids? Written by David Newman and

Robert Benton (who also directed), *Bad Company* crossed the Western with the road movie and, like *John Wayne and the Cowboys*, which had opened during the winter of *Dirty Harry,* concerned a band of teenagers coming of age in the Wild West.*

In the New Sentimental tradition of *Bonnie and Clyde, Bad Company* mixed humor and killing—sometimes in the same scene. The movie's brutal counterculture of kids robbing kids was far tougher than *Bonnie and Clyde*—indeed, the situation of total lawlessness suggests a less malign version of *Night of the Living Dead. Bad Company* was revisionist in other ways as well. Few Westerns had so insisted on the physical discomforts and subsistence-level exploitation of frontier life. The scene in which a defeated homesteader pimps his wife is a marked contrast to the relatively glamorous brothel-on-wheels which unsuccessfully tempts the chaste lads of *The Cowboys.*

If *The Cowboys* can be read as a metaphor for basic training and baptism under fire, *Bad Company* is explicitly about draft dodgers. Two days after the movie opened, the McGovern campaign released a nationwide TV spot offering amnesty for those who chose prison or exile. No matter: The next *New York Times* poll put Nixon ahead 57 to 37 percent. McGovern's own pollster reported the most popular politician in the race was now Thomas Eagleton.†

---

*While *The Cowboys* opened at Radio City, *Bad Company* had its premiere at the 1972 New York Film Festival, only weeks before Election Day. Culturally, the movies were polar opposites. As *The Cowboys* was straightforward family fare, so *Bad Company* came on knowingly absurdist; where *The Cowboys* had a bombastic "Western" score by John Williams, *Bad Company* featured self-consciously period piano music by off-Broadway composer Harvey Schmidt. As the spirit of John Wayne presided over *The Cowboys, Bad Company* was founded upon the absence of authority—a vacuum visualized as the vast Nebraska plains. Like *The Cowboys, Bad Company* endeavored to make violence shocking, albeit by different means. No stars were snuffed, although an actual rabbit is shot dead and the smallest member of the urchin band blown away for stealing a pie.

†Could there be a McGovern Western? He was, after all, a South Dakota native. Was it possible to imagine a multicultural, environmentally conscious, nonviolent reading of American history? As if in search of some impossible cowboy scenario, the Democratic nominee made sixteen campaign visits to Texas (where Bill Clinton was campaign

With fighting reported ten miles from Saigon, Henry Kissinger negotiated with the North Vietnamese in Paris. Two weeks before the election, Kissinger announced that a peace settlement was finally at hand. On November 7, Richard Nixon buried hapless George McGovern in a colossal landslide. But there was no agreement, and so 1972 ended with the prolonged bombing of Hanoi and Haiphong. For the first time, the Strategic Air Command had responsibility for the aerial war. This massive show of force began December 18, resulting in losses including fifteen B-52s. Some crews were reportedly near mutiny; tactical pilots diverted their missions and dumped their payloads. Nevertheless, nearly 20,000 tons of bombs were dropped in eleven days. Such was the context for *Ulzana's Raid*—the last film produced by Ned Tanen's Universal "youth" unit.

After the failures of *Two-Lane Blacktop, The Hired Hand*, and *The Last Movie*, Tanen opted for a traditional Western by a middle-aged director, Robert Aldrich, starring an established action star. The action is set ten years after Custer's Last Stand, at the time of Geronimo's break. The tones are autumnal. There isn't much glory. Fort Lowell, Arizona, is scarcely the bastion of suburban civilization that gave its name to John Ford's *Fort Apache*. Nor is the cavalry engaged in a major operation. The bored commander is hardly a mar-

---

coordinator and Nixon would crush the Democratic ticket with 67 percent of the vote).

Texas was the Democrat's haunted house, and John Connally was the bogeyman. It was Connally who, managing Lyndon Johnson's 1960 bid for the Democratic nomination, had hinted that John Kennedy was kept alive only by "massive doses of cortisone" and certain to die in office. It was Connally who, as Texas governor, begged JFK to come to the state in November 1963 to settle a Democratic squabble, and it was Connally who, next to the President in the motorcade, was wounded in the assassination. With that bullet, Connally entered history. The clothes he wore that day were displayed as sacred relics; running for reelection in 1964, he received more Texan votes than LBJ. Now Connally was fronting Democrats for Nixon while Johnson had become a wraith. Visiting the LBJ Ranch August 22, McGovern was startled to find the former President had shoulder-length hair: LBJ looked like General Custer and, as the Democrats were soon to discover, there was more than one way to wax Custeristic.

tinet, although he does brandish the book perfunctorily at the diffident veteran scout McIntosh (Burt Lancaster).*

Much in *Ulzana's Raid* evokes the last stages of American involvement in Indochina—the demoralized soldiers, the hostility toward the brass, the pervasive cynicism. But Aldrich did not cast the Apache as noble savages nor, as in *Little Big Man*, romanticize their negation of white civilization. If anything, Ulzana's men are a sort of Wild Bunch, and when McIntosh bluntly tells young Lieutenant DeBuin (Bruce Davison, protagonist of *The Strawberry Statement*), who has been sent to chase them, that Ulzana's "probable intention is to burn, kill, rape, maim," the old scout is acting like Dirty Harry. Indeed, the fort commander calls McIntosh a "willful, opinionated man with a contempt for authority."

As in *Fort Apache*, the Indian uprising occurs in response to some white injustice. But here, white injustice and Apache savagery are existential conditions. The Indian war is a dirty, brutal struggle, and the naturalistic Apache atrocities are among the most disturbing in the Western's history. The Indians stab a corpse as if they were members of the Manson family or ghouls from *Night of the Living Dead*, then toss around the internal organs. *Ulzana's Raid* is a post–My Lai Western. Many civilians are doomed to die atrocious deaths; this is one of the few cavalry movies where the white body count outnumbers the Indian.

DeBuin is a minister's son who believes that American treatment of Indians is unchristian—as, of course, is Apache behavior. He soon becomes an Indian-hater even though, as McIntosh tells him, hating the Apaches is "like hating the desert cause there ain't no water on it." After DeBuin interrupts his men's mutilation of Ulzana's dead son, McIntosh suggests that what bothers the lieutenant is the confusing spectacle of "white men behaving like Indians." McIntosh recognizes that morality is not abstract but situational. "You'll learn,"

---

*Elegant and ironic, nuanced yet penetrating in its moral judgments, *Ulzana's Raid* is a Kennedy Western—although, given its tragic realism and underlying sense of loss, it is perhaps a Robert Kennedy Western.

the mortally wounded scout tells the young lieutenant, then sends him off because he wants to die alone and doesn't care whether he's buried. DeBuin protests that "it ain't Christian. . . ." To which McIntosh replies, "You're right. It ain't."

If nothing else, DeBuin has realized that it is impossible to be both a true Christian and a soldier—something that was even then being demonstrated to the world by Nixon's Christmas bombings.

•   •   •

January 1973: On the eve of his second inauguration, Richard Nixon is depressed. "You'd think I'd be elated," he tells *Time*, which has again declared him Man of the Year (albeit in tandem with Henry Kissinger). "You'd think that just when the time comes, you'd have your greatest day. But there is this letdown."

If the President is sick of himself, he is not alone. Released in late December, John Huston's *The Life and Times of Judge Roy Bean* is an anti-Nixon Nixon Western that embraces the Legal Vigilante as the sole alternative to Woodstock depravity and the hypocritical gentility of the corporate state. Here is a movie to fit the President's summer of 1970 mindset. As played by Paul Newman, Roy Bean is a roguish Chisum—or perhaps an authoritarian McCabe—a reformed bandit who liquidates the degenerate Manson Family commune controlling a poor West Texas pueblo and founds civilization on his eccentric notions of law and order.*

As the administration source known as Deep Throat again contacts *Washington Post* reporter Bob Woodward and the Senate establishes a special committee to investigate the Watergate break-in under the chairmanship of North

---

The Life and Times of Judge Roy Bean is the de-greening of America. Although the hard-drinking, poker-playing, gun-slinging Bean embodies the standard Western values of rugged individualism, summary justice, and white male supremacy, he also renders these values ridiculous. The self-proclaimed judge rips inconvenient pages from the legal books on which he bases his rule, wrapping himself (literally) in the American flag to declare that "there's going to be progress, civilization and peace . . . and I don't care who I have to kill to get it."

Carolina's Senator Sam Ervin, a new force for justice stalks the land. A real-life Legal Vigilante named Buford Pusser is immortalized as the hero of Phil Karlson's *Walking Tall*. After being cheated and beaten up in an illegal gambling joint, Pusser made himself sheriff and single-handedly cleaned up McNairy County, Tennessee. When *Walking Tall* is released in late February 1973, *Variety* notes the "body count and meticulous brutality" and predicts the movie will "perform well in further desensitizing the action fans." In fact, *Walking Tall* is tepidly received—with the exception of a few wildly enthusiastic markets. Recognizing the precedent of *Billy Jack*, Cinerama rereleases the movie with a new ad campaign, stressing its demagogic fervor: *When was the last time you stood up and applauded a movie?*

Walking Tall takes off in the South where, in some towns, it becomes an institutionalized local ritual, out-grossing *The Godfather*, en route to earning an eventual $30 million. By April, *Rolling Stone* declares *Walking Tall* "the best American movie so far this year." Like *Judge Roy Bean*, *Walking Tall* imbues the Legal Vigilante with the fiery passion of the Righteous Outlaw. But *Walking Tall* is Judge Roy Bean without irony. Although the hero's trademark weapon is a humongous club, he also maintains, as all vigilantes must, that "there's nothing wrong with a gun in the right hands."

• • •

When *Walking Tall* finally reached New York in early 1974, Pauline Kael used her review to declare the end of an era.

> A few more Westerns may still struggle in, but the Western is dead. Nobody's making even those last-gasp Westerns anymore—the ones about the lonely last cowboy, or the semi-spoofs featuring heavy old movie stars falling off their horses or kinky cowboys going to Mexico or farther south.

But the genre was not quite finished. Clint Eastwood's *High Plains Drifter* had gone into production in late summer 1972—not long after the President appointed the star director to the National Council on the Arts. By time the movie opened on April 18, 1973, the pressure on Eastwood's patron was building. Prices were rising and the dollar falling, but hunkered down in the Oval Office, the President felt a more immediate assault. The previous day, White House Press Secretary Ron Ziegler declared all previous Watergate statements "inoperable." That evening, Nixon went on TV to inform the nation that his personal investigation into the break-in and cover-up had yielded "major" (as yet unspecified) findings.*

Two nights later, Nixon told Ziegler that the Watergate investigation was distracting him from his job: "I sometimes feel like I'd like to resign. Let Agnew be President for a while. He'd love it." Morbidly, Nixon had begun to imagine his own political demise. Meanwhile, having invented the Legal Vigilante, Eastwood reappeared as another sort of Silent Majority avenger: They'd never forget the day he drifted into town, the first print ad promised over a low-angle image of the star cocking a revolver with a barrel even bigger than his *Dirty Harry* magnum.

The ultimate Nixon Western, its sense of exhaustion palpable and premise sufficiently allegorical to remind at least one reviewer of *El Topo, High Plains Drifter* begins with Eastwood's no-name Westerner materializing out of the shimmering heat to enter the High Sierras town of Lago through its grave-yard. The unearthly whine suggests that he has returned from the land of the dead . . . or is it Vietnam? From late winter into early spring, media coverage of the war focused on the returning 25,000 troops and the release of 600 POWs. No one spits in Eastwood's face, but his reception is as hostile as any ever imagined by a returning vet. The citizens of Lago gape as he rides down

---

*"Comeback Time," exulted former Nixon speechwriter William Safire in his new *New York Times* column, "The President did it his way." (The phrase alluded to the same evening's White House dinner for the Italian premier at which Frank Sinatra emerged from premature retirement to sing "My Way.") Nixon, Safire wrote, had neither apologized nor sought an alibi. "Instead he wrote out his announcement, read it in a cold, stern voice, and left no doubt that he had stepped up to the situation and engaged it frontally." Safire had no way of knowing that only hours after Nixon's address, in the course of a gloomy midnight phone chat with his Secretary of State, the President considered "throwing [himself] on the sword."

Main Street; he need only enter the saloon to be insulted as a "flea-bitten range bum." Despite its burgher mentality, Lago is as dangerous as the most godforsaken inner city. Eastwood has to shoot three punks before he can even get a shave. Taunted by a young hussy, he drags her to a stable and rapes her, terming this a "lesson in manners." In much the same spirit, *High Plains Drifter* offers a lesson in civic responsibility.

The annual exhibitor's poll named Eastwood the number-one box-office attraction for 1972—a distinction that, thanks to *High Plains Drifters*'s $7 million in domestic rentals, he would repeat. But although Eastwood had displaced John Wayne as America's reigning male star, he was still associated with exploitation films. "Just as you owe it to yourself to see, say, a porno-chic or nausea-freak flick (i.e. *The Devil in Miss Jones* or *Pink Flamingos*) to see what the strong stomachs, preverts [sic] and/or the Truman Capote set are wallowing in," Judith Crist wrote in *New York* magazine, "so you owe it to yourself to feel a bit of the nation's pulse as it pounds Eastwood-wise." *High Plains Drifter* is

> the Middle America R-rated substitute for *Deep Throat*, its male sexual fantasy restricted, in our grand Puritan tradition, to the rape of a whore and the instant seduction of a 'good' woman and then sublimated in all sorts of virility rites from straight shooting to torture to fire, with an orgy of violence and blood-letting for climax.

Times had changed. Whatever else he might have been, Wayne was not a rapist, although in the course of becoming America's new first—and last—cowboy, Eastwood had to cope with far greater social breakdown. *Coogan's Bluff* and *Dirty Harry* had him tracking murderous psychopaths through the hippie dens of filthy, drug-infested New York and ultra-permissive San Francisco. Lago is even worse. This craven town has no morality. The mine owns everything, the preacher is totally corrupt. These pioneer Americans are truly contemptible.*

---

*Several years later, Wayne took it upon himself to criticize *High Plains Drifter* for maligning the "true spirit of the American frontier."

Judith Crist was right about one thing: *High Plains Drifter* is extremely anti-bourgeois. The good citizens of Lago want everything orderly but lack the guts to enforce the law. Instead, they recruit killers. Initially, Eastwood refuses to save Lago from an approaching criminal gang—he waits to see how avidly the locals will grovel for his protection. To underscore their cowardice, the hussy appears before the council to voice her complaint: "Isn't forcible rape in broad daylight still a misdemeanor in this town?" Evidentially not—if it ever was.

Eastwood accepts the job on the promise of unlimited credit from the local merchants. He appoints his midget mascot (Billy Curtis) both marshal and mayor and agrees to train the townspeople in self-defense. But this is a setup. In preparation for the bloodbath to come, Eastwood has Lago's inhabitants paint their town red and rename it Hell. Then, as in Sergio Leone's *For a Fistful of Dollars*, he contrives to have both sides destroy each other. Thus, Eastwood makes the citizens pay for betraying their former marshal, whipped to death on Main Street because he was set to expose the mine company's theft of government property. And, thus satisfied, he rides back into the twilight zone, disappearing off screen in precisely the manner of *Blowup*'s photographer.*

---

*Although friendly enough to Mexicans, Indians, and the midget, vengeful, contemptuous Eastwood is a cruel hero in a corrupt, degenerate, cowardly civilization. In his prior film, *Joe Kidd*, released during the campaign summer of 1972, the star had played an insolent, inner-directed gunslinger who, although employed by a brutal white establishment, is ultimately radicalized—coming to identify with the local Mexicans as their one-man avenger. It is as though the Dirty Cowboy were attempting to assimilate the lesson of *Billy Jack*. In effect, Eastwood cast himself as a fantasy RFK, a tribune for Chicanos as well as hard-hats. The internal Third World still smoldered. Those reading the *New York Times* the day of *High Plains Drifter*'s premiere learned that the three-week ceasefire had been broken in the siege of Indian insurgents at Wounded Knee, South Dakota; that Black Panther and Chicago conspirator Bobby Seale had finished second to force a run-off in the race for Oakland mayor; and that another new Western called *Charley One-Eye* had opened with the promise that, *Somebody sold out the black man and the red man. Somebody's going to pay.*

Unlike *Dirty Harry*, which directed most of its violence against blacks and women, *High Plains Drifter* is explicitly minority-oriented. The script, by zeitgeistmeister Ernest

As punitive as *Dirty Harry*, *High Plains Drifter* reimagined *The Magnificent Seven* to match the sour aftermath of U.S. disengagement from Vietnam. Finally the Western gave the war a viable myth. *High Plains Drifter* is the spectacle of quasi-divine punishment visited against a gutless, guilty town that hires—or, rather, drafts—men to do its dirty work, and then discards them.

•   •   •

Two weeks into *High Plains Drifter*'s run, Richard Nixon reappeared on TV to announce the resignations of his chief of staff, H. R. Haldeman, his chair of the Domestic Council, John Ehrlichman, and his counsel, John Dean. Nixon was not alone in feeling sorry for himself. *McCabe & Mrs. Miller* could have been titled *The Beautiful Losers* after the experimental Western novel written by Canadian poet Leonard Cohen, who supplied the movie's haunting, if pretentious, score. So, too, Sam Peckinpah's *Pat Garrett and Billy the Kid*, which epitomized the melancholy of the last Westerns, the passing of the Righteous Outlaw, and the demise of the counterculture.

Hip young producer Gordon Carroll claimed the idea of reworking the Billy the Kid scenario in rock 'n' roll terms, although Peckinpah had been trying to make a Billy the Kid film for fifteen years and avant-garde novelist Rudy Wurlitzer had already written a version of *Pat Garrett and Billy the Kid* for Peckinpah's erstwhile editor, Monte Hellman. The script was sold to MGM as the follow-up to Hellman's 1971 *Two-Lane Blacktop*, but after that movie's failure, Carroll redirected the project to Peckinpah.

If the Hellman-Wurlitzer combination was deemed overly arty, the Peckinpah'd result proved hardly more commercial—with weathered James Coburn and baby-faced Kris Kristofferson in title roles turned down by everyone from Charlton Heston to Peter Fonda. Coburn's Garrett is tired and relentless in pursuit of Billy—an unlikely sacred monster, played by Kristofferson as a plump-faced dude with a modified shag and a tight, self-mocking smile. (Kristofferson is fatuous, but Peckinpah works with it; in one antiheroic bit of

---

Tidyman, who wrote the screenplays for *Shaft* and *The French Connection*, was attuned to more than Silent Majority anger in making Eastwood the vehicle for outsider rage.

business, the Kid dons his sombrero, mounts a horse, and gets dumped on his butt in the middle of Main Street.) Nor is this last Righteous Outlaw a heroic social bandit. Discovered by a decrepit deputy in an obscure cantina, beleaguered Billy challenges him to a duel, which he wins by being the first to cheat.

Pat Garrett's abundant violence and leathery camaraderie, ritualistic killing and macho posturing, incidental cockfights and lip-smacking whiskey guzzlers, the rub-a-dub-dub four-whores-in-a-tub partying and the towheaded kids who amuse themselves by swinging on a hangman's noose are pure Peckinpah. Although ultimately disowned by Wurlitzer, *Pat Garrett and Billy the Kid* carries more than a trace of his absurdism and taste for haute-bohemian fashion. Action segueing from one communal crash pad to another, the movie *Garrett* is ridiculously rich in scene-making: In addition to the two nominal stars, it features a pair of then-hot pop icons, Bob Dylan and Rita Coolidge, in supporting roles.*

The same issues of obsolesence, outlaw behavior, corporate chicanery, and the territorial imperative illustrated by *Pat Garrett* were raised in the course of the film's production. Peckinpah originally planned to use the very New Mexico landscapes where the Lincoln County cattle wars occurred a century before. But cash-strapped MGM—whose biggest project, the MGM Grand Hotel under construction in Las Vegas, was behind schedule and overbudget—insisted on sending the project south to Durango, where it could be more economically made.

There was a complication: John Wayne's production company, Batjac, had scheduled its yearly trip to the Cowboy Paradise to shoot *Cahill, U.S. Marshall*,

---

*Both Kristofferson and Wurlitzer took credit for recruiting Dylan; Peckinpah had no clear idea who the singer was. As the Kid's sidekick, Alias, Dylan is something of an embarrassment—he's badly post-dubbed and gets extremely limited mileage out of an angelic smirk. Far more than Kristofferson, Dylan was the signifier of hip. When a character played by Mexican director Emilio Fernández pops up to invite Billy south of the border, Alias portentously presents the Mexican soul brother with a knife: "It has a good edge."

and the town, by now Wayne's private preserve, was only big enough for one movie—as associate-producer Gordon Dawson had discovered when he visited in August 1972. "Guess who'd tied up all of the desirable places?" Dawson reported. "The dreaded one-lunged runaway patriot had struck again." Thus run out of town, Dawson found an alternative location in the nearby pueblo of El Arnal: "I think you'll like it, Sam—hopelessly impoverished, desolate, lifeless earth, bleak desperation, and street just loaded with shit, flies, ants, scorpions, scrawny dogs and sharp rocks. . . ." Dawson wasn't wrong. The movie has the sense of a fond family squabble—Peckinpah packed the cast with an astonishing collection of veteran supporting players and built the narrative on Garrett's inchoate love for his old range buddy.

In some unwholesome way, *Pat Garrett* and *Cahill* merged into *Myra Breckinridge*'s vision of Cowboy degeneracy—"Saturday afternoon for the whole world." Visiting both sets, journalist Lorraine Gauguin was overwhelmed by the horde of secondarios hanging around the plastic-and-Naugahyde dining room at the seedy Campo Mexico bungalow court.

> It is an unbelievable sight to see so many first-rate character actors slobbing around in one room, all working. They are gamy and the smell of leather, sweat, old sheepskin jackets, scruffy worn-down boots, unkempt beards and long, stringy hair blends with the reeking fumes of cigars, chewing tobacco, and last night's booze. They are a crapulent, scrofulous lot.
>
> This is the truss and prostate set for sure, jowls jiggle, bellies sag, yet they all ride like Comanches, gorge like vultures, guzzle like camels, swear like horny cowhands—and after a hard day's work, stink like baboons. The only thing that slows them down is a bad case of jock itch.

Gauguin reported that, for the past few years, Peckinpah had worn the same raggedy outfit. The director was "a thin, gray, tired little man with a dirty bandana twisted into a headband, gray hair sticking out every which way." He looked like a derelict, but, inevitably, his evident madness and psycho-sorcery reminded her of Charles Manson. The *Cahill* set offered a more noble study in self-destruction. Gauguin found Wayne "standing around between scenes in the freezing stone interior of the granary coughing, hawking, spitting" and, too tough to pamper his remaining lung, chain-smoking cigarillos.

MGM decreed Peckinpah's epic be shot in a mere fifty days for a measly $3 million. Production began in mid-November, soon after the Nixon landslide drove a stake through the counterculture's heart. It wrapped—three weeks late—the following March, with American bombers still pounding Indochinese targets (no longer in North Vietnam but Cambodia). Peckinpah had fallen behind schedule almost immediately. The influenza epidemic that carried off thousands in Durango that winter decimated his cast and crew, even as belated discovery of a defective camera lens required extensive retakes. When the first dailies were out of focus, the irate director unzipped his fly and grandly urinated an S across the screen.

Peckinpah claimed to have been brooding over Nixon while making *Pat Garrett*. Given the cutthroat business ethics, rampant corruption, and opportunistic appeals to law-and-order that characterized the Lincoln County wars, New Mexico 1881 seemed nearly contemporary. Garrett, Billy, and their men were pawns manipulated by hidden economic and political powers. The Santa Fe Ring, Peckinpah explained in an on-set interview, was "involved in land-grabbing and shady financial dealings, and Billy and the people around him resented that." Garrett's murderers were the same people who hired him to kill the Kid. It was a conspiracy: "They had already killed a judge and his son in New Mexico and Garrett had indicted people for the murder; so he was assassinated."

"It still happens today," Peckinpah explained. Albert Fall, lawyer for the Santa Fe Ring, later became U.S. Secretary of the Interior. Disgusted with Nixon's America, Peckinpah next planned to make a movie celebrating Mexican revolutionary Pancho Villa. Meanwhile, the director was drinking so heavily *Pat Garrett* had to be shut down for half a week. Paranoia was rampant. Peckinpah routinely taped his phone conversations with production personnel and slept with a Bowie knife on his night table. Members of the crew were threatening each other. The director himself packed a gun and, when the macho mood struck him, would blast a round into the cantina ceiling. After Coburn learned that Peckinpah had shot out his own reflection in a hotel-room mirror, he suggested adding a similar scene to the movie.

One intimates the Orgy's sodden collapse in this dismal saga. Consigned to Mexico by a dying studio, elbowed out of locations by the living god John Wayne, permanently enraged with the "bellhops" at MGM, the half-mad maverick ritualistically medicated himself with whiskey to finish the movie. After the trades reported that *Pat Garrett* was a runaway production with an alcoholic overaged delinquent at the wheel, Peckinpah took out a full-page ad in *Daily Variety* flaunting a photograph of himself on a stretcher being toasted by the movie's cast and crew. One of Peckinpah's drunken inspirations was to sacrifice a horse—shot dead from underneath a stuntman. The Orgy was most definitely over in January 1974, when the director was cited, along with counterculture cine-megalomaniacs Dennis Hopper and Alejandro Jodorowsky—on the *New York Times*'s Sunday Arts and Leisure section front page—as a practitioner of "Death for Art's Sake."*

• • •

As *Dirty Harry* had reduced the Righteous Outlaw to a psychotic, whining punk, Sam Peckinpah's film was not the season's lone Billy the Kid feature. There was also Stan Dragoti's *Dirty Little Billy*. Previously known for his TV commercials, Dragoti wrote the script with fellow adman Charles Moss and pitched it to Jack Warner after hearing that the venerable mogul was returning to film production as an independent. Almost as if Warner were determined to demonstrate his belated now-ness and that he finally dug *Bonnie and Clyde*, the outlaws' backward idiot sidekick Michael J. Pollard was cast as young Billy.

Beginning with a close-up of feet slogging through the muck, *Dirty Little Billy* is the most miserablist of Westerns. The prairie is a sea of mud. Getting

---

*Peckinpah's Hollywood office was nearly incinerated with fiery missives after the *Times* pointed out that, while John Wayne religiously followed American Humane Association guidelines in his treatment of animals, *Pat Garrett and Billy the Kid* received an unacceptable rating from the AHA for the "trip-wiring of horses and casual use of chickens, buried in the ground up to their necks for target practice." Inexplicably, the AHA missed the scene where Billy and a sidekick lasso turkeys in lyrical slow-motion.

off the train, Billy—idiot son of two Irish immigrants—slips and loses his shoe. In a parody of nation-building, the new settlers raise the American flag over this godforsaken dump. It's Freedomland as pure Nixon territory—innocence is exploited, authority is corrupt, and profit rules. Only the day before the movie's belated New York opening, the President issued a White Paper that, albeit releasing information on wiretaps, the Plumbers, and the Huston Plan (all justified as necessary responses to security leaks, campus unrest, and domestic terrorism), continued to deny prior knowledge of the Watergate break-in or cover-up.

Transplanted from New York, *Dirty Little Billy's* eponymous antihero revolts against the hard farm life forced on him by his stepfather, taking up with the hippie degenerates Goldie and Berle. This is the real Bonnie and Clyde! The three establish a ménage à trois—dancing to the music of a metal proto-gramophone, smoking hand-rolled cigarettes like joints, sharing Berle's favors—in a modest little orgy of fun. As in *McCabe & Mrs. Miller*, the barroom commune is crushed by capital. A developer is building a twenty-room hotel across the street and, as he dominates the town, can even offer Billy a cushy civil-service job. Goldie is ambushed and poor Berle shot point-blank. Billy and wounded Goldie make their way to a bad-guy hideout where—even worse than the Mansonoid scum dispatched by Roy Bean—the denizens are ready to kill them for the gold in Goldie's teeth. Here, Billy finds his true nature—going berserk and shooting them all. He and Goldie are busily stripping the bodies as the end credit music comes up.

"Everything is gray: the landscape, the light, the morality. There are no heroes, only villains and victims," *Time* wrote. By comparison, *Pat Garrett and Billy the Kid* is astonishingly glamorous. The colors are ultra magic hour; the score insanely elegiac. The movie is a fiesta of righteous rhetoric: "There's gonna be some hard times coming down." If Billy and his pals are proto-Rolling Stones, the wealthy cattle baron Chisum is their highly unsympathetic idea of the devil. The historical Chisum encouraged Billy's delinquency by cheating him out of his wages; the more paternalistic Chisum played by John Wayne appreciated the Kid as a mixed-up version of himself. Here, Chisum (Barry

Sullivan, whose part would wind up on the cutting room floor) is the embodiment of capital—if not MGM. Unseen but oftened referred to, Chisum dispatches his minions to eliminate Billy for violating corporate property rights. Wurlitzer's original script opened with Billy's escape from prison and covered only the last three months of his life, with the principals not meeting until the final shoot-out. Peckinpah, however, wanted to make their previous friendship obvious and added a scene in which, having sold out to the Sante Fe Ring, the newly civilized Garrett rides to Fort Sumner to warn free-spirited Billy that he's now representing the law. "How does it feel?" the Kid taunts his old buddy. Garrett lets the reference to Dylan's greatest hit hang there for a beat before wearily paraphrasing another old Dylan song: "It feels like times have changed."

Billy is finally cornered, one cold night, back at Fort Sumner. The narrative comes full circle, the set filled with hombres wandering through the fog as Kristofferson and Coolidge bed down with sad hippie smiles, Dylan moaning appreciatively on the track. The real Garrett shot the actual Billy unarmed and asleep. Here, lifting a bit of business from *Two-Lane Blacktop*, Peckinpah revels in the ambiguity of so brutal an execution: Garrett sits impassively outside Billy's window, generously (or voyeuristically) allowing him a last bit of pleasure before he waylays the half-naked and unresisting Kid en route to a post-coital snack. Billy is a sacrificial victim. Indeed, his death necessarily destroys his executioner as well. *Pat Garrett's* spookiest aspect is the sense of America killing an outlaw part of itself and then having it come back as a folk-rock ghost.

Hastily edited, tested, and reedited, *Pat Garrett and Billy the Kid* lurched into theaters for the 1973 Memorial Day weekend, inspiring extremes of praise and (mainly) invective. The televised Ervin Committee hearings had opened six days before and continued throughout the summer. In late June, John Dean testified against the President. July 13, Alexander Butterfield revealed the existence of the Oval Office recording system. Ten days later, Archibald Cox subpoenaed nine tapes. Nixon's approval ratings fell to 40 percent. August 26, Mark Frechette and another member of the Fort Hill commune were arrested attempting to rob a Boston bank. Movie career stalled, Frechette attempted his own *Zabriskie Point* remake, although he later blamed his criminality on the President's. "We didn't want to hurt anyone. We just wanted to hold up Nixon. The bank was the nearest thing that was federally insured."[*]

Two days after Frechette fulfilled his righteous destiny, Abbie Hoffman was busted for selling cocaine to an undercover cop. The Yippie had bought the *Superfly* scenario. "I'm moving into criminality. . . . I'm considering going into movies," he told an interviewer in February. As summer ended, one more outlaw went down. Planned for nearly three years, the coup d'etat in Chile came September 11. Salvador Allende died defending his presidential palace.

Ciné Paranoia: Conspiracies Unmasked, 1973–75

Warren Beatty's proposed solution to the Eagleton fiasco had been to re-convene the DemCon—Together with McGovern Again!—and draft one of the party's unwilling heavies, preferably Ted Kennedy, to run for vice president. A better plan, perhaps, might have been for George McGovern to dem-onstrate his own showmanship, embrace the *Wild in the Streets* scenario, and put Beatty on the ticket. The team could have scarcely garnered fewer votes than did McGovern and Kennedy in-law Sargent Shriver.

Indeed, in October 1973, not quite a year after McGovern's humiliating defeat, *New Times* reported Beatty's contention that a private poll placed his name first among the possible candidates to succeed California governor Ron-ald Reagan. It was an apocalyptic month. Pessimism and anxiety were already evident; September's Gallup poll had 89 percent of Americans concerned with the rising cost of living (a mere 14 percent mentioning Watergate). Now there was war in the Middle East. When the Soviet Union threatened to send troops

---

[*]In April 1974, Frechette pleaded guilty to armed robbery and received a six- to fifteen-year sentence. While in the Norfolk Prison Colony, he directed an inmate production of *The White House Transcripts*, a play based on Richard Nixon's Oval Office tapes. The show was written up in the April 14, 1975, *People*. Less than six months later, Frechette was found dead on the bench press of the prison recreation room, a 160-pound barbell fallen on his throat.

to Egypt, Henry Kissinger ordered the United States on nuclear alert. Worse, the Arab nations imposed an oil embargo that would not only accelerate inflation and hasten recession but blossom into a psychological crisis, replete with panic and conspiracy theorizing.

A sitting vice president had been forced to give up his office to avoid the gangster crime of income-tax evasion; the President suffered the resignation of two attorneys general before finding one to discharge the special Watergate prosecutor, thus goading the House of Representatives to begin an impeachment inquiry. Instead of running for public office, however, Beatty elected to make, first, *The Parallax View*—a paranoid thriller in which an obsessed investigative journalist attempts to solve the assassination of a liberal senator described as the "ideal father, husband, [and] leader of the country"—and then, *Shampoo*.

Was a national narrative being knit together? As in Camelot, American politics was rife with cover-up and conspiracy. The Watergate revelations coincided with a new Hollywood cycle (or, rather, a revival of an old one). The counterculture receded, leaving the sense of living in an alternate universe amid the phantoms of what might have been, a renewed fascination with the Secret Agent of History—the supposedly lone gunmen who made manifest American destiny—and, as suggested in *The Candidate*, an unfulfillable yearning for the ageless Kennedys.

Appropriately, the JFK assassination thriller *Executive Action*—shot in Los Angeles under "unusual security" during the summer's televised Watergate hearings—was the avatar of subsequent conspiracy films, having its premiere November 7, 1973, a year to the day after Richard Nixon's landslide. This first attempt to visualize the Dealey Plaza scenario since Mark Lane's documentary *Rush to Judgment* was financed by wealthy businessman Herbert Magidson, a supporter of the Black Panthers. The production reunited two members of the Spartacist team—producer Edward Lewis and screenwriter Dalton Trumbo—for an independent adaptation of Donald Freed and Lane's speculative novel.

A liberal conspiratorial scenario meant to expose a right-wing conspiratorial scenario, *Executive Action* opens June 5, 1963, several days before JFK made his plea for world peace and, his hand forced by George Wallace, delivered a televised address on civil rights. But something else is blowing in the wind. A Kennedy-hating cabal of anachronistically sideburned honchos is meeting in Texas—an outright fascist (Robert Ryan), a rogue CIA operative (Burt Lancaster), and a cracker-barrel billionaire patterned on Dallas oilman H. L. Hunt (the once-blacklisted Will Geer). Watching this initial scene is like being privy to the Nixon Oval Office—world historical doings plotted by powerful white men in posh surroundings. The Geer character must be persuaded that JFK should be eliminated. Kennedy, the Ryan character maintains in his brief against the President, is planning to lead a Black Revolution, sign a test-ban treaty with the Russians, do away with the oil depletion allowance, and pull our boys out of Vietnam. And so, Lancaster gets another chance to orchestrate the thwarted coup of *Seven Days in May*.

Once the plan becomes operational, potential assassins are shown training in the desert while other agents study Lee Harvey Oswald's file and fabricate the famous photo of him brandishing his rifle. As the conspirators train an Oswald double, so the filmmakers dramatize Oswald's Fair Play for Cuba scuffle on the streets of New Orleans. Throughout, the conspirators biliously study the President's televised activities. Indeed, the entire movie has the sense of a made-for-TV ritual. Extensively rehearsed before the morning of November 22, the assassination (which posits three shooters) is staged without dialogue and set to sad carousel music. The mix of newsreel footage and fictional re-creation is then watched on TV, as if the live feed from some private satellite transmitter, by the trio who authored the show.

In essence, *Executive Action* is the tale of three presidents. The movie draws on the authority of JFK's public image, as well as LBJ's own belief in a conspiracy (only recently articulated in the July 1973 issue of *The Atlantic Monthly*), even as it references the Nixon operation by citing the existence of anti-Castro Cubans available for anything from "picking a lock" to pulling the trigger. Although *Executive Action* was timed to mark the tenth anniversary of Kennedy's death, the favorable *Variety* review mentioned Watergate twice. To the paranoid mind, the connection seemed self-evident. Peter Dale Scott's essay in the November 1973 *Ramparts* suggested that "a full exposure of the Watergate conspiracy will help us to understand what happened in Dallas, and also to understand the covert forces which later mired America in a criminal war in Southeast Asia."

Now the conspiracy theorists are to be found on the Left. As in Watergate, Scott argued, one should "focus on the cover-up rather than the crime." Indeed, ten days after *Executive Action* was released, the President launched Operation Candor, assuring the Associated Press Managing Editors Association convention in Walt Disney World that he was "not a crook." Too bad for Nixon that, sometime in November, the anonymous source code-named Deep Throat tipped *Washington Post* reporters Bob Woodward and Carl Bernstein to "deliberate erasures" on the White House tapes.

•   •   •

The 1973 holiday season was darkened by layoffs, closures, and the absence of traditional displays. Some power plants even cut back on voltage. As angry teamsters blocked interstate highways to protest gasoline prices, service stations were asked to shut down from Saturday night to Monday morning. Dramatizing the need to save fuel, the President, whose approval rating was heading south of 30 percent, took a commercial jet to his San Clemente retreat.

Auto sales, housing starts, and the stock market were plunging as unemployment and oil prices rose. On Christmas Eve, the Iranians doubled the cost of their crude oil for a total increase of 470 percent over the past year. Two days later, *The Exorcist*—a movie in which a twelve-year-old girl is possessed by the devil with extraordinarily graphic effects—was released. Although Warners had decided to open the movie in only a few theaters, the response was so strong (including incidents of fainting, hysteria, vomiting) that the movie grossed over $10 million in its first two weeks. "Director William Friedkin has revolutionized the movie business by going further than anyone had dared," Stephen Farber wrote in the *New York Times*, months into *The Exorcist* craze. Friedkin discovered "the perfect mixture of blood, excrement, perverse sexuality, and religious symbolism to drive audiences wild." Farber called *The Exorcist* a mainstream *El Topo*. Now it was not simply the counterculture that was experiencing its own dissolution.

In February 1974, as lengthening gas lines were increasingly disrupted by acts of desperation and violence, two more long-running disaster scenarios joined Watergate and *The Exorcist*. The best-selling novel and eventual movie blockbuster *Jaws* was published, and the nineteen-year-old college coed Patricia Hearst was violently abducted from the Berkeley house she shared with her fiancé, graduate student Steven Weed. The next Monday, Patty Hearst graced *Newsweek*'s cover—for the first of seven times over the next two years.

Back in November, the day before *Executive Action* opened, a new conspiratorial hit team made its debut when Superintendent Marcus Foster—a popular and dynamic black educator—was ambushed and shot with cyanide-tipped bullets as he left a school-board meeting in Oakland, California. Credit was claimed by a hitherto unknown organization, which, identifying itself as the Symbionese Liberation Army, ended the communiqué sent to Berkeley radio station KPFA with a science-fiction exhortation: DEATH TO THE FASCIST INSECT THAT PREYS UPON THE LIFE OF THE PEOPLE.

February 7, three days after Patty was snatched, the Symbionese Liberation Army, Western Regional Adult Unit, took responsibity for "arresting" the daughter of publisher (and "corporate enemy of the people") William Randolph Hearst. Five days later, KPFA received a tape-recording, soon broadcast across the nation, of Patty herself. "Mom, Dad, I'm OK. I had a few scrapes and stuff, but they washed them up and they're getting OK." A message from a man identified as Cinque, "General Field Marshal in the United Liberated Forces of the Symbionese Liberation Army," explained that before any negotiation for Patty's release, the SLA demanded a "token" of "good faith." Randolph Hearst was to distribute $70 worth of food to each Californian receiving welfare and Social Security payments, as well as to prisoners on probation or parole. The distribution was to begin February 19.

Hearst hurriedly set up the $2 million People in Need program. The first distribution was scheduled for Friday, February 22. In part because the SLA delivered a new tape the day before that demanded more money and denounced the PIN program as "crumbs," the initial giveaway was a debacle—replete with rioting, pilferage, and shortages. Two subsequent distributions were more orderly, although California's governor, Ronald Reagan, created a stir when it was revealed that, in the course of a speech delivered to a closed meeting of high-powered Republicans in Washington, DC, he alluded to the upcoming March 8 PIN distribution and joked that "It's just too bad we can't have an epidemic of botulism." The SLA was not amused. "I'm starting to think no one is concerned about me anymore," bitter Patty complained in a tape released March 10, the day before the *Shampoo* shoot opened.

At the congressional hearings on terrorism held precisely when Patty was confined to a closet in the SLA's San Francisco safe house, Dr. F. Gentry Harris testified that "terrorism ultimately aims at the spectator. The victim is secondary." Dr. Frederick Hacker, hired as an adviser by the Hearst family, was even more blunt: "Terrorism has unfortunately become a form of mass entertainment." A case in point, Patty's abduction was a fantastic pageant in which a gang of crazy, mixed-up, privileged white kids—followers of black ex-con Donald DeFreeze who, like him, took theatrically Third World names and who periodically disguised themselves as blacks—kidnapped a millionaire's daughter and commandeered the media as a platform for their lunatic political rhetoric. Cult or cell, these Outlaws established their celebrity on a scale that, for a few months, surpassed that of Jesse James or Bonnie and Clyde.

As the Watergate hearings purported to reveal the conspiratorial underpinnings of the American government, the SLA replayed the High Sixties, from opening assassination through the free food for all and the bank heist staged to be recorded to their final, televised apocalypse. With the mass movements of the past decade distilled into a single sect, the Patty-thon was ultimate guerrilla theater; not long after the show ended, a clever art historian published a parodic piece terming the SLA a "performance group" who used the media as their medium to demonstrate that "political action itself can be no more than art performance."*

Some years later, German philosopher Peter Sloterdijk would write in re-

---

*The Black Panthers were not the only radicals who believed the SLA a mélange of CIA plants, police agents, and provocateurs, with a few drug-dependent space cadets for window dressing. Mae Brussell—Queen of California conspiracy theorists, whose

gard to the 1977 kidnapping of industrialist Hans-Martin Schleyer that the "political staging of the crime and the spectacular interaction of state and terror group [took] on the significance of an epoch-making event" which, nourished on "powerful catastrophile currents," swelled into an "all-engrossing and prolonged media melodrama." Similarly, the Hearst kidnapping offered what Sloterdijk calls a "substitute for History" avidly consumed by society as the ultimate political spectacular.

Patty achieved full media stardom in the year of the disaster film, when the Sixties were seeking metaphoric representation in traditional Hollywood terms. *Earthquake, The Towering Inferno, The Taking of Pelham One Two Three* were movies—already in production, soon to be touted in the June 10 issue of *Time* as "Coming Afflictions"—that offered the spectacle of all-star casts impersonating ordinary, middle-class people coping with the breakdown of institutions thought to be safe (ocean liners, airplanes, cities, the Constitution). In the case of the Patty Hearst show, that institution was wealth, privilege, power—and youth, with breakdown amply demonstrated by the PIN debacle, the FBI's inability to rescue her (despite the most extensive such operation in the agency's history), and, finally, by Patty's transformation.

It was now taken for granted that Hollywood films might be sociological events—they meant something, and none more than *The Exorcist*, which continued to dominate public discourse as Americans attempted to exorcize Richard Nixon (or rather exorcize something by exorcizing Nixon). Jerry Rubin contributed an appreciation of *The Exorcist* to the *Village Voice*: "When I first saw the movie I was pissed off because I saw it as a return to ancient views about the Devil and the Catholic Church: part of the nostalgic disease of the 1970s." But a second viewing in the company of a clinical psychologist suggested that the movie was in fact an allegory.

---

explication of the Hearst event filled an entire issue of *The Realist*—declared Field Marshal DeFreeze the "first black Lee Harvey Oswald." The Secret Agent of History was a patsy programmed by rogue law-enforcement agencies to discredit the legitimate Left by spreading terror among the populace.

We are all possessed—by our addictions, our loves, our attachments, our habits, our unconscious, our guilts, our needs, our possessions, our social roles. . . .

Movies are therapeutic experiences. After seeing *The Exorcist* I got more in touch with the irrational within me. I am Regan. You are Regan.

But nobody was more Regan than Patricia Hearst.

Rubin's *Voice* piece was still on newsstands April 3 when Patty's latest transmission made her possession apparent. After condemning her parents for their "sham" efforts to secure her release and informing her fiancé that "love doesn't mean the same thing to me anymore," Patty announced that, given the choice of being released or joining the SLA to fight "for my freedom and the freedom of all oppressed people," she opted to "stay and fight."

I have been given the name Tania after a comrade who fought alongside Che in Bolivia. . . . I embrace the name with the determination to continue fighting with her spirit. There is no victory in half-assed attempts at revolution.

Enclosed with the tape was a Polaroid photo of Patty in jumpsuit and beret, posed with resolute expression and an M-1 carbine, before a poster of the seven-headed cobra that was the SLA emblem.

Revolution in hyperreality: Twelve days later, barely disguised in a brown wig, Tania made her carbine-touting debut. Her image captured on film when the SLA held up the Hibernia Bank in San Francisco, Tania Hearst was scarier than Hanoi Jane, a Manson girl with an analysis, Bonnie reborn. Public sentiment turned. Patty's transformation from debutante to Righteous Outlaw—by way of victim—was not the narrative for which America waited. "Consciousness is terrifying to the ruling class," Tania proclaimed. "They will do anything to discredit people who have realized that the only alternative to freedom is death."

In the disaster movies, catastrophe was invariably worsened by mendacious, corrupt, and incompetent leaders. But these films were fundamentally reassuring. Everyone except top public officials demonstrated heroism under stress, establishing the fundamental decency of ordinary people. Disaster movies denied Americans had become permissive or that their traditional values had collapsed. Indeed, they insisted these values not only remained intact but, unlike in *Night of the Living Dead*, continued to help guarantee society's survival. Middle-class virtue prevailed, just as if the Sixties had never happened. Patty's reemergence as Tania, by contrast, suggested the Sixties might go on forever.*

•   •   •

May 17, 1974, the entire SLA, save for Tania and her keepers, Bill and Emily Harris, are trapped in a house in the black ghetto of South Central Los Angeles and obliterated in a firefight with the LA SWAT team. On which planet, in what dimension, is the John Wayne sufficiently committed to Alamo-ize this production? The SLA often predicted, usually through Patty, that the FBI intended to kill them. Now it was death to Bonnie and Clyde, although Bonnie wasn't there. Like the Watts riot, the hour-long battle was televised live and watched by, among others, Patty Hearst, holed up with the Harris couple thirty miles away in a motel room across from Disneyland. "I died in that fire," she announces in the taped June 7 statement that will be her last public utterance as Tania.

A month later, just before the House Judiciary Committee concludes closed hearings, *The Parallax View* opened. The assassination in *Executive Action* had been carried out by rogue elements in the CIA/FBI on behalf of a cabal of right-wing industrialists. In *The Parallax View*—a movie on which the star re-

---

*Which was more incredible, Patty's hyperreal metamorphosis or the desire to believe it? One need only consult the special feature that ran after her capture in two autumn 1975 issues of *Rolling Stone* to see how much a countercultural heroine she had become or how totally she was imagined to internalize her erstwhile captors' worldview: Tania, with her "habit of scanning each morning's *New York Times* with a felt-tip pen, x-ing out pictures of political enemies," personified the delusions of an entire imagined generation. At the height of her invisibility, during her seventeen months underground, Tania was celebrated by the self-consciously Dylanesque ballad that soon became a staple of New York's Pacifica station, WBAI: "Patty dear, I know your sights are on the Milky Way/An' the av-aii-ricious scorpion is a-beggin' you to stay . . ." is the grotesquely solicitous refrain, after which the singer, Sammy Walker, makes the wistful request that "you can tell us all about it someday."

wrote the script and contested Alan Pakula's direction throughout—the perpetrators were a less-personalized, privatized CIA surrogate, and the victim was a generic Robert F. Kennedy presidential candidate, hair over his collar, who in his last words (before being shot and expiring on the floor of a hotel kitchen) declares himself "too independent for [his] own good." To solve this murder, Beatty's journalist commits himself to the madhouse of American politics. Considering that one former mental patient and one future one, Thomas Eagleton and Arthur Bremer, had combined to cost George McGovern the 1972 election, it is appropriate that Beatty's first picture after the McGovern debacle would be an updated *Shock Corridor*. The reporter is scolded by his editor in a line echoing the Fuller film, "I don't care if your self-serving ambition gets you the Pulitzer Prize."

Pauline Kael thought that *Executive Action* concluded with

perhaps the most ludicrous denouement in thriller history. We are presented with the faces of eighteen "material witnesses" who, we are told, have died, against odds of "one hundred thousand trillion to one." But the movie has failed to introduce those witnesses into the action; we haven't discovered what a single one of them witnessed or how he happened to get involved.

But it is with this coincidence, first noted by Mark Lane, that *The Parallax View* takes off. Inspired by the high (and highly unlikely) number of Kennedy assassination eyewitnesses who subsequently died under mysterious circumstances, *The Parallax View* proposes the paranoid scenario—or perhaps new narrative— of an America governed by unfathomable, institutionalized conspiracy.

Beatty is a reporter investigating the deaths of witnesses, consequently everybody wants to kill him—in effect, he is a left-wing Legal Vigilante without a gun. The bland sci-fi mise-en-scène and the absence of establishing shots reinforce the sense of a bleak, empty world. A mysterious entity that eliminates troublesome presidential candidates, the Parallax Corporation is the Secret Agent institutionalized: What purpose do these operations serve? *The Parallax View* leaves only a murky impression of corporate malevolence in positing a talent agency providing assassins required by other companies. If the Parallax ideology can only be explained by the profit motive—well, that's Hollywood.

Just as the hero of *Shock Corridor* catches the killer and is rendered catatonic, so the protagonist of *The Parallax View* solves the murder and is effectively silenced. Beatty's journalist is lured onto the scene of another political assassination, where he can be framed as the perpetrator and then shot. He has penetrated the labyrinth only to find himself blundering onto history's stage. It is the newsman's ambition that enables Parallax to script him a role in their scenario and so cast him out of existence. Did Beatty take such shenanigans seriously? Norman Mailer, in his investigative mode, working for *Life* magazine under his Summer of '69 code name, Aquarius, had encountered the star in McGovern's Senate office shortly after Eagleton was dumped: "It was like talking to a halfback who will explain why his coach, the best coach, can still lose a game." Beatty told Mailer that he had actually been in the room when Frank Mankiewicz questioned McGovern's prospective running mate. "When did word first get to you about Eagleton?" Mailer asked.

[Beatty] shrugged. "A couple of reporters called."

"How did they know?"

"There was a phone call to them from Rochester."

"Was it anonymous?"

He nodded.

Why bother to look for the CIA when there was always the FBI? But, as if the sense of excitement [Aquarius] felt at the possibility quivered across the air and was seized by Beatty, the actor gave a wooden look in return. The interview was abruptly over.

"Are you sure of this?"

"No."

"Is it a secret?"

"No matter. It's not said."

"What do you mean?"

"The rain in Spain."

"What?"

"Doggerel."

Now Beatty got up. The interview was certainly over. Aquarius made small talk with the staff for a minute. Yet, before he left, Beatty tapped him. "It's okay. You can use that story. It's been in print."

Mid-June 1974: *The Parallax View* is dumped in theaters by Paramount only two days before the studio proudly opens Roman Polanski's *Chinatown*. The glossy contemporary thriller is eclipsed by a fastidious period re-creation, a hyperreal film noir, lovingly written by Beatty's alter ego, Robert Towne.

Released even as Charles Colson testifies that Richard Nixon ordered him to ruin Daniel Ellsberg, *Chinatown* is widely understood as another conspiratorial scenario involving government collusion with sinister plutocrats and linked to the Watergate event now approaching its climax. In late July, the House Judiciary Committee begins to consider the President's impeachment. The same day, the movie *Death Wish* opens. A curtain call for the Legal Vigilante, this Charles Bronson vehicle will be festively treated throughout the summer—particularly in New York City, the setting for the story of a "liberal" professional driven by sex crimes committed against his wife and daughter to wreak vengeance on the underclass.*

After a week of televised debate, the House Judiciary Committee adopts three articles of impeachment, and Nixon delivers the so-called smoking-gun tape of June 23, 1972. Three days later, on August 8, the President announces his resignation. Alan Pakula goes on to direct a happier *Parallax View*, namely the story of the Watergate investigation, *All the President's Men*, with Beatty's

---

*As audiences cheered Bronson and *The Parallax View* merged with the final days of the Nixon presidency, other media figures fantasized their own movies. Perhaps there was room for a new Hollywood Freedom Fighter. In early spring, around the time of Patty's conversion, Abbie Hoffman went underground. Like Huey Newton before him, Hoffman hung out in Hollywood, enjoying the available sex, drugs, and socializing. Getting money from Jefferson Airplane and disguise tips from Francis Coppola, Hoffman dreamed he might be a movie star, subject of his own bio-pic. That same summer, Newton and Bobby Seale were planning their blaxploitation film, written by Newton as a vehicle for Seale with Paul Williams directing. Called *I Never Thought of It That Way Before*, the movie was to allegorize Newton's split with Eldridge Cleaver.

rival, Robert Redford. Redford's contribution to the conspiracy cycle is the CIA thriller *Three Days of the Condor*, which will begin production that fall.

As the Orgy dissipates, *Blowup* becomes universal (and hence invisible). It is alluded to in *The Conversation*, the paranoid thriller Francis Coppola makes between the two parts of *The Godfather*, as well as by *Three Days of the Condor*, wherein the Redford character attempts to fathom a photographer's nature by eyeing the "evidence" of the black-and-white landscapes taped to her wall. In *Shampoo*, shot at the height of the Patty Hearst festival, the Orgy is something lost—an object for nostalgia, the strobe-lit locus classicus of *temps perdu*. The Orgy is where George and Jackie get together for the last time as the Beatles sing their LSD ode, "Lucy in the Sky with Diamonds." This inscribed nostalgia for *Sergeant Pepper's Lonelyhearts Club Band*—released only six weeks before *Bonnie and Clyde*—suggests that George and Jackie had their "past" barely a year ago, during the Summer of Love. But this amiable and contained Orgy is also a representation of business as usual—it's not *Night of the Living Dead*, the Manson Family isn't lurking in the bushes at the party's periphery, although, if the truth be known, they were much in evidence during the fall of 1968.

The Orgy has been dispersed and naturalized: The documentary *Janis*, opening soon after *Shampoo*, is a sentimental whitewash of the hippie martyr Janis Joplin. (*Time* calls the film "willfully empty-headed" in portraying its subject as "Little Miss Goodvibes, a wildflower of the love generation who wilted for reasons unspecified.") *Shampoo* is predicated on symbolic freedoms won in the Sixties—its matter-of-fact profanity will inspire a scholarly article on verbal taboo.

Like *Sweet Sweetback's Baadasssss Song*, *Shampoo* blasts off with coitus during the credits—albeit sex quaintly interrupted by a ringing telephone and post-scripted by Felicia's imperious dictum "Christ, get me a Kleenex." The smog of polymorphous perversity is so thick that Lester can't figure out if George is straight or gay, a programmatically anti-establishment rebel or "just a kooky guy who does kooky things." Later, he wonders if George's sexual escapades are some form of revolt—an Oedipal guerrilla war carried out against him.

But it is Lester who is the real swinger. ("I identify sometimes as much with Lester as I do with George," Beatty tells one interviewer.) It's Lester who drives a Rolls-Royce, Lester who keeps a mistress, Lester who strips down to frolic in a hot tub with two compliant hippie girls. It's also Lester who, demonstrating the power to command police or hire muscle, is something of a Legal Vigilante. George may have the deeper wisdom—at least regarding women—but the hairdresser doesn't know how to glad-hand, deal with men in a man's world.*

Humiliated in his request for a small business loan by a bank officer who fails to recognize the significance of then-starlet Barbara Rush as a reference, George impotently hurls a trashcan back toward the bank that he will never be Clyde enough to rob. Illustrating the new forms of the *Blowup* style, *Shampoo* dramatizes a generational restoration. George conducts his business in the boudoir, pledging allegiance to the pleasure principle rather than the marketplace. *Shampoo*'s comic situations are largely based on this confusion. As film critic Chuck Kleinhans will note: "In capitalist terms, as phrased in petit-bourgeois ideology with a hint of Puritanism in the service of primitive capitalist accumulation, George's mistake in life is 'mixing business with pleasure.' "

Mixing business with pleasure is an error Lester repeats in having Jackie brought to the Republican banquet. But that, of course, is the meaning of Hollywood: Their business is our pleasure (and even, to the degree we follow their private lives, vice versa).

•   •   •

It was a brand-new world when *Shampoo* opened February 11, 1975 (the same day Britain's Conservative Party voted Margaret Thatcher its new leader). Al-

---

*Although *Shampoo* is more about the consumers than the producers of glamour, there's an ambiguous moment when George declares, "Baby, I'm a star!" At times, people do treat the hairdresser as if he actually were, and this invites an extratextual reading of the film: Given Beatty's reputation as a lover, *Time* realistically suggested *Shampoo* be retitled *Advertisements for Myself*. "That's what I call real fucking," Lester admiringly announces in the midst of the Orgy, having spotted (without recognizing) George's naked sacroiliac undulating in the clasp of Jackie's thighs.

though the U.S. economy hit bottom in October 1974, the worst postwar recession was still in effect. Unemployment remained close to 9 percent, business spending collapsed. In New York City, which narrowly avoided default, even hard-hats demonstrated against the Republican administration. The disaster-movie mentality was universal. The *New York Review of Books* outlined "The Great World Crisis." *Esquire* featured a "Gala Depression Sneak Preview." "Survivor" was a key word.

The 1976 campaign had already begun—Senator Henry "Scoop" Jackson the designated front-runner in a crowded Democratic field—and *Shampoo*'s reception often made reference to Beatty's political career. One interviewer complained that the actor-producer sounds "like a candidate, dodging the big issues," while, writing in the *New York Times*, Walter Goodman made the Machiavellian suggestion that the absence of Hubert Humphrey in *Shampoo* was a factor of Beatty's current association with candidate Jackson, who was then courting Humphrey's goodwill. True, the world in *Shampoo* is plastered over with images of Nixon-Agnew while Humphrey-Muskie (let alone Wallace-LeMay) are absolutely invisible. But Nixon-Agnew also ran in 1972. And there is no way imaginable that the Beach Boys' plaintive cry "Wouldn't It Be Nice?" could ever possibly apply to Hubert Humphrey's electoral failure.

According to David Thomson, Beatty had blamed McGovern for losing the war of images with Richard Nixon and not only for losing but, perhaps worse, "for extracting such effort and dedication from himself in a losing cause."

> "The most desperate feeling in the world," [Beatty] says, "is to hope people will vote for you." . . .
> People in show business have remarked on Beatty's frustrated search for heroes, and on his remorseless need to prove himself superior to those who might be models. McGovern too falls short, and shows how anyone "right" can still fail.

Idealism only goes so far. "Lester is really great," Jackie tells George, by which she means she feels really great to wake up in the morning with her rent paid. Time for the rinse. "I don't fuck anybody for money—I do it for fun," George lectures Jackie in one of *Shampoo*'s moments of truth, and then, to underscore the depth of his reproach, he criticizes her current hairdo: "It makes you look like a hooker." For her part, Jackie accuses George of having been "too happy." The reason she left him, she says, is because she found his attitude toward life "rather unrealistic." And, in the end, she leaves him again.

If Beatty's relationship with Julie Christie was one more casualty of the 1972 campaign, the name "George" reeks of hostile familiarity—it was Hunter Thompson's observation that no one in the McGovern campaign ever addressed the candidate (or even referred to him) as anything but "Senator." When Thompson suggested that McGovern's was "a Sixties campaign [run] in the Seventies" and McGovern replied that he "might have won in 1968," they might have been dreaming of the George whom Jackie abandons. One notes, with a mixture of contempt and compassion, the forlorn presence of an acoustic guitar amid the debris of George Roundy's dingy apartment.

As George and Lester parlay amid the cheap clutter of George's living room, the televised image of victorious Richard Nixon recalls the anonymous teenager who inspired him by holding up a sign inscribed BRING US TOGETHER. The thought stirs something in Lester, who mutters that "maybe Nixon will be better." Then, as if given a glimpse into the future, he quickly adds: "What's the difference? They're all a bunch of jerks."

Freedomland 1981: Ronald Reagan and the Last Sixties Movie

Shampoo is also a relic—albeit less of Hollywood 1968 than of that brief period in the mid-1970s, coinciding roughly with the post–Oil Shock recession and the reign of America's first unelected president, Gerald Ford. This was the day of Francis Coppola's *The Conversation*, Robert Altman's *Nashville*, Arthur Penn's *Night Moves*, Steven Spielberg's *Sugarland Express*, Terrence Malick's *Badlands*, Sidney Lumet's *Dog Day Afternoon*, Martin Scorsese's *Taxi Driver*, and John Cassavetes's *A Woman Under the Influence*—all small, "serious" movies made from original screenplays and bound neither by genre nor formula. It was also a time when, thanks to Watergate and the new Congress that Watergate helped elect, the vault briefly opened and a few secrets tumbled out, despite—

or, perhaps, because of—the fact that the President was himself a surviving veteran of the Warren Commission (and, indeed, had served as an FBI informant throughout its proceedings).

The year 1974 ended with Seymour Hersh's articles in the *New York Times*, reporting on the CIA's domestic Operation CHAOS, which among other things, included wiretap and break-in surveillance on the Columbia student protests. Two days before *Shampoo* had its premiere, someone leaked the news that former CIA director Richard Helms had told a closed hearing of the Senate Foreign Relations Committee that there was "no doubt" in 1970 that President Nixon wanted Salvador Allende overthrown. A few weeks after *Shampoo* opened, and even before Senator Frank Church's Select Committee to Study Governmental Operations with Respect to Intelligence Activities decided upon its agenda, CBS newsman Daniel Schorr revealed the existence of a secret CIA report to the President on past agency involvement in various assassination plots. It was while *Shampoo* was in release that ABC's *Goodnight America* televised the full Zapruder footage for the first time—the key to the New Totality, albeit forever open to interpretation.

Held during the last half of 1975 and into 1976, the Church Committee hearings would be the source for the information on the Huston Plan, the destabilization of the Allende government, COINTELPRO, the FBI attacks on Martin Luther King, the CIA-Mafia conspiracy against Fidel Castro, and JFK's relationship with Judith Campbell. (Before the Committee could subpoena Sam Giancana, the sixty-five-year-old Chicago mobster was found dead on his kitchen floor, riddled with six slugs.) Brian De Palma's *Blow Out*, released six years after *Shampoo* in the summer of 1981, would recall that heady moment even as it marked a drastic shift in American political life—and, indeed, the corresponding change in Hollywood production, associated with the post–*Star Wars* inflation and recycling of pop-culture imagery.

An independent filmmaker in the late 1960s who had once aspired to be the American equivalent of Jean-Luc Godard, De Palma made movies that epitomized the postmodern craze for pastiche, quotation, and appropriation. *Blow Out* begins as a parody of his previous film *Dressed to Kill*—itself a "remake" of *Psycho*—and, dealing as it does with the problematic nature of mechanical reproduction, goes on to take Michelangelo Antonioni's *Blowup* and transform its premise. The protagonist, Jack Terry (John Travolta) is an audio-surveillance technician who had worked for the Philadelphia police department until an informant whom he wired with a hidden microphone was discovered and killed. Now Jack does sound work for the most egregious of independent movie genres, slasher soft-core porno. De Palma introduces his fallen hero screening one such example and laughing at the feeble scream that issues from the constricted larynx of an even more limited actress.

Antonioni's detached fashion photographer has been drastically reduced in status. In parodying *Blowup*'s pretenses, *Blow Out* criticizes the fashionable illusions of the 1960s as well as particularly American notions of freedom advanced in *Shampoo*. (De Palma, who began making movies in the *Blowup* aftermath, exhibited an earlier taste for political conspiracy in his 1968 *Greetings* and participated in the Orgy by documenting the Open Theater's *Dionysus '69*.) Where the photographer in *Blowup* was a youthful Orgy-master and the hairdresser from *Shampoo* an active, if secondary, participant, *Blow Out*'s techie is a hapless fellow traveler taken for an unexpected ride—the Orgy swirls above his head like a helicopter's rotator blades.

If, each in his way, *Blowup*'s Thomas and *Shampoo*'s George were beauticians, Jack is more of a mortician—he dresses movie corpses in the smelliest of imperial back alleys. That night, while out tape-recording sounds and otherwise eavesdropping in a suburban park, Jack witnesses a speeding automobile suffer a blown tire and consequently career off a bridge and into Wissahickon Creek. Diving in after the car, Jack is able to save the winsome female passenger, Sally (Nancy Allen), but not the driver, who turns out to be presidential candidate Governor George McRyan. "That stiff on the stretcher was probably our next president—hell, he had my vote," a hospital orderly observes. Death renders this never-seen figure Kennedyesque.

Jack has plunged deep into the dream life and salvaged something from the wreck. Immediately, McRyan's icy, high-powered aides take charge of the situation, insisting that the Governor was alone in the car and unsuccessfully pressuring Jack to agree. An extra now in his own drama, Jack befriends Sally, the supporting player written out of the script, discovering that she is a cosmetic-counter salesgirl who moonlights as a decoy for a professional Peeping Tom, blackmail photographer Manny Karp (Dennis Franz). Playing his audiotape of the accident for her, Jack detects two distinct explosions—suggesting that the blowout was the result of a gunshot and hence foul play. Now suspecting that McRyan's death was the result of a political setup, Jack weds his tape to the series of photographs capturing McRyan's fatal ride that Karp has sold to a newsweekly to produce a primitive Zapruder movie of the "accident."

As Jack pieces together one scenario, McRyan's apparent assassin, Burke (John Lithgow), is seen developing a counter-narrative. Burke is making history by destroying evidence, committing a series of murders to prepare a cover for the elimination of the key witness, Sally. His shadowy employers, some unnamed Parallax corporation, have disowned him—like Jack, Burke is a true Secret Agent, forging on alone. Although the police dismiss Jack's "movie," the soundman is contacted by television news personality Frank Donohue, who, representing the fascination that the spectacle has for itself, expresses interest in broadcasting his material. The ubiquitous Burke, however, has been tapping Jack's phone and, by impersonating Donohue, dupes Sally into meeting him. As a precaution, the increasingly paranoid Jack wires Sally with a hidden microphone and is thus nightmarishly positioned to hear that she has actually delivered herself to Burke.

Fighting his way through the garish Liberty Day celebration that clogs the streets of downtown Philadelphia, Jack arrives only to find Sally dead—although he does, in his mania, manage to kill her murderer, his evil double. A brief coda shows the soundman in a desolate landscape, surrounded by phantoms, mourning the woman whose final scream of terror he has incorporated into *Co-Ed Frenzy* and thus immortalized as an echo through the media hall of mirrors. Such is the New Totality: as Daniel Boorstin complained twenty years before, "One interview comments on another; one television show spoofs another; novel, television show, radio program, movie, comic book, and the way we think of ourselves, all become merged into mutual reflections."

• • •

Structurally, *Blow Out* breaks neatly into two parts—the ontology of the assassination and Jack Terry's inability to make this knowledge public. De Palma's circular narrative—a sort of cinematic Moebius strip—hinges upon a series of repetitions. These include not only the reprise of *Co-Ed Frenzy* and the fatal plot device of a bugging gone awry but also a transformation of *Blowup*. Looking back on the Sixties, Brian De Palma makes *Blow Out*'s central crime political and specific rather than vague and existential. (What's existential in *Blow Out* is the sense of an invisible totality.) More rigorous than Antonioni, De Palma flaunts the specifics of filmmaking by insisting on his movie as spectacle and this spectacle as construct.*

Blow Out's images draw attention to the mechanics of the medium. Sound is exposed as a material thing and a source of audience manipulation. The intensity of *Co-Ed Frenzy* is mocked when Jack bursts out laughing. A later scene shows him carefully filing various taped sounds. There are frequent close-ups of tape recorders, and the process of moviemaking is several times deconstructed. A long sequence is devoted to the assembly of a flipbook and the synchronizing of the photographed accident images to Jack's recording. De Palma several times splits the screen to juxtapose the various means of mechanical reproduction with the seamless TV image. (The television newsman is internally split, habitually referring to himself in the third person.) As self-conscious and cinephilic as De Palma

---

*Although the repressed Jack is considerably less libidinal than Thomas, the "innocent" objectification of women in *Blowup* is here something far more sinister. The critic Robin Wood points out that *Blow Out* invites the viewer to make connections between electoral and sexual politics—defining both as male contests founded upon the exploitation of women. Jack's lack of sexual interest in Sally is less the paralyzed equivalent of Thomas's noncommittal cool than an assertion of technical mastery characteristic of all the film's male characters—the manipulative Frank Donohue, sleazy Manny Karp, and, particularly, Jack's sinister doppelgänger, Burke.

is, these conceits seem less a formalist strategy for baring-the-device than a way to further suggest a disintegrating plot. It's as though the social narrative were a form of anesthetic and its tranquilizing effects were wearing off.*

The mod world of 1966 has been corroded by the events of the recent past. Everyone is a potential Zapruder. English chic is replaced by American putrefaction. Swinging London devolves into seedy, downtown Philadelphia, a city of peep shows and porn theaters. The Orgy is packaged as *Co-Ed Frenzy*. This porn-flick fantasy of college dorm as disco—complete with mirrored globe and naked go-go dancing, as well as live sex, masturbation, and inscribed voyeurism—is an image even more lurid than those Ronald Reagan conjured of Berkeley in his first campaign.

At the *Blow Out* climax, Jack drives through a spectacular patriotic parade and literally breaks the glass by crashing through one more tawdry facade— actually John Wanamaker's show window, itself filled with mannequins costumed as the American revolutionaries of 1776. De Palma had been compelled to reshoot this sequence in June after two cartons of his uncut negative footage were stolen from a van parked in midtown Manhattan. Still, no mere Yippie can disrupt the nightmare Freedomland.

The history of the world may be none other than what Hegel called the "progress of the consciousness of Freedom," but the freedom of the Sixties is identified with abuse and murder, as well as the production of soft-core slasher porn. Jack works for Independence Movies; as Burke strangles his first victim, he gazes up at the sign for the Liberty Day Jubilee; when Sally is murdered, the Liberty Bell chimes out in mindless celebration of some ritual pseudo-event. The slow-motion spectacle of her death is accentuated by exploding fireworks, lurid lighting, and the American flag.

Blow Out reiterated the conventional wisdom that recording technology has

---

*Sally in particular is a one-woman distanciation effect: Nancy Allen acts badly and speaks as though auditioning for a high school production of *Guys and Dolls*. In one gratuitous scene, she insists on applying makeup to her co-star—demonstrating, of course, the "no makeup" look. In another, she smashes a ridiculously evident "break-away bottle" over the head of her erstwhile partner, Manny Karp.

rendered reality malleable. The movie proposes that the news media naturally rescripts the scenario in the course of releasing one, two, many parallel accounts. (As Frederic Jameson would observe, "the telltale sound of the assassin's rifle shot can be excised while the documentary soundtrack of a real murder can be spliced into a fictional horror film.") Presenting American social reality as a media circus arranged for the benefit of an image-gorged audience, *Blow Out* is, in essence, De Palma's complaint—perhaps his cynical excuse for doing what he does. Travolta wants to reveal the truth, but people aren't interested; society just keeps pushing him back into his sordid little racket, dubbing the screams for *Co-Ed Frenzy*. (Even here he shows an interest in authenticity.) Oliver Stone before his time, Jack is told by the cops to save his paranoia for public television. Police, politicians, and TV newsmen—or perhaps just the TV—take charge of making History. But can the idiot newsman Frank Donohue really be The Next Voice You Hear?

Who controls the Reality Studio? Whose fantasy is projected on the screen? What does the nation decide to remember and what shall it agree to forget? If *Blow Out*—a commercial failure—struck the imagined community as yesterday's news, the difference was that one citizen's star-spangled hangover was another's glorious "Morning in America." But this is the projection of another narrative.

A retrospective of Sixties concerns, *Blow Out* is less a scenario than a myth. In this overwhelmingly bleak and tawdry film, the Kennedy assassinations, the Watergate scandal, the death car at Chappaquidick, the Son of Sam serial killings that had recently terrorized New York, the life and death of the Orgy, are all conjoined in one ultra-paranoid conspiracy. Our public movie set is governed by an unknowable system whose hidden operations are impossible to name or represent—even as something as vague as the Parallax Corporation—except in the person of a single rogue operative.

Conceived, according to its author, in the aftermath of the Watergate revelations, *Blow Out* was shot and released during the triumph of the Orgy's greatest and most resilient foe. Brian De Palma's most expensive movie to date had gone into production in Philadelphia the weekend before the 1980 election.

The fireworks that illuminated the sky during the climactic killings were staged by the same firm that, only days before, had created a similar display in Washington for the new President's inauguration. Our President at last, Ronald Reagan came through the Sixties with his agenda intact. Reagan would restore a lost authority. He would rewrite the narrative. (Frank Church had been defeated in the same election that brought the former California governor to the White House.)

"It cannot be emphasized too strongly that it was pleasure which was the enemy that Reaganomics was designed to defeat," psychohistorian Lloyd deMause wrote in his media analysis of Reagan's first term.

> During the first few weeks of Reagan's presidency, the [media] imagery of the bloody axing of people and their coming howls of pain seemed to be just what we needed to embody our growing rage. The most important way we asked Reagan to embody our violence was by asking him to effect a military buildup three times as large as that of Vietnam.

The new President had been given a mandate. But first, he would be required to survive his own trial by ordeal. From the day of Reagan's election, Americans articulated a belief that their new and elderly leader would not live out his term. This superstitious scenario originated in the coincidence that, beginning with William Henry Harrison in 1840 and ending with JFK in 1960, every American president elected or reelected in a year ending with a zero had died in office.

The collective fantasy would climax in late March when, deMause pointed out, the media proclaimed a new epidemic of lawlessness in America. Had Bonnie and Clyde risen from the grave? Or Sweetback returned to collect his dues? Did we still need Dirty Harry?*

---

*In late March, both *Time* and *Newsweek* ran near-identical cover stories on this Sixties flashback, while *The New Republic*'s cover represented the Washington Mall as Boot Hill. The hypervigilant members of the Institute for Psychohistory found so many such "hidden messages to shoot the president" in the hundreds of periodicals they analyzed that concern for Reagan's safety was voiced at a meeting that week. DeMause further

• • •

September 1980: John Hinkley Jr.—a twenty-six-year-old college dropout, sometime American Nazi, and obsessed fan of the movie *Taxi Driver* and its disturbed protagonist Travis Bickle—goes out looking for America. Stalking first President Carter and then President-elect Reagan, Hinkley is also trailing actress Jodie Foster, who, nominated for an Oscar after playing a twelve-year-old prostitute in *Taxi Driver*, has begun her freshman year at Yale.

December 8, another crazed fan, twenty-five-year-old ex-security guard and onetime Jesus freak Mark Chapman shoots and kills John Hinkley's idol, John Lennon, as the ex-Beatle enters his New York City apartment. One more Sixties icon fails to survive. Pushed further toward the abyss, Hinkley spends the winter shuttling between New Haven (where he shadows the woman he calls "Jodie Foster, Superstar" around the Yale campus), Washington, DC (where he cases both the White House and the office of Senator Edward Kennedy), New York City (where he visits the site of Lennon's assassination), Dallas (where he buys guns), and his parents' home in Denver. It is while Hinkley is hunkered down in a Denver motel, checked in under the name "J. Travis," that the new President reveals the magnitude of his program. There will be huge "supply-side" tax cuts, along with a correspondingly massive $1.3 trillion boost in defense spending.

March 25, 1981, Hinkley flies to Hollywood, stays one day, and purchases a bus ticket to New Haven, by way of Washington. Arriving in the capital five days later, he picks up the *Washington Star* and sees the President's schedule. This, he will later tell a psychiatrist, was the signal. And so it came to pass that an unhappy young fan, obsessed with a movie that had been inspired in

---

cites an upsurge in violent newspaper headlines and the *U.S. News & World Report* cover on which "Angry Americans" were shown tumbling into an abyss as an indifferent father-figure towered above them, with its "subliminal suggestion" in the headline $60 BILLION OF FEDERAL WASTE—REAGAN'S NEXT TARGET to "waste Reagan." He notes that at least one other person picked up the messages as Secretary of Defense Alexander Haig argued with other administration officials about who would take charge should the President be incapacitated.

part by the case of the would-be George Wallace assassin Arthur Bremer and hoping to impress the actress who had starred in that movie, shoots the first professional movie star to become President of Freedomland, U.S.A.

Instantaneous and ineffable national flashback! Nostalgia for the festival of the JFK assassination gives way to a new festival. The media celebrates Ronald Reagan's remarkable good humor and personal strength as evidence of a new national spirit, if not a divine miracle "Ronald Reagan shot was, in many ways, better than Ronald Reagan unshot," a key presidential adviser, Lyn Nofziger, would recall. Overwhelmed by the President's dramatic reappearance at a joint session of Congress, Democrats line up behind the Reagan economic recovery package. Already, individuals who advocated the destruction of various government agencies have been put in charge of precisely those agencies—including the Departments of Energy, Human Services, and the Interior, the Environmental Protection Agency, and the Occupational Safety and Health Administration. By summer, congressional Democrats sign onto the Reagan defense program, even while the President sends word to sympathetic Central American politicians that he intends to topple the perceived Castro surrogate regime in Nicaragua.

A vacancy has opened and an idea has once again burst out of the darkness. America finds a new leading man. Elvis blurs with Nixon, JFK, and AuH_2O combine. Bonnie and Clyde are dead at the Alamo, but Davy Crockett dances in the dream life with Dirty Harry. Eldridge Cleaver and Patty Hearst will join the Republican Party. The spectacle is reoriented: *A Face in the Crowd* gives way to A Smiley Face in the White House.

While *Blow Out* is in release, the President fires the striking air controllers and, in a no less carefully stage-managed showdown, American F-14 Tomcats shoot down two Libyan jets over the Gulf of Sidra. Reagan had been asleep, perhaps even dreaming, during the incident. But, according to the *Chicago Tribune*, when he awakes and after he is briefed, the President greets his aides with a performance, miming the quick-draw of a Western gunslinger. Thanks to the Secret Agent of History, the Hollywood Freedom Fighter had returned.

There is a new collective memory and a new representation, as well as a new representative, of the national past. America's president is an artist: Ronald Reagan, master of the hyperreal, remaker of history, is Kennedy without tears, John Wayne without Vietnam, a plain-talking Norman Mailer, an affable Dirty Harry, the greatest of all Sixties Survivors.*

---

*In the run up to the 1996 presidential campaign that pit Sixties foe Senator Bob Dole against Sixties personification Bill Clinton, the Ronald Reagan Presidential Library and Museum in Simi Valley, California, created its own Freedomland with an exhibit entitled "Back to the '60s." The logo employed a peace symbol for the zero in "'60s." The day-long "fun-in" that opened the show included Beatles imitators, opportunities to make psychedelic tie-dye T-shirts, and a contest for the best hippie costume. "It was," Jon Weiner reported, "as if the former president's Alzheimer's had spread to his museum as well." Like Reagan's, the library's sense of history was determined by the movies.

Source Notes

INTRODUCTION

Siegfried Kracauer, "The Group as Bearer of Ideas," in Thomas Y. Levin, ed., *The Mass Ornament: Weimar Essays* (Cambridge, MA: Harvard University Press, 1995), 143.

On the "Black Book," Gene Grove, *Inside the John Birch Society* (Greenwich, CT: Gold Medal, 1961), 19–33; *Time*, August 10, 1959, 24–25; Norman Mailer, "Superman Comes to the Supermarket," *The Presidential Papers of Norman Mailer* (New York: Bantam, 1964), 43, 38.

I. MAKING PRE-HISTORY, A.D. 1960

Time, July 11, 1960, 33; "Freedomland in the Bronx," *New York Times*, June 12, 1960, II2, 1ff; "A Satellite From Another World May Be in Orbit, Scientist Says," *New York Times*, June 20, 1960, 1ff; "A 'New Look' on Arms Opposed As a Pointless Propaganda Move," *New York Times*, June 19, 1960, 5; on the Minutemen, William W. Turner, *Power on the Right* (Berkeley, CA: Ramparts, 1971), 68; Tad Szulc, "Shadowy Power Behind Castro," *New York Times Magazine*, June 19, 1960, 5ff; "Autos Jam Roads to Freedomland," *New York Times*, June 20, 1960, 25; Gary Kyriazi, *The Great American Amusement Parks* (Secaucus, NJ: Castle, 1978), 179.

Spartacus ad, *New York Times*, June 19, 1960; Arthur M. Schlesinger, Jr., *The Vital Center: The Politics of Freedom* (Boston: Houghton Mifflin, 1949), 228–29.

FN on p. 4: Naomi Mitchison, "Marxist Rome," *New Statesman and Nation*, March 18, 1939, 436.

Enter the Hollywood Freedom Fighter

On Kennedy and the movies, Garry Wills, *The Kennedy Imprisonment* (Boston: Little, Brown, 1982), 20–25; Kennedy and Grace Kelly, Michael R. Beschloss, *The Crisis Years:*

Kennedy and Khrushchev 1960–1963 (New York: HarperCollins, 1991), 472; Kennedy voted handsomest, Dale Carter, *The Final Frontier* (London: Verso, 1988), 135; "Senator Kennedy Goes A-Courting," *Life*, July 20, 1953; "Sequel: The Senator Weds," *Life*, September 28, 1953; Kennedys on *Person to Person*, J. Fred MacDonald, *Television and the Red Menace: The Video Road to Vietnam* (New York: Praeger, 1985), 149; Kennedy's car mobbed, Carter, 136.

Newsweek, April 18, 1955; Siegfried Kracauer, "The Group as Bearer of Ideas," in Thomas Y. Levin, ed. *The Mass Ornament: Weimer Essays* (Cambridge, MA: Harvard University Press, 1995), 148; financing *The Alamo*, Maurice Zolotow, *Shooting Star: A Biography of John Wayne* (New York: Pocket Books, 1979), 325; Matthews report quoted in Tad Szulc, *Fidel: A Critical Portrait* (New York: Morrow, 1986), 413; Castro's guerrilla theater, Szulc, 409, and Van Gosse, *Where the Boys Are: Cuba, Cold War America and the Making of a New Left* (London: Verso, 1993), 82–83; *Business Week*, October 2, 1954; *Business Week*, November 3, 1956.

FN on p. 8: Margaret J. King, "The Recycled Hero: Walt Disney's Davy Crockett," and Charles K. Wolfe, "Davy Crockett Songs: Minstrels to Disney," *Davy Crockett: The Man, the Legend, the Legacy, 1786–1986* (Knoxville: University of Tennessee Press, 1985), 148, 182; FN on p. 9: Frances Stonor Saunders, *The Cultural Cold War: The CIA and the World of Art and Letters* (New York: The New Press, 1999), 284–85; FN 2 on p. 10: Vosse, 94.

Sputnik and the Specter of Communist Earth Control

Democrats' response to Sputnik and the *New York Times*' response to Johnson, Robert Sherrill, *The Accidental President* (New York: Grossman Publishers, 1967), 125; Gaither report, Martin Walker, *The Cold War: A History* (New York: Henry Holt, 1993), 115; Teller in J. Ronald Oakley, *God's Country: America in the Fifties* (New York: Dembner Books, 1986), 344.

Schlesinger, 230; Wayne as agnostic, Zolotow, 317; *Variety*, September 22, 1959; Richard M. Nixon, *Six Crises* (New York: Pyramid, 1968), 228; William J. Lederer and Eugene Burdick, *The Ugly American* (New York: Crest, 1963), 227.

Time, January 19, 1959, 36–37; *Life*, January 12, 1959; *Life*, January 19, 1959; Castro interviews, Gosse, 110–11; "Castro Biopic via Jerry Wald," *Variety*, April 29, 1959, 1; *Time*, January 26, 1959, 40–41; *Time*, February 2, 1959, 28–29; on Castro's PR firm, Carlos Franqui, *Family Portrait With Fidel* (New York: Random House, 1984), 31; Castro in New Jersey, Aleksandr Fursenko and Timothy Naftali, *"One Hell of a Gamble": Khrushchev, Castro, and Kennedy, 1958–1964* (New York: W. W. Norton, 1997), 10; *Life*, April 13, 1959; *Life*, November 16, 1959; CIA plan, Fursenko and Naftali, 40.

FN on p. 14: *Time*, February 25, 1957; *Time*, March 4, 1957; *Time*, July 8, 1957; FN on p. 15: Dulles, Herbert S. Parmet, *Eisenhower and the American Crusades* (New York: Macmillan, 1972), 540; FN on p. 16: *Newsweek*, March 9, 1959.

When Superman Came to the Supermarket

"Wayne Hits 'Garbage' on Screen," *Hollywood Reporter*, January 11, 1960; Wayne joins John Birch Society, Randy Roberts and James S. Olson, *John Wayne: American* (New York: Free Press, 1995), 568; "Democrats: Man Out Front," *Time*, December 2, 1957, 17; Joseph Kennedy remarks cited, Frank L. Kluckhohn, *America: Listen!* (Derby, CT: Monarch, 1962), 141–42; Rovere on Nixon, Vance Packard, *The Hidden Persuaders* (New York: Pocket Books, 1958), 164.

"Democrats: Jet-Powered Bandwagon," *Time*, July 4, 1960, 12; on cost of Wayne's *Life* ad, *New York Herald-Tribune*, July 5, 1960; Norman Mailer, "Superman Comes to the Supermarket," *The Presidential Papers of Norman Mailer* (New York: Bantam, 1964), 28, 38, 59; Kennedy's rhetoric quoted in "The Convention: To the New Frontier," *Time*, July 25, 1960, 10; Beschloss, 25; Kennedy's Alamo scenario, Kathleen Hall Jamieson, *Packaging the Presidency*, third edition (New York: Oxford University Press, 1996), 132–34; CIA-Mafia plot, Beschloss, 135–37, and Seymour M. Hersh, *The Dark Side of Camelot* (Boston: Little Brown, 1997), 162–68.

"The Weirdest, Jazziest Session," *Newsweek*, September 12, 1960, 39, 36–37; "Polls: The Power of Foreign Affairs," *Time*, July 18, 1960, 14; Khrushchev's press conference, *New York Times*, September 22, 1960, 11, and *Newsweek*, October 3, 1960, 24; Saul Bellow, "Literary Notes on Khruschev," *Smiling Through the Apocalypse: Esquire's History of the Sixties*, Harold Hayes, ed. (New York: Crown, 1987), 173ff; Wayne cited in Roberts and Olson, 473.

David Halberstam, *The Fifties* (New York: Villard, 1993), 732; Theodore White, *The Making of the President 1960* (New York: Pocket Books, 1961), 395, 396.

FN 2 on p. 22: Beschloss, 139–43; Kitty Kelly, *His Way: The Unauthorized Biography of Frank Sinatra* (New York: Bantam, 1986), 295; James Spada, *Peter Lawford: The Man Who Kept the Secrets* (New York: Bantam, 1991), 227. FN on p. 24: Vosse, 151.

October 1960

Worker, December 18, 1960; "Labor Boosterism Aids 'Spartacus,'" *Variety*, January 18, 1961; American Legion attacks and Hedda Hopper quote, Kirk Douglas, *The Ragman's Son, An Autobiography* (New York: Simon & Schuster, 1988), 332; DAR salute to *Spartacus*, Jeffrey Smith, "A Good Business Proposition: Dalton Trumbo, Spartacus, and the End of the Blacklist," *The Velvet Light Trap* 23, Spring 1989, 92; *Time*, October 24, 1960, 102.

Wayne using *The Alamo* to "sell America," Louella Parsons, *Los Angeles Herald-Examiner*, October 23, 1960; Wayne on democracy, Thomas G. Morgan, "God and Man in Hollywood," *Esquire*, May 1963, 124.

For background regarding Kennedy's knowledge about and Nixon's role in U.S. policy toward Cuba, Beschloss, 135–7, Halberstam, 726–9, and Hersh, 178–81; Robert Kennedy's anonymous tip, Hersh, 182; *The Alamo* reviewed *Newsweek*, November 7,

1960, and *Time*, November 7, 1960; Castro's beliefs regarding American attack and statement to *Hoy*, Fursenko and Naftali, 70–71.

FN on p. 30: Giancana bragging, Hersh, 166; FN 1 on p. 31: Chase in Morgan, 124; Gene Grove, *Inside the John Birch Society* (Greenwich, CT: Gold Medal, 1961), 120, 84–85, 114.

The Year's Best Western

Richard Slotkin, *Gunfighter Nation* (New York: Atheneum, 1992), 474. I am indebted to Slotkin's analysis throughout. *Time*, December 12, 1960, 96. Schlesinger in Slotkin, 501–03. For the Peace Corps and the Ugly American see John Hellman, *American Myth and the Legacy of Vietnam* (New York: Columbia University Press, 1966), 4; "Open Letter to John Fitzgerald Kennedy and Fidel Castro," with introduction detailing the circumstances under which it was written, *The Presidential Papers of Norman Mailer* (New York: Bantam, 1964), 63–79. Khrushchev's speech and Kennedy's response, Fursenko and Naftali, 73, 78; Kennedy imagines Castro, Wills, 263; Marx's letter cited by Maria Wyke, *Projecting the Past: Ancient Rome, Cinema, and History* (New York: Routledge, 1947), 47–48; "Kennedy Attends Movie in Capital," *New York Times*, February 5, 1961. CIA invasion plans, Fursenko and Naftali, 84ff.

FN on p. 34: Gingrich on *The Magnificent Seven*, "The Long March of Newt Gingrich," *Frontline* (WGBH, January 16, 1996).

II. GLAMOUR AND ANXIETY

Norman Mailer, "The Leading Man: A review of *JFK: The Man and the Myth*," *Cannibals and Christians* (New York: Dell, 1967), 169-70; Daniel Boorstin, *THE IMAGE; or, What Happened to the American Dream* (New York: Atheneum, 1962), 5, 183, 258; Max Kozloff, " 'Pop' Culture, Metaphysical Disgust, and the New Vulgarians," *Art International* (March 1962), 35; *Newsweek*, October 10, 1960, 24.

Barbie Zelizer, *Covering the Body: The Kennedy Assassination, the Media, and the Shaping of Collective Memory* (Chicago: University of Chicago, 1992), 22; Gore Vidal, *Palimpsest: A Memoir* (New York: Penguin, 1996), 310. Erik Barnouw, *Documentary: A History of the Non-Fiction Film* (New York: Oxford University Press, 1974), 236; Novak cited, Frank L. Kluckhohn, *America: Listen!* (Derby, CT: Monarch, 1962), 142; Documentary Records ad, *New York Times*, February 19, 1961; press conference mise-en-scène, Zelizer, 25; on Drew moving into the White House, Mary Ann Watson, *The Expanding Vista: American Television in the Kennedy Years* (Durham, NC: Duke University Press, 1994), 132.

FN on p. 40: Joyce Hoffman, "How One Brief Shining Moment Became Eternal," *Washington Post National Weekly Edition*, May 29–June 4, 1995, 25.

Camelot Year One

Mailer, "The Leading Man,", 169; Jack Gould, "Disturbing Khrushchev TV Interview," *New York Times*, October 11, 1960; Boorstin, 40.

Peter Kornbluh, ed., *Bay of Pigs Declassified: The Secret CIA Report on the Invasion of Cuba* (New York: The New Press, 1998), 52, 55; Tad Szulc and Karl E. Meyers, *The Cuban Invasion: The Chronicle of a Disaster* (New York: Ballantine, 1992), 8; on Castro's show, see Szulc & Meyers, 144; and Michael R. Beschloss, *The Crisis Years: Kennedy and Khrushchev 1960–1963* (New York: HarperCollins, 1991), 118; McNamara in James W. Hilty, *Robert Kennedy, Brother Protector* (Philadelphia: Temple University Press, 1997), 419; Kennedy on war, Beschloss, 235; well-placed source, Aleksandr Fursenko and Timothy Naftali, *"One Hell of a Gamble": Khrushchev, Castro, and Kennedy, 1958–1964* (New York: W. W. Norton, 1997), 155; Isabelle Moore, *The Day the Communists Took Over America* (New York: Wisdom House, 1961), 7, 10; "Kennedy Calls for 217,000 Men and 3.4 Billion Fund to Meet 'World-Wide' Threat by Soviet," *New York Times*, July 26, 1961, 1.

One, Two, Three, see J. Hoberman, *The Red Atlantis* (Philadelphia: Temple University Press, 1997), 201–03; "war of nerves," *Time*, September 29, 1961; *Life*, September 15, 1961; *U.S. News & World Report*, September 25, 1961; Bradlee and Sulzberger in Beschloss, 308, 320; Robert Lowell, "Fall 1961," *Life Studies and For the Union Dead* (New York: Noonday, 1967), 11; Preminger's promise, "Capitolians Agog, Seek Bit Parts, As Advise & Consent Rolls There Sept. 1," *Variety*, July 19, 1961, 1; *Time*, September 29, 1961, 69; blessing *The Manchurian Candidate* and Condon, Kitty Kelley, *His Way: The Unauthorized Biography of Frank Sinatra* (New York: Bantam, 1987), 319–20; on the "Black Book," Gene Grove, *Inside the John Birch Society* (Greenwich, CT: Gold Medal, 1961), 19–33; Axelrod quoted, *Los Angeles Times*, February 12, 1988; Sinatra interview, *The Manchurian Candidate* (MGM/UA Homevideo) VHS tape.

FN 1 on p. 46: Boorstin, 41; FN 2 on p. 46: CIA plans, Fursenko and Naftali, 84–85. FN on p. 51: President briefed, Beschloss, 309; FN on p. 52: Terry Teachout, "Where Have You Gone, Orrin Knox? The Decline of the Washington Novel," *New York Times Book Review*, August 27, 1995, 17.

Camelot Year Two

"Success Sure for Novel; Khrushchev Is the Hero," *New York Times*, January 28, 1962; Sidey in Watson, 76; "sweetie," Erwin Kim, *Franklin J. Schaffner* (Metuchen, NJ: Scarecrow Press, 1985), 150; Kennedy casting *PT 109*, Pierre Salinger, *With Kennedy* (Garden City, NY: Doubleday, 1966), 103–04; screen tests described, "20 Years After: *PT 109*," *Life*, May 17, 1963, 99; Joseph Laitin, "Brash and Rumpled Star," *Saturday Evening Post*, July 14–21, 1962; Beatty interview, "Politics and Other Dirty Words," *George*, January 1996, 182; Beatty's childhood ambition, David Thomson, *Warren Beatty and Desert Eyes: A Life and a Story* (Garden City, NY: Doubleday, 1987), 32; Beatty on atmosphere, Tag Gallagher, "Warren Beatty: The Stud as a Thoughtful Man," *Village Voice*, February 24, 1975, 60; Beatty's refusal to work with Foy and Foy's remarks, Salinger, 104; Peter Fonda, *Don't Tell Dad: A Memoir* (New York: Hyperion, 1998), 160.

Combat situation, Fursenko and Naftali, 148; timetable, Hilty, 425; "A Death in Georgetown: The Unsolved Killing of Mary Meyer," *Counterpunch*, July 16-31, 1996, 3–6.

Thurmond quoted, *Time*, March 30, 1962, 13; *Sunday Express* review cited, *Variety*, June 6, 1962; *L'Humanité* review cited, "Preminger in the Middle," *New York Herald-Tribune*, June 3, 1962; Murrow in Murray Schumach, *The Face on the Cutting Room Floor: The Story of Movie and Television Censorship* (New York: Morrow, 1964), 114; Fleming on Castro, Beschloss, 134–35; *Newsweek*, April 13, 1964, 94; casting Bond, Alexander Walker, *Hollywood, England: The British Film Industry in the Sixties* (London: Harrap, 1986), 187–88; Alsop and Khrushchev in Beschloss, 371, 373; rumor, *New York Times*, April 5, 1962, and Julian Smith, *Looking Away: Hollywood and Vietnam* (New York: Scribners, 1975), 83.

Khrushchev's fear, Beschloss, 409; Fulbright targeted, William W. Turner, *Power on the Right* (Berkeley, CA: Ramparts, 1971), 71; Lewis quoted in "Traitors (Future) on U.S. General Staff in Screen Version of 'Seven Days,' *Variety*, October 17, 1962; *Time*, October 19, 1962.

LeMay, Ernest R. May and Philip D. Zelikow, eds., *The Kennedy Tapes: Inside the White House During the Cuban Missile Crisis* (Cambridge, MA: Harvard University Press, 1997), 178; Kennedy asks wife, Beschloss, 476; Kennedy calls *Times*, Fursenko and Naftali, 238; Russell in May and Zelikow, 265; *Variety* in Mary Ann Watson, *The Expanding Vista: American Television in the Kennedy Years* (Durham, NC: Duke, 1994), 87; Norman Mailer, "The Big Bite—April 1963," *The Presidential Papers of Norman Mailer* (New York: Bantam, 1964), 159.

FN on p. 63: Totterdale report, Document 93, David Culbert, ed., *Film and Propaganda in America: A Documentary History* (New York: Greenwood Press, 1990), 290–91; FN on p. 64: marijuana, Thomas Brown, *JFK: History of an Image* (Bloomington, IN: University of Indiana Press, 1988), 75; FN on p. 65: *Overseas Weekly* in "Gen. Edwin Walker, 83, Is Dead; Promoted Rightist Causes in 60's," *New York Times*, November 2, 1993; Fulbright's concern, Tristram Coffin, *Senator Fulbright: Portrait of a Public Philosopher* (New York: Dutton, 1966), 155–56.

The Manchurian Candidate

Howard Thompson, "We'll Bury You," *New York Times*, October 15, 1962, 48; "War Clouds Bop B'way B.O. But 'Candidate' Boff 48G," *Variety*, October 31, 1962, 9; Smith, 86; Edward Hunter, *Brainwashing* (New York: Pyramid, 1961); Jacques Ellul, *Propaganda: The Formation of Men's Attitudes* (New York: Vintage, 1973), 313.

"Commie Sheet Joins Am. Legion Attack on Sinatra Film," *Daily Variety*, December 18, 1962; Brendan Gill, *New Yorker*, November 3, 1962; Bosley Crowther, "Twisting Truth," *New York Times*, November 4, 1962, II, 1; 'Manchurian' Not Good Yank Image to Paris Critics,' *Variety*, December 19, 1962; Andrew Sarris, "Film Fantasies, Left and Right," *Film Culture*, Fall 1964, 34; *Time*, July 13, 1959; *Newsweek*, October 1, 1962, 82.

FN on p. 70: *Variety*, October 17, 1962; Frankenheimer in Charles Higham and Joel Greenberg, The *Celluloid Muse: Hollywood Directors Speak* (London: Angus and Robertson,

1969), 81; "anti-anti-Communism gone crazy," *Variety*, October 24, 1962. FN 2 on p. 72: Ronald Reagan with Richard G. Hubler, *Where's the Rest of Me?* (New York: Duell, Sloane, and Pearce), 248. FN on p. 74: Sinatra pulled *Manchurian Candidate*, "1962's 'Manchurian Candidate' to Reopen Via MGM/UA, Sinatra," *Variety*, November 25, 1987; dispute with UA, "'Manchurian Candidate,' Old Failure Is Now a Hit," *New York Times*, February 24, 1988.

Camelot Down

LeMay in Beschloss, 544; Kirk Douglas, *The Ragman's Son, An Autobiography* (New York: Simon & Schuster, 1988), 349; Frankenheimer in Tony Thomas, *The Films of Kirk Douglas* (Secaucus, NJ: Citadel, 1972), 200–1; Herman Kahn, *Thinking About the Unthinkable* (New York: Avon, 1964), 42–43; Eugene Burdick and Harvey Wheeler, "Preface," *Fail-Safe* (New York: Dell, 1964), 6; Sidney Hook, *The Fail-Safe Fallacy* (New York: Stein and Day, 1963), 11, 5; LeMay encourages Bartlett, Suid, 190; "Sick SAC," *Time*, July 22, 1963; Diem's ouster, Hersh, 414.

King on Birmingham, Theodore H. White, *The Making of the President 1964* (New York: Signet, 1966), 204; Dan T. Carter, *The Politics of Rage: George Wallace, the Origins of the New Conservatism, and the Transformation of American Politics* (New York: Simon & Schuster, 1995), 146; *Time*, June 28, 1963, 82; "Boston Responds to a Boston Boy," *Variety*, June 26, 1963; polls cited, Beschloss, 642; For press response to *Crisis*, see Stephen Mamber, *Cinema Verité in America: Studies in Uncontrolled Documentary* (Cambridge, MA: MIT Press, 1974), 106, 111, and Watson, 149–52; Tom Wicker, "Kennedy Focuses Upon Goldwater," *New York Times*, November 21, 1963, 1; Ben Bradlee, *Conversations with Kennedy* (New York: W. W. Norton, 1975), 222.

FN on p. 80: See Suid, 190–92, 210–22; *Time*, May 2, 1955; *Variety*, March 30, 1955.

Coups d'Etat

Frederic Jameson, *Postmodernism, Or, the Cultural Logic of Late Capitalism* (Durham, NC: Duke University Press, 1991), 355; "Kennedy's Death Affects Movies," *New York Times*, November 30, 1963; "Warner to Reissue Film About Kennedy," *New York Times*, February 19, 1964; on *Bishop Show*, Watson, 224; Hazel Flynn, "Was 'Manchurian' Film A Prophet?," *Hollywood Citizen-News*, November 28, 1963; Hunt's radio show, Robert Sherrill, *The Accidental President* (New York: Grossman, 1967), 139; black-bordered ad, David E. Scheim, *Contract on America: The Mafia Murder of President John F. Kennedy* (New York: Zebra Books, 1988), 210–11.

Bosley Crowther, "Seven Days in May," *New York Times*, February 20, 1964, 22.

Dr. Strangelove's Prescription

Committee on Social Issues, *Psychiatric Aspects of the Prevention of Nuclear War* (New York: Group for the Advancement of Psychiatry, 1964), 239; Johnson astonished, Leo Janos, "The Last Days of the President," *Atlantic Monthly*, July 1973, 39; Michael Bechloss,

"The Day That Changed America," *Newsweek*, November 22, 1993, 92; Mumford letter, *New York Times*, March 1, 1964; Robert Brustein, "Out of This World," *New York Review of Books*, February 6, 1964, 3–4; Susan Sontag, "Theater, Etc.," *Partisan Review*, Spring 1964, 291; Andy Warhol, *POPism: The Warhol '60s* (New York: Harcourt Brace Jovanovich, 1980), 69; "ugly guerrilla war," *Time*, March 27, 1964; *Time*, March 20, 1964; Robert Benton and David Newman "The New Sentimentality," *Esquire*, July 1964, 25–31.

SOUTH BY SOUTHWEST

William Walton's mission and Polish intelligence, Aleksandr Fursenko and Timothy Naftali, *"One Hell of a Gamble": Khrushchev, Castro, and Kennedy, 1958–1964* (New York: W. W. Norton, 1997), 344–45, 348–49.

FN on p. 96: Youngstein and Vidal in Joseph McBride, *Frank Capra: The Catastrophe of Success* (New York: Simon & Schuster, 1993), 641–42.

Jet-Age Bronco Busters and Twilight Westerns

"Goldwater Backers Increase in Texas, Along With Republican Strength," *New York Times*, September 17, 1963, 22; *Houston Chronicle* poll, Robert Sherrill, *The Accidental President* (New York: Grossman, 1967), 124; *Women's Wear Daily*, March 2, 1939; Goldwater's "natural step," Robert Alan Goldberg, *Barry Goldwater* (New Haven: Yale University Press, 1995), 587; Goldwater's aim, Richard Hofstadter, *The Paranoid Style in American Politics and Other Essays* (New York: Vintage, 1967), 98; *Time*, April 22, 1957; Goldwater as "salesman," *Time*, June 23, 1961; Hofstadter, 100; Stewart Alsop, "Can Goldwater Win in 1964?," *Saturday Evening Post*, August 24, 1963, 157; *Business Week*, March 25, 1961; *Time*, June 23, 1961; Gore Vidal, "Barry Goldwater: A Chat," *Homage to Daniel Shays: Collected Essays 1952–72* (New York: Vintage, 1973), 107; *New York Times*, May 14, 1962, 32; *Time*, February 10, 1961; *Time*, June 23, 1961; Norman Mailer, "In the Red Light: A History of the Republican Convention in 1964," *Cannibals and Christians* (New York: Dell, 1967), 12.

Philip French, *Westerns* (New York: Viking, 1974), 29–30; *Newsweek*, January 20, 1964.

Variety, October 23, 1963; *Time*, November 15, 1963; Pauline Kael, *I Lost It at the Movies* (New York: Bantam, 1966), 73; Bosley Crowther, *New York Times*, April 1, 1963; French, 138.

Goldwater in Goldman, 260; *Time*, April 10, 1964.

FN on p. 103: *Time*, June 1, 1962; FN on p. 107: Carl Oglesby, *The Yankee and Cowboy War: Conspiracies From Dallas to Watergate* (Kansas City, MO: Sheed Andrews and McMeel, 1976), 5.

The Cowboy Election of 1964

Stan Steiner, *The New Indians* (New York: Delta, 1968), 240; Goldwater on "the so-called liberal," Eric F. Goldman, *The Tragedy of Lyndon Johnson* (New York: Dell, 1969), 259; Robert Benton and David Newman "The New Sentimentality," *Esquire*, July 1964,

30; Wallace solicits support, Jody Carlson, *George C. Wallace and the Politics of Power-lessness: The Wallace Campaign for the Presidency, 1964–1976* (New Brunswick, NJ: Trans-action Books, 1981), 28; Mailer, 34; Theodore H. White, *The Making of the President 1964* (New York: Signet, 1966), 280; "the topic," Hugh Kenner, "Understanding McLuhan," in Raymond Rosenthal, ed., *McLuhan Pro & Con* (Baltimore: Penguin, 1969), 24; Dwight Macdonald, *Book Week*, June 7, 1997; *Time*, July 3, 1964; Leary on LSD, Martin A. Lee and Bruce Shlain, *Acid Dreams: The CIA, LSD and the Sixties Rebellion* (New York: Grove Press, 1985), 108; Marshall McLuhan, *Understanding Media: The Extensions of Man* (New York: Signet, 1964), 275.

White, 252; *"I've Got a Secret* organized by Caligula," White, 337; Johnson's com-plaint, Michael R. Beschloss, "The Johnson Tapes," *Time*, October 13, 1997, 62; Gold-man, 277–77; Youngstein refused assistance, Lawrence H. Suid, *Guts and Glory: The Making of the American Military Image in Film* (Lexington: University of Kentucky, 2002), 236–37; "The Unconscious of a Conservative: Special Issue on the Mind of Barry Gold-water," *Fact*, September–October 1964; Johnson on nuclear casualties, *Time*, September 25, 1964; Humphrey to Moyers, Suid, 239; Mailer, "A Second Open Letter to JFK," *The Presidential Papers of Norman Mailer* (New York: Bantam, 1964), 113; Andrew Sarris, "Film Fantasies, Left and Right," *Film Culture*, Fall 1964, 34.

Clif White memo, Samuel G. Freedman, "The First Days of the Loaded Political Image," *New York Times*, September 1, 1996, 30; Otis Carney letter, *New York Times*, September 22, 1996; "A Time for Choosing," Robert Dallek, *Ronald Reagan: The Politics of Symbolism* (Cambridge, MA: Harvard University Press, 1984), 28.

FN on p. 110: Tom Wolfe, *The Electric Kool-Aid Acid Test* (New York: Bantam, 1969), 69; FN on p. 119: French, 30.

Major Dundee—Great Society Abroad

Bundy memo in Irving Bernstein, *Guns or Butter: The Presidency of Lyndon Johnson* (New York: Oxford University Press, 1996), 344; "Text of the President's Address on U.S. Policies in Vietnam,'" *New York Times*, April 8, 1965, 16; "ugly," "brutal," "gory," "pessimistic," *New York Times*, April 8, 1965, 45.

Commonweal, April 16, 1965; Antonin Artaud, *The Theater and its Double* (New York: Grove Press, 1958), 126; "They Die on Cue for Cash," *Life*, March 26, 1965; Dawson's fear and Heston's intervention, David Weddle, *"If They Move . . . Kill 'Em!" The Life and Times of Sam Peckinpah* (New York: Grove Press, 1964), 236, 240; Heston on the Union, Michael Munn, *Charlton Heston* (New York: St. Martin's, 1986), 126.

Newsweek, May 3, 1965; Johnson to National Security Council, Goldman, 467; Rubin recalls, Hilary Mills, *Mailer: A Biography* (New York: Harper & Row, 1982), 291; Norman Mailer, "A Speech at Berkeley on Vietnam Day," *Cannibals and Christians*, 82; "breaking the glass" and "life-actor," Peter Coyote, *Sleeping Where I Fall* (Washington, DC: Coun-terpoint, 1998), 33; R. G. Davis, "Guerrilla Theater: 1965," *The San Francisco Mime Troup: The First Ten Years* (Palo Alto, CA: Ramparts, 1975), 150; Mailer, "A Speech," 79;

Charlton Heston, *The Actor's Life: Journals 1956–1976*, ed. Hollis Alpert (New York: Dutton, 1978), 228. For other accounts see Goldman, 558-59 and Macdonald 154; Barbara Delatiner, "College Campus Confusing, So Is Show," *Newsday*, June 15, 1965.

FN on p. 125: On L. H. McNelly see Ronnie Dugger, *The Politician: The Life and Times of Lyndon Johnson* (New York: W. W. Norton, 1982), 41–42, 410; FN on p. 127: Richard Slotkin, *Gunfighter Nation* (New York: Atheneum, 1992), 566; FN on p. 128: *Saturday Review*, April 10, 1965; Hamill in Sherrill, 9.

The Chase—Great Society at Home

The New York Times, June 20, 1965; Sherrill, 90; *Newsweek*, February 28, 1966, 91.

Theodore H. White, *The Making of the President 1968* (New York: Pocket Books, 1970), 32; Parker quoted in Jerry Cohen and William S. Murphy, *Burn, Baby, Burn! The Watts Riot* (New York: Avon, 1967), 163; ten-car convoy, yellow school bus, red armbands and *Los Angeles Herald-Examiner* in Robert Conot, *Rivers of Blood, Years of Darkness* (New York: Bantam, 1967), 325, 428; "even slingshots," Cohen and Murphy, 166; Robin Wood, *Hollywood from Vietnam to Reagan* (New York: Columbia University Press, 1986), 25.

Kirkpatrick Sale, *SDS* (New York: Vintage, 1974), 204; Noebel quoted, Benjamin R. Epstein and Arnold Forster, *The Radical Right: Report on the John Birch Society and Its Allies* (New York: Vintage, 1967), 17; Gene Williams, "Don't Throw Rocks at Rock 'n' Roll," *The Worker*, March 9, 1965, 5; *Billboard*, August 21, 1965; David A. Noebel, *Rhythm, Riots and Revolution* (Tulsa, OK: Christian Crusade Publications, 1966), 216, 249; *New York Times*, October 23, 1966; Herbert Marcuse, "Repressive Tolerance," Robert Paul Wolff, Barrington Moore Jr., and Herbert Marcuse, *A Critique of Pure Tolerance* (Boston: Beacon, 1969), 114–15; Philbrick warning cited in Epstein and Forster, 19.

"Arthur Penn Objects," *New York Times*, February 20, 1966; Penn in Rex Reed, "Penn: And Where Did All The Chase-ing Lead?," *New York Times*, February 13, 1966; Richard Schickel, "Small Flop Grows into a Disaster," *Life*, March 4, 1966; Rex Reed, *Status* (March 1966), 12; "An Interview with Arthur Penn," *Cinema* 5, no. 3 (1969), 34; Wood, 25.

FN on p. 136: Thomas Pynchon, "A Journey Into The Mind of Watts," *New York Times Magazine*, June 12, 1966, 84; Murphy in Conot, 426; FN on p. 138: Travis T. Hipp, "Legend of the Red Dog Saloon" *Edging West*, June–July 1995, 18–22.

Vietnam

"We have helped and we will help," Frances FitzGerald, *Fire in the Lake* (New York: Vintage, 1973), 309; Goldman, 458; Johnson invokes Travis and tells NSC, Dugger, 32.

Wayne to Johnson, Document 109, David Culbert, ed., *Film and Propaganda in America: A Documentary History* (New York: Greenwood Press, 1990), 391; Robin Moore, *The*

Green Berets (New York: Avon, 1965), 9; *Time*, April 15, 1966, 84; *Life*, March 4, 1966; *Life*, March 11, 1966; "A Singing 'Duke' Put Patriotism on the Charts," *Washington Post*, February 5, 1978, K1.

Anthony Carthew, "Vietnam Is Like An Oriental Western," *New York Times Magazine*, January 23, 1966, 8; *Variety*, June 29, 1966, 5; "yella bastards," George Carpozi, Jr., *The John Wayne Story* (New Rochelle, NY: Arlington House, 1979).

Loudon Wainwright, *Life*, November 13, 1964, 31; Leo Litwak, "The Ronald Reagan Story; Or, Tom Sawyer Enters Politics," *New York Times Magazine*, November 14, 1965, 46ff; Daniel Boorstin, *THE IMAGE; or, What Happened to the American Dream* (New York: Atheneum, 1962), 5; Litwak, 175; Plog recalls, Garry Wills, *Reagan's America: Innocents at Home* (Garden City, NY: Doubleday, 1987), 295.

Newsweek, July 25, 1966; *Newsweek*, August 15, 1966, 21–22; *Time*, July 8, 1966; *Newsweek*, August 15, 1966; *Time*, August 12, 1966; David Newman and Robert Benton, "Remember the Sixties?," *Esquire*, August 1966; Nixon on split, *Time*, September 5, 1966, 17; Nixon on escalation, *Time*, September 12, 1966, 42; *U.S. News & World Report* cited in *Newsweek*, August 8, 1966; *Time*, November 4, 1966; Barbara Garson, *MacBird!* (New York: Grove Press, 1967), ix; Eastern senator, Sherrill, 8.

Pravda cited in *Time*, October 28, 1965; "vicious and illegal aggression," *Department of State Bulletin*, November 14, 1966, 73; "coonskin to the wall," *U.S. News & World Report*, November 7, 1966, 19; Johnson's "great-great-grandfather," Bernstein, 329.

FN on p. 144: See Dugger, 31–32; FN 1 on p. 146: *Time*, June 25, 1965, 110; *Commonweal*, August 6, 1965; FN on p. 149: Robert Jay Lifton, *Home from the War: Vietnam Veterans Neither Victims nor Executioners* (New York: Touchstone, 1974), 238; Ron Kovic, *Born on the Fourth of July* (New York: Pocket Books, 1977), 112. FN on p. 155: Sidey in Merle Miller, *Lyndon: An Oral Biography* (New York: Putnam, 1980), 456–57.

Gathering the Tribes

Time, September 9, 1966, 28; Todd Gitlin, *The Whole World Is Watching: Mass Media in the Making and Unmaking of the New Left* (Berkeley, CA: University of California Press, 1980), 171; Artaud, 85; Emmett Grogan, *Ringolevio: A Life Played for Keeps* (London: Grenada, 1981), 271; *Time*, September 2, 1966, 16; "drug usage" and "sexual orgies," Joseph Lewis, *What Makes Reagan Run: A Political Profile* (New York: McGraw-Hill, 1968), 146.

David Newman and Robert Benton, "Lightning in a Bottle," Sandra Wake and Nicola Hayden, eds., *Bonnie & Clyde* (New York: Lorrimer, 1972), 19; *Los Angeles Times Calendar*, November 6, 1966, 13; Herbert Gold, "Notes From the Land of Political Pop," *New York Times Magazine*, December 11, 1966, 49; Eldridge Cleaver, *Soul on Ice* (New York: Dell, 1968), 75.

Sunday News, February 5, 1967; *New York Times Magazine*, May 7, 1967, 1; Berg on media and Hoffman transfixed, *Steal This Dream: Abbie Hoffman and the Countercultural*

Revolution in America (New York: Doubleday, 1998), 71–72; Todd Gitlin, *The Sixties: Years of Hope, Days of Rage* (New York: Bantam Books, 1987), 222ff.

FN on p. 159: Producers had difficulty, *New York Times*, January 11, 1967; *New Yorker* refused to list, *New York Times*, February 22, 1967; Dwight Macdonald, "Birds of America," *New York Review of Books*, December 1, 1966; Lionel Abel, *Partisan Review*, Winter 1967.

IV. BORN TO BE WILD

"Reprehensible," "stomach-turning," *Newsweek*, August 21, 1967; "grisly," *Time*, August 25, 1967; "gross and demeaning," *Newsweek*, August 28, 1967; "gruesome" and "dementia praecox of the most pointless sort," *Films in Review*, October 1967; *Variety*, February 2, 1966; Tom Wolfe, "Pornoviolence," *Esquire*, July 1967, 160ff.

Bosley Crowther, *New York Times*, August 7, 1967; Seale's statement, Hugh Pearson, *The Shadow of the Panther: Huey Newton and the Price of Black Power in America* (Reading, MA: Addison-Wesley, 1994), 131; Carmichael in *U.S. News & World Report*, May 29, 1967; Emmett Grogan, *Ringolevio: A Life Played for Keeps* (London: Grenada, 1981), 506; Tom Hayden, *Rebellion in Newark: Official Violence and Ghetto Response* (New York: Vintage, 1967), 32–33; Hughes in Hayden, 32; Hayden, 69; Bosley Crowther, "Another Smash at Violence," *New York Times*, July 30, 1967; Bosley Crowther, *New York Times*, June 16, 1967; *Newsweek*, July 2, 1967; *New York Post*, June 16, 1967; *Daily News*, June 16, 1967; *New Yorker*, July 22, 1967.

Variety, August 9, 1967; Brown quoted, Pearson, 140; Bosley Crowther, *New York Times*, August 13, 1967; "Crowther's 'Bonnie'-Brook," *Variety*, August 30, 1967; anti-Crowther letters and Penn interview, *New York Times*, September 17, 1967; *Films in Review*, October 1967; Penelope Gilliatt, *New Yorker*, August 17, 1967, and Pauline Kael, "Onward and Upward with the Arts: *Bonnie and Clyde*," *New Yorker*, October 21, 1967, 147.

If You Are a Bonnie-and-Clyder . . .

Kael, 147; Jimmy Breslin, "Bonnie and Clyde Revisited," *New York*, July 8, 1968, 31; Henry Miller, "Make Love Not Gore," *Penthouse*, June 1968, 17.

Time, December 8, 1967; *New York Review of Books*, December 8, 1967; *New Republic*, November 4, 1967; Brown quoted, *Time*, August 4, 1967; *Time*, December 8, 1967; *Time*, December 26, 1967; Charles Marowitz, "Dateline London: Bonnie and Clyde: Symptom and Cause," *Village Voice*, December 21, 1967, 43; Benton and Newman quoted in *Mademoiselle*, March 1968; *Women's Wear Daily* cited in *Newsweek*, December 18, 1967; *Mademoiselle*, March 1968; "Bonnie and Clyde Captivates Public, Starts Significant Trends," *Hollywood Reporter*, March 16, 1968, 2; Marowitz, 43.

Andrew Kopkind, "Soul Power," *New York Review of Books*, August 24, 1967; Dunaway interview, *Newsweek*, March 4, 1968; Penn quoted, Cawelti, 19; Tom Wolfe, "Radical Chic," *New York*, June, 1970, the term was first applied to *Bonnie and Clyde* by Peter Collier in *Ramparts*, May 1968; Gerald Long, *National Guardian*, September 9, 1967; Michael Rossman, *The Wedding Within the War* (Garden City, NY: Anchor, 1971), 238; Hoffman 41; Norman Mailer, *Armies of the Night* (New York: Signet, 1968), 108; Lewis quoted, Nancy Zoulis and Gerald Sullivan, *Who Spoke Up? American Protest Against the War in Vietnam 1963–1975* (New York: Holt, Rinehart, and Winston, 1984), 137; Lowell, *!Viva Che! Contributions in tribute to Ernesto 'Che' Guevara*, ed. Marianne Alexandre (New York: Dutton, 1968), 79; *Time*, November 29, 1967, 29, 61; Che to American visitors, David Caute, *The Year of the Barricades: A Journey Through 1968* (New York: Harper & Row, 1988), 45; Zanuck became aware, John Leonard, "Che!—The Making of a Movie Revolutionary," *New York Times Magazine*, December 8, 1968, 65–66.

Paul Williams, *Outlaw Blues: A Book of Rock Music* (New York: Dutton, 1969); *Newsweek*, October 23, 1967; Long, *National Guardian*, September 7, 1967; letter, *National Guardian*, September 16, 1967; John Howard Lawson, "Our Film and Theirs: *Grapes of Wrath* and *Bonnie and Clyde*," reprinted in John G. Cawelti, ed., *Focus on Bonnie and Clyde* (Englewood Cliffs, NJ: Prentice-Hall, 1973), 111–13; Bakunin in E. J. Hobsbawm *Primitive Rebels* (New York: W. W. Norton, 1965), 28; Neil Buckley, "Murdered in Louisiana," *New Left Notes*, January 8, 1968, 4ff.

FN on p. 172: *Time* staffer, Carlos Clarens, *Crime Movies: An Illustrated History* (New York: W. W. Norton, 1980), 259; *Time*, June 4, 1934; FN on p. 173: *New York Times*, March 23, 1968, 25; FN on p. 180: Greene, Read, Sartre, Sontag in Alexandre, 75, 95–96, 105, 106. FN on p. 181: *Newsweek*, August 7, 1967, 51; FN on p. 182: Bosley Crowther, *New York Times*, October 1, 1967; FN on p. 184: Penn in Joseph Gelmis, *The Film Director as Superstar* (Garden City, NY: Doubleday, 1970), 202–03.

Spring 1968

Clifford's thought in Irving Bernstein, *Guns or Butter: The Presidency of Lyndon Johnson* (New York: Oxford University Press, 1996), 473; "Mansfield Says War Hurts Cities," *New York Times*, January 23, 1968; Michael Herr, *Dispatches* (New York: Avon, 1978), 71; Harold Evans in Robert Hamilton, "Image and Context: The Production and Reproduction of *The Execution of a VC Suspect* by Eddie Adams," *Vietnam Images: War and Representation* (New York: St. Martin's, 1988), 178; Cronkite and Johnson quoted in Barbara Matusow, *The Evening Stars: The Making of the Network News Anchor* (Boston: Houghton Mifflin, 1983), 128–29.

Peter Fonda, *Don't Tell Dad: A Memoir* (New York: Hyperion, 1998), 241–42, Hopper quoted in Fonda, 255, and Peter Biskind, *Easy Riders, Raging Bulls: How the Sex-Drugs-and-Rock'n'Roll Generation Saved Hollywood* (New York: Simon & Schuster, 1998), 64; Fonda, 256; *Life*, March 29, 1968, 68, 72.

Theodore White, *The Making of the President 1968* (New York: Pocket Books, 1970), 115; Jack Gould, "TV: Commentators Stunned by President's Action," *New York Times*,

April 1, 1968, Westmoreland quoted in Bernstein, 492; Herr, 158; Kennedy in Michigan, Jules Whitcover, *85 Days: The Last Campaign of Robert Kennedy* (New York: Putnam, 1969), 147.

"Revolutionary action-theater," "huge orgasm," Jerry Rubin, *Do It! Scenarios of the Revolution* (New York: Simon & Schuster, 1970), 161–62; "our own reality," Sloman, 159; *Newsweek*, February 28, 1966; Kael, "Trash, Art and the Movies," *Going Steady* (New York: Warner Books, 1979), 109; James Simon Kunen, *The Strawberry Statement: Notes of a College Revolutionary* (New York: Avon, 1970), 34; Davidoff in Sloman, 124; journalists joke, Lewis Chester, Godfrey Hodgson, and Bruce Page, *An American Melodrama: The Presidential Campaign of 1968* (New York: Viking, 1969), 170; Kennedy calls for jobs, Witcover, 146; White, 215; Renata Adler, "Going 'Wild in the Streets,'" *New York Times*, June 16, 1968, II, 1; Robert Hatch, *Nation*, June 17, 1968, 805; White, 216; *San Francisco Express Times* in Chester, et al., 170.

Hamill and Lowell in Jean Stein, *An American Journey: The Times of Robert Kennedy* (New York: Harcourt Brace Jovanovich, 1970), 335, 340–41; Jack Gould, "TV: Truman Capote Defines His Concept of Justice," *New York Times*, June 15, 1968; Scheer in Stein, 339; "The Psycho-biology of Violence" *Life*, June 21, 1968; Arthur Schlesinger, *Violence: America in the Sixties* (New York: Signet, 1968), 53; Breslin, 31.

FN on p. 188: Kennedy on Tet Photo in Hamilton, 179. FN on p. 191: Fonda, 241; Peter Coyote, *Sleeping Where I Fall* (Washington, DC: Counterpoint, 1998), 100–101, 102; FN on p. 193: Fonda, 254–55; FN on p. 196: "numb and shocked," Roger Morris, *Partners in Power: The Clintons and Their America* (New York: Henry Holt, 1996), 76; FN on p. 197: Fonda, 259–60; FN on p. 201: *Life*, May 10, 1968, 64–69; FN 1 on p. 202: Kennedy openly questioned, Martin A. Lee and Bruce Shlain, *Acid Dreams* (New York: Grove Press, 1985), 93; Ginsberg visits Kennedy, Hayden cited, Stein, 186, 194; "the beards" and FBI, Brian Dooley, *Robert Kennedy: The Final Years* (Staffordshire, UK: Keele University, 1995), 65. FN on p. 203: Jerry Hopkins and Danny Sugerman, *No One Here Gets Out Alive* (New York: Warner, 1980), 184.

Creating Our Own Reality

Peckinpah's set, Marshall Fine, *Bloody Sam* (New York: D.I. Fine, 1991), 138; Dawson in David Weddle, *"If They Move . . . Kill 'Em" The Life and Times of Sam Peckinpah* (New York: Grove Press, 1994), 353–54; Renata Adler, *New York Times*, June 20, 1968; *L'Humanité* cited, *New York Times*, August 2, 1968; "massive falsification" and "racial hatred," Emanuel Levy, *John Wayne: Prophet of the American Way of Life* (Metuchen, NJ: Scarecrow Press, 1988), 323; *Variety*, June 26, 1968, 16; Robbins quoted, "John Wayne as the Last Hero," *Time*, August 8, 1969, 53.

Herr, 46; Wayne quoted, Joan Barthel, "John Wayne, Superhawk," *New York Times Magazine*, December 24, 1967, 29; "The Spokesman: 1968," *Esquire*, May 1968; Kunen, 160; Adler, June 20, 1968.

Humphrey's fear, White, 348–49; Lampe quoted, Sloman, 134; Krassner quoted,

Sloman, 125; Rubin, 167; Rubin telephoned Sanders, Sloman, 126; Zmuda quoted, Slo-
man, 141–42; Rubin, 170; Todd Gitlin, *The Sixties: Years of Hope, Days of Rage* (New
York: Bantam, 1987), 329; Norman Mailer, *Miami and the Seige of Chicago: An Informal
History of the Republican and Democratic Conventions of 1968* (New York: Signet, 1968),
122; Ultra Violet quoted in Sally Beauman, "Norman Mailer, Movie Maker," *New York*,
August 19, 1968, 53; Pennebaker quoted in Hilary Mills, *Mailer: A Biography* (New York:
Empire, 1982), 329; Jean Genet, "The Members of the Assembly," in Harold Hayes, ed.,
Smiling Through the Apocalypse: Esquire's History of the Sixties (New York: Crown, 1987),
94; White, 360; Wexler quoted, *New York Times*, September 7, 1969.

Mailer, 175; Cronkite in Thomas Whiteside, "Corridor of Mirrors: The Television Editorial Process, Chicago," *Columbia Journalism Review*, Winter 1968/1969, 165; Mailer, 204.

Fouratt in Sloman, 156; Hoffman, 101.

FN on p. 210: Joseph McBride, "Drums Along the Mekong," *Sight and Sound*, Autumn 1972; FN on p. 211: Richard Slotkin, *Gunfighter Nation* (New York: Atheneum,
1992), 532; Frankel in George McT. Kahin, *Intervention: How America Became Involved in
Vietnam* (New York: Knopf, 1986), 290–91; FN on p. 212: Renata Adler, *New York Times*,
June 20, 1968; FN on p. 214: Chester, et al., 654; FN on p. 217: Carl Rollyson, *The Lives
of Norman Mailer: A Biography* (New York: Paragon House, 1991), 210–11; FN on p. 221:
White, 373.

The Election

"The Defiant Voices of S.D.S.," *Life*, October 18, 1968, 80ff; "aggressive confrontation
politics" Sale, 490ff; Rubin quoted, Sloman, 159; "What They Believe," *Fortune*, January
1969; Omar Sharif, with Marie-Thérèse Guinchard, *The Eternal Male*, Martin Sokolinsky,
trans. (Garden City, NY: Doubleday, 1977), 155; Richard F Shepard, "Film About Guevara a Boon to Puerto Rico," *New York Times*, November 12, 1968, 52; John Leonard,
"Che!—The Making of a Movie Revolutionary," *New York Times Magazine*, December
8, 1968, 62; Fleischer quoted, Leonard, 66; *Variety*, June 4, 1969.

Don Siegel, "The Anti-Heroes," *Films and Filming*, January 1969, 22; Bosley Crowther,
"Another Smash at Violence," *New York Times*, July 30, 1967; Joseph Gelmis, *Newsday*,
May 6, 1969; Andy Warhol and Pat Hackett, *POPism: The Warhol '60s* (New York:
Harcourt Brace Jovanovich, 1980), 261; FBI and Warhol, Margia Kramer, *Andy Warhol
et al.: The FBI File on Andy Warhol* (New York: UnSub Press, 1988), iv.

"Socially irresponsible," Richard Schickel, *Clint Eastwood* (New York: Knopf, 1996),
201; Chester, et al., 667; "Wallace is the only guy" and "I've been waiting," *New York
Times*, October 25, 1968, 32; "educate students" and "turn this country over to the
police," Caute, 293; "We don't have a sick society" and "We don't have riots," Carter,
366; "register Communists, not guns," T.R.B., *New Republic*, November 9, 1968, 3.

Gore Vidal, "The Twenty-Ninth Republican Convention," *Homage to Daniel Shays:
Collected Essays 1952–1972* (New York: Vintage, 1973), 315.

FN on p. 232: Nixon's line, "Candidates Take Show to the Airwaves," *Washington Post*, September 26, 2000.

No Future

National Commission on the Causes and Prevention of Violence report, Jerome H. Skolnick, *The Politics of Protest* (New York: Ballantine, 1969), xi; "Press Violent About Film's Violence; Prod Sam Peckinpah Following Bunch," *Variety*, July 2, 1969, 15; Andrew Sarris, *Village Voice*, July 31, 1969.

The New Republic, September 27, 1969; "Will 'Easy' Do It for Dennis Hopper?" *New York Times*, July 20, 1969; Archer Winsten, *New York Post*, July 15, 1969; *Saturday Review*, August 30, 1969; Herndon and Manduke in "Alice's Restaurant: The Ballad of Arlo the Litterbug comes to the Silver Screen," *Eye*, March 1969, 32.

Penn in Gelmis, *The Film Director as Superstar*, 205; Polonsky in Eric Sherman and Martin Rubin, *The Director's Event: Interviews with Five American Film-Makers* (New York: Atheneum, 1970), 25; *Variety*, October 22, 1969.

Steven Lerner, "Antonioni Audition: How I Slipped on the First Step to Stardom," *Village Voice*, June 27, 1968, 1; scout report, Lawrence M. Bensky, "Antonioni Comes to the Point," *New York Times*, December 15, 1968, II, 23; phones tapped and mail opened, Louise Sweeney, "Zabriskie Lives!," *Show*, February 1970, 42ff; Antonioni quoted, *Rolling Stone*, March 1, 1969, 17.

Feldman quoted, *Variety*, July 2, 1969, 15.

FN on p. 241: Pauline Kael, *New Yorker*, December 27, 1969. FN on p. 245: Frechette in David Felton, *Mindfuckers: A Source Book on the Rise of Acid Fascism in America* (San Francisco: Straight Arrow, 1972), 250.

V. NIXON TIME

"The way civilizations begin to die," *New York Times*, March 23, 1969, 54; Nixon at General Beadle State College, *New York Times*, June 4, 1969, 31; Reagan's declaration, Nancy Zaroulis and Gerald Sullivan, *Who Spoke Up? American Protest Against the War in Vietnam* (New York: Holt, Rinehart and Winston, 1985), 306; Morrison's taunts, Jerry Hopkins and Danny Sugerman, *No One Here Gets Out Alive* (New York: Warner, 1980), 231.

The End of the Sixties

Norman Mailer, *Of a Fire on the Moon* (New York: Press Grove, 1985), 435; *New York Times*, August 3, 1969; Mailer, 111; Abbie Hoffman, *Woodstock Nation* (New York: Vintage, 1969), 13; Nietzsche, *The Birth of Tragedy*, 124; Ayn Rand, *The New Left: The Anti-Industrial Revolution* (New York: Signet, 1971), 81; "all systems go" and Nixon's threat, Jeffrey Kimball, *Nixon's Vietnam War* (Lawrence: University of Kansas, 1998), 160, 153; Kissinger's threat, Richard Nixon, *RN: The Memoirs of Richard Nixon* (New York : Grosset

& Dunlap, 1978), 396; Hoffman, 13; Peter Collier, "Apollo 11: The Time Machine," *Ramparts*, October 1969, 56.

Stew Albert, "Flicker Flashes," *Berkeley Tribe*, August 1–7, 1969, 6; Joan Didion, *The White Album* (New York: Pocket Books, 1980), 46.

America's Night of the Living Dead

U.S. economy and *Business Week* in Gabriel Kolko, *Anatomy of a War: Vietnam, The United States, and the Modern Historical Experience* (New York: The New Press, 1994), 346.

"Mae West Still Gets Top Billing," *Los Angeles Times*, August 13, 1969; *Time*, November 29, 1968; Sarne quoted, *Hollywood Reporter*, February 3, 1969; Sarne interview cited, Rex Reed, "Myra Goes Hollywood," *Playboy*, August 1970; not "subtlety" but "vulgarity," Joyce Haber, *Los Angeles Times Sunday Calendar*, October 19, 1969; "Interview with Michael Sarne," *Inter/View*, January 1969; Sarne quoted, *Variety*, October 1, 1969; "intellectual pygmies, " Calvin Trillin, "Through the Muck with Myra," *Life*, March 6, 1970, 50; Reed op.cit.; Welch quoted, *Look*, March 24, 1970, 48; "vast piranha pool," *Women's Wear Daily*, January 14, 1970; "dying for me all over town," Harry Clein, "Getting 'Myra' to Production . . ." *Entertainment World*, October 3, 1969, 16; Sarnes entertain Sharon Tate, consider dropping by Cielo Drive, Ed Sanders, *The Family: The Story of Charles Manson's Dune Buggy Attack Batalion* (New York: Dutton, 1971), 262, 265; *Women's Wear Daily*, January 14, 1970.

Nixon's speech, *New York Times*, November 4, 1969, 16.

Richard McGuiness, *Village Voice*, December 25, 1969; "white riot" and Dohrn in Kirkpatrick Sale, *SDS* (New York: Vintage, 1974), 627, 628.

Free Press column, *Tuesday's Child* declaration, Rubin quote, and Manson as cause, Vincent Bugliosi with Curt Gentry, *Helter Skelter: The True Story of the Manson Murders* (New York: Bantam, 1975), 296; "Life with Manson," *Berkeley Barb*, January 16–22, 1970; "Fourteen Ways to Make Out Manson," *Berkeley Barb*, February 13–19, 1970.

Time, January 5, 1970; Pauline Kael, *New Yorker*, December 27, 1969; Paul Zimmerman, *Newsweek*, December 21, 1970; *Look*, December 1, 1970; Candice Bergen, *Knock Wood* (New York: Simon & Schuster, 1984), 221; *Time*, February 2, 1970.

FN on p. 254: Coburn quoted in Peter Manso, *Brando* (New York: Hyperion, 1994), 636. FN on p. 256: "reality and fantasy," Clein, 14; Sarne agreed, *Variety*, October 1, 1969; FN 1 on p. 264: *Berkeley Barb*, February 13–19, 1970. FN 2 on p. 264: Edwin Kennebeck, *Juror Number Four: The Trial of Thirteen Black Panthers as Seen from the Jury Box* (New York: W. W. Norton, 1973), 137.

Spring 1970

Vincent Canby, *New York Times*, February 5, 1970; *Time*, January 5, 1970; Stanley Kauffmann, *New Republic*, March 7, 1970; Vincent Canby, *New York Times*, February 8, 1970, II, 1; Kauffmann, op.cit.

Times of London, May 10, 1970; the most detailed account of Nixon screening *Patton* is Ronald A. Carpenter and Robert V. Seltzer, "Nixon, Patton, and the Silent Majority Sentiment About the Viet Nam War: The Cinematographic Bases of a Rhetorical Stance," *Central States Speech Journal* 25 (1974), 105–110; see also Hugh Sidey, "Anybody See *Patton*?" *Life*, June 19, 1970, Rowland Evans and Robert Novak, *Nixon in the White House: The Frustration of Power* (New York: Random House, 1971), 252, and Philip D. Beidler, "Just Like in the Movies: Richard Nixon and *Patton*," *Georgia Review*, Fall 1995; Evans and Novak, 252; Madman Theory, H. R. Haldeman, *The Ends of Power* (New York: Times Books, 1978), 83; Agnew in Henry Kissinger, *The White House Years* (Boston: Little, Brown, 1979), 491; Kissinger's understanding, Zaroulis and Sullivan, 338; "Nixon Sends Combat Forces Into Cambodia to Drive Communists From Staging Zone," *New York Times*, May 1, 1970, 1; Nixon's appearance on TV and language at the Pentagon, William Shawcross, *Sideshow: Kissinger, Nixon and the Destruction of Cambodia* (New York: Washington Square Press, 1977), 147, 152.

Rhodes and Haldeman in Shawcross, 153,157–58.

"Thousands of Americans," Shawcross, 158; Arthur Irving, "Mae West at the Myra Premiere," *East Village Other*, June 30, 1970; *New York Times*, June 23, 1970; *Time*, July 6, 1970, 70; "dazzling directorial debut," *Time*, November 29, 1968; Young's suit, *The Last Days of the Zanuck Dynasty at Twentieth Century-Fox* (Secaucus, NJ: Lyle Stuart, 1988), 232.

FN on p. 267: Wayne confessed, Lawrence H. Suid, *Guts and Glory: The Making of the American Military Image in Film*, revised and expanded edition (Lexington: University Press of Kentucky, 2002), 266; FN on p. 271: Sidey interviewed, Suid, 264; Garry Wills, *The Kennedy Imprisonment* (Boston: Little, Brown, 1982), 194. FN on p. 273: Kissinger, 498; Max Frankel, "Behind the President's Decision," *New York Times*, May 2, 1970, 6. FN on p. 277: *Los Angeles Times*, June 25, 1970; *Los Angeles Herald-Examiner*, June 25, 1970; *Time*, July 6, 1970; *Newsweek*, July 6, 1970; *New York*, July 13, 1970; *Life*, July 4, 1970. FN on p. 280: *Hollywood Reporter*, June 10, 1969.

Generational War in the Dream Life

Time, January 5, 1970; Hoover in Mario Van Peebles, Ula Y. Taylor, and J. Tarika Lewis, *Panther: A Pictorial History of the Black Panthers and the Story Behind the Film* (New York: Newmarket Press, 1995); Sarandon in *New York Post*, December 9, 1982).

Time, July 24, 1970; Stanley Kauffmann, *New Republic*, August 29, 1970; "Reluctant Hero of the Hardhats," *Life*, October 16, 1970, 69–70; "kids are standing up," Judy Klemesrud, "His Happiness Is a Thing Called 'Joe,'" *New York Times*, August 2, 1970, II, 9.

"Nixon's Remarks on Manson and Statement in Washington," *New York Times*, August 4, 1970, 16; " 'Chisum,' Nixon and Frontier Justice," *New York Post*, August 5, 1970, 5; "Impulsive Nixon Action," *New York Times*, August 5, 1970; Schneider quoted, Peter Biskind, *Easy Riders, Raging Bulls: How the Sex-Drugs-and-Rock'n'Roll Generation Saved*

Hollywood (New York: Simon & Schuster, 1998), 124; Leary statement, Abe Peck, *Uncovering the Sixties* (New York: Pantheon, 1985), 254.

Power's summer, "Return of the Fugitive," *New Yorker*, June 13, 1994, 50; Dotson Rader, *New York Times*, September 20, 1970, II, 13; *New York Times*, October 27, 1970; Agnew asked, Jonathan Schell, *The Time of Illusion* (New York: Vintage, 1976), 120; Reich, 320; Manson's leap, Bugliosi, 500–501; "the mark of being 'with it'," Schell, 120; Nixon's taunt, Zaroulis and Sullivan, 338; police chief's claim, "Pres Nixon's San Jose Jorseshit," *Berkeley Barb*, November 6–12, 1970.

"A thousand incoherent hippies," Kimball, 237; Krogh's memo, "The Nixon-Presley Meeting: The Documentation," National Security Archive, Gelman Library, George Washington University; Elvis's declaration etc., "The F.B.I. and the King Both Had Suspicious Minds," *New York Times*, August 17, 1997.

FN on p. 284: Kevin Phillips, *The Emerging Republican Majority* (New Rochelle, NY: Arlington House, 1969), 140; FN on p. 285: Vincent Canby, *New York Times*, June 16, 1970, 54. FN on p. 291: Dotson Rader, *New York Times*, September 20, 1970, II, 13; "Call for a Revolutionary People's Constitutional Convention," in Philip S. Foner, ed., *The Black Panthers Speak* (New York: Da Capo, 1995), 268. FN on p. 292: Agnew on Duffy, David Maraniss, *First In His Class* (New York: Touchstone, 1996), 231.

The Last Round-Up

Melvin Van Peebles, *Sweet Sweetback's Baadasssss Song* (New York: Lancer Books, 1971), 6, 13; "cultural genocide," "Sez Pic Code a White Plot, And He 'Might Sue' MPAA, *Variety*, March 24, 1971, 5; King's description, "White Distrib Blur on Blacks," *Variety*, March 24, 1971, 5; *The Militant, Women's Liberation*, and *Muhammad Speaks*, cited in Jon Hartman, "The Trope of Blaxploitation in critical responses to Sweetback," *Film History*, Autumn 1994, 387–90; Van Peebles, 21; Lerone Bennett and Don L. Lee, "The Emancipation Orgasm: Sweetback in Wonderland," *Ebony*, September 1971; Newton in *Time*, August 14, 1971; *JET* cited, Hartman, 390; Van Peebles quoted, Brad Darrach, "Sweet Melvin's very hot, very cool black movie," *Life*, August 13, 1971.

Agnew in Jerry Lembcke, *The Spitting Image: Myth, Memory, and the Legacy of Vietnam* (New York: New York University Press, 1998), 99; Tom Laughlin, "Introduction," *Billy Jack: A Screenplay by Frank and Teresa Christina* (New York: Avon, 1973), 9; Tom Topor, "The Saga of 'Billy Jack' Is One of Rage to Riches, *New York Post*, December 8, 1973, 40; Pauline Kael, *New Yorker*, November 27, 1971, 151; Rex Reed, "'Billy Jack's' Message: Peace Through Sacrifice," *Daily News*, July 30, 1971, 52; Reed paid to endorse, Topor, 40; Kael, 151; Stuart Byron, *The Real Paper*, May 15, 1974, 26.

Reich, 244; Fonda's desire, Howard Junker, "Maui Boogie," *Rolling Stone*, May 13, 1971; Peter Fonda, *Don't Tell Dad: A Memoir* (New York: Hyperion, 1998), 315; "largest western town ever built," Rex Reed, "The Pain and Strain of Filming in Spain," *Sunday News*, October 18, 1970; *Variety*, August 11, 1971; *Life*, September 17, 1971; Andrew Sarris, *Village Voice*, August 26, 1971; Penelope Gilliatt, *New Yorker*, August 21, 1971, 60.

Newsweek, August 30, 1971; Hopper's inspiration, J. Hoberman, *Dennis Hopper: From Method to Madness* (Minneapolis: Walker Art Center, 1988), 23; Tanen quotes, Biskin, 134–35.

FN on p. 298: Lennon interview, Jon Wiener, *Come Together: John Lennon in His Time* (New York: Random House, 1984), 153. FN on p. 301: *Variety*, April 21, 1971; Clayton Riley, "What Makes Sweetback Run?" *New York Times*, May 9, 1971, II, 11. FN on p. 305: Laughlin, 5,6; FN on p. 309: *Village Voice*, August 12, 1971.

The Legal Vigilante

Harrington in "Capital Police Rally Links A.C.L.U. and Court to Radical Violence," *New York Times*, October 15, 1970; "up against an enemy," in Stanley I. Kutler, ed., *Abuse of Power: The New Nixon Tapes* (New York: Free Press, 1997), 8; Stein's recollection, Allen J. Matusow, *Nixon's Economy: Booms, Busts, Dollars, & Votes* (Lawrence: University of Kansas, 1998), 150; Donald Kirk, "Who Wants to Be the Last Man Killed in Vietnam," *New York Times Magazine*, September 21, 1971; Colonel Robert D. Heinl Jr., "The Collapse of the Armed Forces," *Armed Forces Journal*, June 7, 1971, 31.

Frank Chin, "Real West Pictorial," *Helix*, October 23, 1969, 17, 18; Vincent Canby, "Sheriff Eastwood Tangles With the Big City," *New York Times*, October 3, 1968, 56; Pauline Kael, *New Yorker*, January 15, 1972, 78; "torrent of legalistic rhetoric," Gerard W. O'Connor, "Dirty Harry: 'The Law is Crazy,'" *Civil Liberties*, March 1972, 2.

David Marc, *Comic Visions: Television Comedy and American Culture* (Boston: Unwin Hyman, 1989), 181–82.

Muskie and Buchanan in Theodore H. White, *The Making of the President 1972* (New York: Atheneum, 1973), 82n, 220; "frequent displays of short-term memory loss," Michael Simmons, "Marx and Duchamp for Beginners," *LA Weekly*, July 24–30, 1998; Rubin's explanation, Wiener, 202.

Foster Hirsch, *Crawdaddy*, March 5, 1972, 22; Paul Nelson, *Rolling Stone*, March 2, 1972, 66; Kael, 79; Larry Cole, "Clint's Not Cute When He's Angry," *Village Voice*, May 24, 1976, 124.

FN on p. 317: Kutler, 6; FN on p. 320: Siegel in Stuart Kaminsky, "Don Siegel," *Take One*, vol. 3, no. 4 (1972), 15; FN on p. 326: "Bush Boasts of Turnaround From 'Easy Rider' Society," *New York Times*, October 7, 1988, B7. FN on p. 331: Nelson, 66; Siegel's letter, *Rolling Stone*, April 13, 1972. FN on p. 332: ultimate endorsement, *Variety*, December 16, 1981, and *Newsweek*, June 15, 1992.

VI. AFTER THE ORGY

Garry Wills, *The Kennedy Imprisonment* (Boston: Little, Brown, 1982), 278; orgies "so vile," Lou Cannon, *Reagan* (New York: Putnam, 1982), 148; Reagan to women's club, Bill Boyarsky, *Ronald Reagan: His Life and Rise to the Presidency* (New York: Random House, 1981), 82; Rubin and presidential task force, David Zane Mairowitz, *The Radical*

Soap Opera: Roots of Failure in the American Left (New York: Avon, 1976), 223, 218; Pauline Kael, "Southwestern: *The Chase*," *Kiss Kiss Bang Bang* (New York: Bantam, 1969), 186.

FN on p. 336: Sinclair in Mairowitz, 224–25.

Flash-forward to 1968

Pauline Kael, "Beverly Hills as a Big Bed," *New Yorker*, February 17, 1975; Kael, "Tourist in the City of Youth: *Blowup*," *Kiss Kiss Bang Bang* (New York: Bantam, 1969), 44.

Antonioni in Alexander Walker, *Hollywood, England: The British Film Industry in the Sixties* (London: Harrap, 1986), 315; *Time*, April 16, 1966, 33; London critics in Walker, 328–29; *Life*, January 27, 1965.

Arthur Knight, "Three Encounters with *Blowup*," *Film Heritage*, Spring 1967, 3; *Variety*, December 21, 1966; *Life*, January 27, 1967, 64–65; "not unusual to see Americans freezing in line," Jean Clair, "The Road to Damascus: *Blowup*," *Focus on Blowup*, ed. Roy Huss (Englewood Cliffs, NJ: Prentice-Hall, 1971), 53.

Daily Express in Robert Joseph, "Britain Balmy Over Bonnie, Clyde," *Los Angeles Times*, December 3, 1967; "royal premiere of *Doctor Dolittle*," *Hollywood Reporter*, January 18, 1968, 1; *Los Angeles Times*, December 3, 1967; *Time*, February 24, 1975.

FN 1 on p. 338: Kael, "Tourist in the City of Youth," 40; FN 2 on p. 338: *Time*, February 24, 1975; David Ehrenstein, *Film Quarterly*, Summer 1975, 63; FN on p. 339: Walker, 316.

The 1972 Campaign

Dr. Hunter S. Thompson, *Fear and Loathing on the Campaign Trail '72* (New York: Popular Library, 1973), 142; *Rolling Stone* photograph, Thompson, 179.

New York Times, May 4, 1972.

Richard Reeves, "The Stars Shone Bright on George McGovern," *Saturday Review*, July 8, 1972, 5, 6; "orgy for celebrities," Abbie Hoffman, Jerry Rubin, and Ed Sanders, *Vote!* (New York: Warner, 1972), 68; Reeves, 6; "Robert Redford's hits," *New York Post*, February 15, 1975; David Thomson, *Warren Beatty and Desert Eyes: A Life and a Story* (Garden City, NY: Doubleday, 1987), 301; Redford in Jerry Talmer, "This Would Make a Movie," *New York Post Magazine*, July 1, 1972, 2; *Newsweek*, July 17, 1972.

Louise Sweeney, "Speeding 'The Candidate' to the box office," *Christian Science Monitor*, July 13, 1972, 2; "a multi-media psychedelic experience," Hoffman et al., 65; Hart in David Maraniss, *First in His Class: The Biography of Bill Clinton* (New York: Touchstone, 1995), 266; "the hairiest convention," Hoffman, et al., 74; Norman Mailer, *St. George and the Godfather* (New York: Signet, 1972), 26; "no ego-tripping," Roger Morris, *Partners in Power: The Clintons and Their America* (New York: Henry Holt, 1996), 157; Levin and Philbin in Larry Sloman, *Steal This Dream: Abbie Hoffman and the Countercultural Revolution in America* (New York: Doubleday, 1998), 262–63; "calling the role call," Hoffman, et al., 79; Thompson, 319; McGovern in Thompson, 470–71.

"Why Is Bella Bored?" Congresswoman Bella S. Abzug, *New York Times*, July 23, 1972, II, 7; *Newsweek*, July 17, 1972; *Commonweal*, August 25, 1972; *Life*, July 28, 1972; Thompson, 329.

Colson and Gergen in John Anthony Maltese, *Spin Control: The White House Office of Communications and the Management of Presidential News*, second edition (Chapel Hill, NC: University of North Carolina Press, 1994), 93; BBC reporters, Hoffman, et al., 173–74; Thompson, 382; self-described liberated zone, Mailer, 211; Joseph Morgenstern, "The Dick & Spiro Show (Rerun)," *Newsweek*, September 4, 1972, 89; Mailer, 179.

Mailer, 112, 156; *Life*, April 23, 1971, 51; *Playboy*, May 1971, 75ff; *Life*, April 23, 1971; Vivian Gornick, "I don't want anyone over me, I don't need anyone under me," *Village Voice*, March 30, 1972, 38; Fonda to "passively" support McGovern, Gary Arnold, "'F.T.A.': The Fonda Way," *Washington Post*, June 28, 1972, E9; Newton's paradigm, David Hillard and Lewis Cole, *This Side of Glory: The Autobiography of David Hillard and the Story of the Black Panther Party* (Boston: Little, Brown, 1993), 339; *Variety*, October 4, 1972, 3.

FN on p. 348: "A left-winger by the time we get through," in Stanley I. Kutler, ed., *Abuse of Power: The New Nixon Tapes* (New York: Free Press, 1997), 38. FN on p. 353: Jeremy Larner, "Politics Catches Up to 'The Candidate,' " *New York Times*, October 23, 1988; FN on p. 356: Gail Sheehy, *Character: America's Search for Leadership* (New York: Bantam Books, 1990), 209. FN on p. 359: Mailer, 218 and Thompson, 381; FN on p. 361: Mailer, 188.

The Nixon Western

"Unglamorous, lonely, miserable existence," Kathleen Carroll, *Daily News*, April 17, 1972; Kissinger felt, William Bundy, *A Tangled Web: The Making of Foreign Policy in the Nixon Presidency* (New York: Hill and Wang, 1998), 315; incapacitate Ellsberg, Steve Weissman, *Big Brother and the Holding Company: The World Behind Watergate* (Palo Alto, CA: Ramparts, 1974), 38–39; "international outlaws," Jonathan Schell, *The Time of Illusion* (New York: Vintage, 1976), 241.

Thompson, 409–10; McGovern's pollster in Kathleen Hall Jamieson, *Packaging the Presidency: A History and Criticism of Presidential Campaign Advertising*, third edition (New York: Oxford University Press, 1996), 307.

Time, January 19, 1973; *Variety*, February 28, 1973; *Rolling Stone*, April 26, 1973, 64.

Pauline Kael, *New Yorker*, February 25, 1974; all previous Watergate statements "inoperable," Len Colodny and Robert Gettlin, *Silent Coup: The Removal of a President* (New York: St. Martin's, 1993), 280; Nixon to Ziegler, Kutler, 349; Judith Crist, "Git 'Em Up, Move 'Em Over," *New York*, April 30, 1973.

Dawson's report, Marshall Fine, *Bloody Sam* (New York: D.I. Fine, 1991), 246; Lorraine Gauguin, "One Size Fits All: December 1972," *Views & Reviews*, December 1973, 11, 12; irate director, Fine, 248; Peckinpah interview, Jan Aghed, "Pat Garrett and Billy the Kid," *Sight and Sound*, Spring 1973, 65, 68–69. Coburn in David Weddle, *"If They*

Move . . . Kill 'Em" The Life and Times of Sam Peckinpah (New York: Grove Press, 1994), 479; "bellhops," Garner Simmons, *A Portrait in Montage: Peckinpah* (Austin: University of Texas, 1982), 171; T.E.D. Klein, "They Kill Animals And They Call It Art," *New York Times*, January 13, 1974, 13.

Time, November 13, 1972; Frechette, "In Prison, An Ex-Actor Stages the Watergate Tapes," *People*, April 14, 1975, 22.

FN on p. 366: Roger Greenspun, *New York Times*, April 17, 1972; FN 2 on p. 369: Connally hinted, Robert Sherrill, *The Accidental President* (New York: Grossman, 1967), 121. McGovern in Maraniss, 272; FN on p. 374: William Safire "Comeback Time," *New York Times*, April 18, 1973, 47; "throwing [himself] on the sword," Anthony Summers, *The Arrogance of Power: The Secret World of Richard Nixon* (New York: Viking, 2000), 451; FN on p. 381: Klein, 13.

Ciné Paranoia

Peter Dale Scott, "From Dallas to Watergate: The Longest Cover-up," in Steve Weissman, ed., *Big Brother and the Holding Company: The World Behind Watergate* (Palo Alto, CA: Ramparts Press, 1974), 108.

Reagan in Vin McLellan and Paul Avery, *The Voices of Guns* (New York: Putnam, 1977), 251; Harris and Hacker in Michael Selzer, *Terrorist Chic: An Exploration of Violence in the Seventies* (New York: Hawthorne, 1979), 181–82; "political action itself can be no more than art performance," Cheryl Bernstein, "Performance as News: Notes on an Intermedia Guerrilla Art Group," in Michel Benamou and Charles Caramello, eds., *Performance in Postmodern Culture* (Madison, WI: Coda Press, 1977), 83; Peter Sloterdijk, *Critique of Cynical Reason*, trans. Michael Eldred (Minneapolis: University of Minnesota, 1987), 123; Jerry Rubin, "I am Regan, you are Regan," *Village Voice*, May 2, 1974; "my freedom and the freedom of all oppressed people," McLellan and Avery, 299.

"I died in that fire," McLellan and Avery, 368; Pauline Kael, *New Yorker*, November 19, 1973; Mailer, 103–104.

Thomson, 279.

FN on p. 384: "Moving into criminality" and "going into movies," Sloman, 285, 287; FN on p. 389: "Mae Brussell's Conspiracy Newsletter," *The Realist*, February 1974; FN on p. 392: *Rolling Stone*, October 23, 1975, and November 20, 1975; FN on p. 397: *Time*, February 24, 1975.

Freedomland 1981

FBI informant, Bob Callahan, *Who Shot JFK? A Guide to the Major Conspiracies* (New York: Simon & Schuster, 1993), 52; Daniel Boorstin, *THE IMAGE; or, What Happened to the American Dream* (New York: Atheneum, 1962), 258.

Frederic Jameson, *The Geopolitical Aesthetic: Cinema and Space in the World System* (Bloomington: University of Indiana Press, 1992), 19.

Lloyd deMause, *Reagan's America* (New York: Creative Roots, 1984), 63, 11.

Lyn Nofziger in *New York Times* documentary *Bulletproof: Reagan After Hinkley* (Showtime, December 9, 2001).

FN on p. 406: DeMause, 12-13; FN on p. 409: Jon Weiner, "Hippie Day at the Reagan Library," *LA Weekly*, September 20–26, 1996, 16.

Index